EYEWITNESS HISTORY

World War I

Rodney P. Carlisle

Facts On File
An imprint of Infobase Publishing

NOTE ON PHOTOS

Many of the illustrations and photographs used in this book are old, historical images. The quality of the prints is not always up to modern standards, as in many cases the originals are damaged. The content of the illustrations, however, made their inclusion important despite problems in reproduction.

World War I

Copyright © 2007 by Rodney P. Carlisle
Maps copyright © 2007 by Infobase Publishing

Facts On File, Inc.
An imprint of Infobase Publishing
132 West 31st Street
New York NY 10001

Library of Congress Cataloging-in-Publication Data
Carlisle, Rodney P.
   World War I / Rodney P. Carlisle.
      p.   cm.—(Eyewitness history)
   Includes bibliographical references and index.
   ISBN 0-8160-6061-4
   1. World War, 1914–1918. 2. World War, 1914–1918—Sources. I. Title: World War One. II. Title: World War 1. III. Title. IV. Series.
   D521.C4355 2006
   940.3—dc22   2005027236

Facts On File books are available at special discounts when purchased in bulk quantities for businesses, associations, institutions, or sales promotions. Please call our Special Sales Department in New York at (212) 967-8800 or (800) 322-8755.

You can find Facts On File on the World Wide Web at http://www.factsonfile.com

Text design by Joan M. McEvoy
Cover design by Cathy Rincon
Maps by Sholto Ainslie

Printed in the United States of America

VB JM 10 9 8 7 6 5 4 3 2 1

This book is printed on acid-free paper.

CONTENTS

ACKNOWLEDGMENTS

My debts of gratitude for help in conceptualizing this work are owed to quite a variety of sources. I certainly am indebted to Professors Richard Abrams, Lawrence Levine, and Walton Bean at the University of California, who required, in the 1960s, that their graduate students think deeply about historical cause and effect in the 20th century. As I sought to instill in my own students at Rutgers University in Camden over a period of three decades a similar desire to penetrate beneath the surface events to deeper causes, I benefited from hundreds of questions that came up in discussion that I found myself unable to answer without further reading and thinking. In particular, American college students always seemed to find it difficult to unravel both the causes of the war that began in 1914 and the causes of American entry into it in 1917. From such concerns, I drew the focus for many of the chapters of this book, and I attempted to cull through the rich body of memoirs, diaries, and secondary literature to find the answers. The scholars who have for decades sought to unravel the tragedy and the lessons of the war have produced a vast library, a fraction of which I was able to review and consult.

Discussions over the years with colleagues at Rutgers also helped develop my thinking about the relations of the Great Powers and the war they fought. Bernard Dehmelt, James Muldoon, Joseph Held, Gerald Verbrugghe, Edgar Rice-Maximin, and Andrew Lees each directed me to sources and materials I might not otherwise have consulted in my efforts to teach the subject. Colleagues at History Associates Incorporated since the 1980s have plied me with suggestions about how to make historical writing come home to the reader, and I owe thanks to Philip Cantelon, Richard Hewlett, James Lide, James Rife, and Brian Martin for such advice. I hope they can discover in this work some evidence of their good critiques of earlier works. At Facts On File, support and a good dialogue by e-mail with Nicole Bowen and Laura Shauger helped bring this manuscript to completion.

I owe to my wife, Loretta, more than I can say in a few lines. She heard many of the anecdotes and tales, both ironic and tragic, that I discovered in the research for this work, and her patience in hearing me out helped me pick the eyewitness selections that make up about a third of this work. In addition, after being immersed for a year in discussions of this distant war, she suffered through the painful process of helping to edit the final manuscript.

AUTHOR'S PREFACE

Every age has seen some great event that marks the ending of an earlier era, a watershed in history. In the early 21st century, we speak of the time before September 11, 2001, and the changed world since then. For the generations who lived through the early years of the 20th century, the Great War of 1914–18 was their defining catastrophe. Even after a second world war loomed and the Great War had become known as World War I, the events of 1914–18 were seen as the end of an age of innocence, the end of a way of life identified with the 19th century, and the time of transition to the age of modernity. For decades, the phrase *before the war* meant "before 1914," and those words carried echoes of a time that was lost forever.

In retrospect, it became clear that the outcome of World War I planted the seeds of disillusionment and bitterness that led to World War II. All the romantic claims that war was a glorious expression of national loyalty seemed smashed by the senseless slaughter. The ideals for which a generation fought, from God and country to a war to end war and to make the world safe for democracy, seemed overblown, naïve, or simply foolish. Despite widespread disillusionment with patriotism, idealism, and nationalism, the war left legacies of unjust boundary settlements and bitter territorial disputes. The peace settlements fanned the coals of intense national and ethnic hatreds that glowed, ready to flare up into further conflict.

The survivors of World War I left thousands of memoirs and diaries and collections of papers and letters, and historians continued to debate the war's strange origins, gruesome and tragic battles, and lasting legacy of crisis and conflict. Serious scholarship followed on the heels of the personal eyewitness accounts, generating hundreds, then thousands of examinations of every aspect of the war.

Now, in the early 21st century, in our post–September 11 world, as a new generation looks back at World War I, it may begin to ask new questions that amplify and build on the questions asked a few decades ago. The war itself started when a group of seven young terrorists smuggled themselves into Bosnia, then under the jurisdiction of their hated enemy, and targeted Archduke Franz Ferdinand, heir to the Austro-Hungarian throne, in an act of violence. To modern eyes, the terrorists' act of assassinating the archduke as a symbol of the regime they despised has a haunting resemblance to the suicide mission of the 19 young men who, in 2001, attacked America's symbols of power, the World Trade Center and the Pentagon. In 1914, as in 2001, a group of fanatically dedicated youths, acting as part of a broader, international terrorist plot, launched a series of events that changed the world.

Other parallels to the world of the early 21st century abound. As the Great Powers launched into their death struggle, they found allies around the world. As they did so, many of the new allies fought with what we now call asymmetric warfare methods, in which lightly armed insurgent groups or individuals sought to gradually wear down the superior conventional armies of their enemies. The British helped Arabs overthrow the rule of the Ottoman Turks, while Germany tried to help the Irish and the South African Boers rebel against British rule. Germany, England, and Portugal recruited Africans to fight on their side in hit-and-run tactics that bore little resemblance to the head-on conflict between the Great Powers in Europe. The dynamite planted near railroad tracks to destroy Turkish troop trains by T. E. Lawrence and his camel-mounted Arab rebels in 1917 bears a striking, and not altogether accidental, resemblance to the improvised explosive devices planted as roadside bombs in Iraq in 2004 and 2005.

For generations, historians have explored the many ways that the Versailles Peace Treaty at the end of the war sought to reshape the maps of Europe and the Middle East and to impose the cost of the war on Germany and thereby set the stage for World War II. However, long after World War II, many continuing international disputes and smaller wars clearly trace their origins to the raised expectations and failed promises of 1914–18. Middle East conflicts in the 21st century in Iraq, Palestine, and Syria are best understood in the light of British and French efforts to undermine Turkish rule in the region in World War I. The struggle over the doctrine of self-determination of peoples, which seemed so revolutionary in 1918, has continuing echoes in nation after nation around the world as ethnic minorities and religious groups fight, sometimes in costly local wars, to define their own identity in the form of a national political entity. The bombs planted by Basques in Spain, by Irish in Ulster, by Aceh in Sumatra, and by Tamils in Sri Lanka echo the asymmetric techniques and ethnic self-determination goals of that earlier age. Furthermore, in our times, international peacekeepers maintain uneasy calm in Bosnia and Kosovo, at the very heart of the Balkan region that spawned World War I.

Running through the story of World War I is another haunting set of lessons. The generation of senior officers who led troops into that war had been trained in an earlier era, one without submarines, barbed wire, telephones, or dozens of other inventions that changed how war could be fought. The failure of that generation to understand how technology inevitably changes the nature of warfare seems familiar as we see modern armored vehicles destroyed by hand-held weapons and concrete and steel buildings demolished by truckloads of high explosives or airplanes loaded with jet fuel and face the haunting threats of postal envelope–borne anthrax and missile-borne or suitcase-sized nuclear weapons.

Although the war began as a European conflict and its origins can be traced to the uneasy balance of power and the aspirations for national identity among peoples of the Austro-Hungarian Empire, from the perspective of Americans, the causes of the war were quite different. The United States stayed aloof from the conflict from August 1914 to April 1917, generally supporting President Woodrow Wilson's plea for neutrality. Nevertheless, American businessmen and government officials defined that neutrality to mean that the American right to trade with belligerents should continue. As Britain used mines and warships to blockade Germany and as Germany used submarines to try to close off trade with Britain and France, that neutral position of the United States became more and more untenable. For Americans, the story of how the country was taken into World War I requires a focus on the struggle to maintain neutrality in the face of those blockades.

For Europeans, the war lasted four years and cost millions of lives, but for Americans, the war lasted only 19 months and cost less than 110,000 dead. For the families of those who fell and for the additional 200,000 wounded Americans, the war was as deep a personal tragedy as for the European survivors. However, at the end of the war, the most dramatic impact for the American nation as a whole was not the human cost of the war, but the immense social, political, and cultural transformation to a new time. It was difficult to define that new age, and labels abounded, including the Jazz Age, the Lost Generation, and the conservative politicians' term, the New Era.

This book is written for the reader who would like to search out the fundamental questions about the war that have been asked by prior generations, as well as the newer questions that the events of the new and post-9/11 era have raised. In this treatment, the reader will learn how the war started, why its cost in lives was so immense, why the United States became involved, and how the war became the point of origin, not only for World War II, but also for many of the conflicts of the later 20th and early 21st centuries. The national aspirations of the Serbs living under Austro-Hungarian rule, which lay behind the plot of the archduke's assassins, are given new focus here, partly because of contemporary understanding of how a few dedicated young fanatics can alter the course of history and also because the Balkans remain one seat of today's conflicts.

The book is structured like the others in this Eyewitness History series. A narrative chapter is followed by a chronicle of events covered in the chapter, and then by a selection of direct eyewitness testimony, consisting of quotations from participants and observers. The choice of eyewitness accounts includes not only statesmen and cabinet members but also journalists, frontline tourists, soldiers in the field, sailors and survivors of torpedoed ships, and ordinary citizens whose lives were changed by the conflict. Most of these eyewitness selections are long enough to present a complete account of an episode, a typical event, or a crucial turning point. For reference, Appendix A includes a rich selection of official documents that speak to the causes and outcomes of the war, and Appendix B presents biographies of more than 50 individuals who played a role in the events. A short glossary defines some of the technical and informal expressions of the era, and a selection of maps will help in locating some of the battles on land and sea and in identifying the boundary changes that the war brought about. For the student of the war, such materials may present useful starting points for further reading or research into sources.

The vast and still accumulating literature on World War I has evolved in its interpretation, slowly moving away from the prejudices and bitterness of the war to more objective analysis. Immediately after the war, it was difficult for historians writing in the Allied nations to show any understanding for the decisions and methods of the Central Powers, while German memoirists blamed their defeat on betrayal at home, rather than on the illusions or short-sightedness of the officer class. Overlaid with such natural inclinations was the fact that massive amounts of propaganda generated during the war distorted reality, exaggerating the brutality and creating accounts of atrocities that never occurred. Even so, the gruesome and real details of slaughter in the trenches haunted many writings, often making close accounts of the war into convincing arguments that future generations should bend every effort to negotiate settlements and find solutions to international crises short of armed conflict.

Some of the classics and newer historical works that have contributed to the evolving understanding, together with full publication data of included eye-witness quotations, are listed in the bibliography at the end of this volume. As later generations wrote about the war and its aftermath, they reexamined many assumptions, looking more deeply into the issue of war-guilt, the failure of the officer generation of 1914–18 to adjust to the changed nature of the conflict, and the long-range international consequences of the war and the peace conference that followed. The facts of the story are presented here in the light of these deeper understandings developed by scholars over the nearly 100 years since the tragic events began to unfold.

1

The Spark and the Fuel
1903–August 1914

The sun shone down brightly on Sarajevo, Bosnia, on Sunday, June 28, 1914. Archduke Franz Ferdinand, heir to the Habsburg throne of the Austro-Hungarian Empire, together with his wife, Sophie, duchess of Hohenberg, rode in the third car of a seven-car procession from the train station to the town hall. Resplendent and probably a bit warm in his full dress uniform and plume-topped helmet, the archduke graciously waved to the sparse crowds that lined the route. Gavrilo Princip, a Bosnian-born Serb, and six fellow conspirators had stationed themselves along the Appel Quay that fronted on the River Miljacka with plans to assassinate either the Austro-Hungarian governor of the province or the archduke and duchess. Although armed with pistols and small grenade-like bombs (and carrying cyanide suicide pills), the youthful plotters nearly failed in their mission. The first two lost their nerve and did nothing as the caravan passed by. The third would-be assassin, Nedjelko Čabrinović, threw his grenade, but it bounced harmlessly off the back of the archduke's car, then exploded behind, knocking out the oil pan on the following car and slightly injuring an officer.

Čabrinović took his cyanide pill (with a dosage far too small to kill him) and then jumped into the shallow river, where police waded in to pull him out. The procession stopped to examine the damage and observe the arrest. As the archduke's car started up again, the remaining armed youths in the conspiracy stood by, too shocked to fire their guns, and Princip found his line of fire blocked. The archduke arrived at Town Hall, where the mayor, in his prepared remarks, extended the welcome of the citizens of Sarajevo to the visiting dignitaries. Franz Ferdinand at first responded: "To hell with your speech! I have come to visit Sarajevo and am greeted with bombs, it is outrageous." But then he recovered his composure and graciously accepted the welcome.[1]

After the visit to the town hall, the small procession left, with a slight change of route to visit the hospital and check on the injured officer. The archduke's chauffeur, apparently uninformed about the change in plans, made a wrong turn off the quay instead of speeding on to the hospital. As he shifted gears to back up and turn around, the dark-haired and sallow-faced young Princip, who had paused at a café at the corner, found he had a straight shot. Closing his eyes, he fired twice. In those few seconds, the history of the world changed. Both shots

1

This photo shows Sarajevo on the eve of the assassination. Gavrilo Princip fired his pistol at the archduke from a café just to the right of the fourth bridge over the river Miljacka in this prewar view of the city. *(Library of Congress)*

found their mark, one hitting the archduke and the other his wife. Within minutes, by 11:30 A.M., both died.

This event set in motion, over the next month, a steadily mounting crisis that produced, in the first week of August 1914, the Great War, known to later generations as World War I. To many American and Canadian citizens and British subjects, the causes of World War I seemed on the surface to be rather simple. Germany had invaded Belgium and France, and thus became remembered as the aggressor. Britain and Canada came to Belgium's aid, and after Germany extended its aggression to ruthless war at sea, that action involved the United States. But this simple view of the causes of the war begs the question: What led Germany to march into Belgium and France? The German invasion of Belgium and France did not produce the first shot of the war. Indeed, young Princip had fired the first shots on that hot day in June, fully a month before the war. To understand how those first pistol shots led to artillery on the Belgian and French border a month later requires a closer look into affairs in the Balkans.

Moving from the immediate causes to the deeper ones leads beyond individuals to long-range developments that show how rational people could make individual decisions that ultimately produced a war that seemed irrational and wrong-headed even at the time. For the eyewitnesses, as well as for later generations, the tragic events flowed like an irresistible dark river, strange and unstoppable. The statesmen who tried to arrest the flow of tragedies seemed powerless in the face of forces too strong for any individual, and often they too stood by like the crowds in the street, recording their observations as eyewitnesses to what seemed the inevitable flow of history.

Competition for world power between the British Empire and the newly emerging German Empire surely lay at the heart of the problems. More than once through the first decade of the 20th century, the two great powers and their allies almost launched into war over other issues, some of which sprang from the same troubled region of southeastern Europe that included the Balkan province Bosnia and its capital, Sarajevo. Another set of forces put pressures on the political structures of Europe, forces created by the ideology of nationalism and the anarchist doctrine of propaganda by deed that justified direct actions such as assassination to change the course of history. Employing what a later generation would call the asymmetric technique favored by terrorists, powerless youths who resorted to political assassination felt attracted to the possibility that individual acts of violence could provoke governments by generating crises. In southeastern Europe, young terrorists using these methods fought against the rigid political structure of the Habsburg empire, a clumsily built state incapable of resolving the national aspirations of unrepresented peoples.

Several nationalities speaking related languages, known as South Slavs, had their homelands on the Balkan Peninsula, much of it under Habsburg rule. The political ideas that led Gavrilo Princip to fire his pistol on June 28, 1914, and which sparked off the conflagration, derived from the history and politics of the South Slavs, and the changing map of the Balkans. The reasons why a group of Serbian college and secondary-school dropouts stood waiting for the archduke on June 28, 1914, and why their actions sparked the fire are deeply rooted in the prior decades of Balkan history.

Borrowing a term from the Italian movement for national unification in the 19th century, the Serbian-led pan–South Slav movement called itself *irredentism,* referring to the effort to bring fellow nationals living under the rule of foreign states, the "unredeemed," into the same national government. Princip and his fellow conspirators, in the language of the day, believed in propaganda by deed to achieve *irredentist* goals.

EUROPE: THE POWDER KEG

One broader reason why Europe had become an unstable pile of explosive fuel waiting for a spark is found in the position of the German Empire. Germany emerged late as a unified state, one of the last major European powers to form, for the unified German Empire itself dated back only to 1871. German leaders quickly tried to build a world empire that would match those of Britain and France, acquiring through the 1880s and 1890s a string of colonies and overseas possessions in Africa and the Far East and on strategically located Pacific islands.

The empire patched together by Germany ranged from some of the most primitive and undeveloped parts of the world to some very modern and developed regions of Europe. The bits and pieces assembled lay scattered around the globe, some in places overlooked in the earlier grab for territory by Portugal, Spain, Britain, and France. Germany annexed the primitive northeastern quarter of Papua New Guinea, in 1884. And in the same year Germany acquired, by negotiation with the British and French, Togoland and the Cameroons in West Africa and German East Africa, now Tanzania. Germany acquired other colonies by purchase, as for example when Spain, after losing the Philippines and Guam in the Spanish-American War of 1898 to the United States, agreed to sell small holdings of Pacific outposts in the Caroline and Mariana Islands to Germany. German colonists and troops settled another overseas colony, South-West Africa (later known as Namibia), in 1890. In Europe Germany had acquired the formerly French provinces of Alsace and Lorraine in the Franco-Prussian war of 1870–71, a transfer bitterly resented by the French. French desire for revenge and return of the lost provinces remained a threat to Germany through the following decades, and Germany treated the acquired European territories more as colonies than as integrated parts of the German Empire. For the French it added insult to injury to realize that former French citizens in Alsace and Lorraine had been given the same status as tribesmen in South-West Africa or Papua New Guinea.

Britain, France, and Russia viewed the upstart colonial power of Germany with its worldwide and European ambitions as a threat to the status quo. To the east, Germany faced the Russian Empire, and the German province of East Prussia nudged uncomfortably close to the Russian border province of Lithuania.

Britain dominated the high seas, and after 1906, with Britain's construction of the all-big-gun battleship, *Dreadnought,* Germany emulated the design and struggled to catch up. Both nations built more dreadnought-style battleships, as well as fast cruisers and other ships in an arms race. With some justification, the leaders of the German Empire believed they had few friends in Europe and felt hemmed in by potential enemies: France to the west, Russia to the east, and Britain on the oceans. Consequently, Germany entered an alliance with the ungainly Habsburg empire to its south, the Austro-Hungarian Empire with its main capital in Vienna. Italy joined the two empires in the so-called Triple Alliance. But tensions and territorial disputes between Italy and Austria led German leaders to believe that they had to keep a strong relationship with Austria-Hungary or face complete isolation without allies on the continent of Europe. So the German Empire, despite its own superiority, supported the survival of the Habsburg Austro-Hungarian Empire as an aspect of its own strength.

The Austro-Hungarian Empire or Dual Monarchy consisted of an awkward assemblage of governments with a single monarch wearing two crowns: those of emperor of Austria and king of Hungary, under a compromise constitution of 1867. Through the Austrian crown, Franz Josef I ruled the lands on "this side" of the Leitha River, or Cisleithania. In modern geography, these territories include the seven provinces of the Czech Republic, all the provinces of modern Austria, and parts of the modern states of Poland, Ukraine, Slovenia, and Trieste, a province now part of Italy. Out of Budapest in Hungary, or Transleithania, the emperor ruled over the kingdom of Hungary, which included Transylvania (now in Romania), what is now the republic of Slovakia, the kingdom of Croatia and Slovenia, and the separate little state of Rijeka, now called Fiume. The Hungarian side of the empire, with its separate aristocracy and legislature, jealously guarded its claim to a distinct identity from the Austrian side of the empire, making for a clumsy match. The empire directly ran only the Ministries of War, Foreign Affairs, and Finance; all other ministries concerned with internal affairs operated in either Vienna, for the Cisleithenian side, or in Budapest, for the Transleithenian side. The Habsburg empire was not a nation in the modern sense of the word, but a collection of jurisdictions held together by a dual crown.

In 1909, by secret agreement between the military staffs, the German Empire and the Dual Monarchy agreed that the existing purely defensive treaty between the two empires be converted to a treaty of commitment in case either state should initiate an offensive or preemptive war. Oral and written understandings ratified this secret agreement annually through 1914. From the point of view of the Dual Monarchy, such an agreement, coming in 1909, served as a form of insurance against the mounting irredentist troubles encountered on its southern frontier. If any of the crises faced by the Habsburg empire led to war, the assurance that Germany would be an ally strengthened the hand of those in the Habsburg regime who argued for military, rather than diplomatic, solutions to the threats to stability. Later historians made much of the fact that the secret alliance represented a blank check from Germany, guaranteeing support to Austria-Hungary, no matter what crisis the Habsburg empire caused itself. And after Gavrilo Princip killed the archduke and Vienna sought to suppress the Serbs, Germany explicitly reinforced in an official note that it would back the Habsburg decision, confirming the blank check once again.

BACKGROUND OF THE BALKAN CRISIS

As a patchwork of some 15 linguistic groups, many of whom desired their own national identity, the Dual Monarchy grew more unstable in the first decade of the 20th century. Rather than moving in the direction of a multinational federation, the Dual Monarchy attempted to retain the domination of the elites of two groups, Germans in Austria and Magyar-speaking Hungarians in the eastern, Hungarian-ruled part of the empire. The other nationalities ranged from the generally more prosperous and well-educated Czechs, some of whom served in government bureaucratic positions, to mostly peasant populations in outlying regions of the empire, including among smaller groups Italians, Poles, Ukrainians or Ruthenians, Romanians, Bulgarians, Croats, and Serbs.

The province of Bosnia-Hercegovina visited by the crown prince that sunny June day in 1914 had a strange and unique political history, peculiar even in the complex patchwork that made up the Austro-Hungarian Empire. The transfer of the Bosnian province from the Ottoman Empire into the Austro-Hungarian Empire had taken place through two steps, the origins of which go back to a settlement that followed the Balkan War of 1877–78.

In that Balkan war, Russia defeated the Ottomans and imposed a pro-Russian state of Greater Bulgaria that extended through present-day Macedonia and Albania to the Adriatic Sea across from Italy. The next year, however, the Congress of Berlin reduced the territory controlled by Bulgaria. Some of the Bulgarian lands that Russia had joined together into Greater Bulgaria went back under Turkish jurisdiction, with Bosnia and Herzegovina retained under nominal Turkish sovereignty but mandated for military control by the Habsburg empire. Rather than assigning the territory to either the Austrian or Hungarian crown as with the rest of the kingdoms, duchies, counties, and states within the Dual Monarchy, however, the empire decided that Bosnia's civil affairs would be administered by one of the three joint ministries of the empire, the Finance Ministry. Thus, Bosnia-Hercegovina's status within the empire differed from that of all of the other territories of the Dual Monarchy because from 1878 to 1908 the Habsburgs administered that province much like a colony, under the nominal sovereignty of the Ottoman Empire. Things would change in 1908 when Vienna annexed Bosnia-Hercegovina, while still running its civil affairs out of the joint Finance Ministry.

SERBIAN NATIONALISM, IRREDENTISM, AND YOUTHFUL TERRORISTS

Gavrilo Princip was by no means the first Serbian youth who resorted to assassination and terror to draw attention and support to his cause. Serbian nationalism took the violent form chosen by the politically powerless because most Serbs lived under the rule of Turks, Hungarians, or Austrians. Serbs had a long-standing dream to create a united South Slav state that would incorporate all those speaking the Serb language into one nation. But that dream seemed nearly impossible to realize given the powerful governments dedicated to preventing such an outcome.

The small nation of Serbia with its capital in Belgrade had been recognized as a separate and independent state since 1856, but many ethnic Serbs remained under Turkish control in Macedonia. In fact the majority of ethnic Serbs lived outside of Serbia, either under the jurisdiction of the Ottoman Turks or in the jurisdiction of the Dual Monarchy. In the 1878 settlement, the Dual Monarchy retained control over a narrow strip of land that separated two ethnic Serbian nations in order to prevent collaboration and direct contact between the Serbs of the kingdom of Serbia and the principality of Montenegro. That strip pointed like an arrow southward toward Ottoman-controlled Kosovo, the legendary homeland of the Serbs and called by them "Old Serbia." The strategic strip of land, the Sanjak of Novi Pazar, was a sore point with the Serbs, one of many. Serbs protested when Austria began to develop support for a scheme to build a railroad through the sanjak designed to provide a railroad link from Vienna to the Aegean Sea, right through the Serbian heartland and right through the narrow strip that separated Serbia from Montenegro.

The early rise of Serbian nationalism and irredentism, aspiring for national unification of Serbs living under these various jurisdictions, had its beginnings as a reaction to the Berlin Congress of 1878. In that year, Nikola Pašić, a Serbian intellectual living in exile in Switzerland, helped establish the Radical Party in Serbia, devoted to greater Serb nationalism. He aimed for the liberation of Serbs in both the Ottoman and the Austro-Hungarian Empires. As Austrian troops moved into Bosnia following the terms of the Berlin Congress to occupy Bosnia as a mandate, they soon encountered resistance, suffering an estimated 5,000 casualties in the face of guerrilla attacks and snipers. The armed resistance continued in 1882 with a Dalmatian and Bosnian uprising against Austrian occupation of Bosnia-Hercegovina, known as the Upheaval of Civoscie; as a result of the stern measures to repress the insurgents, some 10,000 Serbs emigrated from Bosnia over the border to independent Montenegro.

In 1882, the European powers recognized Serbia as an independent kingdom. In Serbia, two families, the Obrevenovich dynasty and the Karageorgevich dynasty, remained rivals for power, with the Obrevenovich dynasty being somewhat pro-Austrian and the Karageorgevich line more sympathetic to the Radicals and irredentists. In 1885, King Milan (of the Obrevenovich dynasty) proposed the annexation of Serbia to the Habsburg empire, but the empire rejected his proposal. King Milan ruled until 1889 when his son King Alexander succeeded him. In 1900 King Alexander of Serbia married his mistress Draga, one of his mother's former ladies-in-waiting, and a notoriously promiscuous widow. The wedding, as well as the pro-Austrian stand of the Obrevenoviches, angered Serbian army officers as well as the Radicals. Throughout Serbia rumors spread that the ambitious Draga sought promotions and revenues for her relatives, increasing popular discontent with the regime.

The Radical politics of greater Serbian nationalism turned genuinely radical in method in 1903, with the regicide of King Alexander. In addition to the general discontent with King Alexander and his wife, Alexander's 1903 imposition of an autocratic constitution and absolutist rule served to unite a group of plotters behind the idea of a coup. On June 10, 1903, the conspirators, mostly army officers, murdered Alexander and his queen, together with two cabinet ministers, one officer, and two brothers of Queen Draga. The Skupshtina (the Serbian legislature) then installed on the Serbian throne King Peter, from the Karageorgevich dynasty, and granted immunity to the regicides. Peter returned from exile and accepted the crown; he did not overrule the legislative amnesty for the murderers. The targeted murders represented the central act of a successful Serbian nationalist coup d'état.

The army then promoted the regicides, while some officers who had not participated in the coup or who had attempted to warn Alexander of the rumored plot committed suicide. Peter's wife came from the royal family of the Serbian principality of Montenegro, representing a dynastic way of linking the two Serbian states. With a couple of minor interruptions, the Radical Party, under the leadership of Nikola Pašić, formed the cabinet that governed Serbia from 1903 through 1918. Although Pašić disapproved of the violent methods of the regicides, he shared their long-range goal of Serbian unification and the installation of the Karageorgevich dynasty.

So the 1903 Serbian coup represented a major change in the Balkans, both in bringing about more constitutional rule in Serbia and in establishing precedents for larger developments that the coup set in motion. This successful use of assassination in 1903 in gaining the goals of greater Serbian nationalism was well remembered over the next few years. Coupled with the anarchist writings of the Russian Michael Bakunin, who advocated propaganda by deed, the concept of assassination as a means of effecting change had a sort of intellectual underpinning and could serve as a shining example of success, with the nationalist Karageorgevich takeover of Serbia.

King Peter of Serbia dreamed of uniting all Serbs, Croats, and Slovenes in a South Slav national state. *(Library of Congress)*

FROM RESOLUTIONS TO MORE ASSASSINATIONS

Over the following years, pan-Serbian and pan-Jugo Slav or South Slav movements picked up in intensity. Between 1903 and 1914, many episodes, some of them parliamentary and legal in nature and others showing a resort to direct action, demonstrated how enthusiastic Serbian nationalists sought to bring a greater Serbian nation to fruition. In October 1905 the Resolution of Fiume called for unification of the provinces of Dalmatia and Croatia. Then on

Thriving market stalls stand outside the palace in the sleepy provincial city of Zagreb (or Agram), the capital of Croatia. In 1908 the Austro-Hungarian governor, Baron Rauch, arrested members of the legislature here. *(Library of Congress)*

November 18, 1905, a declaration of a meeting at Zara in Dalmatia accepted the Resolution of Fiume on the condition of equality of Serbs and Croats and declared Serbs and Croats one nationality; Croat and Serb parties formed coalitions in both the local legislative bodies in Dalmatia and in Zagreb. In the summer of 1906 delegates who had signed the Fiume and Zara declarations visited Serbia and there they received a warm welcome from a new pan-Serbian organization, Slovenski Jug.

The new Hungarian governor of Croatia, Baron Paul Rauch, imposed absolutist rule to put down anti-Hungarian disturbances that arose from the betrayal of the principles of the Resolution of Fiume and the proposed unification of Dalmatia with Croatia. In the summer of 1908, Governor Baron Rauch arrested 53 Serbian members of the Croatian Diet on grounds of working with Serbia. Some historians have assumed this arrest and the disturbances served as a pretext for the Habsburg decision to change the status of Bosnia-Hercegovina that year to a province of the empire, not merely a Habsburg mandate of an Ottoman province.

As a practical matter, the change meant almost nothing in terms of administration, since the Ottoman Empire had earlier retained only nominal sovereignty over the territory. The same Austrian troops remained, and civil affairs continued to be administered by the Habsburg finance ministry and a Habsburg-appointed governor. Despite the fact that the change of status had little local effect, World War I nearly began in 1908–09 as a result of what newspapers around the world soon called the Bosnian crisis. Serbia used the annexation as grounds for a major international protest, demanding Austria grant Bosnia autonomy and withdraw from the small Novi Pazar strip that barred the way between Serbia and Montenegro. In fact, at a secret meeting earlier in 1908, the Austrian and Russian foreign ministers had agreed to a compromise solution, the annexation of Bosnia to the Dual Monarchy and the Habsburg withdrawal from the Sanjak of Novi Pazar. In exchange for accepting this arrangement, the Russians hoped to gain Austrian support for an agreement allowing Russian warships the right of passage from the Black Sea through the Dardanelles to the Mediterranean Sea. Behind the scenes, Germany, Britain, and France took a hands-off position on the Serbian question.

The Great Powers probably averted a world war in 1908 because Austria did not then have a pledge of support from Germany, acquired only later in 1909. Furthermore, the Russians refused to support Serbia in its demands, so the two adversaries chose not to risk full armed conflict. Nevertheless, world newspapers carried bulletins from the obscure provinces, and attentive readers in New York and London searched their atlases for the location of Belgrade, Sarajevo, and the Sanjak of Novi Pazar. Austria agreed to withdraw from the sanjak and give up its railway scheme to connect Sarajevo south through the strip to link up with Greek railroads. By March 1909 the tempest over the annexation of Bosnia seemed to die away. The Turks accepted a large cash payment, Germany proposed an exchange of notes accepting the change to the 1878 Treaty, and the annexation of Bosnia by the Dual Monarchy went ahead. Bosnia moved out of the headlines, but the Balkans continued to simmer during the next few years.

As result of the 1908 Bosnian crisis and Bosnia's change into a province of the Habsburgs, groups all over Serbia joined a new organization in 1910, Narodna Odbrana (National Defense). Narodna Odbrana, on the surface, seemed to act as a national movement of local committees devoted to raising national consciousness. But behind this innocuous-seeming purpose lay a commitment to use force. The army officers who had participated in the 1903 assassination figured prominently among the new organization's members and helped organize irregular militia groups known as *comitadjis,* ready to take up arms to achieve Serbian goals.

On another level, the Bosnian crisis of 1908–09 helped sow seeds for the later crisis that produced World War I. Italy, which had belonged to a Triple Alliance with Germany and the Dual Monarchy, had reason to be insulted that it had not been informed of the Bosnian annexation ahead of time and feared the extension of Austrian power on the other side of the Adriatic Sea. Russian public opinion simmered as well, as pan-Slavists there claimed that Russia should have backed up Serbia against the extension of Habsburg and Roman Catholic influence among the fellow Slavs of Bosnia.

But the most trouble came among the Slavs of the southern provinces of the Habsburg empire. Over the years 1910–14, the Austro-Hungarian rulers of the various South Slav states under their jurisdiction attempted to control the rising tide of protest. In a vicious cycle, the authoritarian rule provided even more justification to the more radical and conspiratorial of the Serbian nationalists, scattered across provinces ruled by Austria-Hungary: Croatia and Slovenia, Fiume, Dalmatia, Slovenia, and Bosnia-Hercegovina. At the same time, within Serbia itself, those officers who had engaged in the 1903 coup continued to organize, planning to seize the last Ottoman provinces, Kosovo (Old Serbia) and Macedonia, which housed large Serb populations.

The symptoms of the ongoing crisis mounted month by month. In May 1910, agents reported that two assassination plots had been uncovered against Emperor Franz Josef during a planned trip to Bosnia scheduled for May 20 to June 5 of that year. Austrian intelligence attributed one of the plots to South

Slav anarchists, the other to Slovenski Jug, the pan-Serbian secret society. Warned of the plots, the police in Sarajevo carefully cleared the parade route and sealed the windows overlooking it. Franz Josef successfully completed the state visit without incident. However, a few days after his visit, on June 15, 1910, a law student, Bogdan Žerajić, attempted to kill the governor of Bosnia, Feldzeugmeister (General) Marjan Veršanin. The would-be assassin Žerajić then committed suicide. According to a rumor that only enhanced the story of the failed attempt, General Veršanin kicked the corpse of the attempted assassin. Throughout the South Slav provinces, Žerajić instantly won lasting fame as a martyr to the cause. His legend would influence a whole generation of young students, including Gavrilo Princip and others. Princip, on the day before the assassination of Archduke Ferdinand, placed flowers on the grave of his hero, Žerajić.

Eleven months after Žerajić attempt, on May 9, 1911, a group of 10 army officer members of Narodna Odbrana signed the statutes of *Ujedinjenji ili Smrt,* Union of Death. The organization became known to history as Crna Ruka, the Black Hand. The founders of Crna Ruka modeled it on a secret society of 19th-century irredentists in Italy, the Carbonari or charcoal-burners. Within a couple of years, the Black Hand group reputedly controlled the Serbian army, the Serbian frontier guards, and the state police. The organization had the open and explicit goal of uniting Serbs then under foreign rule with Serbia. One of the leaders of the group, Dragutin Dimitrijević, nicknamed Apis, had been a young member of the 1903 conspiratorial plotters who had killed King Alexander. The Black Hand demonstrated its success in gaining influence two years later when Apis became head of intelligence on the Serbian General Staff. In light of the later assassination of the archduke in Sarajevo, the promotion of Apis, a known assassination plotter, to the head of Serbian intelligence struck many close observers of the Balkan scene as quite significant.

As one of its early goals the Black Hand sought to establish contacts with student societies in Bosnia and Herzegovina. The Central Committee of the Black Hand held places for delegates from Bosnia-Hercegovina, Croatia, Dalmatia, the province of Voivodina in Hungary, and from Macedonia and Montenegro, as well as from Serbia. In 1911, the Black Hand established its own newspaper, *Pijemont* or "Piedmont," so named in honor of Italian nationalists, which gave voice to the pan-Serbian movement.

After the December 1911 electoral victory of a Serb-Croat coalition party in Croatia, the new Habsburg governor of that province, Baron Slavko von Cuvaj, banned all political meetings. He soon faced a student uprising, then enhanced by a student sympathy strike in Sarajevo in Bosnia. Among the 20 students expelled for participating in the strike in Sarajevo, Gavrilo Princip gave up school and moved to Belgrade where he attempted to continue his studies. In Serbia, Princip tried to join the Serbian paramilitary organization that operated guerrilla raids into Ottoman-controlled Macedonia, and, according to his own testimony, Princip received training in one of those free corps or *comitadji,* before being turned down as too young and inexperienced at age 16. A delegation of student strikers from Croatia visited Belgrade, where Apis of the Black Hand showed them around, and where the *Pijemont* published inflammatory eulogies to the earlier martyred but unsuccessful assassin Žerajić.

In the light of such developments and many other signs of unrest, the Austrian government suspended the local constitution in Croatia early in 1912, and

In this photo, newsmen interview Serbian-American volunteers aboard ship in New York Harbor. They were about to depart to serve in the First Balkan War. *(Library of Congress)*

Governor Cuvaj ruled by decree there. That summer, he faced an attempted assassination by a Croat student from Bosnia, Luka Jukić, who killed a policeman in the attempt. Jukić came to trial in the summer of 1912. Defiant in the face of his conviction, he used the trial as a forum to cry for Serbian liberty.

BALKAN WARS

In 1912 and 1913, the success of Serbia in two Balkan wars further emboldened not only the officials of the Serbian state but also their fellow nationals who remained under the control of Vienna, Budapest, and Constantinople. In the First Balkan War of 1912–13, Bulgaria, Serbia, Montenegro, and Greece allied to drive out the Turks from their European holdings, pushing them back to Edirne (Adrianople) in Thrace. Serbs throughout the southern provinces of the Austro-Hungarian Empire celebrated the Serb advances and many crossed the porous frontiers to join the advancing armies. Aided by the flood of volunteers, Serbs occupied territory all the way to the Albanian coast and the port of Durazzo (Durrës, the port serving Tirana, the capital of modern Albania), but they had to pull back after pressure from European powers. Bulgaria got as its booty the province of Macedonia, which did not sit well with the Serbs or the Greeks who rankled at seeing fellow nationals fall under Bulgarian rule.

In the Second Balkan War, of February–May 1913, the Serbs, Romanians, and Greeks defeated their former ally, the Bulgarians. As a consequence of this war, the winners divided Macedonia between Greece and Serbia; Bulgarian nationalists felt stunned and embittered at the loss of that province. In the two back-to-back Balkan Wars, Serbia had made the gains that the Radical Party, Slovenski Jug, Narodna Odbrana, and the Black Hand had been demanding. It seemed to such advocates that Greater Serbia came closer to realization through these short and successful wars.

THE ARCHDUKE'S TRIP TO SARAJEVO

In September 1913 Archduke Franz Ferdinand, who had recently been appointed as inspector general of the Austrian army, began to plan his ill-fated trip to Bosnia, where he intended to inspect the corps of Austrian troops and observe their maneuvers. He hoped to raise the morale of the troops in the Bosnian outpost and sought to marshal some local support and popular enthusiasm for the Austrian presence in the face of local Serbian discontent. A royal progress had become a tried and true means of whipping up supporters through the simple public relations method of getting a crowd to watch the spectacle.

The local governor, Oskar Potiorek, set up the agenda for the trip. He, like the authorities in Vienna, believed that the display of the imperial presence with a parade and reception in Sarajevo would help unite local Muslims behind the monarchy and would serve to offset the troublesome Serbian nationalist sentiment. Potiorek did not call up the same degree of security as had been used during the state visit of Franz Josef in the summer of 1910, which had foiled two assassination attempts against the emperor on that visit. Franz Ferdinand himself thought that traveling in an open car and waving to welcoming crowds might have a better effect on public opinion than would a trip behind masses of armed guards. After all, excessive security forces could tarnish any hopes of using the state visit as a demonstration to the local population of the personal power of the Crown.

On May 28, 1914, three of the young would-be assassins, Princip, Čabrinović, and Grabež, traveled by river steamer from Belgrade part way to Sarajevo, carrying bombs, pistols, and cyanide obtained in Serbia. After dropping Čabrinović for being too talkative to strangers, the other two continued on foot, sneaking at night across the border into Bosnia with the connivance of border guards. After several meetings and some target practice with the unfamiliar weapons, the assassins were waiting in place with their fellow plotters in Sarajevo by mid-June.

FROM SARAJEVO TO EUROPE

Following the assassination of Franz Ferdinand and Sophie on June 28, 1914, authorities in Sarajevo and in the capitals of Europe reacted with shock and horror, which soon turned into a growing recognition that the event might provoke another Balkan crisis. From the point of view of newspaper readers in New York and London, however, the events may have seemed familiar—probably, they assured each other, just another dustup in the Balkans. After the 1903 assassination of King Alexander, obscure debates over the Sanjak of Novi Pazar, the 1908 takeover of Bosnia by the Dual Monarchy, minor riots and student strikes, and the short and bloody Balkan Wars of 1912 and 1913, British and American readers probably grew used to the idea that Serbia and its neighbors would make the headlines for a few weeks, then recede again.

Behind the scenes, however, this Balkan crisis rapidly matured into something much more dangerous. One of the reasons lay in the secret 1909 agreement between the German Empire and the Habsburg empire that each would come to the other's assistance, not only in a defensive war, but also in case either made a preemptive strike on another nation. With this blank check, the Dual Monarchy could use the assassination as the tool to finally suppress Serbian irredentism, not only in its South Slav provinces but also by striking at Serbia itself.

In Bosnia, a rather slow and amateurish investigation by a local judge, Leon Pfeffer, into the assassination soon revealed that Princip and Čabrinović had worked with other accomplices. Although the young men did not at first come forth with much information, authorities rounded up all seven, most of them under 20 years of age: Trifko Grabež, Nedjelko Čabrinović, Gavrilo Princip, Danilo Ilić, Veljko Čubrilović, Miško Joavanović, and Jakov Milović. Looking back, the authorities realized the assassination was part of a broader scheme of terrorism—at least the fifth attempt at an assassination by South Slav nationalists in four years. There had been two planned against Franz Josef in June 1910, and there had been the martyred attempt by Bogdan Žerajić against Bosnian governor Veršanin. Then in 1912 Luka Jukić, the Croat student from Bosnia, had tried to kill the governor of Croatia, Cuvaj. The murder of the archduke and the duchess may have seemed like isolated events to distant observers who did not follow Balkan affairs closely, but to the authorities in Vienna, the killings clearly seemed part of a pattern of terrorist acts.

The recent promotion of Apis, who had been one of the officers who killed King Alexander and was a cofounder of the Black Hand, to the position of head of Serbian Intelligence certainly looked suspicious. When investigators learned that some of the youths involved in the assassination had acquired their weapons in Serbia and that they had crossed with the weapons from Serbia to Bosnia under the noses of Serbian border guards, the connection to the Serbian government seemed at least plausible. What a later generation would call state-sponsored terrorism lay behind the killing of the archduke, at least in the firm opinion of the government of the Dual Monarchy.

The assassins had been armed and otherwise supported by officers in the Serbian army, known members of the Black Hand. The assassins supported the explicit political goals of all of the irredentist movements, from the Serbian Radical Party, which used parliamentary methods, through Slovenski Jug and Narodna Odbrana to the murderous Black Hand. By July 23, the Habsburg Imperial Crown Council decided to send an official diplomatic note to Serbia that could result in war, that is, a note with an ultimatum including at least one clause to which the Serbs might not be able to agree. At the time, however, many critics in Britain and France believed that the Austrians lied when they charged the Serbian government and Black Hand with involvement in the assassination. Many viewed the claims as false propaganda cooked up by Vienna to provide an excuse for war. Austria took the official position that it simply could not tolerate a small and warlike country on its southern borders harboring and training terrorists who would cross into Austrian territory to kill the heir to the imperial throne. If the conspirators went unpunished, who knew what could happen next among Poles, Czechs, Ruthenians, and even Italians living under Habsburg rule?

On July 23, Austria issued its ultimatum to Serbia, giving the Serbs 48 hours to agree to all demands. The ultimatum demanded suppression of nationalist groups and Austrian presence in an investigation into the linkages between Serbian security forces and the assassins. By this action Austria set the date of the war. The German government, which received a copy of the note 24 hours into the 48-hour period, took no action to stop its ally.

Historians have explored in depth why the Austrian government took such a provocative step, knowing it would probably precipitate a war against Serbia and probably also war against Serbia's self-appointed protector, Russia. Some students of the subject have regarded the steps as mistakes in judgment by Austrian leaders. However, in light of the difficulty of controlling the southern provinces of the empire and the activities of assassins there, the link of the assassination to authorities in Belgrade provided Habsburg leadership with just the precipitating cause for the decisive move, apparently with justice on its side, that it sought.

In a deeper sense, the leap to war derived from the long-running social, constitutional, and political crisis that, after 40 or more years in the making, had brought the Habsburg empire to a fragile state. If irredentism unraveled Austrian control of the Balkans, soon the centrifugal forces of national aspirations could pull the other restless national groups out of the Habsburg orbit and destroy the empire. From the point of view of Germany, such a collapse would mean the end of its only solid ally in Europe. The state that harbored and armed the assassins deserved to be punished, if not destroyed, or so the leadership in Vienna and Berlin believed.

Serbian Americans hoped to rally American support for their cause, with a poster showing soldiers and refugees together. *(Library of Congress)*

On July 25, with one hour to go in the ultimatum period, Serbia accepted all but one clause (Article 6) of the ultimatum. Article 6 required Austrian presence in the investigation and trial of any Serbian officers found to support the Bosnian conspirators. This request, the official Serb reply politely indicated, would violate the Serbian constitution. Receiving and reading the note, Baron Vladimir Giesl, the Austrian ambassador to Serbia, following instructions, left Belgrade, breaking off diplomatic relations. That evening, Austria issued its mobilization order, bringing its troops to high alert and calling up reserves. Three days later, on July 28, the Austro-Hungarian Empire declared war against Serbia and started shelling Belgrade across the Danube River from the Hungarian side on July 29.

The alliances that had represented the balance of power in Europe and that had been designed to preserve the peace now served to throw the continent into a death grip. Declarations of war fell like dominoes over the following week. Berlin, Vienna, and St. Petersburg rejected last-minute efforts to resolve the crisis by negotiation as suggested by different statesmen including the British foreign minister, Edward, Lord Grey. Between July 28 and August 4 the mobilizations of troops and then declarations of war blared forth in the headlines. The rapid sequence of war declarations suggests that all the great powers in Europe, not only Germany and the Dual Monarchy, were eager for an excuse to go to war.

In Paris and Vienna, people accepted the mobilization with stoic resolve and sometimes with warm displays of national feeling. Eyewitnesses noted the quiet patriotism of the crowds, and the eager support of the troops who left behind their sweethearts and wives to march to band music and board the trains for the mobilization points. The irresistible flow to war began.

On August 1, Germany declared war on Russia and Russia on Germany. Knowing that France had a commitment by alliance to come to Russia's aid, Germany immediately demanded that the Belgians allow passage of their troops through Belgium to the French border. Under the Schlieffen Plan, the German war plan to be invoked in case of war with France, which had been spelled out in detail before 1906, the army would skirt the heavy French defenses on the French–German border by passing to the west through Belgium and Luxembourg. Although Schlieffen's successor, Count Helmuth von Moltke, had modified the plan, he retained the concept of the flanking sweep in a bold attack through Belgium, which German leaders agreed seemed the best way to achieve a quick victory against France. When the Belgians refused passage, Germany anticipated that it would be simple to march through Belgium with or without that consent. On August 2, German troops moved through Luxembourg.

On August 3 Germany declared war on France and the next day invaded Belgium. Ruled by a politically divided group of cabinet ministers, Britain wavered for a few hours and then declared war on Germany late on August 4, on the grounds of a long-standing pledge to protect Belgian sovereignty. As their first action, the British mounted the British Expeditionary Force (B.E.F.), an 80,000-man group of four divisions of highly trained troops, and readied them for transport to France and Belgium. In light of the fact that the Germans had committed more than 150 divisions to the western front, the British effort seemed only a token commitment to the cause of both Belgium and France, yet it had a symbolic and strategic importance, even if not likely in itself to stem the German advance.

Historians have speculated that even if the assassins in Sarajevo had failed in their attempt, some other precipitating crisis would have been enough at some point in mid- or late 1914 to start the conflagration. But in fact, as a result of the June 28 assassination on the Appel Quay in Sarajevo, within a little more than five weeks, the guns of August had sounded. They would not fall silent for another four years.

CHRONICLE OF EVENTS

1903

Deputies from Dalmatia and Istria ask for an audience with Emperor Franz Josef I to protest the policies of the Hungarian governor of Croatia, Count Khuen Hédeváry. Khuen is replaced.

Macedonian uprising against the Turks is suppressed.

King Alexander imposes an autocratic constitution and absolutist rule in Serbia.

June 10: Officer conspiracy successfully stages coup in Serbia; the officers murder King Alexander and Queen Draga; the Skupshtina (Serbian legislature) installs King Peter.

1905

October: The "Resolution of Fiume" calls for unification of Dalmatia and Croatia.

November 18: Declaration of Zara is issued in Dalmatia, accepting the Resolution of Fiume on condition of equality of Serbs and Croats and declaring Serbs and Croats to be one nationality. Croat and Serb parties form coalitions in both Dalmatia and in Zagreb, Croatia.

1906

In the so-called Pig War between the Dual Monarchy and Serbia over customs, Vienna refuses to accept live cattle imports into the Habsburg empire from Serbia.

The new governor of Croatia, Baron Paul Rauch, imposes absolutist rule to put down anti-Hungarian disturbances that derive from the betrayal of the principles of the Resolution of Fiume and the rejection of the proposed unification of Dalmatia with Croatia.

February: The emperor dissolves the Hungarian parliament unconstitutionally, then accepts reinstatement of the oligarchic electoral system, as a way of winning support for the future annexation of Bosnia-Hercegovina.

summer: Delegate signatories of the Fiume and Zara declarations visit Serbia and are warmly received by new pan-Serbian organization, Slovenski Jug.

1908

summer: The absolutist regime in Croatia arrests 53 Serbian members of the Croatian Diet on grounds of working with Serbia, setting a pretext for the takeover of Bosnia-Hercegovina.

fall: In the "Bosnian crisis" Serbia and Austria nearly go to war; Russia refuses to support Serbia; Austria declares sovereignty over Bosnia-Hercegovina, previously a mandate with military occupation since 1878 at the Congress of Berlin, while the Ottoman Empire had retained nominal suzerainty over the territory.

fall: As result of the Bosnian crisis, a group of Serbian officers, made up of those who had participated in the 1903 coup, form a paramilitary and broad-based organization known as Narodna Odbrana (National Defense—or People's Defense).

1909

In Croatia, 53 legislators are tried in a manifestly corrupt trial.

By secret agreement between their military staffs, Germany and Austria-Hungary agree that the purely defensive treaty between the two empires be converted to a treaty of commitment in case either state should initiate an offensive or preemptive war. This agreement is ratified by oral and written understandings annually through 1914. The treaty emboldens the war party in Vienna. This is the so-called Blank Check of Germany to Austria.

March 4: Serbia backs down under Russian pressure after Vienna drops claim to Novi Pazar and Serbia drops demand for Bosnian autonomy, ending the Bosnian crisis.

March 25: Dr. Heinrich Friedjung publishes charges in *Neue Freie Presse,* a Viennese newspaper, that members of the Serbo-Croat coalition in the Croatian parliament were acting as agents of the Serbian government.

1910

In a libel trial held in Vienna against historian Friedjung, the plaintiffs prove their innocence and demonstrate that the documentary evidence against them had been fabricated by the Austrian minister to Belgrade, Count Forgach. Forgach is promoted.

May: Two assassination plots against Emperor Franz Josef are reported on his planned trip to Bosnia scheduled May 20–June 5; one plot is attributed to South Slav anarchists, the other to Slovenski Jug (the Serbian secret society).

June 15: Law student Bogdan Žerajić attempts to kill the governor of Bosnia, Feldzeugmeister Marjan Veršanin, then commits suicide. He is later regarded as a martyr to the cause. Others later claim he sought to kill the emperor. His legend influences Princip and others.

Sarajevo, in Bosnia, was peaceful before the Great War, but with trouble brewing beneath the surface. *(Library of Congress)*

1911

May 9: A subgroup of 10 officers of Narodna Odbrana signs the statutes of *Ujedinjenji ili Smrt* (Union of Death), later known as the Crna Ruka, the Black Hand. Black Hand officers hold key positions in the Serbian army, as frontier guards, and as police, with the goal of uniting Serbs now under foreign rule with Serbia.

May 10: Austria appoints Feldzeugmeister Oskar Potiorek as governor of Bosnia-Hercegovina to replace Marjan Veršanin. Potiorek urges a visit from the archduke to help solidify popular support, despite warnings from others.

September 3: New newspaper appears in Belgrade, *Pijemont,* reflecting the position of, and financed by, the Black Hand.

December: Serb-Croat coalition party wins electoral victory in Croatia. In response, the new governor, Baron Slavko von Cuvaj, bans all political meetings.

1912

Lord Haldane offers to arrange an Anglo-German rapprochement, but it fails.

January 31: Student uprisings break out in Croatia against Governor von Cuvaj.

February 18–19: Student uprisings take place in Sarajevo, Bosnia, in support of students in Croatia. Gavrilo Princip is expelled along with 19 others.

spring: 150 students from Croatia, hosted by the Black Hand, are welcomed at the Officer's Club in Belgrade. The Black Hand newspaper, *Pijemont,* publishes eulogies to Bogdan Žerajić, attempted assassin of Bosnian governor.

April 4: Austria suspends the constitution in Croatia. Governor von Cuvaj rules by decree.

June 8: Luka Jukić, Croat student from Bosnia, attempts to kill the governor of Croatia, Cuvaj. He fails but kills a policeman and wounds others.

August: Luka Jukić, along with 11 other young men, is brought to trial. Jukić is found guilty.

fall: Princip attempts to volunteer for *comitadjis,* the irregular Serbian military force commanded by Black Hand officers, headed by one of the 1903 regicides. Princip is rejected.

October: First Balkan War begins. Balkan countries (Bulgaria, Serbia, Montenegro, Greece) drive the Turks back to Edirne in Thrace.

1913

Dragutin Dimitrijević (Apis), one of the 1903 regicides and cofounder of the Black Hand, is appointed head of intelligence on the Serbian General Staff.

First Balkan War ends.

High school of Mostar in Bosnia is closed for a whole year due to student strike.

February–March: Archduke Franz Ferdinand agrees to the agenda set by Bosnian governor Potiorek for a visit to Sarajevo in June. Potiorek does not mount the same degree of security as used during the state visit of Franz Josef in the summer of 1910.

February–May: Second Balkan War is fought in which Serbs, Romanians, and Greeks defeat the Bulgarians. Serbia makes the gains that are the object of the Radical Party, Slovenski Jug, Narodna Odbrana, and Black Hand.

September: Archduke Franz Ferdinand, recently appointed as inspector general of the Austrian army, plans a trip to inspect the corps of troops and its maneuvers in Bosnia to raise morale.

1914

May 28: Princip, Čabrinović, and Grabež travel by river steamer from Belgrade partway to Sarajevo, carrying bombs, pistols, and cyanide obtained in Serbia. Two continue on foot after sneaking across the border with the connivance of border guards.

June 28: Austrian archduke Franz Ferdinand is assassinated by a group headed by Princip in Sarajevo, Bosnia. The assassins appear to have been armed by officers in the Black Hand. Suspicion immediately centers around Apis, head of Serbian Intelligence and a leader in the Black Hand.

June 28–July 9: Local judge Leon Pfeffer investigates Princip and other assassins.

July 7: The Imperial Crown Council decides to send a note to Serbia. It includes stiff demands.

July 11–13: Friedrich von Weisner, Austrian representative, visits Sarajevo to report on the progress of the investigation. He sends a mixed report on Serbian complicity.

July 13–23: During this period, the Austrian prime minister Count Tisza decides to send a note that the Serbs cannot accept. Whether it was intentionally written to be unacceptable remains a subject of historical debate.

July 20–23: French president Raymond Poincaré visits St. Petersburg on a previously scheduled state visit.

July 23: Austria issues a 48-hour ultimatum to Serbia demanding suppression of nationalist groups. By this action Austria sets the date of the war.

July 25: Serbia accepts all of the ultimatum but one clause, which Serbs claim would violate the Serbian constitution.

July 25: Baron Vladimir Giesl (Austrian ambassador to Serbia) leaves Belgrade, breaking off diplomatic relations.

July 25: Austria issues mobilization order.

July 28–August 4: Following the Austro-Hungarian declaration of war against Serbia, the alliances are invoked and multiple declarations of war immediately follow. The shooting war begins on the western front on August 4.

July 28: Austria-Hungary declares war on Serbia. Serbia declares war on Austria-Hungary in return.

July 29: Austrians bombard Belgrade.

July 31: British foreign minister Edward Grey proposes a conciliation plan to involve a five-power conference, which is rejected in Vienna.

July 31: Germany demands that Russia demobilize its fleet and army.

August 1: France orders general mobilization.

August 1: Germany declares war on Russia because Russia did not respond to ultimatum to demobilize.

August 1: Germany begins mobilization.

August 2: Germany issues a 12-hour ultimatum, delivered at 7 P.M. to Belgium, to allow German passage to France. Germany invades Luxembourg, implementing the Schlieffen Plan.

August 3: 7:00 A.M. The Belgian reply is "no!" Germany declares war on France.

August 4: 8:02 A.M. German troops cross into Belgium. That evening Britain declares war on Germany for violating Belgian neutrality.

August 6: Austria declares war on Russia.

Eyewitness Testimony

There were a number of us. Whether it was I or another who fired the first shot is simply conjecture. The chief point for us is that our work was successful. We have rendered the Fatherland a tremendous service, and we are highly satisfied at our success. The first shot at [General Lazar] Petrovich [the king's adjutant] was from the revolver of Capt.[Milan] Ristice, who is a noted marksman. Petrovich was hit in the forehead and fell dead instanteaneously.

Lieutenant Colonel Alexander Misitch, one of the leaders of the coup and successful assassination that deposed King Alexander, from a Berlin report of June 12, 1903, quoted by the New York Times, Details of the Belgrade Tragedy, *June 13, 1903, p. 1.*

It is true that my partisans have a complete organization in Servia, with which I am in frequent communication. I know from other sources that the discontent of the Servian people had reached its height, but I could not possibly have foreseen the events of the other night. I in no way contributed to their preparation, and I took no part, direct or indirect, in them. On the contrary their perpetration surprised me.... I was first informed of the royal tragedy enacted at Belgrade the following morning by a telegram from a cousin of mine in Vienna. Later a Montenegro friend confirmed the news, which till then I had regarded as quite unofficial. I have received numerous messages of congratulation, but that is all. I calmly await the trend of events. So long as no formal proposals reach me I have no reason to leave Geneva, and I will remain here. No one has yet asked me to return to Servia. No one has yet offered me the crown. I am even without news of the members of my family, who reside in Belgrade. My opinion of the execution of the King and Queen of Servia is this. I deeply regret that it has been thought necessary to shed streams of blood. I formally disapprove of the violent measures, and I especially deplore the fact that the army has had recourse to such measures—an army which has nobler tasks to accomplish than assassination. It would have sufficed to force King Alexander to sign his abdication. He could have been bound, as has been done in other circumstances. It is a horrible thing to shed blood.... Regarding foreign relations, it has been alleged that I am systematically hostile to Austria. That is false. May be I am in special sympathy with Russia, to which

country, I sent my boy in the hope that he would take service there.

Prince Peter Karageorgevich, to be chosen as king of Serbia on June 15, 1903, on hearing of the coup d'état and murder of King Alexander of Serbia in Belgrade, in a statement issued from his home in Geneva, Switzerland, on June 13, 1903, as quoted in the New York Times, *in "Interview with the New king of Servia," June 13, 1903, p. 1.*

It has been well known that there have been two parties in Servia, the one struggling to maintain King Alexander on the throne, and the other to set up somebody else. The advocates of the pretender's claims have been occupying practically the same position as the Carlists in Spain. They have naturally been working to bring about their ends, but that they would resort to such tactics was never dreamed of.... No countries in Europe are more desirous of having peace in Servia than Russia and Austria. In fact, all the countries of Europe would pre-

Kaiser Wilhelm reassured his fellow emperor, Franz Josef of Austria-Hungary, of his support in dealing with the troublesome South Slav provinces. *(Library of Congress)*

fer to see conditions peaceful in Servia. . . . The nations of Europe don't think [Servia] worth gobbling [up]. However, the questions of Servia never will be settled until all the nations have a part in its solving. Peace will be kept just now, anyway. There is nothing for the powers to do over the present crisis in the country's affairs except to let it go, although taking good care that peace is maintained. A European war would be too great and terrible a thing to start of an affair like this.

U.S. ambassador to Austria-Hungary Bellamy Storer, giving his views on the coup d'état in Serbia that deposed and killed King Alexander, as quoted in an interview in the New York Times, *"Bellamy Storer's Views," June 14, 1903, p. 11.*

Dear Franzi,
The Slav danger has revealed itself amazingly in its delusions and violence within the last months. According to your presentation Belgrade and Prague conspire on the basis of a fixed programme. . . . Behind both of them stands Moscow; how far Cracow and Lemberg are in the game I cannot judge. But apparently the Pan Slav danger is the greater one for Austria, since it pulls the lever in your own country through the Czechs. . . . It endangers the preservation of the Monarchy because she has recently incorporated Slavonic lands, and thus is in the process of becoming a second Slavonic Great Power.

Kaiser Wilhelm in a letter to Emperor Franz Josef, February 12, 1909, regarding the Balkan Crisis, quoted in Lavender Cassels, The Archduke and the Assassin, *p. 98.*

Two months ago . . . on the opening day of the Diet of Bosnia and Herzegovina, a young Servian, the student Bogdan Žerajić, made an attempt in Sarajevo to kill the Governor of Bosnia and Herzegovina, General Marian Veresanin. Žerajić fired five shots at this renegade, who had assured his career by pouring out the blood of his brothers in the famous insurrection in Rakovica, but owing to a remarkable accident, did not succeed in killing him. Whereupon the brave and composed Žerajić fired the sixth and last bullet through his own head, and immediately fell dead. In Vienna, they know very well that it was not the reading of Russian and revolutionary writings which had induced Žerajić to make this attempt, but that he acted thus as the noble scion of a race which wished to protest against foreign rule in this bloody way. . . . In Vienna, it was desired that every

memory of Žerajić should be extinguished, and that no importance should be attached to his attempt; but just this fear of the dead Žerajić, and the prohibition against mentioning his name throughout Bosnia and Herzegovina, brought it about that his name is spoken among the people as something sacred today, on the 18th of August, perhaps more than ever.

Editorial in Politika *(a Serbian newspaper), August 18, 1910, quoted in Supplement I, Opinions of the Serbian Press,* The Austro-Hungarian Red Book, *in* Collected Diplomatic Documents Relating to the Outbreak of the European War, *p. 472.*

The investigation of Jukic's assassination attempt in Agram has led to the discovery of a secret South Slav youth organisation extending throughout Croatia and Dalmatia and possibly into Bosnia. The statutes of this organisation, which were drawn up in 1909, are not subversive, but during the past year schoolboys in Dalmatia have formed a new secret revolutionary off shoot of it—"Jugoslavia"—whose declared objective is the establishment of a republican state consisting of Croatia, Dalmatia, Bosnia, Hercegovina and Macedonia, in conjunction with Serbia and Montenegro.

Col. Karl Bardolff, in a memorandum, August 1912, to Franz Ferdinand, quoted in Lavender Cassels, The Archduke and the Assassin, *p. 134.*

Already in the First Balkan War I could have let it come to an European war, in order to acquire Bosnia and Herzegovina: but as I feared that we should then be forced to make large concessions to Bulgaria in Macedonia, I wanted first of all to secure the possession of Macedonia for Serbia and only then to proceed to the acquisition of Bosnia.

Nikola Pašić, prime minister of Serbia, in a note to the Serbian chargé d'affaires in Berlin, following the March 1913 peace conference that ended the Second Balkan War, quoted in Sidney Bradshaw Fay, The Origins of the World War, *vol. I, p. 446.*

Five years ago today an imperial decree extended the sovereignty of the Habsburg sceptre over Bosnia and Herzegovina. The Servian people will feel for decades yet the grief that was that day inflicted on them. Shamed and shattered, the Servian people groaned in despair. The people vow to take vengeance in attaining freedom by a heroic step. This day has aroused the energy that had already sunk to sleep, and soon the refreshed here will strive for freedom. Today when Servian graves adorn the ancient Servian territories, when the Servian cavalry has trod the battlefields of Macedonia and old Servia [Kosovo], the Servian people having ended their task in the South turn to the other side, whence the groans and tears of the Servian brother are heard, and where the gallows has its home. The Servian soldiers who today in Dušan's kingdom fight those Albanians who were provoked against us by the state which took Bosnia and Herzegovina from us, vowed to march against "the second Turkey" [i.e., Austria-Hungary] even as with God's help they had marched against the Balkan Turkey. They make this vow and hope that the day of revenge is drawing near. One Turkey vanished. The good Servian God will grant that the "second Turkey" will vanish too.

Editorial in Pijemont *(organ of the Black Hand), October 8, 1913, quoted in Supplement I, Opinions of the Serbian Press,* The Austro-Hungarian Red Book, *reprinted in* Collected Diplomatic Documents Relating to the Outbreak of the European War, *pp. 474–475.*

I do not remember whether it was at the end of May or the beginning of June, when one day, Mr. Pašić said to us (he conferred on these matters more particularly with Stojan Protitch, who was then Minister of the Interior; but this much he said to the rest of us) that certain persons were making ready to go to Sarajevo to murder Franz Ferdinand who was to go there to be solemnly received on St. Vitus' Day. As they told me afterwards, this plot was hatched by a group of secretly organized persons and by patriotic Bosno-Hercegovinian students in Belgrade. M. Pašić and the rest of us said, and Stojan agreed, that he should issue instructions to the frontier authorities on the Drina [River] to prevent the crossing over of the youths who had already set out from Belgrade for that purpose. But the frontier "authorities" themselves belonged to the organization, and did not carry out Stojan's instructions, but reported to him (as he afterwards told us) that the instructions had reached them too late, because the youths had already crossed over.

Recollection of Ljuba Jovanovitch, Serbian minister of Education (and cofounder of the Black Hand) regarding foreknowledge of the assassination plot by Serbian officials in early June 1914, published in a 1924 Serbian journal, and because of its sensational nature, reprinted in English publications in 1925, quoted in Sidney Bradshaw Fay, The Origins of the World War, *vol 2, p. 62.*

Your Imperial and Royal Highness! Your Highness! Our hearts are filled with joy over your most gracious visit. . . . Your Highnesses can read in our countenances our feelings of love and devotion, unshakeable loyalty and obedience to His Majesty our Emperor and King. . . . All the citizens of Sarajevo, overwhelmed with happiness, greet your Highnesses' most illustrious visit with the utmost enthusiasm, convinced that Your Highnesses' stay in our beloved city of Sarajevo will still further increase Your Highnesses' most gracious interest in our progress and well being, and deepen that gratitude and loyalty which is for ever rooted in our hearts.

Speech by Mayor Fehim Čurčić to Franz Ferdinand and Sophie at town hall, Sarajevo, after the first assassination attempt had failed, June 28, 1914, as cited in Lavender Cassels, The Archduke and the Assassin, *p. 176.*

What moved me primarily was revenge for the oppression which the Serbs in Bosnia and Herzegovina had had to suffer, especially the "Exceptional Laws" which last year continued for two full months. . . . I regarded revenge as the holy duty of a moral civilized man, and therefore I planned to take vengeance. . . . I knew that there existed at the Ballplatz [the Austro-Hungarian Foreign Office] a clique, the so called war-party, which wanted to conquer Serbia. At its head stood the Heir to the Throne. I believed that I should take vengeance on them all in taking vengeance on him . . . I hated him because he was an enemy of Serbia. . . . All the injustices of which I read in the newspapers—all this had collected in me until it burst forth on St. Vitus's Day.

Confession of Nedjelko Čabrinović, assassination plot member, referring to motives on June 28, 1914, cited in Sidney Bradshaw Fay, The Origins of the World War, *vol 2, p. 130.*

As the car quickly reversed a thin stream of blood spurted out of his Imperial Highness's mouth on to my right cheek. With one hand I got out my handkerchief to wipe the blood from the Archduke's face, and as I did so Her Highness called out, "In God's name what has happened to you?" Then she collapsed, her face between the Archduke's knees. I had no idea that she was hit and thought she had fainted from fear. His Imperial Highness then said, "Sopherl! Sopherl! Don't die! Live for my children." I took hold of the collar of his tunic in order to prevent his head sinking forward and asked him "Is

Your Imperial Highness in great pain?" He answered distinctly "It is nothing." Then he turned his face a little to one side and said six or seven times, more faintly as he began to lose consciousness, "It is nothing." There was a very brief pause, then the bleeding made him choke violently, but this stopped when we reached the Konak.

Deposition by Count Franz Harrach, a member of Franz Ferdinand's entourage, who had been riding on the running board of the car in which Franz Ferdinand was assassinated, June 28, 1914, cited in Lavender Cassels, The Archduke and the Assassin, *p. 179.*

About 5 P.M. an official from the Press Bureau rang me up on the telephone and told me what had happened that morning at Sarajevo. Although I knew what was being prepared there, yet, as I held the receiver, I felt as though someone had dealt me an unexpected blow; and a little later, when the first news was confirmed from other quarters, I began to be overwhelmed with grave anxiety. I did not doubt for a moment that Austria-Hungary would make this the occasion for a war on Serbia. I saw that the position of our Government and our country in regard to the other Powers would now become very difficult, in every way worse than after [June 11, 1903, the day of the assassination of King Alexander], or than at the time of our later conflicts with Vienna and Budapest. I was afraid that all the European Courts would feel themselves the targets of Princip's bullets, and would turn away from us with the approval of the monarchist and conservative elements in their countries. And even if it did not come to that, who would dare to defend us? I knew that neither France, nor, still less, Russia, was in a position to match herself with Germany and her ally on the Danube [Austria-Hungary], because their preparations were not to be complete until 1917. This especially filled me with anxiety and fear.

Ljuba Jovanovich, minister of Education in the Serbian cabinet [and founding member of the Black Hand], recalling his receipt of the news of the assassination on June 28, 1914, quoted in Sidney Bradshaw Fay, The Origins of the World War, *vol 2, pp. 63–64.*

Nedeljko Čabrinović, a compositor by profession, was full of anarchical ideas, and well known as a restless spirit. Until twenty days ago, he lived in Belgrade, whither he came after the war and was employed in the State printing works. Before his departure he announced that he was going to Trieste, where he would get work in a new printing works. Gavrilo Princip also was living at Belgrade until a short time ago. During the war he offered his services as a volunteer, but was not accepted, and therefore he left Belgrade. He returned, however, at Christmas last year to Belgrade, attended the gymnasium for a time, and left Belgrade almost at the same time as Čabrinović, though in a different direction. Princip was a silent nervous, hard-working student, and associated with some fellow students who came, like himself, from Bosnia-Herzegovina, as well as latterly with Čabrinović. He inclined towards socialistic ideas although he had originally belonged to the Young Men Progressive Party. Princip, like Čabrinović, was brought up at Serajevo; the two have been bound by ties of the closest friendship since their childhood.

Report in newspaper Balkan, *June 29, 1914, reprinted in Section 2, Appendix 9,* Austro-Hungarian Red Book, *in* Collected Diplomatic Documents Relating to the Outbreak of the European War, *p. 494.*

Your Excellency has been good enough to communicate to me the impressions which have been collected by our Ambassador at Berlin with regard to the démarche which the Austro-Hungarian Minister is proposing to make at Belgrade. These impressions have been confirmed by a conversation which I had yesterday with the Secretary of State for Foreign Affairs. Sir Edward Grey told me that he had seen the German Ambassador, who stated to him that at Berlin a démarche of the Austro-Hungarian Government to the Servian Government was expected. Prince Lichnowsky assured him that the German Government were endeavouring to hold back and moderate the Cabinet of Vienna, but that up to the present time they had not been successful in this, and that he was not without anxiety as to the results of a démarche of this kind. Sir Edward Grey answered Prince Lichnowsky that he would like to believe that, before intervening at Belgrade, the Austro-Hungarian Government had fully informed themselves as to the circumstances of the conspiracy to which the Hereditary Archduke and the duchess of Hohenburg had fallen victims, and had assured themselves that the Servian Government had been cognisant of it and had not done all that lay in their power to prevent the consequences. For if it could not be proved that the Servian Government were responsible and implicated to a certain degree, the intervention of Austria-Hungary would not be justified and would arouse against them the opinion of Europe.

The communication of Prince Lichnowsky had left Sir Edward Grey with an impression of anxiety which he did not conceal from me. The same impression was given me by the Italian Ambassador, who also fears the possibility of fresh tension in Austro-Servian relations.

This morning the Servian Minister came to see me, and he shares the apprehensions of Sir Edward Grey. He fears that Austria may make of the Servian Government demands which their dignity, and above all the susceptibility of public opinion, will not allow them to accept without a protest. When I pointed out to him the quiet which appears to reign at Vienna, and to which all the Ambassadors accredited to that Court bear testimony, he answered that this official quiet was only apparent and concealed feelings which were most fundamentally hostile to Servia. But, he added, if these feelings take a public form (démarche) which lacks the moderation that is desirable, it will be necessary to take account of Servian public opinion, which has been inflamed by the harsh treatment to which the Austrian Government have constantly subjected that country, and which has been made less patient by the memory of two victorious wars which is still quite fresh. Notwithstanding the sacrifices which Servia has made for her recent victories she can still put 400,000 men in the field, and public opinion, which knows this, is not inclined to put up with any humiliation.

Sir Edward Grey, in an interview with the Austro-Hungarian Ambassador, asked him to recommend his Government not to depart from the prudence and moderation necessary for avoiding new complications, not to demand from Servia any measures to which she could not reasonably submit, and not to allow themselves to be carried away too far.

PAUL CAMBON.

Paul Cambon, French ambassador in London, in a report to M. Bienvenu-Martin, acting minister for Foreign Affairs. London, July 22, 1914, cited as document no. 19 in the French Yellow Book, *in* Collected Diplomatic Documents Relating to the Outbreak of the European War, *pp. 151–152.*

As among the Entente Powers, Great Britain might be easily led to form an impartial judgment on the step which we are today taking at Belgrade, I request Your Excellency in the conversation which you will have on the 24th instant on the occasion when you hand in our circular note at the Foreign Office, to point out among other matters that it would have been within the power of Servia to render less acute the serious steps which she must expect from us, by spontaneously doing what is necessary in order to start an inquiry on Servian soil against the Servian accomplices in the crime of 28th June, and by bringing to light the threads, which as has been proved, lead from Belgrade to Servia [Sarajevo.] Up to the present time, although a number of notorious indications point to Belgrade, the Servian Government have not taken any steps in this direction; on the contrary they have attempted to wipe out the existing traces. . . . With regard to the short time limit attached to our demand, this must be attributed to our long experience of the dilatory arts of Servia.

Count Berchtold (foreign minister of Austro-Hungarian Empire) in a telegram to Count Mensdorff (imperial ambassador to Great Britain), July 23, 1914, reprinted as document no. 9, in Austro-Hungarian Red Book, *in* Collected Diplomatic Documents Relating to the Outbreak of the European War, *pp. 454–455.*

According to information collected by the French Ambassador at Vienna, the first intention of the Austro-Hungarian Government has been to proceed with the greatest severity against Servia while keeping eight army corps ready to start operations. The disposition at this moment was more conciliatory; in answer to a question put to him by M. Dumaine, whom I instructed to call the attention of the Austro-Hungarian Government to the anxiety aroused in Europe, Baron Macchio stated to our Ambassador that the tone of the Austrian note, and the demands which would be formulated in it, allow us to count on a peaceful result. In view of the customary procedure of the Imperial Chancery I do not know what confidence ought to be placed in these assurances. In any case the Austrian note will be presented in a very short space of time. The Servian Minister holds that as M. Pashitch [Pašić] wishes to come to an understanding, he will accept those demands which relate to the punishment of the outrage and to the guarantees for control and police supervision, but that he will resist everything which might affect the sovereignty and dignity of his country.

In diplomatic circles at Vienna the German Ambassador is in favour of violent measures, while at the same time confesses that the Imperial Chancery is perhaps not entirely in agreement with him on this point; the

Russian Ambassador, trusting to assurances which have been given him, has left Vienna, and before his departure confided to M. Dumaine that his Government will not raise any objection to the punishment of the guilty and the dissolution of the revolutionary associations, but that they could not accept requirements which were humiliating to the national sentiment of Servia. BIENVENU-MARTIN.

M. Bienvenu-Martin, acting minister for foreign affairs, in a formal note to London, Berlin, St. Petersburg, and Rome. From Paris, July 23, 1914. Cited as document no. 20 in the French Yellow Book, *in* Collected Diplomatic Documents Relating to the Outbreak of the European War, *pp. 152–153.*

. . . just handed the circular note to Sir Edward Grey, who read it carefully. At the fifth heading, he asked what it meant; to introduce officials of our Government in Servia would be equivalent to the end of Servian political independence. I answered that cooperation of, e.g. police officials, in no way affected the sovereignty of the State. He regretted the time-limit, as in this way we should be deprived of the possibility of quieting the first outbreak of excitement and bringing pressure to bear upon Belgrade to give us a satisfactory answer. It was always possible to send an ultimatum if answer not satisfactory. I developed our point of view at length. (Necessity of defense against continued revolutionary undertakings which threaten the territory of the Monarchy; protection of our most vital interests; complete failure of the conciliatory attitude which we had hitherto often shown to Servia, who had had more than three weeks to set on foot of her own accord investigations as to accomplices in outrage, &c.) The Secretary of State repeated his objections to the short time limit, but recognized that what was said as to complicity in the crime of Sarajevo, as well as many of our other requirements, was justified. He would be quite ready to look on the affair as one that only concerned Austria-Hungary and Servia. He is, however, very "apprehensive" that several Great Powers might be involved in a war. Speaking of Russia, Germany and France, he observed that the terms of the Franco-Russian Alliance might be more or less to the same effect as those of the Triple Alliance [the alliance between the German Empire, the Austro-Hungarian Empire, and Italy]. I fully explained to him our point of view and repeated with emphasis that in this case we must stand firm as to gain for ourselves some

sort of guarantees, as hitherto Servian promises have never been kept.

Count Mensdorff (imperial ambassador to Great Britain) in a telegram to Count Berchtold (Austro-Hungarian foreign minister), telegraphic communication, July 24, 1914, reprinted as document no. 10 in Austro-Hungarian Red Book, *in* Collected Diplomatic Documents Relating to the Outbreak of the European War, *pp. 455–456.*

As point 5 of our demands, namely, the participation of representatives of the Imperial and Royal Government in the suppression of the subversive movement in Servia has given rise to special objection on the part of M. Sazonof, your Excellency will explain in strict confidence with regard to this point that this clause was interpolated merely out of practical considerations, and was in no way intended to infringe on the sovereignty of Servia. By "collaboration" in point 5, we are thinking of the establishment of a private "Bureau de Sûreté" at Belgrade, which would operate in the same way as the analogous Russian establishments in Paris and in cooperation with the Servian police and administration.

Count Berchtold in a telegram to Count Szápáry at St. Petersburg. Vienna, July 25, 1914, reprinted as document 27, Section 2, Appendix, The Austro-Hungarian Red Book, *in* Collected Diplomatic Documents Relating to the Outbreak of the European War, *p 503.*

I thank You cordially for Your mediation which permits the hope that everything may yet end peaceably. It is technically impossible to discontinue our military preparations which have been made necessary by the Austrian mobilization. It is far from us to want war. As long as the negotiations between Austria and Servia continue, my troops will undertake no provocative action. I give You my solemn word thereon. I confide with all my faith in the grace of God, and I hope for the success of Your mediation in Vienna for the welfare of our countries and the peace of Europe. Your cordially devoted NICOLAS.

Czar Nicholas II of Russia in a telegram to Kaiser Wilhelm of Germany, July 31, 1914. This telegram crossed with the message from Wilhelm, below, as cited in the German White Book, *in* Collected Diplomatic Documents Relating to the Outbreak of the European War, *p. 411.*

Upon Your appeal to my friendship and Your request for my aid I have engaged in mediation between Your Government and the Government of Austria-Hungary. While this action was taking place, Your troops were being mobilized against my ally Austria-Hungary, whereby, as I have already communicated to You, my mediation has become almost illusory. In spite of this, I have continued it, and now I receive reliable news that serious preparations for war are going on on my eastern frontier. The responsibility for the security of my country forces me to measures of defense. I have gone to the extreme limit of the possible in my efforts for the preservation of the peace of the world. It is not I who bear the responsibility for the misfortune which now threatens the entire civilized world. It rests in your hand to avert it. No one threatens the honour and peace of Russia which might well have awaited the success of my mediation. The friendship for You and Your country, bequeathed to me by my grandfather on his deathbed, has always been sacred to me, and I have stood faithfully by Russia while it was in serious affliction, especially during its last war. The peace of Europe can still be preserved by You if Russia decides to discontinue those military preparations which menace Germany and Austria-Hungary.

Kaiser Wilhelm in a telegram to Czar Nicholas, 2 P.M. July 31, 1914, cited in The German White Book, *in* Collected Diplomatic Documents Relating to the Outbreak of the European War, *pp. 411–412.*

Germany endeavored to act as mediator in the Austro-Russian conflict. In this effort she was supported by England, France and Italy, because all these Powers, as is clearly shown by the attitude of their Governments and also by the expressions of public opinion, wished to avoid a great European war. But it appears that the localization of the Austro-Serbian conflict cannot be secured and that we are at the beginning of that great European war of which there has been so much talk, but in which no one seriously believed until today.

Editorial in Frankfurter Zeitung, July 31, 1914, as quoted in Munroe Smith, ed., Out of Their Own Mouths, *p. 81.*

Paris went on steadily about her mid-summer business of feeding, dressing, and amusing the great army of tourists who were the only invaders she had seen for nearly half a century. All the while, every one knew that other work was going on also. The whole fabric of the country's seemingly undisturbed routine was threaded with noiseless invisible currents of preparation, the sense of them was in the calm air as the sense of changing weather is in the balminess of a perfect afternoon. Paris counted the minutes till the evening papers came. They said little or nothing except what every one was already declaring all over the country. "We don't want war—*mais it faut pie vela finisse!*" This kind of thing one heard. If diplomacy could still arrest the war, so much the better: no one in France wanted it. All who spent the first days of August in Paris will testify to the agreement of feeling on that point. But if war had to come, then the country, and every heart in it, was ready. At the dressmaker's, the next morning, the tired fitters were preparing to leave for their usual holiday. They looked pale and anxious—decidedly, there was a new weight of apprehension in the air. And in the rue Royale, at the corner of the Place de la Concorde, a few people had stopped to look at a little strip of white paper against the wall of the Ministère de la Marine. "General mobilization" they read—and an armed nation knows what that means. But the group about the paper was small and quiet. Passers-by read the notice and went on. There were no cheers, no gesticulations: the dramatic sense of the race had already told them that the event was too great to be dramatized. Like a monstrous landslide it had fallen across the path of an orderly laborious nation, disrupting its routine, annihilating its industries, rending families apart, and burying under a heap of senseless ruin the patiently and painfully wrought machinery of civilization. That evening, in a restaurant of the rue Royale, we sat at a table in one of the open windows, abreast with the street, and saw the strange new crowds stream by. In an instant we were being shown what mobilization was—a huge break in the normal flow of traffic, like the sudden rupture of a dyke. The street was flooded by the torrent of people sweeping past us to the various railway stations. All were on foot, and carrying their luggage; for since dawn every cab and taxi and motor-omnibus had disappeared. The War Office had thrown out its drag-net and caught them all in. The crowd that passed our window was chiefly composed of conscripts. . . .

Writer Edith Wharton observing the effects of mobilization in Paris, August, 1914, The War on All Fronts: Fighting France, 1918, *pp. 7–9.*

We reached Vienna on August first. A startling change had come over the city since I had left it only a few weeks before. Feverish activity everywhere prevailed. Reservists streamed in by thousands from all parts of the country to report at headquarters. Autos filled with officers whizzed past. Dense crowds surged up and down the streets. Bulletins and extra editions of newspapers passed from hand to hand. Immediately it was evident what a great leveler war is. Differences in rank and social distinctions had practically ceased. All barriers seemed to have fallen; everybody addressed everybody else. I saw the crowds stop officers of high rank and well-known members of the aristocracy and clergy, also state officials and court functionaries of high rank, in quest of information, which was imparted cheerfully and patiently. The imperial princes could frequently be seen on the Ring Strasse surrounded by cheering crowds or mingling with the public unceremoniously at the cafés, talking to everybody. Of course, the army was idolized. Wherever the troops marched the public broke into cheers and every uniform was the center of an ovation. . . .

I saw in an open café a young couple, a reservist in field uniform and a young girl, his bride or sweetheart. They sat there, hands linked, utterly oblivious of their surroundings and of the world at large. When somebody in the crowd espied them, a great shout went up, the public rushing to the table and surrounding them, then breaking into applause and waving hats and handkerchiefs. At first the young couple seemed to be utterly taken aback and only slowly did they realize that the ovation was meant for them. They seemed confused, the young girl blushing and hiding her face in her hands, the young man rising to his feet, saluting and bowing. More cheers and applause. He opened his mouth as if wanting to speak. There was a sudden silence. He was vainly struggling for expression, but then his face lit up as if by inspiration. Standing erect, hand at his cap, in a pose of military salute, he intoned the Austrian national hymn. In a second every head in that throng was bared. All traffic suddenly stopped, everybody, passengers as well as conductors of the cars, joining in the anthem. The neighboring windows soon filled with people, and soon it was a chorus of thousands of voices. The volume of tone and the intensity of feeling seemed to raise the inspiring anthem to the uttermost heights of sublime majesty. We were then on our way to the station, and long afterwards we could hear the singing, swelling like a human organ.

What impressed me particularly in Vienna was the strict order everywhere. No mob disturbances of any kind, in spite of the greatly increased liberty and relaxation of police regulations. Nor was there any runaway chauvinism noticeable, aside from the occasional singing of patriotic songs and demonstrations like the one I just described. The keynote of popular feeling was quiet dignity, joined to determination, with an undercurrent of solemn gravity and responsibility.

Musician Fritz Kreisler, August 1, 1914, observing mobilization in Vienna, Four Weeks in the Trenches: The War Story of a Violinist, *pp. 4, 5, 7.*

Gentlemen, we are now in a state of necessity of self-preservation and necessity knows no law. Our troops have occupied Luxembourg and perhaps have already entered Belgian territory. Gentlemen, that is a breach of international law. It is true that the French Government declared at Brussels that France would respect Belgian neutrality so long as her adversary respected it. We knew, however, that France stood ready for an invasion. France could wait, we could not. A French attack on our flank on the lower Rhine might have been disastrous. So we were forced to ignore the rightful protests of the governments of Luxembourg and Belgium. The wrong—I speak openly—the wrong we thereby commit we will try to make good as soon as our military aims have been attained. He who is menaced as we are and is fighting for his highest possessions can only consider how he is to hew his way through.

Chancellor von Bethmann-Hollweg speaking to the Reichstag, August 4, 1914, quoted in Munroe Smith, ed., Out of Their Own Mouths, *p. 18.*

I found the Chancellor very agitated. His Excellency at once began a harangue, which lasted for about twenty minutes. He said that the step taken by His Majesty's Government was terrible to a degree; just for a word— "neutrality," a word which in war time had so often been disregarded—just for a scrap of paper, Great Britain was going to make war on a kindred nation who desired nothing better than to be friends with her. All his efforts in that direction had been rendered useless by this last terrible step, and the policy to which, as I knew, he had devoted himself since his accession to office had tumbled down like a house of cards. What we had done was unthinkable; it was like striking a man from behind while he was fighting for his life against two assailants.

He held Great Britain responsible for all the terrible events that might happen.

British ambassador in Berlin reporting to British foreign secretary Edward Grey, regarding his conversation with Chancellor von Bethmann-Hollweg, August 4, 1914, cited in Munroe Smith, ed., Out of Their Own Mouths, *pp. 19–20.*

On August 5 . . . I was received by the Under Secretary of State. Herr Zimmermann expressed to me, with much emotion, his profound regrets for the cause of my departure. . . . He sought no pretext to excuse the violation of our neutrality. He did not invoke the supposed French plan . . . of passing through Belgium in order to attack Germany on the lower Rhine. . . . [He] simply replied that the Department for foreign affairs was powerless. Since the order for mobilization had been issued . . . all power now belonged to the military authorities. It was they who had considered the invasion of Belgium to be an indispensable operation of the war.

Baron Beyens, Belgian minister in Berlin, reporting to the Belgian foreign minister, August 5, 1914, Second Belgian Grey Book, *document numbers 25, 51, 52, cited in Munroe Smith, ed.,* Out of Their Own Mouths, *pp. 18–19.*

2

First Battles and the Western Front Stalemate

August 1914–November 1915

The first year of the Great War revealed several shocking aspects to the troops, to the leadership, and to the general public of the world. Although Germany and Austria-Hungary expected rapid victories over the small countries of Serbia and Belgium, the ferocious resistance they encountered in both countries stunned them. German leaders also expected that after passing through Belgium, they would be able to outflank French defenses and march on Paris, bringing a rapid French capitulation. That notion made up the essence of the Schlieffen Plan.

Leaders on all sides chose not to inform their people of what they learned in the battlefronts. In most cases such manipulation of the truth could be carried out easily, for correspondents did not gather news at the front, but usually compiled it from official announcements, thoroughly reviewed by military officers for propaganda value as well as to protect the security of the troops. Minor advances would be characterized as victories; disastrous defeats would be presented as strategic retreats to better-defended positions. And, in general, the public learned of the scale of slaughter only slowly, as the realization grew on the home fronts that troops who signed up for a few months' duty had died, been wounded, captured, or remained at war a year later.

A Shocking War

The German plans did not unfold as expected. Since Germany had to employ troops on the eastern front to defend against Russian attacks on East Prussia and from Poland into Germany, fewer troops than needed could be thrown against the Belgians and the French. The original Schlieffen Plan had been modified to strengthen defenses against a French attack into Alsace-Lorraine. Furthermore, the Belgian resistance, although futile, slowed the German advance by a month, allowing time for the small British Expeditionary Force (B.E.F.) to arrive and participate and for the French to bolster their defenses. Even with German armies totaling about 1.5 million men launched into the attack through Belgium and France, the retreating defenders eventually began to hold off the German advance. Instead of a rapid and mobile war in the west, the armies ground on to a strange halt within a few months. Early on, the generals learned that although

As the French pulled back, they sought cover in ruins to set up machine guns. *(National Archives)*

they had expected a war of movement, they entered a war of position, as the defense usually proved capable of holding back the offense, on both sides. Many developments conspired to convert the classic Napoleonic warfare of movement into the new and nearly static confrontation of forces.

By the end of 1914, parallel lines of trenches and fortifications, separated by a pockmarked terrain known to soldiers as no-man's-land, full of unburied bodies and tangles of barbed wire, ran from the English Channel near Nieuport to the Swiss border. That line would remain virtually unchanged within a few miles through all of 1915 and the first half of 1916. Despite battles in which hundreds of thousands of men threw themselves into withering defensive fire, neither side made very much headway. The great stalemate, at first only dimly recognized, presented a shocking reality to the nations of the world and became a slaughterhouse for a generation of young European men, known as the Lost Generation. Hundreds of thousands of potential writers, artists, engineers, scientists, and teachers born in the years between 1890 and about 1900 fell dead among the millions of casualties, lost to the history of the human race. Some lost arms or legs, yet counted themselves lucky to have survived.

The tragedy of death in war became even more horrible because of the grotesque nature of the new means of slaughter, as eyewitness accounts revealed through letters home, in diaries, and in reports by travelers to the front. Gruesome tales came back from Belgium and France, detailing the mangled corpses that littered the stretch of land between the trenches and hung in shreds to rot from splintered trees and barbed wire. Artillery barrages always served as preludes to ground assaults once the lines became set, and they wreaked fearsome destructive power. Even concrete fortresses gradually crumbled to rubble under artillery pounding. The trenches became knee-deep and sometimes neck-deep in water, mud, and body parts.

In this photo British troops take a defensive position along a railroad embankment. *(National Archives)*

New weaponry and new civilian-based technologies had changed the face of the war. Entrenched positions would be defended by masses of troops armed with machine guns and rapid-fire rifles, behind tangles of barbed wire to slow any advance. The Germans introduced the use of chlorine poison gas in April 1915, and, in September of that year, the British began employing it. Both sides found poison gas of several types unreliable and difficult to employ, but its use represented the dawn of a new age in which the tools of modern science would be used to terrible effect in warfare. But even without this first of the weapons of mass destruction, the war took a terrible toll in killed and injured.

A combination of several factors made the defense stronger than the offense. An artillery barrage, often lasting several days, would generally be employed to soften defenses, including the entrenched lines and machine-gun nests on the sector targeted for attack. The shelling, however, not only destroyed some of the defenders; it also allowed the defense to prepare reinforcements behind the lines. With the artillery concentration, the defenders would know where to expect an attack and could move reserves close to the point by rail and road over a period of days. Commanders pressed trucks, busses, and even taxis into service, allowing the rapid movement of troops without the need for massive amounts of feed for horses that had slowed the armies of the past. When the artillery barrage stopped to allow the attack, the defenders could bring the reserves forward from the rail and road head to plug the hole. Thus quite frequently a battle lasting two to six weeks simply resulted in a change of the front line by less than three miles, with a loss of anywhere from 50,000 soldiers to more than 300,000 soldiers on *each* side. Whenever an advance broke through into the enemy trenches, the defending forces would simply pull back to a new line of trenches and throw in more reserves at the point of penetration.

Looking back, it is only natural to wonder why the generals did not learn their lesson and try something different. In fact, they did. Not only did the armies try poison gas, but they also introduced many other innovations to change the awful deadlock of effective defense. Tethered balloons sent aloft carried observers who were able to direct artillery to the precise point needed. The Germans employed self-propelled rigid airships, developed by Count Ferdinand Zeppelin, to bomb enemy positions. Both sides equipped small aircraft to shoot down the balloons, to raid the trenches, and, eventually, to bomb enemy supply points and strafe the troops as they moved along approach roads.

In the zeppelin, the Germans had a formidable aircraft. Although it flew slowly, it could fly at extremely high altitudes, well above the reach of either ground fire or guns mounted on airplanes. First in Belgium in September 1914, and then early in 1915 against Great Britain, the zeppelins bombed civilian targets, the first employment of aircraft in what later became known as strategic bombing.

Only after British developers conceived, invented, manufactured, and deployed an armored self-propelled gun platform with caterpillar treads did the offense gain some degree of mobility. Tanks began to play an important role in 1917 and 1918. Even as new methods were tried, the most common response of generals to the strength of the defense consisted of a cry for more and more artillery, more and more shells. Over and over, officers blamed the failure to take much territory on the need for more troops and more ammunition. As a consequence, the battlefields consumed men and shells, both in vast quantities never before imagined.

Officers simply had not anticipated the stalemate on the western front and the terrible slaughter that resulted from fruitless assaults against defended positions. The reasons go far deeper than the ignorance, stubbornness, or stupidity of specific individual officers. The tendency by contemporary critics and later historians to place blame on those men reflected the long tradition of associating the outcome of a battle with the competence of its leaders, rather than looking into the culture, training, and heritage that shaped a generation's ideas of battle. Despite a few conflicts engaging the countries of Europe in the 19th century, the period since the end of the era of Napoleon in 1815 had been an extended European peace. Between the major powers, that peace had been broken briefly by colonial jostling and by the Crimean War of 1853–56, the brief Franco-Prussian conflict of 1870–71, and the Balkan War of 1877–78 between Russia and the Ottoman Empire.

Yet even those few wars had been fought with weapons and technology quite outmoded by 1914. The 1870s had seen the civilian introduction of barbed wire (1873), the telephone (1876), and gelignite, a high-explosive nitroglycerine-

The idea of dropping a bomb from an aircraft developed in stages, as this early German photograph demonstrates. *(National Archives)*

nitrocellulose combination (1876). Western European armies and navies had not confronted each other since the development of the machine gun (1885), smokeless powder (1888), the internal combustion propelled vehicle (1890s), the submarine (1898), the zeppelin (1900), the wireless telegraph (1902), the airplane (1903), and the all-big-gun dreadnought battleship (1906). Although military leaders, with different degrees of enthusiasm, adapted each of these and other new technologies to warfare, it would take their application to real combat situations to develop an understanding of how each of them would change the ways wars would be fought. A weapon system must be accompanied by what officers call doctrine, the scheme and method of its employment and use, and it would take years of experience to create good doctrine. Officers trained in military schools tended to use the old tactics of shoulder-to-shoulder advance, employed in the days when troops used muskets. They eventually learned that in the face of barbed wire and trench defenses, each soldier had to move forward as an individual, taking advantage of cover, cutting through wire, or finding passages through the maze, and fighting on a hand-to-hand basis if and when he reached the enemy position. Frequently, newly appointed officers, who had been businessmen, teachers, or other professionals without military training, adapted far better to the new kind of war than did the officers who had studied the battles of Napoleon in officer-training academies or who had used the older methods in prior wars. As in every trade, learning on the job had its value.

Contemporary and later studies of the deadlock have often focused on the defense tools themselves as a cause of the slaughter: the trench, barbed wire, and the machine gun. But the less dramatic infrastructure of rail and motorized roads behind the lines, connected by rapidly strung telephone and telegraph lines, also became crucial to the rapid reinforcement of any perceived weak spot. Those transport and communication innovations, common in everyday civilian life, brought changes with consequences little understood by the generals of the day. Although they employed the infrastructure for their advances and for their own defense, they seemed unaware that the new methods of moving men, materiel, and information provided an overwhelming advantage to the defense, by allowing the rapid movement of reserves to points under attack. Whenever one side made a small breakthrough, the lack of transport to the other side of no-man's-land, with its discontinuity in rail and road, usually slowed any attempt to push forward more than a walking distance of a few miles before the advance would be stopped. In the battlefields of western Europe and in some of the engagements on the eastern front and in the Middle East, the war turned into a process of slow attrition, with little hope on either side of a complete victory.

The stalemated battles on the western front in World War I represented the true consequences of symmetric warfare, in which the forces confronting each

As they slowly retreated while defending their homeland, some wounded Serbs received treatment in Red Cross dressing stations near the front. *(Library of Congress)*

other had similar weapons, similar numbers, and used similar tactics against each other. Even the smaller forces, like those of Belgium and Serbia, utilized many of the same tactics and weapons as the major powers. The Serbs eventually retreated to the Albanian mountains where they held the advantage of difficult terrain. As the war spread beyond Europe to Africa and the Near East, here and there individual officers would show their mastery of new ideas, such as camouflage from air observation, deception, and alliance with irregular troops fighting in guerrilla style far behind the front lines. At the time, military specialists called asymmetric guerrilla tactics Boer-style warfare, after the methods employed by the South African Boers in their long uprising against the British in 1899–1902. That style of war required innovative officers, able to think outside the traditions of the military by using highly mobile forces to operate without regard to front lines, and such tactics had little place on the battlefields of western Europe.

When Italy joined the war in May 1915, as an ally of Britain and France against the Dual Monarchy, it already had many proofs, from the terrible disasters in Flanders and on the approaches to Paris, that the war would not be easy. The Italians had a 300-mile, mostly mountainous, border with the Austro-Hungarian Empire that saw repeated bitter engagements, some with trenches dug into snow banks and glaciers. But the logical place to advance appeared to be on their northeastern frontier across a 60-mile stretch of the River Isonzo. After four extensive battles on the Isonzo, through 1915, the Italians advanced no more than 10 miles, with the Austrian forces still holding bridgeheads on the Italian side of the river.

FROM THE BALKANS TO A GREAT WAR

In August 1914, the war became Europe-wide and the press immediately labeled it the Great War. The interlocking alliances resulted in rapid declarations of war by Russia in support of Serbia against Austria-Hungary and Germany, followed by France in support of Russia and Britain in support of Belgium. In Africa and the Far East, German colonies came under attack by British and British Dominion troops. The war expanded to include other major combatants within months. The Ottoman Empire joined in against Russia and Britain, and Japan abruptly issued an ultimatum to Germany and then declared war, seizing the opportunity to gain German territories in China and the Pacific. The British and French backed Japanese aspirations with a secret agreement to honor those gains at the end of the war. Britain and France also wooed Italy into the war with a secret alliance that pledged those powers to back territorial demands by Italy against Austria-Hungary. The Central Powers enticed Bulgaria in 1915 to join them by the offer of a territorial concession from the Turks along the Maritsa River and by a loan from Germany and Austria of some 400 million francs. If Bulgaria could defeat Serbia, it could regain all or part of the Macedonian province it had lost in 1913 in the Second Balkan War. As the various nations joined in, by late 1915, the alliances looked as follows:

ALLIANCES, LATE 1915

The Central Powers	Date Joined	The Entente and Allied Powers	Date Joined
Austria–Hungary	August 1914	France	August 1914
Germany	August 1914	Britain	August 1914
		Russia	August 1914
		Serbia and Montenegro	August 1914
		Belgium	August 1914
		Japan	September 1914
Ottoman Empire	October 1914	Italy	May 1915
Bulgaria	October 1915		

Both sides tried to negotiate with Greece and Romania to join with them, but, by the end of 1915, both of these Balkan states remained neutral. Romania would join the Allied side August 27, 1916.

The conflict between the Austro-Hungarian Empire and Serbia, which might have been resolved by negotiation or fought on a strictly local basis, had become a tragic war engaging the Great Powers for numerous underlying reasons. The interlocking alliances and the fragile balance of power lay at the root of the escalation from local conflict to an all-Europe war. The prewar alliances had been signed with a defensive purpose, but, like ultimate weapons, they immediately lost their effectiveness as deterrents to war once employed. The secret offensive treaty between Austria and Germany probably emboldened Vienna to make the first move. Russia's alliance with France, intended to prevent Austrian or German adventurism by threatening the Central Powers with the possibility of a two-front war, had a certain logic to it. When Russia came to the assistance of Serbia against Austria, the house of cards fell.

The sequence of mobilizations and declarations of war that followed through the last weeks of July and into early August seemed inevitable or unstoppable once they had occurred. Clearly, however, more lay behind the conflict than simply the unfolding of legal-diplomatic obligations. Scholars of diplomatic history have studied those interlocking alliances and the related treaties in great detail as a source of understanding how a Serbian irredentist incident could escalate to a global war. Yet such a focus may not answer the question of *why* the leaders of the nations decided to honor the treaties by ultimatums and war rather than seeking a negotiated settlement.

Leaders and their peoples alike seemed almost eager for the war in July and August 1914. That eagerness revealed itself by the vast numbers of volunteers who signed up to join the armies of Britain, France, Germany, and Austria-Hungary. German troops sang as they marched, to the amusement of American newspaper reporters; other eyewitnesses reported the deeply moving patriotic singing among the Austrians, the Russians, and the British as they trooped to war. So many joined in 1914 in all of these countries that the armies could not absorb them at first, housing them in tents and training them with wooden rifles and often in civilian clothes. Not only governments, but also the populations seemed eager to jump off the precipice.

One of the underlying reasons why leaders and peoples chose war rather than negotiation and conciliation can be traced to deep-seated resentment at some specific border rearrangements that had emerged from the 19th and early 20th century jockeying for power and dominance, both in Europe and in the overseas colonies. Serbian irredentist territorial ambition lay behind the spark that caused the war in Bosnia. The Austro-Hungarian government presented its cause for war against Serbia as just and proper to the people of the Dual Monarchy on the grounds that it had every right to maintain order on its southern frontier. The government believed it proper to punish Serbia for its support of assassins, rioters, and dissident politicians inside Austro-Hungarian territory. Other geographic issues also had deep roots. The French hoped to recover the provinces of Alsace and Lorraine lost to Germany in the Franco-Prussian War of 1870–71. The French motive of revenge, or *revanche,* clearly made the French eager to honor their commitment to the Russians.

No matter the spark that set off the war, once underway it could provide other powers with opportunities for long-desired border adjustments. Thus Italy eyed Trieste and the Tyrol while Austria found continued Italian holdings in the Dalmatian islands disturbing; South Africa looked at South-West Africa, then a colony of Germany; Japan eyed the German holdings in the Far East. Turkey remembered that Russia had supported Bulgaria in its whittling away at Turkish holdings.

Germany made a concerted effort to win Turkish support with military assistance. Decades of insult and opposition from both Russia and Britain also contributed to the decision of the Turks to participate, although, in retrospect, that decision can only be characterized as foolhardy. When Britain refused to turn over warships that Turkey had paid for in Britain, it only added to Turkish anger. Turkey, of all the Central Powers, came in the least prepared and the most politically unstable.

Although the British had no territorial ambitions in Europe, the naval arms race between Britain and Germany, Germany's support for Boer resistance to British rule in South Africa, and German control of large colonies in Africa all presented challenges to Britain's overseas empire. Britain, however, had relied on a superior navy for defense of its homeland and mounted only a small professional army for maintaining order in its colonies and India. While Germany,

Invading Belgium, the Germans encountered more resistance than on their easy pass through Luxembourg. After taking Brussels, they marched and rode down the Boulevard Bolwerk. *(Library of Congress)*

France, Russia and the Dual Monarchy maintained huge armies of draftees, British leaders had favored a small, highly trained, and well-equipped group of professionals. Hence, Britain's first contribution to the war appeared almost minuscule by contrast to the forces mounted by the other major powers.

In the past, wars had often rearranged the borders of Europe, the positions of ethnic minorities, and the holdings of colonial powers in favor of the victors. So part of the initial eagerness for war seemed to spring from the belief that the war provided a chance to settle old scores, readjust borders, suppress troublesome minorities, and arrange some transfers of territory in the spirit of national expansion. Leaders and the masses of the general population had little understanding that 20th-century war technology would prevent the quick victories that they anticipated and the transfer of territories and peoples they sought. The optimism of August 1914 sprang from ignorance of how the new tools of war and transport would change the nature of battle, once those tools were employed on a massive scale.

Many aspects of modern warfare that grew out of the new technologies of aircraft and long-range artillery and out of the problems of assault from sea to land, obvious to later analysts and students of the subject, could not be anticipated when the Great War began. Naval officers had little understanding of the limitations and potentialities of the ocean-going submarine. So at the heart of the scramble to join in war that unfolded in August of 1914, a scramble that seems so strange to later generations, lay simple optimism. People and governments alike believed that the conflict would resolve outstanding grievances, leading to quick readjustment of the boundaries of Europe and the distribution of colonial holdings around the world. Only as the war unfolded and the new technologies led to slaughter on a previously unimaginable scale did the optimism subside. Yet even as the destruction gradually became obvious, the temptations of territorial gain and resolution of ethnic issues led to participation by Italy, Bulgaria, and later even Romania and Greece, which had both struggled to maintain neutrality.

FROM GREAT WAR TO WORLD WAR

The victors in Europe stood to gain the overseas holdings of the losers. The war almost immediately spread far beyond Europe to Africa, the Middle East, the Far East, and on to the islands of the Pacific. Germany had been late in joining the scramble of European powers for holdings in Asia and Africa. Colonial possessions contributed to the spread of the conflict, as possible prizes for the victors. In Africa, for example, the German colonies of Togoland, Cameroons, German East Africa (later Tanganyika), and South-West Africa (Namibia) offered tempting and ready targets for British, French, and South African ambitions. These colonies soon fell to British, French, and South African troops. Only German East Africa put up a fight, one that lasted until after the war ended in Europe in 1918.

The Japanese wanted the Kiaochow peninsula of China, also known as Shantung, some 200 square miles that had been under a 99-year German lease since 1898. Japan also eyed the Caroline and Northern Mariana Islands of the Pacific acquired by Germany in 1899 by purchase from Spain at the end of the 1898 Spanish-American War. After Spain lost the Philippines to the United States, it had little use for the lonely outpost islands, and Spain gladly sold them to Germany for much-needed cash. Japan had joined the European powers in hopes of building an empire. It had taken over Formosa in 1895, Port Arthur (from Russian occupation) in 1905, and Korea in 1910. Further, Japan participated with the European powers in the semicolonial control of the corrupt and collapsing Chinese empire through the use of treaties and spheres of influence. Germany was unable to defend Kiaochow and its Pacific islands because they were so remote from Europe. These additional prizes seemed there for the taking, and Japan seized the opportunity. To induce Japan to side with them, Britain and France secretly agreed to support Japan's takeover of German territories in the Pacific region, but only north of the equator, which included Kiaochow, the Caroline Islands, and the Northern Marianas. The British Empire planned to acquire German holdings south of the equator, so that New Zealand could move troops into German-held northeastern Papua New Guinea.

With the battles in the Pacific, German attacks on British holdings in the Indian Ocean, and the British move from the Persian Gulf into the Ottoman province of Mesopotamia (now Iraq), the war took on a truly global nature in 1915. Only the continents of South America and Antarctica remained uninvolved. Even North America engaged in the war from the beginning. Although the United States immediately announced its neutrality, Canada quickly came to the support of Britain, passing a war budget through its Parliament and eventually committing more than 600,000 troops to the fight. The declarations of war by Britain obliged all the British dominions—Canada, New Zealand, Australia, and the Union of South Africa—to join in the war. Troops from British and French colonies and from India also fought as part of the alliance against the Central Powers.

Among the major powers of the world, only the United States remained neutral through 1915 and 1916. However, that neutrality would be severely tested through those years.

THE WAR ON THE GROUND: AUGUST–DECEMBER 1914

With the German advance into Belgium on August 4, the shooting war began in earnest on the western front, and the opening of the war is commonly dated from this day despite the shelling of Belgrade in Serbia the week before. The Belgians, under the leadership of King Albert I, decided to fight, relying on numerous concrete fortresses with heavy guns, placed on the outskirts of major cities, with dispersed units of light troops around the country. The spirited defense by Belgium came as a surprise not only to the Germans but also to world opinion, which expected that the Belgians would simply surrender as hopelessly outmanned and outgunned. Hoping for British and French reinforcements and relying on the fortresses, the Belgian decision may have seemed rational. As it turned out, the German army brought up heavy guns with greater range than the cannon in the Belgian fortresses, and simply fired on the targets for a period of weeks, gradually reducing them to rubble and killing the defenders. German artillery brought down the 11 Belgian forts near Liège through extended bombardment; German guns pounded the last forts at Loncin into silence on August 17. The first air raid in history occurred in these first attacks on Belgium, when bombs were dropped from zeppelins on the city of Liège, with a few civilian casualties.

Horrified by the outbreak of the war, and aware how ethnic loyalties divided the American people, President Wilson announced on August 4 that the United States would remain neutral. Two weeks later, on August 19, Wilson urged the American people to be neutral in thought as well as in deed. However, Wilson would find it difficult to maintain neutrality not only because of the affinity of different recent immigrants and their descendants to one or another European power, but also because, traditionally, neutral states asserted and defended their rights to commercial trade with belligerent nations. Although the United States advocated that stand in 1914, as events unfolded in 1915 and 1916, the issue of maritime trade with Europe would embroil Americans in one crisis after another.

When the Belgians refused to yield passage to the German troops, the British Expeditionary Force (B.E.F.) began landing at Le Havre and Boulogne, and put some forces inland at Rouen. Meanwhile, the Germans repulsed the expected French invasion of Lorraine, with heavy French losses. In the west, the Belgians retreated to Antwerp, and, by August 20, the Germans had occupied Brussels. Gradually, the German forces advanced, defeating the French at Charlerois and the British at the Battle of Mons, in Belgium, the first major clash between German and British troops. Since the military did not allow newspaper correspondents anywhere near the front, newspapers in Britain carried no news of the defeat of the B.E.F. at Mons. Similarly, however, the German public did not learn that the Schlieffen Plan had failed and that the grand strategy soon resulted in near stalemate.

The Germans took Namur in Belgium, using the same long-range artillery previously employed at Liège. By the end of August, the British and French desperately tried to stop the German advance, with a British force at Le Cateau and the French surrendering the fortress at Longwy. The Germans moved on to take Amiens and crossed the River Oise on the path to Paris. By August 31, they arrived within 15 to 30 miles of the outskirts of Paris, near Chantilly.

As the stalemate set in, both sides developed more elaborate emplacements, like this German defensive line. *(National Archives)*

On the eastern front, Russian forces moved into East Prussia and advanced through Poland into Germany. However, at a major battle at Tannenberg, the Germans turned back the Russian advance. The Russians occupied Lvov in the Ukraine, and the battles on the eastern front seesawed over the next months. In October and November, the Germans advanced through Poland to Warsaw, but retreated from a massive Russian counterattack westward to Cracow.

With the Germans within shelling range of Paris, the French government moved to Bordeaux on September 3. On September 4, Britain, Russia, and France signed the Triple Entente, the agreement each made not to sign a separate treaty with the Central Powers. One of the first massive and long battles, the Battle of the Marne, lasting the week of September 5 to 12, 1914, began to give the shape of things to come, yielding only a small French advance with great losses. The first battles near Verdun began in September, and the Germans took the French fortress of St. Mihiel. The Germans retained a salient, or advanced position, into French territory at St. Mihiel well into 1918.

In September and October 1914, the Germans defeated the British and Belgian defenders of Antwerp and turned south, advancing along the Channel into Flanders, slowly pushing down through Ghent, Lille, Bruges, and Ostend. The British and French finally held the German advance at the First Battle of Ypres, which lasted more than three weeks: October 30 to November 24, 1914.

Meanwhile, the Ottoman Empire joined the Central Powers, and Britain declared war on that empire. Britain brought in Egypt as an ally to protect the Suez Canal. The British moved up from Kuwait into Iraq. The Austrians temporarily invaded Serbia, taking Belgrade in early December but evacuating it after intense Serbian counterattacks two weeks later. On the all-important western

One use for aircraft was aerial spotting and surveillance photography, which remained important throughout the war. *(National Archives)*

front, the French and British attempted to push back the German advances but made no important gains.

By the end of the year, Germany had lost 675,000 soldiers, and the French had lost about 850,000. The British had lost more than half of the original British Expeditionary Force.

In 1915, there would be a series of long, bloody engagements on the western front. These so-called battles, named for the nearest village, fort, river, or city, were actually long-drawn-out and fruitless attempts to assault well-defended positions. More men were sometimes killed in one of these battles than in entire past or future wars. Major engagements, some lasting more than a month, cost thousands of casualties. The major western front battles in 1915 included Soissons (January–February), St. Mihiel (March–April), Ypres (April–May), Artois (May–June and September–October), and Champagne-Argonne (September–November). Although casualties in these engagements ran as high as 300,000 troops, one side or the other achieved only very minor gains or none at all.

THE WAR IN THE AIR

From the perspective of later history, the introduction of aircraft in World War I has been the subject of great interest, romantic exaggeration, and fascination with the airplanes themselves and with the pilot-aces who flew them. But, in reality, the war in the air represented only a minuscule aspect of the whole war in terms of the total number of men involved or the total damage to land forces. At first the armies employed light aircraft along with tethered observation balloons for artillery spotting and observation. Some of the first air-to-air engagements consisted of one side's spotter aircraft firing a rifle at the other side's tethered balloon.

Soon, however, the aircraft mounted machine guns instead of rifles, and one- or two-man crews engaged in hundreds of spectacular dogfights. Some of the pilots, who displayed a real killer instinct or hatred of the enemy, accounted for many deaths. In the last months of the war in 1918, air forces of the British, French, and Germans began supporting ground troops in both offense and defense, playing more of a role as commanders gradually recognized the value of integrating the air arm into their battle plans.

The most famous of the aces, Manfred von Richthofen, accounted for 80 enemy planes shot down. He maintained a set of trophies at his quarters. He sent investigators to examine enemy planes that had crashed behind German lines. They would try to establish the identity of the downed pilots from papers found on the corpses. They would cut from the wreckage pieces of canvas, often with the serial number of the plane, which Richthofen then mounted on the wall of his room.

Mick Mannick, a hero of the British Royal Flying Corps, shot down 73 German aircraft. Mannick and Richthofen both died in action. Other aces included the American, Eddie Rickenbacker (who lived to the ripe old age of 83), and the Canadian, Billy Bishop, who became a national hero in his own country. The American pilot Frank Luke developed a specialty of bringing down enemy observation balloons.

In 1918, as the Germans, French, and British introduced larger aircraft, the future of warfare could be dimly perceived; bombing raids involving hundreds of aircraft supported ground action and dropped hundreds of tons of bombs on industrial targets. In the period 1914–15, however, only a few officers recognized the potential of the airplane, and, as with the submarine, effective employment had to evolve gradually.

American pilot Frank Luke developed a special talent for shooting down German observation balloons. Here he poses with one he knocked out over Allied-held territory. *(National Archives)*

THE POLITICS OF BLAME

Contemporaries and later generations have struggled to understand the seemingly mysterious reasons for the outbreak and early course of the Great War. The slaughter of literally millions of young men by the most advanced and most civilized nations of the world flew in the face of logic. Much of the American public and the American political leadership at first insisted that some common formula for peace should immediately be discussed and that the war should be brought to a quick end by negotiation. Woodrow Wilson continued to plead with both sides to accept mediation, without success. Britain, France, Germany, and the Dual Monarchy all saw victory as the only way out. The persistence of the conflict seemed incomprehensible. Then and later, outsiders asked questions about the origin of the war, the extent of the slaughter, and the failure of international diplomacy. Above all, it seemed someone should be blamed for the tragedy.

Most contemporary observers tended to blame the individual leaders, from Helmuth von Moltke in Germany, to Winston Churchill and General Kitchener and later General Haig in Britain, to Marshall Foch in France. Clearly all these men made decisions that in the light of events turned out to be disastrous. Simply put, they made mistakes. But the tendency to focus on grand leaders and to place the blame on them as individuals leaves unanswered the more profound problem of why the best military, diplomatic, and political minds of the most advanced nations in the world made so many mistakes, so repeatedly.

That generation of leaders did not have a particularly high proportion of irrational or ignorant individuals, no worse and probably no better than generations that came before and later. Rather, it seems that their decisions, which seemed perfectly sensible to them, grew out of assumptions and values that had become outmoded by a reality that had changed around them without their recognizing it. Traditional military strategy had correctly relied on surprise, concentration of force, overwhelming power, mobility, adequate logistics, and good intelligence about the disposition of the enemy. Earlier wars, which were fought with lightning cavalry charges and fast overland marches that relied on the element of surprise, afforded many textbook examples of the war of motion. While officers understood those strategic methods and theories very well, they only gradually came to recognize the changes that the new tools of war and new inventions from the civilian sector collectively made in warfare and how those developments produced the stalemate on the front.

A CHANGED WORLD

Slowly developing social phenomena undermined the logic and some of the political assumptions of the leadership generation. Throughout the multiethnic empires of the Habsburgs, the Russian czars, and the Ottoman sultans, in the smaller nations of the Balkans, and even within the home territory of all the major powers, ethnic-based nationalism had become an extremely powerful force by the early 20th century. The leaders of the empires found it difficult to assess seriously, to harness, or to contain the ties of language, heritage, and religion that motivated Armenians and Arabs against Turks and that caused the Serbs to struggle against the Dual Monarchy of Vienna and Budapest.

Another subtle social change lay in the degree of public awareness, involvement, and commitment to the affairs of state. This factor worked powerfully in the relatively open democracies of France and Britain, but it also played a significant role within the autocratic regimes of Germany, Austria-Hungary, Russia, and the smaller states. That is, leaders tended to think that the decisions of enemies and allies alike would be made by clusters of other leaders in isolation from their peoples. The kings, premiers, presidents, princes, foreign ministers, chiefs of military staffs, and generals at first made their calculations based on their assessment of their foreign counterparts in positions of power. As the war ground on, they grew more and more aware of the importance of the reactions of the people, now shaped by mass psychology, propaganda, and the combined effect of widespread literacy and mass-circulation print media. Even in remote and semiliterate regions, such as the mountains of the Balkans or the villages of Russia, literate local leaders would pass around and read to eager clustered listeners from newspapers containing passionate editorials, news of atrocities, and calls to patriotism.

When millions of men eagerly volunteered to fight, and later, as millions became disillusioned in the quality of their leadership, had to be driven into battle at gunpoint, and even mutinied, the world seemed turned upside-down. Clumsily, the leaders tried to affect public opinion by withholding news of some of the greatest tragedies, by fabricating stories of enemy cruelties, exaggerating the crimes of enemy soldiers, or by concealing their own tactical and strategic mistakes. They appealed to national heritage, to religion, to prejudice, or fear. Sometimes such efforts had apparent short-term success, but often the leadership failed to predict the reaction of people at home and abroad.

Such a miscalculation of public impact allowed the German command to ignore the neutral status of Belgium. As a military calculation, or as a pattern on a map, the invasion might have made some sense; as a political or propaganda event, it became a disaster for Germany. The German execution of the British nurse Edith Cavell in 1915 for assisting more than 130 allied prisoners to escape across the Dutch frontier also created an unanticipated international outcry. While clearly guilty of playing a military role under the cover of a civilian assignment, she died a martyr. Her execution caused an outpouring of anger not only in Britain, but also in the United States and around the world. When stories leaked out from Belgium of German troops executing priests, burning homes, or bombing civilians, the British and French tried, with considerable success, to depict the invaders as barbarians.

The Germans seemed far less capable than the British in building international sympathy based on the enemy's misdeeds. The British execution of Sir Roger Casement, the leader of Irish rebels against British rule, or the French execution of an accused female Dutch spy for the Germans, the dancer-turned-courtesan Mata Hari, while notorious, had little long-range effect on American, Canadian, or British public opinion. By contrast, the English-speaking world was shocked and horrified by the German execution of Edith Cavell in Belgium, partly because she seemed to represent the plight of innocent noncombatant women.

The seemingly irrational behavior or decisions of leaders that in hindsight proved disastrous could be construed as immoral or near-criminal. In Britain, France, and Germany, individual generals, admirals, and heads of ministries regularly faced demands for resignation, or their superiors simply sacked and replaced them. In Russia, Marxist revolutionary leaders tapped mass sentiments that blamed the slaughter of the war front and the war's consequent shortages of food and fuel on a corrupt conspiracy of aristocrats, capitalists, and landowners. In the United States, a growing suspicion of war profiteers and munitions-makers at home and greedy imperialists in Europe emerged and became focused during the period of American neutrality from 1914 through the end of 1916. Such sentiments fed into America's later isolationism from the affairs of Europe and the world.

Among the suppressed or politically unrepresented ethnic groups of Europe and the Middle East, including, among many others, Serbs, Poles, Irish, Ukrainians, Armenians, Arabs, and Kurds, the deadly struggles between the great powers seemed to hold out hope for national liberation. This ethnic resistance to the imperial powers only complicated the picture for the leaders in London, Vienna, and Constantinople.

Tensions in the Balkans, the powder-keg of Europe, had set off the chain reaction of ultimatums, mobilizations, and declarations of war. Troops paraded, civilians flocked to enlist and then marched with enthusiasm to war, and cavalry forces prepared their mounts and lances. Within months, however, as battles cost casualties in the tens and hundreds of thousands and as single torpedoes launched from submarines took the lives of thousands of sailors, the horror began to sink in. Worse was yet to come.

CHRONICLE OF EVENTS

1914

August 4: Germany invades Belgium; Britain declares war on Germany. The British declaration of war includes the dominions: Canada, South Africa, New Zealand, and Australia. Belgium decides to fight although vastly outnumbered, relying on heavily built concrete fortresses equipped with artillery; German guns have greater range.

August 4: United States of America declares its neutrality.

August 5: Montenegro declares war on Austria-Hungary.

August 5: First air raid, with zeppelins dropping bombs on Liège, kills nine civilians.

August 5–6: German troops pass Liège.

August 6: Austria declares war on Russia, and Serbia declares war on Germany.

August 6–17: German artillery reduces the Belgian forts of Liège through extended bombardment; 11 forts are destroyed by August 16 and Loncin reduced on August 17.

August 8: Montenegro declares war on Germany.

August 12: Britain and France declare war on Austria-Hungary

August 12: First Russian Army invades the German province of East Prussia.

August 12–14: Austria-Hungary begins its offensive against Serbia.

August 12–17: The British send four divisions, about 80,000 men, to Le Havre, to Boulogne, and up the Seine to the river port of Rouen.

August 14–25: The French invasion of Lorraine is repulsed by Germany with heavy French losses.

August 15: The Japanese issue an ultimatum to Germany to withdraw from the Far East and the German-held Kiaochow peninsula in China (Shantung).

August 16: Germans take Liège; the Belgian army retreats to Antwerp.

August 17: The Russian army advances into Germany.

August 17–21: In Serbia, at Battles of the Tser and the Jadar, Serbian forces drive Austrians back from their territory.

August 18: Canada votes a war budget; eventually 425,000 Canadians will serve overseas and nearly 61,000 will be killed.

August 19: Woodrow Wilson appeals to the American people to be neutral in thought as well as in action.

August 20: Germany occupies Brussels, Belgium.

August 21–24: French armies are defeated at Charleroi and driven out of Luxembourg.

August 22–24: The Germans defeat the British at the Battle of Mons, Belgium.

August 23: Japan declares war on Germany.

August 25: The Germans take Namur, Belgium, after a two-day bombardment using the same artillery used at Liège and devastate Louvain.

August 25: Japan declares war on Austria-Hungary.

August 26: In West Africa, German Togoland surrenders to the British and French.

August 26–September 2: On the eastern front, the Austrian army defeats the Russians at Zamosc.

August 26: The British fight a delaying action at Le Cateau.

August 27: The Germans take the French fortress at Longwy.

August 27–30: At the Battle of Tannenberg, Germans defeat the Russians. Tannenberg is regarded as the turning point in the early war on the eastern front.

August 28: Austria-Hungary declares war on Belgium.

August 29: New Zealand occupies German Samoa.

August 30: The Germans take Amiens, France.

August 30–31: The Germans advance in France, taking Givet and Montmedy, and cross the River Oise.

August 31: The Germans take Compiègne and advance to within about 30 miles of Paris, then move another 15 or so miles down the Oise to the northern edge of Chantilly, within 15 miles of Paris, their most advanced position.

September 1: German armies take Soissons.

September 2: Britain and France divide German Togoland according to the Lomé Convention.

September 2: German armies take Laon.

September 3: German armies take Rheims.

September 3: The French government leaves Paris and transfers to Bordeaux.

September 3–4: The Germans cross the Marne and advance toward Paris.

September 4: France, Britain, and Russia sign a treaty not to make a separate peace, an agreement known as the Triple Entente.

September 5–12: At the Battle of the Marne, the French advance; the battle will later be regarded as the one that saves France.

September 8–17: In Serbia, an Austrian army forces a Serbian retreat after crossing the Drina River.

September 12: Japan takes control of several German island holdings in the Pacific.

September 13: After the Battle of the Marne, German armies retreat north of the River Aisne.

September 15–18: At the Battle of the Aisne, the Germans hold their position.

September 21: New Zealand troops take the German-controlled section of New Guinea.

September 22–25: At battles near Verdun, St. Mihiel is taken by the Germans. Battles are fought near the English Channel. St. Mihiel remains a German salient into French territory for nearly the whole war.

September 27: Battles are fought in the Artois region between Picardy and Flanders.

October 1–9: German troops defeat Belgian and British forces in Antwerp; German troops are freed to advance down the English Channel into Flanders on the westernmost flank of the British-French defense.

October 7: The Japanese take the German-held island of Yap in the Carolines.

October 11: The Germans take Ghent.

October 12: The Germans take Lille.

October 13–November 12: Troops from the Union of South Africa suppress the pro-German rebellion of the Boers in the Transvaal.

October 14: The Germans take Bruges.

October 15: The Germans take Ostend.

October 18: The Battle of Yser begins.

October 30: The Ottoman fleet bombards Odessa on the Black Sea. The Ottoman Empire declares war on Britain and Russia.

October 30–November 24: First Battle of Ypres is fought. The British and French hold back the German advance through Flanders.

This photo shows the wreckage of St. Martin's Church at Ypres. The British stopped the German advance through Belgium near the French border, in Ypres. The British Tommies called the city "Wipers." *(National Archives)*

November 5: Britain declares war on the Ottoman Empire and annexes Ottoman-held Cyprus.

November 6: Egypt declares war on the Ottoman Empire.

November 22: The British occupy Basra in southern Iraq, thus invading the Ottoman Empire.

December 2: The Austrian Army takes Belgrade, the capital of Serbia.

December 9: The British accept the surrender of Ottoman/Turkish forces at Kurna in Iraq.

December 14–24: The Allied armies push on the whole western front but make no significant gains.

December 15: The Serbians retake their capital at Belgrade, forcing Austrians out of Serbia.

December 17: The British declare a protectorate over Egypt.

December 20: The first Battle of Champagne is fought.

December 31: By the end of the year, there are 675,000 German deaths and 850,000 French deaths. The British have lost more than 40,000 of the original 80,000 sent in the British Expeditionary Force. The war in the west turns static; from the end of 1914 to July 1916 the battle line in the west from Nieuport on the Channel in a curve to Soissons and on to St. Mihiel will remain virtually unchanged.

1915

"Battles" on the western front in 1915 last from two to six weeks, all resulting in great casualties but with very minor gains by either side. When one side advances, its forces are too exhausted or commanders too cautious to push the advantage for a breakthrough. The major engagements are at Ypres, Artois, Soissons, Champagne-Argonne, and St. Mihiel. On the southern front, after Italy joins as an ally of Britain and France, there are three deadlock battles on the Isonzo River frontier with Austria-Hungary near Gorizia, with no advance greater than 12 miles. All such battles in Europe claim casualties in a range from 50,000 to more than 300,000.

January 8–February 5: Heavy fighting near Soissons and La Bassée Canal area yields minor German gains.

February 16–March 30: The French attempt to attack with bombardment and infantry charges in the eastern Champagne, making only minor gains.

March 30–April 15: The French fail in an attempt to reduce the German salient at St. Mihiel.

March 31–April 5: The Germans launch zeppelin raids against southern Britain, the first strategic bombing against civilian targets in history.

April 20: British and French troops take Mandera in the German colony of Cameroons in West Africa.

April 22–May 25: The British plan a major offensive at the second Battle of Ypres, but the offensive is turned back by German use of chlorine poison gas, one of the first uses of what will later be called WMD. The Germans make little advance, not pushing their advantage.

April 26: Italy signs the secret Treaty of London with the Entente.

May 9–June 18: The second Battle of Artois is fought. The French advance only three miles after suffering great losses. The total Allied casualties in this battle are 300,000 men.

May 12: South African troops take the German city of Windhoek in Southwest Africa.

May 23: Italy declares war on Austria-Hungary. Italy holds off declaring war on Germany until 1916.

June 29–July 7: Italians attempt to push beyond the Isonzo River, the northeasternmost frontier with Austria-Hungary. The first Battle of Isonzo is fought in an attempt to establish bridgeheads across the river. The Austro-Hungarian troops engage the Italians with more enthusiasm than they do the Russians.

July 18–August 10: The second Battle of Isonzo is fought with no significant gains.

August 20: Italy declares war on the Ottoman Empire.

September 8: Zeppelins bomb London and other areas in Britain.

September 22–November 6: The French attack between Argonne and Rheims in the second Battle of Champagne, using intense artillery bombardment and infantry advance. They make only minor gains.

September 25–October 15: The British push the Germans back slightly at Loos, but do not break out in the third Battle of Artois. In this battle, the British use poison gas for the first time. Champagne and Artois casualties for the Allies are more than 250,000.

October 13–November 3: The third Battle of Isonzo is fought with no important gains.

October 29: Aristide Briand becomes the French prime minister.

November 10: The fourth Battle of Isonzo is fought with no major gains.

Eyewitness Testimony

[Woodrow Wilson] and I had often discussed the war and its effect upon our own country, and one day in August, 1914, just after the Great War had begun, he said to me: "We are going through deep waters in the days to come. The passions now lying dormant will soon be aroused and my motives and purposes at every turn will soon be challenged until there will be left but few friends to justify my course. It does not seem clear now, but as this war grows in intensity it will soon resolve itself into a war between autocracy and democracy. Various racial groups in America will seek to lead us now one way and then another. We must sit steady in the boat and bow our heads to meet the storm." Bound as he was by the responsibilities of trusteeship to adhere to a policy of neutrality, personally he saw that the inevitable results would be only bitter disappointment. "We cannot remain isolated in this war," he said, "for soon the contagion of it will spread until it reaches our own shores. On the one side Mr. Bryan will censure the Administration for being too militaristic, and on the other we will find Mr. Roosevelt criticizing us because we are too pacifist in our tendencies."

Joseph Tumulty, the president's personal secretary and political confidant, recalling Woodrow Wilson's neutrality position, August 1914, in his Woodrow Wilson as I Know Him, *pp. 227–228.*

Even when the news of the first ephemeral successes in Alsace began to come in, the Parisians did not swerve from their even gait. The newsboys did all the shouting—and even theirs was presently silenced by decree. It seemed as though it had been unanimously, instinctively decided that the Paris of 1914 should in no respect resemble the Paris of 1870, and as though this resolution had passed at birth into the blood of millions born since that fatal date, and ignorant of its bitter lesson. The unanimity of self-restraint was the notable characteristic of this people suddenly plunged into an unsought and unexpected war. At first their steadiness of spirit might have passed for the bewilderment of a generation born and bred in peace, which did not yet understand what war implied. But it is precisely on such a mood that easy triumphs might have been supposed to have the most disturbing effect. It was the crowd in the street that shouted "A Berlin!" in 1870; now the crowd in the street continued to mind its own business, in spite of showers of extras and too-sanguine bulletins. I remem-ber the morning when our butcher's boy brought the news that the first German flag had been hung out on the balcony of the Ministry of War. Now, I thought, the Latin will boil over! And I wanted to be there to see. I hurried down the quiet rue de Martignac, turned the corner of the Place Sainte Clotilde, and came on an orderly crowd filling the street before the Ministry of War. The crowd was so orderly that the few pacific gestures of the police easily cleared a way for passing cabs, and for the military motors perpetually dashing up. It was composed of all classes, and there were many family groups, with little boys straddling their mothers' shoulders, or lifted up by the policemen when they were too heavy for their mothers. It is safe to say that there was hardly a man or woman of that crowd who had not a soldier at the front, and there before them hung the enemy's first flag—a splendid silk flag, white and black and crimson, and embroidered in gold. It was the flag of an Alsatian regiment—a regiment of Prus-sianized Alsace. It symbolized all they most abhorred in the whole abhorrent job that lay ahead of them; it sym-bolized also their finest ardour and their noblest hate, and the reason why, if every other reason failed, France could never lay down arms till the last of such flags was low. And there they stood and looked at it, not dully or uncomprehendingly, but consciously, advisedly, and in silence: as if already foreseeing all it would cost to keep that flag and add to it others like it: foreseeing the cost and accepting it. There seemed to be men's hearts even in the children of that crowd, and in the mothers whose weak arms held them up. So they gazed and went on, and made way for others like them, who gazed in their turn and went on too. All day the crowd renewed itself, and it was always the same crowd, intent and under-standing and silent, who looked steadily at the flag, and knew what its being there meant. That, in August, was the look of Paris.

American writer Edith Wharton, commenting on the reaction of the Parisian populace to news of first advances on the Alsace front, August 1914, in her The War on All Fronts: Fighting France, *pp. 27–29.*

The Germans are going to war smiling, singing, and cheering. Company after company of reservists marches across Berlin from hour to hour without a suggestion of unwillingness to shoulder the unknown burdens which await the Kaiser's sons. Yesterday, while riding tediously across Prussia from Berlin to the Dutch fron-tier, we encountered countless troop trains. *"Die Wacht* am Rhein," and *"Deutschland, Deutschland, uber Alles"* echoed unceasingly from them. The men are going to war in the liveliest good spirits. They embellished the cattle-car coaches in which they travel with such inscriptions as, "Special train to Moscow and St. Petersburg," "Excursion to Paris," and "Never mind, we'll soon be chewing English Beefsteak." At every station crowds of men, women, and children assembled to throw posies to the troops and sing the national anthems as the trains pass along. The Social Democrats are for the war. They cheered the Imperial Chancellor's speech on Tuesday to the echo, unanimously voted the war credits, and will shoulder rifles cheerfully when the time comes. The Kaiser's people are a united nation.

Reporter Frederick Wile, in a cable to the
New York Times, *August 8, 1914, p. 1.*

I spoke with an elderly woman who came to a nearby door. Cool and definite she was as a French soldier, bringing home the character of the women of France which this war has made so well-known to the world.

"Were you here during the fighting?"

"Yes, monsieur, and during the shelling and the burning. The shelling was not enough. The Germans said that some one fired on their soldiers—a boy, I believe—so they set fire to the houses. One could only look and hate and pray as their soldiers passed through, looking so unconquerable, making all seem so terrible for France. Was it to be '70 over again? One's heart was of stone, monsieur. *Tiens!* They came back faster than they went. A *mitrailleuse* was down there at the end of the street, our mitrailleuse! The bullets went cracking by. They crack, the bullets; they do not whistle like the stories say. Then the street was empty of Germans who could run. The dead they could not run, nor the wounded. Then the French came up the street, running, too—running after the Germans. It was good, monsieur, good, good! My heart was not of stone then, monsieur. It could not beat fast enough for happiness. It was the heart of a girl. I remember it all very clearly. I always shall, monsieur."

Frederick Palmer, on an elderly woman's reaction to a
battle in her village September 1914, in My Year of the
War, *pp. 71–73.*

The British were fighting with their last reserves on the Ypres-Armentieres line. The French divisions to the south were suffering no less heavily, and beyond them the Belgians were trying to hold the last strip of their land under Belgian sovereignty. Cordons of guards which kept back the observer from the struggle could not keep back the truth. Something ominous was in the air. It was worth while being in that old town as it waited on the issue in the late October rains. Its fishermen crept out in the mornings from the shelter of its quays, where refugees gathered in crowds hoping to get away by steamer. Like lost souls, carrying all the possessions they could on their backs, these refugees. There was numbness in their movements and their faces were blank—the paralysis of brain from sudden disaster. The children did not cry, but munched the dry bread which their parents gave them mechanically. The newspaper men said that "refugee stuff" was already stale; eviction and misery were stale. Was Calais to be saved? That was the only question. If the Germans came, one thought that Madame at the hotel would still be at her desk, unruffled, businesslike, and she would still serve an excellent salad for *dejeuner;* the fishermen would still go out to sea for their daily catch.

What was going to happen? What might not happen? It was human helplessness to the last degree for all behind the wrestlers. Fate was in the battle-line. There could be no resisting that fate. If the Germans came, they came. Belgian staff officers with their high-crowned, gilt-braided caps went flying by in their cars. There always seemed a great many Belgian staff officers back of the Belgian army in the restaurants and cafes. Habit is strong, even in war. They did not often miss their *dejeuners.* On the Dixmude line all that remained of the active Belgian Army was in a death struggle in the rain and mud. To these *shipperkes,* honour without stint, as to their gallant king. Slightly wounded Belgians and Belgian stragglers roamed the streets of Calais. Some had a few belongings wrapped up in handkerchiefs. Others had only the clothes on their backs. Yet they were cheerful; this was the amazing thing. They moved about, laughing and chatting in groups. Perhaps this was the best way. Possibly the relief at being out of the hell at the front was the only emotion they could feel. But their cheerfulness was none the less a dash of sun-light for Calais. The French were grim. They were still polite; they went on with their work. No unwounded French soldiers were to be seen, except the old Territorials guarding the railroad and the highways. The military organization of France, which knew what war meant and had expected war, had drawn every man to his place and held him there with the inexorable hand of military and racial discipline. Calais had never considered caring for wounded, and the wounded poured in. I saw an automobile with a wounded man stop at a crowded corner, in the midst of refugees and soldiers; a doctor was leaning over him, and he died while the car waited.

Frederick Palmer, on observing Belgian and French troops retreating to Calais, October 1914, in My Year of the War, *pp. 74–75.*

I entirely believed that France and England had been drawn into a war which they had never contemplated and for which they were entirely unprepared. It never occurred to me that newspapers and statesmen could lie. I forgot my pacifism—I was ready to believe the worst of the Germans. I was outraged to read of the cynical violation of Belgian neutrality. I wrote a poem promising vengeance for Louvain. I discounted perhaps twenty per cent. of the atrocity details as war-time exaggeration. That was not, of course, enough. Recently I saw the following contemporary newspaper cuttings quoted somewhere in chronological sequence:

"When the fall of Antwerp got known the church bells were rung" (i.e. at Cologne and elsewhere in Germany). *Kolnische Zeitung.*

"According to the *Kolnische Zeitung,* the clergy of Antwerp were compelled to ring the church bells when the fortress was taken."—*Le Matin* (Paris).

"According to what *The Times* has heard from Cologne, via Paris, the unfortunate Belgian priests who refused to ring the church bells when Antwerp was taken have been sentenced to hard labour."—*Corriere della Sera* (Milan).

"According to information to the *Corriere della Sera* from Cologne, via London, it is confirmed that the barbaric conquerors of Antwerp punished the unfortunate Belgian priests for their heroic refusal to ring the church bells by hanging them as living clappers to the bells with their heads down."—*Le Matin* (Paris).

British writer Robert Graves, on the spread of propaganda, October 1914, Goodbye to All That, *pp. 88–89.*

19th November, 1914. Urgent message from Sir Reginald Brade asking me to call at the War Office. He says that Kitchener is much disturbed by failure of English newspapers to give adequate publicity to doings of the French Army and that they are taking all the credit to the English. K. tells him that there is a very strong feeling in France about this. K. had instructed him to see me and ask my advice. Brade said K. was very keen about the matter and had asked him about it six times

during the day. I advised that Major Swinton ("Eye-Witness") or Hilaire Belloc should be instructed to write a two-column *communique* describing the respective performances of the two armies and that the writer should be supplied with details of French gallantry, etc. I also suggested that the *communique* should be issued through the Press Bureau.

Lord George Riddell, on French demands that British press present the French in a better light, November 1914, Lord Riddell's War Diary, *p. 41.*

First the graves were scattered, for the boys lie buried just where they fell—cradled in the bosom of the mother country that nourished them, and for whose safety they laid down their lives. As we advanced they became more numerous, until we reached a point where, as far as we could see, in every direction, floated the little *tricolore* flags, like fine flowers in the landscape. They made tiny spots against the far-off horizon line, and groups like beds of flowers in the foreground, and we knew that, behind the skyline, there were more. Here and there was a haystack with one grave beside it, and again there would be one, usually partly burned, almost encircled with tiny flags which said: "Here sleep the heroes." It was a disturbing and a thrilling sight. I give you my word, as I stood there, I envied them. It seemed to me a fine thing to lie out there in the open, in the soil of the fields their simple death has made holy, the duty well done, the dread over, each one just where he fell defending his mother-land, enshrined forever in the loving memory of the land he had saved, in graves to be watered for years, not only by the tears of those near and dear to them, but by those of the heirs to the glory—the children of the coming generation of free France. You may know a finer way to go. I do not. Surely, since Death is, it is better than dying of old age between clean sheets.

American resident in France, Mildred Aldrich, on a visit near the Chambray front, December 5, 1914, in her On the Edge of the War Zone, *pp. 75–76.*

On Christmas morning we stuck up a board with "A Merry Christmas" on it. The enemy had stuck up a similar one. Platoons would sometimes go out for twenty-four hours rest.—It was a day at least out of the trench and relieved the monotony a bit—and my platoon had gone out in this way the night before, but a few of us stayed behind to see what would happen. Two of our men then threw their equipment off and jumped on the parapet with their hands above their heads. Two of the Germans done the same and commenced to walk up the river bank, our two men going to meet them. They met and shook hands and then we all got out of the trench. Buffalo Bill [the Company Commander] rushed into the trench and endeavored to prevent it, but he was too late: the whole of the Company were now out, and so were the Germans. He had to accept the situation, so soon he and the other officers climbed out too. We and the Germans met in the middle of no-man's-land. Their officers was also now out. Our officers exchanged greetings with them. One of the German officers said that he wished he had a camera to take a snapshot, but they were not allowed to carry cameras. Neither were our officers. . . . Officers on both sides clinked glasses and drunk one another's health. The officers came to an understanding that the unofficial truce would end at midnight. At dusk we went back to our respective trenches . . . During the whole of Boxing Day (December 26) we never fired a shot, and they the same, each side seemed to be waiting for the other to set the ball a-rolling.

Private Frank Richards of the Royal Welsh Fusiliers, commenting on Christmas fraternization in the trenches, December 25, 1914, in his Old Soldiers Never Die, *pp. 45–46.*

In the window, at the back of the half dark room, sat the *concierge,* whom I had known for nearly twenty years, a brave, intelligent, fragile woman. She was sitting there in her black frock, gently rocking herself backward and forward in her chair. I did not need to put a question. One knows in these days what the unaccustomed black dress means, and I knew that the one son I had seen grow from childhood, for whom she and the father had sacrificed everything that he might be educated, for whom they had pinched and saved—was gone. I said the few words one can say—I could not have told five minutes later what they were—and her only reply was like the speech of the woman of another class that I had met at Esbly. "I had but the one. That was my folly. Now I have nothing—and I have a long time to live alone." It would have been easy to weep with her, but they don't weep. I have never seen fewer tears in a great calamity. I have read in newspapers sent me from the States tales of women in hysterics, of women fainting as they bade their men goodbye. I have never seen any of it. Something must be wrong with my vision or my lines must have fallen in brave places. I can only speak of what I

see and hear, and tears and hysterics do not come under my observation.

Mildred Aldrich, observing the response of civilians to the loss of loved ones in Paris, December 30, 1914, in her On the Edge of the War Zone, *pp. 84–85.*

Who started it? Who is to blame? . . . When the quarrel is between nations, the neutral world turns to the diplomatic correspondence which preceded the breaking-off of relations; and only one who is a neutral can hope to weigh impartially the evidence on both sides. For war is the highest degree of partisanship. Every one engaged is a special pleader. I, too, have read the White and Blue and Yellow and Green Papers. Others have analyzed them in detail; I shall not attempt it. One learned less from their dignified phraseology than from the human motives that he read between the lines. Each was aiming to make out the best case for its own side; aiming to put the heart of justice into the blows of its arms. Obviously, the diplomatist is an attorney for a client. Incidentally, the whole training of his profession is to try to prevent war. He does try to prevent it; so does every right-minded man. It is a horror and a scourge, to be avoided as you would avoid leprosy. When it does come, the diplomatist's business is to place all the blame for it with the enemy. One must go many years back of the dates of the State papers to find the cause of the Great War. He must go into the hearts of the people who are fighting, into their aims and ambitions, which diplomatists make plausible according to international law. More illumining than the pamphlets embracing an exchange of dispatches was the remark of a practical German: "Von Bethmann-Hollweg made a slip when he talked of a treaty as a scrap of paper and about hacking his way through. That had a bad effect." Equally pointed was the remark of a practical Briton: "It was a good thing that the Germans violated the neutrality of Belgium; otherwise, we might not have gone in, which would have been fatal for us. If Germany had crushed France and kept the Channel ports, the next step would have been a war in which we should have had to deal with her single-handed." I would rather catch the drift of a nation's purpose from the talk of statesmen in the lobby or in the club than from their official pronouncements. Von Bethmann-Hollweg had said in public what was universally accepted in private. He had let the cat out of the bag. England's desire to preserve the neutrality of Belgium was not altogether ethical. If Belgium's coast had been on the Adriatic rather than on the

British Channel, her wrongs would not have had the support of British arms. Great moral causes were at stake in the Great War; but they are inextricably mixed with cool, national self-interest and racial hatreds, which are also dictated by self-interest, though not always by the interests of the human race. One who sees the struggle of Europe as a spectator, with no hatred in his heart except of war itself, finds prejudice and efficiency, folly and merciless logic, running in company. . . . Europe is a very small section of the earth's surface, indeed. Yet at the thought of a great European war, all the other peoples drew their breath aghast. When the catastrophe came, all were affected in their most intimate relations, in their income, and in their intellectual life. Rare was the mortal who did not find himself taking sides in what would have seemed to an astronomer on Mars as a local terrestrial upheaval.

Frederick Palmer, commenting on war causes, diplomats, and neutrality, 1915, in his My Year of the Great War, *pp. 1–3.*

I still have the roll of my first platoon of forty men. The figures given for their ages are misleading. When they enlisted all the over-age men had put themselves in the late thirties and all the under-age men had called themselves eighteen. But once in France the over-age men did not mind adding on a few genuine years. No less than fourteen in the roll give their age as forty or over and these were not all. Fred Prosser, a painter in civil life, who admitted to forty-eight, was really fifty-six. David Davies, collier, who admitted to forty-two, and Thomas Clark, another collier who admitted to forty-five, were only one or two years junior to Prosser. James Burford, collier and fitter, was even older than these. When I first spoke to him in the trenches, he said: "Excuse me, sir, will you explain what this here arrangement is on the side of my rifle?" "That's the safety-catch. Didn't you do a musketry course at the depot?" "No, sir, I was a re-enlisted man and I had only a fortnight there. The old Lee-Metford didn't have no safety-catch." I asked him when he had last fired a rifle. "In Egypt in 1882," he said. "Weren't you in the South African War?" "I tried to re-enlist but they told me I was too old, sir. I had been an old soldier when I was in Egypt. My real age is sixty-three." He spent all his summers as a tramp and in the bad months of the year worked as a collier, choosing a new pit every season. . . . The other half of the platoon contained the under-age section. There were five of these boys; William Bumford, collier, for instance, who

gave his age as eighteen, was really only fifteen. He used to get into trouble for falling asleep on sentry duty. The official penalty for this was death, but I had observed that he could not help it. I had seen him suddenly go to sleep, on his feet, while holding a sandbag open for another fellow to fill. So we got him a job as orderly to a chaplain for a while, and a few months later all men over fifty and all boys under eighteen were combed out and sent to the base. Bumford and Burford were both sent; but neither escaped the war. Bumford was old enough to be sent back to the battalion in the later stages of the war, and was killed; Burford was killed, too, in a bombing accident at the base-camp. Or so I was told—the fate of many of my comrades in France have come to me merely as hearsay.

Robert Graves, commenting in his memoir on the eagerness of British men to enlist, 1915, Goodbye to All That, *p. 118.*

The troop-train consisted of forty-seven coaches and took twenty-five hours to arrive at Bethune, the railhead. We went via St. Omer. It was about nine o'clock in the evening and we were hungry, cold and dirty. We had expected a short journey and so allowed our baggage to be put in a locked van. We played nap to keep our minds off the discomfort and I lost sixty francs, which was over two pounds at the existing rate of exchange. On the platform at Bethune a little man in filthy khaki, wearing the Welsh cap-badge, came up with a friendly touch of the cap most unlike a salute. He was to be our guide to the battalion, which was in the Cambrin trenches about ten kilometers away. He asked us to collect the draft of forty men we had with us and follow him. We marched through the unlit suburbs of the town. We were all intensely excited at the noise and flashes of the guns in the distance. The men of the draft had none of them been out before, except the sergeant in charge. They began singing. Instead of the usual music-hall songs they sang Welsh hymns, each man taking a part. The Welsh always sang when they were a bit frightened and pretending that they were not; it kept them steady. They never sang out of tune.

We marched towards the flashes and could soon see the flare-lights curving over the trenches in the distance. The noise of the guns grew louder and louder. Then we were among the batteries. From behind us on the left of the road a salvo of four shells came suddenly over our heads. The battery was only about two hundred yards away. This broke up *Aberystwyth* in the middle of a verse and set us off our balance for a few seconds; the column of fours tangled up. The shells went hissing away eastward; we could see the red flash and hear the hollow bang where they landed in German territory. The men picked up their step again and began chaffing. A lance-corporal dictated a letter home: "Dear auntie, this leaves me in the pink. We are at present wading in blood up to our necks. Send me fags and a life-belt. This war is a booger. Love and kisses."

Robert Graves, commenting in his memoir on traveling by train and foot to the front, 1915, Goodbye to All That, *pp. 119–120.*

Our guide took us up to the front line. We passed a group of men huddled over a brazier. They were wearing water-proof capes, for it had now started to rain, and cap-comforters, because the weather was cold. They were little men, daubed with mud, and they were talking quietly together in Welsh. Although they could see we were officers, they did not jump to their feet and salute. I thought that this was a convention of the trenches, and indeed I knew that it was laid down somewhere in the military textbooks that the courtesy of the salute was to be dispensed with in battle. But I was wrong; it was just slackness. We overtook a fatigue-party struggling up the trench loaded with timber lengths and bundles of sandbags, cursing plaintively as they slipped into sump-holes and entangled their burdens in the telephone wire. Fatigue-parties were always encumbered by their rifles and equipment, which it was a crime ever to have out of reach. When we had squeezed past this party we had to stand aside to let a stretcher-case past. "Who's the poor bastard, Dai?" the guide asked the leading stretcher-bearer. "Sergeant Gallagher," Dai answered. "He thought he saw a Fritz in No Man's Land near our wire, so the silly b—r takes one of them new issue percussion bombs and shoots it at 'im. Silly b—r aims too low, it hits the top of the parapet and bursts back. Deoul! man, it breaks his silly f—ing jaw and blows a great lump from his silly f—ing face, whatever. Poor silly b—r! Not worth sweating to get him back! He's put paid to, whatever." The wounded man had a sandbag over his face. He was dead when they got him back to the dressing-station.

Robert Graves, reacting to troops in the trenches, 1915, in his Goodbye to All That, *p. 124.*

I was hot and sweaty; my hands were sticky with the clay from the side of the trench. C Company headquarters was a two-roomed timber-built shelter in the side of a trench connecting the front and support lines. Here were tablecloth and lamp again, whisky-bottle and glasses, shelves with books and magazines, a framed picture of General Joffre, a large mirror, and bunks in the next room. I reported to the company commander. I had expected him to be a middle-aged man with a breastful of medals, with whom I would have to be formal; but Dunn was actually two months younger than myself. He was one of the fellowship of "only survivors." Captain Miller of the Black Watch in the same division was another. Miller had only escaped from the Rue du Bois massacre by swimming down a flooded trench. He has carried on his surviving trade ever since. Only survivors have great reputations. Miller used to be pointed at in the streets when the battalion was back in reserve billets. "See that fellow. That's Jack Miller. Out from the start and hasn't got it yet."

Robert Graves, commenting in his memoirs on survivors of the trenches, 1915, in Goodbye to All That, *p. 125.*

For a while, in September and October, the streets were made picturesque by the coming and going of English soldiery, and the aggressive flourish of British military motors . . . But there is another army in Paris. Its first detachments came months ago, in the dark September days—lamentable rear-guard of the Allies' retreat on Paris. Since then its numbers have grown and grown, its dingy streams have percolated through all the currents of Paris life, so that wherever one goes, in every quarter and at every hour, among the busy confident strongly-stepping Parisians one sees these other people, dazed and slowly moving—men and women with sordid bundles on their backs, shuffling along hesitatingly in their tattered shoes, children dragging at their hands and tired-out babies pressed against their shoulders: the great army of the Refugees. Their faces are unmistakable and unforgettable. No one who has ever caught that stare of dumb bewilderment—or that other look of concentrated horror, full of the reflection of flames and ruins—can shake off the obsession of the Refugees. The look in their eyes is part of the look of Paris.

Edith Wharton, commenting on refugees in Paris, 1915, in her The War on All Fronts: Fighting France, *pp. 32–33.*

We arrived in London at 5:15 P.M. and, in accord with English custom, had tea at once in the Corner House, Piccadilly, where many soldiers congregated. At the Corner House we received sixty-one invitations to the theater and dinner for the next day. That night we attended the Princess Theater where, as we entered, the orchestra played the Canadian anthem, "The Maple Leaf Forever." The audience cheered and we were forced to make a speech. You see, we were the first Canadians the English people had seen who had come to do their bit. . . .

Albert Franklin Edwards, 1st Division Canadian Infantry, remembering his brief London furlough, January 1915, in Henry L. Fox, editor, What the "Boys" Did over There—By "Themselves," *p. 50.*

We passed through more deserted villages, with soldiers lounging in the doors where old women should have sat with their distaffs, soldiers watering their horses in the village pond, soldiers cooking over gypsy fires in the farm-yards. In the patches of woodland along the road we came upon more soldiers, cutting down pine saplings, chopping them into even lengths and loading them on hand-carts, with the green boughs piled on top. We soon saw to what use they were put, for at every cross-road or railway bridge a warm sentry-box of mud and straw and plaited pine-branches was plastered against a bank or tucked like a swallow's nest into a sheltered corner. A little farther on we began to come more and more frequently on big colonies of "Seventy-fives." Drawn up nose to nose, usually against a curtain of woodland, in a field at some distance from the road, and always attended by a cumbrous drove of motor-vans, they looked like giant gazelles feeding among elephants; and the stables of woven pine-boughs which stood near by might have been the huge huts of their herdsmen. The country between Marne and Meuse is one of the regions on which German fury spent itself most bestially during the abominable September days. Half way between Chalons and Sainte Menehould we came on the first evidence of the invasion: the lamentable ruins of the village of Auve. These pleasant villages of the Aisne, with their one long street, their half-timbered houses and high-roofed granaries with espaliered gable-ends, are all much of one pattern, and one can easily picture what Auve must have been as it looked out, in the blue September weather, above the ripening pears of its gardens to the crops in the valley and the large landscape beyond. Now it is a mere waste of rubble and cinders, not one threshold distinguishable from another. We saw many other ruined villages after Auve, but this was the first, and perhaps for that reason one had there, most hauntingly, the vision of all the separate terrors, anguishes, uprootings and rendings apart involved in the destruction of the obscurest of human communities. The photographs on the walls, the twigs of withered box above the crucifixes, the old wedding-dresses in brass-clamped trunks, the bundles of letters laboriously written and as painfully deciphered, all the thousand and one bits of the past that give meaning and continuity to the present—of all that accumulated warmth nothing was left but a brick-heap and some twisted stove-pipes!

As we ran on toward Sainte Menehould the names on our map showed us that, just beyond the parallel range of hills six or seven miles to the north, the two armies lay interlocked. But we heard no cannon yet, and the first visible evidence of the nearness of the struggle was the encounter, at a bend of the road, of a long line of grey-coated figures tramping toward us between the bayonets of their captors. They were a sturdy lot, this fresh "bag" from the hills, of a fine fighting age, and much less famished and war-worn than one could have wished. Their broad blond faces were meaningless, guarded, but neither defiant nor unhappy: they seemed none too sorry for their fate. Our pass from the General Head-quarters carried us to Sainte Menehould on the edge of the Argonne, where we had to apply to the Head-quarters of the division for a farther extension. The Staff are lodged in a house considerably the worse for German occupancy, where *offices* have been improvised by means of wooden hoardings, and where, sitting in a bare passage on a frayed damask sofa surmounted by theatrical posters and faced by a bed with a plum-coloured counter-pane, we listened for a while to the jingle of telephones, the rat-tat of typewriters, the steady hum of dictation and the coming and going of hurried despatch-bearers and orderlies. The extension to the permit was presently delivered with the courteous request that we should push on to Verdun as fast as possible, as civilian motors were not wanted on the road that afternoon; and this request, coupled with the evident stir of activity at Head-quarters, gave us the impression that there must be a good deal happening beyond the low line of hills to the north. How much there was we were soon to know. We left Sainte Menehould at about eleven, and before twelve o'clock we were nearing a large village on a ridge from which the land swept away to right and left in ample reaches. The first glimpse of the outlying houses showed nothing unusual; but presently the main street turned, and dipped downward, and below and beyond us lay a long stretch of ruins: the calcined remains of Clermonten-Argonne, destroyed by the Germans on the 4th of September. The free and lofty situation of the little town—for it was really a good deal more than a village—makes its present state the more lamentable. One can see it from so far off, and through the torn traceries of its ruined church the eye travels over so lovely a stretch of country! No doubt its beauty enriched the joy of wrecking it.

Edith Wharton, visiting the front and observing the damage to French villages, February 28, 1915, in her War on All Fronts: Fighting France, *1918, pp. 56–61.*

... when we left Verdun we took the road to Bar-le-Duc. It runs south-west over beautiful broken country, untouched by war except for the fact that its villages, like all the others in this region, are either deserted or occupied by troops. As we left Verdun behind us the sound of the cannon grew fainter and died out, and we had the feeling that we were gradually passing beyond the flaming boundaries into a more normal world; but suddenly, at a cross-road, a sign-post snatched us back to war: *St. Mihiel, 18 Kilometres.* St. Mihiel, the danger-spot of the region, the weak joint in the armour! There it lay, up that harmless-looking bye-road, not much more than ten miles away—a ten minutes' dash would have brought us into the thick of the grey coats and spiked helmets! The shadow of that sign-post followed us for miles, darkening the landscape like the shadow from a racing storm-cloud. . . . A little way beyond Bar-le-Duc we came on another phase of the war-vision, for our route lay exactly in the track of the August invasion, and between Bar-le-Duc and Vitry-le-Francois the high-road is lined with ruined towns. The first we came to was Laimont, a large village wiped out as if a cyclone had beheaded it; then comes Revigny, a town of over two thousand inhabitants, less completely leveled because its houses were more solidly built, but a spectacle of more tragic desolation, with its wide streets winding between scorched and contorted fragments of masonry, bits of shop-fronts, handsome doorways, the colonnaded court of a public building. A few miles farther lies the most piteous of the group: the village of Heiltz-le-Maurupt, once pleasantly set in gardens and orchards, now an ugly waste like the others, and with a little church so stripped and wounded and dishonoured that it lies there by the roadside like a human victim.

Edith Wharton, on the devastation near Verdun, March 1915, in her The War on All Fronts: Fighting France, *pp. 80–82.*

In the second line trenches we live the lives of convicts at hard labor. Either we have to dig more trenches or carry heavy logs, iron bars, bales of hay, etc., from the outside, along the communication-trench to where we are "lodged," a distance of about half a mile. As the communication-trenches are always congested with men coming and going, this work is all the more irksome. We live like swine. There is no water, so we never wash or even brush our teeth. We are not allowed to drink water. We simply live in filth. At night we are huddled together in a small bomb-proof or covered trench. Though we are pretty well protected from the weather and bullets, we have hardly room enough to turn around in. We use candles to light up this terries [underground den], but nevertheless everything gets lost or hopelessly dirty. We eat from the pail, and can get or send for all the red or white wine we want. In the morning, besides tepid coffee, we are given a swig of rum which warms our stomach and starts the blood going. This small pleasure and continued pipe smoking are about our only joys—but hold—there is also our mail, which we get fairly regularly.

A. C. Champollion, Harvard class of 1902, serving with the French army, in a letter home, March 20, 1915, three days before being killed, in Mark Anthony De Wolfe Howe, editor, The Harvard Volunteers in Europe: Personal Records of Experience in Military, Ambulance, and Hospital Service, *pp. 21–22.*

In that charge I enjoyed the experience of getting my first German. I crashed into him, a big burly six-footer, and now that my wish to meet one had been gratified, and I stood there before him, I did not know whether to shoot him, punch him, kick him or stick him as you would a pig. Not having much experience with the bayonet, I acted on impulse and rammed it right through his stomach. Oh boy! What a squeal he let out. Putting my foot on his breast I pulled the bayonet from out his vitals, taking along with it his bowels. This nerved me, and I rushed forward like a raving maniac stopping for nothing. I plowed my way through them using first my butt and then the bayonet until I had rushed right into their second line, and Holy Jerusalem!! right smack into a whole nest of them. We were proceeding rather methodically in cleaning them out, when a shell from a "Jack Johnson" burst in the midst of our gallant little company, killing five outright and separating two from their legs and arms, I myself losing a leg and having my shoulder put out of commission. I was conscious all the time of what had happened, and managed to crawl into a shell-hole, and slap a bandage about my leg. With my shoulder I could do nothing and after lying exposed for two hours the company stretcher bearers picked me up and carried me back to the dressing station.

Sgt. Frederick Muir, 10th Battalion, Canadian Expeditionary Force, on being wounded April 21, 1915, in What the "Boys" Did over There—By "Themselves," *pp. 103–104.*

It appeared that at the particular line of trenches where he was they had agreed only to fire at each other with rifles! In several places here the trenches are only fifteen or twenty metres apart and the French and Germans are on quite good terms. They exchange tobacco for wine and paper for cigarettes and then return and shoot at each other quite merrily. About Christmas or February, I am told, by soldiers who were then here, they used to walk into each other's trenches and exchange stories, etc., but now they have become *"méchant."*

Leslie Buswell, American ambulance driver, in a letter written home about first impressions at the front in France, June 1915, in his Ambulance No. 10: Personal Letters from the Front, *p. 22.*

We have been kept well occupied, supplying working parties to assist "sappers." The work we have been doing has been mostly on one small part of the line, where there is a very pronounced local salient. Across this salient a second line of trenches is being made in case of any need of giving up the apex of the salient. A line of this sort is known as a "switch," and it more or less cuts along the salient and joins up with the present fire-trenches on either side. Most nights we have been working on this switch, either digging or improving trenches, or putting up wire or carrying up material. Some of the ground covered by this line can be seen from the German line, so work cannot be carried on there by day; moreover, an aeroplane would soon spot any working party and have it shelled right away. Being able to work only by dark has meant regular hours, almost like the routine hours of a peace-time job. We start off in the evening in time to get our digging tools and get up to the work just as sufficient darkness arrives to afford cover, and leave again as the first light begins to show itself. This "switch" is by no means healthy, as it is very liberally distributed by all the bullets coming over our fire-trenches from the other side. Such fire is called "overs," and, of course, is not aimed at one, but is just as good at doing damage, when it hits, as aimed fire might be. Being a salient, the middle part of the ground gets "overs" from the flanks as well as the front. If there is a lot of fire coming from the German trenches, we have to quit work until it cools down a bit. It is rather a thankless job, it seems to me, as we are losing quite a few men at it, and get very little in return but candid criticism from rather self-satisfied R.E. [rear-echelon] subalterns.

F. C. Baker, Harvard class of 1912, serving with the Cyclist Service of the British Army, published in Harvard Graduate's Magazine *of December 1915, recording observations on trench work, "about" June 10, 1915, in Mark Anthony De Wolfe Howe, editor,* The Harvard Volunteers in Europe: Personal Records of Experience in Military, Ambulance, and Hospital Service, *pp. 105–106.*

It was a sad trip for me—a boy about nineteen had been hit in the chest and half his side had gone,—"tres pressé" they told me,—and as we lifted him into the car, by a little brick house which was a mass of shell holes, he raised his sad, tired eyes to mine and tried a brave smile. I went down the hill as carefully as I could and very slowly, but when I arrived at the hospital I found I had been driving a hearse and not an ambulance. In made me feel very badly—the memory of that faint smile which was to prove the last effort of some dearly loved youth. All the poor fellows look at us with the same expression of appreciation and thanks; and when they are unloaded it is a common thing to see a soldier, probably suffering the pain of the damned, make an effort to take the hand of the American helper. I tell you tears are pretty near sometimes.

Leslie Buswell, American ambulance driver, on transporting the wounded, June 28, 1915, in his Ambulance No. 10: Personal Letters from the Front, *p. 22.*

The Press soon became furious regarding the censorship arrangements. The Cable Censor's Department was chiefly responsible. It had been created secretly and was officered by half-pay *officers,* many being of the antiquated type afterwards christened "dug-outs." There was, and is, considerable misunderstanding regarding the Press censorship. The Regulations prohibited the Press from publishing certain things—for instance, the movements of troops, ships, or aircraft, or plans for the conduct of the war. The newspapers were under no obligation to submit their "copy" to the Censor's Department, although that plan was generally adopted in the case of doubtful material. . . . The original intention was that war correspondents should go to the Front. When war broke out, the correspondents selected by the papers were called together and acquainted with the arrangements. Each was to be provided with a horse. After the horses had been champing in their stables for six weeks it became apparent that the correspondents were not to be allowed to go to the Front. Thereupon the War Office notified their willingness to buy the horses which had been purchased, it being stated that the experience gained in the last few weeks had convinced the Army Council that owing to the long distances that had to be covered horses would be useless for war correspondents, if and when they were permitted to take the field. Meanwhile unauthorised correspondents had made their way to France and had been arrested by the French or sent back to England. The authorities adopted the alternative of appointing Major E. D. Swinton as official "Eye-Witness." He went to France on September 14th and continued his functions until the middle of July 1915. Grave dissatisfaction existed not only among newspaper men, but also among the public and in some sections of the Army, regarding the inadequate information published concerning the progress of the war and the doings of the British troops in particular. I continually urged the War Office to allow correspondents to go to the Front. Eventually, during March and April, three parties of correspondents were permitted to make short tours in France. . . . The correspondents' dispatches did much to stimulate the nation and enable it to realise the nature of the struggle in which it was engaged. The authorities, however, were resolute in declining to allow the correspondents to describe the doings of the different regiments by name. . . . The Australian and Canadian Publicity Departments, however, adopted the plan of describing the doings of their troops, with the result that the doings of the Home Army were perhaps inadequately appreciated in comparison. It is not for me to say whether the authorities were right in the view they took. The Press urged that the enemy already knew in most instances what units were fighting on the various fronts, but this was denied by the Intelligence Department. . . . Many foolish mistakes were made by the censors, but perhaps these were inevitable. Looking back, it is somewhat surprising that the system worked as well as it did, considering that the work was done by people without any previous experience and without any prin-

ciples to guide them. A series of disjointed prohibitions was evolved, but, as far as I am aware, no general principles were laid down. On the one hand the Press were always fighting for more freedom, while on the other mysterious and unknown personages acting through the medium of the Press Bureau and the censors at G.H.Q. were always insisting on the necessity for secrecy.

George Allardice, Lord Riddell, commenting on press censorship, July 1915, in Lord Riddell's War Diary, *pp. 16–18, 24–25.*

The Germans dared not shell us as we were so close to their trenches that they were afraid of hitting their own men. The shell craters through which our trenches ran were only thirteen yards from the trenches of the enemy, and we could hear the Saxons who opposed us singing songs in English which they all seemed to speak fluently. One night I was on patrol when our party passed a German patrol not five yards distant. Neither side dared fire for fear of starting the machine gun fire. One of the Saxons called out, "Hello, Canuck, how's Quebec, Winnipeg, and Vancouver?" Evidently he had been in Quebec as he spoke of the St. Regis Hotel.

Private Albert Franklin Edwards, 1st Division, Canadian Infantry, July 1915, in Henry L. Fox, editor, What the "Boys" Did over There—By "Themselves," *p. 53.*

I went over some of their trenches the other day and have never seen anything so horrible. Although, as prisoners have told us, they knew they were to be attacked, they had no idea that the attack would be anything like so severe as it was. Those I have talked to said it was awful, and that they were glad to be out of it. Their trenches were very elaborately constructed, many of the dug outs being fitted up with considerable furniture, the dwellers evidently having no notion they would be hurriedly evicted. After the bombardment there was nothing left of all this careful work. The whole earth was torn to pieces. It looked as though some drunken giant had driven his giant plough over the land. In the midst of an utterly indescribable medley of torn wire, broken wagons, and upheaved timbers, yawned here and there chasms like the craters of small volcanoes, where mines had been exploded. It was an ashen gray world, distorted with the spasms of death—like a scene in the moon. Except for the broken guns, the scattered clothing, the hasty graves, the dead horses and other signs of human passage, no one could have believed that such a place had

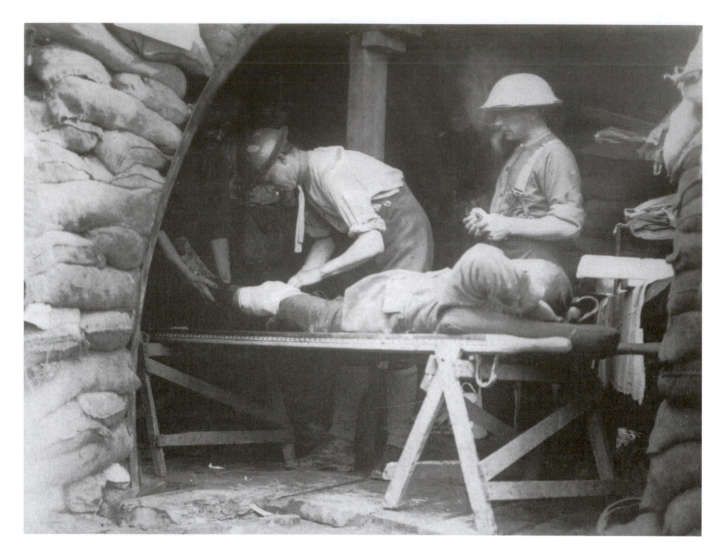

Often the first care for the seriously wounded was in a frontline bunker like this one in the British sector of the front near Menin Road in Belgium. *(National Archives)*

ever been anything but dead and desolate. The rubbish still remained when I was there, but masses of material had already been gathered up and saved.

Richard Norton, Harvard class of 1902, ambulance driver, observations on the German trenches, October 14, 1915, in Mark Anthony De Wolfe Howe, editor, The Harvard Volunteers in Europe: Personal Records of Experience in Military, Ambulance, and Hospital Service, *pp. 101–102.*

It was this night, while carrying up sand bags, a bullet struck my right arm. I made the front line all right, but as soon as I was dressed by the stretcher bearer I was sent back to the dressing station to the medical officer to receive attention. I was then sent to the field hospital, and the next day I was removed on an ambulance train, and sent to the base hospital in Etaples. I might state that this hospital was an American hospital. How wonderful it was to me to find myself back in a nice white bed again. I was there for two weeks and then sent to a convalescent hospital for another week. At the beginning of December I found myself on the way back to the front line. Of course all my pals who were still there were glad to see me again; but, believe me, it was hard to leave that nice white bed and go back "somewhere in the mud." I made the best of it. I knew it was doing my duty, as every soldier does.

Sergeant Jack Winston on being wounded, November 1915, in Henry L. Fox, editor, What the "Boys" Did over There—By "Themselves," *p. 28.*

3

The Early War on and beneath the Sea

August 1914–December 1916

THE WAR AT SEA

The war at sea, like that on land, changed because of new technologies: wireless communication, the airplane, the mine, the self-propelled torpedo, the submarine, and a host of minor improvements in explosives, propellants, armor, and electrical equipment. These new inventions and systems, not only required naval officers to think creatively and break out of the confines of their early training and experience, but also the mine and the submarine especially seemed to challenge the very principles of proper conduct and morality. Regularly the French and British press called submarine captains brigands or pirates, while the German press regarded the use of mines to stop the flow of food to Germany as tantamount to an atrocity directed at the defenseless civilians, including children, who depended on food imports.

Naval officers and men fought the war at sea at both extremes of the style of the World War, the civilized and the barbaric. Many naval officers had great respect for the seamanship and fighting ability of their enemies, and the maritime war yielded hundreds of gallant stories of gentlemanly treatment of prisoners, the rescue from the sea and medical care of enemy combatants and neutral civilians, and high adventure and clever deceptions of officers and men who carried the war literally around the world to the islands of the Pacific and the distant shores of Africa and Asia. At the same time, the war at sea frequently turned brutal and treacherous, with cold-blooded slaughter and the death by drowning or fire not only of tens of thousands of enemy sailors, but of more than 5,000 innocent civilians, including many women and children unlucky enough to be caught aboard merchant or passenger ships that submarines sank in the open ocean.

From the American perspective, the new kind of maritime war made American neutrality increasingly difficult because both the Central Powers and the Allies sought to cut off the rich supply of food and other goods to their enemies that flowed by ship from the United States and from other neutral countries. Both sides used ruthless, impersonal, and drastic means to interdict the flow of commerce by merchant ships. Although international law laid down ambiguous standards on some points, both sides clearly violated established legal traditions

After submarines successfully sank capital ships such as cruisers, small subchasers like this one became even more valuable. *(National Archives)*

and humane practices in their blockade methods. Britain, no less than Germany, sought to use starvation of civilians as a weapon of war, and turned its sea power to that end.

As the maritime war unfolded through 1915 and 1916, tensions between the United States and Germany over German use of the submarine or *Unterseeboot,* the notorious U-boat, brought relations close to the breaking point. But British tactics of declaring food contraband, interdicting shipping to neutral Holland and Denmark, and setting up minefields to assist in the blockade, all drew criticism not only from the Central Powers, but from neutral observers as well. In the long run, the German use of the submarine, both the official policy and the violations of standards of decency by individual submarine commanders, eventually brought the United States into the war.

With the submarine especially, the changing technology of warfare created a new environment in which policies and ethics lagged behind. Although the submarine and its consequences would arouse the American public and American press, from the perspective of naval officers around the world, the engagements of the surface battle fleets against each other also showed very clearly that the nature of war at sea had changed drastically even without considering the impact of the submarine. Like the army officers of the major powers, naval officers at first naturally followed the principles that were inculcated in them in their youth.

In the age of sail, ships had formed a line, sailing with the prevailing winds. Consequently, when the engagement took place, ships would often be in parallel lines, and would fire from their sides at each other, providing the logic behind such terms as *battle ship of the line* and *broadside*. However, with the advent of steam and independence from wind that came with the all-steam vessels of the 1870s and later, some of those older tactics became obsolete. Yet the culture died hard. Battles fought at night, in fog or mist, with independently steaming surface ships that moved in all directions did not quite match the conditions under which Lord Horatio Nelson had fought more than a century before. When small torpedo boats engaged, and commands dealt with intercepted radio messages, secret codes, and tangled communications, naval war seemed unrecognizable.

Some of the navies adapted better to the new technologies than others. The German High Seas Fleet had less tradition behind it. Perhaps that very lack of heritage meant that German officers and crew could grow more proficient at night fighting and at adapting new devices and techniques such as electric searchlights and illuminating shells. Admiral John Jellicoe of the British Grand Fleet thought it fruitless to drill for night battles, since he believed it would be nearly impossible to distinguish friendly ship from enemy ship in the confusion of the night. But the lack of experience and tradition could also work against the Germans. The German naval command remained reluctant to commit their surface ships against the superior numbers of British ships; both the British and the Germans believed that the long naval tradition of Britain and the longer service and experience of its enlisted men gave the British an advantage. In fact, in the few battles in which the groups of the surface fleets met each other, British experience and seamanship seemed to meet its match in German engineering, equipment, and gunnery.

DREADNOUGHTS AND SUBMARINES

When the war started, Britain clearly dominated the sea. The first all-big-gun battleship, the British *Dreadnought,* had been launched in 1906, supplemented by another 23 built by mid-1914, including three funded with generous contributions from Canada. Before the war, Germany attempted to catch up in the strategic arms race, building about 16 dreadnought-type battleships before the guns of August signaled the beginning of the war. Even with the British naval superiority, however, Britain had cause to be concerned about the naval balance of power.

Despite the numerical advantage of the Grand Fleet over Germany's High Seas Fleet, the British clearly had more responsibilities than did the German navy. Although Germany could launch ground assaults on the continent without a navy, Britain relied on the Grand Fleet to protect its merchant shipping. Two-thirds of the food supply for Britain came by sea, and the British merchant fleet carried more than half of the world's total maritime commerce. In addition, the Grand Fleet had to make sure the British Expeditionary Force (B.E.F.) sailed under escort safely to Europe, and it had to protect the food supply to the British Isles and guard against any invasion or bombardment of its coastal ports. Furthermore, as passenger ships transported troops from India and the Dominions of Australia and New Zealand through the Suez Canal to Egypt, the Mediterranean, and Europe, they had to be protected. In addition to these duties, the fleet had to mount a blockade of German ports and, if possible, bottle up the German fleet.

Although the dreadnought with its heavy guns represented a new type of ship, the logic of its employment became clear from the beginning. It could be used in attacks on enemy warships and could serve to bombard shore facilities, to escort other ships, or could be pressed into blockade duty. However, the submarine represented a revolution in military affairs that, like the aircraft, took warfare off the surface of the planet. Yet naval officers did not know exactly how it would be employed in 1914.

The submarine, however, demonstrated its potential for changing the nature of war at sea when the German U-boat *U-9* under Lieutenant Otto Weddigen attacked three British cruisers off the Dutch coast. One reason for the loss of all three ships derived from adherence to a fine heritage. Following tradition, when *Aboukir* went down, the other two cruisers closed in to rescue sailors from the sea, exposing themselves to further attack. Weddigen, in his eyewitness account of the episode, recognized that he confronted a unique targeting opportunity that would probably not recur. In later engagements, only ships capable of attacking submarines, such as destroyers, would come to the rescue of sailors, while the heavier capital ships such as cruisers, battleships, and dreadnoughts fled to safer waters. British and Germans alike learned the lessons of *Aboukir, Hogue,* and *Cressy,* paid for at such a tragic cost.

Another German submarine, *U-24,* sank the British battleship *Formidable* on December 31, 1914, with the loss of 547 officers and men. The early success of the *U-9* in sinking three British warships and then the loss of *Formidable* added to Jellicoe's concerns, leading him to station both his reserve fleet and the ships to blockade Germany at great distances from the German ports, relying on mine-fields in the North Sea and the Channel to restrict the movements of commercial ships. Dreadnoughts, battleships, and even fast cruisers could no longer be risked to submarine attack and needed to be protected by destroyers, torpedo boats, and other small craft while at sea or protected in harbor by strong defenses. Within months, the British Admiralty applied the lessons in the wake of the loss of heavy warships to the small submarines.

Questions remained. Could the submarine be used to raid against civilian merchant ships? According to traditional practice, when a warship seized a merchant ship at sea in the course of a blockade, the naval vessel would confiscate the freighter and would make every effort to save the noncombatant sailors and even work to repatriate them to their home nation. Usually submarines did not carry enough men to put prize crews aboard the merchant ships they stopped at sea, and, in the cramped quarters of a submarine, there would be little room for guests, although many submarine captains did take prisoners aboard rather than let them drown. So if a submarine destroyed a merchant ship at sea, the question of humane treatment of the civilian crew and passengers presented a problem. The traditions of the sea and the conditions of the submarine did not make a good match, and submarine captains found them especially difficult to reconcile. Nevertheless, many German U-boat officers developed reputations for extreme care for the crews of the ships they sank. Some would wait nearby until rescue vessels approached the lifeboats, and, in some cases, the U-boats would tow lifeboats to within sight of land.

As submarine policy changed in Germany several times, the final decision on humane practices varied, frequently depending on the values and character of individual submarine captains. Some, like Lothar von Arnauld de la Perière, proved consistently gracious and helpful to the crews and passengers of ships they attacked, warning them before sinking their vessel and making provisions for their safety. Arnauld only rarely used his torpedoes, but, instead, after warning a ship and evacuating its crew and any passengers to seaworthy lifeboats, he would sink the ship with delayed charges placed aboard or with shells from his deck gun. The British listed other more ruthless captains as war criminals, like Wilhelm Werner of *U-55*, who more than once torpedoed clearly marked hospital ships in defiance of official German policy and the rules of war. The British press played up such atrocities with great fanfare and several such incidents inflamed American opinion. Yet only a very few German submarine captains were charged with such war crimes by the British, and the vast majority of them did their best to act within the spirit and even the letter of the international cruiser rules even though their submarines could be rammed by ordinary freighters or shot and sunk by armed merchant ships. Some of the most crucial episodes that angered American public opinion and which prompted American diplomatic responses remained surrounded by ambiguity. In some cases, U-boat captains claimed that the merchant ships that they torpedoed appeared as if making threatening runs to ram them; in other cases, a merchant ship may have been mistaken for a warship. Newspapers sometimes reported an attack on the front pages as if the merchant ship had been given no warning and many of the crew had been killed, only to give a fuller report in a much smaller story on interior pages a few days later when lifeboats full of survivors began to be picked up or reach land. Even so, U-boats made attacks without warning on defenseless civilian merchant ships frequently enough through the period 1914–17 to give plenty of cause for distress in the United States and Britain.

Not until Germany launched into an official policy of unrestricted submarine warfare in 1917 did the practice of sinking without warning become commonplace, however. In 1915, German submarines gave no warning to only 21 percent of ships attacked; in 1916, the number sunk without warning climbed to 29 percent.

The British confronted the question of how they might maintain a blockade against Germany in the face of land-based aircraft for spotting the blockading ships and the possibility of torpedo-equipped submarines that could dart out from port to destroy the blockaders. For the Germans, it seemed unwise to risk their smaller surface fleet in a major engagement with the British Grand Fleet, yet, if most of the German fleet could not break out to sea, its effectiveness would be nullified.

Naval strategists had entered the war believing that the surface ship and the great fleet engagements could determine the outcome of the war. But the course of the war nearly erased that illusion, with the consequences of the use of submarines and aircraft at least partially demonstrated.

These maritime issues would come to the fore in 1915, all of them requiring new solutions because of the changes in the technology of war at sea. Before the submarine emerged as the weapon that might decide the war, three battles of the surface fleets tested the British and German navies in the seas between Britain and the western coast of Europe: Heligoland Bight, Dogger Bank, and Jutland, while far off in the Pacific, Indian, and South Atlantic oceans, a few German surface raiders, sailing independently or in small squadrons of a few ships, demonstrated that the war had indeed spread across the whole planet, becoming truly a worldwide war.

HELIGOLAND BIGHT

The Battle of Heligoland Bight, on August 28, 1914, less than a month into the war, gave hints of the perils of a surface fleet engagement. Concerned that the ships carrying the British Expeditionary Force to Belgium might fall victim to German cruisers, the British Admiralty sent the light cruiser *Arethusa* and the destroyer *Lurcher* to look for any large German warships that might attack the troop carriers. Maintaining radio silence, the Admiralty did not inform *Arethusa* and *Lurcher* that another light cruiser, *Fearless,* together with a group of 16 destroyers, had been dispatched to assist them. Consequently, when the two British groups met in the mist off the Belgian coast, *Arethusa* narrowly avoided making the mistake of firing on the supplementary British force. Soon, six more cruisers and a total of 31 destroyers assembled, available to make a raid on German forces.

The British ships encountered German destroyers on the move and a German cruiser, *Stettin,* at anchor off the Heligoland Bight. At 0650 hours Greenwich Mean Time (that is, at 6:50 A.M. in London), a furious 25-minute action began between *Arethusa* and *Stettin. Frauenlob,* another light cruiser, soon joined *Stettin.* Several of the guns aboard the British ship jammed and a German shell put another out of action, but with one remaining six-inch gun, the *Arethusa* hit the command bridge of the *Frauenlob.* As the ships broke off action, *Fearless* joined the damaged *Arethusa,* and then together both cruisers encountered a heavy German destroyer, *V 187.* The British cruisers trapped the destroyer and sank her. As boats from British destroyers and a submarine stopped to pick up German survivors struggling into lifeboats, *Stettin* arrived to interrupt them. Displaying some of the gallantry that characterized these early days of the war, the British provided the Germans in lifeboats with water, food, a compass, and directions back to shore, themselves taking off with British survivors and only a few German prisoners aboard the British submarine.

Off and on during the morning, German and British ships encountered each other, with numerous cases of mistaken identity as British officers often spotted another British ship in the mist and assumed it to be a German one. Several of the British destroyers took severe damage from shells from the German cruiser *Mainz,* and then the *Mainz* sank under a battering from five heavy British cruisers. After several more engagements, the British broke off the battle. Altogether, the British lost about 35 men killed and another 40 wounded, with *Arethusa* severely damaged, but not sunk. The Germans lost three light cruisers, the large destroyer, and about 1,000 men killed, wounded, or captured.

A clear British victory, the Battle of Heligoland Bight had the effect of encouraging the British to think that they could maintain control of the surface, while ignoring their own deficiencies in communication, gunnery, and the near-tragedies of mistaken identity. Meanwhile, the loss of the German ships to the superior British force left an immediate and conclusive effect on the German command. The kaiser concluded that the valuable German High Seas Fleet should not risk exposure to British attacks. Believing in late August 1914—with the Russian advance stopped, the French and British retreating in Belgium and France, and Paris within reach—that the war would be over soon, it seemed wise to simply preserve the German fleet from needless losses. The first origin of the German policy to largely bottle up their fleet in port can be traced to the outcome of Heligoland Bight.

SURFACE COMMERCE RAIDERS IN THE PACIFIC AND INDIAN OCEANS

In the early months of the war, several other engagements between British and German ships around the world showed the British that German gunners fired their weapons with high accuracy and that the smaller German fleet represented a serious threat. A German squadron of five ships under Count von Spee destroyed a British cable station in the central Pacific, sent the cruiser *Emden* off on a separate course toward the Indian Ocean, and then moved on for reinforcements to a rendezvous near Easter Island in the South Pacific. On November 1, 1914, the German squadron sank two British ships off the west coast of South America—the armored cruiser *Good Hope* and the light cruiser *Glasgow,* which went down with 1,600 men. In response, the British launched a stronger unit, including two battle cruisers, *Inflexible* and *Invincible,* that caught up with the German group near the Falkland Islands in the South Atlantic. In the ensuing battle, the British sank four of the German ships, and Spee and 1,800 German sailors died in the engagement. The British chased the fifth German ship, *Dresden,* around Cape Horn to the Pacific, where her crew scuttled the ship off the Juan Fernandez Islands (the site of the marooning of the real-life Robinson Crusoe, Alexander Selkirk).

Two German surface commerce raiders, the *Emden* and the *Koenigsberg,* together destroyed 41 allied merchant ships, and the British and Australians mounted search parties that eventually tracked them down. The exploits of *Emden* became the stuff of maritime legend. Steaming through the Dutch East Indies after getting orders from Spee, *Emden* cruised past Java and Sumatra into the Indian Ocean, where between September 10 and October 24, it sank or captured 23 merchant ships. *Emden* also destroyed a British cruiser and a destroyer, shelled a British oil depot at Madras, India, and cut a vital undersea cable in the Cocos Islands. Altogether, the ship inflicted more than £15 million damage. After the *Emden* was pursued by at least 14 major Allied warships, the Australian navy caught the ship in the Indian Ocean, where, after being outgunned and damaged, the captain ordered it run aground to save his surviving crew. Even British and pro-Allied newspapers in neutral countries recognized the captain, Karl von Müller, for his chivalrous treatment of the enemy. He had worked to remove all the crews and passengers from merchant ships before sinking them, then transferred the crews to neutral ships or to safety in ports, making him one of the legendary gentlemen-heroes of the conflict at sea. After similar exploits and knocking out some 18 ships, the *Koenigsberg* took refuge in a river in German East Africa, where the captain finally scuttled the ship and joined German forces in the colony to continue the fight through 1918. The surviving crew and officers surrendered only after word reached them of the armistice in Europe.

DOGGER BANK

Although the British and Germans fought very few engagements between their surface fleets, a second major clash developed on January 14, 1915, off Dogger Bank. The largest sea battle up to that time during the war, Dogger Bank saw five British cruisers engage four German ones. In a confused battle, several British weaknesses became apparent. In particular, the British did not communicate well, allowing three of the German ships to escape, leaving only *Blücher* to be destroyed by superior British guns. German guns severely damaged the British *Lion,* and, due to British confusion, the three other German cruisers escaped while British ships poured fire into the already sinking *Blücher.* Although the British press touted the battle as a victory, professionals within the Admiralty worried about

Crew evacuate from the sinking *Blücher* during the Battle of Dogger Bank, January 14, 1915. *(National Archives)*

not only the failure of command and communication, but other questions as well. Superior German fire control, or aiming of naval ordnance, showed that the Germans could put more shells on their targets. Furthermore, the possibility of a flash explosion traveling down the gun loading hoists or elevator shafts to the ammunition magazines required design and training improvements. Despite the fact that one of the British ships, *Tiger,* had a new direction finder, none of its shots hit their target, while another, *Southampton,* regularly overshot its targets by some 3,000 yards.

JUTLAND

In a sense, Germany lost an opportunity to win World War I against Britain in one day, May 31, 1916. By early 1916, the British blockade against Germany had cut off most overseas neutral trade with the Central Powers, and the British could fairly believe they had begun to win the maritime war. A change in German policy came with the appointment of Vice Admiral Reinhard Scheer in February 1916 as head of the German High Seas Fleet. Scheer showed a bit more daring than his predecessors did, but, like them, he recognized that his fleet represented no match in numbers or size for the British fleet. He adopted the strategy however, of trying to lure out small British forces, by offensive movements and bombardments of the British coast, into a position where the British Grand Fleet could be attacked piecemeal. Furthermore, by mining and submarine attacks, he hoped to engage such small forces, knowing that a full-scale traditional battle of the main fleets would be too hazardous for Germany.

The battle off the coast of Denmark, called the Battle of Jutland by the British and the Battle of Skagerrak by the Germans, had been provoked by Scheer's strategy. The battle lasted through the night of May 31 and into the next day, and in many ways it demonstrated once again the superior German gunnery. The German use of searchlights and illuminating shells, their highly accurate spotting shells, and their methodical firing even from ships already damaged and dead in the water all impressed their British counterparts. The British dreadnoughts pounded some of the smaller German ships, however, and, in general, the British had heavier guns and heavier armor available. Although both sides suffered great losses, three of the British losses revealed that they had not solved the problem of protecting the ammunition magazines. The *Indefatigable, Queen Mary,* and *Invincible* all blew up from magazine explosions, taking nearly all hands to the bottom of the sea. From *Invincible,* only six members of the crew survived from a total of more than 1,000. An incoming round destroyed a gun turret aboard *Lion,* and a mortally wounded Royal Marine officer, Major F. W. Harvey, ordered the magazine doors closed, thereby saving his ship from a similar fate. The British Grand Fleet lost 14 ships, with a total of 110,000 tons, while the Germans lost 11 ships totaling 62,000 tons. More than 6,000 British officers and men died in the engagement, while the Germans lost 2,551.

Although these figures of lost ships and staggering losses of human life suggest a British defeat, they account for only part of the story. At the end of the battle, Britain's Admiral Jellicoe still had 24 dreadnoughts ready to fight, while Germany's Admiral Scheer had only 10 dreadnoughts left. Furthermore, the British repaired their damaged ships much more rapidly than did the Germans. For example, British yards repaired three British battle cruisers, *Lion, Tiger,* and *Princess Royal,* by mid-July; German repair facilities could only accommodate one battle cruiser per month, bringing *Moltke, von der Tann, Seydlitz,* and *Derfflinger* up to readiness gradually between July 30 and October 16.

One of the German cruisers, *Seydlitz,* although severely damaged, limped back to port by dint of excellent patching and repair work at sea, all well documented later in a published eyewitness account by Captain von Egidy. Von Egidy took particular pride in the technical ability of electrical engineers, mechanics, and the crew in general, suggesting the degree to which German officers regarded seamanship as a set of modern engineering skills, rather than a collection of maritime traditions inherited from the days of sail. His account of the struggle caught the imagination and interest of even dedicated pro-British maritime specialists.

Despite the heavier British losses, most accounts of the battle, especially those published in Britain and the United States ranked the battle as a draw. That viewpoint reflected some justice, because after Jutland the German High Seas Fleet did not venture forth again for a major engagement. It appeared, even though the Germans had shown a number of superior tactics and some superior use of equipment, that the battle had decisively immobilized the German surface fleet almost as effectively as if it had been all destroyed. In later months and years, naval historians minutely reviewed the Battle of Jutland, studying each turn of the ships and each decision, from cleverly executed maneuver through tragic mistake and failure of communication. Participants and later generations of naval officers of many nations including the United States pored over detailed, shot-by-shot accounts of the engagement.

For naval engineers and architects the lessons of Jutland included the need to adapt to torpedoes, radio, and the conditions of night fighting. In the United

States over the next decades, even though working on reduced peacetime budgets, technical researchers, officers, and crews sought to bring American surface ships up to the standards displayed by the Germans in the battle that they almost won.

MEDITERRANEAN ACTION

While the German High Seas Fleet remained bottled up in harbor, Jellicoe did not order the British Grand Fleet into action against the exposed coast of Germany because of the joint fear of submarines, torpedo boats, and aircraft. In addition to the early loss of several major warships to submarines, another submarine victory helped convince the British that the surface fleet should not be exposed unprotected to the deadly combination of submarine and self-propelled torpedo. German captain Otto Hersing took *U-21* on a voyage from the North Sea south around France and Spain and through the Straits of Gibraltar. Although refueled once at sea from the Hamburg America steamer *Marzala,* the offloaded oil supply turned out to be too thick to fire in *U-21* diesel engines, and Hersing carefully motored across the Mediterranean, harboring the sub's last reserves, some 26 tons of good diesel fuel. *U-21* arrived at the Austrian port of Cattaro (Kotor, Montenegro) on the Adriatic with 1.8 tons of fuel left.

After refitting and refueling, *U-21* slipped around the Greek islands and approached the battlegrounds of Gallipoli. There, Hersing sank the battleship *Triumph* on May 27, 1915, and, two days later, torpedoed the even larger battleship *Majestic,* both within sight of the troops battling ashore. Both battleships had bombarded the Turkish trenches, but, after Hersing's attacks, the British pulled all their major warships away from the coast, leaving the landing troops without the major gun power the battleships had brought to bear. Turkish and Allied troops watched the sinking and the flight of heavy ships with a visible improvement to Turkish spirits. However, for the Australian and New Zealand troops in the

The German fleet left port only rarely in World War I. In this photo the second battleship squadron steams out into the North Sea. *(National Archives)*

trenches, a sense of being abandoned by the British navy soured morale, foreshadowing the eventual failure of that effort.

Although the U-boats had won spectacular victories against British sea power during the early months of the war, it soon became evident that the submarine threat to the surface fleet could be controlled. Twice as many warships sank during the first year of the war as in all the three remaining years. After the victories by Weddigen and Hersing, submarine captains rarely found an opportunity to mount a successful attack on a major naval ship of the rank of heavy cruiser or battleship. Although the subs had proven quite deadly in those attacks, the British and French learned the lessons of the sinking very quickly. The simplest method to avoid submarine attack was to keep the major capital ships in harbor. The British tended to shelter them in the inlets of Scotland, closely guarded by nets made of steel cable, screens of mines, and fleets of patrol craft.

At sea, fast lightly armored cruisers that could zigzag and thus usually avoid submarines, together with destroyers, whose mission became hunting and killing submarines, were the ships of choice for the British. Furthermore, in the later years of the war, improved methods of attacking submarines developed, with depth charges, set to explode at pre-set depths, dropped over the last sighted submerging point of a submarine being very effective. Although scientists did not develop echo ranging sonar until much later, they did introduce a primitive system of hydrophones during the war, which allowed a surface ship to locate a submarine's bearing by listening for its underwater electric motor and propeller noises. And, in a few cases, land-based aircraft spotted submarines at sea, either on the surface or lurking in clear water at a shallow depth and radioed their locations for hunting down by destroyers or bombed them directly.

BRITISH BLOCKADE METHOD

With the German coast protected from close-in blockade by submarines and aircraft, the British adopted a technique of mining the approaches to the European coast and blocking the Straits of Dover with submarine nets and a string of blockade ships. Although some submarines could slip through the nets and minefields, merchant ships bound for the continent could be stopped. Under traditional rules of blockade, only ships bearing contraband destined for the enemy would be seized and brought to port for adjudication. Contraband usually consisted of war materiel, transport equipment, and other items that had a clear war-use. The British, however, redefined contraband to include food, after Germany began managing its food supply and agriculture as part of an effort to direct manpower from farms to factories and into the front lines.

Furthermore, Britain stated that shippers sending goods to neutral Holland or Denmark in excess of prewar amounts probably intended them for further transmission into Germany, and so the Royal Navy interdicted ships flying neutral flags such as that of the United States destined for a neutral port, such as Copenhagen. The Germans protested loudly that the blockading of goods to a neutral on the claim that they might have been intended to go on to Germany represented clear violations of the rules of war. The rules, they claimed, allowed only interdiction of vessels on a single leg of a voyage, rather than when destined for such an overland transshipment route by way of a neutral port, called a "continuous voyage." In fact, the rule against applying the concept of continuous voyage in blockades had been agreed on in a prewar conference held in London, but the British had never signed that Declaration of London. Even so, declaring food to be contraband shocked many even in the United States and aroused German popular anger at Britain to a fever pitch. Starvation of besieged children held echoes of the barbaric methods of warfare of prior centuries.

German Methods

But for many Americans and other neutrals not directly involved in the business of shipping, such British violations appeared to be matters of technical international law. The complaints against the British involved obscure rules of blockade and levels of international trade and seemed to have no immediate effects except the confiscation of ships followed by long-drawn-out Admiralty proceedings in British ports. The submarine, however, and its method of employment, had a more immediate and dramatic quality, with all the horrors of narrow escapes in lifeboats, sinking ships, and death by drowning.

Early in 1915, Germany decided to experiment with using the submarine to attack Britain's commerce on a large scale, in the first so-called unrestricted submarine blockade. Announced in February 1915, Germany declared a war zone around the British Isles, in which any ship might be sunk without warning. Since the Germans sought to avoid sinking neutral ships, Britain made it official policy to urge merchant captains to fly a false flag of a neutral as a *ruse de guerre*. As a result, Germany warned that from time to time, a neutral ship might fall victim to torpedoing. Although most of the submarine captains continued to warn merchant ships and to evacuate passengers and crew before sinking a ship despite the official "no-warning" order, some captains simply followed the orders and sank obvious British or French ships without warning.

The most disastrous such attack, and one that enraged American opinion, occurred on May 7, 1915, when Captain Walther Schwieger of *U-20* ordered the firing of a single torpedo against the huge, four-stack Cunard British flag liner, *Lusitania*. The ship went down with 1,198 passengers and crew, including many women and children. The death toll included 128 American passengers. Until that sinking, American public opinion, although divided, had been fairly neutral toward the war. To the American public, British interference in trade,

Great excitement always surrounded the arrival and departure of the four-stack *Lusitania* as well-wishers arrived by auto and carriage. *(Library of Congress)*

the stopping of food supplies to Germany, limitations on journalists, and censoring of the mail had all been tallied against Britain. Reports of German atrocities in Belgium seemed horrible, but many believed the British had fabricated such tales or cooked up exaggerations as part of their propaganda. *Lusitania,* however, changed the minds of many. The British and pro-British publicists in the United States constantly reminded the American public of the tragedy, making it easy to believe that the Germans officially adopted intentionally inhumane methods of warfare.

German U-boat commander Schwieger reacted with horror when he saw the *Lusitania* sink so rapidly. Peering through the telescope, he noted, ". . . there was a terrible panic on her decks. Desperate people ran helplessly up and down while men and women jumped into the water and tried to swim to empty overturned lifeboats. The scene was too horrible to watch and I gave orders to dive to 20 metres and away."[1] Schwieger operated under somewhat vague or open-ended orders that did not clarify exact procedures: "Hostile merchant ships are to be destroyed." Another standing order indicated that the safety of the U-boat had to be a first consideration. Despite the confusion or vagueness in his orders, the British vilified Schwieger as a murderer and Germans hailed him as a hero.

The *Lusitania* tragedy helped recruit pro-British Irishmen to the Allied effort, as in this poster. *(Library of Congress)*

The German government stressed the fact that the *Lusitania* suffered a secondary explosion, suggesting the explosion as evidence that the ship had been carrying a cargo of munitions. Indeed *Lusitania* did carry a shipment of small arms and ammunition aboard. However, many experts concluded at the time that a boiler explosion accounted for the secondary blast, and later investigations suggested that it might have been due to a detonation of coal dust in the coal storage compartment.

Although some naval officers and some of the public understood that the U-boat could not follow the traditional method of warning when in fear of being rammed, part of the worldwide shock of the *Lusitania* sinking derived from the jubilation expressed in Germany. Suffering food shortages from the British blockade, the German public saw Schwieger's act as an appropriate revenge against the British, and even religious ministers called for Germans to take pride in the attack. Postcards showing the ship and Schwieger's picture became favorite collectibles in Germany, as did a newly minted medal commemorating the victory. The British press simply described the sinking as cold-blooded murder and a disgrace.

Only about 760 *Lusitania* survivors reached land. In Britain, U.S ambassador Walter Hines Page sent President Woodrow Wilson a telegram, asking him to respond to the tragedy with a declaration of war against Germany. Page stated that public opinion in Britain held that unless the United States did so, it would forfeit all respect from the European population and governments. According to legend, Wilson burned the telegram and thereafter tended to ignore any messages from Page. Page himself noted the coldness in Wilson's response to his notes, and began to realize that he had lost the president's confidence. Wilson did not take kindly to advice from U.S. ambassadors on how to conduct foreign policy; indeed, he often paid little attention to advice from his own secretary of state.

The sinking of the *Lusitania* and other submarine attacks on freighters, passenger liners, and other noncombatant ships would eventually lead to more crises between the United States and Germany. The United States however, continued to strive for a strictly neutral position during the war, and Wilson and many of his advisers continued to hope that the war could be resolved by negotiation. They believed that the United States, as the world's most powerful and important neutral power in the war, should continue to press for a peace conference.

The British fought back against the submarine attack on their merchant ship lifeline, with one of their most successful efforts consisting of merchant ships and schooners that carried concealed guns, known as Q-ships. After encountering a submarine and appearing to be disabled in the water, with "panic parties" scurrying for lifeboats, the Q-ship would hoist the British white battle ensign and drop movable panels to reveal cannons and machine guns. With gunfire, they would sink the attacking U-boat, even if it had stopped to pick up survivors from the attacked merchant ship. U-boat captain Baron von Spiegel survived such a Q-ship attack and left a vivid account of the attack on *U-93,* and a British officer, Gordon Campbell, wrote an account of the strategies used aboard his own Q-ship to sink *U-68.*

The British continued to enforce their blockade against Germany with their powerful surface fleet. Germany used its submarines selectively, successfully avoiding the sinking of any American-registered vessels in the period from early 1915 to early 1917. Meanwhile, German U-boat captains continued to seek out isolated British warships, battle against the disguised Q-ships, and destroy as many Allied merchant ships as possible without further angering Wilson or American public opinion.

Meanwhile, the war in Europe, in the Middle East, and on the eastern front with Russia ground on through 1915 and 1916.

CHRONICLE OF EVENTS

1914

August 9: The British light cruiser HMS *Birmingham* rams and sinks the German submarine *U-15* in the North Sea.

August 28: The Battle of Heligoland Bight takes place, in which British cruisers *Fearless* and *Arethusa* sink the German destroyer, *V 187*. In addition, the Germans lose three light cruisers, *Mainz, Ariadne,* and *Köln,* and about 1,000 sailors.

September 10–October 24: The German cruiser *Emden* sinks or captures 23 merchant ships and two British warships in the Indian Ocean and shells a British oil depot at Madras, India.

September 22: The German submarine *U-9* sinks three British heavy cruisers, *Aboukir, Cressy,* and *Hogue.*

November 1: In the Battle of Coronel off the west coast of South America, a German naval squadron headed by *Scharnhorst* and *Gneisenau* sinks the British armored cruiser *Good Hope* and the light cruiser *Monmouth.* The British lose 1,000 sailors.

November 9: After an exchange of gunfire with the Australian cruiser *Sydney,* the German cruiser *Emden* is severely damaged, and the captain orders the ship run aground on coral reefs in the Cocos Islands in the Indian Ocean.

November 14: *Scharnhorst* and *Gneisenau* are sunk at the Falkland Islands in the South Atlantic by British battle cruisers *Inflexible* and *Invincible;* the fleeing German light cruisers *Nürnberg* and *Leipzig* are tracked and sunk by British cruisers *Kent, Cornwall,* and *Glasgow.* With the loss of this squadron, the Germans lose 1,800 sailors.

December 31: German submarine *U-24* sinks British battleship *Formidable.*

1915

January 24: The Battle of Dogger Bank is fought, during which German admiral Franz von Hipper directs a battle cruiser squadron against a superior British fleet. The Germans lose the battle cruiser *Blücher.* The British fleet, although outnumbering the German fleet, breaks off the engagement out of concern that German submarines might be in the area.

February 4: Germany announces a submarine blockade of Britain in response to a prior British blockade of Germany in which Britain adopted the doctrine of "continuous voyage."

February 10: The U.S. response to the German announcement is to declare that in the event that American ships or the lives of U.S. citizens are destroyed by Germany in international waters, the United States will regard such an act as "an indefensible violation of neutral rights," and Germany will be held strictly answerable for the violation. German ambassador von Bernstorff urges that the United States explicitly warn Americans against traveling on belligerent ships. His advice is ignored.

February 18: The German submarine blockade goes into effect. At first German submarine crews employ cruiser rules, stopping merchant ships with a shot across the bows, allowing evacuation by lifeboat (and sometimes German crews notify by radio rescue vessels of the state of the crew), then sinking the ship, usually with shell fire or placed charges. However, as merchant ships often outrun or ram submarines, German practice shifts to unannounced torpedo attack.

March 14: The German cruiser *Dresden* is scuttled by its crew at Juan Fernández Island in the southeastern Pacific.

March 28: The German submarine *U-28* sinks the *Falaba,* a British liner, in the Irish Sea, with the loss of Leon Thrasher, the first American killed by submarine attack in World War I.

May 1: Off the Scilly Islands (southwestern Britain), during an engagement between a British naval patrol and a German submarine, a torpedo damages the American oil tanker *Gulflight,* with two American fatalities. Germany later offers full compensation for the loss.

May 1: The German embassy in Washington issues a warning that Americans entering the war zone around the British Isles will do so at their own risk. Specific warnings are published in New York City papers regarding sailing aboard the *Lusitania,* a liner operated by the British-owned Cunard line. The *Lusitania* departs New York harbor.

May 7: U-boat *U-20,* under command of Walther Schwieger, sinks the liner *Lusitania* off the Irish coast en route from New York to Liverpool, with the loss of 1,198 lives, including some 128 Americans. About 760 survivors reach land. The shock in the United States is immense. From Britain, U.S. ambassador Walter Hines Page urges Wilson to respond with a declaration of war.

August 16: The British Q-ship *Inverlyon* sinks German U-boat *U-4.*

August 19: The German U-boat *U-24* sinks without warning the 15,800-ton *Arabic,* a British steamer bound

Photographs like this one of some of the bodies of the 1,198 civilians killed aboard the *Lusitania* shocked public opinion among Allies and neutrals. *(Library of Congress)*

from Liverpool to New York, and two Americans are among the 44 killed. The number of lives saved is 389. Submarine commander Schneider claimed the steamer's zigzagging seemed an attempt to ram.

October 5: The German government offers apologies and indemnity for the loss of American lives in the sinking of the *Arabic.*

November 21: Germany issues a secret order authorizing submarine commanders to regard as troop transports all ships crossing the English Channel at night, as Britain uses commercial liners to send troops to the Continent.

1916

February 21: Germany advises the U.S. government that armed merchantmen are to be treated as cruisers beginning March 1. This action is in response to British use of Q ships in large numbers and to open arming of merchant vessels.

March: Admiral Alfred von Tirpitz resigns and is replaced by Admiral Reinhard Scheer. Scheer is more successful than Tirpitz in advancing a more aggressive policy, involving U-boat construction, raids on British coastal towns, and use of armed merchant ships as commerce raiders.

March 24: A German U-boat torpedoes the *Sussex,* a French cross-channel passenger ship. Several Americans aboard are injured.

April 24–25: A German naval squadron bombards the British ports of Yarmouth and Lowestoft.

May 31: In the Battle of Jutland (Skagerrak to the Germans), the British lose 14 ships, including the *Invincible* and the *Queen Mary,* both to spectacular explosions. The Germans lose 11, but British loss in tonnage is nearly double that of the Germans. Superior German fire-control yields a loss of 117,000 tons of British ships, compared to only 61,000 tons of German ships lost.

June: *Deutschland* crosses the Atlantic, the first crossing by a submarine; it carries cargo and stops at Baltimore and New London. Its cargoes are insufficient for commercial success.

December: The German commerce raiders *Moewe* and *Wolf* and the sailing vessel *Seeadler* set forth to attack Allied shipping with numerous successes.

EYEWITNESS TESTIMONY

The greatest anxiety constantly confronting me was the defenceless nature of the base at Scapa, which was open to submarine and destroyer attacks. Whilst the fleet was fuelling the only protection that could be afforded was to anchor light cruisers and destroyers off the various entrances and to patrol outside the main entrance: but these measures were no real defences against submarines, and the position was such that it was deemed most inadvisable to keep the Fleet in harbour longer than was necessary for fuelling purposes. Accordingly, at 6:30 P.M. on the same day, the Battle Fleet again proceeded to sea, being screened through the Pentland Firth to the westward until dark by the 4th Flotilla [of destroyers], and the course being then shaped to pass round the Orkneys into the North Sea. In order to provide some protection against destroyer attack, a request was forwarded to the Admiralty asking that two of the older battleships might be sent up to defend the main entrances. This measure was approved. . . .

British admiral John Jellicoe, recalling submarine danger to warships noted by August 7, 1914, as quoted by Thomas Goddard Frothingham, Naval History of the World War, *pp. 72–73.*

I had been going ahead partly submerged, with about five feet of my periscope showing. Almost immediately I caught sight of the first cruiser and two others. I submerged completely and laid my course so as to bring up in the centre of the trio, which held a sort of triangular formation. I could see their grey-black sides riding high over the water. When I first sighted them they were near enough for torpedo work, but I wanted to make my aim sure, so I went down and in on them. I had taken the position of the three ships before submerging, and I succeeded in getting another flash through my periscope before I began action. I soon reached what I regarded as a good shooting point.

Then I loosed one of my torpedoes at the middle ship. I was then about twelve feet under water, and got the shot off in good shape, my men handling the boat as if she had been a skiff. I climbed to the surface to get a sight through my tube of the effect, and discovered that the shot had gone straight and true, striking the ship, which I later learned was the *Aboukir,* under one of her magazines, which in exploding helped the torpedo's work of destruction. There were a fountain of water, a burst of smoke, a flash of fire, and part of the cruiser rose

in the air. Then I heard a roar and felt reverberations sent through the water by the detonation. She had been broken apart, and sank in a few minutes. The *Aboukir* had been stricken in a vital spot and by an unseen force; that made the blow all the greater.

Her crew were brave, and even with death staring them in the face kept to their posts, ready to handle their useless guns, for I submerged at once. But I had stayed on top long enough to see the other cruisers, which I learned were the *Cressy* and the *Hogue,* turn and steam full speed to their dying sister, whose plight they could not understand, unless it had been due to an accident. The ships came on a mission of inquiry and rescue, for many of the *Aboukir*'s crew were now in the water, the order having been given, "Each man for himself." But soon the other two English cruisers learned what had brought about the destruction so suddenly.

As I reached my torpedo depth I sent a second charge at the nearest of the oncoming vessels, which was the *Hogue.* The English were playing my game, for I had scarcely to move out of my position, which was a great aid, since it helped to keep me from detection. On board my little boat the spirit of the German Navy was to be seen in its best form. With enthusiasm every man held himself in check and gave attention to the work in hand.

The attack on the *Hogue* went true. But this time I did not have the advantageous aid of having the torpedo detonate under the magazine, so for twenty minutes the *Hogue* lay wounded and helpless on the surface before she heaved, half turned over and sank. But this time, the third cruiser knew of course that the enemy was upon her and she sought as best she could to defend herself. She loosed her torpedo defence batteries on boats, starboard and port, and stood her ground as if more anxious to help the many sailors who were in the water than to save herself. In common with the method of defending herself against a submarine attack, she steamed in a zigzag course, and this made it necessary for me to hold my torpedoes until I could lay a true course for them, which also made it necessary for me to get nearer to the *Cressy.*

I had come to the surface for a view and saw how wildly the fire was being sent from the ship. Small wonder that was when they did not know where to shoot, although one shot went unpleasantly near us. When I got within suitable range I sent away my third attack. This time I sent a second torpedo after the first to make the strike doubly certain. My crew were aiming like sharpshooters and both torpedoes went to their bulls-eye. My luck was with me again, for the enemy was made useless and at once began sinking by her head. Then she careened far over, but all the while her men stayed at the guns looking for their invisible foe. They were brave and true to their country's sea traditions. Then she eventually suffered a boiler explosion and completely turned turtle. With her keel uppermost she floated until the air got out from under her and then she sank with a loud sound, as if from a creature in pain.

The whole affair had taken less than one hour from the time of shooting off the first torpedo until the *Cressy* went to the bottom. Not one of the three had been able to use any of its big guns. I knew the wireless of the three cruisers had been calling for aid. I was still quite able to defend myself, but I knew that news of the disaster would call many English submarines and torpedo boat destroyers, so, having done my appointed work, I set my course for home. . . .

I reached the home port on the afternoon of the 23rd, and on the 24th went to Wilhelmshaven, to find that news of my effort had become public. My wife, dry eyed when I went away, met me with tears. Then I learned that my little vessel and her brave crew had won the plaudit of the Kaiser, who conferred upon each of my co-workers the Iron Cross of the second class and upon me the Iron Cross of the first and second classes.

German Lieutenant Otto Weddigen, recalling his part in the sinking of the Aboukir, Cressy, *and* Hogue *by U-9 in September 1914, cited in* Source Records of the Great War, *vol. 2, pp. 297–300.*

Iron Duke 30th October, 1914. The experience gained of German methods since the commencement of the war makes it possible and very desirable to consider the manner in which these methods are likely to be made use of tactically in a fleet action.

8. . . . it is necessary to consider what may be termed the tactics of the actual battlefield. The German submarines, if worked as expected with the battlefleet, can be used in one of two ways: With the cruisers, or possibly with destroyers. With the battlefleet. In the first case the submarines would probably be led by the cruisers to a position favourable for attacking our battlefleet as it advanced to deploy, and in the second case they might be kept in a position in rear, or to the flank, of the enemy's battlefleet, which would move in the direction required to draw our own Fleet into contact with the submarines.

9. The first move at (a) should be defeated by our own cruisers, provided we have a sufficient number present, as they should be able to force the enemy's cruisers to action at a speed which would interfere with submarine tactics. The cruisers must, however, have destroyers in company to assist in dealing with the submarines, and should be well in advance of the battlefleet; hence the necessity for numbers.

10. The second move at (b) can be countered by judicious handling of our battlefleet, but may, and probably will, involve a refusal to comply with the enemy's tactics by moving in the invited direction. If, for instance, the enemy battlefleet were to turn away from an advancing Fleet, I should assume that the intention was to lead us over mines and submarines, and should decline to be so drawn.

11. I desire particularly to draw the attention of Their Lordships to this point, since it may be deemed a refusal of battle, and, indeed, might possibly result in failure to bring the enemy to action as soon as is expected and hoped.

12. Such a result would be absolutely repugnant to the feelings of all British Naval Officers and men, but with new and untried methods of warfare new tactics must be devised to meet them. I feel that such tactics, if not understood, may bring odium upon me, but so long as I have the confidence of their Lordships I intend to pursue what is, in my considered opinion, the proper course to defeat and annihilate the enemy's battlefleet, without regard to uninstructed opinion or criticism.

Admiral John Jellicoe, notifying the British Admiralty by letter that the traditional tactics of engaging the enemy cannot be used because of the danger posed by submarines to warships on October 30, 1914, from A. Temple Patterson's The Jellicoe Papers, *vol. 1, pp. 75–76.*

Turning about and breasting the waves we faced the oncoming steamer and signaled to her to stop; but hardly had she espied us than she also turned about in the hope to escape. She showed no flag to indicate her nationality, so surely we had sighted an English vessel. Even after we had fired a warning shot, she tried by rapid and tortuous curves to return to her former course, and endeavor thereby to reach her home port. Meantime she sent up rockets as signals of distress in quick succession to draw the attention of British patrol ships that must be hovering in the neighborhood.

This obliged us to fire a decisive shot, and with a loud report our first shell struck the ship close to the captain's bridge. Instead of resigning himself to his fate, the Englishman sent up more signals and hoisted the British flag. This showed us he was game, and the fight began in dead earnest. All honor to the pluck of these English captains—but how reckless to expose in this manner the lives of their passengers and crew, as we shall see in the present instance. . . .

The fight had lasted four hours without our being able to deliver the death stroke. Several fires had started on the steamer, but the crew had been able to keep them under control; big holes gaped open in the ship's side, but there were none as yet below the water line, and the pumps still sufficed to expel the water. . . .

It was now essential for us to put an end to this deadly combat, for English torpedo-boat destroyers were hurrying on to the calls of distress of the steamer. Big clouds of smoke against the sky showed they were coming towards us under full steam. The ship was by this time listing so heavily that it was evident we need waste no more of our ammunition. . . . We cast a last look on our courageous adversary who was gradually sinking, and I must add it was the first and last prey whose end we did not have the satisfaction to witness. We had been truly impressed by the captain's brave endurance, notwithstanding his lack of wisdom, and we knew that the men-of-war were coming to his rescue. We read in the papers, on our return to a German port, that the "Vosges" had sunk soon after we had departed, and what remained of the passengers and crew were picked up by the English ships. The captain was rewarded for his temerity by being raised to the rank of Reserve officer, and the crew were given sums of money; but all the other officers had perished, as well as several sailors and a few passengers, who had been forced to help the stokers in order to increase the speed of the flying steamer.

German U-boat commander G. G. von Forstner, remembering the sinking of the British Moss Line steamer Vosges, *March 27, 1915, in Forstner, G. G. von (translated by Mrs. Russell Codman),* The Journal of Submarine Commander von Forstner, *pp. 100–102.*

We ran blindly under water for a while without daring to show our periscope. I did not like the idea of showing any asparagus again in that neighbourhood for the present. Our course lay north from the tip of the peninsula, toward Ga-Tepe. There the periscope showed another battleship in front of the northern beaches. My reference showed the vessel to be of the Triumph class. Again the inevitable swarm of patrol boats and destroyers circling around to protect it from submarine attack, like pigmies guarding a giant.

"In periscope!" And we dived to seventy feet and headed toward the monster, passing far below the lines of patrol craft. Their propellers, as they ran above us, sounded a steady hum. For four and a half hours after I caught sight of the ship, which was in fact H.M.S. *Triumph* itself, I maneuvered the *U-21* for a torpedo shot, moving here and there and showing the asparagus on the smooth surface of the sea for only the briefest moments.

In the conning tower my watch officer and I stood with bated breath. We were groping toward a deadly position—deadly for the magnificent giant of war on the surface above.

"Out periscope!" H.M.S. *Triumph* stood in formidable majesty, broadside to us, and only three hundred yards away. Never had an under-sea craft such a target.

"Torpedo—fire!" My heart gave a great leap as I called the command.

And now one of those fearfully still, eventless moments. Suspense and eagerness held me in an iron grip. Heedless of all else, I left the periscope out. There! And I saw the telltale streak of white foam darting through the water. It headed swiftly away from the point where we lay, and headed-straight—yes, straight and true. It streaked its way swiftly to the bow of our mammoth adversary. A huge cloud of smoke leaped out of the sea. In the conning tower we heard first a dry, metallic concussion and then a terrible, reverberating explosion.

It was a fascinating and appalling sight to see, and I yearned with every fibre to keep on watching the fearful picture; but I had already seen just about enough to cost us our lives. The moment that dread white wake of the torpedo was seen on the surface of the water, the destroyers were after me. They came rushing from every direction.

"In periscope!" And down we went. I could hear nothing but the sound of propellers above me, on the right and on the left. Why hadn't I dived the moment after the torpedo left? The two seconds I had lost were like years now. With that swarm converging right over our heads, it surely seemed as if we were doomed. Then a flash crossed my brain.

"Full speed ahead," I called, and ahead we went right along the course the torpedo had taken, straight toward the huge craft we had hit.

It was foolhardy, I admit, but I had to risk it. Diving as deeply as we dared, we shot right under the sinking battleship. It might have come roaring down on our heads—the torpedo had hit so fair that I rather expected it would. And then the U-boat and its huge prey would have gone down together in an embrace of death. That crazy maneuver saved us. I could hear the propellers of destroyers whirring above us, but they were hurrying to the place where we had been. Our maneuver of ducking under the sinking battleship was so unexpected that no hint of it ever occurred to the enemy. We were left in tranquil safety. Keeping as deep as possible and showing no tip of periscope, we stole blindly but securely away. When I ventured to take a look through the asparagus, we were far from the place where the *Triumph* had met her disaster.

> *May 25, 1915, account by German captain Hersing,*
> *recalling the May 25, 1915, action by Germany's*
> *U-21* in the sinking of the Triumph, *as quoted in*
> *Lowell Thomas,* Raiders of the Deep, *pp. 64–65.*

It was at 6.40 that I was aroused by men rushing by me, and someone trod on or stumbled against my chest. This awoke me, and I called out, "What's the matter?" A voice replied from somewhere, "There's a torpedo coming." I just had time to scramble to my feet when there came a dull heavy explosion about fifteen feet forward of the shelter deck on the port side. The explosion must have been very low down, as there was no shock from it to be felt on deck. The old *Majestic* immediately gave a jerk over towards port and remained with a heavy list. Then there came a sound as if the contents of every pantry in the world had fallen at the same moment. I never before heard such a clattering, as everything loose in her tumbled about. You could tell at once she had been mortally wounded somewhere in her vitals, and you felt instinctively she would not long stay afloat. . . . I was swept down the ladder to the main deck by the crowd rushing by me, and from there made my way aft to the quarter-deck.

The quarter-deck was crowded with men nearly all dressed, and many wearing lifebelts who were climbing over the side and jumping into the sea, all determined to get clear before she went down. Just after the explosion of black smoke came up and got down my throat and in my eyes, so that all this time I seemed to be in

semi-darkness. I looked over the side and saw that I was clear of the torpedo nets and then climbed over, intending to slide down a stanchion into the water and then swim clear. But again my programme was upset by unforeseen events, for just as I had both legs over the rail there came a rush from behind and I was pushed over the side, falling with considerable force on to the net shelf, which is where the nets are stowed when not out. I made no long stay on the net shelf, but at once rebounded into the sea and went under. I came up at once still holding my useless belt, and having got some of the water out of my eyes, took a look round.

The sea was crowded with men swimming about and calling for assistance. I think that many of these old reservists, who formed the majority of the crew, had forgotten how to swim or else had lost all faith in their own powers. A few yards from me I saw a boat, towards which everyone in the water seemed to be making. She was already packed with men, whilst others were hanging on to her gunwale. I swam towards her, mixed up with a struggling crowd, and managed to get both hands firmly on the gunwale, but it was impossible to drag myself on board. I looked round at the *Majestic,* which was lying only a few yards away at an acute angle, and I remember thinking that if she turned right over, our boat would probably be dragged under with her. . . .

The *Majestic* now presented an extraordinary spectacle. She was lying over on her side, having such a list that it was no longer possible to stand on her deck. About one-third of the crew still seemed to be hanging on to the rails or standing on her side as if hesitating to jump into the sea. . . . All of the vessels in the neighbourhood were lowering boats and many steam launches were hastening to pick up survivors, but they did not dare stand in too close for fear of being dragged under in the final plunge. . . . A very few seconds later the *Majestic* rolled right over to port and sank bottom upwards like a great stone, without any further warning. There came a dull, rumbling sound, a swirl of water and steam, for a moment her green bottom was exposed to view and then the old flagship disappeared forever, except for a small piece of her ram which remained above water as her bows were lying on a shallow sandbank.

As she turned over and sank a sailor ran the whole length of her keel and finally sat astride the ram, where he was subsequently taken off without even getting a wetting. . . . The loss of life was small, numbering only fifty. This was due to the fact that most of the men had lifebelts. The majority had time to clear before she turned over; we were anchored in shallow water, so the suction was small, and above all, assistance was promptly forthcoming from the numerous ships, boats and launches which hastened to pick up those struggling in the water. The final plunge was watched by thousands of troops on shore and by thousands of men afloat. It was a sight which will not easily be forgotten.

British survivor E. Ashmead-Bartlett recalling the sinking of the Majestic, *May 27, 1915, as described in his memoir,* Some of My Experiences in the Great War, *pp. 130–131.*

On the 25th and 27th of May the recently arrived German submarines scored two great successes in that Lieutenant Hersing torpedoed the British battleships *Triumph* and *Majestic* off the outer coast of the peninsula. The enemy now temporarily withdrew the greater part of his battleships to the protected ports of Imbros and Lemnos and during the next few weeks the artillery support of the landed army came chiefly from the destroyers and torpedo boats. At the same time, however, all the effective means of defense against submarines were put in operation by the enemy who had at his disposal every kind of material he wanted. Thereafter the German submarines were unable, during the next seven months of the campaign, to score any success against the hostile fleet, except that they torpedoed a transport.

German commanding officer of Turkish army, Liman von Sanders, commenting on Hersing's sinking of Triumph *and* Majestic, *May 25, 27, 1915, in his memoir,* Five Years in Turkey, *p. 77.*

Daylight on March 12, 1916, found us steering up the west coast at eight knots, representing a collier flying no coulours bound for the north, and keeping just at the extreme submarine visibility range from the coast.... At seven o'clock ... the track of a torpedo was seen approaching, which we made no attempt to avoid. It was fired from our starboard quarter—a bad position from the submarine point of view. The bubbles of the track passed under the focsle which meant that the torpedo had just missed us ahead. We therefore maintained our course and took no outward notice, as a tramp steamer (at that time) could not be expected to know what a torpedo track looked like, and in any case, the lookouts would neither be numerous nor very bright at that hour of the morning.

We could have escaped with ease if we had been an ordinary steamer by putting our stern towards him and steaming off at full speed. He might have opened fire with his gun, but under the weather conditions prevailing the steamer would have got away....

One young seaman was whistling at his gun, because, as he explained when asked what he was doing, "if he didn't whistle he would get scared." A few minutes after the torpedo had missed us, the submarine came to the surface astern of the ship and steamed up on our port side. As he came up, his gun was manned and he fired a shot across our bows as a signal to stop. After firing his shot he closed down and partially submerged again, obviously ready to dive in a few seconds if we attempted to ram. But in the meantime we had proceeded with our pantomime as prearranged, and as soon as the shot fell, the engines were stopped, steam was blown off and the panic party got busy.

They entered into the spirit of it with more zeal than ever—a great scrambling for boats took place, which apparently satisfied the submarine as to our bonafides for he came right on the surface again and closed towards the ship—this was before we had even got to the stage of lowering the boats. I was still rushing about the bridge and had not yet been relieved of my cap by the navigator. The submarine was evidently in a hurry to get on with the business and go after another prey, as he fired a shot at us which fell just short of the magazine, a matter of a few feet....

...I therefore blew my whistle. At this signal the White Ensign flew at the masthead, the wheel-house and sideports came down with a clatter, the hen-coop collapsed; and in a matter of seconds, three 12-pounder guns, the Maxim and rifles were firing as hard as they could.

... Our after gun was leaving nothing to chance and put a few more rounds in at point blank range. A couple more depth-charges were released and the surface of the sea became covered with oil and small pieces of wood—but there was no living soul.

This boat, it was ascertained afterwards, was *U-68,* and by destroying her before she got to her hunting ground, we had done exactly what we set out for. The great feeling of rejoicing and relief to all on board showed itself in the whole crew rushing to the bridge and cheering.

British Q ship captain Gordon Campbell of Farnborough (Q-5), detailing his encounter with a U-boat on March 12, 1916, from Rear Admiral Gordon Campbell, My Mystery Ships, *as quoted in Bernard Fitzsimmons, ed.,* Warships and Sea Battles of World War I, *pp. 136–137.*

An incident occurred at about 6.47 p.m. which was an indication of the spirit prevailing in the Fleet, of which it is impossible to speak too highly. The destroyer *Acasta*, which had been badly hit aft during her attack on enemy light cruisers in company with the *Shark* and had her engines disabled, was passed by the Fleet. Her commanding officer, Lieut.-Commander J.O. Barron, signalled the condition of his ship to the *Iron Duke* as that ship passed, leaving the *Acasta* on her starboard or engaged side. The ship's company was observed to be cheering each ship as they passed. It is satisfactory to relate that this destroyer and her gallant ship's company were subsequently brought into Aberdeen, being assisted by the *Nonsuch*.

Shortly after 6.55 p.m. the *Iron Duke* passed the wreck of a ship with the bow and stern standing out of the water, the centre portion apparently resting on the bottom, with the destroyer *Badger* picking up survivors. It was thought at first that this was the remains of a German light cruiser, but inquiry of the *Badger* elicited the lamentable news that the wreck was that of the *Invincible*. It was assumed at the time that she had been sunk either by a mine or by a torpedo, and in view of the safe passage of other ships in her vicinity, the latter appeared to be the more probable cause of her loss. Subsequent information, however, showed that she was destroyed by gunfire, causing her magazines to explode, as already recorded.

British admiral Jellicoe, recalling the Battle of Jutland on May 31, 1916, in his memoir, The Grand Fleet, 1914–1916 *(1919), as cited in Jere Clemens King,* The First World War, *p. 167.*

Towards midnight our destroyers were overtaken by several three- and four-funnel German ships (cruisers, they thought) hurrying home. At this stage of the game anybody might have been anybody—pursuer or pursued. The Germans took no chances, but switched on their searchlights and opened fire on *Gehenna*. Her Acting Sublieutenant reports: "A salvo hit us forward. I opened fire with the afterguns. A shell then struck us in a steampipe, and I could see nothing but steam. But both starboard torpedoes were fired."

Eblis, *Gehenna*'s next astern, at once fired a torpedo at the second ship in the German line, a four-funneled cruiser, and hit her between the second funnel and the mainmast, when "she appeared to catch fire fore and aft simultaneously, heeled right over to starboard, and undoubtedly sank." *Eblis* loosed off a second torpedo and turned aside to reload, firing at the same time to distract the enemy's attention from *Gehenna*, who was now ablaze fore and aft. *Gehenna*'s Acting Sublieutenant (the only executive officer who survived) says that by the time the steam from the broken pipe cleared he found *Gehenna* stopped, nearly everybody amidships killed or wounded, the cartridge boxes round the guns exploding one after the other as the fires took hold, and the enemy not to be seen. Three minutes or less did all that damage.

Eblis had nearly finished reloading when a shot struck the davit that was swinging her last torpedo into the tube and wounded all hands concerned. Thereupon she dropped torpedo work, fired at an enemy searchlight which winked and went out, and was closing in to help *Gehenna*, when she found herself under the noses of a couple of enemy cruisers. . . . The enemy did her best. She completely demolished the *Eblis*'s bridge and searchlight platform, brought down the mast and the forefunnel, ruined the whaler and the dinghy, split the foc's'le open above water from the stern to the galley which is abaft the bridge, and below water had opened it up from the stern to the second bulkhead. She further ripped off *Eblis*'s skin plating for an amazing number of yards on one side of her, and fired a couple of large calibre shells into *Eblis* at point-blank range narrowly missing her vitals. Even so, *Eblis* is as impartial as a prize court. . . .

After all that *Eblis* picked herself up, and discovered that she was still alive, with a dog's chance of getting to port. But she did not bank on it. That grand slam had wrecked the bridge, pinning the commander under the wreckage. By the time he had extricated himself he "considered it advisable to throw overboard the steel chest and dispatch box of confidential and secret books." [These] are never allowed to fall into strange hands, and their proper disposal is the last step but one in the ritual of the burial service of His Majesty's ships at sea. *Gehenna*, afire and sinking, out somewhere in the dark, was going through it on her own account. This is her Acting Sublieutenant's report: "The confidential books were got up. The First Lieutenant gave the order: 'Every man aft,' and the confidential books were thrown overboard. The ship soon afterwards heeled over to starboard and the bows went under. The First Lieutenant gave the order: 'Everybody for themselves.' The ship sank in about a minute, the stern going straight up into the air."

British writer Rudyard Kipling, describing in a newspaper account for the London Daily Telegraph *the encounter of HMS destroyers* Tipperary *and* Spitfire *with enemy ships between 11:30 and midnight in the Battle of Jutland on May 31, 1916, published October 19–31, 1916. For reasons of security, Kipling used fictitious names for the destroyers, calling* Tipperary Gehenna, *and* Spitfire Eblis.

Our repair parties were very efficient, the efforts of the electricians eclipsing all the others. They found solutions for the trickiest problems, invented new connections, created electric bypasses, kept all necessary circuits going and crowned their achievements by repairing the electric baking-oven so that on the morning we got pure wheat bread, a rare treat for us.

Our aerials were soon in pieces, rendering our ship deaf and dumb until a sub-lieutenant and some radio operators rigged new ones. The anti-torpedo net was torn and threatened to foul the propellers, but the boatswain and his party went over the side to lash it. They did it so well that later, in dock, it proved difficult to untie it again. According to regulations our paymasters were expected in a battle to take down and certify last wills, but we preferred them to prepare cold food forward and aft, and send their stewards round to battle-stations with masses of sandwiches. . . .

Now darkness fell, and we had to make preparations for the next morning—for we were sure to meet the British again. Searchlights were repaired, night recognition signals were rigged, and ammunition carried to the undamaged guns. At first, we could continue to follow the battle-cruiser SMS *Moltke,* but soon we had to slow down, for water began to come over the forecastle as our bows settled. Steering was difficult, as was finding the right course, for the main gyro compartment was flooded and the after gyro unreliable. Its normal circuit had been destroyed, and the new connection short-circuited off and on. The shocks had made the magnetic compass entirely undependable. Sounding had its problems, too. The sounding machines in the casemates were scrap, while the hand-leads fouled the torn nets and then parted. Our charts were covered with blood and the spare charts were inaccessible in a flooded compartment. Under the circumstances it was not at all easy to make the correct course for the Horns Reef lightship. Moreover, all coal near the boilers had been used up,

and bringing up more supplies from the more distant bunkers became increasingly difficult as a result of damage and the amount of water in the ship. Fortunately, our boilers could also burn oil, and supplies of this continued to flow, although the oil-pipes needed constant attention to keep them from clogging. . . .

. . . A buoy gave us our position, and at the lightship we got in touch with the rest of our fleet, the light cruiser SMS *Pillau* being detached to pilot us to the Jade river. Now a dogged fight to save the vessel began. The entire forecastle was riddled like a sieve. Through rents, holes, leaky seams and rivets water entered one room after the other until only the forward torpedo flat could be held. The big "swimming bladder" gave the forward part of the ship just enough buoyancy. But she was so much down by the bows that the sea started getting into the forward casemates. Their covers were destroyed or bent, and the wood for shoring up leaks was somewhere under the forecastle. We used everything we could get our hands on, mess tables, benches, eventually even the empty shelves from the shell-rooms to the dismay of the head gunner.

Quite a number of compartments had to be kept clear by incessant bailing over a period of two days. Some bulkheads had to be watched carefully and shored up again from time to time. The whole ship's company was kept busy, and so sleep was possible only in snatches. . . .

. . . We made it and arrived in the early morning of June 3 off Wilhelmshaven locks, where we were welcomed by hurrahs from the crews of the battleships anchored there. The *Seydlitz* had been hit by 21 heavy shells and one torpedo, lost 98 men killed and 55 injured and had four heavy and two medium guns put out of action.

Kapitan zur See von Egidy, in a speech, describing the at-sea repairs June 1, 1916, to the German cruiser Seydlitz, *as quoted in* Warships and Sea Battles of World War I, *p. 102.*

I recall the afternoon when we received a bulletin announcing that at last the German fleet had come out and was in action against the British fleet in the battle of Jutland. We knew only that some British ships had been sunk, that the battle continued. . . . If the German fleet should win then Britain would cease to be mistress of the seas. Germany would control the English Channel; the B.E.F. would be cut off from its home base, the artery that gave it life severed, the weapon struck from its hand; no one of the Allies could receive further sup-

This photo shows the German Fleet in port at Kiel. It rankled officers in the German navy that their fleet was rarely allowed to venture out in World War I. *(National Archives)*

plies from America. The whole Allied structure would fall, and its parts each seek a separate peace.

What would outraged Belgium, or Rheims, or the *Lusitania,* matter against this stroke of German propaganda? The British Empire would be the spoil of the victor though he had only a quarter of his fleet afloat and firing when the last British battleship was sunk.

We said little as we waited for the decisive word. When we learned that the German fleet had been driven limping to the cover of its mine fields we did not dance nor shout nor sing. Minds that had been numb glowed with relief, lungs that had been congested breathed free air again, shoulders had the light feeling of release from a crushing load.

American journalist Frederick Palmer, recalling his reaction to the news accounts of the Battle of Jutland, June 1916, in his memoir, With My Own Eyes, *pp. 328–329.*

4
Gallipoli and Arabia
October 1914–November 1918

Turkey, heart of the Ottoman Empire, had joined the Central Powers in October 1914. Through a combination of botched diplomacy, neglect, and underestimation of the ability of Turkey to put up much of a fight, leaders in England and France rather suddenly found themselves confronted with a new set of major problems growing out of the Turkish decision. If the Ottoman Empire attempted to send its massive but ill-equipped army to reclaim its jurisdiction over Egypt, the Allies could lose the vital Suez Canal link between the Indian Ocean and the Mediterranean Sea. More imminently, Turkey controlled access to the Black Sea, where Russia had its only ice-free ports in winter, through the waterways connecting to the Mediterranean Sea.

The Bosporus flowed as a narrow but unbridged waterway dividing Europe from Asia at the city of Constantinople, then the capital of the Ottoman Empire. That waterway passed south to the Sea of Marmara, enclosed by land in the 100-mile-long neck known as the Gallipoli Peninsula, where the water again narrowed in the Dardanelles passage (itself 38 miles long), before emptying into the Mediterranean. With ships, minefields, and shore-mounted artillery, the Turks found it quite easy to monitor all water-borne traffic and to prohibit the passage of any enemy warships or merchant ship traffic. With the Ottoman declaration of war, Turkey suddenly cut off the traditional Black Sea ports of Russia from Allied traffic. By closing the single strategic choke point of the Dardanelles passage, Turkey could prevent supplies from the Allies ever reaching Russia. Some of Russia's other ports were icebound in winter, and the Pacific port of Vladivostok, although linked by rail to European Russia, offered a very poor substitute for the Black Sea ports closed by the Ottoman decision.

The Turkish threat to the Suez Canal seemed only slightly less imminent. Turkey had nominal rule over Egypt, although British troops had occupied that region since the 1880s to help guarantee British and friendly access through the canal, one of the world's most crucial maritime choke points. If Turkish troops in nearby Palestine, then under Ottoman rule, marched across the 120-mile-wide Sinai Peninsula and closed the canal, the Central Powers could effectively block the best route for transport of troops from Australia, New Zealand, and India to

Only a few Armenian refugees enjoyed conditions as good as ones like these, encountered by those who made it into Russian territory, at Novorossiisk. *(Library of Congress)*

assist Britain in Europe. The lightly manned garrison in Egypt had to be immediately strengthened against this very real threat.

Despite the strategic importance of the Ottoman Empire, with its ability to control these crucial waterways, policy makers in Britain and France and the public in those countries tended to think that any battles fought against the Turks would represent a "sideshow." Western Europeans often jokingly spoke of the Ottoman Empire as the "sick man of Europe" for its ineffectual control of the Balkans and its losses of territory to smaller nations like Greece, Serbia, and Bulgaria during the 1912–13 First Balkan War. The Ottoman acquiescence in the British occupation of Egypt, coupled with the seizure of the North African territory of Libya by Italy in 1911, all seemed to suggest that the empire verged on collapse and that its remaining territories would readily fall as spoils of war to the victors. Such expectations also rested on a racist view that Turks could not possibly stand up against British or other European troops. This illusion, in particular, died hard.

In Britain, some saw Turkish weakness as an opportunity. Winston Churchill, serving as First Lord of the Admiralty, believed that a British naval expedition to force the Dardanelles and take Constantinople could quickly open the way to aiding Russia and allow encirclement of the Central Powers. This concept would grow into a somewhat muddled plan to take the Dardanelles and the Gallipoli Peninsula, subdue Constantinople, and knock the Turks out of the war quickly.

The battles of World War I fought in the Middle East turned out not to be a sideshow at all, but rather a series of grand engagements that shaped the history of the region for the rest of the 20th century and left a legacy of lessons about how warfare would be fought in the new era. World War I in the Middle East revealed the difficulties of mounting a major invasion of troops from the sea and showed how out of date the traditional tactics of war had become. It also showed how a racial holocaust could transpire during a major war. And, in a lasting legacy, it left behind redrawn maps of the region that sowed the seeds of conflict for at least a century.

DISASTROUS LESSONS

The effort against the Dardanelles and the landings of troops at Gallipoli led to more than 250,000 Allied casualties, and demonstrated many of the problems of coordinating army and navy forces in "combined operations." A Royal Commission in Britain reviewed the mistakes almost immediately, and, over the next decades, a host of published studies dissected the campaign. The commission reviewed and studied every detail of the failed operation, from chain of command, to personality of officers, tactics on the ground, supply systems, and use of aircraft, ships, and submarines. Although the Allies made many mistakes, in some cases they simply suffered the bad luck of the accidents of war. In retrospect, the history of Gallipoli became one of the great tragedies of World War I.

While the great powers in western Europe engaged in war, Turkey unleashed a massive genocidal holocaust against the Armenian population of Turkey. At first, journalists and neutral diplomats like those connected with the American legation assumed the Turkish authorities simply wanted to repress any political dissent among the Christian Armenians who might feel more sympathy for the Russians than for their Muslim government. Such observers could not believe the early accounts of the horrors of extermination of the civilian population. However, before the slaughter subsided, upwards of 1 million Armenian civilians had been viciously murdered. This mass atrocity in itself served as a precedent, in several ways, for the later holocaust against the Jewish people conducted by the Nazi regime in the 1930s and under the cover of World War II. From the perspective of potentially victimized minority ethnic groups around the world, the Armenian tragedy far exceeded in importance the military defeat of the Allies during the Gallipoli campaign.

As the British attacked at Gallipoli, defended the Suez, and invaded the Mesopotamian provinces (now the nation of Iraq) of the Ottoman Empire, they came to realize that the Turkish army, although ill-equipped and although defeated in the Balkan Wars of 1912 and 1913, put up a formidable fight, especially when on the defensive. In fact, the principles that produced stalemate on the western front also served to stymie British and French advances at Gallipoli, in Mesopotamia short of Baghdad, and in the British effort to advance from the Sinai Peninsula through Gaza into Palestine. Entrenching shovels and the machine gun proved as effective in the hands of the Turks as in the hands of the French and Germans on the western front. The theory of massed attack by troops against defenders, inherited from the age of Napoleon, worked no better in the Middle East than it had in Europe. That method of war seemed equally disastrous at Gallipoli, on the Tigris River in Mesopotamia, and in Palestine. Although most Allied officers failed to learn that lesson during the war, a few did.

Success eventually came to the Allies against the Turks because several Allied leaders adopted two techniques of war fighting that they rarely used in Europe: deception and asymmetric warfare. In Palestine, General Edmund Allenby employed several ruses that led the Turkish defenders and their German advisers to reinforce the wrong points. Furthermore, Allenby got assistance from the Arabs, led by Prince Feisal and advised by T. E. Lawrence (later remembered as Lawrence of Arabia), who used harassing guerrilla tactics to hold down Turkish troops and to sever crucial Turkish supply lines. Both these methods of warfare, deception and the use of irregular bands of mobile troops in civilian clothes who lived off the land, ran counter to some of the long-established traditions of the British and French regular armies. However, both techniques would become characteristic of later wars in the 20th century, and the lessons from these successes would be closely studied, not only in World War II by the Allies, but also by leaders such as Tito in Yugoslavia, Mao Zedong in China, and Ho Chi Minh in Vietnam.

The war against the Ottoman Empire left the legacy of a completely changed map of the Middle East. The British, in this region as well as in Europe and the Far East, worked to gain allies by making secret promises of territorial adjustment. That concept might have been reasonable, except for the fact that in the Middle East the British made at least three separate contradictory groups of promises—to the French, to leaders of the world Jewish community, and to the Arabs. The British partially fulfilled other promises to the Russians, Italians, and Greeks, while assurances to the Kurdish people vanished into history. As the Allies cut up the Ottoman Empire and occupied parts of it in the postwar world, those contradictory promises would come back to haunt the British and would sow the seeds of future conflicts that would last into the 21st century. Many of the burning issues that occupied headlines in later decades, such as the status of Palestine and Israel, the nature of Iraqi nationality, and the relationship of Arabic-speaking states with Europe and the West, had their origins in the breakup of the Ottoman Empire. What seemed to the Arabs and even to British critics of the policy to be duplicity probably resulted from the fact that different statesmen and officers made various promises at different times. In that way they created a muddle of affairs not fully known until after the war when all the commitments began to surface.

OTTOMAN EMPIRE AND YOUNG TURKS

Although the Ottoman Empire had shrunk and its military forces seemed weakened in the years before World War I, the country had been modernizing fairly rapidly. In a seizure of power, a group of military men and political leaders known as the Young Turks took over in 1908, retaining the sultan in name, but working to reduce the influence of Islamic clergy. In their efforts to westernize the country, they brought in military advisers from Europe and built up the armed forces. Reforms in the status of women, in education, and in other areas of life proceeded more slowly than the improvement in the military. The leaders, Enver Pasha, Talaat Bey, and Djemal Pasha proclaimed the official equality of all faiths, Jewish, Christian, and Muslim, within the state. In some of the Arabic-speaking areas of the Empire, such as Syria, Palestine, and the Arabian Peninsula, resentment at the Turks for their movement away from traditional Muslim values simmered beneath the surface.

Several factors pushed Turkey in the direction of allying with Austria-Hungary and Germany. Although the Young Turks admired both German and British modernity, British Liberals had openly criticized Turkish policies and the regime. Russia and Turkey had a long history of conflict, and Russia had made no secret of its ambitions to control the Bosporus and the Dardanelles. Meanwhile, Germany had tried to build up friendly relations with Turkey by sending military advisers. The effort lead to a secret treaty signed just before the war, in which Enver Pasha, the Young Turk war minister, agreed to assist Germany in event of war. Nevertheless, Turkey appeared to waver and remained officially neutral through the first three months of the war.

Several events made it easier for Turkey to meet its treaty obligations. First, the British decided, given the well-known pro-German stand of Turkey, to refuse to deliver two new battleships that had been ordered by Turkey, paid for, and built in British yards. The Young Turks played up the British offense to their sovereignty in the press and public opinion took a decidedly anti-British turn.

Another maritime development provided the final push. Germany had two battleships in the Mediterranean when the war started, the battle cruiser *Goeben* and the light cruiser *Breslau*. After some inconclusive engagements with British warships, the commander of this small German force, Admiral Wilhelm Souchon, decided to proceed to Constantinople. After some negotiations, the Turks agreed to let the German ships proceed through the Dardanelles, on condition that the Turkish navy purchase them. The purchase went ahead, with the German officers remaining in charge to train Turkish sailors, and Turkish vessels escorted the ships through the minefields of the Dardanelles to the safety of Constantinople. The Turks assured the Germans that no combatant warships, such as those of the British or French, would be allowed to pass the officially neutral waterway.

By the end of October, the German command decided the time had come to bring Turkey into the war. In order to provide the precipitating incident, the two German warships left Constantinople, under nominal Turkish control and flags but officered and partially crewed with the original German sailors, and steamed across the Black Sea, where they shelled three Russian ports. Russia, with its long-standing interest in controlling the route to the Mediterranean, needed no further provocation for a war with the sick man of Europe. Russia declared war on Turkey, dreaming of the day when the Bosporus would become a permanent Russian transit route.

CHURCHILL AND THE DARDANELLES DECISION

The German-Turkish raids on the Black Sea ports led directly to the British decision to open a campaign against the Dardanelles straits and the Gallipoli Peninsula. That campaign in 1915 turned out to be one of the most controversial efforts of all of World War I. The idea developed at first in response to a request from Count Nicholas, who commanded the Russian armies, in which he asked for some pressure on the Turks to draw them off from potential attacks into Russian Armenia and to prevent further German-Turkish naval raids on Russian ports.

Winston Churchill got support for the idea of a combined operation of naval and army forces against the Dardanelles from First Sea Lord John Fisher. However, as the advocates advanced the plans, Field Marshal Herbert Kitchener, who served as minister of war in the cabinet of Herbert Asquith, at first opposed them. Kitchener argued that he could not spare troops from the battles on the western front. Reluctantly, Kitchener came to accept the idea of a naval operation to force the straits and take Constantinople. Although later analysts have scoffed at the idea that a naval force could take a city, others have argued that the Turkish government had so little popular support and mounted such poor defenses that if British naval warships had bombarded the capital, the whole Turkish state would have collapsed.

Like other plans in that and other periods, the concept of a Dardanelles operation began to grow in acceptance, without a clear and full analysis of exactly what forces and equipment would be required and without good charts and maps of the sea approaches and the lay of the land. The Dardanelles strait narrowed to less than a mile in width in some areas. The presence of shore batteries along both sides, together with mine emplacements, put any Allied ships that tried to move up the strait at severe risk.

The British War Council finally agreed to a joint operation in February 1915, and the Allies ordered that Australian, New Zealand, and Indian troops be forwarded from Egypt to the island of Lemnos, off the Dardanelles, where they could assemble and prepare an invasion. While the British general Sir Ian Hamilton organized the troop shipments from Egypt, the French agreed to provide four battleships and a small army to help in the invasion. Unfortunately, the British conducted the transfers of troops so openly that General Liman von Sanders, the German officer in charge of Turkish troops, got word of the movements from a variety of sources, including private Greek shipping contractors, and even from London newspapers. With the advance warnings, Sanders promptly ordered reinforcement of the defenses on the land along the Dardanelles Peninsula as well as new minefields in the straits themselves.

PREMATURE FIRING ON THE DARDANELLES

To prepare the way for a run of ships through the Dardanelles, the Allied fleets began bombardment of the Turkish shore batteries on February 19, 1915, and, after a bit of bad weather, landed several small commando detachments to demolish some of the guns defending the opening of the strait. Although these efforts succeeded, the attack, combined with the obvious larger movement of troops, gave further warning to the Turks and Sanders of the impending attack. The full-scale attack would not begin for another two months, so the February shelling served as an added warning to the Turks to prepare.

In Constantinople, the February bombardment had other effects. Now that the British and French had opened fire, the Turkish government viewed resident British and French, not just as technical enemy aliens, but also as potentially hostile spies and saboteurs. U.S. ambassador Henry Morgenthau, who had been trying to arrange the departure of British and French civilians, suddenly found that the Turkish government and police put all sorts of harassing obstacles in their way, and the Turks began to intern some civilians in detention centers. Even more ominously, the Turks pledged to kill two Christians for every Turk killed. Although the French and British seemed likely targets for this blood-revenge, the Turks turned instead to a more defenseless Christian people, the Armenians.

BEGINNING OF THE ARMENIAN PERSECUTION

After the group of secular Muslims (together with a few Jewish and Armenian leaders) who called themselves Young Turks had established control in Turkey in 1908, they had changed the practice of the Turkish army, which had previously excluded Armenians from service. Committed to modernizing the state and reducing the influence of the Islamic clergy, the Young Turks tried to rule the Ottoman Empire in a more efficient, European style, which meant overlooking religious differences in favor of secular unity. In fact, during the Balkan War of 1912–13, with the new policy, Christian Armenian troops had fought alongside other Ottoman Empire troops in numerous battles. During World War I, however, the Turkish army began to convert the Armenian troops from armed soldiers into unarmed work or labor battalions, known as *ameles*. The Turks gave as their ostensible reason for disarming the Armenian soldiers a concern that they would desert and then use their arms to fight with the Russians against the Turkish regime.

When word of this disarmament spread, Armenian civilians feared the worst. The Turkish regime then ordered the confiscation of all weapons belonging to Armenian civilians, because, they claimed, of pro-Russian sentiments among them. This seizure soon became a basis for raids on homes, forced searches, and executions of Armenians who denied having any weapons. Stories leaked out that some Armenian households would purchase weapons just in order to have some to turn in, rather than facing a charge of concealment that would lead to an unjustified execution.

Muslim civilians slaughtered several large groups of *ameles* as they marched into Muslim communities, and, in response, the population of the large Armenian town of Van, on the eastern side of the large lake by the same name, openly rebelled against the Turks. Turkish troops then surrounded and besieged Van as well as several other holdout Armenian communities. In April, the Turkish gov-

In this photo British troops hold out in caves on W beach at Gallipoli, a "terrible place." *(National Archives)*

ernment began a program announced as relocation, but which amounted in fact to mass murder. Turkish troops rounded up all able-bodied men from Armenian communities, took them out of town, tied them in groups of four, and then shot them to death. Turkish authorities ordered the Armenian women, children, sick, and aged to immediately pack their belongings and begin an overland march southward to theoretical but nonexistent relocation destinations in the Syrian and Mesopotamian deserts, several hundred miles away over grueling mountain territory through hostile Muslim communities. Marched on foot, some with livestock, these groups soon encountered the worse horrors of rape and slaughter. Only gradually did word of the atrocity seep out, through missionaries, consular officers, journalists, and a few surviving refugees. Meanwhile, the battle at Gallipoli began in earnest.

GALLIPOLI: BAD PLAN OR BAD EXECUTION?

During the war and through the decades after the war, analysts reviewed the Gallipoli campaign. Some argued that the plan reflected serious flaws from the start, with no real understanding of the hazards, with poor security, and with no sense of what would be required to eject or cut off entrenched troops who held the high ground along the peninsula. Others argued that the plan made good sense, but that leadership simply executed it poorly, reflecting incompetent or inexperienced officers, bad communication, and multiple episodes of bad luck and missed opportunities.

As an example of opportunities that might have made a difference, several British submarines penetrated through minefields and protective nets to torpedo Turkish supply ships in the inland Sea of Marmara. A few troops landed from submarines in a fast behind-the-lines commando raid could have cut vital supply roads to the defending Turks farther down the peninsula and prepared the way for larger landings behind the Turkish front. But the Allies made no such effort. Furthermore, although the British began to employ seaplanes for observation, they never exploited the opportunity to use aircraft in close support of the ground troops. In later years, such uses of submarines and aircraft would become commonplace; in 1915, with both technologies of war just being explored, Allied commanders developed neither concept.

Instead, Allied officers and the Turkish leadership continued to think along traditional lines, much as the generals on the western front did. They believed that masses of troops, supported by heavy artillery, should be deployed to take positions and either to drive back the enemy or to defend against being driven back. In Europe, the policy already seemed a disaster, leading to excessive casualties and immobilized fronts facing each other, but at Gallipoli no commanders thought of a means to break out of that pattern.

The first landings on April 25 put thousands of men ashore at several points in the face of severe fire. But crossing the beaches came at the price of great casualties, and, once ashore, the diminished ranks of invading troops, sometimes with all or most officers slaughtered, failed to move very far inland. Without good maps and struggling over terrain that consisted of multiple ridges and canyons, many troops simply became lost. Soon equipment, stores, food, mules, and water supplies began to pile up on the beaches in a terrible jumble, still under sniper fire from the enemy.

The invading troops dug into the rocky ground, eventually creating networks of trenches, some of which came within a few yards of the defending Turkish trenches. For a month, older British dreadnoughts and other capital ships pounded the Turkish positions with heavy shells, but the sinking of the two British ships, the *Triumph* and the *Majestic,* in late May by Hersing's U-boat led to the withdrawal of this heavy supporting fire.

Dozens of diaries, collections of letters, and memoirs of eyewitnesses reported the horror of trench conditions. The diet for the Allies consisted of bully beef (canned beef), biscuits (crackers), and plum and apple jam. Troops found the diet intensely boring, and later analysis showed it nutritionally quite bad for the weather and the living conditions. Flies that gathered on dead mules and human corpses clouded the air and immediately covered any exposed food before a soldier could eat it. A plague of dysentery resulted, which left its victims almost too exhausted to move. Troops slept curled up in narrow shelves cut into the face of trenches, and, if they survived, would live for weeks in conditions of intense heat with no shade during the daylight.

When relieved from service at the trench-fronts, troops would bathe in the ocean, even though exposed to sniper fire from the hills still within rifle range. Mules and horses tied in ranks on the shore did not realize that the gunfire represented a hazard, and, when one among them would fall from a sniper's shot, the

Turkish prisoners of war were held behind their own barbed wire during the Dardanelles campaign. *(National Archives)*

others would hardly react. Often, the dead mules floated out to sea, where sailors sometimes mistook their stiffened legs for enemy periscopes, creating temporary panic aboard supply ships.

On the beach known as Anzac, for the Australian–New Zealand Army Corps, troops spent hours digging trenches. So the nickname "diggers" became attached to the men from down under. The Anzac troops tended to scoff at authority, and British officers found it scandalous that the troops would not always salute properly, that they would not wear a full uniform, and that they would expect a rest after an eight-hour day. But as the surviving Anzacs hardened, their bitter determination to hold onto the territory gained and their courage under fire earned them the name, the "imperishable" Anzacs. Tales of individual heroism, tragic or gruesome death, and desperate battles that emerged from the hills of Gallipoli rivaled those of the western front.

Troops from Britain frequently remarked on the strange and haunting contrast between the beautiful clear weather and the horrors of the battlefield. Fragrant wildflowers and spice plants like thyme and sage, swooping birds, and powder-puff clouds against an intensely blue sky, with a view out over the sparkling Aegean Sea seemed almost like an outing to the beach at home on a rare balmy British summer day. The illusion vanished with the constant sound of gunfire, the screams of the wounded, and the stench of death.

Despite all the agony, the April landings gained only a foothold on several beaches and a few hills nearby, while the Turks under Kemal continued to reinforce the high ground and kept the Allied forces pinned down. The Turks clearly recognized the importance of keeping the Allied troops from reaching the shore batteries and preventing the Allied warships from reaching Constantinople.

After several debates between the command at Lemnos and the War Cabinet in London over how to alter the situation, the War Cabinet finally authorized the simple solution of sending in more troops. In August, fresh divisions arrived, with a major landing at Suvla Bay, just north of the Anzac beachhead. This landing force, however, despite its improved landing craft, resulted in another failure, largely because the officers in charge believed they needed artillery support to advance inland. That, after all, seemed to be the lesson of Belgium, Flanders, and the Marne.

In fact, the Turks had mounted only light defenses in front of the invading forces at Suvla Bay, and, if the landings had followed the original plan, the new Allied troops could have seized the high ground in a few hours. Instead, they waited on the beach and salt flat without advancing, while the Turks gradually realized the enemy disposition and began to reinforce their own lines. Meanwhile, communications between Ian Hamilton, in command on Lemnos, and officers on shore dissolved into a confused tangle of misunderstandings, missed or undelivered messages, and contradictory interpretations of the best course of action.

Mustafa Kemal, the Turkish officer who recognized the threat and defended against the Allied attacks, had expressed aggressive opinions in the past, earning him some political disfavor in the Turkish army. Liman von Sanders recognized Kemal's leadership qualities, however, and endorsed his command of the defense. Under Kemal's command, the Turks held the front, and Kemal became an instant national hero. Kemal later would go on to lead a revolt against the sultan, establish the Turkish Republic, and become universally recognized as the father of his country with the honorary name "Ataturk."

The eventual victory over the invaders cost the Turks more than 250,000 casualties. On the Allied side, the losses amounted to a similar number, with Britain and the "colonies," as Australia, New Zealand, and India were called, suffering about 214,000 casualties, with the French casualties numbering about another 37,000. In a pattern like that in other battles and in other nations, blame fell on key individuals, some later demoted or quietly shifted to other assignments. First Sea Lord Fisher resigned in disgust at the multiple failures. General Charles Monro replaced Ian Hamilton. The War Cabinet and others regarded Hamilton as too optimistic and criticized him for his inability to cooperate in detailed planning with the Admiralty. The failure of the Dardanelles expedition even brought down the Herbert Asquith Liberal-led government, replaced by a union or multiparty government under Lloyd George. Winston Churchill lost his post as First Lord of the Admiralty and left England to command a battalion of infantry in France. Monro, as Hamilton's replacement, recommended that all the troops on the peninsula be evacuated.

Considering all the mistakes made at Gallipoli, when it seemed whatever could go wrong did go wrong, the evacuation turned out as the one great exception, coming off as a quite smooth operation. Despite the fact that commanders anticipated terrible losses, the troops, aided by diversionary artillery barrages, successfully departed without any casualties at all in several operations in December 1915, and culminating January 8 and 9, 1916, under cover of fog. In this situation, the troops invented numerous clever deceptions to create the impression that they still held the trenches they abandoned. One method consisted of leaving behind loaded rifles rigged with weights to fire long after the troops had left. The soldiers muffled their footsteps by binding their feet with rags. Pre-timed mines left the impression of a pending attack against the Turkish

At Anzac beach, Australians charged Turkish trenches just prior to the evacuation from the peninsula. *(National Archives)*

trenches. Despite efforts to demolish equipment and to kill the remaining mules and horses, the Allies had to abandon immense quantities of supplies that fell into the hands of the Turks.

The attempt to attack Constantinople would have changed the course of the war if it had succeeded, just as Churchill had predicted and as Kitchener had reluctantly concluded. Although a failure in many respects, the long-drawn-out campaign through 1915 did draw Turkish forces off the Russian front, allowing the Russians to advance into Turkish Armenia and western Persia (now Iran). By taking pressure away from the Russians, the expedition had the benefit of delaying the collapse of the Russian effort by at least a few months.

The British and French troops who evacuated from the peninsula transferred to Salonika, in Greek Macedonia. There they joined forces with Serbian troops and attempted to push the Austrians, Germans, and Bulgarians out of Serbia.

In later wars, when planners contemplated combined operations involving troops landed from the sea, they reviewed closely the lessons of the Dardanelles expedition. Later operations put in practice ideas such as deception, commando raids behind the lines, close air support, coordination of naval and army forces, improved command and control communication, rapid mobility, and attention to supply organization (logistics), most of which had been sorely lacking at the Dardanelles. The effective evacuation itself provided some lessons later employed at Dunkirk in May and June 1940, when more than 300,000 troops successfully escaped to Britain in the face of German attacks.

Armenian Holocaust

While the battles on the Gallipoli Peninsula raged over the summer of 1915, the Armenian holocaust intensified. When a Turkish officer asked Enver Pasha for a clarification of the destination to which the refugees should be marched in Mesopotamia (now Iraq), Pasha told him that the destination was "nowhere." The Turkish guards ostensibly provided to protect the Armenian women and children appeared to join enthusiastically in the massacres. As the columns approached a town, local toughs would be invited to have their pick of the women and girls, raping some and kidnapping others to be sold. Villagers along the way stole all the belongings of the marching refugees, sometimes even including the clothes they wore. When a family group stopped to assist fallen sick or elderly members, troops would force the marchers at bayonet point to abandon them. Guards cut food rations back to the point where only a small percentage of the refugees could have any, and the guards regarded their struggles over the remnants as entertainment.

Mothers begged passersby to take their children that they might survive. Missionaries and consular officials attempted to intervene, but the Turks usually prevented them from assisting the survivors. Although the local German authorities took the official position that handling the Armenians was a strictly Turkish issue, some individual German missionaries felt sufficiently shocked at the massacres to complain to the Turkish government.

The protests of Ambassador Morgenthau and America consular official Lewis Einstein fell on deaf ears, as did the reports from missionaries. When Morgenthau protested to the Turkish government about the episodes, Enver Pasha asked him why, as a Jew, should he care what happened to Christians? Morgenthau replied that he represented the U.S. government, not the Jewish race, and that all civilized peoples felt appalled at the atrocity. Enver pointed out that the Armenians were Turkish citizens and that the American government had no jurisdiction over a strictly internal Turkish matter.

In May, the Russian army advanced to Van to relieve the Armenian community there, but the Turks drove the Russians back in August. Eventually the holocaust seemed to wear itself out in the late summer of 1915. By that time, the slaughter had run its course. Of an estimated 2 million Armenians resident in Turkey earlier that year, about 1 million remained. Although the extermination proceeded with the obvious cooperation of the government authorities, its origin appeared to spring from a backlash against both the secularizing influence of the Young Turks and the threat posed by the Allied invasion.

FROM CAIRO TO DAMASCUS

The British grand strategy for the defeat of the Ottoman Empire beyond the Gallipoli-Dardanelles thrust toward Constantinople relied on a two-pronged attack through the outlying reaches of the Ottoman Empire. The plan called for a western prong attack from Egypt to cross the Sinai Peninsula and then pass through Palestine toward Damascus in Syria. The other thrust would be northward from the Persian Gulf through Iraq, to link up with the Russians advancing southward through Persia (now Iran). As a grand strategy, the plan made sense, although nothing turned out quite as hoped.

After the Turks joined the war, the British hastily brought troops to Egypt in December 1914 from Australia, New Zealand, and India. They faced threats from two directions. In the Sudan, an uprising of Senussi tribesmen tied down British forces in the Darfur region, and Turkish moves from Palestine suggested the risk of an immediate attack on the Suez Canal. Drawing troops off from Egypt for the Gallipoli campaign had always been dangerous, but the local British command in Egypt held off both local threats. In addition to dealing with the Senussi uprising, when the British forces tried to advance from Egypt into Palestine, they encountered severe resistance by Turkish troops in the Gaza region, frustrating any thoughts of a lightning raid through Jerusalem to Damascus.

In Iraq, as British troops advanced northward toward Baghdad in hopes of meeting the Russian forces advancing southward through Persia (now Iran), they found their way stopped at the city of Al Kut, southeast of Baghdad. Turks surrounded a British force at Kut, and, despite three attempts to relieve the besieged troops and an attempt to bribe the Turkish command into releasing them, the Turks captured some 10,000 British soldiers in April 1916 in one of the major defeats for the British in the region. British forces finally took Baghdad in March of 1917, but only after receiving support from an unexpected source that drew off Turkish resources, the Arab Revolt.

THE ARAB REVOLT, T. E. LAWRENCE, AND LEGACIES

Arabia, the site of the Muslim holy cities of Mecca and Medina, rumbled with popular discontent at the official Turkish policy of religious equality even before the war started. Secularization of the Turkish regime angered devout Muslims throughout the Arab-speaking regions. Rumors that the Turkish governor of Syria had mistreated Syrian Arabs reached Hussein, the sheriff of Mecca, who claimed descent from Muhammad. Hussein sent one of his sons to investigate, and the Syrian governor ordered his arrest. This incident precipitated an uprising of Arabs against the local Turkish authorities in Arabia, which grew into the larger Arab Revolt. Hussein declared the independence of Hejaz from Turkish rule in June 1916 and sent out several armies under the command of his sons to drive out the Turks.

Hussein's forces soon controlled Mecca, but under the leadership of the local commander, Fakhri Pasha, the Turks held off Hussein's attack on their garrison at Medina. In order to restore command of the situation through intimidation, Fakhri ordered Arab prisoners executed under torture. Contrary to his expectations, word of the atrocity only increased the fighting spirit of the Arabs. The Turks believed that if they could hold the railroad link from Syria to Medina, they would be able to bring in needed reinforcements and repress the Arab uprising.

In October 1916, the British authorities in Cairo decided to work with the Arabs, hoping that they would tie down enough Turkish troops to allow the original two-pronged plan of attack, through Palestine and through the Tigris-Euphrates plains of Iraq, to go forward. In order to open liaison with the Arab leaders, the Cairo headquarters sent Ronald Storrs, a scholarly Arabist attached to the British Agency in Cairo, together with a young captain, T. E. Lawrence, also fluent in local Arab dialects, to meet with Hussein. In the Hejaz, while Storrs conferred with one of Hussein's sons, Abdullah, Lawrence met with another son, Feisal, who commanded an army outside of Medina. After the two reported back, Lawrence got orders to serve with Feisal's army as a political and military liaison officer.

Lawrence had gained fluency in Arabic in prewar archaeological explorations and intelligence missions and soon earned the confidence of Feisal and the other

Arab commanders. Unlike other British officers, he willingly ate and dressed like the Arab rebels and rode camels alongside them. His short height helped him fit right in with the local population. Furthermore, his education had not been in military history or at a war college, but at Oxford, so he tended not to be bound by traditional officer-corps views of how war should be conducted. He advised Feisal to abandon the concept of a siege around Medina, but to move his units to the north of the city and to launch hit-and-run attacks on the rail line connection.

Beginning in March 1917, Lawrence and Arab forces under Feisal began blowing up troop and freight trains, cutting off the Turkish garrison at Medina from its support. An Egyptian force under British command took the minor port of Wejh (Al Wajh) on the Red Sea, and, at Lawrence's urging, Feisal marched his army to link up with the port, where it could receive supplies, money, and arms from Egypt.

In summer 1917, Lawrence accompanied a force of Arab camel cavalry on an expedition across desert country to the port of Aqaba at the northern end of the Red Sea. The Turkish garrison there did not expect an attack from the south, and the city quickly fell to the Arab forces. Lawrence then rode on to Cairo, and, after dealing with bureaucrats who thought he had no right to cross the canal, reported back to headquarters. There, General Archibald Murray had been replaced by General Edmund Allenby, who had won distinction with the British cavalry in Europe. Allenby listened to Lawrence, who met with him barefoot and still in his desert robes, and, although Allenby found Lawrence's ideas unconventional, he agreed to provide further support to the Arab Revolt. Allenby ordered Lawrence promoted, and Lawrence then returned to Arabia with further commitments of arms and money.

Meanwhile, the British attempt to advance through the Sinai into Palestine had been stopped by a combined Turkish and German force at Gaza. Eventually one of Allenby's generals, Guy Dawnay, proposed a deception plan to Allenby. Suggested by Dawnay's intelligence officer, "Meiner" Meinertzhagen, the plan called for an officer to lose a knapsack in no-man's-land. Meiner concocted a set of false papers that indicated incorrect positions for Allenby's main formation of troops, a planned attack in the wrong direction, and a date several days later than the actual one. Meiner walked out into no-man's-land, dropped the knapsack and his rifle, and ran for cover. The Turks recovered the documents and provided them to the German staff for study and interpretation. Several messages sent by radio in code that the Germans had already deciphered enhanced the deception. Allenby then drove past the Turkish troops as they reinforced a point closer to the seacoast, and the Meinertzhagen deception entered British espionage lore as precedent for later operations.

When Lawrence returned to Aqaba, he worked with Arab forces, now backed up by armored cars and with some air support, in moving northward through the Dead Sea region of Palestine. On December 8, Allenby marched into Jerusalem, and during the next weeks, with the Arabs operating in unseasonably cold weather, Lawrence helped blow up rail connections near the city of Dar'a in southern Syria, which were crucial to the Turkish supply of their front in northern Palestine. While he operated near Dar'a, the Turks captured Lawrence, then raped and whipped him before he escaped back to his lines. Further deceptions on Allenby's part led the Germans and Turks to believe he intended to attack in

British troops captured these Germans serving with the Turks in Palestine. *(Library of Congress)*

the Jordan Valley while he drove up the coast. The British pushed on to Damascus and Aleppo in October 1918. In a little more than a month, the British advanced some 300 miles and took 75,000 prisoners. The campaign led to the surrender of the Ottoman Empire a few days before the armistice in Europe.

On the eastern prong of the grand two-pronged attack, after long battles again at Kut in early 1917, the British moved into Baghdad in March and then took Ramadi and Tikrit in the Sunni Triangle by September. Meanwhile, the Russians had advanced through western Persia (now Iran) until the revolution in Russia brought all the Russian fronts to a standstill.

Immediately after the war, Lawrence protested the fact that the Allies did not honor the promises made to the Arabs by the British. In particular, he believed that the British should never have given jurisdiction over Syria to the French under the secret Sykes-Picot agreement of May 1916. Later, when Prince Feisal got the reward of the nominal monarchy of Iraq for agreeing to leave Damascus and then British troops moved into Iraq to attempt to establish order, Lawrence criticized the British government. He also believed the promises made by Foreign Secretary Arthur Balfour to Lord Rothschild to accept the establishment of a Jewish homeland in Palestine represented a betrayal of promises made to the Arabs that they would be rewarded for their assistance in the liberation of Palestine from Turkey. Lawrence attended the peace conference convened in Paris to present his views, with no notable impact.

Bitter over these issues, he resigned from the service, although he had been promoted to lieutenant colonel and offered other positions of honor. Lawrence later changed his name twice, once to join the tank corps as an enlisted man, and then to join the newly established Royal Air Force, also as an enlisted man. His death in a motorcycle accident a few years later added to the legends surrounding him. Before he died, however, Lawrence wrote a thorough memoir of his adventures, first published in an abbreviated version, and then later released under the title *Seven Pillars of Wisdom*. The work established his place in history, served as a popular critique of British Middle East policy, and endures as a major contribution to English literature.

The air of mystery and romance that Lawrence evoked tended to obscure his practical advocacy of what later generations of soldiers recognized as asymmetric warfare. Viewed at the time as the way in which the Boers had fought against the British in the period 1899–1902, the method involved the use of lightly armed and mobile guerrilla bands that would operate with no clear front in mind to harass and wear down regular forces. Lawrence, like Generals Guy Dawnay and Edmund Allenby, also recognized the crucial value of deception as a tool of modern war.

The lessons of the Gallipoli beachheads, of the sieges of Medina and Kut, the surprise attack on Aqaba, the success of irregulars against regular troops, and the Meinertzhagen deception would echo in the calculations of military leaders through the rest of the century. For politicians and peacemakers, the conflicts between rival claimants to the spoils of the Ottoman Empire would prove that the Middle East had been no sideshow to World War I but crucial in its outcomes for future generations.

CHRONICLE OF EVENTS

1914

October 29: Turkish warships, provided by Germany and officered by Germans, bombard the Russian port of Odessa on the Black Sea.

November 2: Russia declares war on Turkey.

November 5: Britain and France declare war on Turkey.

November 14: The sultan of Turkey proclaims a jihad against all those warring on Turkey or its allies.

November 22: British forces invade Mesopotamia (now Iraq), landing at Basra and moving north toward Baghdad.

December 17: Turks advance toward Kars in Armenia.

December 18: The British declare a protectorate over Egypt, formerly a province of the Ottoman Empire but occupied by Britain since 1882.

December 29–January 2: Turks advance into Persia (now Iran) and occupy Tabriz.

1915

January 30: Russians retake Tabriz in Persia (now Iran).

February: U.S. ambassador to Turkey Henry Morgenthau attempts to secure safe passage to Greece for French and British diplomats and civilians in Turkey.

February 3–4: The British turn back a Turkish advance in Sinai on the Suez Canal.

February 19: The British prematurely shell defenses at the Dardanelles. The Turks vow to kill two Christians for every Turk killed.

February 23: The British occupy the Greek island of Lemnos as a base for operations against the Dardanelles.

March 1: Five British battleships and several torpedo boats enter the Dardanelles strait and engage Turkish shore batteries in a gun battle.

March 4: Russia sends a note to Britain and France claiming that at the end of the war Russia should control Constantinople, the western side of the Bosporus, and the Dardanelles.

March 12: The British and French accept the Russian planned annexation of Constantinople, but with the proviso it should be a free port and that the straits should remain open to merchant ships of all nations. Britain is to occupy Mesopotamia (now Iraq).

March 18: The British attempt to force the Dardanelles with an older fleet of warships. They are turned back by shore batteries and mines.

April–August: The Turks begin the deportation of Armenians from their homeland region. An estimated 750,000 to 1 million Armenians will be killed in genocidal slaughters.

April 20: Armenians in Van (in eastern Turkey) conduct an uprising against the Turks. The scattered resistance of Armenians to Turkish repression is generally ineffective.

April 23: A young British poet, Rupert Brooke, dies of infection on his way to Gallipoli. He becomes a symbol of a "lost generation."

April 25: British, Australian, and New Zealand troops land in Gallipoli. The forces are held at the beaches and first hills by Turkish defenses. The troops dig in. They suffer from dysentery, snipers, and ill-planned trench warfare.

May 13: A Turkish torpedo boat sinks the British battleship *Goliath* near Morto Bay in the Dardanelles.

May 19: Russian forces relieve besieged Armenians at Van.

May 25–27: The German submarine *U-91,* after a long voyage from the Belgian coast around Spain and across the Mediterranean, sinks the British battleships *Triumph* and *Majestic.* The British withdraw capital ships from the bombardment of the Gallipoli Peninsula.

June 3: British forces advance toward Baghdad and take Amara on the Tigris River.

July 4: American consular official reports on the Armenian resistance to the massacre by Turks at Karahissar. The murder and starvation of Armenian civilians while being marched overland continues.

July 13: A heavy British and French attack at Gallipoli is repulsed by the Turkish army. General Liman von Sanders will later admit that the Allies could have won the battle if they had persisted one more day.

July 25: British forces advance to Nasariya on the Euphrates River in Mesopotamia (now Iraq).

August 5: Van, in Turkish Armenia, is retaken by the Turks.

August 6: The British attempt further landings at Suvla Bay on the Gallipoli Peninsula but are held in check by a counterattack.

August 6–10: The British are kept from advancing at the Battle of Sari Bair on the Gallipoli Peninsula.

August 21: Italy declares war on Turkey.

September 28: The British army, under General Vere Townshend, take the city of Kut, Mesopotamia (now Iraq), southeast of Baghdad.

October 6: British and French land troops at Salonika in Macedonia, a province of Greece. The Greek king dismisses pro-Allied premier Venizelos.

November 15: Austrian artillery batteries arrive at Gallipoli to support the Turks.

November 22–24: In inconclusive battles, British forces engage Turks at Ctesiphon, about 25 miles from Baghdad. The British retreat to Kut.

December 7–April 29, 1916: Turkish forces besiege British troops at Kut. Several relief expeditions are defeated or stalemated.

December 19–20: The British begin to withdraw troops from Gallipoli under cover of fog.

1916

January 8–9: The British complete the withdrawal of troops from Gallipoli. Despite predictions, the troop withdrawal is conducted without casualties, although masses of equipment, horses, and mules are abandoned to the Turks.

January 15: Elements of the Serbian military flee to the Greek island of Corfu, occupied by the French. The Greek government protests.

January 18: Russians begin an offensive in Turkish Armenia.

January 18–21: The British attempt to relieve besieged forces at Kut but fail.

February 13–16: The Russians take Erzerum in Turkish Armenia.

February 26: The Russians take Kirmanshah in western Persia (now Iran).

March 8: The British attempt and fail to relieve besieged Kut.

April 1–9: The last British attempt to relieve Kut fails.

April 26: A British-French-Russian secret agreement regarding division of the Ottoman Empire is reached. England is to retain southern Iraq and Baghdad, with ports in Syria. France is to have Syria and a section of Kurdistan. Russia is to obtain the Armenian section of Turkey (including Van, Trebizond, and Erzerum), as well as control of Constantinople and the straits.

May 9–16: The secret Sykes-Picot agreement is signed in which the British and French agree on the division of the Ottoman Empire. Both countries agree to recognize an independent Arab state or federation of states.

June 27: The Arab Revolt against Turkey begins with the declaration of the independence of Hejaz by Sharif Hussein of Mecca. Arabs attack the Turkish garrison at Medina but do not occupy the city.

August 4: Turkish forces attempting to take the Suez Canal are defeated at Rumani, about 10 miles east of the canal.

August 20: Turkey declares war on Romania.

September 29: Venizelos, with Admiral Paul Condouriotis, sets up a provisional Greek government in British-occupied Crete, in support of the Allies.

October: Ronald Storrs, secretary to the British agency in Cairo, and Captain T. E. Lawrence, both fluent in Arabic and enthusiasts for Arab culture, are sent on a mission to meet with Sharif Hussein and his sons.

October 25: Mecca is captured by Hussein's forces and declared the capital of Hejaz.

October 29: Hussein, the grand sharif of Mecca, is proclaimed king of the Arabs.

November 20: The British under Archibald Murray begin to advance in Suez.

November 23: The Greek provisional government headed by Venizelos declares war on Germany and Bulgaria.

December 15: The British recognize Hussein as king of Hejaz.

1917

January: A British-led army of Egyptian troops takes Wejh (now Al Wajh) in Arabia, providing a port for supplies to Arab Revolt forces.

March: Lawrence begins blowing up railway lines north of Medina.

March 11: The British occupy Baghdad.

March 26–27: At the Battle of Gaza, the British fail to take the city from the Turks.

April 17–19: At the Second Battle of Gaza, the Turks drive the British back.

April 19–21: According to the Agreement of Saint Jean de Maurienne, Italy will agree to the terms of the Sykes-Picot Agreement, in exchange for concessions at the ports of Alexandretta (Iskenderun), Turkey, and Haifa and Acre in Palestine.

May 9–July 4: Lawrence, with Sheikh Auda Aba Taya, leads a Huwaitat camel force north from the port of Wejh in Arabia toward the port of Aqaba, traversing extremely difficult territory and subsisting on dates and camel meat.

June 28: Archibald Murray is replaced by Edmund Allenby as commander of British forces in Egypt.

July 6: The Huwaitat camel force, with T. E. Lawrence, takes Aqaba (now in Jordan) on the Red Sea.

July 8: The Russians begin to pull back from western Persia (now Iran).

July 10: Lawrence meets with Allenby, is promoted to major, and gets a commitment of more funds and arms for the Arab Revolt. Lawrence advances his theories of guerrilla-style warfare and wins some support among the British.

September 29: The British take Ramadi in the Sunni Triangle area of Iraq.

November 2: British foreign secretary Arthur Balfour sends a note to Baron Rothschild, a British leader of the international Jewish community. This "Balfour Declaration" notes that the British government views with favor the establishment in Palestine of a national home for the Jewish people. The note also states that such a homeland is not to prejudice the rights of the non-Jewish population in Palestine, nor diminish the rights and political status of Jews residing in or citizens of other countries.

November 7: The British force the Turkish evacuation of Gaza.

December 8: British forces under Allenby take Jerusalem.

1918

September 17: Prince Feisal's forces, with Lawrence, blow up a vital rail link at Dar'a, Syria, interrupting the Turkish supply line to troops opposing Allenby's advance through Palestine.

October 1–2: After a masterful deception by Allenby's forces, British and Arab forces take Damascus, Syria. Lawrence protests French plans to establish a Syrian governing body. He later regards Damascus as properly under Prince Feisal's leadership and the award of the Iraq throne to him as a sop.

General Edmund Allenby enters Jerusalem on horseback, providing a photo-op. *(Library of Congress)*

October 7: French naval forces land and take Beirut, Lebanon.

October 14: The Turkish government appeals to Woodrow Wilson to establish an armistice.

October 26: Aleppo in northern Syria is taken by Allied forces. The sultan dismisses the Young Turks' cabinet headed by Enver Pasha.

October 30: At Moudros, on the island of Lemnos, Turkey and the Allies conclude an armistice.

November 12: The Allied fleet goes through the Dardanelles to Constantinople.

EYEWITNESS TESTIMONY

At this meeting Talaat frankly told me that Turkey had decided to side with the Germans and to sink or swim with them. He went again over the familiar grounds, and added that if Germany won—and Talaat said that he was convinced that Germany would win—the Kaiser would get his revenge on Turkey if Turkey had not helped him to obtain this victory. Talaat frankly admitted that fear—the motive, which as I have said, is the one that chiefly inspires Turkish acts—was driving Turkey into a German alliance. He analyzed the whole situation most dispassionately; he said that nations could not afford such emotions as gratitude, or hate, or affection; the only guide to action should be cold-blooded policy.

"At this moment," said Talaat, "it is for our interest to side with Germany; if a month from now, it is our interest to embrace France and England we shall do that just as readily."

"Russia is our greatest enemy," he continued; "and we are afraid of her. If now, while Germany is attacking Russia, we can give her a good strong kick, and so make her powerless to injure us for some time, it is Turkey's duty to administer that kick!"

And then turning to me with a half-melancholy, half-defiant smile, he summed up the whole situation.

"*Ich mit die Deutschen,*" he said, in his broken German.

Because the Cabinet was so divided, however, the Germans themselves had to push Turkey over the precipice. The evening following my talk with Talaat, most fateful news came from Russia. Three Turkish torpedo boats had entered the harbour of Odessa, had sunk the Russian gunboat *Donetz,* killing a part of the crew, and had damaged two Russian dreadnaughts. They also sank the French ship *Portugal,* killing two of the crew and wounding two others. They then turned their shells on the town and destroyed a sugar factory, with some loss of life. German officers commanded these Turkish vessels; there were very few Turks on board, as the Turkish crews had been given a holiday for the Turkish religious festival of Bairam. The act was simply a wanton and unprovoked one; the Germans raided the town deliberately, in order to make war inevitable. The German officers on the *General,* as my friend had told me, were constantly threatening to commit some such act, if Turkey did not do so; well now they had done it.

U.S. ambassador to Turkey Henry Morgenthau, reflecting on his meeting on October 29, 1914, with Turkish cabinet member Mehmed Taalat regarding Turkey's course in the war, as noted in his memoir, Ambassador Morgenthau's Story, *pp. 124–125.*

As contrasted with Enver's palace, with its innumerable rooms and gorgeous furniture, Talaat's house was an old, rickety, wooden, three-story building. All this, I afterward learned was part of the setting which Talaat had staged for his career. Like many an American politician, he had found his position as a man of "the people" a valuable political asset, and he knew that a sudden display of prosperity and ostentation would weaken his influence with the Union and Progress Committee, most of whose members, like himself, had risen from the lower walks of life. The contents of the house were quite in keeping with the exterior. There were no suggestions of Oriental magnificence. The furniture was cheap; a few coarse prints hung on the walls, and one or two well-worn rugs were scattered on the floor. On one side stood a wooden table, and on this rested a telegraph instrument—once Talaat's means of earning a living, and now a means by which he communicated with his associates. In the present troubled conditions in Turkey Talaat sometimes preferred to do his own telegraphing!

Amid these surroundings I awaited for a few minutes the entrance of the Big Boss of Turkey. . . .

"Well, Talaat," I said, realizing that the time had come for plain speaking, "don't you know how foolishly you are acting? You told me a few hours ago that you had decided to treat the French and English decently and you asked me to publish this news in the American and foreign press. I at once called in the newspaper men and told them how splendidly you were behaving. And this at your own request! The whole world will be reading about it tomorrow. Now you are doing your best to counteract all my efforts in your behalf; here you have repudiated your first promise to be decent. . . . Now let's have a real understanding. The thing we Americans particularly pride ourselves on is keeping our word. We do it as individuals and as a nation. We refuse to deal with people as equals who do not do this. You might as well understand now that we can do no business with each other unless I can depend on your promises." . . .

I could see that this argument was having its effect on Talaat. He remained quiet for a few moments, evidently pondering my remarks. Then he said, with the utmost deliberation,

"I am going to help you."

He turned around to his table and began working his telegraph instrument. . . . Evidently the ruler of Turkey was having his troubles, and as the argument went on over the telegraph, Talaat would bang his key with increasing irritation. . . . It took Talaat some time to locate Enver, and then the dispute apparently started all over again. A piece of news which Talaat received at that moment over the wire almost ruined my case. After a prolonged thumping of his instrument, in the course of which Talaat's face lost its geniality and became almost savage, he turned to me and said:

"The English bombarded the Dardanelles this morning and killed two Turks!"

And then he added:

"We intend to kill three Christians for every Moslem killed!"

For a moment I thought that everything was lost. Talaat's face reflected only one emotion—hatred of the English. Afterward, when reading the Cromer report on the Dardanelles, I found that the British Committee stigmatized this early attack as a mistake, since it gave the Turks an early warning of their plans. I can testify that it was a mistake for another reason, for I now found that these few strange shots almost destroyed my plans to get the foreign residents out of Turkey.

Ambassador Morgenthau, commenting in his memoir on meeting with Talaat on February 19, 1915, from his Ambassador Morgenthau's Story, *pp. 139–144.*

April 23, 1915

The first boat of the fleet leaves, named the *River Clyde,* an old tramp steamer, painted khaki. She contains the Dublin and Munster Fusiliers. Fore and aft on starboard and port the sides are cut away, but fastened like doors. She will be beached at "V" Beach, and immediately that is over, her sides will be opened and the troops aboard will swarm out on to the shore. Good luck to those on board! She slowly passes the battleships, and turning round the boom, is soon out of sight.

A British officer, Major Graham Gillam, recording in his diary the transport of Dublin and Munster Fusiliers at the Gallipoli Peninsula, April 23, 1915, Gallipoli Diary, *p. 29.*

April 24, 1915

Half Battalion Royal Fusiliers and Headquarters went on board H.M.S. *Implacable* about 7 p.m., from which ship we had been practicing getting into boats, and so on; the other Half Battalion, under Brandreth, spent the night on two Fleet mine-sweepers. At about 10.30 p.m. the brigade and warships all sailed for the peninsula, arriving there by night. We had a good breakfast on *Implacable* at 3.30 a.m. We then proceeded to load up the boats, four tows of six boats each and a steam pinnace, twenty-five men in each boat, besides the six bluejackets to row when the pinnace cast us off.

Lieutenant-Colonel Henry Newenham, commander of the 2nd Royal Fusiliers, describing the landing of troops at X beach, April 23, 1915, in a letter quoted in Rev. O. Creighton, With the Twenty Ninth Division in Gallipoli: A Chaplain's Experiences, *p. 55.*

Our packs were crammed to bursting, we had blankets and a waterproof sheet outside, picks, shovels, entrenching tools, rifles, and 200 rounds of ammunition, besides a bundle of firewood and a haversack full of rations. If the triumphal march into Constantinople had come off I am afraid a good many Government articles would have been lost on the road. . . . The time passed slowly after dark as we lay below in an orgy of equipment. At length we imagined we heard artillery fire, and began to get saddled up. Then the *Gezreih* stopped, and we knew we were there. . . . At length the unwieldy craft began to move. Then we crawled out, tottered gingerly down a slippery gangway on which two men were constantly flinging sand and landed ankle deep in shingle. We had arrived at the Dardanelles!

We formed up on the beach, and then being ordered to stand easy (but not to talk or smoke) we sat down and reviewed the situation. The ugly lighter was still disgorging its human beasts of burden. Behind lay the *Gezreih*. Beyond that again lay a brilliantly lighted hospital ship. Behind us we could distinguish little. . . . There was a steady interchange of compliments from the local artillery rivals all day, but no shrapnel came near us, although the Brigade was not without casualties on that first day. We thus got a nice quiet introduction to the song of the shells, but about dusk we were rather startled by a sudden terrific burst of rifle fire. That day we had our first introduction to the Gallipoli fly. That abominable insect is anything but shy or fastidious. When we opened a tin of jam the air grew black with them. We hung our mosquito nets from our helmets, and endeavoured to sneak our precious mess-tin of tea away unpolluted. But nothing could keep them back. We never grew really reconciled to them, but in a short time we were messing more or less contentedly on sand and flies. Thus in a few days I had become acquainted with two things of which I had no previous knowledge, viz. Thirst and flies. . . . But our greatest treat while in these reserve trenches was getting down in small parties to the beach for a bathe. It was a boon beyond words in the hot weather.

Trooper L. McCustra, recalling the conditions on landing at Gallipoli on April 25, 1915, in his Gallipoli Days and Nights, *pp. 54–65.*

April 25, 1915
Was awakened at four by the noise of the distant rumbling of guns, and coming to my senses, I realized that the great effort had started. I dressed hastily and went on deck, and there found the Essex and Royal Scots falling in on parade, with full packs on, two bags of iron rations, and the unexpended portion of the day's rations (for they had breakfasted), entrenching tools, two hundred rounds of ammunition, rifle and bayonet. I stood and watched—watched their faces, listened to what they said to each other, and could trace no sign of fear in their faces and no words of apprehension at forthcoming events in their conversation.

It was a simple fall in, just as of old in the days of peace parades, with the familiar faces of the N.C.O.'s and officers before them, like one big family party.

They seemed to be rather weighed down with their packs, and I pity them for the work that this parade is called for. The booming of the guns grows louder. It is very misty, but on going forward I can just see land, and the first officer points out to me the entrance through the Dardanelles. How narrow it seems; like the Thames at Gravesend almost. I can see the *Askold* distinctly. A Tommy said, "There's the old packet of Woodbines [Russian cruiser, *Askold*] giving them what-ho!" She is firing broadsides, and columns of dust and smoke arise from shore. The din is getting louder. I can't quite make out which is the Asiatic side and which Gallipoli. It is getting clearer and a lovely day is developing. Seagulls are swooping over the calm sea above the din, and a thunderous roar bursts out now and again from *Queen Bess.* Her 15-inch guns are at work, and she is firing enormous shrapnel shells—terrible shells, which seem to burst 30 feet from the ground. . . .
8:30 am.

On a hopper which somehow or other has been moored in between the *River Clyde* and the shore I see khaki figures lying, many apparently dead. I also see the horrible sight of some little white boats drifting, with motionless khaki freight, helplessly out to sea on the strong current that is coming down the Straits.

Major John Graham Gillam, recording in his diary observations on the landings of the troops at Gallipoli, April 25, 1915, in Gallipoli Diary, *p. 29.*

One exposed knoll, which the snipers were paying particular attention to, we were compelled to rush over singly. As it came to my turn, I bolted, pick in one hand and rifle in the other as hard as my legs would carry me. One had simply to claw one's way up the soft, yielding bank. No sooner had I reached the top than a dozen bullets kicked up the dirt all around me. An officer who followed me said, "What's the matter, laddie?" "Drop," I shouted. He did so, only just in time to miss a perfect fusilade of snipers' bullets.

Side by side we wriggled over the knoll, slid down the opposite side, regained our feet, and put up a record sprint to where the rugged hill afforded some little cover. At the top of the hill we were in the full blast of the enemy's fire. It was a perfect Inferno; a score of machine guns filled the air with their rat-a-tat; just like a hundred noisy motor bicycles; while the Turkish artillery threw a curtain of shrapnel along the ridge that looked as if it would stop any further effort to advance. But knowing that our only safety lay in victory, one had to forget self and fight like the very devil.

But many of the boys never passed that shrapnel-swept ridge. . . . Right and left men were being hit, and a fellow had to just clinch his teeth and keep going, with the vague thought somewhere in the back of your cranium that you might be the next. It was just here that my chum, Howard Proctor, was killed. A shrapnel burst right in the midst of the platoon in front of me; it cut the haversack from the side of Corporal Turton, and splashed two or three others, but poor Proctor was struck with a piece of the shell, which inflicted a fatal wound.

The lads close at hand, after shaking hands with him, offered a few words of cheer, and then had to advance. A few minutes later, when my platoon advanced, I knelt by his side, but he was going fast; I tried to cheer him, but somehow I got a big lump in my throat, my eyes were dimmed, and after a few incoherent words I was silent. Then, in spite of the fact that he was paralyzed by his wound, and almost at his last gasp his face brightened, and with a smile he said, "Don't worry about me, Cav.; I feel quite satisfied: I feel I have done my bit; take my glasses and try and return them to my mother." And so brave Proctor passed away. . . .

The few remaining hours of daylight were spent in such fierce, unequal fighting that I remembered little else until, about an hour before dusk, something hit me. I thought at first that I had been struck by a shell. After picking myself up, and regaining a sitting position, I put my hand down to feel if my leg was still there; I was really scared to look, for fear it had gone. Feeling that that really useful member was still attached to my body, I started to discover the extent of the damage. . . . The bullet—for such it was—had gone right through, coming out behind the knee, severing, en route, some of the important nerves of the leg, thus paralyzing the leg. This was temporarily useful, as it saved me any intense pain.

It was just at this stage that the Turks, heavily reinforced, counter-attacked, and compelled our sadly-diminished force to fall back; so knowing that if I stayed five minutes longer I should fall into their hands, I jumped to my feet to retire—only to collapse, my leg was as useless as though there was no bone in it. The only thing to avoid capture was to crawl, and crawl pretty quick; so on one knee and two hands I started, faced with a three-mile journey over as rough country as it would be possible to find.

How I accomplished the distance safely I shall never know. At least a dozen snipers wasted a cartridge on me—the bullets clipping twigs in front of my nose, whistling through my hair, and kicking the dirt up in my face. On one occasion a platoon of Australians passed on their way to the firing-line. One man, dropping out, half carried me back about a hundred yards, and with a sincere, "Good luck mate, I'm needed up above," raced away to assist the hard pressed exhausted men in the firing line.

H. W. Cavill, an Australian private, recounting his experiences at Gallipoli on April 25, 1915, in a firsthand account published during the war, Imperishable Anzacs: A Story of Australia's Famous First Brigade, *pp. 70, 78–80.*

As the boats touched the shore a very heavy and brisk fire was poured into us, several officers and men being killed and wounded in the entanglements, through which we were trying to cut a way. Several of my company were with me under the wire, one of my subalterns was killed next to me, and also the wire-cutter who was lying the other side of me. I seized his cutter and cut a small lane myself through which a few of us broke and lined up under the only available cover procurable, a small sand ridge covered with bluffs of grass. I then ordered fire to be opened on the crests, but owing to submersion in the water and dragging rifles through the sand, the breech mechanism was clogged, thereby rendering the rifles ineffective. The only thing left to do was to fix bayonets and charge up the crests, which was done in a very gallant manner, though we suffered greatly in doing so. However, this had the effect of driving the enemy from his trenches, which we immediately occupied. . . . During the night a violent counter-attack was made by the enemy against us. But we stood firm and drove them back again. Our casualties were very heavy. In my company alone I had 95 casualties out of 205 men. One of my platoons captured 13 Turks in one trench. The officers and men who were killed were buried together, close to the beach in an enclosure. We are now much reduced in strength, but the spirit of the old corps is just as strong as ever it was.

Major George Stopford Adams, who was later killed and buried on the beach, describing the conditions during a landing, ca. April 25, 1915, in a letter quoted in Rev. O. Creighton, With the Twenty Ninth Division in Gallipoli: A Chaplain's Experiences, *pp. 57–58.*

April 25, 1915
On the right of me on the cliff was a line of Turks in a trench taking pot shots at us, ditto on the left. I looked back. There was one soldier between me and the wire, and a whole line in a row on the edge of the sands. The sea behind them was absolutely crimson, and you could hear the groans through the rattle of musketry. A few were firing. I signalled to them to advance. I shouted to the soldier behind to signal, but he shouted back, "I am shot through the chest." I then perceived they were all hit. I took a rifle from one of the men with me and started in at the men on the cliff on my right, but could only fire slowly, as I had to get the bolt open with my foot—it was clogged with sand. About this time Maunsell was shot dead next to me. Our men now began to scale the cliffs from the boats on the outer flanks, and I need only add it was a capital sight. They carried the

trenches at the top at the point of the bayonet; there was some desperate work up there.

Major Harold Shaw, who was later killed at Gallipoli, describing the X-beach landing in a letter, April 25, 1915, quoted in Rev. O. Creighton, With the Twenty Ninth Division in Gallipoli: A Chaplain's Experiences, *pp. 62–63.*

We appear to have been forgotten altogether. On the cliffs in front of us Tommies are limping back wounded. One comes perilously near the edge of the cliff, stumbling and swaying like a drunken man. We shouted loudly to him as time after time he all but falls over the edge. Two R.A.M.C. [Royal Army Medical Corpsmen] grabbed him eventually and led him safely down. I have a smoke, and view the scenes on shore. Gradually the beach is becoming filled with medical stores and supplies. It is gruesome seeing dozens of dead lying about in all attitudes. It becomes eerie as it gets darker. . . . Midshipmen and Naval Lieutenants were in charge of the pinnaces towing strings of boats, and as they approached the shore, fired for all they were worth with machine guns mounted forward, protected by shields. Then swinging round, they cast the boats adrift. Each boat had a few sailors, who rowed for shore like mad, and many in so doing lost their lives, shot in the back. To row an open boat, unprotected, into murderous machine gun and rifle fire requires pluck backed by a discipline which only the British Navy can supply. Some of the sailors grabbed rifles from dead and wounded soldiers and fought as infantrymen. I can see many such dead Naval heroes before my eyes now, lying still on the bloody sand. I am sitting on the boxes now, and "ping" goes something past my head, and then "ping-ping" with a long ringing sound, follows one after the other. The crackle of musketry begins again, and faster and faster the bullets come. At last I know what bullets are like.

The feeling at first is weird. We get behind the pile of boxes, and bullets hit bully beef and biscuit boxes or pass harmlessly overhead. . . . I run into the Brigade quartermaster-sergeant and ask him, "How's the Brigadier?" He replies, "Killed sir." I can't speak for a moment. "And the Brigade Major?" "Killed also, sir." That finishes me. It is my first experience of the real horrors of war—losing those who had become friends, whom one respected. . . . "How did it happen, Leslie?" I ask. The General was shot in the stomach while in the pinnace, before he could step on to the hopper along-side the *River Clyde,* and died shortly after. The Brigade Major got it walking along the hopper. The *River Clyde* was to have been Brigade H.Q. and the Brigade was to have taken "V" Beach that day. So far, "V" Beach was still Turkish. Their machine guns kept our men at bay.

Major John Graham Gillam, describing in his diary entry for April 26, 1915, 4 P.M., *his landing on the beach, in* Gallipoli Diary, *p. 86.*

April 26, 1915
Old men in rags; women in red calico pantaloons, red waists, red shawls, and some of them in red veils; children of all ages, dressed like their elders; the halt, the blind, the sick made up this miserable column.

Stoically they drudged on. Some of the men glanced at me furtively. The older women begged for bread, the younger ones pulled either their veils or their shawls over their faces. They seemed to fear that I might hurt them.

The crowd stepped readily out of the way of the carriage, and I had trouble keeping the driver from going off at a trot. I could see that the road ahead was very narrow, especially in the gate, and I was not minded to have an accident on my hands. . . . A few highwheeled ox-carts hove in sight. They were packed with light baggage and children. I saw some cows in the train. Children rode on them. On other cows and steers packs were carried.

The spectacle was pitiful. The rain was still coming down in cold drizzle. It was cold up in that elevation—a sort of March weather. Few of the exiles had shoes; all of them were soaked to the skin, the clothing hanging to the weary bodies limp and wet. All faces showed suffering—hunger, exposure to the cold and wet, together with mental anguish about their kin and the future. . . .

In the wet grass by the roadside lay an old woman. I halted the *yailah* to see if anything could be done for her. She was still alive, I found. I poured some brandy between her teeth. She opened her eyes and with them motioned me away. I suppose she wanted to die in peace. . . .

Five miles I had gone, and still there was no break in the column. Since the exiles walked in groups and preserved no uniform marching order, I could not estimate their number. All I can say is that the exiles numbered no less than 4,000.

Then I came to the stragglers. The picture grew yet more harassing. It was composed of men and women trying to help some sick relative or friend along. Some of them sat by the wayside, tired and disconsolate, while the object of their care lay in the wet grass, resting or asleep. Two men were digging a grave.

George Abel Schreiner, an American journalist, recalling in his memoir of the war the flight of Armenian deportees on the road, April 6, 1915, From Berlin to Bagdad: Behind the Scenes in the Middle East, *pp. 200–202.*

Diary. Monday, April 26th. At 5 o'clock yesterday our artillery began to land. It's a very rough country; the Mediterranean macchia everywhere and steep, winding valleys. We slept on a ledge a few feet above the beach . . . Firing went on all night. In the morning, it was very cold, and we were all soaked. The Navy, it appeared had landed us in the wrong place. This made the Army extremely angry, though as things turned out it was the one bright spot. Had we landed anywhere else, we should have been wiped out.

I believe the actual place decided on for our landing was a mile farther south, which was an open plain, and an ideal place for a hostile landing from the Turkish point of view. . . .

At noon we heard the rumour that the 29th were fighting their way up from Helles, and everybody grew happy. We also heard that two Brigadiers had been wounded and one killed.

The Australians had brought with them two ideas, which were only eliminated by time, fighting, and their own good sense. The "eight hours' day" was almost a holy principle, and when they had violated it by holding on

The so-called irrepressible Anzacs took care of their wounded mates personally. *(National Archives)*

for two or three days heroically, they thought that they deserved a "spell." The second principle was not to leave their pals. When a man was wounded his friends would insist upon bringing him down, instead of leaving him to the stretcher-bearers. When they had learned the practical side of war, both these dogmas were jettisoned.

Herbert Aubrey, a British scholar (and later member of Parliament) acting as translator, recording in his diary entry for April 26, 1915, the experiences of Anzac troops in their landing at Gallipoli in Mons, Anzac and Kut, *pp. 82–83.*

April 27, 1915
It was a work of some difficulty to explain to the Colonial troops that many of the prisoners that we took—as for instance, Greeks and Armenians—were conscripts who hated their masters. On one occasion, speaking of a prisoner, I said to a soldier: "This man says he is a Greek, and that he hates the Turks." "That's a likely story, that is," said the soldier; "better put a bayonet in the brute."

The trouble that we had with the native interpreters is even now a painful memory. If they were arrested once a day, they were arrested ten times. Those who had anything to do with them, if they were not suspected of being themselves infected by treachery, were believed to be in some way unpatriotic. It was almost as difficult to persuade the officers as the men that the fact that a man knew Turkish did not make him a Turk. There was one moment when the interpreters were flying over the hills like hares.

Herbert Aubrey, commenting in his diary entry for April 27, 1915, regarding prejudice against interpreters at Gallipoli, in Mons, Anzac and Kut, *pp. 86–87.*

May 1. B. has lunched. He says that Rupert Brooke died at Lemnos. I am very sorry; he was a good fellow, and a poet with a great future. . . . While we lunched a man had his head blown off 20 yards away. . . .

Sunday May 2nd. 6 a.m. Shrapnel all round as I washed. Beach opinion is if this siege lasts they must be able to get up their heavy guns. The Indians have gone to Helles, and the Naval Division is being taken away from us. New Turkish Divisions are coming against us. There are no chaplains here for burial or for anything else. . . . We are to attack tonight at seven. We have now been here a week, and advanced a hundred yards farther than the first rush carried us. There is a great bombardment going on, a roaring ring of fire and the Turks are being shelled and shelled.

At night the battleships throw out two lines of searchlights, and behind them there gleam the fires of Samothrace and Imbros [Islands]. Up and down the cliffs here, outside the dugouts, small fires burn. The rifle fire comes over the hill, echoing in the valleys and back from the ships. Sometimes it is difficult to tell whether it is the sound of ripples on the beach or firing.

Tuesday May 4th. The sea like a looking-glass, not a cloud in the sky, and Samothrace looking very clear and close. The moon is like a faint shadow of light in the clear sky over the smoke of the guns. Heavy fighting between us and Helles. A landing is being attempted. Pessimists say it is our men being taken off because their position is impossible. The boats coming back seem full of wounded. It may have been an attempt at a landing and entrenching, or simply a repetition of what we did the other day at Falcon Hill or Nebronesi, or whatever the place is.

The attack has failed this morning. Perfect peace here, except for rifles crackling on the hill. Smith and I wandered off up a valley through smilax, thyme, heath and myrtle, to a high ridge. We went through the Indians and found a couple of very jolly officers, one of them since killed. There are a good many bodies unburied. Not many men hit. We helped to carry one wounded man back. The stretcher-bearers are splendid fellows, good to friend and enemy.

Herbert Aubrey, recording the conditions at Gallipoli in his diary entries for May 1, 2, and 4, 1915, in Mons, Anzac and Kut, *pp. 93–94.*

May 6, 1915

The Twenty-ninth Division went forward under these conditions on the 6th of May. They dashed on, or crawled for a few yards at a time, then dropped for a few instants before squirming on again. In such an advance men do not see the battlefield. They see the world as the rabbit sees it, crouching on the ground, just their own little patch. On broken ground like that, full of dips and rises, men may be able to see nothing but perhaps the ridge of a bank ten feet ahead, with the dust flying in spouts all along it, as bullets hit it, some thousand a minute, and looking back or to their flanks they may see no one but perhaps a few men of their own platoon lying tense but expectant, ready for the sign to advance while the bullets pipe over them in a never-ending birdlike croon. They may be shut off by some all important foot of ground from seeing how they are fronting, from all knowledge of what the next platoon is doing or suffer-ing. It may be quite certain death to peep over that foot of ground in order to find out, and while they wait for a few instants shells may burst in their midst and destroy a half of them. Then the rest, nerving themselves, rush up the ridge and fall in a line dead under machine gun fire. The supports come up, creeping over their corpses, get past the ridge, into scrub which some shell has set on fire. Men fall wounded in the fire and the cartridges in their bandoliers explode and slowly kill them.

British poet John Masefield, describing the battle conditions at Gallipoli, May 6, 1915, in a contemporary published account, Gallipoli, *pp. 99–101.*

The mules, most admirable animals, had now begun to give a good deal of trouble, alive and dead. There were hundreds of them on the beach and in the gullies. Alive, they bit precisely and kicked accurately; dead, they were towed out to sea, but returned to us faithfully on the beach, making bathing unpleasant and cleanliness difficult. The dead mule was not only offensive to the Army; he became a source of supreme irritation to the Navy, as he floated on his back, with his legs sticking stiffly up in the air. These legs were constantly taken for periscopes of submarines, causing excitement, exhaustive naval maneuvers and sometimes recriminations.

Herbert Aubrey, commenting about the mules at Gallipoli in his diary entry for May 7, 1915, in Mons, Anzac and Kut, *p. 97.*

. . . owing to congestion at Lancashire Landing, we steered for "V" Beach. An aeroplane away towards Achi Baba was surrounded by little white puffs of enemy shrapnel, clearly notched against the blue of the sky. She dropped a smoke ball, making a perpendicular line to mark an enemy position of our artillery. Then with a magnificent swoop she sped away to the south and safety. A small steam pinnace was having a rousing time out towards Kum Kale, the shells from an Asian gun plunging around her in the most exciting fashion. . . . We passed under the lee of the stranded *River Clyde,* and over the lighters to the beach which only a few days before had been the scene of such horror and agony. Traces of that conflict were pretty well removed, and now the sand was a litter of supplies, empty tins, packing cases and straw, with piles of equipment.

British chaplain William Ewing, recounting in his memoir his arrival at "V" Beach, Gallipoli, after the landing battle, on May 16, 1915, From Gallipoli to Baghdad, *p. 49.*

Our sport was bathing and the Brotherhood of the Bath was rudely democratic. There was at Anzac a singularly benevolent officer, but for all his geniality a strong disciplinarian, devoted to military observances. He was kind to all the world, not forgetting himself, and he had developed a kindly figure. No insect could resist his contours. Fleas and bugs made passionate love to him, inlaying his white skin with a wonderful red mosaic. One day he undressed and, leaving nothing of his dignity with his uniform, he mingled superbly with the crowd of bathers. Instantly he received a hearty blow upon his tender and white shoulder and a cordial greeting from some democrat of Sydney or Wellington: "Old man, you've been amongst the biscuits!" He drew himself up to rebuke this presumption, then dived for the sea, for as he said, "What's the good of telling one naked man to salute another naked man, especially when neither have got their caps?"

Herbert Aubrey, commenting in his diary on the democracy of nudity while bathing in the sea at Anzac beach in Gallipoli, May 19, 1915, in Mons, Anzac and Kut, *pp. 109–110.*

Early in July, 2,000 Armenian *"ameles"*—such is the Turkish word for soldiers who have been reduced to workmen—were sent from Harpoot to build roads. The Armenians in that town understood what this meant and pleaded with the Governor for mercy. But this official insisted that the men were not to be harmed, and he even called upon the German missionary, Mr. Ehemann, to quiet the panic, giving that gentleman his word of honour that the ex-soldiers would be protected. Mr. Ehemann believed the Governor and assuaged the popular fear. Yet practically every man of these 2,000 was massacred, and his body thrown into a cave. A few escaped, and it was from these that news of the massacre reached the world. A few days afterward another 2,000 soldiers were sent to Diarbekir. The only purpose of sending these men out in the open country was that they might be massacred. In order that they might have no strength to resist or to escape by flight, these poor creatures were systematically starved.

Ambassador Henry Morgenthau, commenting on the Armenian massacres, July 1915, in his Ambassador Morgenthau's Story, *p. 303.*

Just now the lot of the Armenians is especially sad, though Talaat has promised betterment. They are taking it out on peaceful people, because of Armenian volunteers with the Russian armies at Van, and in the Caucasus. Only a few months ago Enver threatened the Patriarch that if there should be an Armenian rising during this war, he would destroy the entire people, and the recent policy of removing populations from their homes and scattering them penniless among hostile Moslem communities aims at nothing else. . . .

The plot seems rather to be one which aims to uproot every compact Armenian settlement in the interior, scatter the population, and create conditions which must lead to the death of many and to the impoverishment and misery of all. The Armenians had been injudicious enough before Turkey entered the war to express sympathy for the Entente. A small minority among them have been revolutionaries. Others have aided the Russians. But as is usual here, punishment is visited on the inoffensive. The vast depots of arms and bombs found in Armenian villages is a myth. . . . In some few localities the Armenians have now revolted to avoid massacres. At Karahissar they have seized the ancient stronghold of Mithridates and cut the road between Sivas and Erzingian. The Turks have been compelled to send troops with artillery against them. But all this persecution indicates confidence on the part of the Government. They have seized the moment when Europe is distracted by war. They would hardly have dared do so if they felt less certain of their position.

Lewis Einstein, a staff member of the American legation in Constantinople, describing Armenian conditions in his diary entry for July 4, 1915, in his Inside Constantinople: A Diplomatist's Diary during the Dardanelles Expedition, April–September 1915, *pp. 160–161, 163–164.*

All the novelty had worn off the trench life. Instead of six noncoms, there were only three. Each of us was doing the work of two men. Our ration had been the eternal bully beef, biscuit, and jam. Our cooks did their best to make it palatable by cooking the beef in stew with some desiccated vegetables, but these were hard and tasteless. Most of us had got to the stage where the very sight of jam made us sick. That night, looking down through the ravine, I saw, winking and blinking cheerfully, the only light that brightened the Stygian darkness, the Red Cross of the hospital ships. I have wondered since if the entrance to heaven is illuminated with an electric Red Cross. There was not a man in the whole battalion who was really fit. Most of them had had a touch of one or more of the prevalent diseases. . . . By sickness and snipers' bullets we were losing thirty men a day. Nobody in the front line trenches or on the shell-swept area behind ever expected to leave the Peninsula alive. Their one hope was to get off wounded. . . . The best thing one could wish a man was a "cushy wound," one that would not prove fatal, or a "Blighty one." But no one wanted to quit. Men hung on till the last minute. Often it was not till a man dropped exhausted that we learned from his comrades that he had not eaten for days.

John Gallishaw, a noncommissioned officer, describing food and trench conditions August 6, 1915, in his Trenching at Gallipoli: The Personal Narrative of a Newfoundlander with the Ill-Fated Dardanelles Expedition, *pp. 87–89.*

The reports about the Armenians have now come in from every Consul in the interior; no longer hearsay, but direct—terrible in their grim tragedy. At Harpoot our Consul lately saw the deported during the halt there, and related that nothing could equal their misery. He spoke to three sisters educated here and speaking English. They belonged to the richest family of Erzeroum, and when ordered to go they had with them horses and valuables. At that time their family consisted of twenty-five members. Eleven of these had already been murdered before their eyes on the roadside, and the oldest remaining male representative was only eight years of age. They had been stripped of everything by the Kurds and left literally naked, till their very guards had to borrow shirts for them from the women of a Turkish village. About five hundred formed this caravan, mostly women and children, for nearly all the men had already been killed. They had been two months on the road. The Government doled them out a pittance of food, for which they fought like wild beasts. The women would beg passers-by to take their children, so that they at least might not starve. And at every halt Turks would be invited to select such women as they preferred, and would often come attended by physicians to inspect these. The fate of the men is simpler. They are led away at night into neighbouring valleys and shot down in cold blood by their guards, who finish them with their bayonets. The whole policy of extermination transcends one's capacity for indignation. It has been systematic in its atrocious cruelty, even to the extent of throwing the blame for the murders on the Kurds, who are instigated by the Government to lie in wait in order to kill

and pillage. Its horrors would be unbelievable if less universally attested.

Lewis Einstein, describing Armenian conditions in his diary entry for August 11, 1915, Inside Constantinople: A Diplomatist's Diary during the Dardanelles Expedition, April–September 1915, *p. 230.*

The first thing we were told to do was to march—an effort which kept us continuously moving for nearly twelve hours—from six o'clock on the evening of March 7th to 5:30 the following morning. . . . We had stood still for weeks, waiting for generals and the weather to make up their minds. Now we were going to move. . . . Presently, when it was dark. We halted. Across our front an endless succession of Ghurkas passed, silent but for the rhythmic click of swinging equipment. On our right, guns and transport rattled along incessantly. They had the continuous sound of a rotary press or big engineering works heard from a distance. On our left more Indian troops file noiselessly into position, approaching no one knew whence. From every direction troops, guns and transport secretly appeared and were allotted a place in the column. Somebody seemed to be controlling all this by pressing buttons; it was all inhuman; it was an enormous machine. "Just go down and tell them to shut making such a row," Tarrant rapped out to me, hearing a noise in his company.

I went down to my platoon and shut them up, and we moved on again past the starting point. The night was dark and moonless, and the lightning, constantly flickering, lit up the clouds in jagged black outlines. Occasionally it was so brilliant there seemed a possibility of our being discovered. The whole desert was alight with blinding blue flames. Suppose we *were* discovered! Suppose heavy fire were suddenly opened on us, without warning, or one of the land mines were to blow up we had been told about? You cannot help thinking of these eventualities. . . .

The first thing we heard next morning was that the attack had been a failure and that the Force was to retire. It sounded incredible after these weeks of preparation. Why was it a failure? Why couldn't the advance be continued and Kut relieved? Why was the attack cancelled we had been ordered to make the previous day? As soon ask the moon the nearest way to heaven!

At eight o'clock that morning we could already see brigades beginning the withdrawal. It was unusually hot for that time of year, and a heavy mirage enveloped all distant objects in quivering layers of air. . . . Trees assumed blurred and trembling outlines, and it was impossible to say in which direction our columns were moving. But there was no sound of battle now; there was nothing to battle for. Nothing.

Our Brigade was detailed to act as rear-guard to the Division, and we were therefore held back until one o'clock. By this time the heat was intense, and the Turks, well aware of its shattering effect and of the heavy blow they had dealt us themselves, were not slow to add the finishing touches. At the appropriate moment, when the whole force was retiring, they brought their guns into play. The fire was heaviest at about four o'clock, when our Division was careering along in a rolling column of yellow dust towards the river. To add to our difficulties we were now without water, and despite every effort to maintain march discipline, numbers of men fell out to drink from the stagnant pools we were passing. Mad with thirst, the danger of so poisonous a remedy escaped them. It mattered not what they drank, so long as they drank. One or two paid dearly for this folly afterwards. But how distinguish between folly and madness in such circumstances? It was surprising so few lost their self-control. . . .

We wanted to get away, and we did get away—with all our guns, effectives, and personnel. It was undignified, no doubt, but war is not a dignified affair. It was hurried to an ungentlemanly degree, but we were not thinking of being gentlemen. We considered the retreat an achievement, a thing well done. And it was.

Ernest Betts, a British soldier, recounting the failed effort on March 7–8, 1916, to relieve the British troops besieged by the Turks at Kut, southeast of Baghdad, in his memoir, The Bagging of Baghdad, *pp. 51–53, p. 68.*

We threw our baggage across our camels on the instant and set out over the rolling downs of this end of the tableland of Syria. Our hot bread was in our hands, and as we ate, there mingled with it the taste of the dust of our large force crossing the valley bottoms, and some taint of the strange keen smell of the worm-wood which overgrew the slopes. In the breathless air of these evenings in the hills, after the long days of summer, everything struck very acutely on the senses: and when marching in a great column, as we were, the front camels kicked up the aromatic dust-laden branches of the shrubs, whose scent-particles rose into the air and hung in a long mist, making fragrant the road of those behind.

The slopes were clean with the sharpness of worm-wood, and the hollows oppressive with the richness of their stronger, more luxuriant growths. Our night-passage might have been through a planted garden, and these varieties part of the unseen beauty of successive banks of flowers. The noises too were very clear. Auda broke out singing, away in front, and the men joined in from time to time, with the greatness, the catch at heart, of an army moving into battle.

We rode all night, and when dawn came were dismounting on the crest of the hills between Batra and Aba el Lissan, with a wonderful view westwards over the green and gold Guweira plain, and beyond it to the ruddy mountains hiding Akaba and the sea.

Lawrence of Arabia (T. E. Lawrence), describing the ride with Arabian camel cavalry on the road to the conquest of Aqaba in Arabia from the Turks, in June 1916, in his memoir, Revolt in the Desert *(1927), p. 107; expanded and republished as* The Seven Pillars of Wisdom *(1935), p. 309.*

. . . in the hotel, I tried to find clothes less publicly exciting than my Arab get-up; but the moths had corrupted all my former store, and it was three days before I became normally ill-dressed.

Before I was clothed the Commander-in-Chief sent for me, curiously. In my report . . . I had stressed the strategic importance of the eastern tribes of Syria and their proper use as a threat to the communications of Jerusalem. This jumped with his ambitions, and he wanted to weigh me.

It was a comic interview, for Allenby was physically large and confident, and morally so great that the comprehension of our littleness came slow to him. He sat in his chair looking at me—not straight, as his custom was, but sideways puzzled. . . . He was full of Western ideas of gun power and weight—the worst training for our war—but as a cavalry-man, was already half persuaded to throw up the new school, in this different world of Asia, and accompany Dawnay and Chetwode along the worn road of maneuver and movement; yet he was hardly prepared for anything so odd as myself—a little bare-footed silk-skirted man offering to hobble the enemy by his preaching if given stores and arms and a fund of two hundred thousand sovereigns to convince and control his converts.

Allenby could not make out how much was genuine performer and how much charlatan. The problem was working behind his eyes, and I left him unhelped to solve it. He did not ask many questions, nor talk much, but studied the map and listened to my unfolding of Eastern Syria and its inhabitants. At the end he put up his chin and said quite directly, "Well, I will do for you what I can," and that ended it. I was not sure how far I had caught him; but we learned gradually that he meant exactly what he said; and that what General Allenby could do was enough for his very greediest servant.

Lawrence of Arabia, describing his meeting with General Allenby when he secured Allenby's support for the Arab Revolt, July 6, 1917, in his memoir, Revolt in the Desert *(1927), pp. 121–122; expanded and republished as* The Seven Pillars of Wisdom *(1935), pp. 319–322.*

The Turkish fire sounded heavy, and I wondered with how many men we were going to have affair, and if the mine would be advantage enough for our eighty fellows to equal them. I would have been better if the first electrical experiment had been simpler.

However, at that moment the engines, looking very big, rocked with screaming whistles into view around the bend. Behind them followed ten box-wagons, crowded with rifle-muzzles at the windows and doors; and in little sandbag nests on the roofs Turks precariously held on, to shoot at us. I had not thought of two engines, and on the moment decided to fire the charge under the second, so that however little the mine's effect, the uninjured engine should not be able to uncouple and drag the carriages away.

Accordingly, when the front driver of the second engine was on the bridge, I raised my hand to Salem. There followed a terrific roar, and the line vanished from sight behind a spouting column of black dust and smoke a hundred feet high and wide. Out of the darkness came shattering crashes and long, loud metallic clangings of ripped steel, with many lumps of iron and plate; while one entire wheel of a locomotive whirled up suddenly over our heads to fall slowly and heavily into the desert behind. Except for the flight of these, there succeeded a deathly silence, with no cry of men or rifle-shot, as the now-dewy mist of the explosion drifted from the line towards us, and over our ridge until it was lost in the hills.

In the lull, I ran southward to join the sergeants. Salem picked up his rifle and charged out into the murk. Before I had climbed to the guns the hollow was alive with shots, and with the brown figures of the Bedouin leaping forward to grips with the enemy. I looked round

to see what was happening so quickly, and saw the train stationary and dismembered along the track, with its wagon sides jumping under the bullets which riddled them, while Turks were falling out from the far doors to gain the shelter of the railway embankment.

As I watched, our machine-guns chattered out over my head, and the long rows of Turks on the carriage roofs rolled over, and were swept off the top like bales of cotton before the furious shower of bullets which stormed along the roofs and splashed clouds of yellow chips from the planking. The dominant position of the guns had been an advantage to us so far. . . . The enemy in the crescent of the curving line were secure from the machine-guns; but Stokes slipped in his first shell, and after a few seconds there came a crash as it burst beyond the train in the desert.

He touched the elevating screw, and his second shot fell just by the trucks in the deep hollow below the bridge where the Turks were taking refuge. It made a shambles of the place. The survivors of the group broke out in a panic across the desert, throwing away their rifles and equipment as they ran. This was the opportunity of the Lewis gunners. The sergeant grimly traversed with drum after drum, till the open sand was littered with bodies. Mushagraf, the Sherari boy behind the second gun, saw the battle over, threw aside his weapon with a yell, and dashed down at speed with his rifle to join the others who were beginning, like wild beasts, to tear open the carriages and fall to plunder. It had taken nearly ten minutes.

Lawrence of Arabia, describing the destruction of a Turkish troop and freight train on September 19, 1917, in his memoir, Revolt in the Desert *(1927), pp. 145–146; expanded and republished as* The Seven Pillars of Wisdom *(1935), pp. 367–368.*

On our return to Akaba domestic affairs engaged the remaining free days. My part mostly concerned the bodyguard which I formed for private protection, as rumour gradually magnified my importance. On our first going up country from Rabegh and Yenbo, the Turks had been curious: afterwards they were annoyed; to the point of ascribing to the English the direction and motive force of the Arab Revolt, much as we used to flatter ourselves by attributing the Turkish efficiency to German influence.

However, the Turks said it often enough to make it an article of faith, and began to offer a reward of one hundred pounds for a British officer alive or dead.

As time went on they not only increased the general figure, but made a special bid for me. After the capture of Akaba the price became respectable; while after we blew up Jemal Pasha they put Ali and me at the head of their list; worth twenty thousand pounds alive or ten thousand dead.

Of course, the offer was rhetorical; with no certainty whether in gold or paper, or that the money would be paid at all. Still, perhaps, it might justify some care. I began to increase my people to a troop, adding such lawless men as I found, fellows whose dash had got them into trouble elsewhere. I needed hard riders and hard livers; men proud of themselves, and without family. By good fortune three or four of this sort joined me at the first, setting a tone and standard.

Lawrence of Arabia, describing the Turkish price on his head and his decision to set up a personal bodyguard January 1918, in his memoir, Revolt in the Desert *(1927), p. 93; expanded and republished as* The Seven Pillars of Wisdom *(1935), p. 462.*

Our war was ended. Even though we slept that night in Kiswe, for the Arabs told us the roads were dangerous, and we had no wish to die stupidly in the dark at the gate of Damascus. The sporting Australians saw the campaign as a point-to-point, with Damascus the post; but in reality we were all under Allenby, now, and the victory had been the logical fruit solely of his genius. . . .

He hoped we would be present at the entry, partly because he knew how much more than a mere trophy Damascus was to the Arabs, partly for prudential reasons. Feisal's movement made the enemy country friendly to the Allies as they advanced, enabling convoys to go up without escort, towns to be administered without garrison. In their envelopment of Damascus the Australians might be forced, despite orders, to enter the town. If anyone resisted them it would spoil the future. One night was given us to make the Damascenes receive the British Army as their allies.

This was a revolution in behaviour, if not in opinion; but Feisal's Damascus committee had for months been prepared to take over the reins when the Turks crashed. We had only to get in touch with them, to tell them the movements of the Allies, and what was required. So as dusk deepened Nasir sent the Rualla horse into the town, to find Ali Riza, the chairman of our committee, or Shukri el Ayubi, his assistant, telling them that relief would be available on the morrow, if they constructed a government at once. As a matter of fact it had been done at four o'clock in the afternoon, before we took action. Ali Riza was absent, put in command at the last moment by the Turks of the retreat of their army from Galilee before Chauvel: but Shukri found unexpected support from the Algerian brothers, Mohammed Said and Abd el Kader. With the help of their retainers the Arab flag was on the Town Hall before sunset as the last echelons of Germans and Turks defiled past. . . .

When dawn came we drove to the head of the ridge, which stood over the oasis of the city, afraid to look north for the ruins we expected: but, instead of ruins, the silent gardens stood blurred green with river mist, in whose setting shimmered the city, beautiful as ever, like a pearl in the morning sun.

Lawrence of Arabia, commenting on the Arab seizure of power in Damascus prior to his entry to the city September 31–October 1, 1918, in his memoir, Seven Pillars of Wisdom, *pp. 643–644.*

5

The Eastern Front and Russia

August 1914–March 1918

During the rule of Nicholas II as czar of the Russian Empire since 1894, the country showed some signs of modernizing. By 1905, the Trans-Siberian Railroad, although poorly built and maintained in sections and with a gap at Lake Baikal, tied the capital in St. Petersburg with the Pacific Ocean port city of Vladivostok. Industries flourished, particularly near the capital and in the Polish, Lithuanian, and White Russian provinces of the empire. Economic progress did not bring political or social modernization, however. When the czar's secret police, the Okhrana, infiltrated and broke up labor unions, the heavy-handed treatment provided a fertile ground for agitation by radical socialists, organized into the Social Democratic Party and the Social Revolutionary Party. Both these parties, although small, further split into left and right wings. After 1903 the Social Democrats divided between the more moderate Mensheviks and the radical Bolsheviks, whose leader, Lenin, argued that the party should not attempt to become a mass party, but should be open only to a dedicated revolutionary elite. He continued to run the Bolshevik branch of the Social Democratic Party in exile from Switzerland after 1912.

Although some of the czar's advisers and government ministers worked to modernize the administrative structure of government, Nicholas believed himself chosen by divine right to make crucial decisions and to lead the country. The Duma, an elected body representing the propertied classes, could make recommendations, but remained relatively powerless to oppose or modify the decrees of the czar.

Like his predecessors, Nicholas II took his commitment to the empire seriously, hoping to resolve its international security questions by territorial gain or by concessions from traditional opponents. Blocked from access to the Mediterranean by Turkish control of the Bosporus and Dardanelles, Russia sought influence on the Balkan Peninsula, among the Serbs, and among the Armenian population of Turkey. Throughout the 19th century, Britain had opposed Russian expansion in the Black Sea and had encouraged the Ottoman Empire to block Russia's entry via the Bosporus to the Mediterranean Sea, but the czar had welcomed the alliance with France and Britain.

When Nicholas declared war on Germany and Austria-Hungary in August 1914, the Russian arms industry stumbled along, disorganized and unproductive. Yet shipments of weapons from the Allies, together with the vast reserves of Russian manpower should be sufficient, the czar and his advisers believed, to put up a credible showing against the Central Powers. If Germany and Austria were quickly defeated, Russia might gain its longtime objective of security on its southern frontier with Turkey. When Turkey joined the Central Powers and the Allies promised to support Russia in its goals to gain control of the Bosporus, it appeared Russia would achieve some long-standing aspirations.

With Germany engaged with France, and Austria struggling to suppress Serbia, each of the Central Powers would be at the disadvantage of fighting on two fronts. Geographically, it made good sense, as Russian troops could push into the East Prussian province of Germany from Russian Poland. Looked at from a simple strategic or geopolitical viewpoint, the alliance of Russia with France and Britain against the German Empire appeared brilliant.

The czar and his advisers could make a similar evaluation regarding the Austro-Hungarian Empire. Germany's Habsburg ally controlled restless populations of Ukrainians and Poles in Bukovina and Galicia, frontier provinces directly on the doorstep of Russia. With a rapid push through these provinces into the Carpathian Mountains, Russian armies could come to the aid of Serbia by threatening the heartland of Austria-Hungary itself. The prospects for an early victory, in Russian eyes, seemed imminent.

However, the Russian generals and aristocrats, like their counterparts in the rest of Europe, had very little understanding of the many ways in which warfare had changed. They predicted victory based on the outmoded and faulty premise of simple calculations of available manpower and distances to be traversed, making the sort of Napoleonic-era calculations common among their counterparts in the west.

Just as in Germany, France, and Britain, millions of Russian volunteers offered their services to the army, and the politically divided country appeared united and ready for a patriotic war. Even the socialists, including the Menshevik wing of the Social Democrats and both the Right and Left Social Revolutionaries, joined in endorsing the war against the Central Powers. Only the Bolsheviks protested. They reluctantly followed the advice of Lenin from exile to oppose going to war. He believed that all working people in Russia should join with their brothers in the Central Powers in resisting the war, in a socialist-led front against the capitalist powers. However, Lenin's cry for class solidarity in the face of the war met no response either in Russia or among socialists in Germany. Russian liberals, other socialists, and of course conservatives widely decried Lenin and his followers for lack of patriotism in time of war. Some accused Lenin of working as a German agent. Meanwhile peasants, workers, and the middle class thronged into army recruiting offices.

In spite of Russian popular optimism, the war turned out to be neither short nor easy. For the Russian people, World War I and its aftermath of continuing armed conflict brought immense tragedy in loss of life on land and sea, of men wounded in battle, and in those held prisoners of war by the enemy. Russia suffered some 8 million casualties when all these categories are considered together. Many of the battles and much of the devastation of homes, farms, businesses, and factories of World War I took place on lands that had long been part of the Russian Empire, including the Kingdom of Poland, White Russia, and Ukraine, all of which lay under the rule of the czar.

While the front lines mutinied and the capital seethed with riots, life in Yaroslav, Russia, went on as before. *(Library of Congress)*

World War I brought fundamental changes to Russia in politics and social structure. As in the Austro-Hungarian Empire and the Ottoman Empire, the war broke apart the Russian Empire and destroyed it as a political entity. After the war, parts of the former Russian Empire immediately emerged as independent countries: Finland, Latvia, Lithuania, Estonia, and Poland. Yet the changes ran deeper than mere territorial loss. The war in Russia ended the regime of the czars and contributed to the formation of a government after November 1917 dominated by the Bolsheviks. The story of World War I on the eastern front for this reason is much more than an account of armed clashes but runs far deeper, to culminate in a rapid social and political transformation, characterized by American eyewitness John Reed as "Ten Days that Shook the World."

BATTLES 1914–1916

Following the battles across the face of eastern Europe is made difficult for the modern student of the subject, because the boundaries of the various countries in eastern Europe have changed several times over the decades since the war. Frequently a city or fortress located in the provinces of Russian Poland, White Russia, or Ukraine in World War I is now found under a new national jurisdiction. Many cities and provinces have different names than they had then. Russian troops moved first into the German province of East Prussia, located now in the northeastern region of Poland and in the Russian province of Kaliningrad Oblast, geographically separate from the rest of Russia.

Two Russian armies, expecting a quick victory, marched from Russian Poland into German East Prussia. The First Army made a strong advance across what is now the border between Lithuania and the Kaliningrad Oblast toward the city of Kaliningrad, then known as Koenigsberg. The German forces fell back in August, yielding German territory to this first success. Farther to the south, the Russian Second Army took up positions near the town of Tannenberg inside East Prussia after meeting light resistance. Although the territorial gains in East Prussia represented only a small advance in the estimation of Britain and France, the rapid Russian offensive drew off German troops, in effect saving Paris from the German onslaught in the west in the first weeks of the war.

Although it cost valuable resources Germany would have preferred to pour into Belgium and France on the western front, German commanders rapidly moved forces by rail to Tannenberg where they drove back the Russians in an extended battle, August 26–30. A week later, the Battle of Masurian Lakes drove the Russian First Army back across the frontier, there marked by the Nieman River. By mid-September, the Russian invasion of East Prussia had come to an ignominious end. The Germans took more than 90,000 Russian prisoners. General Alexander Samsonov, commander of the Russian Second Army, retreating on foot with his troops, became lost in the woods on the retreat, and then, by some accounts, committed suicide on August 29.

Farther to the south, Russian forces advanced into the province of Bukovina, now in the nation of Ukraine, but then a frontier province of the Austro-Hungarian Empire, running along the Carpathian Mountains that presented a barrier to invasion into Hungarian-ruled Transylvania. The Russian forces threatened to advance through the Carpathians into those lands at the core of the Austro-Hungarian Empire. In another advance, the Russians besieged an Austrian-held fortress city at Przemysl, now on the Polish side of the southern border with

Austrian prisoners were taken to the rear and housed well behind Russian lines in rough structures like this A-frame. *(Library of Congress)*

Ukraine. Cut off from Austrian supply lines, the defenders and citizens, mostly sympathetic to the Russians, began to starve before finally capitulating.

German and Austrian forces mounted a counterattack in early October that drove the Russians back through Russian Poland toward the Vistula River, with the Germans driving toward Warsaw itself. In southern Poland through November and December, the Russians held back the Austrian advance at Cracow, although the Germans took the city of Lodz in Poland, about 60 miles southeast of Warsaw.

By the end of 1914, German forces had pushed Russian troops well back into Russian Poland, halting the threat to the eastern German province of Silesia; farther south, the Austrians held a line against the Russians in the Carpathian Mountains between Galicia and Hungarian Czech lands. That line held through the 1914–15 winter, and the Russians did not attempt to pass through the Carpathians until March 1915. By the end of April 1915, the Russian advance ground to a stop. Meanwhile, in the winter months of February and March, the Germans advanced to take the Baltic coastal city of Memel, in what is now Lithuania. After bitter back and forth fighting, the Germans gained Memel by the end of March and then made further advances into Lithuania.

By the summer of 1915, the Germans and Austrians began a gradual advance, pushing back the Russian troops first in Galicia and southern Poland. By the end of June, Austrians had regained control over their provinces of Galicia and Bukovina. They recaptured the fortress at Przemysl and moved on to the city of Lemberg (now L'vin) in Russian Ukraine. In a major offensive, German and Austrian troops continued to push forward. By August, they had taken Warsaw and, by the end of the month, moved on to Brest-Litovsk in eastern Poland (now right on the border between Poland and Belarus). With these advances, the Central Powers had moved well into the Russian Empire by fall 1915.

With these events, even ordinary citizens in Russia realized that the empire would have no easy victories, that the officers gave poor leadership, and that the Central Powers by contrast had well-organized and determined forces. In September 1915 Czar Nicholas II relieved his nephew, Grand Duke Nicholai, of command of the Russian military. The czar took over the position of minister of war for the remainder of his reign. Like his nephew, however, the czar faced problems of troop morale, supply, and lack of imagination and experience among officers that he could not do very much about. By the end of September the Germans had moved well into Lithuania. German forces controlled a line running north and south between the cities of Minsk and Pinsk in Belarus; the line continued southward under Austrian control, taking in almost all of Galicia, including the city of Czernowitz in the Ukraine.

After the Battle of Tannenberg in the first month of the war, the front had moved slowly to the east. Compared to the western front that remained stalemated in a narrow band stretching from the North Sea to Switzerland, the eastern front showed a gradual wearing down of the Russian forces and the loss of territory to the Central Powers. Even though the defense had a natural advantage under the conditions of World War I combat, with trenches, strong points, and machine guns holding the line against artillery bombardment and marching troops armed only with rifles and grenades, the defense could hold only if well-supplied with ammunition and manned by willing troops. However,

Russia remained plagued with incompetent officers leading dispirited troops who lacked weapons and ammunition.

Russian factories could not produce modern weapons, and, with the only access for Allied shipments through the ports of Murmansk and Archangel frozen in during the winter, weapons from the west could not augment the meager Russian supply. Efforts to modernize the Russian arms industry proceeded, but slowly and with very meager results.

Nicholas appointed the one officer with a record of success, General A. Brusilov, as commander of the forces on the Russian Southern Front, in April 1916. In a last push forward, known as the June Offensive or the Brusilov Offensive, Russian troops spent the summer of 1916 in an attempt to retake Lemberg in the Ukraine and Lublin in Poland. Before their advance stopped, some in the west took encouragement, believing that the tide had turned on the eastern front. Brusilov's forces regained some lost ground in Galicia.

Whole units of Czech troops in the Austro-Hungarian army deserted to the Russian side. Not a huge army by the standards of the day, nevertheless, the Czech Legion of experienced and dedicated soldiers, numbering about 50,000, represented an impressive addition to Allied strength. Furthermore, under Brusilov's command, the Russian forces took more than 350,000 prisoners, mostly from the Austro-Hungarian forces. As a consequence of the Russian successes against the Austrians, the Germans convinced the Austro-Hungarian officers to accept a unified command under German control, noted with some satisfaction by General Erich von Ludendorff.

In Russia at the end of 1916, the leadership still believed that, if they held their line, with an eventual Allied victory, Russia would emerge with territorial gains and access to the Mediterranean through the Bosporus and Dardanelles,

The Kaiser (center) consults with Paul von Hindenburg (left) and Erich von Ludendorff (right) beneath trophies at a hunting lodge. They agree that the Austro-Hungarian forces should come under German control. *(National Archives)*

as promised by the British in their secret treaty. However, the Brusilov offensive cost the Russians more than a million casualties and made only modest advances toward its objectives. Although the Russian army had suffered severe casualties, as yet no major mutinies among the troops had erupted. The Russian military position had grown difficult, but not desperate.

Brusilov moved the battle lines back somewhat to the west. Encouraged by the Russian advances, Allied promises of support, and pledges to endorse the acquisition of the territory of Transylvania from Austria-Hungary, Romania joined the Allies in August 1916. At first the Romanian forces advanced and took the city of Sibiu in Transylvania, but, by September, Austrian forces surrounded the advanced salient of Romanian troops there. To add to these problems faced by Romania, its southern neighbor, Bulgaria, a member of the Central Powers since October 1915, had designs on Romanian territory. Even though French and British forces withdrawn from Gallipoli assembled at Salonika to threaten Bulgaria from the south, they made no advance. Soon the Central Powers nearly overran Romania, with German and Bulgarian forces moving through the Romanian coastal lands on the Black Sea and taking most of the province of Dobrudja. By November, German forces advanced on the Romanian capital, which the Romanian government abandoned in December, taking refuge in the provincial town of Jassy near the Russian border.

MORALE, MYSTICS, AND MURDER

In the Russian capital, Petrograd, morale wavered between hope for victory and a search for scapegoats for the many defeats. With a censored press, the city had become a hotbed of rumor. Czar Nicholas, as minister of war, chose to leave the capital to work at the General Headquarters more than 400 miles to the south in Mogilev (now Mohilyow, Belarus), and rumors spread of the increasing influence of his wife and her adviser, the holy man Grigory Rasputin. Mystic, hypnotist, and official necromancer to the court, Rasputin, some claimed, had planned the assassination of the somewhat liberal prime minister, Pyotr Stolypin, in 1911. Other rumors swirled around Rasputin concerning his influence at the court, some due to his own bragging of his close connections to the royal family. An adherent of an obscure Russian sect that claimed the only way to purge the soul of sin was to indulge in it, he gained notoriety for participating in drunken sexual orgies with admiring women of the aristocracy and with prostitutes.

The czarina made Rasputin a court favorite despite his unsavory reputation, peasant manners, and unkempt, food-smeared beard. Alexandra admired him because he seemed able to relieve her son Alexis's symptoms of hemophilia. Due to Rasputin's closeness to Alexandra, liberals within the government believed he secured the appointment, not only of clergy, but also of ministers of government favorable to a reactionary position or even of working to undermine the war effort. As the czar dismissed competent ministers and replaced them with incompetents on the advice of Rasputin and the czarina, members of the royal family and members of the state Duma grew more and more desperate to bring an end to his influence. Opposition to the apparently collapsing management of the government sprang from politicians on both the right and left of the political scale.

Other suspicions centered around Alexandra herself, and many Russians thought she had divided loyalties because of her German birth. The spread of stories about court corruption and the hypnotic powers of the dissolute Rasputin seriously weakened popular support for the czar, and many even in the aristocracy came to believe that the country would be better led by a new regime. As for the urban workers, gross mismanagement of grain prices had led to severe shortages of bread in the cities. Meanwhile, peasants hoarded grain in hopes of a price rise or converted it into cheap vodka. Urban residents who could afford it bought train tickets to the countryside where they visited farm markets in the villages to purchase grain or bread and bring it back to the city.

Some members of the aristocracy and some politicians conspired to rid themselves of Rasputin and the czarina and their reputed hold on the government. Prince Felix Yussupov (a nephew of the czar) and a small group of fellow aristocrats invited Rasputin to a private party where they poisoned him on December 30, 1916. Rasputin proved extremely difficult to kill. When the poison did not work, the conspirators shot him several times, tied up his arms, and then threw him in the frozen Neva River, where he finally drowned below the ice.

MUTINY, MONARCHY, AND THE FEBRUARY REVOLUTION

Within the Duma, liberals hoped that the czar would institute reforms that would make the executive responsible to the legislature, along the lines of western parliamentary systems. But instead of replacing the minister of war with one of the liberals, the czar took that post himself. Although he refused to make the ministries answerable to the Duma, the czar did dismiss some of the most reactionary ministers and empowered a War Industries Committee to take over central control of weapons production, which seemed a step in the right direction. After the assassination of Rasputin, however, the czar and czarina went into seclusion, apparently emotionally shattered by the news that members of the extended royal family had been involved in the murder. Then, at the beginning of 1917, the liberals found that their hopes to reduce the power of the czar seemed further undermined by new disorders that could serve as an excuse for him to enhance his grip on the state.

A wave of strikes in the capital and elsewhere broke out in January and early February 1917. Agitation by both Menshevik and Bolshevik Social Democrats and possibly by German agents among the factory workers of Petrograd attempted to turn the popular discontent over economic conditions into revolutionary fervor. However, the regime had dealt with strikes and protests before, and the czar and his ministers did not view the disturbances very seriously.

The fall of the monarchy, known as the February Revolution, came about so quickly and spontaneously that it almost seemed accidental. The strikes in Petrograd did not turn particularly violent at first, and, on February 22, the czar left the capital to return to the general headquarters at Mogilev, leaving instructions with the minister of interior to disperse the last remaining strikers. The Petrograd army garrison had become a sort of staging area for raw peasant recruits prior to their further training and shipment to the front. The interior minister, A. D. Protopopov, demonstrated his incompetence by ignoring warnings that the large garrison of troops in Petrograd, mostly poorly trained and ill-disciplined, could not be trusted. Even so, Protopopov refused to work closely with the czar's secret police, the Okhrana, who had experience in breaking revolutionary organizations and strikes, and chose to rely on the demoralized and raw garrison troops for security.

When Protopopov ordered the Petrograd garrison troops to march on the strikers on February 27, they refused. Four regiments of troops mutinied and shot a few of their officers who tried to stop them. The armed but disorganized soldiers joined the workers in the streets, then seized armories and provided more arms to the massed civilians. Within days the city police could no longer control the partially armed mobs, and groups of soldiers turned their machine guns, armored cars, and rifles on the weak police forces. The rebelling troops broke into the prisons and city jails, freeing political prisoners as well as common criminals. During these armed clashes, the first meeting of the Petrograd Soviet, or council of workers and soldiers dominated by socialists of the various wings of those parties, convened. The ministers of government fled their offices, in fear that the rioters would wreak their anger on them.

The czar heard of these difficulties, and, from Mogilev, he ordered the Duma dissolved, apparently believing the liberal leaders in that body responsible for the crisis. A small group of representatives in the Duma defied the order, and, when they heard that the czar planned to return to Petrograd with loyal troops, the rump group of the Duma demanded that the czar abdicate. Railway workers cooperated by shunting the czar's train aside. Within a few days, the czar agreed to the demands of the Duma. He named Prince Lvov as prime minister and abdicated at the same time. He named his only son, the czarevich Alexis, the young boy with hemophilia, as his successor, with the provision that the czar's brother, Mikhail Aleksandrovich, should be regent until the son came of age. He later altered the succession so that the crown was to go directly to his brother. In a passionate statement, he abdicated officially on March 3, 1917 (in the older Julian calendar, but March 16 in the western or Gregorian calendar). The Petrograd Soviet and the Duma agreed that the crown should pass to the czar's brother, Mikhail, but Mikhail refused, at the urging of Alexander Kerensky and others of the Duma. Mikhail indicated he would serve if called by an official constituent assembly, but in the meantime he refused to assume the "Supreme Power." Suddenly, as the result of a few days of rioting and disorder and chaotic meetings of the Duma, the monarchy had ended. Surprisingly, the Russian Revolution that destroyed the monarchy had cost only 169 people killed and another 996 wounded. Far worse casualties followed, however.

Almost as suddenly as the collapse of the czar's rule, two governing bodies replaced the monarchy: the Petrograd Soviet and a Temporary Committee of the Duma. Together they agreed in supporting a Provisional Government. The only member of the Duma to be a member of the Soviet was the popular socialist lawyer Alexander Kerensky. The Petrograd Soviet appointed him as one of two vice-chairmen, and he served the Provisional Government first as minister of justice and later in other posts. He readily worked as a liaison between the Soviet and the Duma over the next months. His reputation as a defender of political dissidents and wrongly accused victims of the czar's secret police had earned him support among both liberals and socialists, and, as an effective speaker, he seemed an ideal go-between for the liberals and others in the Duma and the Soviet, dominated by Social Revolutionaries, Mensheviks, and Bolsheviks. Prince Lvov served as the first chairman of the council of ministers in the Provisional Government. Despite his initial popularity and his position in both the Duma and in the Soviet, Kerensky soon made political enemies on every side.

From March to November 1917, the uneasy balance of power continued between the Petrograd Soviet, increasingly supported by other urban and regional soviets, and the Duma. The revolution that established the Provisional Government seemed to observers in the West to represent the replacement of the monarchy by a republic of sorts. Many signs of liberal reform gave credence to that view, such as increasing freedom of the press, labor reforms, and promises of equality for women. From Britain, Lloyd George congratulated Prince Lvov, noting that Russia now stood with the nations that based their institutions on responsible government, allowing him to characterize the war as one of a fight for freedoms against Prussian military autocracy. During the next few months, the Bolshevik leaders Lenin and Leon Trotsky, both in exile overseas, returned to Russia to be a part of the revolutionary situation.

Lenin traveled from Switzerland in a sealed train, with the permission of the German authorities. Although his enemies used that fact to suggest that Lenin actually worked for the Germans, his trip had been funded by several Bolsheviks who had made fortunes using their underground connections to arrange the smuggling of western products into wartorn Russia. When Lenin arrived in Petrograd, an enthusiastic crowd greeted him at the Finland Station of the railway. After his impassioned speech, they seemed eager for him to seize power and install the proletariat revolution. Lenin, however, held back, seeking better timing.

Even in Russia, the press mattered a great deal. This Russian "newsboy" carries quite a variety of publications. *(Library of Congress)*

THE COLLAPSE OF THE FRONT

The Provisional Government presided over the beginnings of the breakup of the Russian Empire. In March and April, the government recognized the independence or autonomy within the empire of Finland, Poland, and Estonia.

At the same time, the Provisional Government continued to prosecute the war. Kerensky became minister of war on May 16, and, six weeks later, General Brusilov began an offensive in Galicia with the objective of retaking Lemberg. However, Kerensky and Brusilov faced a major mutiny among the troops in mid-July, partly brought on by the breakdown of morale and encouraged by radical newspapers circulated to the front and passed from hand to hand and read out loud for the majority of illiterate soldiers. Hundreds of troops shot their officers, abandoned the front line, and retreated in disorganized, but still armed bands into the Ukraine by mid-July. The Provisional Government put down an unsuccessful attempt of armed workers, supported by the Bolsheviks, to seize power in Petrograd as the troop mutiny began. After the put-down during these July days, the Provisional Government had Trotsky arrested. Finland declared complete independence from Russia, and Lenin found refuge from Russian arrest there. In the Executive Committee of the Soviet, N. N. Sukhanov, an astute and independent socialist, kept a close diary of the events, while at the French embassy, a young diplomat, Count Louis de Robien, observed events with sympathy for the oppressed workers, the brave revolutionaries, and the dispossessed members of the middle class and elite.

FROM DUMA TO SOVIET

Faced with the mutiny of soldiers, the abortive Bolshevik coup attempt, and constant agitation, the liberal prince Lvov resigned as head of the government, to be replaced by Kerensky, who remained in that office from July 20 until November 1917. Kerensky did not round up the mid-level and rank-and-file Bolsheviks, a tactical mistake, for it allowed Lenin to maintain contact with his supporters from his nearby Finnish exile. Despite his reputation as a sympathetic socialist, Kerensky had no success in restoring troop morale, and, by the end of July, the mutiny among troops had spread. Austrian and German forces retook all of Galicia. The disorganized retreat of the Russian army gave up all the territory Russia had gained over the previous two years of fighting.

Although Kerensky won admiration in the west for his pronouncements of civil liberties, the unrest among the populace began to outstrip even the socialist prime minister's reforms, while continuing losses on the war front and desertions of troops worsened his position. In August, factory workers went on strike in a demand that the war be ended. Kerensky replaced General Brusilov with General Lavr Kornilov. To restore order in Petrograd, Kerensky ordered Kornilov to bring reliable troops to the city. However, rumors reached Kerensky that Kornilov planned a military coup to seize power, so Kerensky dismissed Kornilov and rescinded the order. Bolshevik union members cooperated in diverting Kornilov's train, and organized factory workers poured into the streets to protect the revolution from the threat of Kornilov's counterrevolutionary troops. The Bolshevik party took some credit for forestalling the expected Kornilov coup attempt. Meanwhile, the Bolsheviks continued to maneuver in the Petrograd Soviet, and by October they had established a majority there. Pressured from both the left and the right, Kerensky found himself increasingly isolated. His talents as a speaker soon proved inadequate to provide answers to the dilemmas of the Provisional Government.

THE OCTOBER REVOLUTION

In the days of November 6 and 7 (October 24–25 in the Old Style calendar), the Bolsheviks organized a coup of their own in Petrograd to seize power in the name of the Soviet. Under Lenin's leadership, the Central Committee of the Bolshevik Party agreed to launch the revolution. Trotsky spread a rumor that Kerensky planned to bring troops into the city to suppress the Soviet, and the Soviet, including members of the Menshevik and Social Revolutionary parties, supported Trotsky in arming factory workers. Very quickly, the organized Soviet armed groups took key points such as the telephone exchange, bridge crossings, rail stations, and government buildings. A small bloody skirmish developed in the Winter Palace, where some officer cadets and a unit of women troops briefly stood off Trotsky's forces. Armed guards escorted the remnants of the Provisional Government out of their quarters and then released them. On the whole, the vaunted October Revolution, although it would have long-lasting historical

During the foreign intervention, U.S. Signal Corps cameramen have time to stop for some tourist photos of the Monastery Church in Archangel. *(National Archives)*

class and condemned them to forced labor. The civil war raged on through 1918 and 1919.

The Communist government, which formed the Russian Soviet Federated Socialist Republic in 1918, regained control of some of the territories formerly ruled by the czar. Then, as the Union of Soviet Socialist Republics, the regime extended control to some of the other lands of the Russian Empire, including Ukraine, White Russia (Belarus), and countries in Central Asia and the Caucasus region: Georgia, Armenia, Azerbaijan, Uzbekistan, Turkmenistan, Tajikistan, Kyrgyzstan, and Kazakhstan. Poland, Finland, and the Baltic states, however, remained independent in the two decades following World War I. Today, each of these countries is an independent nation, although some maintain close diplomatic, economic, and cultural ties to modern Russia.

The profound changes that swept through Russia affected not just Eastern Europe and Central Asia but the whole world for the rest of the 20th century. The foreign intervention, although eventually a failure, only hardened the Soviet view that the new government faced a world of enemies and would have to be prepared to fight them again in the future. In the decades after World War I, Lenin and his successors would use many of the same ruthless methods they employed during their revolution and civil war to extend the reach of Soviet power, both within their country and beyond.

For the western powers, the timing of the Russian February Revolution with its apparent shift to a form of democracy briefly allowed parliamentary Great Britain and republican France to present the alliance with Russia as an alignment of democratic regimes against the authoritarian empires of Germany, Austria–Hungary, and the Turks. That shift in March 1917 came just at the time when the United States faced a mounting crisis in its attempt to remain neutral.

consequences, had been carried off as a well-organized coup d'état within the capital city.

With the city in the hands of the Soviet, the next day the Congress of Soviets, including representatives from outlying cities and towns, convened. Bolsheviks made up about half its membership, and most of the others, including Mensheviks and right-wing Social Revolutionaries, walked out of the meeting in protest at the high-handed Bolshevik control. The remaining members of the Congress appointed a Council of People's Commissars, mostly Bolshevik, with a few Left Social Revolutionaries. Through such leveraging of the Bolshevik domination of the Petrograd Soviet, Lenin had in fact created a Bolshevik government.

Despite dissent within the Soviet, counterrevolution, civil war, counter-coup, and assassination attempts, the Bolsheviks would retain control of the Russian state for the next 70 years. Although the coup took place in early November it became known to history as the October Revolution because Russia still operated under the Julian calendar.

Kerensky at first fled the city, then attempted to raise loyal troops. When that failed, he left the country in disguise, going into exile, first in France and later in the United States.

The Bolsheviks had opposed the war with Germany from the beginning, and the new government immediately undertook to end it. As foreign minister of the new regime, Trotsky proposed an armistice with the Central Powers, and, on November 22, 1917, fighting stopped all along the eastern front, from the Baltic Sea in the north to the Black Sea in the south. The Soviet government then offered peace terms to the Germans, and negotiations began formally near the front line, at the city of Brest Litovsk.

While negotiations proceeded, the Bolshevik-dominated Soviet regime, like Kerensky's Provisional Government earlier, faced further erosion of territorial control and threats from the right. General Kornilov, together with General Kaledin, organized a counterrevolutionary force and took control of the Don River region in the south. Lithuania and Moldava declared their independence, and the Soviet government accepted Finland's full national independence. Within the Soviet regime, political control required further adroit manipulation on the part of Lenin. Voters elected delegates to a constitutional convention to be convened in January. The Bolsheviks secured only about 25 percent of the seats at these elections, and Lenin recognized that if the convention ever met, Bolshevik control of the state would be endangered by the Socialist Revolutionary majority. Partly to begin a clampdown on other socialists, Lenin established a new secret police in December, the Cheka, run by the Polish Bolshevik, Felix Dzerzhinsky. Then, when the Constituent Assembly convened in January 1918, the guards sent by the Bolsheviks to maintain order simply closed down the meeting, turned off the lights, and locked the doors. The simple maneuver eliminated that threat to

The Lazian Militia with which these men served was only one of a variety of forces in the Russian Civil War. *(National Archives)*

Bolshevik control. Lenin continued to hold that his party alone understood the true demands of the people and represented the only means to implement the dictatorship of the proletariat that he envisioned.

THE TREATY OF BREST LITOVSK

Even with political control established, however, the Soviet regime faced continuing crises with the loss of territory, German military advances, and organized counterrevolutionary forces. In late January the Ukraine declared its independence, and a few days later a Ukrainian government signed a separate peace treaty with the Central Powers. Frustrated with German demands for territorial concessions in a formal treaty, on February 10, 1918, Trotsky simply announced that the war ended without a treaty. He called his formula "neither peace nor war." Trotsky and others in the Bolshevik leadership hoped that a wave of socialist revolutions in Germany and the Austro-Hungarian Empire would lead to collapse of the regimes there. No such revolutions materialized while the Russians stalled at the Brest Litovsk negotiations, and the Germans refused to accept the "neither peace nor war" concept. The German army, under General Ludendorff, resumed battle.

On March 3, 1918, the Russian delegates at Brest Litovsk grimly accepted the terms of the treaty, which recognized the loss of the Ukraine and directly ceded to Germany control of former Russian territories in all Poland and Lithuania and the southern half of Latvia. With these concessions, Russia lost one-third of its population, more than half its industry, and about 90 percent of its mines. German troops occupied White Russia (Belarus), all of Ukraine, the rest of Latvia, and Estonia as well. More ominously for the other Allies, Germany withdrew whole armies from the eastern front and began to shift them to France, anticipating a final push on Paris in the spring and summer of 1918.

At a Bolshevik Party congress called on March 8, 1918, to ratify the treaty of Brest Litovsk, the party also officially changed its name to the Communist Party (Bolshevik). As the Communist government moved from Petrograd to Moscow, Germany continued its advance into the Ukraine, meeting only spotty resistance from disorganized bands. In the south, Turkish troops took over Armenia and the territories that Russia had gained in Persia.

AFTERMATH

Although the war formally came to an end for Russia by March 1918, the killing did not stop. So called White Armies, units of counterrevolutionary troops, organized in the Don River region of the south of Russia continued to fight against the Soviet regime in the Russian Civil War that continued for another year after the end of World War I on the western front.

International intervention began in the spring of 1918, with Japanese landings at Vladivostok and British landings at Murmansk. The Czech Legion, which had deserted from Austria-Hungary to fight on the Allied side with the Russians, now turned against the Bolshevik regime and demanded passage back to help establish a Czech republic. When they could not obtain transport, they seized control of whole sections of the Trans-Siberian Railway, hoping to secure pas-

sage to the Far East and then voyage by Allied ships to return to the fight against Austria-Hungary.

Although troops from France and the United States joined those from Britain and Japan inside Russia, the intervening powers could not agree on their objectives and could not cooperate militarily. Britain sought to gain dominance in the Caspian Sea region, seat of rich Russian oil reserves. France sought to strengthen Poland by transferring Russian lands to that new country, so that it would represent a counterbalance to any postwar German threat. Japan sought control of rail lines and former Russian concessions in Chinese Manchuria. The United States hoped to end the Bolshevik regime itself, but not at the expense of Russian territorial control. By 1919 after most of these goals had proven illusory, the intervening powers withdrew their troops.

Lenin's regime faced an abortive effort to stage a coup, led by the Left Socialist Revolutionaries, and an assassination attempt on his own life, which left him wounded. Under Dzerzhinsky, an officially sanctioned Red Terror began in which the Cheka secret police rounded up and shot political opponents. Soldiers and Cheka detained many members of the middle class and proprietor

Troops of the United States, Japan, France, and Britain landed in Vladivostok with very different motives. *(National Archives)*

CHRONICLE OF EVENTS

A note on the calendar change:

In western Europe and in most of the world, the calendar reform instituted by Pope Gregory XIII in 1582 had been widely accepted. In Britain and the British colonies, the change to this Gregorian calendar was made in 1752. In Russia, however, the older Julian calendar remained in use despite efforts for reform in the 19th century. The change to the Gregorian calendar was not made until February 1918, when to bring the Russian calendar into conformity with the rest of the world, Lenin ordered that January 31 was to be followed by February 14. In the following chronology, the Gregorian calendar commonly used in western Europe and the United States is used for all events. Conventional dating refers to Julian dates as Old Style or O.S. and Gregorian dates as New Style or N.S. The 13-day difference means that the revolution that occurred in early March 1917 N.S. was known as the February Revolution, and the Bolshevik coup, which occurred November 7, 1917, N.S. was known as the October Revolution.

1914

August: Russian first and second armies invade German East Prussia.

August 26–30: In the Battle of Tannenberg, the Russian Second Army is surrounded and defeated.

September 6–15: In the Battle of Masurian Lakes, German forces defeat the Russian First Army and drive across the border at the Nieman River into Russian territory.

September 21: Russians make advances into Bukovina and besiege the fortress at Przemysl, now on the Polish side of the southern border with Ukraine.

September 24: Russians begin an advance toward the Carpathian Mountains and into northern Hungary.

October 4: A combined German and Austrian attack drives Russians back toward the Vistula River in Poland.

October 12: The Germans advance toward Warsaw.

November 16–December 2: The Battle of Cracow begins.

December 5–17: The Russians hold the Austrian advance at Cracow.

December 6: The Germans take Lodz.

December 31: By the end of the year, German forces have regained all of East Prussia and have pushed Russian troops well into Russian Poland, halting the threat to the German province of Silesia. Austrians hold a line against the Russians at the Carpathian Mountains between Galicia and Hungarian Czech lands.

1915

February 17: German troops take Memel in Lithuania.

March 18: The Russians retake Memel.

March 21: The Germans drive the Russians out of Memel.

March 22: The Russians advance through the Carpathian Mountain passes into Hungary.

April 1–25: Austrian forces drive Russians back through the Carpathian Mountains.

April 26: The Germans make advances in Courland (Lithuania).

May 2: In a major German-Austrian offensive, troops advance into Galicia.

May 3–5: A German-Austrian drive crosses the Dunajec River.

May 15–23: German-Austrian forces cross the San River in southern Poland.

June 3: German-Austrian troops retake the fortress of Przemysl.

June 22: German-Austrian forces take Lemberg (now L'vin, Ukraine).

June 23–27: German-Austrian troops cross the Dniester River; Galicia and Bukovina are restored to Austrian control.

July 1: The second major offensive by German-Austrian troops begins, with advances against weakening Russian resistance.

August 4–17: The German army advances through Poland and takes Warsaw.

August 25: Germans take Brest Litovsk.

September 5: Grand Duke Nicholai is relieved of command of the Russian forces by his uncle, Czar Nicholas II, who takes the post of minister of war himself.

September 19: Germans take Vilna on the Neris River in Lithuania.

November: By November, German forces have pushed beyond Vilna (Vilnius) and Brest Litovsk to a north-south line running between Minsk and Pinsk in what is now Belarus. Austrian forces have regained nearly all of Galicia from the Russians and have advanced to continue the line southward through Ukraine to Czernowitz.

1916

April 4: General A. Brusilov is appointed as commander on the Russian southern front.

June 4: General Brusilov begins the June, or Brusilov, Offensive against the Austrians. This is the last advance of Russian troops against the Central Powers. The Russians make a small advance against the Austrians in a drive toward Lemberg in Austria-Hungary and toward Lublin, Poland.

August 17: Russian advances over the summer stop before Lemberg.

August 27: Romania joins the Allies and declares war on Austria-Hungary.

August 28: Romania invades Transylvania and occupies Sibiu.

September 27–29: Austrian forces surround the Romanians at Sibiu.

October 22–25: German-Bulgarian forces take territory in the Romanian Dobrudja province along the Black Sea.

November 23: German forces push toward Bucharest, Romania.

December 6: The Romanians are defeated at Bucharest. They abandon the capital and move to Jassy in the extreme northeast section of Romania near the Ukrainian border, still under Russian control.

December 30: Grigory Rasputin is assassinated by Prince Yussupov (nephew of the czar) and a group of fellow aristocrats.

1917

January 15: The Central Powers, including Bulgaria, occupy almost all of Romania.

February–March: There is a general collapse of Russian troop morale. The czar's government loses control of the streets of Petrograd and many other cities. Ministers of government flee their positions; local soviets emerge. The fall of the czar's government is called the February Revolution.

March 10: (February 25, Old Style) Troops at the Petrograd garrison mutiny in response to a routine order from Czar Nicholas to suppress the riots.

March 11: A group of delegates at the Duma refuse the czar's order to disband.

March 12: The Socialists organize the Petrograd Soviet, a council of workers and soldiers. The Duma sets up a provisional government with Prince George Lvov as prime minister, with Alexander Kerensky as a minister in the Provisional Government and

Although not motorized, Bulgarian artillery units like this one were still a factor in battles on the eastern front. *(Library of Congress)*

serving simultaneously as vice chairman of the Petrograd Soviet.

March 15: (March 2, Old Style) Czar Nicholas II, at the demand of the Duma, abdicates in favor of his son, who abdicates to Nicholas's brother Michael.

March 16: Michael abdicates, giving power to the Provisional Government.

March 21: The independence of Finland is recognized.

March 30: The independence of Poland is recognized.

April 12: The autonomy of Estonia is recognized.

April 16: Vladimir Lenin arrives in Petrograd by sealed train from Switzerland. He is accompanied by Grigori Zinoviev, Karl Radek, and Anatoly Lunarcharski.

May: Leon Trotsky arrives in Russia from exile. The Poles demand an independent and united Poland.

May 14: In a shake-up of the Russian Provisional Government cabinet, the minister of war is dismissed.

May 16: Kerensky is appointed minister of war in the Russian Provisional Government.

June: German troops occupy Georgia. They will remain until end of the war.

July 1: General Brusilov begins a major offensive in Galicia, with initial advances toward Lemberg.

July 16–17: Russian troops mutiny, refuse to resume the offensive, abandon the front in Austrian territory, and retreat into the Ukrainian side of the border. Hundreds of troops are shot by their officers as they flee to the rear.

July 16–18: The Bolsheviks attempt to seize power; Lenin escapes to Finland; Trotsky is arrested.

July 20: Finland declares complete independence.

July 20: Prince Lvov resigns as prime minister and is replaced by Kerensky.

July 20–28: Austrian-German forces drive back the advance of the Russians in Galicia. Russian troop mutinies over the prior two weeks lose all the territory gained in Galicia in two years of fighting.

August: Factory workers in Moscow go on strike demanding an end to the war.

August 1: General Brusilov is replaced by General Lavr Georgievich Kornilov.

September 2–5: In the Battle of Riga, Germans surround and capture the city.

September 8–10: Kornilov marches on Petrograd, at first at Kerensky's order; then is dismissed by Kerensky who fears Kornilov plans a military coup. The Bolshe-viks get some credit for assisting in the resistance to Kornilov.

October: Bolsheviks secure their majority in the Petrograd Soviet.

October 11: Germans take Latvia and off-shore islands in the Baltic.

November 6–7: (October 24–25 Old Style): During the October Revolution, Bolsheviks conduct a coup and Kerensky escapes.

November 7: An all-Russian congress of Soviets approves the Bolshevik coup. The Soviets organize a new government: the Council of the People's Commissars, which includes Lenin and Trotsky.

November 22: Trotsky proposes an armistice; fighting stops on the front from the Baltic to the Black Sea.

November 25: A constituent assembly is elected in Russia; 420 Socialist Revolutionaries are elected and 225 Bolsheviks. A meeting is scheduled for January 1918.

November 28: The Bolsheviks offer peace terms to the Germans.

December 5: The Bolshevik government reveals the secret treaties under which Britain and France promised Russia control of the Bosporus and Dardanelles and the annexation of Turkish Armenia at the end of the war. A formal armistice is declared between Russia and the Central Powers. Negotiations begin at Brest Litovsk.

December 9: Cossacks under General Kaledin and General Kornilov begin a counterrevolutionary takeover in the Don River region.

December 11: Lithuania sets up an independent government.

December 15: Moldava declares independence.

December 20: The Cheka, a Bolshevik-run secret police, is formed under Dzerzhinsky.

December 28: Negotiations at Brest Litovsk are suspended.

1918

January 10: Cossacks declare an independent republic of the Don.

January 18: When the Russian constituent convention convenes, it is dispersed by its guards, who are members of the Red Army.

January 28: Ukraine declares independence.

February 9: Ukraine concludes a separate peace with the Central Powers.

February 10: The Bolsheviks declare the war over without a treaty.

February 14: Lenin brings the Russian calendar into conformity with the western Gregorian calendar by decreeing that January 31 (O.S.) will be followed by February 14 (N.S.).

February 18: German troops resume battle, but reorganized Red Army forces take Kiev in the Ukraine.

March: British troops advance from Murmansk and Archangel in northern Russia.

March 3: The Treaty of Brest Litovsk is signed; Russia gives up control of Ukraine, Poland, and the independent states of Finland, Latvia, Lithuania, and Estonia.

March 8: The Seventh Special Party Congress changes the name of the Bolshevik Party to the Communist Party (Bolshevik). The congress also approves the Brest Litovsk Treaty.

March 9: The Communist (Bolshevik) government moves the capital from Petrograd to Moscow.

March 13: The Germans occupy Odessa on the Black Sea and most of Ukraine and remain in Georgia. Turks occupy Armenia and northwestern Persia (now Iran).

EYEWITNESS TESTIMONY

Tannenberg! A word pregnant with painful recollections for German chivalry, a Slav cry of triumph, a name that is fresh in our memories after more than five hundred years of history. . . . On the way from Marienburg to Tannenberg the impression of the miseries into which war had plunged the unhappy inhabitants were intensified. Masses of helpless refugees, carrying their belongings, pressed past me on the road and to a certain extent hindered the movements of our troops which were hastening to meet the foe.

General Paul von Hindenburg in official dispatch, reporting on the lead-up to the Battle of Tannenberg, August 24, 1914, from Source Records of the Great War, *vol. 1, p. 179.*

I beg most humbly to report to Your Majesty that the ring round the larger part of the Russian Army was closed yesterday. The 13th, 15th, and 18th Army Corps have been destroyed. We have already taken more than 60,000 prisoners, among the Corps Commanders of the 13th and 15th Corps. The guns are still in the forests and are now being brought in. The booty is immense though it cannot yet be assessed in detail. The Corps outside our ring, the 1st and 6th, have also suffered severely and are now retreating in hot haste through Mlawa and Myszaniec.

General von Hindenburg, describing in his report the defeat of the Russian army at Tannenberg, August 31, 1914, from Source Records of the Great War, *vol. 2, p. 179.*

Night fell. Samsonoff, accompanied by five other staff officers, was guiding himself through the thick forest towards the Russian Frontier. Their motor-cars had been abandoned, for it was too risky to use the roads. The little party mounted on horseback, passing out of the forest, despite the darkness were seen by a party of German infantry armed with machine guns. Amidst a hail of bullets the party dismounted and continued their way on foot, into another belt of forest. Utter darkness surrounded them. The sounds of fighting died away, and all that could be heard was the trampling of the undergrowth and an occasional voice as members of the little party called out to each other in order to keep together. From time to time a halt was called and all drew closer to make sure that nobody was missing.

General Samsonoff, who suffered from heart trouble, and found his breathing more and more difficult, lagged behind. There came a time when everybody had been called and all had answered but Samsonoff. General Postovski, the Chief of his Staff, immediately called a halt and in the thick darkness led a search for the missing general. It was fruitless.

Russian general Basil Gourko, describing the confused retreat from Tannenberg, in which General Samsonoff was killed, later presumed to have committed suicide, August 31, 1914, from Charles Horne and Walter Austin, editors, Source Records of the Great War, *vol. 1, pp. 188–189.*

Surrender was the last thing in the world that the Russians against whom our men were advancing with fixed bayonets had in mind. I went over the top, clambering over the body of a man whose brains were sticking out of his head, and signed to them to surrender—they were at most 200 yards away. But they still continued to call to us without attempting to move. I thereupon gave the command, "Fire!" and held my own rifle at the ready. At this point my calculations broke down. My Rumanians refused to fire, and what was more, prevented me from firing either. One of them put his hand on my rifle and said: "Don't fire, sir; if we fire, they will fire too. And why should Rumanians kill Rumanians?" (He was thinking of the Bessarabians.)

I accordingly refrained, but beside myself with rage, tried to rejoin my right wing, where incredible things were happening. The schoolmaster Catavei and Cizmas barred my way, exclaiming: "Stop, don't go and get yourself shot, too!" Our men were advancing towards the Russians, and then with their arms at the slope, were shaking hands with them; and the fraternizing business started again.

"Surrender, and we will surrender, too. We're quite ready."

Our men were bringing in Russians, and vice versa. It was a touching sight. I saw one of my Rumanians, towards Saliste, kiss a Russian and bring him back. Their arms were round each other's necks as though they were brothers. They were old friends, who had been shepherd boys together in Bessarabia.

We took ninety Russians as prisoners in this way, while they took thirty of our men.

Octavian Taslaunu, a Romanian officer with the Hungarian army, describing a joint surrender at the front in the Carpathian Mountains, November 20, 1914, from Charles Horne and Walter Austin, editors, Source Records of the Great War (1915 Volume), *pp. 117–118.*

It was Petrov, a volunteer and friend of Pavel's who informed me about his death. To spare his mother and Sashenka a sudden shock, Pavel must have arranged with his friend to write to my office address in case of need, so that I should be the one to break the terrible news to his nearest and dearest. I shall never forget the envelope marked "on Active service," and addressed in an unfamiliar hand, a fact which in itself foreboded evil, and read the few lines it contained. . . . The men in our office were very sympathetic, but what did their sympathy matter to me? I went home at once, wondering, in agony, how I was to break the news to mother and Sashenka. . . . I would sooner die a thousand deaths than have to tell any woman that her son has been killed. Rather than go through the experience a second time, to gaze into trusting, innocent eyes, I would sooner lay hands on myself. Grieved as I am over Pavel's death, I can't help rejoicing that the ordeal is behind me and will never have to be repeated again. Death would be easier. . . . And now Pavel is dead and we do not know where he is buried. I cannot picture the place, no matter how hard I try. I am dazed; I don't understand what is happening; I don't understand the war. I feel only that it crushes us, and there is no salvation for any of us, big or small.

Minor government bureaucrat and diarist Leonid Andreyev, recounting in his diary notification of the death of his son, January 18, 1915, in his The Confessions of a Little Man during Great Days, *pp. 81–88.*

The day before the surrender . . . 2,000 beautiful horses were killed, not for meat for the starving soldiers be it noted, but that they might not fall into the hands of the Russians. Perhaps I can best illustrate what happened by quoting the words of a Russian officer who was among the first to enter the town. "Everywhere," he told me, "one saw the bodies of freshly-killed saddle horses, some of them animals that must have been worth many thousand roubles. Around the bodies were groups of Hungarian soldiers tearing at them with knives; with hands and faces dripping with blood, they were gorging themselves on the raw meat. I have never seen in all my experience of war a more horrible and pitiable spectacle than these soldiers, half crazed with hunger, tearing the carcasses like famished wolves." My friend

paused and a shadow crossed his kindly face. "Yes," he said, "it was horrible." Even my Cossack orderly wept—and he—well, he has seen much of war and is not overdelicate. . . .

The fall of Przemysl strikes one as being the rarest thing possible in war—namely a defeat, which seems to please all parties interested. The Russians rejoice in a fortress captured, the Austrians at a chance to eat and rest, and the civilians, long since sick of the quarrel, at the city once more being restored to the normal.

Stanley Washburn, an official British observer, describing the effect of the Russian siege of Przyemysl as he entered with Russian troops, March 22, 1915, in Charles Horne and Walter Austin, editors, Source Records of the Great War, *vol. 1, pp. 103–104.*

On February 23 at 9:00 A.M., the workers of the plants and factories of the Vyborg district went on strike in protest against the shortage of black bread in bakeries and groceries; the strike spread to some plants located in the Petrograd, Rozhdestvenskii, and Liteinyi districts, and in the course of the day 50 industrial enterprises ceased working, with 87,534 men going on strike.

At about 1:00 P.M. the workmen of the Vyborg district, walking out in crowds into the streets and shouting "Give us bread," started at the same time to become disorderly in various places, taking with them on the way their comrades who were at work, and stopping tramcars; the demonstrators took away from the tram drivers the keys to the electric motors, which forced 15 tramway trains to quit the lines and retire to the Petrograd tramway yard.

The strikers who were resolutely chased by police and troops summoned [for this purpose], were dispersed in one place but quickly gathered in other places, showing themselves to be exceptionally stubborn; in the Vyborg district order was restored only toward 7:00 P.M.

Official document of the czar's secret police, the Okhrana, reporting on disturbances in St. Petersburg that precipitated the February revolution, February 23, 1917, from Browder and Kerensky, The Russian Provisional Government 1917, *vol. 1, p. 34.*

Next day, early in the morning, I intended to go as usual to my battalion. Suddenly I heard the telephone ring, and on behalf of Kerensky I was informed that the Duma was dissolved, that Protopopov was proclaimed dictator, that the Volynskii regiment had revolted, had killed its officers, had walked out carrying rifles into the streets, and was making its way toward the Preobrazhenskii barracks (my battalion was stationed in these barracks). Without losing a moment, I grabbed my combat equipment and rushed toward the battalion. On the corner of the Liteinyi and Kirochnaia [Street] I saw a mob, which watched attentively what happened on Kirochnaia Street. I approached; at the end of the Kirochnaia, right in front of the Preobrazhenskii barracks, was deployed a gray, disorderly crowd of soldiers who were slowly proceeding toward the Liteinyi Prospekt. Above their heads two or three dark banners made out of rags were visible. I made my way toward the crowd, but was stopped by an N.C.O., who was running rapidly from the crowd:

"Your honor! Don't go, they'll kill you! The commander of the battalion is killed. First Lieutenant Ustreugov is killed, and some officers are lying by the gate. The rest have run away."

I was frightened and went into the school for ensigns located at the beginning of Kirochnaia [Street]; I tried by telephone to contact my battalion and the State Duma, but did not get any reply . . .

The director of police, General Vasil Vasilev, reporting on the riots on February 27, 1917, in St. Petersburg, from Browder and Kerensky, The Russian Provisional Government 1917, *p. 40.*

I was aroused by strange noises. I realized at once where I was but could not explain these sounds to myself.

I got up and saw two soldiers, their bayonets hooked into the canvas of Repin's portrait of Nicholas II, rhythmically tugging it down from both sides. A minute later, over the chairman's seat in the white Hall of the Duma there was an empty frame which for many months continued to yawn in this revolutionary hall . . . Strange! It never came into my head to worry about the fate of this portrait. To this day I don't know what happened to it; I was more interested in other things.

A number of soldiers were standing on the upper levels of the chamber, at the height of my gallery. Leaning on their rifles they watched what their comrades were doing, and quietly made their own comments. I went over to them and listened eagerly. . . . Twenty-four hours before, these rank-and-file soldiers had been the dumb slaves of the despot who was now thrown down, and at this moment the outcome of the revolution depended on them. What had taken place in their heads during those twenty-four hours? What would they say to the shameful treatment of the portrait of the "adored monarch" of yesterday? It evidently made no strong impression: there was neither surprise, nor any sign of intense intellectual activity, nor a shadow of the great enthusiasm from which even I myself was ready to catch fire. They were making remarks in a tranquil and matter-of-fact way, so down-to-earth they can't be repeated.

The break had been accomplished with a sort of fabulous ease. No better sign was needed of the definitive rottenness of Tsarism and its irremediable ruin.

The hands of the large clock over the entrance doors of the hall pointed to 7:30. It was time to begin the second day of the revolution.

N. N. Sukhanov, an independent socialist member of the Soviet Executive Committee, remembering the end of the monarchy and the establishment of the Provisional Government on February 28, 1917, in his memoir, The Russian Revolution, *p. 74.*

It was already about 11 o'clock [February 28] when the Ex.Com. session opened. I have the impression that during these first days its work went on almost uninterruptedly around the clock. But what work it was! They were not meetings but a frenzied and exhausting obstacle race.

The agenda had been set up in relation to the urgent tasks of the moment. But neither at that session nor in general during the days that followed could there be any questions of fulfilling a programme of work.

Every five or ten minutes business was interrupted by "urgent announcements," or "emergency reports," "matters of exceptional importance" which couldn't "tolerate the slightest delay," and on which the "fate of the revolution depended," etc. These emergency questions were for the most part raised by the Ex.Com. members themselves, who kept getting some sort of information on the side, or prompted by people who were besieging the Ex.Com. But again and again the petitioners, delegates, and messengers from every possible organization and agency, or simply from the nearby crowds, would themselves burst into the meeting.

In the great majority of cases these emergency matters were not worth a barley-corn. I don't remember what the Ex.Com. did during these hours. I remember only unimaginable hubbub, tension, hunger, and the feeling of irritation at these "exceptional reports." There was simply no way of stopping them.

There was no order even in the meeting itself. There was no permanent chairman. Chkheidze, who later performed the chairman's duties almost permanently, didn't do much work in the Ex.Com. during its first days. He was constantly being summoned—either to the Duma Committee or the Soviet sessions, or above all, "to the people," the constantly-changing crowd standing in front of the Tauride Palace. He spoke practically without stopping both in the Ekaterinskii Hall and in the street, sometimes to workers and sometimes to soldiers. He would scarcely have time to return to the meeting of the Ex.Com. and take his things off before some delegate would burst in with a categorical demand for Chkeidze, sometimes even reinforced by threats—that the mob would break in. And the tired and sleepy old Georgian would get his fur coat on again and with a resigned look, put on his hat, and disappear from the Ex. Com.

. . . On the writing desk of the chairman of the former Finance Committee there appeared from somewhere or other tin mugs of tea with crusts of black bread and other eatables. Someone was looking after us. But there was not much food, or else there was simply no time to get it. A feeling of hunger remains in my memory. . . .

N. N. Sukhanov, recalling the chaos as the new Provisional Government attempted to get started, February 28, 1917, from his memoir, The Russian Revolution, *pp. 83–84.*

It is with sentiments of the most profound satisfaction that the peoples of Great Britain and of the British Dominions across the seas have learned that their great Ally Russia now stands with the nations which base their institutions upon responsible government.

Much as we appreciate the loyal and steadfast cooperation which we have received from the late Emperor and the armies of Russia during the past two and a half years, yet I believe that the revolution whereby the Russian people have based their destinies on the sure foundation of freedom is the greatest service which they have yet made to the cause for which the Allied peoples have been fighting since August, 1914.

It reveals the fundamental truth that this war is at bottom a struggle for popular government as well as for liberty. It shows that, through the war, the principle of liberty, which is the only sure safeguard of peace in the world, has already won one resounding victory. It is the sure promise that the Prussian military autocracy which began the war, and which is still the only barrier to peace, will itself, before long, be overthrown.

Freedom is the condition of peace, and I do not doubt that as a result of the establishment of a stable constitutional Government within their borders the Russian people will be strengthened in their resolve to prosecute this war until the last stronghold of tyranny on the Continent of Europe is destroyed and the free peoples of all lands can unite to secure for themselves and their children the blessings of fraternity and peace.

Lloyd George, giving his opinion that the Russian Revolution of February 1917 transforms the World War into one of democracy against autocracy, March 23, 1917, in a telegram to Prince Lvov, quoted in the London Times, *"Great Britain to Free Russia: A Resounding Blow for Liberty," March 23, 1917, p. 7.*

Unfortunately the government has not much armed force at its disposal, as the great majority of the troops do not want to take sides either for or against it. It appears too that the Bolsheviks are in the same situation . . . the soldiers are quite prepared to walk about with rifles, but they do not want to be regimented and have to fight as units. In their independent state, they can always resort to running away and joining the side which wins. In spite of everything, according to Tatichev the government can still count on the Preobrajensky regiment (half of which has unfortunately been dispersed to mount guard on the banks, the ministries, etc.), on Rehbinder's two cannon, on two or three cavalry regiments, two Cossack regiments and sixteen armored cars. On the rioters' side are the regiment of Grenadiers, the sailors of Kronstadt, the Paul regiment, seven or eight armoured cars and, it is said, four cannon. Nevertheless, Tatichev is fairly confident, because they expect the arrival of troops who support the government.

As I was coming back from the Ministry I saw a large mob of soldiers along the branch of the Moika Canal which joins the Neva after passing under the Hermitage Bridge: I walked up to them. They were soldiers of all arms, who had got together to rescue a little cat which had fallen into the canal and was mewing despairingly and floundering about, with its white body showing up in the black water of the canal. All these people, who were shooting each other a few hours ago, had come together to save the poor beast and to give a leg up to one of their number who had not hesitated to jump in the water to effect the rescue . . . what worthy people they are, basically.

Count Louis de Robien, a young French diplomat, noting in his diary his observations of the abortive Bolshevik-led uprising of July 17, 1917, in The Diary of a Diplomat in Russia, 1917–1918, *pp. 86–87.*

This I have seen. I could not believe it unless I had seen it through and through. For several weeks I lived with it; I went all about it and back of it; inside and out of it was shown to me—until finally I came to realize that the incredible was true. It is monstrous, it is unthinkable, but it exists. It is the Prussian system. A year ago I went to Poland to learn its facts concerning the remnant of a people that had been decimated by war. The country had been twice devastated. First the Russian army swept through it and then the Germans. Along the roadside from Warsaw to Pinsk, the present firing line, 230 miles, nearly half a million people had died of hunger and cold. The way was strewn with their bones picked clean by the crows. With their usual thrift, the Germans were collecting the larger bones to be milled into fertilizer, but finger and toe bones lay on the ground with the mud-covered and rain-soaked clothing.

Wicker baskets were scattered along the way—the basket in which the baby swings from the rafter in every peasant home. Every mile there were scores of them, each one telling a death. I started to count, but after a little I had to give it up, there were so many.

That is the desolation one saw along the great road from Warsaw to Pinsk, mile after mile, more than two hundred miles. They told me a million people were made homeless in six weeks of the German drive in August and September 1915. They told me four hundred thousand died on the way. The rest, scarcely half alive, got through with the Russian army. Many of these have been sent to Siberia; it is these people whom the Paderewski committee is trying to relieve. . . . In that situation, the German commander issued a proclamation. Every able-bodied Pole was bidden to Germany to work. If any refused, let no other Pole give him to eat, not so much as a mouthful, under penalty of German military law.

This is the choice the German Government gives to the conquered Pole, to the husband and father of a starving family: Leave your family to die or survive as the case may be. Leave your country which is destroyed, to work in Germany for its further destruction. If you are obstinate, we shall see that you surely starve. . . . Germany will set him to work that a German workman may be released to fight against his own land and people. He shall be lodged in barracks, behind barbed wire entanglements, under armed guard. He shall sleep on the bare ground with a single thin blanket. He shall be scantily fed and his earnings shall be taken from him to pay for his food.

That is the choice which the German Government offers to a proud, sensitive, high strung people: Death or slavery.

When a Pole gave me that proclamation, I was boiling. But I had to restrain myself. I was practically the only foreign civilian in the country and I wanted to get food to the people. That was what I was there for and I must not for any cause jeopardize the undertaking.

Frederick C. Walcott, a member of the U.S. Commission for Polish Relief, reporting on his visit to Poland in September 1917, from Source Records of the Great War, *pp. 426–427.*

It was just 8:40 when a thundering wave of cheers announced the entrance of the presidium, with Lenin—great Lenin—among them. A short, stocky figure, with

Bolshevik leader Vladimir Ilyich Lenin seized the opportunity to implement the "dictatorship of the Proletariat." *(Library of Congress)*

a big head set down in his shoulders, bald and bulging. Little eyes, a snubbish nose, wide, generous mouth, and heavy chin; clean shaven now, but already beginning to bristle with the well-known beard of his past and future. Dressed in shabby clothes, his trousers much too long for him. Unimpressive, to be the idol of a mob, loved and revered as perhaps few leaders in history have been. A strange popular leader—a leader purely by virtue of intellect; colourless, humourless, uncompromising and detached, without picturesque idiosyncrasies—but with the power of explaining profound ideas in simple terms, of analyzing a concrete situation. And combined with shrewdness, the greatest intellectual audacity.

Kamenev was reading the report of the actions of the Military Revolutionary Committee; abolition of capital punishment in the Army, restoration of the free right of propaganda, release of officers and soldiers arrested for political crimes, orders to arrest Kerensky and confiscation of food supplies in private store-houses. . . . Tremendous applause.

John Reed, American radical journalist, observing the entrance of Lenin to a meeting of the Congress of Soviets on October 26, 1917, in his contemporary memoir, Ten Days That Shook the World (1960 edition), *pp. 170–171.*

I spent a great deal of time at Smolny. It was no longer easy to get in. Double rows of sentries guarded the outer gates, and once inside the front door there was a long line of people waiting to be let in, four at a time, to be questioned as to their identity and their business. Passes were given out, and the pass system was changed every few hours; for spies continually sneaked through.

One day as I came up to the outer gate I saw Trotsky and his wife just ahead of me. They were halted by a soldier. Trotsky searched through his pockets, but could find no pass.

"Never mind," he said finally. "You know me. My name is Trotsky."

"You haven't got a pass," answered the soldier stubbornly. "You cannot go in. Names don't mean anything to me."

"But I am president of the Petrograd Soviet."

"Well," replied the soldier, "if you're as important a fellow as that you must at least have one little paper."

Trotsky was very patient. "Let me see the Commandant," he said. The soldier hesitated, grumbling something about not wanting to disturb the Commandant for every devil that came along. He beckoned finally to

the soldier in command of the guard. Trotsky explained matters to him. "My name is Trotsky," he repeated.

"Trotsky?" The other soldier scratched his head. "I've heard the name somewhere," he said at length. "I guess it's all right. You can go in, comrade."

John Reed, observing Trotsky entering a meeting of the Congress of Soviets during the November Revolution, November 1917, in his memoir, Ten Days That Shook the World (1960 edition), *p. 77.*

Kerensky's supporters have laid down their arms. His General Staff have given themselves up, and he himself has fled. So now we are rid of this grotesque character, and with him the regime which issued from the revolution has collapsed too: it only succeeded in alienating everyone and in becoming an object of ridicule, defended by a few Cossacks, a battalion of women and some children.

The Bolshevik government has not yet been constituted, but it is thought that by tomorrow this will be an accomplished fact.

I am waiting impatiently to see the "workers' and peasants' government" at work. How will these people with an ideal translate their dream into reality? In any case they cannot do worse than the puppets of the "provisional government." Let us hope that the International, which to a certain extent had been realized by the aristocracy before and which was destroyed by the nationalist bourgeois, can be reconstituted by democracy and the proletariat. The workman and the peasant have something in common, no matter in what country they are thus classified, just as there was something in common between a peer of France and prince of the Holy Roman Empire.

It is the bourgeois, vain, selfish and grasping, who created that nationalism which encourages their ignorance of foreigners and fills their coffers. They are the people who are responsible for the policy of imperialism, as much in Germany as anywhere else. It is their newspapers which during peacetime dreamed only of drums and flags, and which are still blowing the trumpet to prevent the voice of the people being heard. . . .

Since the International of the Church has gone bankrupt and that of the intelligentsia is too weak to make itself heard, let us put our trust in the International of democracy, while at the same time we regret the good old days of the aristocratic International, and the elegant solution which consisted of stopping a massacre with the wedding of a princess.

Count Louis de Robien, a young French diplomat, noting in his diary the end of the Kerensky regime and waiting to see how the Bolshevik government will work out, in his entry for Saturday, November 17, 1917, in The Diary of a Diplomat in Russia, 1917–1918, *p. 141.*

The town is still quiet and it is impossible to get any idea of what is happening from the look of the streets, where the trams and izvozchiks are circulating as usual, where everyone is going quietly about their business, and where customers line up in long queues outside the bakeries and food shops. The almost total absence of motorcars is due to the petrol shortage. At night fires burn at the main cross-roads, where soldiers and Red Guards bivouac adding a picturesque touch to the dark streets. The town has been put in charge of a military commandant subordinate to the Soviet, a Colonel Muraviev, who has shown himself to be forceful. . . .

Sunday 18th November, 1917

The Bolsheviks, moreover, are in a difficult position . . . the populace already blames them for having not yet made peace or distributed bread. They are also accused of using old regime methods, prejudicial to liberty, by suspending the newspapers which are hostile to them and prohibiting meetings. . . . It is being said that "their hands are drenched in blood." It's true that they don't wear kid gloves.

Besides, they are having trouble among themselves, and this very day several People's Commissars have resigned. The new regime depends entirely on two men, Lenin and Trotsky. But the extremists, especially among the sailors, are already accusing them of not acting . . . since the war is still going on and the age of plenty has not returned. Some day perhaps these two apostles of Bolshevism will seem very Menchevist in relation to men of more advanced ideas.

Count Louis de Robien, commenting in his diary on life under the Bolsheviks in the first few days of the Bolshevik government, November 17–18, 1917, in The Diary of a Diplomat in Russia, 1917–1918, *pp. 142–145.*

Constant burglaries and murders and the inadequacy of police protection under the new demoralized anarchical regime compelled citizens to organize civil vigilance companies with compulsory attendance on the part of all able-bodied males. Last night I performed my duty as a guardsman for the first time. Aside from a big fire somewhere beyond the city limits, nothing of notice happened during the night. Relieved of my duties at 7 A.M., I hurried to the bakery with the intention of taking advantage of my guardsman's privilege and getting my loaf ahead of the bread line, but found a notice on the door to the effect that there would be no bread before 9 A.M.

On returning home I took [the dog] out for a walk, went to bed and did not get up until nearly eleven o'clock. When my maid failed to answer several of my bells I went to the kitchen, but found it empty. The landlady, whom I approached on the matter, explained to me that the maid had gone to see a lynching. It turned out that about 10 A.M. three robbers got into a house nearly opposite ours. The inmates managed to raise an alarm, one of the robbers was killed outright, one ran away, and one was caught by soldiers. The crowd that had assembled in front of the house roared for the last named—and our maid hastened there to see the execution. . . .

The crowds are said to become perfectly frantic on such occasions and invariably demand immediate execution. A pious and charitable old lady who happened to be present at the lynching of a housebreaker goaded on the crowd, though under ordinary circumstances she would not hurt a fly.

Alexis Babine, an apolitical Russian civilian, commenting on the disorders following the November Revolution, in his diary entry for December 28, 1917, in A Russian Civil War Diary. Alexis Babine in Saratov, 1917–1922, *p. 38.*

January 5, 1918

A delegation of about twenty officers' wives came to the Embassy to ask the Allies for help. It was pathetic to see these unfortunate women, who have been used to a certain comfort, still wearing fur coats and decent clothes, but reduced to begging as most of them have no knowledge of any profession. Their husbands are prisoners in the barracks, where they lead the life of convicts and only get a private soldier's pay of about fifteen roubles, and the soldiers prevent them from working outside and earning more money. One of these ladies told me that her husband, who is a Guards officer, had managed to escape and had spent the night unloading sacks of coal at the station; but the *tovariches* found out, and confiscated the few roubles which he had earned with such difficulty. . . . The Ambassador received these poor women and said a few words of comfort to them. . . . But there were tears in his eyes as he talked about it.

One wonders how the "bourgeois" can live at all. All property has been confiscated in actual fact, and all bank deposits seized, and salaries and pensions stopped. It means utter destitution. A few days ago near the Cinizelli Circus I saw an old general and a priest—the old Russia itself—clearing the streets of snow in order not to die of starvation. A gang of soldiers, in the prime of life, stood and mocked them.

Count Louis de Robien, commenting on the plight of the bourgeoisie after the revolution in his entry for January 5, 1918, in The Diary of a Diplomat in Russia, 1917–1918, *pp. 185–186.*

19 January, 1918:
The Constituent Assembly will not have lasted long. . . . When the deputies belonging to the Bolshevik minority left the hall, the government considered that the Assembly no longer represented national opinion, and decided purely and simply to forbid it to reassemble from then on. It is being said that the Revolutionary Socialists intend to organize big demonstrations the day after tomorrow, but I doubt if they will take place after yesterday evening's incidents. While we were near the Taurid Palace, the Red Guards did in fact open fire in the Liteiny Prospekt in order to stop a column of demonstrators which was trying to reach the palace of the Constituent Assembly. Several people were killed and many wounded, especially among the musicians and standard-bearers who were marching at the head.

It seems therefore that the Constituent Assembly will not reassemble. . . . they tried to elect a president. There were two candidates, or rather a candidate and a candidatess: M. Chernov, supported by the Revolutionary Socialists and Mlle Spiridonova, put forward by the Bolshevik minority. Chernov was elected, with a rather weak majority. The session continued until rather late into the night with palavering. The military had taken charge of the hall and towards two o'clock in the morning one of the sailors on guard having had enough of it, beckoned to the Comrade President that it was time to stop, and at his injunction, everyone had to clear out.

So that was the famous Constituent Assembly, which people in France were relying on to force Lenin and Trotsky to go on with the war!

In consequence, we should have no illusions: whether the policy of "All power to the Soviets" or "All power to the Assembly" wins, the result will be exactly the same from our point of view, that is to say from the point of view of the war. . . .

Count Louis de Robien, commenting on the Bolshevik closure of the Constituent Assembly in his entry for January 19, 1918, in The Diary of a Diplomat in Russia, 1917–1918, *pp. 197–198.*

6

Debacles on the Western Front

December 1915–December 1916

After the initial advance of German troops through Belgium and into France to the Marne in 1914–15, the war on the western front had settled down to a line from the North Sea coast to Ypres in Belgium, then to the east of the towns of Arras and Albert in the Somme region of France and roughly along the course of the Aisne River in France. The British held a sector between Ypres and the Somme, while the French defended from the Somme in a broad sweep that protected Paris. To the south of Luxembourg in France the line then took a large double curve. That is, the French held the forward fortress city of Verdun, and, just to the southeast of that city, the Germans held the salient at St. Mihiel.

In 1916, each side tried to break the other's lines along this long front in two places. Even though called the Battle of Verdun and the Battle of the Somme, each of these grand campaigns lasted many months and each consisted of many separate attacks. At the end of the year, the lines had changed very little, but at the cost of more than a million dead, wounded, missing, or captured. With these two disastrous battles, 1916 became a year of the greatest debacles on the western front, and the period that convinced all sides that the war could not end quickly.

In order to provide the manpower needed in any attempt to break the German lines, the British turned from a volunteer army to conscription in January

The city of Ypres in Flanders was devastated after years of bombardment. *(Library of Congress)*

1916. On January 27 the British put into effect the Military Service bill, ordering conscription of single men between the ages of 18 and 41. The law provided for exemption from service for ministers, essential war-workers, the medically unfit, and conscientious objectors. The British extended conscription to married men in April and rapidly trained the new inductees, selected new officers, and shipped the New Army to bolster the British line in Belgium and Flanders. The conscription act excluded the Irish, although units of volunteers from both the largely Protestant Ulster counties and from the Catholic southern counties continued to serve. The Irish exemption from conscription somewhat backfired in the southern counties of Ireland, where the most strongly pro-British young men volunteered for service, leaving behind those most opposed to Britain and the war and most inclined to a more radical nationalist viewpoint.

The Germans began the Battle of Verdun in February 1916 and did not break off the effort completely until November 1916. Farther to the north and west, where the French and British sectors of the lines met at the Somme, the Allies began a massed attack near the town of Albert, pushing toward Bapaume on the British sector and Péronne in July. General Kitchener had planned that the New Army of conscripts would be ready for action in 1917, but he had fallen into disfavor over questions of supply and over the Gallipoli campaign. Then, in June 1916, Kitchener drowned when a British cruiser on which he was steaming to the Russian front struck a German mine and sank. Demands for more troops from the French and political pressure for more aggressive conduct of the war sped up Kitchener's original timetable, so that conscripts began to appear in the British lines after a few weeks' training in mid-1916.

General Douglas Haig had been appointed as commander of British forces on the western front in December 1915, and many of the failures and successes of British campaigning over the next two years have been attributed to him. It seemed to many observers then and later that Haig obstinately refused to understand the emerging conditions on the front, and, unlike the French, he and his officers refused to adapt their view that masses of courageous men, advancing in determined waves and supported by artillery, could eventually break the German defenses.

Both sides had concluded that the process of attrition, exhausting the enemy's manpower and material resources by wearing them down, would be the only way to win the war. What the British called attrition, the French called *la guerre d'usure* and the Germans thought of as *Materialschlachten,* or battles of material. By this logic, the attackers hoped to lose fewer men, taking acceptable losses in order to gain territory and to inflict more severe damage on the defending enemy. Of course, in order to do that, the attackers had to sacrifice manpower and material. The question became who would break first. For the troops, the phrase *acceptable losses* summed up the gulf of understanding between officers and men; only very rarely would an enlisted man regard the loss of his own life as acceptable.

VERDUN

At Verdun, the German commander, Erich von Falkenhayn, made the decision to draw the French infantry into a destructive defense of that fortress city in early 1916. Sitting on the River Meuse, Verdun had been bypassed in the earlier German advances through Belgium and Luxembourg to the Marne, and Falkenhayn

The machine gun contributed greatly to defense. *(National Archives)*

and other German commanders may have believed that the French had under-defended the fortress. In front of the Verdun fort itself, the French manned several smaller forts, notably Douaumont and Vaux. The German attack began with a bombardment on February 21, 1916, in the heaviest artillery barrage of the war to that date. The guns homed in on two French divisions that held a section of eight miles along the Meuse River. After falling back and bringing new troops up to Verdun, the French held a line of trenches connecting the forward forts of Douaumont and Vaux.

General Philippe Pétain, commanding the defense at Verdun, ordered heavy artillery fire in defense and soon organized a massive resupply of Verdun with men and material. In order to bring in the vast quantities of transport, he ordered the widening of the road from Souilly. Crowded with trucks and guns, the high-way soon became known as *La Voie Sacrée* or the Sacred Way. The Germans took Douaumont in February, and the Germans captured the fort at Vaux after heavy losses on both sides on June 6. Verdun itself consisted of a strongly built fort rela-tively impervious to direct shell hits, surrounded with smaller outlying civilian structures that the German shelling soon demolished. The fort itself, however, withstood attack and could have been defeated only if German troops had cut it off from the rear and placed it under siege. The French lines, although pushed back, held in front of the fort.

With Allied attacks on the Somme that required German troops to bolster defense in that sector, Falkenhayn had fewer troops to call upon, but the attacks and counterattacks at Verdun continued into the late fall. By the time the battles had died down at Verdun, with the lines more or less restored to their original position, it had become the longest and most disastrous land battle in history. Although the figures have never been precisely established, the losses on both the French and German side exceeded 300,000 each. If it had been Falkenhayn's intention to bleed France of resources, he had partially succeeded, but only at the cost of depleting German human and material resources to an equal or greater extent. *Materialschlachten* had met *la guerre d'usure* in a virtual stalemate.

The Germans tended to overestimate the casualties inflicted on the French with their artillery. Pétain rotated units through the defense of Verdun, so that the casualties, although severe, did not destroy whole regiments. Meanwhile, the Germans, who kept the same units at the front, found them weakened and diminished. German officers reported that troop morale had severely declined, with many of the men regarding Verdun as a lost cause as early as March or April.

Despite the horror of Verdun, many neutral and French observers saw the attack at Verdun as somehow more honorable than the swinging attack through neutral Belgium and Luxembourg that had started the war on the western front in August 1914. A military attack by Germany directly across the German-French border, against the line of French forts from Verdun to Belfort, seemed, in the values of the day, more decent than attacking France through neutral Belgium. If the German attack at Verdun had succeeded, neutral observers noted, it would demonstrate that the German dishonorable attack through Belgium had not been necessary. From the German point of view, the strong defense at Verdun, even though it had been undermanned at the opening of the attack, only proved that the original concept of the Schlieffen plan had been based on a logical premise, that the direct route to Paris by way of Verdun or the other French fortress sites of Toul and Belfort that faced toward the German border presented too high a risk.

The contemporary leadership on both sides tended to place credit or blame regarding Verdun on individuals, rather than on the fundamentals of strategic balance between offense and defense. The command removed Falkenhayn and sent him to lead on the eastern front, where, in fact, his troops had rapid successes against the Romanians, who entered the war on the side of the Allies in August. Pétain, who had led the early defense at Verdun and who had planned the supply route along the Sacred Way, came to be hailed as the hero who had saved Verdun, but the government replaced him with General Robert Nivelle, who led the counterattacks against the Germans. After the campaign, the French removed by promotion the commander of all forces, General Joseph Joffre, and replaced him with Nivelle, who promised a more aggressive method of warfare.

THE SOMME

By mid-1916, the British sector of the front extended from around Ypres in Belgium down through Flanders to the Somme. There on the rolling hills on both sides of the River Somme, the British and French planned a major offensive. After a lengthy artillery barrage, British troops advanced on July 1. Due to inexperience and poor planning, the artillery shelling, with more than a million shells expended, did little to dislodge the German defenders. Shrapnel shells, useful against exposed personnel, had little effect on the deep German dug-outs, and they served only to throw the barbed wire entanglements into even worse tangles. When the artillery preparation stopped, the German defenders emerged from their bunkers and dugouts and took defensive positions in the damaged trenches and in new shell holes. The British advanced in three lines, almost shoulder to shoulder, only to quickly fall under machine-gun fire and shelling by German artillery. The slaughter increased to the point that in some sectors the Germans offered an informal truce and stopped firing to allow some of the surviving wounded to crawl back to their trenches. At the end of the first day, British deaths amounted to almost 20,000, the greatest single day's disaster for the British in all their military history. Later, as British troops advanced to take various small wooded sections, they sometimes suffered from what a later generation would call friendly fire, in which their own artillery pounded into their own ranks.

The French made slightly greater advances, and, here and there, took sections of the German line. However, when the Allied forces attempted to follow up with cavalry charges, disaster ensued. The German defenders, at first astonished to see mounted lancers with plumed helmets charging across no-man's-land, soon recovered their composure and struck down horse and rider alike with machine-gun and rifle fire. As at Verdun, the Battle of the Somme seesawed back and forth. In September, the British introduced a small number of tanks, thrown into the front at Flers and Courcelette, where their initial surprise value collapsed, as numbers broke down and others were knocked out by German shell fire. The British generals in particular earned criticism for lack of intelligent planning, simply falling back on the concept of pouring more men against machine-gun emplacements and attempting to wear down the enemy. By November, when the Battle of the Somme died down because of impenetrable mud, the British and French had lost some 600,000 casualties total. The British had advanced about six or seven miles on an 18-mile front, and the French had taken only slightly

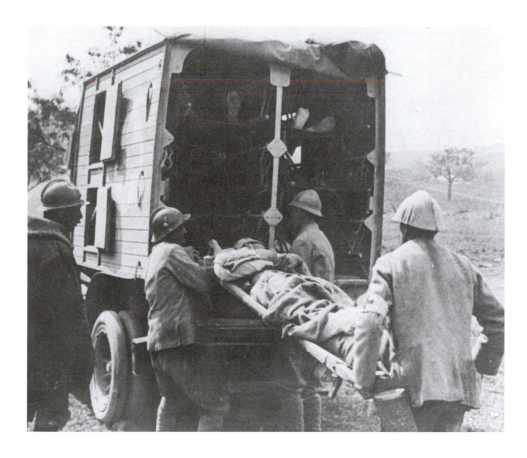

Wounded soldiers in the Somme were evacuated by motor ambulance. *(Library of Congress)*

more ground. No significant or strategic objectives or resources changed hands, and the dent made in the German lines had no lasting importance.

Even though no strategic advantage had been achieved by either side in the Somme or at Verdun, the German command reacted to the two great battles with a reassessment of tactics and leadership. At the end of August, when Hindenburg and Ludendorff took over the administration of the German war effort, they concluded that fundamental changes in how to handle defense, offense, and the management of the civilian war effort had to be undertaken.

TROUBLES ON THE HOME FRONTS

All of the major powers on the western front suffered from rebellion, mutiny, or uprisings on the home front during 1916. In Dublin, about 2,000 Irish Nationalists rose in a fruitless, ill-conceived, ill-executed rebellion against British rule on April 23. After the rebels took control of a few buildings, British troops subdued them and arrested and quickly executed some of the leaders. This Easter Rebellion and the swift retribution by the British had echoes in Irish and American public opinion, although Irish regiments, including those from the Catholic counties, continued to perform bravely on the western front. The Ulster Division of 15,000 men took part in the initial advance on the Somme, and some 5,000 died in the first two days of that battle.

In Germany and Austria, the British blockade and failing harvests due to the lack of agricultural manpower and loss of some producing regions in Galicia led to severe food shortages. As food prices climbed, only the wealthy could afford meat, dairy products, or decent bread, and the consequent gulf in diet between rich and poor and the presence of a thriving black market and smuggling operations fueled popular resentment. Food riots in both empires erupted over and over throughout 1916.

In August, the officer corps viewed a walkout by German sailors from the *Prinzregent Luitpold* as a major Socialist-led uprising. The few executions that followed only rankled the sailors, whose complaints about poor food, ill treatment by well-fed officers, and arbitrary punishment went unaddressed. These discontents would continue to simmer beneath the surface in the German navy, weakening morale.

In October, the assassination of the president of Austria and then the death of Emperor Franz Josef in November signaled the end of an era. Franz Josef's successor, Karl, sought to find a political strategy that would allow the empire to hold together. However, Franz Josef had already joined with the kaiser of Germany in promising that Poland would become an independent kingdom after the war; the Czechs had already risen in organized rebellion against the empire, and, throughout the Balkan provinces, south Serbs continued to demand a new South Slav state. Reconciliation with the empire's diverse populations and restoration of the glory days of the Dual Monarchy would be impossible. Austria and Hungary had become too tied to German policy to pursue an independent course, and signs surfaced that the Hungarian side of the empire rankled at control from Vienna in Austria.

The French too faced difficulties, with mounting resentment among the troops at foolish orders to advance in hopeless charges. As food and wine froze in the trenches, and as wounded men not fully recovered from their battles in the

Somme and Verdun returned to the fronts, morale dropped. When officers asked soldiers to subscribe to a new loan drive, many simply refused, sending back the forms with curses scrawled on them. By the end of 1916, the French had lost some 950,000 men either dead or captured.

France also faced a major uprising against its colonial rule in the Volta region of French West Africa. In that colony, when the French attempted to conscript men for their army on the western front in November 1915, a group of villages formed a league pledged to fight against colonial rule. After failing to exert control over the town of Bona, the French mounted an army of some 800 troops that soon confronted 10,000 determined rebel warriors. Despite superior firepower, the French had to retreat and the struggle continued into 1916. Through February and March 1916, the Volta–Bani war spread, with the French adopting ruthless tactics of taking hostages, slaughtering civilians, poisoning wells, and driving off livestock. Final "pacification" of the region came at the cost of 30,000 African rebels and noncombatants killed.

CHANGES IN THE CENTRAL POWERS

After his disappointments at Verdun, Falkenhayn took command on the Romanian front, where, by early December, German and Austrian forces drove Romanian defenders from the capital of Bucharest. General Paul von Hindenburg became head of the German General Staff and, along with General Erich von Ludendorff as quartermaster general, took charge of all German war planning. With victory over Romania assured, the Germans offered to negotiate a peace based on the status quo in December 1916, but the Allies made it clear they would not accept such terms. Hindenburg developed plans to mobilize the total German civilian population in war production.

He hoped to extend the so-called Hindenburg Program to Austria-Hungary as well, but there the young emperor Karl showed signs of resisting the scheme. Under the program, the total civilian industrial economy went on a war footing, regulated by the state. In effect, the system represented a type of war socialism rather than a free enterprise or market system, with planning of priorities, allocation of raw materials, and labor contracts all set by the state. Meanwhile, Hindenburg and Ludendorff secretly planned that if the Allies rejected the offer of a negotiated peace, by early in 1917 a campaign of unrestricted submarine warfare to isolate Britain would be put in place.

GERMAN INNOVATIONS

The debacles of Verdun and the Somme demonstrated to some officers and most survivors in the trenches the futility of existing tactics. The concept of destruction by attrition, in which the attacking side would set a standard of acceptable losses in order to gain a small section of the front, clearly did not work. However, despite dogged persistence in the old ways, signs could be detected that all three of the major combatants on the western front were beginning to experiment with or consider new weapons and new tactics.

The Germans pushed several technological innovations in their search for a way out of the disastrous paradoxes of the western front. Building larger zeppelins with longer range and capable of flying well above defending aircraft, the

Germans increased their air raids over Britain, bombing midland counties and London. Although such raids killed very small numbers of people by contrast to the losses on the western front, the raids required that Britain divert antiaircraft guns and troops from the front to areas around London to reassure workers. In order to control public panic, the British government prevailed on newspapers to refrain from publishing photographs of bomb destruction in London or reporting civilian casualties from the air raids.

In addition, Germans attempted other innovations. They continued to develop and employ poison gas, often combining it in artillery barrages with shrapnel and high-explosive shells to wreck morale. Meanwhile, they turned to new defensive methods on the front, using engineered construction rather than shovel-built fortifications. They planned and began building the Siegfried line, a heavily fortified defense in depth with concrete bunkers and machine-gun emplacements, constructing the line in secret in 1916 and preparing to withdraw to it in early 1917. The new line lay some 25 miles to the rear of their front with the Allies on the Somme. To assist in building the Siegfried line fortifications, the Germans recruited forced labor conscripted from conquered French and Belgian towns. When the Allies heard rumors of the construction, they dubbed the new defense the Hindenburg Line, but they remained unsure of its exact nature and location.

The fact that the Germans would eventually withdraw without a fight from regions the French and British had sacrificed hundreds of thousands of men to win only further demonstrated the folly of the Battle of the Somme. On the other hand, the German concern that their lines had been penetrated and that battles of attrition wore down their forces led them to adopt several other new methods, including not only more carefully engineered defensive lines but also

After 1916, aircraft of both sides participated in close ground support. Machine gunners on the ground brought down this German plane. *(National Archives)*

modified offensive tactics. They developed light-machine-gun companies and trained specialized units in the use of grenades and field mortars.

Germany continued to pour resources into other technologies. The Germans developed the new twin-gun Albatross D-1 biplane that played an important role in their defense in the Somme. In numerous dogfights on the Somme there, the German aviators outgunned their British opponents, although neither side established complete command of the air on that front. Increasingly, the Germans used aircraft in direct support of ground operations, not simply in artillery spotting, photo-reconnaissance, and attacks on enemy aircraft. Of course, the U-boat, another technologically advanced weapon system not used to its fullest capacity, represented another asset. Through 1916, German policy had restricted submarines by adhering to cruiser rules for the most part, requiring the warning of a target ship before sinking it. By August 1916, German strategists seriously considered using the submarine to its fullest advantage, without restrictions, enforcing a blockade with unannounced attacks on both Allied and neutral shipping.

ALLIED INNOVATIONS

The British seemed apparently the slowest to learn the lessons of the war on the western front. Some analysts have attributed the failure to adapt to the built-in conflict between the older Regular Army units that had made up the B.E.F. and the New Army of conscripts and new, hastily trained officers. Traditionally trained professional soldiers may have believed that rapidly trained officers and enlisted men could not handle the complexities of tactics and could understand only the simplest of procedures. Furthermore, officers with experience in the trenches rarely survived to take their lessons to the rear. In any case, the British persisted in the method of artillery barrage followed by massed attacks across the torn-up no-man's-land with troops carrying full, heavy packs against machine-gun emplacements. It would not be until later in 1917 that the British began to follow the German and French examples of open-formation advances, lightly equipped troops for fast movement, and combined attacks using close coordination with artillery and aircraft.

One innovation upon which the British did rely came with the invention of the tank, kept secret until its first deployment in September 1916 at Flers. That particular battle did not prove the usefulness of the tank, since the slow-moving monsters with top speeds of about three miles per hour could be easily sought out by small cannon and frequently broke down on their own; nevertheless, British officers planned larger tank attacks for 1917, with the advance to be followed up with rapid infantry movement. The glimmer of the concept of combined-weapon attack, using aircraft, tanks, and more intelligent use of mobile foot soldiers began to develop in 1916. The Germans emulated the tank, developing a huge vehicle with a 12-man crew, but limited resources and a lack of faith in the new device kept the number of German tanks extremely low, while both Britain and France rushed hundreds into production.

The French began to introduce a new tactic in October at Verdun, one that held promise for a new approach. Under General Nivelle, French artillery blasted enemy lines in a rolling barrage that moved forward at a set rate. Behind the accurate and advancing detonations, troops moved forward, not in shoulder-to-shoulder massed lines, but in smaller units, with specialists. Some carried machine

The British introduced tanks in 1916, and soon the Allies began employing them in numbers. *(National Archives)*

guns, while grenadiers rushed forward in open formation, taking cover individually as they advanced. The Germans had introduced a similar method, but when the French coupled it with extremely precise artillery barrages, the new tactics held promise of breaking the defensive lines far more effectively than the older, massed advance of waves of troops up and over the trench parapets into withering machine-gun fire after the cessation of an artillery barrage.

In both the French and British case, the home country sought to spare its own population the devastation by reaching out to its empire for manpower for the front lines. To make up for the losses of manpower, the French sought to bring in more African troops. At the same time, the British transferred from Gallipoli the Australian and New Zealand troops and sought more from Canada. Troops from India were usually used in supporting roles, and, when committed to battle, British officers expressed concern that the Indian veterans would return to India after the war with aspirations for independence, coupled with military experience that would make British control there difficult.

The new French commander in chief, Nivelle, like the new prime minister in Britain, David Lloyd George, committed himself to a more aggressive campaign to defeat Germany. Although the lessons of 1916 had suggested that the war would not end soon, the Allies faced the new year with a determination not to compromise but to fight vigorously and achieve a German surrender. The Germans, for their part, had decided that if no compromise would be forthcoming, the U-boat would be released to bring about British collapse. Hindenburg's plan for mobilization of the economy represented the conversion of the German state to a status of total war. So the fundamental lesson of the debacles of the battles of the Somme and Verdun, that the war itself had proven a useless and disastrous folly, seemed lost on both sides, as each faced 1917 with a determination to pour more resources, new weapons, and new methods into the effort to win.

CHRONICLE OF EVENTS

1915

December 19: The Germans make the first use of phosgene gas on the British front at Ypres and to the south of Ypres. Like prior efforts to use other gases as the primary weapon in attack, it fails.

December 19: General Douglas Haig is appointed commander in chief of British forces on the western front.

1916

January 27: The British promulgate the Military Service bill, ordering conscription of single men between the ages of 18 and 41, with exemptions for ministers, essential war-workers, the medically unfit, and conscientious objectors. Conscription is extended to married men in April. The Irish are excluded from conscription.

January 31: German zeppelin raids bomb towns in Lincoln, Leicester, Derby, and Stafford counties north of London; 70 people are killed.

February–March: The French suppress a widespread rebellion in the colony of French West Africa, killing as many as 30,000 rebels and defenseless civilians.

February 10: Rumors of a massive zeppelin attack cause panic in Britain as workers leave factories. The British will establish a home defense system with searchlight stations, antiaircraft weapons, and airplane bases for defense during the rest of the year.

February 21: The German offensive toward Verdun begins; French general Philippe Pétain declares, "They shall not pass." The Battle of Verdun will continue with German advances until July and with French counterattacks into November.

February 24: The Germans advance toward Verdun on the River Meuse.

February 25: The Germans take Fort Douaumont near Verdun.

April 9: Pétain orders a counterattack at Verdun, with the words *Courage, on les aura!* ("Courage, we'll get them!")

April 19: General Joseph Joffre orders Pétain replaced by General Robert Nivelle at Verdun.

April 23: The Easter Rising takes place in Dublin; about 2,000 Irish nationalists take on the British government. The rebellion is suppressed by artillery and its leaders will be executed.

June 2: Germans take Fort Vaux in their advance at Verdun.

June 5: Horatio Herbert, Lord Kitchener, is drowned while on a military advisory mission to Russia when the cruiser *Hampshire* sinks after striking a German mine off the Orkney Islands.

June 22: British aircraft bomb the German cities of Karlsruhe, Cologne, and Trier.

June 23: Germans take Thiaumont near Verdun.

July 1: The British begin attacks on the Somme River; the Battle of the Somme will continue until November. The British lose 20,000 troops on the first day of the battle, the single deadliest day in British military history.

July 16: The Germans reach the point of the greatest advance toward Verdun.

August 2: German sailors aboard the *Prinzregent Luitpold* stage a walkout that is treated as a mutiny, resulting in courts-martial and a few token executions. Officers react by treating it as an abortive socialist-led uprising rather than addressing the men's complaints about rations and treatment.

August 27: Romania declares war on Austria.

August 29: Paul von Hindenburg is appointed chief of the General Staff. Erich Ludendorff is appointed quartermaster general; in effect, he is in charge of all German military strategy.

September: Hindenburg states "Whoever does not work shall not eat."

September: Advances in the Somme take the British a total of three to four miles since the beginning of the offensive, reaching Delville Wood, known by the troops as Devil's Wood.

September 15: The British make their first use of tanks in a battle between the villages of Flers and Courcelette on the Somme front; the initial advance is driven back. The British believe this secret weapon holds the key to breaking the western front stalemate.

October 19: The French begin a series of counterattacks at Verdun. Under General Nivelle the French introduce the rolling barrage, followed by open formation advances at Verdun.

October 21: Austrian minister-president, Count Karl Stürgkh, is assassinated in Vienna.

October 24: Using new tactics, Moroccan and Senegalese troops in the French colonial army drive the Germans from Douaumont on the Verdun front.

November: Extensive food riots break out in Austria due to shortages caused by the conscription of peasant farmers and the loss of supplies from Galicia. The winter of 1916–17 is known as the turnip winter in Germany because potatoes become scarce; there are numerous food riots as well.

November 2: The French retake Fort Vaux after the Germans evacuate. Total French casualties at Verdun in 1916 are about 375,000; total German casualties are about 335,000. Verdun is the longest field battle in history, lasting more than eight months.

November 18: The British and French end their advance on the Somme, with total advances of about six to seven miles on a 30-mile front. The total Allied casualties during the Battle of the Somme are more than 600,000. The total British casualties on the Somme amount to about 1 percent of the total British population. The French take twice as much territory as the British, with fewer losses.

November 21: Emperor Franz Josef dies; Karl (Charles) Franz Josef succeeds him. Karl resists Hindenburg's plans to totally mobilize the Austro-Hungarian economy along German lines.

December 1–5: German forces capture 70,000 Romanian prisoners.

December 5: Germany mobilizes its civilian population with the Auxiliary Service law, adopting a form of war socialism. The scheme is known as the Hindenburg program and is coordinated by a supreme war office.

December 6: The Romanian capital, Bucharest, is taken by German troops.

December 7: A coalition government under David Lloyd George takes over in Britain, pledged to a more vigorous conduct of the war.

December 12: An offer of negotiated peace is made by the Central Powers to be based on the current status quo.

December 13: General Robert Nivelle replaces General Joseph Joffre as commander in chief of the French

This British Red Cross orderly aids a captured and wounded German trooper to a field hospital. *(Library of Congress)*

armies due to the losses at Verdun; Nivelle is pledged to a more aggressive approach.

December 30: The British and French cabinets decide against accepting the offer of the Central Powers for a negotiated peace based on the current status quo.

EYEWITNESS TESTIMONY

Then out of the blue came the German attack on Verdun, with the capture of fort Douaumont. Would the Crown Prince break through? What was the British new army doing—the French partizans were asking—why didn't it help the French? I received telephone calls asking me if the French could hold. After the third day I said that I thought they could; the German attack had slowed down as all major offensives had against the siege line. A new hero had flashed into fame, Pétain, with his "They shall not pass," with no mention of Castlenau who saw the danger in time and planned the defense.

Frederick Palmer, commenting on the German attack on Verdun on February 5, 1916, in his With My Own Eyes, *p. 327.*

I have a feeling that the attack at Verdun must succeed—succeed, not because of the number of guns and attacking troops, but because of the more general reason that war must be directed in the last resource, not against positions and armies, not against a State, but against human weaknesses. When they appear there is no more hope. The French are abandoning absolutely impregnable positions. No trip to Rome, no council of War, no talk of glory, and no Army Order can prevail against that.

It may take a long time yet. Of course this feeling does not portend the end of the War by a long way, particularly against a coalition. Thanks to her command of the seas England will take less notice of it than anyone. That cannot be helped at present. But when Verdun falls—and I believe, subject to reserves, that it will fall—the Frenchman will lose the butter off his war-bread to say the least; and I doubt whether he will still care to eat it then.

German officer Rudolf Bunting, commenting on the German chances of success at Verdun on February 26, 1916, in his collection of letters, A Fatalist at War, *p. 94.*

We are living these days in the atmosphere of the great battle of Verdun. We talk Verdun all day, dream Verdun all night—in fact, the thought of that great attack in the east absorbs every other idea. Not in the days of the Marne, nor in the trying days of Ypres or the Aisne was the tension so terrible as it is now. No one believes that Verdun can be taken, but the anxiety is dreadful, and the idea of what the defence is costing is never absent from the minds even of those who are firmly convinced of what the end must be. . . .

You have only to look on a map to know how important the position is at Verdun, the supposed-to-be-strongest of the four great fortresses—Verdun, Toul, Epinay, and Belfort—which protect the only frontier by which the Kaiser has a military right to try to enter France, and which he avoided on account of its strength.

Verdun itself is only one day's march from Metz. If you study it up on a map you will learn that, within a circuit of thirty miles, Verdun is protected by thirty-six redoubts. But what you will not learn is that this great fortification is not yet connected with its outer redoubts by the subterranean passages which were part of the original scheme. It is that fact which is disturbing. Every engineer in the French army knows that the citadel at Metz has underground communications with all its circle of outer ramparts. Probably every German engineer knows that Verdun's communication passages were never made. Isn't it strange (when we remember that, even in the days of walled cities, there were always subterraneans leading out of the fortified towns beyond the walls—wonderful works of masonry, intact today, like those of Provins, and even here on this hill) that a nation which did not want war should have left unfinished the protection of such a costly fortress?

You probably knew, as usual, before we did, that the battle had begun. We knew nothing of it here until February 23, three days after the bombardment began, with the French outer lines nine miles outside the city, although only twenty-four hours after was the full force of the German artillery let loose, with fourteen German divisions waiting to march against the three French divisions holding the position. Can you wonder we are anxious? . . .

When communications were opened the news we got was not consoling. First phase of the battle closed six days ago—with the Germans in Douaumont, and the fight still going on—but the spirit of the French not a jot changed. Here, among the civilians, they say, "Verdun will never fall," and out at the front, they tell us that the *poilus* simply hiss through their clenched teeth, as they fight and fall, "They *shall* not pass." And all the time we sit inactive on the hilltop holding that thought. It's all we can do.

Mildred Aldrich, in a letter dated March 2, 1916, describing reaction of the French people to the defense of Verdun, On the Edge of the War Zone, *pp. 183–185.*

There is nothing for anyone to do but wait for news from the front. It is the same old story—they are see-sawing at Verdun, with the Germans much nearer than at the beginning—and still we have the firm faith that they will never get there. Doesn't it seem to prove that had Germany fought an honest war she could never have invaded France?

Mildred Aldrich, in a letter dated April 28, 1916, in her From the Edge of the War Zone, *p. 189.*

On the first of July 1916, an offensive on the Somme was started and our division was now in the thick of it. This was a change from the previous engagements, as our munition and armament factories in Britain had been working at top pressure for months and we had ample supplies of guns and ammunition and could give "Fritz" shell for shell.

I had left the stretcher bearers and during the Somme offensive I was fighting in the ranks and went "Over the Top," this time with rifle and bayonet. After severe fighting we took Friecourt, our first objective, and after entering the village the prisoners were collected, and I was detailed to escort prisoners to the cages and to remain as one of the sentries until relieved.

Canadian lance corporal Edmund Hall, 2nd Scottish Rifles, B.E.F., during the Somme offensive, July 1, 1916, in What the "Boys" Did over There by "Themselves," *p. 175.*

It looked like victory, because of the German dead that lay there in their battered trenches and the filth and stench of death over all that mangled ground, and the enormous destruction wrung by our guns, and the fury of fire which we were still pouring over the enemy's lines from batteries which had moved forward.

I went down flights of steps into German dugouts, astonished by their depth and strength. Our men did not build like this. This German industry was a rebuke to us—yet we had captured their work and the dead bodies of their laborers lay in those dark caverns, killed by our bombers, who had flung down hand-grenades. I drew back from those fat corpses. They looked monstrous, lying there crumpled up, amid a foul litter of clothes, stick-bombs, old boots, and bottles. Groups of dead lay in ditches which had once been trenches, flung into chaos by that bombardment. They had been bayoneted. I remember one man—an elderly fellow—sitting up with his back to a bit of earth with his hands half raised. He was smiling a little, though he had been stabbed through the belly and was stone dead....Vic-tory! . . . some of the German dead were young boys, too young to be killed for old men's crimes, and others might have been old or young. One could not tell, because they had no faces, and were just masses of raw flesh in rags and uniforms. Legs and arms lay separate, without any bodies thereabouts....

Victory? . . . Well, we had gained some ground, and many prisoners, and here and there some guns. But as I stood by Montauban I saw that our line was a sharp salient looped round Mametz village and then dipping sharply southward to Fricourt. O God! had we only made another salient after all that monstrous effort.

Philip Gibbs, English war correspondent on July 2, 1916, describing his encounter with German dead after a minor advance on the Somme, in Now It Can Be Told, *pp. 364–365.*

July 2

After the night's roar of bombardment we waited for the zero hour when the infantry should go over the top. How often I have waited for that! In spite of the long leaping sheets of flame from the guns and mortars I had no sense of the glamour of war, as I had in Greece looking out on the spectacle on the Thessalian plain. There might have been a touch of the old glamour if this new army, after a few weeks' drilling, had gone against another force as little trained, in the catch-as-catch can that would have ended the struggle in a few hours, but not in the agony of the minds of soldiers as the seconds ticked off to the zero second, not in the thought of figures in khaki breasting artillery barrages and machine-gun fire across No Man's Land.

We know the long battle of the Somme; we know how in the initial attack the British left was murderously checked and the British right took some ground, and how the French, who had still less opposition, took more. The privilege of being a correspondent at the front allowed me to go over captured No Man's Land and captured trenches and villages and see the English faces of youth I had seen drilling at Aldershot now white and still in death. This they had known might be their portion in the mill with none of the compensations of the romance of the wars of old before they fell.

Frederick Palmer, July 2, 1916, commenting on the initial advances on the Somme, in With My Own Eyes, *p. 330.*

A taste, just a taste, of action the cavalry was to have, owing to the success of the attack of July 14, which manifestly took the Germans by surprise between High and Delville Woods and left them staggering with second-line trenches lost and confusion ensuing, while guns and scattered battalions were being hurried up by train in an indiscriminate haste wholly out of keeping with German methods of prevision and precision. The breach was narrow, the field of action for horses limited; but word came back that over the plateau which looked away to Bapaume between Delville and High Woods there were few shell-craters and no German trenches or many Germans in sight as day dawned.

Gunners rubbed their eyes at the vision as they saw the horsemen pass and infantry stood amazed to see them crossing trenches, Briton and Indian on the way up the slope to the Ridge. How they passed the crest without being decimated by a curtain of fire would be a mystery if there were any mysteries in this war, where everything seems to be worked out like geometry or chemical formulae. The German artillery being busy withdrawing heavy guns and the other guns preoccupied after the startling results of an attack not down on the calendar for that day did not have time to "get on" the cavalry when they were registered on different targets—which is suggestive of what might come if the line were cleft over a broad front. A steel band is strong until it breaks, which may be in many pieces. . . .

The cavalry had done everything quite according to tactics, which would only confuse the layman. The wonder was that any of it had come back alive. On that narrow front it had ridden out toward the German Army with nothing between the cavalry and the artillery and machine guns which had men on horses for targets. In respect to days when to show a head above a trench meant death the thing was stupefying, incredible.

Frederick Palmer, reporting on a cavalry charge of July 14, 1916, in the Battle of the Somme, in his memoir, My Second Year of the War, *pp. 183, 186.*

On July 17th I stood in a tent by a staff-officer who was directing a group of heavy guns supporting the 3rd Division. He was tired, as I could see by the black lines under his eyes and tightly drawn lips. On a camp table in front of him, upon which he leaned his elbows, there was a telephone apparatus, and the little bell kept ringing as we talked. Now and then a shell burst in the field outside the tent, and he raised his head and said: "They keep crumping about here. Hope they won't tear this tent to ribbons. . . . That sounds like a gas-shell."

Then he turned to the telephone again and listened to some voice speaking.

"Yes I can hear you. Yes, go on. 'Our men seen leaving High Wood.' Yes. 'Shelled by our artillery.' Are you sure of that? I say, are you sure they were our men? Another message. Well, carry on. 'Men digging on road from High Wood southeast to Longueval, I've got that. 'They are our men and not Boches.' Oh, hell! . . . Get off the line. Get off the line, can't you? . . . Our men and not Boches.' Yes I have that. 'Heavily shelled by our guns.'"

The staff officer tapped on the table with a lead-pencil a tattoo, while his forehead puckered. Then he spoke into the telephone again.

"Are you there, 'Heavies'? . . . Well, don't disturb those fellows for half an hour. After that I will give you new orders. Try and confirm if they are our men."

He rang off and turned to me.

"That's the trouble. Looks as if we had been pounding our own men like hell. Some damn fool reports 'Boches.' Gives the reference number. Asks for 'Heavies'. Then some other fellow says, 'Not Boches. For God's sake cease fire!' How is one to tell?"

I could not answer that question, but I hated the idea of our men sent forward to capture a road or a trench or a wood and then "pounded" by our guns. They had enough pounding from the enemy's guns. There seemed a missing link in the system somewhere. Probably it was quite inevitable.

Philip Gibbs, July 17, 1916, describing an episode of casualties from friendly fire, in Now It Can Be Told, *pp. 382–383.*

When the battle of the Somme began the Entente had a tremendous superiority both on land and in the air. General Headquarters was surprised at first. Reinforcements were thrown in, but it had never succeeded in wiping out the enemy's superiority in artillery, munitions, and aircraft, even to a limited extent.

The Entente troops had worked their way farther and farther into the German lines. We had heavy losses in men and material. At that time the front lines were still strongly held. The men took refuge in dugouts and cellars from the enemy's artillery fire. The enemy infantry, coming up behind their barrage, got into the trenches and villages before our men could crawl out from their shelters. A continuous yield of prisoners to

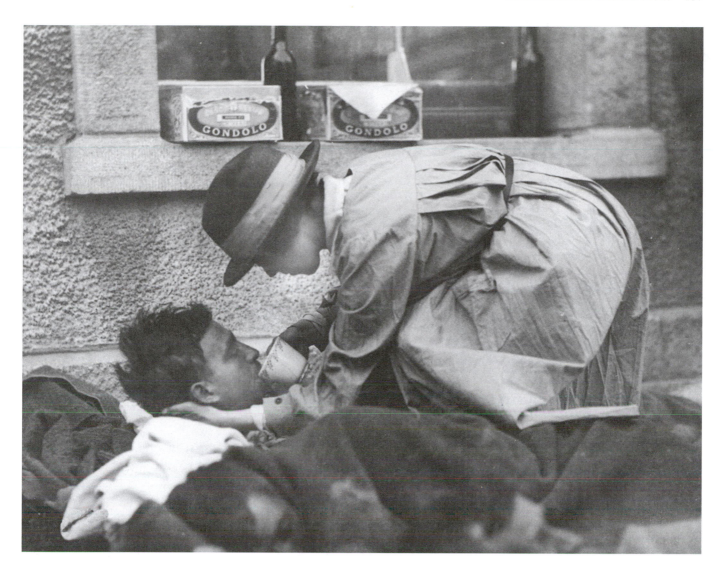

An American Red Cross worker provides water to a wounded British soldier awaiting evacuation at a French railroad station. *(National Archives)*

the enemy was the result. The strain on physical and moral strength was tremendous, and divisions could be kept in the line only for a few days at a time. They had to be frequently relieved and sent to recuperate on quiet fronts. It was impossible to leave them behind the line—we had not enough men. The number of available divisions was shrinking. In view of the shortage of artillery, it was now kept in the line, even when the divisions were relieved. Divisions which were released by battle-worn divisions had, in turn, to leave their artillery behind them and come up behind the battle-front. The result was that units were hopelessly mixed up.

Erich von Ludendorff's assessment of problems when he took office as quartermaster general on August 29, 1916, in Ludendorff's Own Story, *pp. 289–290.*

The course of the Somme battle had also supplied important lessons with respect to the construction and plan of our lines. The very deep underground forts in the front trenches had to be replaced by shallower constructions. Concrete "pill-boxes," which, however, unfortunately, took long to build, had acquired an increasing value. The conspicuous lines of trenches, which appeared as sharp lines on every aerial photograph, supplied far too good a target for the enemy artillery. The whole system of defense had to be made broader and looser and better adapted to the ground. The large, thick barriers of wire, pleasant as they were when there was little doing, were no longer a protection. They withered under the enemy barrage. Light strands of wire, difficult to see, were much more useful. Forward infantry positions with a wide field of fire were easily seen by the enemy.

Erich von Ludendorff, commenting on conclusions reached at a conference at Cambrai, September 7, 1916, in Ludendorff's Own Story, *p. 322.*

Officers and crew were sealed up in a steel box, the sport of destiny. For months they had been preparing for this day, the crowning experiment and test, and all seemed of a type carefully chosen for their part, soldiers who had turned land sailors, cool and phlegmatic like the monsters they directed. Each one having given himself up to fate, the rest was easy in these days of war's super-exaltation, which makes men appear perfectly normal when death hovers near. Not one would have changed places with any infantryman. Already they had *esprit de corps.* They belong to an exclusive set of warriors.

Lumberingly dipping in and out of shell-craters, which sometimes half concealed the tanks like ships in a choppy sea, rumbling and wrenching they appeared out of the morning mist in face of the Germans who put up their heads and began working their machine guns after the usual artillery curtain of fire had lifted. . . .

A tactical system of coordinated action had been worked out for the infantry and the untried auxiliary, which only experienced soldiers could have applied with success. According to the nature of the positions in front, the tanks were set definite objectives or left to find their own objectives. They might move on located machine gun positions or answer a hurry call for help from the infantry. Ahead of them was a belt of open field between them and the villages whose capture was to be the consummation of the day's work. While observers were straining their eyes to follow the progress of the tanks and seeing but little, corps headquarters eagerly awaited news of the most picturesque experiment of the war, which might prove ridiculous, or be a wonderful success, or simply come up to expectations.

No more thrilling message was ever brought by an aeroplane than that which said that a tank was "walking" up the main street of Flers surrounded by cheering British soldiers, who were in possession of the village. "Walking" was the word officially given; and very much walking, indeed, the tank must have seemed to the aviator in his swift flight. An eagle looked down on a tortoise which had a serpent's sting. This tank, having attended to its work on the way, passed on through Flers bearing a sign: "Extra Special! Great Hun Victory!" Beyond Flers it found itself alongside a battery of Ger-

man field guns and blazed bullets into the amazed and helpless gunners.

The enemy may have heard of the tanks, but meeting them was a different matter. After he had fought shells, bullets, bombs, grenades, mortars, bayonets and gas, the tank was the straw that broke the camel's back of many a German. A steel armadillo laying its bulk across a trench and sweeping it on both sides with machine guns brought the familiar complaint that this was not fighting according to rules in a war which ceased to have rules after the bombing of civilian populations, the sinking of the *Lusitania,* and the gas attack at Ypres. It depends on whose ox is gored. . . .

Germans surrendered to a tank in bodies after they saw the hopelessness of turning their own machine gun and rifle fire upon that steel hide.

Frederick Palmer, commenting on the first tank attack through Flers, September 25, 1916, in his memoir, My Second Year of the War, *pp. 347–350.*

Rushed out of the pleasant atmosphere of an English hospital into France, thence to Arras, to help extend the British front, was my next little bit of adventure. Arras at that time was a sort of resting place, as the fighting there was not half so severe as at Gallipoli, and besides it was held on a fifty-fifty basis, the Germans holding one-half the village and the British the other.

Vimy Ridge, nearby, and Arras were well sown with mines, and this being known to the enemy, we were not molested by surprise attacks as we otherwise would have been. Close upon Arras stood Devil's Wood, a point of vantage to whichever side could hold it. It was a much sought after place and had recently been wrested from the British. It was up to the newcomers, mostly from the 1st King's Liverpool Regiment, to regain it. Needless to say we did this thoroughly and kept on advancing to Fleurs [Flers].

At this stage of the game a great surprise was sprung on us. We were keyed up to the highest point, ready for battle, and it was to be our first attack on Fleurs, when of a sudden we were drenched by a deluge of tear shells. A tear shell is one of the meanest of all shells as it gives out a poison that causes the tear ducts to turn almost inside out and the tears, which continually flow, change to a sickly looking green fluid. On top of that, we were also treated to a breakfast of liquid gas and believe me, I got my fill on that memorable morning. . . .

It was "Zero Hour" and we were nervously awaiting the word to go over, when five huge, lumbering

This photo shows two men in a Whippet tank. The turret could be turned manually. *(National Archives)*

monsters crept forward from our lines. Could this be a bad dream, or were we seeing things. But look! They are spitting fire! They don't stop! Down into a trench and over they go. Barbed wire is like a spider's web to them! God! how they travel, these animated blocks of steel. They look like caterpillars or frogs. They look like every living thing that crawls, and the enemy's shells fall from them like water from a duck's back. Onward they go and we are told to follow them. The rest is history. They were the first five "tanks" used in the war and, at once, were recognized as the most terrible of all engines of destruction. Their presence revived our fellows as though an electric current had passed through them. These first "tanks" were a symbol of our strength and determination to win and when we saw them sweep forward majestically, literally eating up the Hun devils, my heart was glad, and the pain of my wounds vanished. The boys now had a fighting chance against the wicked machinations of the foe. We had gone the enemy one better, at his own game of inventions, and Victory was only a question of building more "tanks" behind which the infantry could find shelter in the attack.

Account by British sergeant Mark L. Nicholson, September 25, 1916, describing his first view of tanks, in Henry Fox, editor, What the "Boys" Did over There by "Themselves," *pp. 140–141.*

The battle of the Somme was the biggest offensive during 1916. Considerable ground was taken, and thou-

sands of Germans captured. We were sent to the Bethune front, which was at the time a quiet sector in comparison to the Somme, and there we did trench duty for six weeks before being returned once again to the Somme.

On the 23rd of October we again attacked and gained more ground. By this time the Somme battlefield was a land of shell-holes and mud. The hardships we had to undergo were terrible. The bombardments never ceased, and some times it increased to drum fire. For the next few months we remained on this front, this being my third winter in the trenches, I was beginning to be "fed up" with the whole thing.

Canadian lance corporal Edmund Hall, 2nd Scottish Rifles, B.E.F., October 23, 1916, describing his experiences on the Somme in Henry Fox, editor, What the "Boys" Did over There by "Themselves," *p. 177.*

Verdun was German valor at its best and German gunnery at its mightiest, the effort of Colossus shut in a ring of steel to force a decision; and the high-water mark of German persistence was where you stood on the edge of the area of mounds that shells had heaped and craters that shells had scooped by the concentration of fire on Fort Souville. A few Germans in the charge reached here, but none returned. The survivors entered Verdun, the French will tell you with a shrug, as prisoners. Down the bare slope with its dead grass blotched by crater the eye travels and then up another slope to a crest which you see as a cumulus of shell-tossed earth under an occasional shell-burst. That is Douaumont, whose taking cost the Germans such prolonged and bloody effort and aroused the Kaiser to a florid outburst of laudation of his Brandenburgers who, by its capture, had, as Germany then thought, brought France to her death-gasp. . . .

Fort Vaux, on another crest at the right was still in German hands, but that, too, was to be regained in the next rush. Yes it was good to be at Verdun after Douaumont had been retaken, standing where you would have been in range of a German sniper a week before. Turning as on a pivot, you could identify through the glasses all the positions whose names are engraved on the French mind. Not high these circling hills, the keystone of a military arch, but taken together it was clear how, in this as in other wars, they were nature's bastion at the edge of the plain that lay a misty line in the distance.

Either in front or to the rear of Souville toward Verdun the surprising thing was how few soldiers you saw and how little transport within range of German guns; which impressed you with the elastic system of the French, who are there and are not there. Let an attack by the Germans develop and soldiers would spring out of the earth and the valleys echo with the thunder of guns. A thrifty people, the French.

When studying those hills that had seen the greatest German offensive after I had seen the offensive on the Somme, I thought of all that the summer had meant on the Western front, beginning with Douaumont lost and ending with Douaumont regained and the sweep over the conquered Ridge [on the Somme].

Frederick Palmer, reflections at Verdun in November 1916, in My Second Year of the War, *pp. 395–397.*

The struggle of men from one low ridge to another low ridge in a territory forty miles wide by more than twenty miles deep, during five months of fighting, was enormous in its intensity and prolongation of slaughter, wounding, and endurance of all hardships and terrors of war. As an eye-witness I saw the full scope of the bloody drama. I saw day by day the tidal waves of wounded limping back, until two hundred and fifty thousand men had passed through our casualty clearing stations, and then were not finished. I went among these men when the blood was wet on them, and talked with hundreds of them, and heard their individual narratives of escapes from death until my imagination was saturated with the spirit of their conflict of body and soul. I saw a green, downy countryside, beautiful in its summer life, ravaged by gun-fire so that the white chalk of its subsoil was flung above the earth and grass in a wide, sterile stretch of desolation pitted with shell-craters, ditched by deep trenches, whose walls were hideously upheaved by explosive fire, and littered yard after yard, mile after mile, with broken wire, rifles, bombs, unexploded shells, rags of uniform, dead bodies, or bits of bodies, and all the filth of battle. I saw many villages flung into ruin or blown clean off the map. I walked into such villages as Contalmaison, Martinpuich, Le Sars, Thilloy, and at last Bapaume, when a smell of burning and the fumes of explosives and the stench of dead flesh rose up to one's nostrils and one's very soul, when our dead and German dead lay about, and newly wounded came walking through the ruins or were carried shoulder high on stretchers, and consciously and subconsciously the living, unwounded men who went through these places knew that death lurked about them and around them and above them, and at any second might make

its pounce upon their own flesh. I saw our men going into battle with strong battalions and coming out of it with weak battalions. I saw them in the midst of battle at Thièpval, at Contalmaison, at Guillemont, by Loup-art Wood, when they trudged toward lines of German trenches, bunching a little in groups, dodging shell-bursts, falling in single figures or in batches, and fighting over the enemy's parapets. I sat with them in their dugouts before battle and after battle, saw their bodies gathered up for burial, heard their snuffle of death in hospital, sat by their bedside when they were sorely wounded. So the full tragic drama of that long conflict on the Somme was burned into my brain and I was, as it were, a part of it, and I am still seared with its remembrance, and shall always be.

Philip Gibbs, British war correspondent, describing his horror at conditions during the Battle of the Somme in December 1916, in Now It Can Be Told, *p. 394.*

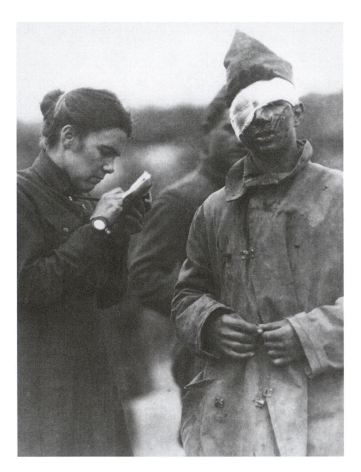

A Salvation Army worker helps a blinded soldier write home to his family. *(National Archives)*

The battle here is the epitome of everything which the War represents to-day; that is to say, constantly repeated destruction, constant putting forth of effort, development of power and means, employment of masses of men and material, constant physical and mental strain.

For me, too, this is the greatest effort of the War. It takes hours to cover even a portion of our position at night. One wades waist deep through shell-holes filled with mud; one crawls through the passages of dug-outs, cut thirty feet deep in the rock, under fallen trees, over plank bridges of the most damnable slipperiness, often in sight of the enemy, and every now and then caught in a burst of shell-fire or held up by a barrage.

The transport has to plough its way with horses and wagons through the mud at night in order to take the troops their rations, the guns their ammunition. Their way is marked by dead horses; many of them fall without being hit, and the mud closes over them. But ammunition, rations, trenching material, and all the rest has to be got up; there's no rest at night. In the morning we crawl home, plastered with mud, horse and rider stiff with cold, our heads sunk on our chests, dead tired and worn out. Every few yards along the roads, which are now worn deep below their edges, are posted Russian prisoners, who are supposed to shovel the mud aside. Day after day they stand helpless, for, however much they shovel, the mud bath never grows less.

German officer Rudolf Binting, commenting on conditions on the western front on December 26, 1916, in A Fatalist at War, *pp. 140–141.*

7

Woodrow Wilson and the Dilemmas of Neutrality
August 1914–January 1917

American neutrality might have at first seemed a simple matter at the outbreak of war in Europe. The United States had no alliances that required siding with any of the belligerent powers. The nation had remained neutral in the several wars that had swept Europe since 1815, including the Austro-Prussian War, the Franco-Prussian War, and the Crimean War. From the perspective of the United States, the Great War that broke out in August 1914 appeared as another in a series of conflicts spurred on by the corrupt European system of balance of power, one that should be resolved by negotiation, possibly arbitration, border adjustment, and other diplomatic means, not by force of arms. Certainly the United States had no reason to become involved in the senseless slaughter that swept Europe, or so it seemed at first.

NEUTRALITY: TRADITIONAL, PRACTICAL, AND ETHICAL

George Washington, in his Farewell Address in 1796, had warned Americans against becoming involved in alliances, and, although he never used the phrase *entangling alliances* in that speech, he had indeed advised against such alliances in slightly different phrasing. Washington had said, "Why quit our own to stand upon foreign ground? Why, by interweaving our destiny with that of any part of Europe, entangle our peace and prosperity in the toils of European ambition, rivalship, interest, humor, or caprice? It is our true policy to steer clear of permanent alliances with any portion of the foreign world. . . ."[1] That concept had become so much a basis for American foreign policy that no president had varied from it in the nearly 120 years since Washington had declared it, and Wilson had no intention of breaking with that tradition.

However, American neutrality would face numerous challenges in the period between August 1914 and February 1917. Many Americans had ethnic ties with one side or the other; the diverse origins of the American population made neutrality appear not only traditional but also very practical. But American trade with Europe, either with the Allies or with the Central Powers, threatened to involve the United States in the conflict. The diplomatic and legal pathway through this trade dilemma would consume much of the time of Wilson and the

State Department during the first 32 months of World War I. Wilson's attempt to find a strictly neutral course of action through both the ethnic loyalties and the shipping and trade issues worked for a while, but his position angered both those who favored entering the war and those who opposed it.

As a population of immigrants and their descendants, the American people certainly had reason to have divided loyalties. Although a majority could trace their ancestry to one of the nations of the Allies, including Britain, France, Russia, and Italy, many regions and cities of the United States were heavily populated by people of German ancestry. Furthermore, Irish-Americans, like the population of the southern counties of Ireland, resented British failure to grant Home Rule to Ireland. With German Americans, Irish Americans, and other groups such as Hungarians feeling affinity to the Central Powers or at least animosity to Britain, many feared that favoring either side in the European conflict could lead to civil war in the United States. Both Wilson and American statesman and politician William Jennings Bryan stated that the diverse ethnic roots of Americans were a leading reason to choose neutrality.

Many Americans were shocked at the news from the war zones and horrified at rumors of atrocities and destruction of cities. The ravaging of neutral Belgium and the French countryside by Germany appalled newspaper readers. The British established an official propaganda agency at Wellington House in London, where staff members diligently collected stories of atrocities, both real and fabricated, to help convince American public opinion that German soldiers systematically raped, pillaged, and burned their way across Belgium. With British control of undersea cables, nearly all news of the war flowed through British censors, and editors and writers often generated stories with the intent to win America to the Allied side. At the same time, as Wilson sought to establish even-handed neutral policies, critics charged him with being too tolerant of British transgressions of international law. British censorship of the news, refusal to allow newspaper correspondents to approach the front, and the British blockade of Germany, which by 1915 led to food shortages and malnutrition, all shocked American sensibilities. The death of innocent women and children, caused by German submarine torpedo attacks on merchant and passenger ships, the bombing of civilians in Antwerp, the shelling and burning of churches, the execution of civilian enemy collaborators by both sides, all caused consternation in the United States. The 1915 holocaust against Christian Armenians in Turkey seemed unbelievable and added to the disgust and horror Americans felt at the war. With grotesque acts being committed by both sides, to many thoughtful Americans, it seemed wise to steer clear of engagement, for idealistic and moral, as well as traditional and practical self-interest reasons.

While many Americans believed that Wilson advised the best course, a strict neutrality, others believed that the United States had a more appropriate choice: build up arms, ships, and military training so as to be able to participate effectively, probably on the side of the democracies of Britain and France against the autocratic regimes of Germany and Austria-Hungary. Although the precise causes of the war in the conflict between Serbia and Austria-Hungary appeared murky and difficult to unravel with objectivity, some of Wilson's closest advisers came to accept the British view that Germany committed serious crimes in its ruthless refusal to recognize Belgian neutrality and in brutally crushing Belgian resistance. Advocates of preparedness included many Republican Progressives, like

Many woman leaders were pacifists who adopted protest methods to demonstrate for their rights and their beliefs. *(National Archives)*

Theodore Roosevelt, and they pushed a program of voluntary training. At the other extreme, many politically active leaders, especially in the women's movement, were advocates of pacifism, and they urged Wilson to act as peacemaker to convene a peace conference at which to bring about a negotiated settlement.

Despite the pressures from militarists and pacifists, from pro-British and pro-German advocates, and from businesspeople who were able to increase employment and revenues by increased sales of manufactured goods to Britain and France, especially transport equipment and explosives, as long as trade with the Allies could be maintained, Wilson steered a neutral course for two and a half years, from August 1914 through February 1917. As he did so, the American people became familiar with the quirks of his personality, his precise and formal manner of speaking, his moral certainty, and his stern idealism. For some, those traits were endearing; for others, they were infuriating. A symptom of how divisive Wilson's own personality and decisions became showed up with his narrow electoral victory in the presidential election of 1916, when a switch of less than 2,000 votes in California would have resulted in his losing to his Republican opponent, Charles Evans Hughes. One of the closest elections in American history, it took several days to fully tally the vote and reveal Wilson as the winner.

William Jennings Bryan, Wilson's secretary of state, aroused equally controversial responses. Noted as a powerful orator in the style of evangelical preachers, Bryan had crusaded in the 1890s against monopolies, banks, and corporations, advocating an inflationary doctrine of increased coinage of silver to raise prices of farm commodities and diminish the power of vested capital. He had been the Democratic nominee for the presidency in 1896, 1900, and 1908. Wilson had chosen Bryan, as he did many of his cabinet and other high-level appointments, as a pay-off for political support in the 1912 elections, not for any special competence, and Bryan had never shown much interest in foreign affairs or defense policy. Bryan had handled Wilson's nomination at the Democratic national convention in 1912 and had delivered an average of 10 speeches a day during Wilson's campaign for the presidency. Bryan showed little interest in the legal minutiae of memoranda, precedent, and international law, but, like Wilson, Bryan expressed a firm commitment to a strict isolation from the entanglement of European war.

Even before Wilson announced his official neutral policy in a speech to Congress, Bryan quietly indicated to the banking community that it would be inappropriate to loan money to any belligerent nation or purchasing agency in those countries. With his August 15, 1914, letter to J. P. Morgan, he set a policy that, had it been strictly adhered to, would have limited American sales of goods to the warring European powers to the amount of American funds they already held. In explaining his policy to Wilson, Bryan stated that he believed a refusal to loan money to the belligerents would help shorten the war. He also pointed out that if the citizens of the United States made loans to the countries they favored, the country would be further divided into two camps. Expressions of sympathy based on ethnic connections would become combined with what he called "pecuniary interests," his rather old-fashioned way of referring to economic motivation. Furthermore, the powerful banking interests, he argued, would make an effort through newspapers to influence public opinion in favor of the country to whom they loaned the money. Bryan's position on this score carried echoes of earlier campaigns he had fought against the banking interests. However, the "ban" that he placed on loans to the belligerent powers took the shape of a simple request from the secretary of state to the bankers, not an official law or executive order. The informally stated policy worked effectively for a period of about one year, from August 1914 to September 1915.

Four days after Bryan requested the bankers to refrain from loaning money to the belligerents, Wilson addressed Congress. He made a strong plea for impartiality.

Every man who really loves America will act and speak in the true spirit of neutrality, which is the spirit of impartiality and fairness and friendliness to all concerned. The spirit of the nation in this critical matter will be determined largely by what individuals and society and those gathered in public meetings do and say, upon what newspapers and magazines contain, upon what ministers utter in their pulpits, and men proclaim as their opinions upon the street.

The people of the United States are drawn from many nations, and chiefly from the nations now at war. It is natural and inevitable that there should be the utmost variety of sympathy and desire among them with regard to the issues and circumstances of the conflict.... Such divisions amongst us would be fatal to our peace of mind and might seriously stand in the way of the proper performance of our duty as the one great nation at peace, the one people holding itself ready to play a part of impartial mediation and speak the counsels of peace and accommodation, not as a partisan, but as a friend.... We must be impartial in thought, as well as action, must put a curb upon our sentiments, as well as upon every transaction that might be construed as a preference of one party to the struggle before another.[2]

Despite Wilson's often convoluted speaking and writing style, from time to time, his formal prose would result in a very memorable phrase, sometimes lifted by the press in order to encapsulate his thinking in a few words. From this address, the public remembered the advice to "be impartial in thought, as well as action," and, although ethnic groups found it difficult to always heed the warning, it set the tone for Wilson's effort to steer through the dilemmas presented by the war. Those dilemmas soon deepened.

BLOCKADE AND RESPONSE

As the British began their blockade of shipping to Germany, they adopted the rule of "continuous voyage." In international maritime law and practice, this meant that in addition to stopping ships directly destined for German ports, the British were allowed to stop and confiscate goods and ships bound for Germany by way of neutral Denmark or Holland.

Throughout the last decades of the 19th century, warring nations had agreed that in order for a blockade to be legal, it had to be effective; that is, it had to involve ships stationed off the ports of destination rather than at some remote point. By this traditional rule, Britain could not blockade Germany by blockading intermediate ports like Copenhagen in Denmark or Rotterdam in Holland. An unsigned Treaty of London had outlawed the continuous voyage concept. However, when Britain adopted the rule of continuous voyage, such intermediate destinations would be regarded as on the way to Germany and hence cargoes directed through such ports could be confiscated.

At the U.S. State Department, advisers prepared a strong protest to this British announcement. Before dispatching the note, however, Woodrow Wilson's personal adviser, Colonel Edward House, notoriously pro-British, suggested that it be altered. Instead of protesting the violation of the laws of war or an infringement on American rights, the note simply suggested that the British practice might have an adverse effect on American public opinion.

Within a month after the weak American protest, the British extended the blockade. The British announced that they were mining the North Sea and that all shipping to Denmark, Holland, or into the Baltic would have to go by way of the Dover Strait for the sake of safety. Further, to avoid the mines, ships would be required to take on Admiralty pilots in British ports. Neutral Scandinavian and American shipping companies, without backing from a strong neutral navy, had to accept these terms. In effect, the requirement for picking up an Admiralty pilot from a British port allowed Britain to blockade all German and northern European neutral ports without unduly risking warships. While awaiting the pilot, inspectors would examine cargoes and manifests to make sure no contraband goods were aboard destined for eventual transshipment to Germany, even if the announced destination was Copenhagen or Rotterdam. The policy was rounded out with an announcement declaring the whole North Sea a military area subject to mining.

The British practice continued, with Wilson finally issuing a note on December 29, 1914, complaining that ships had been detained while British inspectors searched for contraband. In the Senate, Henry Cabot Lodge, a Republican member of the Foreign Relations Committee since 1895, had grown highly irritated at what he regarded as a weak-kneed reaction to the British transgressions of international law. Wilson reciprocated Lodge's hostility. Both Wilson and Lodge held doctoral degrees, and, until Wilson had taken office, Lodge had regarded himself as the leading intellectual in the government when it came to issues of foreign policy. Wilson, however, made it clear that he intended to set foreign policy personally and that he would simply inform Congress of that policy, rather than letting Congress have any role in setting it. In January 1915, Secretary of State Bryan undertook to explain to Lodge and the Democratic chair of the committee, Senator William J. Stone, how U.S. policy had been strictly neutral and even-handed.

Bryan pointed out to Senators Stone, Lodge, and the other members of the committee that the United States could hardly protest against the doctrine of continuous voyage, since the United States itself had used that doctrine during the Civil War to prevent British goods from reaching the Confederacy. As to the fact that Britain held up goods destined for neutral countries, Bryan pointed out that this practice had already been protested in a formal note to the British. At that point, no contraband destined for the Central Powers had been seized from an American ship, he claimed. It appeared the British blockade succeeded so well that it had discouraged any American business from attempting to sell weapons or transport equipment to Germany and her allies. Other complaints had come to the attention of the State Department, pointing out that the United States had not interfered in the sale of arms, ammunition, and transport equipment to the Allies. Bryan pointed out that no law had been passed to prohibit such trade, and that neutrals traditionally sold such goods to belligerents. Germany had done so during the Russo-Japanese war in 1905, for example. After pointing out the loan ban, Bryan concluded by indicating that if Britain and France, using their own resources, could purchase more goods and weapons than Germany, it was because Britain had a more effective blockade of Germany; the effectiveness of the blockade, Bryan claimed, did not derive from American acquiescence, but from the British command of the sea.

In a strictly legal sense, therefore, U.S. trade with Britain and France, although it helped them advance the Allied cause, did not involve the United States in any violation of neutrality. Several developments over the next few weeks heightened the problem, however. On January 26, 1915, Germany announced that food supplies within Germany and within the conquered regions of France, Belgium, and Poland would be managed by the military. As Germany redirected manpower from agriculture to industry and directly into the military, German food production declined, and increased supplies of food from the conquered regions would have an impact on the manpower requirements by reducing the need for German farm labor. Although this policy made sense from an economic management point of view, it opened the door for Britain to regard food as contraband. Clearly, if Germany imported vast quantities of food from neutral countries, by Germany's own planning and admission, this practice would free up German manpower for the military. German doctrine had established the economic equation that food equaled manpower and that manpower equaled a military force; by such logic food could be considered part of the war effort as much as weaponry, mules, trucks, or ammunition. Within a week of the German announcement, Britain responded by declaring food products contraband and began confiscating any food destined for the Central Powers found aboard ships in British harbors.

This practice meant that the food supply of German-occupied Belgium began to decline in early 1915. The American engineer-turned-administrator, Herbert Hoover, would head a Belgian Relief Commission to arrange imports of food to offset the decline of supply in Belgium. The British opposed Hoover's Relief Commission effort because they believed it only played into the hands of the Germans, who seized Belgian-produced food for German consumption while the Allies provided food to the Belgians. However, the British did allow ships for the Relief Commission through to Belgium.

In response to the increasingly severe British blockade and the American acceptance of it, Germany attempted to impose a kind of blockade, enforced by U-boat, around Ireland and Britain in February 1915. However, stopping a ship at sea and then sinking it had a far different effect than the British method of escorting a ship into a British harbor where it would be examined at leisure. The German blockade necessitated the sinking of ships, rather than their sequestration in harbor, because it was nearly impossible for a submarine to escort a detained ship into a German port. The immediate American response to the announcement of a submarine blockade came in a warning to Germany that it would be held strictly accountable for any loss of life of Americans aboard ships sunk at sea. The German ambassador to the United States, Count Bernstorff, suggested that the U.S. government should warn Americans not to travel on ships owned by belligerent nations.

The strict-neutrality advocates in the United States regarded Wilson's refusal to issue such a warning as an indication of his pro-British leaning. Thus, Bryan, in an even-handed fashion, sent a note to all the belligerents, urging that they not use mines or submarines against commercial freighters or passenger ships and that they prohibit their own merchant ships from falsely flying neutral flags. The note had no effect, as Britain continued to mine the North Sea, Germany continued to send out U-boats against merchant ships, and British sea-captains often adopted the *ruse de guerre* of flying American or other neutral flags. With food on the list of contraband, Britain simply announced a complete blockade of all trade in any sort of goods with German ports on March 11, 1915.

FALABA, GULFLIGHT, LUSITANIA

Over the next few months, the German use of the U-boat led to several American deaths. One American, Leon Thrasher, died when the *Falaba* was sunk in the Irish Sea by *U-28* on March 28, 1915, probably the first American to be killed at sea in World War I as a consequence of armed conflict. On May 1, 1915, *U-30* torpedoed the American tanker *Gulflight,* off the Scilly Islands, near the tip of Cornwall in southwestern Britain. Although the ship made it to port, two Americans aboard the tanker died. Of course, these episodes came to seem minor compared to the disastrous sinking of the *Lusitania,* with the loss of nearly 1,200 lives, including 128 Americans, off the coast of Ireland on May 7, 1915.

Wilson sent three protest notes to Germany over the *Lusitania,* the second and third slightly more angry than the first. On May 13, over the objections of Secretary of State William Jennings Bryan, Wilson insisted on the right of Americans to sail in international waters and stated that Germany should be held to strict accountability for any loss of civilian lives. Two weeks later, Germany responded officially, noting that the *Lusitania* had carried ammunition and war cargo. The German press claimed that Britain had used civilians as human shields to protect such cargos. Wilson regarded that response as evading the central issue of the right to travel on the high seas. Stunned by an international outcry, the kaiser endorsed a confidential order in June 1915 to submarine captains not to sink any passenger liners, no matter what flag they flew, without warning. He did not specify such a warning notice for merchant freighters, however, and many freighters carried a few supercargo passengers or were crewed by international crews. In any case, the kaiser did not announce the change in policy publicly.

The *Lusitania* tragedy created such a newsworthy sensation that, for a generation, Americans remembered it, mistakenly, as one of the major causes of American entry into the war. In fact, the strong American protests over the *Lusitania* sinking resulted in a change in German policy and in a gradual improvement in German-American relations over the issue of sea transport during the following months.

Despite the popular outcry over the loss of American lives and of the lives of more than 1,000 other civilians aboard the *Lusitania,* Wilson delivered an appeal for calm in a speech in Philadelphia on May 10, in which he pointed out "There is such a thing as a man being too proud to fight." Cartoonists and critics immediately used the speech to suggest that Wilson lacked the spine to defend American rights.

Troubled by his conscience, William Jennings Bryan finally decided to resign as secretary of state. *(Library of Congress)*

William G. McAdoo had just arrived home for lunch on Saturday, June 5, 1915, when Secretary of State William Jennings Bryan stopped in unexpectedly. Bryan's haggard face reflected a visible nervousness, and McAdoo, his colleague in the cabinet, had never seen the Great Commoner so agitated.

Bryan began by saying that he had come to McAdoo because of their personal friendship and because of McAdoo's intimacy with Woodrow Wilson, McAdoo's father-in-law.

Bryan explained that if Wilson were to send a second note to Germany regarding the *Lusitania,* it would surely lead to war. As a profound believer in peace, Bryan could not conscientiously follow the president in that course of action. When McAdoo asked what should be done instead, Bryan suggested arbitration, but McAdoo regarded that as out of the question, and an impossible solution. He did not argue that point with Bryan, however.

Bryan went on to say that he regarded his usefulness as over; he planned to resign, and he sought advice on how to make the resignation create the least possible embarrassment.

Later on Saturday, McAdoo related the conversation to Wilson, and the president expressed no surprise at Bryan's intended resignation but said that he would prefer him to stay on, so that the Germans would not get the wrong impression. McAdoo tried again to convince Bryan, but Bryan was steadfast. On June 8,

Bryan put his resignation in the hands of the president. McAdoo was surprised at the "hurricane of abuse that was to howl around" Bryan for his action.[3]

Bryan's resignation at the height of the *Lusitania* crisis sprang directly from the dilemmas of neutrality. Although Bryan was wrong and the stronger notes to Germany did not lead to war, the crisis showed the difficulty American statesmen encountered in trying to find a neutral path. Bryan could not accept the paradox that to defend neutrality required actions that could take the United States closer to war.

The issues between the two men ran deeper, for it had become clear to Bryan that Wilson intended to be his own secretary of state and that Bryan's role had been reduced to simply signing the notes and stating the positions decided upon by the president. Wilson replaced Bryan with Robert Lansing, a specialist in international law who had served as counselor to the State Department and who had worked on arbitration commissions as a professional international lawyer for more than a decade prior to the war. Bryan, by contrast, had been an established leader of the Democratic Party, had run for president three times, and had a clear reputation as a pacifist. Lansing, who had no independent political following or reputation, seemed far more suited to the position as conceived by Wilson than Bryan had been.

ECONOMIC AND TECHNOLOGICAL IMPERATIVES

The difficulties went far beyond those of personalities, however. The world economy had become so intertwined by the early 20th century that a major manufacturing and food-exporting nation such as the United States found it nearly impossible to remain uninvolved in a conflict on the scale of the Great War. At the root of the problem lay the fact that by control of the sea, Britain could purchase vast supplies from the United States and thus could transfer its manpower from agriculture and industry to the war front while maintaining a flow of food and manufactured goods from overseas. At the beginning of the war, the United States owed more to Europe than Europe owed to the United States, which was, in effect, a net debtor. British and French bankers and investment houses held outstanding investments equivalent to about a billion dollars in American firms and institutions. By simply cashing in these amounts, the British and French had ample resources to begin buying munitions and transport equipment without asking for additional credit.

As American industry geared up to produce the ordered items, employment picked up, and American business began to thrive as a consequence of the new flow of exports. Although Bryan had asked that no loans be made to the belligerent nations, no loans were necessary to meet the requirements of British and French purchasing agents from August 1914 through August 1915. Through the simple process of international trade filtered by the blockades of the two major belligerents and the difference in their effectiveness, the United States had become an economic ally of Britain and France, regardless of Wilson's policies and Bryan's protestations.

Britain could enforce a blockade against Germany through its control of the sea, with mines and with surface ships channeling trade through British ports. But if Germany sought to blockade Britain through the use of the submarine, the demands of that technology required submarines to sink a large number of blockade-running ships in order to effectively interdict the trade. A few of the German U-boat captains seemed quite careless of human life, although the majority apparently tried to honor the traditions of the sea by ensuring the safety of passengers and crew of the vessels they sank. The British press, however, portrayed them all as ruthless pirates, and a few episodes such as the attacks on the *Falaba,* the *Gulflight,* and the *Lusitania* sustained that impression. American acceptance of the British style of blockade and anger at the German method using the submarine meant that although the United States remained neutral in a technical or legal sense, its resources had flowed disproportionately to the Allies, hardly a neutral economic stand.

The impersonal forces of technology and the geographic structure of the British blockade created a situation that made it nearly impossible for the United States to be neutral in economic terms. The injunction to be neutral in thought as well as action reflected a deeply felt American tradition and attitude, but it had little effect in stopping the natural flow of commerce. The British government understood the strength of its position. On August 4, 1915, it sent a note to the United States explaining that its blockade operated in full conformity with extant international law. If any problems came up, the British stated, they would agree to submit cases of confiscation to arbitration. Of course, very few problems did arise, since American companies, for the most part, did not attempt to sell goods to Germany, and most had no ethical problem as they tried to supply the large demand for goods in Britain and France.

The commercial involvement of the United States evolved. By September 1915, it became clear that the Allies had come close to exhausting the financial resources available for purchase of U.S. goods and that either short-term loans or long-term financing would be required if American companies continued to supply goods and food. Lansing and his advisers realized that to cut off European orders would cause a major recession in the United States, with factories laying off newly hired workers and farm prices plummeting. Furthermore, the loan ban that had been established by Bryan had had little or no effect in preventing purchases, and the "pecuniary interest" that Bryan had originally feared in 1914 had by now become well established in supporting continued trade. On September 6, Lansing recommended to Wilson that the banks be notified that the U.S. government no longer believed it inconsistent with the spirit of neutrality for Americans to make loans to belligerents. Quietly, in this fashion, Bryan's policy vanished, and on September 25 a consortium of bankers made the first loan of $500 million to Britain and France. Over the next 18 months, American institutions made loans of more than $2 billion to the Allies. In the spirit of impartiality, loans could also be made to Germany and Austria-Hungary, but since the trade to those countries amounted to a mere trickle, the Central Powers borrowed less than $20 million in 1915 and 1916.

ARABIC AND SUSSEX

German submarine captains, however, continued to attack merchant ships through the summer of 1915, usually warning the crews to evacuate, but not always. The policy varied with the personality and character of the submarine captain and with the particular situation. For example, on August 19, 1915, Captain Rudolf Schneider of *U-24* sank without warning a British steamer, *Arabic,* bound from

Liverpool to New York City. Although most of the 433 passengers and crew were rescued, two Americans were among the 44 dead. Schneider claimed that the steamer took an evasive zigzagging course and that he interpreted that action as an attempt to ram, but few believed the claim. The ship sank in 10 minutes.

World outrage mounted again, and this time the kaiser issued explicit orders that not only should a liner be fully warned before being sunk, but that the submarine captain must observe that both crew and passengers safely boarded lifeboats before sinking the ship. Orders went to Count von Bernstorff, the German ambassador in Washington, to give assurances to the U.S. government, and he did so September 1 in a statement that Americans interpreted as the "*Arabic* Pledge." "Liners will not be sunk by our submarines without warning and without safety of the lives of non-combatants, provided that the liners do not try to escape or offer resistance."[4] Backing off from attacking liners, German submarine commanders found themselves restricted to attacking freighters or warships. As a result of the changed submarine tactics, from the late summer of 1915 until early 1917, German-American relations gradually improved.

On February 21, 1916, Germany advised the U.S. government that armed merchantmen were to be treated as cruisers beginning March 1. This action came in response to British use of Q ships in large numbers, to the use of neutral flags by British merchant ships, and to the open arming of merchant vessels.

Realizing that Americans traveling on an armed merchant ship could easily be killed by either side, and that such an event could draw the United States into the conflict, in early March 1916, members of Congress introduced congressional resolutions designed to preserve neutrality. The resolutions came in direct response to the German announcement that their submarines would sink armed merchantmen as warships. The resolutions openly challenged Wilson's policies. Again, Wilson reacted firmly, believing that no one, including ambassadors, secretaries of state, and legislators, should infringe on his ability to set foreign policy.

Member of Congress Jeff McLemore of Texas introduced a resolution requesting that the president warn Americans not to travel on armed vessels. Senator Thomas P. Gore of Oklahoma introduced a separate bill that would deny passports to Americans traveling on armed vessels and demanded Allied respect for non-contraband trade with the Central Powers.

Following the votes closely, and seeing them as congressional challenges to his prerogatives as president, Wilson called on his party regulars to have both resolutions stopped. The Gore and McLemore measures, although they failed, showed strong public and congressional opinion that Wilson's policies could put the United States in a position to be drawn into the war.

Improved relations between the United States and Germany were threatened in the period March 24–May 4, 1916, over one more U-boat attack. On March 24, 1916, a German U-boat torpedoed *Sussex*, a French cross-channel passenger ship, and several Americans aboard were injured. The United States regarded the attack as a violation of the *Arabic* Pledge, but Germany claimed the submarine captain mistook *Sussex* for a minelayer. In fact, U-boat captain Herbert Pustkuchen of *U-29* acted wantonly, simply ignoring the orders about warnings, and he sank several other ships on his March cruise with no regard for the safety of passengers or crew. Wilson dismissed the minelayer story, and, on April 18, 1916, in response to the sinking of *Sussex,* Secretary of State Robert Lansing suggested to Wilson that the United States should break diplomatic relations with Germany.

Instead, Wilson sent an ultimatum that unless Germany abandoned its method of submarine warfare, the United States would sever diplomatic relations. The next day, Wilson explained to Congress his decision to issue an ultimatum to Germany in response to the *Sussex* sinking, stating that "unless the Imperial German Government should now immediately declare and effect an abandonment of its present methods of warfare against passenger and freight carrying vessels this Government can have no choice but to sever diplomatic relations with the Government of the German Empire altogether."[5]

On May 4, 1916, Germany agreed to the U.S. demands issued after the *Sussex* sinking but imposed a counter-condition that the United States compel the Allies to respect the rules of international law with regard to shipping, in reference to mines, continuous voyage blockade, and rules of contraband. Traditionally, food had never been regarded as contraband, and shortages were affecting Germany. Wilson accepted the German response as a pledge but refused to accept the counter-condition. This so-called *Sussex* Pledge remained in effect, and German U-boat captains generally refrained from sinking passenger ships or American merchant ships over the next months. However, the pledge continued to leave the decision as to war in German hands, because, if Germany openly moved to violate the pledge, the United States had almost committed itself to entering the war against Germany. So from mid-1916 onward, in this sense, Germany held the power to keep America in or out of the war.

DOMESTIC PRESSURES

The American people continued to be severely divided by the horrifying events of the war. As journalists, famous authors, and various eyewitnesses, including American volunteers serving with the Red Cross as ambulance drivers, sent back reports from the front, much of the reaction in the United States coalesced around two poles. At one extreme, a variety of pacifists, led by prominent Progressives, sought to pressure the president to continue a strictly neutral stand and, at the same time, bring the belligerents together for a negotiated peace. One article of Progressive faith had been a belief that conflict could be resolved by intelligent compromise rather than by force, and a few activist advocates like Jane Addams and Henry Ford worked to achieve such negotiation whether or not the president went along with them. Cynics, however, pointed out that such idealism had become naive and misplaced, and they criticized such private efforts as almost ludicrous in the face of the blood that had been spilled and of the hard-headed leaders who were locked in a struggle for power.

On May 1, 1915, the American social worker and political activist Jane Addams met in the Netherlands with representatives from 12 countries to advocate permanent peace. The women delegates included a group from Germany. In December, Henry Ford sailed aboard the "peace ship" *Oskar II,* on a separate, privately funded mission to end the war with a negotiated peace. The British and American press ridiculed these and other efforts, depicting the pacifists as wooly-minded idealists. Nevertheless, such efforts reflected a major sentiment in the United States, as many politically active Progressives believed that Wilson either did not do enough to bring about negotiations, or that he accepted advice

Although mostly pacifists, women suffrage advocates supported national goals, winning support for their cause. *(National Archives)*

from his pro-British advisers and acted with pro-British partiality in his handling of the blockade issues.

At the other extreme from the pacifists, practical businessmen and political leaders believed that the United States missed an opportunity to build up the manpower of the nation in readiness for war. Following in the footsteps of Theodore Roosevelt, who believed that the experience of war instilled manly virtues such as courage, hardiness, physical fitness, and a robust approach to public affairs, many urged the establishment of training camps. In August, organizers established the American Defense Society to set up such camps. The preparedness movement, like the pacifist movement, went forward without official government sanction. On August 10, the first Citizens Military Camp opened up at Plattsburg, New York; it attracted 4,000 young men who received military training, despite the late start for the summer. In 1916 the number attending such camps rose to 16,000. The camps, known as the Plattsburg Idea, later extended to include separate camps for black officer trainees and for women. Theodore Roosevelt joined other Progressives in supporting the Plattsburg Idea, and advocates of the camps spread the notion of preparing for war through speeches, films, and publications.

At one level, the disparity between the pacifist movement and the preparedness movement reflected two sides of the Progressive ideology, which seemed to spring from contemporary gender values. The pacifist movement drew upon many of the ideas and ideals supported by the leaders of the women's movement, suggesting a humanism that rejected violence and force in favor of rational resolution of differences in national as well as international affairs. On the other hand, the preparedness movement reflected the "strenuous life" concept of exaggerated masculinity promoted by Theodore Roosevelt, emphasizing a hard-headed practicality and a concern with physical fitness, outdoor living, and sportsmanship.

Through 1915 and 1916, Wilson and his administration continued to be pulled in conflicting directions by popular and political pressures. Gore and McLemore in Congress had tried to take a more neutral policy that would avoid conflict with Germany. Advisers like Page and House continued to urge a pro-British position. Facing an election in November, Wilson attempted to address these mutual concerns simultaneously by developing a stronger military preparedness stance and at the same time working toward a negotiated peace.

Wilson gave a nod to the growing support for the preparedness movement by developing a comprehensive plan for national defense. On December 7, 1915, he put the plan before Congress, and over the next months several bills passed that fundamentally changed the antiquated system of state-controlled National Guard units into an effective reserve for the regular army and established government agencies for the coordination of the economy on a war footing. At first, however, Wilson approached these ideas cautiously, forcing the resignation of Secretary of War Lindley Garrison, who had supported nationalizing the Guard and placing all military training under a centralized administration. His replacement, Newton Baker, would go on to become a strong secretary of war. To build support for the defense plan, on January 27, 1916, Wilson began a nationwide tour to urge preparedness.

After several attempts, Colonel Edward House got the British foreign secretary to sign on to an agreement for an international peace conference. However, the House-Grey Memorandum, issued in February 1916, seemed to strict-neutrality critics to be a decidedly pro-British statement, since it indicated that if Germany refused to agree to a peace conference, the United States would probably enter the war on the Allied side.

In June 1916 Wilson signed the National Defense Act, the first step in his preparedness program. The plan called for expansion of the army to 223,000 regular troops and the National Guard to 450,000. Following a plan much like that suggested by the dismissed secretary, Garrison, the act placed the funding of the National Guard on the federal government. Furthermore, the act established the first Reserve Officer Training Corps (ROTC) programs at universities across the nation. The act also authorized the establishment of civilian training camps similar to those already begun without government sanction under the Plattsburg Idea. One major difference between the defense plan adopted and that suggested by Garrison lay in the fact that Garrison had insisted that the troops be raised, trained, officered, and controlled by the national government, but the adopted defense plan left much authority for the Guard in state hands. Garrison had also favored universal compulsory military training, and the need for a draft or conscription system did not figure in Wilson's 1916 plans.

FOREIGN PRESSURES

Even as Wilson worked to get his defense legislation enacted, outside events continued to press on public opinion. On Easter Monday, April 24, 1916, the British suppressed the bloody and poorly planned uprising in Dublin, Ireland. Roger Casement, an Irish statesman who had attempted to recruit an army of anti-British troops from among Irish prisoners of war held in Germany, landed in Ireland from a submarine. British warships interdicted a freighter carrying weapons sent to Ireland from Germany and destroyed them. The British quickly apprehended Casement and brought him to trial. Casement's rapid hearing and execution, together with the suppression of the Easter Rebellion, the execution by firing squad of nearly 100 of the rebels, and deportation of more than 1,700 others, further angered Irish Americans. In an effort to increase the public's antagonism to Casement, the British published his diaries, which detailed his prior homosexual activity while serving as a British diplomat in South America and Africa.

Anti-British feelings rose to a new level in the United States when Britain announced a blacklist of individuals and companies that had been trading with neutrals in Holland and Denmark, who in turn transshipped goods to Germany. Companies on the blacklist were denied access to British banking and cable facilities.

German and Austro-Hungarian agents working under cover for members of the diplomatic missions continued to attempt a variety of sabotage and labor-organizing efforts to block shipments of goods from America to the Allies. Although investigators uncovered several such plots, no one ever determined the facts behind a massive explosion at the docks at Black Tom, New Jersey, in New York harbor on July 30, 1916. The early morning detonations shattered windows in Manhattan, and people heard the explosion more than 100 miles away. The explosion destroyed a large shipment of ammunition destined for the Allies, causing damage estimated at $22 million. Although no proof ever emerged that Black Tom had resulted from sabotage, the public and press logically enough assumed that German agents lay behind the detonation. All such events put pressure on American neutrality, but through the course of 1915 and 1916, it appeared that Wilson would be able to steer through the dilemmas and keep the United States out of the war.

PREPAREDNESS LEGISLATION AND THE ELECTION

Three pieces of legislation enacted in the late summer of 1916 implemented Wilson's defense plan. On August 29, 1916, the Army Appropriation Act authorized the Council of National Defense. The council consisted of six cabinet members, working with Secretary of War Newton Baker and responsible for coordinating planning for transportation, labor, munitions, and medical facilities. This council and other war agencies were later regarded as setting the precedents for national agencies involved in economic management during the Great Depression, in World War II, and in later years. On September 7 Wilson signed the Shipping Act—creating a five-person commission empowered to build, purchase, lease, or requisition ships through the Emergency Fleet Corporation—which received an initial funding of $50 million. The next day, Wilson signed the 1916 Revenue Act, which, among other powers, gave the president the ability to withhold port facilities in retaliation for acts of discrimination against American commerce. Although Wilson never used the provision, supporters claimed that its mere threat resulted in the British relaxing the Black List limitations on American companies.

In the summer of 1916, the political season heated up. On June 7, 1916, the Republican national convention in Chicago nominated Supreme Court Justice Charles Evans Hughes for president. Hughes began to win support among Irish Americans, who traditionally voted with the Democrats. In a more serious threat to Wilson, however, Hughes showed great strength in East Coast states that leaned in a pro-Allied direction, including New York and New Jersey, states usually found in the Democratic column. Wilson eventually lost New York state by some 7 percent of the popular vote. Many cross-currents reflected the difficulty of running for the presidency in the heated atmosphere of war and neutrality. Wilson supporters charged Hughes with failure to repudiate "hyphenate" support from the Irish and German voters, so-called because of the hyphen in expressions like "Irish-American" and "German-American," at the very time that Wilson's neutrality stand appealed to those same voters. Campaign speaker Ollie James supported Wilson by reciting a litany of the crises the president had faced. "What happened when the Germans torpedoed the *Lusitania?*" James chanted. "He kept us out of war!" The crowd shouted. "What happened when the British confiscated American ships?" "He kept us out of war!"[6]

The slogan and the chant captured the American sentiment for neutrality very well, but, nevertheless, the country remained evenly divided. Many Progressive voters in the West who had supported Roosevelt in 1912 apparently shifted to Wilson in 1916, partly because of his firm neutrality stand and also perhaps because of Wilson's support for woman suffrage and Prohibition and because Bryan campaigned for him tirelessly in the West, despite his earlier resignation from the State Department. On November 7, with early results from the East Coast states in, newspapers in New York predicted a Hughes victory. The next morning, the vote seemed to be turning in Wilson's direction with pro-Wilson returns from midwestern and western states that usually voted Republican. Wilson won the election, but the results did not become known until the final tally of the vote in California two days after the election, where Wilson took the state's electoral college vote by 3,773 popular votes.

President Woodrow Wilson faced an insoluble set of dilemmas as he tried to maintain neutrality. *(Library of Congress)*

LAST EFFORTS AT NEGOTIATION

From early in the war, Wilson had hoped that the United States could play the role of mediator, and he hoped to bring the warring parties to the negotiating table. For this purpose, he sent his personal adviser Edward House on several missions to Europe. In February 1916, House signed a secret agreement with British foreign secretary Edward Grey, known as the House-Grey Memorandum. In that document, House promised on Wilson's behalf that when England and France thought the moment was opportune, the United States would issue a call for a peace conference. If Germany were to refuse to attend, the memo indicated, the United States would probably enter the war against Germany. Wilson endorsed the memorandum in March, but Britain refused to agree to a call for a peace conference, especially since the Central Powers continued to hold territory through 1916 that they had taken by force of arms, and the Allies had little bargaining power. Britain and France insisted that Germany state its war goals before agreeing to a conference.

Finally, in December 1916, Germany notified the neutral countries of a willingness to enter peace negotiations, but the Allies continued to demand a statement of German war goals. Wilson in turn asked for such a statement from the Allies, and they responded in January 1917 with a list of goals that clearly would be unacceptable to the Central Powers. In effect, they demanded that the Austro-Hungarian Empire be dissolved and that the Ottoman Empire give up all territory in Europe. Technically, this would include the western shore of the Dardanelles and the Bosporus waterway. Further demands included the evacuation of all the lands conquered by Germany in Russia, France, and Romania. In short, the demands amounted to acceptance of defeat by the Central Powers when they were not militarily defeated and evacuation of territory they controlled politically and militarily.

Wilson responded by calling for a peace without victory. He hoped to be able to at least begin discussions on the basis of competing proposals. The Germans responded with a list of their own goals early in 1917. The terms the Germans proposed included restitution and funding by them for areas damaged in war and the establishment of an economic and strategic buffer state to separate Germany from Russia. Further, they expected the restoration of German overseas possessions and the establishment of rules of international use of the sea. However, while these apparently reasonable suggestions were being offered, Germany developed a plan for winning the war. With the growing collapse of Russian resistance through mutinies and desertions of Russian troops on the eastern front, German leaders believed that a transfer of German armies to the west, coupled with a severely tightened submarine blockade, could force the Allies to surrender. The risk of bringing America into the war seemed worth it, as Wilson's military planning had only just gotten started, in a fashion that Germany could only view as half-hearted.

If America could be tied down by a conflict with Mexico, even at a low level, Germany believed this would delay any American help to the Allies for long enough to secure a solid victory for the Central Powers. Decisions taken by Germany in January 1917 to unleash unrestricted submarine warfare, not only against Allied shipping, but also against neutral shipping carrying goods to Britain and France, would put a sudden end to the long and difficult search for a neutral position that the American people and Wilson had sought since August 1914. The German high command planned in this fashion to snuff out the American supply line to the Allies, knowing, since Wilson's *Sussex* note, that unrestricted submarine warfare would lead to war with the United States. In effect, the decision that the United States should enter World War I took place, not in the White House, but in a castle in Germany.

CHRONICLE OF EVENTS

1914

August 15: Secretary of State W. J. Bryan notifies J. P. Morgan that making loans to belligerents would be "inconsistent with the true spirit of neutrality"; Bryan hopes to avoid investors' having a stake in either side's victory.

August 19: President Woodrow Wilson announces a neutrality policy in a message to Congress. Wilson asks Americans to be neutral in thought as well as action.

September 26–28: A strong protest against British violation of traditional rules of blockade prepared in the State Department is suppressed at the suggestion of presidential adviser Edward House; a substitute memorandum suggesting the ill effect on American public opinion, rather than violation of rights, is sent instead.

October: The British blockade is extended after the weak American protest to include the doctrine of continuous voyage. The blockade requires ships to take on Admiralty pilots (after putting in to a British port on the way to Germany or to a continental neutral port). The British also announce mining of the North Sea. Neutral Scandinavian and American shipping companies agree to these terms, which in effect allow Britain to blockade all German and northern European neutral ports.

November 3: The British declare the North Sea a military area and announce that it is mined.

December: The National Security League, a preparedness organization, is founded in the United States.

December 29: Wilson protests the British detention of ships in searches for contraband.

1915

January 20: Secretary of State Bryan spells out for the Senate Foreign Relations Committee a detailed account of how the U.S. policy of neutrality has not been partial to the Allies or unfriendly to the Central Powers.

January 26: Germany puts foodstuffs under military control.

February 2: Britain places food and all other goods on the contraband list.

February 4: Germany declares a war region around Britain and Ireland effective February 18, announcing a "restricted" submarine blockade.

February 10: A U.S. note states that Germany will be held to strict accountability for the loss of life of any Americans traveling on the high seas. German ambassador Bernstorff suggests the U.S. government warn Americans not to travel on ships registered to belligerent nations. His advice is ignored.

February 20: Bryan sends a note to all belligerents urging no mines, no use of submarines against merchant ships, and no misuse of neutral flags.

March 11: A complete British blockade barring all neutrals from German ports goes into effect; the British declare all ships bound for any German port liable for seizure and confiscation.

March 28: One American is killed when the *Falaba* is sunk in the Irish Sea after a German U-boat attack.

April 11: The German ambassador to the United States asks the American people to end the sale of arms to the Allies.

May 1: Jane Addams meets in the Netherlands with representatives from 12 countries to advocate permanent peace. Women delegates include a group from Germany.

May 1: Off the Scilly Islands (southwestern Britain), during an engagement between a British naval patrol and a German submarine, a torpedo damages the American oil tanker *Gulflight,* with two American fatalities. Germany later offers full compensation for the loss.

May 1: The German embassy in Washington issues a specific warning, published in New York City newspapers, regarding sailing aboard the *Lusitania,* a liner operated by the British-owned Cunard line.

May 7: The U-boat *U-20* sinks the liner *Lusitania* off the Irish coast: 1,198 are dead, including some 128 Americans.

May 10: Wilson delivers an address in Philadelphia in which he declares, "There is such a thing as a man being too proud to fight. There is such a thing as a nation being so right that it does not need to convince others that it is right."

May 13: The first *Lusitania* note is sent by Wilson; it insists on the right of Americans to sail in international waters and reiterates the principle that Germany will be held to strict accountability for any loss of life.

May 28: The German response to the first *Lusitania* note points out that the vessel carried contraband, including rifles, ammunition, and other war cargo.

June 7: A second *Lusitania* note, using stronger language, is drafted by Wilson, but Secretary of State Bryan threatens to resign if it is sent; he will resign on June 8.

June 9: Robert Lansing, Bryan's successor, signs the second *Lusitania* note. Bryan then lunches with colleagues from the cabinet and explains his reasoning.

The crew of a German U-boat prepares to fire a torpedo. *(National Archives)*

Lansing is Bryan's interim successor until June 23, when he is formally appointed.

July 21: The third *Lusitania* note warns Germany that a repetition of the sinking of an ocean liner will be regarded as "deliberately unfriendly."

August: The American Defense Society, a preparedness organization, is founded.

August 4: The British send a note to the United States claiming their blockade is in conformity with international law but agree to submit disputed cases of confiscation to arbitration.

August 10: The First Citizens Military Camp is set up at Plattsburg, New York; it attracts 4,000 young men who receive military training. In 1916 the number attending such camps will total 16,000. The camps become known as the Plattsburg Idea. Theodore Roos-

evelt is among national leaders supportive of the Plattsburg Idea.

August 19: The British steamer *Arabic* is sunk by a German submarine. Two American lives are lost.

September 1: German ambassador von Bernstorff issues the *Arabic* Pledge.

September 6: Secretary of State Lansing recommends changing the position that loans to belligerents are inconsistent with the spirit of neutrality.

September 8: Because of the exposure of his involvement in sabotage, Austro-Hungarian ambassador Constantin Dumba is sent home.

September 25: A first loan of $500 million is made to Britain and France by a consortium of bankers. Over the next 18 months, more than $2 billion will be loaned to the Allies, less than $20 million to the Central Powers.

October 5: In response to *Lusitania* protests, Germany agrees not to sink merchant ships without warning. U.S.-German relations improve over next six months; Germany offers compensation for the loss of American lives in the *Arabic* sinking.

December 1: German attachés Franz von Papen and Karl Boy-Ed are sent home on suspicion of engagement in sabotage.

December 4: Henry Ford embarks aboard the "peace ship" *Oskar II* on a private mission to end the war with a negotiated peace.

December 7: Wilson puts a comprehensive plan for national defense before Congress.

1916

January 27: Wilson begins a tour of the country to urge preparedness.

February 10: Secretary of War Lindley Garrison, who had advocated a drafted national army instead of a state-controlled National Guard, resigns. He will be replaced by Newton Baker on March 7. Assistant Secretary of War Henry Breckinridge also resigns.

February 17: Congressman Jeff McLemore of Texas introduces a resolution requesting the president to warn Americans not to travel on armed vessels.

February 22: The mission of Edward House to Britain leads to the House-Grey memorandum, which suggests a peace conference and states that, if Germany refuses to attend, the United States will probably enter on the Allied side.

February 25: Senator Thomas P. Gore of Oklahoma introduces a resolution denying passports to Americans traveling on armed vessels and demanding Allied respect for non-contraband trade with the Central Powers.

March 3–7: Wilson succeeds in having the Gore resolution tabled; in the House the McLemore resolution is defeated 276 to 142.

March 24: The French cross-channel ship the *Sussex* is torpedoed; Secretary Lansing urges severance of diplomatic relations with Germany. Instead, Wilson sends a note with an ultimatum.

April 19: Wilson explains to Congress his decision to issue an ultimatum to Germany in response to the *Sussex* sinking.

April 24–28: The British suppress an Irish uprising, in Dublin and elsewhere, led by Sean Connolly of Sinn Féin and Patrick Pearce of the Irish Republican Brotherhood. The uprising will be suppressed by April 28.

May 4: Germany agrees to the U.S. demands issued after the *Sussex* sinking, but imposes a counter-condition that the United States compel the Allies to respect the rules of international law with regard to shipping, in reference to mines, continuous voyage blockades, and rules of contraband.

May 8: Wilson accepts the German response as a pledge, but refuses to accept the counter-condition. This so-called *Sussex* Pledge will remain in effect over the following seven months, reducing German-American tensions. However, the pledge leaves the decision as to war in German hands.

June 3: The National Defense Act (the first aspect of Wilson's preparedness program) calls for the expansion of the army (to 223,000) and the National Guard (to 450,000), places responsibility for funding the National Guard on the federal government, establishes ROTC programs at universities, and authorizes the establishment of civilian training camps.

June 7: The Republican national convention in Chicago nominates Supreme Court Justice Charles Evans Hughes for president. Hughes is supported by Irish-American and German-American groups, and his failure to repudiate such "hyphenate" support is used against him in the campaign by Wilson supporters.

July 18: The British announce a blacklist of individuals and companies, including U.S. firms. American companies that had been trading with Dutch and Danish firms that reexported goods to Germany are officially boycotted by the British government and denied access to British cable and banking facilities. Blacklist, censorship of news, and suppression of the Irish uprising combine to sour American-British relations.

July 30: The Black Tom explosion, an apparent sabotage attack, destroys ammunition stored on New Jersey docks ready to be loaded for shipment to the Allies. German saboteurs are suspected. The damage is estimated at $22 million.

August 3: Roger Casement is executed for his part in the Easter Rebellion in Dublin.

August 29: The Council of National Defense is authorized under the Army Appropriation Act. It will be organized on October 11, under Secretary of War Newton Baker, and will include six cabinet members responsible for coordinating industry. A seven-member advisory committee will plan transportation, labor, munitions, and medicine.

September 7: The Shipping Act is signed, creating a five-person body empowered to build, purchase, lease,

To expand American shipping required completely new shipyards like Hog Island shipyard in Pennsylvania, along the Delaware River (shown here). *(National Archives)*

or requisition ships through the Emergency Fleet Corporation. The corporation is funded with an initial capitalization of $50 million.

September 8: The Revenue Act authorizes the president to withhold port facilities from any ship declared guilty of discrimination against American commerce. Although not implemented, the threat results in some British relaxation of the black list.

November 7–10: Woodrow Wilson is reelected on the basis of the campaign slogan, "He Kept Us Out of War." The election is one of the closest in U.S. history; the result is not known until the final vote in California is tallied, where Wilson wins by less than 4,000 votes and the Republicans concede the state on November 10.

December 12: After an exchange of notes with the United States, Germany notifies all neutrals that Germany and the other Central Powers are ready to enter peace negotiations. The Allies reject the offer until the German war aims are stated.

December 18: Wilson asks all the Allies to state the terms on which peace could be concluded.

December 26: Germany suggests to Wilson that peace negotiations between belligerents should take place in a neutral nation. Germany does not state its war goals.

1917

January 10: The Allied war aims are announced in response to Wilson's repeated requests. The terms are clearly unacceptable to the Central Powers: restoration of Belgium, Serbia, and Montenegro with indemnities for damages; evacuation of territories taken in Russia, Romania, and France; liberation of Italians, Slavs, and Czechs from Austro-Hungarian control; expulsion of the Ottoman Empire from Europe; reorganization of European boundaries. In effect, the goal calls for dissolution of the Austro-Hungarian Empire and the retreat of Germany from all conquered territories.

January 11: Sabotage is suspected in an explosion at the Canadian Car and Foundry plant in Kingsland, New Jersey. Estimated damage exceeds $30 million.

January 22: Wilson proposes a peace settlement based on "peace without victory."

January 29: Germany sends to Wilson the list of German war goals. They include restitution of areas damaged in war, the establishment of an economic and strategic buffer state to separate Germany from Russia, the restoration of German overseas possessions, and the establishment of rules of international use of the sea.

EYEWITNESS TESTIMONY

While President Wilson was giving his whole thought and effort to the solution of exacting domestic tasks, the European war broke upon him and thus turned his attention and study to the age-long and complicated political struggle between Germany, France, and England.

Fully conscious from the very beginning of the difficulties that lay in his path, he was aware of the eventualities the war now beginning might lead to. As a profound student of history he saw with a clear vision the necessity of neutrality and of America remaining disentangled in every way from the embroilments of Europe. To the people of the country it at first appeared that the war was one more in a long series of European quarrels and that we must play our part in the great conflict as mere spectators and strictly adhere to the American policy of traditional aloofness and isolation, which had been our immemorial custom and habit. Although we were bound to maintain a policy of isolation, Woodrow Wilson from the beginning foresaw its futility. . . .

He knew how difficult it would be to keep a people so variously constituted strictly neutral. No sooner was his proclamation of neutrality announced than the differences in points of view in racial stocks began to manifest themselves in language both intemperate and passionate, until his advice to his country "to be neutral in fact as well as in name" became a dead and spiritless thing.

I have often been asked if the policy of neutrality which the President announced, and which brought a fire of criticism upon him, represented his own personal feelings toward the European war, and whether if he had been a private citizen, he would have derided it as now his critics were engaged in doing.

As an intimate associate of Woodrow Wilson during the whole of the European war, and witnessing from day to day the play of his feelings, especially after the violation of the neutrality of Belgium, I am certain that had he been free to do so he would have yielded to the impulse of championing a cause that in his heart of hearts he felt involved the civilization of the world. But it was his devotion to the idea of trusteeship that held him in check, and the consciousness that in carrying out that trusteeship he had no right to permit his own passionate feelings to govern his public acts.

It would have been a dramatic adventure to accept Germany's assault on Belgium as a challenge to the humane interest of America, but the acceptance would have been only a gesture, for we were unable to transport armies to the theatre of war in time to check the outrage. Such action would have pleased some people in the East, but the President knew that this quixotic knight errantry would not appeal to the country at large, particularly the West, still strongly grounded in the Washingtonian tradition of non-interference in European quarrels. . . .

I recall the day he prepared his neutrality proclamation. At the end of one of the most strenuous days of his life in Washington, he left the Executive offices where he was engaged in meeting and conferring with senators and congressmen, and I found him comfortably seated under an elm tree, serenely engaged with pad and pencil in preparing his neutrality proclamation, which was soon to loose a fierce storm of opposition and ridicule upon him. He and I had often discussed the war and its effect upon our own country, and one day in August, 1914, just after the Great War had begun, he said to me: "We are going through deep waters in the days to come. The passions now lying dormant will soon be aroused and my motives and purposes at every turn will soon be challenged until there will be left but few friends to justify my course. It does not seem clear now, but as this war grows in intensity it will soon resolve itself into a war between autocracy and democracy. Various racial groups in America will seek to lead us now one way and then another. We must sit steady in the boat and bow our heads to meet the storm."

Bound as he was by the responsibilities of trusteeship to adhere to a policy of neutrality, personally he saw that the inevitable results would be only bitter disappointment. "We cannot remain isolated in this war," he said, "for soon the contagion of it will spread until it reaches our own shores. On the one side Mr. Bryan will censure the Administration for being too militaristic, and on the other we will find Mr. Roosevelt criticizing us because we are too pacifist in our tendencies."

Joseph Tumulty, Woodrow Wilson's private secretary, commenting on the dilemmas facing Woodrow Wilson after the outbreak of World War I, in mid-August 1914, in his memoir, Woodrow Wilson as I Know Him, *pp. 225–228.*

The note which you propose will, I fear, very much inflame the already hostile feeling against us in Germany, not entirely because of our protest against Germany's action in this case, but in part because of its contrast with our attitude toward the Allies. If we oppose the use of the submarine against merchantmen we will lay down a law for ourselves as well as for Germany. If we admit the right of the submarine to attack merchantmen but condemn their particular act or class of acts as inhuman we will be embarrassed by the fact that we have not protested against Great Britain's defense of the right to prevent foods reaching non-combatant enemies.

William Jennings Bryan objecting to the tone of the Gulflight *note, April 23, 1915, in William Jennings Bryan and Mary Baird Bryan,* The Memoirs of William Jennings Bryan, *p. 296.*

Along about noon on May 7th, as we were skirting the Irish coast, I went up on the hurricane deck to get a bit of exercise, and the purser and I were tossing a medicine ball. Standing alongside me, playing ball with some one else, was Elbert Hubbard. That was the last I saw of him.

We went down to lunch rather late, and were sitting at the table when the explosion came. Shattered glass from the porthole windows splattered all around us. I got up and hurried on deck. The purser rushed off to his office. That was the last that I saw of him.

When I got on deck the passengers were milling around, running in all directions, but there was no panic, no screaming. The ship had already started to list to starboard and the crew were trying to lower the boats. One boat got halfway down. But one end gave way and dumped all her crowd of passengers into the sea. A second boat got down part way, then something happened to the ropes. Down it fell, right on top of the first crowd—smashing them, of course. Seeing the way things were going, and that not many had on life preservers, I decided to go after mine. As I went down the companionway I passed Alfred G. Vanderbilt. He was sitting calmly on a sofa—just sitting, thinking, not a bit excited. That was the last I ever saw of him.

I carried seven life belts back on deck and passed them around. Near by stood a gentleman and his daughter who also had been at the purser's table. She had none, so I fastened a belt about her. It saved her life. Then I tried to get over to the port side of the ship. But by then the list was so great that I couldn't make it and slid back. The liner was going over fast. I saw how hopeless it was to attempt to get away in a boat. So I waited until the deck rail was within eight feet or so of the water. Then I jumped.

I had always been keen about sports and was a fair swimmer. But never before had I tried swimming with my clothes on. I struck out, but kept glancing back, keeping one eye on the ship. In another moment or two she would be flat on her side, and I saw that unless I made more speed I would be crushed by one of the huge stacks. A few moments after that it looked as if I might get hit by the main mast. So I slowed up a bit and it fell right in front of me. Clambering over it, I headed for an empty lifeboat. Before I reached it I saw the nose of the *Lusitania* disappear. Her stern rose high in the air. She seemed to poise there for a moment and then, with a lunge, she vanished. Instead of causing a vortex and sucking us down, as I had always heard would happen, the sea seemed to hump up like a big hill. Then, as it flattened out, I was carried farther away.

One of the ship's officers clambered into the lifeboat with me. She was half full of water, and we tried to bale her out with our hands. Then we spent the next few hours diving in and out of the water, rescuing as many as we could. Most of the people we got hold of were already dead, but we got some twenty safely into the boat. Later, we were picked up by a trawler.

Account by surviving passenger C. W. Bowring of his experiences aboard the Lusitania, *May 7, 1915, from Lowell Thomas,* Raiders of the Deep, *pp. 102–103.*

Anyone who cannot bring himself to approve from the bottom of his heart the sinking of the *Lusitania,* who cannot conquer his sense of the monstrous cruelty to countless perfectly innocent victims . . . and give himself up to honest joy at this victorious exploit of German defensive power—such an one we deem no true German.

German pastor D. Baumgarten, commenting on the German attitude to the sinking of the Lusitania, *about May 10, 1915, "Deutsche Reden in schwerer Zeit," no. 25, p. 7, cited in* Out of Their Own Mouths, *p. 68.*

On May 10, 1915, [President Wilson] made a speech in Philadelphia, which contained the regrettable and much-criticized phrase, "Too proud to fight." Unfortunately, the headlines of the papers carried only the phrase, "Too proud to fight," and little or no attention was paid to the context of the speech in which the phrase was lodged. As a matter of fact, there was nothing unusual about the character of this speech. The phrase, "Too proud to fight," was simply expressive of the president's policy since the outbreak of the war. It was not a new thought with him. Some weeks before he had said the same thing, only in different words, in a speech delivered at a banquet of the Associated Press in New York. "My interest in the neutrality of the United States is not a petty desire to keep out of trouble. I am interested in neutrality because there is something so much greater to do than fight. There is a distinction awaiting this nation that no nation has ever yet got. That is the distinction of absolute self-control and mastery." The phrase, "Too proud to fight," was simply expressive of the idea that was close to his heart; a reliance upon means of settling our difficulties with Germany other than a resort to war.

On our way to Philadelphia on the day of the delivery of this speech I read a copy of it which the President handed to me, and when I ran across the phrase, "Too proud to fight," I scented the political danger in it and warned him, but he declined to be admonished because he was confident in the moral strength of his position, namely, that self-mastery is sometimes more heroic than fighting, or as the Bible states it, "He that ruleth his own spirit is greater than he that taketh a city," and trusted the people to understand his full meaning. The President himself was so above the petty tricks by which politicians wrest words from their context and force upon them unfavourable meaning that he sometimes incautiously played into the hands of this type of foe. Nor did he fully realize that his gift for making striking and quotable phrases added to the danger.

Joseph Tumulty, Wilson's personal secretary, recalling the Too Proud to Fight *speech, May 10, 1915, from his* Wilson as I Know Him, *p. 237.*

Dear Archie: There is a chance of our going to war; but I don't think it is very much of a chance. Wilson and Bryan are cordially supported by all the hyphenated Americans, by the solid flubdub and pacifist vote. Every soft creature, every coward and weakling, every man who can't look more than six inches ahead, every man whose god is money, or pleasure, or ease, and every man who has not got in him both the sterner virtues and the power of seeking after an ideal, is enthusiastically in favor of Wilson; and at present the good citizens, as a whole, are puzzled and don't understand the situation, and so a majority of them also tend to be with him. This is not pardonable; but it is natural. As a nation, we have thought very little about foreign affairs; we don't realize that the murder of the thousand men, women and children on the *Lusitania* is due, solely, to Wilson's

abject cowardice and weakness in failing to take energetic action when the *Gulflight* was sunk but a few days previously. He and Bryan are morally responsible for the loss of the lives of those American women and children—and for the lives lost in Mexico, no less than for the lives lost on the high seas. They are both of them abject creatures and they won't go to war unless they are kicked into it, and they will consider nothing but their own personal advantage in the matter. Nevertheless, there is a chance that Germany may behave in such fashion that they will have to go to war. Of course, I will notify you at once if war is declared; but I hope in any event, that it won't be until you and Quentin have had your month in camp. . . .

Former president Theodore Roosevelt to his son Archie, giving his views on Wilson's neutrality policies, May 19, 1915, in Elting E. Morison and John M. Blum, The Letters of Theodore Roosevelt, *vol. 8, pp. 922–923.*

Theodore Roosevelt became thoroughly angry over Wilson's policies. *(Library of Congress)*

When the Cabinet next assembled to consider the final draft of the note to Germany, the seat of the Secretary of State on the President's right was vacant. The President's face was grim and unsmiling, and he said as he took his seat: "Mr. Bryan has resigned as Secretary of State. The resignation was brought to me twenty minutes ago to become effective the moment this note is put on the cables to Germany. I have, with regret, accepted. Mr. Bryan feels a delicacy in attending this meeting."

To the majority of the members of the cabinet it was a complete surprise. Bryan had left the Cabinet meeting when it adjourned at six o'clock the preceding evening. He had insisted that the note be modified, but had given no intimation that his protest would go to the length of resignation. Unanimously the Cabinet suggested that he be asked to attend, and the President sent for him. He was affectionately greeted. All felt regret at the separation. At its conclusion most of the members accepted Bryan's invitation to lunch. In a private dining room he opened his heart. To his colleagues Bryan unbosomed himself with deep feeling. Unable to suppress the emotion which almost shook his frame, he said in substance: "Gentlemen: this is our last meeting together. I have valued our association and friendship. I have had to take the course I have chosen. The President has had one view. I have had a different one. I do not censure him for thinking and acting as he thinks best. I have had to act as I have thought best. I cannot go along with him in this note. I think it makes for war. The President still hopes for peace and I pray, as earnestly as he, that Germany may do nothing to aggravate further the situation. Because it is the duty of the patriot to support his government with all his heart in time of war, he has a right in time of peace to try to prevent war. I shall live up to a patriot's duty if war comes—until that time I shall do what I can to save my country from its horror. I believe that I can do more on the outside to prevent war than I can on the inside. I think I can help the President more on the outside. I can work to direct public opinion so it will not exert pressure for extreme action which the President does not want. We both want the same thing—peace."

Bryan's eyes were not the only ones dimmed with tears in that quiet room.

Impulsively and emotionally and sincerely [Franklin K.] Lane said: "You are the most real Christian I know," and others shared that sentiment.

Controlling himself after this expression of admiration by his old associate, Bryan added: "I must act according to my conscience. As I leave the Cabinet I go out in the dark, though I have many friends who would die for me. The President has the prestige and the power on his side."

Josephus Daniels after Bryan's resignation, June 9, 1915, in his The Wilson Era: Years of Peace—1910–1917, *pp. 431–432.*

I did not like these last expressions. They did not run on all fours with his earlier ones. They did not square with his statement that he and the President wanted the same thing. The President wanted peace, but an honourable peace. Bryan apparently wanted peace at any price. He was, in effect, telling Germany and the world that we had not meant what we had said, and that we would not stand up for our rights. He was quitting under fire. Of course, he could not logically refuse to sign the proposed note after signing the first one. If he was in doubt, he ought to have resigned when the first note was agreed upon. The only explanation is that he had not thought that the first note was dangerous, while this one, in his judgment meant trouble—that is, that Germany would not accept our view and, in effect, back down. Therefore, we must back down.

Bryan is mistaken if he thinks that he can promote his programme on the outside and not be drawn into opposition to the President.

Secretary of Agriculture David F. Houston, on Bryan's resignation, June 9, 1915, in his Eight Years with Wilson's Cabinet: 1913 to 1920, *vol. 1, pp. 146–147.*

"What do you think of our new Secretary of State?" was the question Postmaster General Burleson asked me on the morning of the announcement. I answered, "I do not like it. Lansing is a good international lawyer and a fine gentleman. He obtained nearly all his practice in the State Department and in service on government commissions from his Republican father-in-law, ex-Secretary of State Foster. He is wholly unknown in the country except as a son-in-law of Foster and a beneficiary of Republican favors. I suppose he is a Democrat by inheritance, but if he has ever turned his hand over to strengthen the party I never heard of it, and if all Democrats were of his type, Taft instead of Wilson would be President. His appointment will add no strength to the administration or the party. He lives in the District of Columbia and is unknown outside a small circle of Washington city lawyers."

"You are wrong," replied Burleson. "Woodrow Wilson is going to be his own Secretary of State. Lansing is the very man he wants—a good lawyer, without outstanding personality, who will be able to carry on the regular duties of the office and be perfectly willing to let the 'Old Man' be the real Secretary of State."

Josephus Daniels, on Lensing as secretary of state, June 23, 1915, in his The Wilson Era: Years of Peace— 1910–1917, *p. 436.*

It was a cowardly attack, considering the women and children on board. We were about three and a half miles from the *Dunsley,* and the only thing that I or any of the crew saw was a few bubbles of air from the torpedo that was fired at the *Arabic* from off the starboard bow. It struck her abaft the engine room, with an explosion that even shook the bridge. The bottom was ripped clean out by the torpedo, and no vessel, however built, could have stood up against it. With the weight of water pouring in, she went down by the stern.

I remained on the bridge until she sank under me, and I was drawn into the vortex as the ship disappeared in 300 feet of water. She was a fine ship and a good sea boat in all kinds of weather, and I was sorry to see her career ended in such a way.

In time of peril women can give some men a long lead in pluck and presence of mind and still win. Facing death on the deck of the *Arabic* women were as cool as martyrs of old. Some of them even asked what they could do toward getting the boats lowered. A woman in the water with her baby was magnificent in her courage. In the lifeboat I was in, one of them wanted to take an oar, and it's a pretty hard pull. . . .

Captain of the Arabic *William Finch, in an interview with reporters, regarding the attack of August 19, 1915, in* New York Times, *December 4, 1915, "Arabic's Captain Brings in Adriatic," p. 7.*

Captain Finch headed the *Arabic* toward the sinking steamer, and we realized that she had been torpedoed, and the majority of those on deck put on their life preservers, ready for anything that might happen. When we got within half a mile of the *Dunsley* we saw her crew getting into the boats and one of the officers told us afterward they wanted to warn us, but were prevented from doing so by the Germans on the submarine alongside their ship. Nobody on our ship saw the submarine and did not know what was going to happen until Second Officer Steele shouted out from the bridge,

"Look out! Here comes a torpedo!" The next moment it struck the *Arabic* on the starboard side in number five hold, just abaft the engine room, and the shock of the explosion nearly threw us off our feet. The discipline maintained on the ship was excellent and there was no confusion of any kind.

Playwright Zellah Covington, a survivor of the Arabic, *describes the torpedo attack on the ship, August 19, 1915, in "45 Arabic Survivors Here on Two Liners,"* New York Times, *September 3, 1915, p. 2.*

The President was advised by the Cabinet officers with whom he conferred regarding the matter that it would be a hopeless task on his part to attempt to stem the tide that was now running in favour of the passage of the McLemore resolution, and that were he to attempt to prevent its passage it might result in a disastrous defeat of his leadership, that would seriously embarrass him on Capitol Hill and throughout the nation.

At the conclusion of this conference the President asked me whether my information about affairs on Capitol Hill and the attitude of the members of the House and Senate toward the McLemore resolution was in accord with the information he had just received from his Cabinet officers. I told him that it was, but that so far as I was concerned I did not share the opinion of the Cabinet officers and did not agree with the advice which they had volunteered to the effect that it would be useless for him to throw down the gage of battle to those who sought to pass the McLemore resolution. I informed him that regardless of what the attitude of those on Capitol Hill was toward the resolution, he could not afford to allow the matter to pass without a protest from him, and that, indeed, he could afford to be defeated in making a fight to maintain American rights upon the high seas. The discussion between the President, the Cabinet officers, and myself became heated. They were reluctant to have the President go into the fight, while I was most anxious to have him do so.

February 1916. Joseph Tumulty recalling discussion with Wilson over the McLemore resolution, in his memoir, Wilson as I Know Him, *p. 203.*

I consider the reliance upon the militia for national defense an unjustifiable imperiling of the nation's safety. It would not only be a sham in itself, but its enactment into law would prevent, if not destroy, the opportunity to procure measures of real, genuine national defense. I could not accept it or acquiesce in its acceptance. I am obliged to make my position known immediately upon each of these questions—in a speech on Thursday afternoon upon the national defence question and in a communication to the House committee having charge of the Philippine question. If with respect to either matter, we are not in agreement upon these fundamental principles, then I could not, with propriety, remain your seeming representative in respect thereto. Our convictions would be manifestly not only divergent, but utterly irreconcilable.

On February 9, 1916, Secretary of War Lindley Garrison states his disagreement with Wilson regarding defense planning and a change in policy toward the Philippines, the day before submitting his resignation, "Garrison to Wilson," in David F. Houston, Eight Years with Wilson's Cabinet: 1913 to 1920, vol. 1, pp. 174–175.

If we settle the *Lusitania* question by compromising in any way your original demands, or if we permit it to drag on longer, America can have no part in bringing the war to an end. The current of allied opinion will run so strongly against the Administration that no censorship and no friendly interference by an allied government can stem the distrust of our Government which is now so strong in Europe. We shall gain by any further delay only a dangerous, thankless, and opulent isolation. The *Lusitania* is the turning point in our history. The time to act is now.

February 15, 1916, U.S. ambassador to Britain Walter Hines Page, advising Wilson to continue to take a hard line with Germany, in Burton J. Hendrick, editor, The Life and Letters of Walter H. Page, vol. 2, p. 52.

It is important to reflect that if in this instance we allowed expediency to take the place of principle the door would inevitably be opened to still further concessions. Once accept a single abatement of right, and many other humiliations would follow, and the whole fine fabric of international law might crumble under our hand piece by piece. What we are contending for in this matter is of the very essence of the things that have made America a sovereign nation. She cannot yield them without conceding her own impotency as a nation and making virtual surrender of her independent position among the nations of the world.

On February 25, 1916, Wilson writes to Senator William J. Stone opposing the Gore and McLemore resolutions and publishes the letter "Wilson to Stone," quoted in Joseph Tumulty, Wilson as I Know Him, p. 205.

Two men and a girl were pushing a raft over the rail. She had been on the boat train, accompanied by her mother, and I had noticed how beautifully dressed she was. Now her thin, yellow blouse was dripping wet and she wore over it a lifebelt. She turned from the raft toward me and threw out her arms with a most desperate gesture. The raft went over with a great splash. Whether they leaped after it I do not know. I crossed to the other side of the boat. The last lifeboat had just been made ready. At first women were allowed to get in rather faster than men. But toward the end men began to jump for it, and there were many still on board. As the boat hit the water half a dozen men slid down the ropes after it. Some landed on the heads of those already in, while others missed. It was impossible to stop them and get more women in. The boat got away. Some of the people waved to us, and a Belgian soldier started to free the oars. Gazing down over the side, I saw a face in the water. It was deadly white with terror written on every feature. For a moment we gazed at each other, but neither spoke.

Wilder Penfield, a passenger aboard the Sussex, *reporting on the torpedo attack of March 24, 1916, in "Brave and Calm on Sussex," New York Times, April 29, 1916, p. 3.*

When the *Sussex* was sunk in March 1916, there was a long discussion in the Cabinet on April 4 over the course to pursue. Lansing declared that the time had come "to quit writing notes" and "for action." There was a difference of opinion in the Cabinet, the President not being as ready for war as Lansing and some others. The warlike note drawn up by Lansing was not sent, but a somewhat modified note was approved. It gave notice to Germany that "unless the Imperial German Government should now immediately declare its intention to abandon its present practice of submarine warfare and return to a scrupulous observance of the practice clearly prescribed by the law of nations, the Government of the United States can have no choice but to sever diplomatic relations with the German government altogether." Lansing wanted to close the door at once. Considering the previous vigorous notes to Britain over freedom of the seas and defense of neutrality and against entrance into the war and trying to avert it, I could not reconcile Lansing's belligerency with his previous attitude.

The position of the President in keeping the door open was approved by the Cabinet. I took the ground that, aside from other questions, if Wilson brought on war with Germany except after exhausting every possible means to avert it, the country would rise up against him in the 1916 election.

On April 4, 1916, Josephus Daniels comments on Lansing's suggested note in response to the Sussex *incident, in his* The Wilson Era: Years of Peace— 1910–1917, *p. 439.*

There is one thing I feel quite certain about, and that is, no formal reply should be made to the German note. I believe, too, it would be better for you to let Lansing make any statement to the public that is considered proper.

None of the papers have brought out the real concessions that the Germans have made. This I think, should be done, and then I believe a rather curt statement should be made to the effect that we will deal with the other belligerents who violate international law as we see fit.

I do not see how we can break with Germany on this note. However, I would make it very clear to the German Government, through both Gerard and Bernstorff, that the least infraction would entail an immediate severance of diplomatic relations; and I would let the public know unofficially that this had been done. We will then have to wait and hope for the best.

At my conference with Bernstorff yesterday, I suggested that he caution his Government against any further transgression. He said he would, but he did not believe any would occur. The disagreeable parts of the note, he told me, were necessary because of German public opinion, but he confessed that he knew it would be impossible for us to make Great Britain conform to international law in regard to the blockade. He thought you could make peace easier than you could do this. . . .

Colonel Edward House writes to Wilson advising him to ignore the conditions that the Germans put in their Sussex *Pledge, "House to Wilson," May 6, 1916, in Charles Seymour, editor,* The Intimate Papers of Colonel House, *p. 243.*

The English do not see how there can be any mediation, nor (I confess) do I see. German militarism must be put down. I don't mean that the German people should be thrashed to a frazzle nor thrashed at all. I find no spirit of revenge in the English. But this German military caste caused all the trouble and there can be no

security in Europe as long as it lives in authority. That's the English view. It raped nuns in Belgium, it took food from the people, it even now levies indemnities on all towns, it planned the destruction of the *Lusitania,* and it now coos like a suckling dove in the United States. It'll do anything. Now, since it has become evident that it is going to be beaten, it wants peace . . . on terms which will give it a continued lease of life. . . . In another year or two the German military caste will be broken as the rulers of that country. And that caste will not be trusted in Europe with any professions of repentance that it will make. That's the long and short of it.

On May 23, 1916, the U.S. ambassador to Great Britain, W. H. Page, confides to Colonel House his feelings about Germany, in Charles Seymour, editor, The Intimate Papers of Colonel House, *p. 256.*

I lunched with Mr. Asquith. One does not usually bring away much from his conversations, and he did not say much to-day worth recording. But he showed a very eager interest in the Presidential campaign, and he confessed that he felt some anxiety about the anti-British feeling in the United States. This led him to tell me that he could not in good conscience interfere with Casement's execution, in spite of the shoals of telegrams that he was receiving from the United States. This man, said he, visited Irish prisoners in German camps and tried to seduce them to take up arms against Great Britain—their own country. When they refused, the Germans removed them to the worst places in their Empire and, as a result, some of them died. Then Casement came to Ireland in a German man-of-war (a submarine) accompanied by a ship loaded with guns. "In all good conscience to my country and to my responsibilities I cannot interfere." He hoped that thoughtful opinion in the United States would see this whole matter in a fair and just way.

On August 1, 1916, Ambassador W. H. Page notes his discussion with the British prime minister regarding the sentence of death on Roger Casement for his part in the Irish Easter Rebellion, in Burton J. Hendrick, editor, The Life and Letters of Walter H. Page, *vol. 2, p. 168.*

It has seemed to me that it might be advisable to pursue this method at the present time in bringing home to the British Government the growing irritation in this country at the blacklisting, censorship of mails and other measures adopted by Great Britain and the indifference shown by the British Government in failure to make prompt reply to our notes. I am afraid that London does not appreciate that the tide of resentment is rising very high in this country, and that there is a tendency to demand drastic action by this Government. The British Government ought to be fully advised of this menace to our cordial relations, because the removal of it lies with them. I do not think that their representatives here have correctly pictured the state of the public mind in this country or impressed them with the conditions which are rapidly approaching a critical stage.

Secretary of State Robert Lansing suggesting to Wilson that a set of informal protests should be sent to Britain regarding British violations of neutrality, "Lansing to Wilson," September 22, 1916, in Arthur Link, et al., eds., The Papers of Woodrow Wilson, *vol. 38 (August 7–November 19, 1916), p. 202.*

Last night at Peoria I had a long talk with Mr. Pindell. His paper is making a straw vote in Illinois and Iowa in connection with the New York Herald. He is not surprised that the tendency in Illinois and Iowa, both rock-ribbed Republican States, is to Hughes, although he said that a most significant fact was the straw ballots of the Illinois women, who had, by two to one, voted for you. Their vote was not included in the straw ballot made public by the Herald today. It is the conviction of everyone I have met out here that a strong appeal to the women, who vote for President the first time this year in Illinois, on the peace issue, would bring large support and arouse them to the importance of voting in November. I think attention should be given to this and that an early opportunity ought to be made to address a body of women on this subject.

Wilson's son-in-law and secretary of the treasury, William Gibbs McAdoo, discussing the upcoming election in a letter to Wilson, advising him to be aware of the women's vote, "McAdoo to Wilson," September 24, 1916, in Arthur Link, et al., eds., The Papers of Woodrow Wilson, *vol. 38 (August 7–November 19, 1916), p. 260.*

Laughingly, he [Wilson] said, "Well, Tumulty, it begins to look as if we have been badly licked." As he discussed the matter with me I could detect no note of sadness in his voice. In fact, I could hear him chuckle over the phone. He seemed to take an impersonal view of the whole thing and talked like a man from whose shoulders a great load had been lifted and now he was happy and rejoicing that he was a free man again. . . . "Tumulty,

you are an optimist. It begins to look as if the defeat might be overwhelming. The only thing I am sorry for, and that cuts me to the quick, is that the people apparently misunderstood us. But I have no regrets. We have tried to do our duty." So far as he was concerned, the issue of the election was disposed of, out of the way and a settled thing. . . .

Just about the break of day on Wednesday morning, as David Lawrence, Ames Brown, and my son Joe, were seated in my office, a room which overlooked a wide expanse of the Atlantic Ocean, we were notified by Democratic headquarters of the first big drift toward Wilson. Ohio, which in the early evening had been claimed by the Republicans, had turned to Wilson by an approximate majority of sixty thousand; Kansas followed; Utah was leaning toward him; North Dakota and South Dakota inclining the same way. The Wilson tide began to rise appreciably from that time on, until state after state from the West came into the Wilson column. At five o'clock in the morning the New York *Times* and the New York *World* recanted and were now saying that the election of Mr. Hughes was doubtful.

Without sleep and without food, those of us at the Executive offices kept close to the telephone wire. We never left the job for a minute. . . .

Mr. Wilson arose the morning after the election, confident that he had been defeated. He went about his tasks in the usual way. The first news that he received that there had been a turn in the tide came from his daughter, Margaret, who knocked on the door of the bathroom while the President was shaving and told him of the "Extra" of the New York *Times,* saying that the election was in doubt, with indications of a Wilson victory. The President thought that his daughter was playing a practical joke on him and told her to "tell that to the Marines," and went on about his shaving.

On November 7–8, 1916, Joseph Tumulty discusses the reaction to the delayed results of the November 1916 presidential election, in his Wilson as I Know Him, *pp. 218–219, 222–223.*

Soon after the note was published, when I returned to Washington, I saw Maurice Low, correspondent of the London Morning Post. He was very much disturbed and angry about the note. He said to me that it would be resented by the Allies; that it was a peace move, that the President had played into the hands of the Germans, and that he had created a very delicate situation which might become serious. I replied that he was unduly excited. I protested that I could not speak for the President, that I did not know all that was in his mind or that lay behind the note, but that I presumed he had a faint hope that, if the Allies and the Central Powers stated to the world what they were fighting for, it might be discovered that they were not far apart in what they would be willing to set forth, and that a basis for a conference and peace might be reached. I added that I had no such hope, but that I was confident that the note would place the Allies in a favourable tactical position. They would be able to make a statement of their purposes, one which would appeal to our own people and to the conscience of the world. The Germans could not make any statement whatever, or, at any rate, one which would not cause world-wide resentment. The further result would be the education or enlightenment of the American people. They would be brought to a fuller realization of the fact that the Allies were waging a just war and fighting for a higher civilization. As we were profoundly affected, it was not inappropriate that both sides should tell us directly and concretely what they stood for in their own way. Each evidently valued our good opinion and wanted at least our moral support.

Low assented to this last statement but asserted that we knew what each was fighting for and that the Allies had stated their terms—"full reparations, complete restitution, and adequate guaranties." I agreed that they were fighting for those things and that they ought to have them. "Certainly," I said, "the Allies are in the right—that is, Great Britain, France, and Belgium are. I have been on their side since the first day the Germans moved. They ought to win, and I believe they will win, in the end; but I am not so blind as not to know that they are not fighting merely for the three things they proclaim. Their motives and purposes are very complex. The British for a long time have been very jealous of the growing commercial as well as of the growing naval power of the Germans. Not unnaturally, they have watched with apprehension the development of German colonies. They are anxious about the Dardanelles, Asia Minor, Egypt, and India. Great Britain intervened in 1878 to prevent the Turks from being driven out of Constantinople by the Russians. Great Britain, France, and Belgium have acted nobly, but they have not acted from single or simple motives, and when the war is over we shall see evidence of the truth of it. If they win, we shall see a great scramble. There have been other wars, and in all of them there were complex motives and loud protestations of unselfish gains." . . . The American people, I added, would not welcome dictation even from one of the Allies, and this nation itself did not wish to dominate anybody. It was sick of all that sort of mad business. It merely wanted a clean national house for itself, peace and law everywhere in the world, so that people everywhere might prosper and nations might live together in neighbourly fashion. . . . The reply of Germany, as well as that of the Allies confirmed my view.

On December 20, 1916, David Houston, Wilson's secretary of agriculture, discusses with a British journalist Wilson's arguments for a statement of war goals, in his Eight Years with Wilson's Cabinet: 1913 to 1920, *vol. 1, pp. 221–223.*

8

U.S. Entry into the War
November 1916–April 1917

In the period between the reelection of Woodrow Wilson as president of the United States in November 1916 and his inauguration for a second term March 5, 1917, a variety of decisions and actions by the German government had brought the United States to the verge of war. Wilson continued to believe that the United States should remain neutral and should be able to act as an impartial mediator between the belligerents, but as events unfolded through the remaining weeks of March 1917 that peaceful path seemed less and less possible. A combination of German decisions and actions, revelations of the Zimmermann plans for lining up allies against the United States, and mounting public opinion were at work during the event-filled weeks of early 1917 to bring an end to American neutrality.

THE GERMAN DECISION

On January 9, 1917, at a secret conference held at Pless Castle in Germany, Chancellor Bethmann-Hollweg discussed the war situation with his leading generals, Hindenburg and Ludendorff. The generals pushed for a decision to launch unrestricted and "ruthless" submarine warfare against Great Britain on February 1. They believed that sinking all shipping to and from Britain would cripple the British war effort to the point that the British would sue for peace within a few months. At the conference, the chancellor questioned whether the submarine blockade, enforced against neutrals including Denmark, Holland, Switzerland, and the United States, would bring the neutrals into the war. The generals weighed that possibility but decided they could handle any action by the small European countries. As to American participation, they believed it would be limited to a corps of volunteers, some aircraft, and financial credits to Britain. However, if the amounts of food and supplies flowing to Britain could be drastically reduced by the submarine blockade, the war would be over before American aid could affect the outcome. The chancellor finalized the decision to launch the blockade but did not announce it until January 31, 1917, to go into effect the next day.

From the German perspective, the submarine blockade seemed to represent the best chance to bring the war to a successful end. A negotiated peace or a victory for the Allies would mean that Germany would have to pay indemnification, sacrifice territory, give up its colonies, and limit its arms. The Allied war goals, the German leadership believed, would reduce Germany to a second-rate power in Central Europe. A victory would leave Germany a major nation and world power, ranking as an equal to France and Britain. In a rather organized and mathematical calculation, the German high command recognized that if they could reduce the tonnage flowing to Britain by 600,000 tons a month, Britain would have to capitulate within a year and perhaps within a few months, if the British recognized the situation they faced. The United States did not have a large, trained army, and it would take months to transport troops and equipment to Europe. With submarine control of the sea-lanes, even that transport would be endangered. With starvation in Germany among the civilian population, and with the troops in strong positions outside the German frontiers, a push to victory through full use of the submarine weapon, even with the risk of American hostility, made logical sense by these calculations.

Even so, the German leadership knowingly took on a clear risk to use the submarine against American shipping. Wilson had threatened Germany with the severance of diplomatic relations over the sinking of the British ships *Lusitania* and *Arabic* and the French packet *Sussex;* with the violations of the pledge to respect liners and not to attack unarmed ships, a blockade enforced by submarines, especially one against neutral American ships, even with warnings to the crews, would have serious consequences.

THE NAVY NEEDS YOU! DON'T READ AMERICAN HISTORY — MAKE IT!

The shipping crises in the news stimulated naval recruiting. *(Library of Congress)*

WILSON: PEACE WITHOUT VICTORY

Meanwhile, Wilson, unaware of the German decision, continued to advocate a negotiated peace during January 1917, and, in a speech delivered on January 22, he called for a "peace without victory." He argued that a war that resulted in victors and vanquished would lead to an uneasy peace, in which the defeated nations would want revenge, leading to another round of war. If the war were to result in a lasting peace, he argued, the nations of the world would have to organize in a league to preserve the peace. His remarks, as so often in the past, became reduced to slogans and headlines. While those advocating continued neutrality and pacifists applauded his ideas, the concept of peace without victory infuriated those like Theodore Roosevelt who advocated American participation on the Allied side. A war fought to preserve a lasting peace would become, in a slogan of the era, "a war to end wars."

While pro-British Americans, like Walter Hines Page, the U.S. ambassador in Britain, believed that the war should bring about a lasting peace, they believed that only a sound defeat of Germany could ensure such a peace. Wilson's position, they argued, treated Britain as if it were on an equal footing with Germany in terms of war guilt and responsibility.

For Americans who had been stunned by the brutality of the German invasion of Belgium and France, the German tactics of ruthless suppression of irregular resistance, and the destruction of resources when Germans retreated, such as the poisoning of wells, burning of homes and farms, and the slaughter of livestock, it seemed incredible that Wilson would suggest that neither side should win. All of those acts had been reported and exaggerated by the British propaganda agencies, convincing at least some of the public in the United States by January 1917 that Germany was simply barbaric when compared to Britain, France, and Belgium. Furthermore, the fact that autocratic regimes ruled the Central Powers and that the British and French regimes had democratic forms of government made it seem that the United States should be a natural member of the Allies. Pro-Allied Americans believed that the war should not only bring a lasting peace but also that it should be a peace that spread and preserved democracy. If Germany were to emerge undefeated after the war, they argued, it would continue to dominate Europe and would continue to expand its overseas empire.

Page and other pro-Allied Americans, like Theodore Roosevelt seethed with outrage at Wilson's continued insistence on neutrality, and, in their private correspondence and sometimes in their public statements, they attacked him not only for his ideas but also for the personality traits they found offensive. To such men, Wilson's idealism appeared muddle-headed, and his refusal to fight seemed un-masculine and cowardly. Some found his attitude of peacemaker condescending and insulting to the Allies. Wilson, however, and much of American public opinion held to a position of strict neutrality through January 1917. The German decision to unleash the submarines quickly changed some minds, however, although others still hoped to find a course that would preserve neutrality.

Wilson explained to Congress his decision to break relations with Germany on February 3, 1917. *(National Archives)*

The announcement of the German submarine blockade on January 31 brought a storm of protest from the pro-Allied camp in the United States. Even the provisions that the Germans made for allowing free passage for one ship a week for passengers to and from Britain, a safety zone in the North Sea for trade with neutrals Holland and Denmark, and a lane through the Mediterranean for trade with Greece appeared to such critics as insulting and dictatorial, a clear set of infringements on the concept of freedom of the seas. As Wilson discussed the matter with his cabinet, some members insisted that the announcement that German ships would attack American shipping amounted to an act of war in itself. At the very least, they argued, the United States had to break diplomatic relations with Germany. Reluctantly, Wilson agreed to break relations, holding off declaring war at least until Germany committed an overt act of war, and, on February 3, the State Department notified Ambassador Johann von Bernstorff that the United States had severed diplomatic relations. In the expression of the day, the U.S. government "handed his passports" to Bernstorff. The United States arranged with Britain that Bernstorff and his staff could sail safely from New York by way of Halifax, Canada, and Holland on his return to Germany.

ZIMMERMANN AND HIS TELEGRAM

Meanwhile, however, the foreign minister of Germany, Arthur Zimmermann, had decided that, in the event of war with the United States, Germany should seek new allies. His predecessors had little luck in building alliances, and the Central Powers fighting alongside Germany included only three states: the severely divided Austro-Hungarian Empire, the weak and corrupt Turkish-run Ottoman Empire, and Bulgaria, whose primary motive appeared to be revenge against Serbia for the loss of Macedonia in the Second Balkan War in 1913 and the opportunity to gain some territory there and later in Romania. Italy, once an ally of Germany, had joined the Allies in May 1915.

Zimmermann's plans to approach Mexico to join in an alliance against the United States, may have seemed quite logical, since Mexico already had severely strained relations with the United States. Furthermore, Zimmermann hoped that Mexico would be able to convince the Japanese to break their alliance with the Allies and join against the United States. With the United States threatened on its southern border, and needing to protect its island possessions in the Pacific and its West Coast against Japanese attack, any American participation in the war in Europe would be strictly limited. Like a number of other apparently logical decisions made by leaders on both sides during the war, it would backfire against its creator.

Secretly, Zimmermann sent the telegram outlining the proposed alliance to Bernstorff on January 16, with instructions that Bernstorff should forward the message to the German minister in Mexico, H. von Eckhardt. The German foreign ministry sent the message encoded over undersea cable. The cable system they employed had been provided by the United States to allow Germany to respond to peace negotiations made by Wilson. Unknown to the United States, the British listened in on the line, and, furthermore, the British Naval Intelligence service had made great progress in cracking the German codes. In their crowded Room 40 in the British Admiralty building, Director William "Blinker" Hall and his team of code-crackers worked day and night on such intercepts. Thus, on January 17, Nigel de Grey began to learn the content of the Zimmermann telegram sent the day before, including the plan for unrestricted submarine warfare, the proposed alliance with Mexico, and the feelers to Japan that Zimmermann requested that Eckhardt undertake in Mexico.

The secret Zimmermann telegram, the British assumed, would infuriate the Americans once they heard about it and would help convince Wilson of German underhanded tactics. However, revealing the message and the fact that the Admiralty had deciphered it would lead the Germans to adopt new and tougher diplomatic codes. Furthermore, it would be irritating and perhaps insulting to Americans to learn that the British tapped the Americans' own line. Thus, Hall worked at first to develop a full transcription of the Zimmermann telegram and to plan a strategy for its revelation to the Americans. He realized that Bernstorff would have forwarded a version to Mexico, and he worked to recover that version, so that it would appear that the leak came out of Mexico City.

While Hall worked on decoding the telegram and developing a cover story that would conceal how it had been obtained, Germany proceeded with the submarine blockade. German U-boats began to stop any vessel in the seas around Britain, evacuating the crews and destroying the ships with planted explosives, gunfire, or torpedoes. In some cases U-boats simply torpedoed the target ship without warning. How the submarines would deal with American ships remained to be seen.

THE SUBMARINE BLOCKADE—FIRST EPISODES

The sinking of a total of nine American ships prior to April 6 constituted the specific casus belli, or cause of war, the overt acts Wilson required before declaring war. However, when submarines sank the first of these ships, the humane practices of the submarine commanders and the fact that the seamen survived made it possible for the United States to remain at peace with Germany, at least for a few weeks.

With the announced blockade, most U.S. ships stayed in port, although a few that had already departed began to arrive in European ports. The first two American ships to be destroyed under the new blockade were the steam-propelled freighter *Housatonic* on February 3 and a schooner, the *Lyman M. Law,* on February 12. In both cases, the submarine commander ensured that the crews evacuated the ships before sinking them, and no one died in these two sinkings.

The *Housatonic* carried a cargo of wheat consigned to the British government and encountered the submarine off the Scilly Islands, in the designated war zone off the tip of Cornwall in Britain. A former German-registered, 3,143-ton steamship of the Hamburg American line that had been sold in April 1915 to an American firm, *Housatonic* sailed under a special provision of the American maritime law that allowed such ships built in Germany to be transferred to American registry. In the case of the *Housatonic,* the submarine captain gave the crew a full hour to evacuate into lifeboats, and, after sinking the ship, he towed the lifeboats toward land for an hour and a half.

Under these circumstances, even the pro-Allied *New York Times* observed, the sinking of the *Housatonic* did not represent an overt act of war, since the goods aboard were consigned to the British government and were thus clearly contraband, and since the submarine captain had followed traditional cruiser rules in warning the ship and providing for the safety of the crew. Indeed, it appeared from this episode that the Germans would be quite scrupulous in applying cruiser rules to American ships in their new blockade. Furthermore, even anti-German observers believed that the German U-boat captains carefully followed correct procedure with American ships that had left port prior to the January 31 announcement of the blockade.

Less than 10 days later, another submarine stopped the four-masted, 1,300-ton American schooner the *Lyman M. Law*, with a crew of 10, off Sardinia in the Mediterranean, not too far from the lane that the Germans had designated as the safety zone for trade to Greece. The ship carried lumber and a good supply of live chickens, which apparently caught the eye of the submarine captain. After the schooner crew evacuated to two lifeboats, the submarine crew rescued several dinners worth of fowls, then planted a bomb aboard the schooner, setting fire and destroying it. The U.S. State Department did not regard this attack as an overt act of war. It appeared that the submarine might have accosted the schooner within the protected safety lane, but since the exact location remained unclear, official reaction in Washington stayed muted. Captain S. W. McDonough and the other nine members of the crew landed safely in Cagliari, Sardinia. McDonough had set sail before the blockade announcement had been made, and he had not expected any difficulty.

Following the announcement on January 31, American shipping companies began to limit their departures, and the U.S. cabinet met several times through February to discuss the effect of the blockade on trade. Cabinet members discussed the fact that as long as the United States did nothing in response to the blockade except sever diplomatic relations, the blockade would be effective, both from occasional sinking and from the voluntary "interning" of U.S. ships in American ports.

Cabinet members urged Wilson to give some guidance to the shipping companies. After all, several companies had government contracts to deliver mail, but did not sail because of fear of destruction. William Gibbs McAdoo, the son-in-law of Wilson, insisted on setting a policy of at least "armed neutrality" in which U.S. merchant ships would be provided with antisubmarine guns to defend themselves. Wilson expressed impatience at the warlike suggestions, but others supported the idea.

Meanwhile, in Britain, Ambassador Page and officials of the British government grew increasingly worried that Wilson would simply accept the submarine embargo and limit his reaction to breaking diplomatic relations with Germany. Blinker Hall had succeeded in obtaining a copy of the Zimmermann telegram as received in Mexico and, on February 22, he delivered it to Ambassador Page. Page immediately recognized that the telegram might be the tool he and the British needed to convince Wilson to take stronger measures. Page sent a copy of the telegram with assurances of its authenticity back to the United States on February 24, and Wilson read it. He first thought that it should be made public but agreed to wait a few days until Secretary of State Lansing returned to Washington from a short trip out of town.

From the perspective of Page, the telegram gave sufficient cause for war, but Wilson responded more cautiously. The telegram, however, might prove useful in getting support in Congress for the move demanded by members of the cabinet, a form of protection for U.S. ships passing through the submarine blockade.

THE ARMED SHIP BILL

Convinced by the insistence of cabinet members and emboldened by the shocking suggestion of a German alliance with Mexico in the telegram, Wilson asked Congress to pass the Armed Ship bill on February 26. Even though he had read the telegram, he did not at first release it, nor did he mention it in his request to Congress. Ignoring the Austrian sinking of the schooner *Lyman M. Law* and the earlier German sinking of the steamship *Housatonic*, he said that, as yet, Germany had made no overt act of war. Furthermore, he said, he had the constitutional authority to arm merchant ships without asking Congress for approval but that he hesitated to take such a momentous step without congressional endorsement of the action. A clear majority in the House of Representatives supported the armed ship concept, but in the Senate the Democratic chair of the Foreign Relations Committee, Senator Stone, opposed it, and a group of neutralist senators planned a filibuster to prevent passage of the bill.

From the German perspective on international law, if merchant ships were armed, it made them equivalent to warships, justifying attacks without warn-

Enforcing freedom of the seas remained a rallying cry. *(National Archives)*

ing. Lansing and Wilson knew and understood this interpretation and realized that arming merchant ships could move the United States closer to war. However, neither in his speech nor in his correspondence did Wilson make clear whether he expected that the arming of civilian ships would provoke the overt act that would be necessary to move to war or whether he believed that armed neutrality would prevent full-scale war. Those in the cabinet who supported the Armed Ship bill included some, like McAdoo, who believed it would take the United States closer to belligerency, and others, like Daniels, who hoped it would keep the United States out of war at least for a period. Both hawks and doves agreed that providing arms to merchant ships seemed better than simply shutting down trade with the Allies, and perhaps Wilson sought to win support from both sides by sidestepping either the hawkish or dovish implications of the bill.

Within the State Department, the counselor for the department, Frank L. Polk, worked to find a copy of the original encrypted version of the telegram received by Bernstorff. Finally, he obtained the text and showed it to Wilson, who expressed dismay at the discovery that the secure cable line that he had personally arranged for Bernstorff's use in working toward a negotiated peace had been used to attempt a Mexican-German-Japanese alliance against the United States. It seemed a rather ungentlemanly betrayal of a trust. Wilson agreed with Lansing that the telegram should be made public, and Lansing gave a copy to the Washington bureau chief of the Associated Press on the evening of February 28.

The timing of the release worked well, but many critics believed it had been stage-managed. Members of Congress in the House of Representatives were debating the Armed Ship bill when the news broke, and they voted overwhelmingly to support the bill in a vote of 403 to 13. However, the Associated Press story contained an error, indicating the telegram had been in the president's hands since early February, when in fact he had seen the first copy only four days previously, on February 24. If it had been true that he withheld release of the telegram for several weeks, it would appear that Wilson had carefully timed the news in order to maximize its effect on Congress to win support for his measure.

A storm of indignant debate broke out in the Senate, as some doubted the authenticity of the telegram, and others thought Wilson had pulled off a bit of trickery by timing the release to coincide with the congressional action. After heated argument over these points between supporters and opponents of Wilson, the Senate passed a resolution requesting more information about the telegram. Wilson and Lansing immediately replied that they had had the note for less than a week and that they could attest to its authenticity. Beyond that, however, they stated that it would be inconsistent with the national interest to describe how the note had been obtained. That hint left many with the impression that it had been secured by American espionage, and Blinker Hall gladly let that impression remain, rather than spread suspicion that British intelligence had been cracking the German codes.

Across the country, for two days, the Zimmermann telegram caused a sensation. The German-American press condemned the note as a fraud, as did many neutralists, pacifists, and pro-German advocates. In the Midwest and West, regions that had been staunchly opposed to getting involved in the war and whose popular vote in the presidential election had swung to Wilson in November 1916 because voters saw him as a convinced advocate of American neutrality, the thought of a Mexican army, officered by Germans and supported with Japanese ships and arms, invading the country suddenly began to break down resistance to involvement in the war. In the Senate, however, a group of die-hard neutralists continued to filibuster, and Congress reached the end of its session on March 4 without passing the Armed Ship bill. Wilson gave vent to a rare burst of temper and released a peevish remark to the press, noting that the United States had been immobilized by "a little group of willful men representing no opinion but their own."[1]

That same day, news reached the United States that German foreign minister Zimmermann admitted to reporters that he had indeed sent the telegram as reported. Although he never explained why he admitted its authenticity, it may very well have been because, since he did not know how it had been revealed, he thought that proof of its authenticity might be published within a few days, and that if he had denied it his honor and credibility would be further damaged. In any case, he and many Germans believed that Germany had every right to seek further allies if the United States entered the war. They saw nothing so very terrible in admitting that Germany sought to protect its own interests. Zimmermann and the other German leadership had no understanding of how the American public would react to such an arrangement, or perhaps they simply did not care.

Since the United States had been engaged for more than a year with troops sent deep into Mexico in a fruitless effort to find and capture the Mexican

General John J. Pershing returned from his expedition in Mexico after failing to track down Pancho Villa. He had earned the nickname "Black Jack" for his prior command of an African-American unit. *(Library of Congress)*

rebel chieftain, Pancho Villa, against the protests of the Mexican government, the relations between the United States and Mexico had deteriorated almost to the point of war. Wilson had recalled General Pershing and his forces from Mexico only a few weeks earlier. Furthermore, in the western states, anti-Japanese feelings ran strong, representing a mix of racial prejudice and economic jealousy. Several states had attempted to legislate against the sale of land to Japanese immigrants, and all had favored immigration restriction to prevent Japanese from entering the United States. Instead of intimidating the United States, even the hint of a German-Mexican-Japanese alliance could have the effect of swaying the neutralist Midwest and anti-Japanese West to a more pro-Allied position.

Even the German-American press found Zimmermann's admission that he had sent the telegram appallingly insensitive to the American political situation. One of the leaders of German-American opinion in the United States, Bernard Ridder, of the newspaper *Staats-Zeitung,* regarded Zimmermann's telegram and Zimmermann's admission of its authenticity as a "mistake so grave that it renders the situation almost hopeless." He believed Germany had lost forever its chance to redeem itself in the eyes of the American public.[2]

Wilson took the oath of office for his second term on March 5, and in his inauguration address he alluded to the desire to remain neutral but hinted that it might no longer be possible to avoid taking a more active part in the conflict. Events continued to move the nation and the president closer to such an active role.

With Congress adjourned and no action on the Armed Ship bill, and without authorization from Congress, Wilson ordered on March 9 that the navy begin providing guns and trained gun crews for civilian merchant ships. The controversies over the Armed Ship bill and the telegram itself, however, did not provide the final push that tipped the United States into war. That push came from the actions of German U-boat captains over the next four weeks.

SUBMARINES AND U.S. SHIPPING

Through the rest of March 1917, the sinking of American ships by German submarines continued. On March 12, a submarine sank the single-screw, three-masted steamship *Algonquin,* loaded with 2,800 tons of food consigned by Swift company of Chicago to Britain, at the approaches to the English Channel. All members of the crew safely evacuated in lifeboats and landed in Penzance.

What seemed to tip American public opinion and many newspaper editorialists in favor of war came in a single announcement on March 18 of the sinking of three more American-registered and American-crewed ships: the *City of Memphis,* the *Illinois,* and the *Vigilancia.* The ships had actually been sunk over the previous two days, and in the case of the *Vigilancia,* 15 members of the crew died, including five Americans. Considering the fact that the *Lusitania* sailed under British registration, the *Vigilancia* sinking brought the first war casualties aboard an American-registered ship since the admittedly accidental killing of two Americans aboard the *Gulflight* in 1915. Between February 1 and March 18, 1917, six American ships had been sunk, but in every case, the crews had been able to escape in lifeboats, sometimes assisted by the submarine crews. In the case of the *Vigilancia,* however, one lifeboat had been swamped and the men in it drowned.

The *Vigilancia* had sailed for Le Havre from New York on February 28, carrying a general cargo of iron, fruit, asbestos, and straw; a submarine fired two torpedoes at the ship without warning, about 145 miles from land, on March 16. F. A. Middleton, who captained the steamship, had a crew of 45, including 20 American citizens. (Usually in this period, American-registered ships had crews made up of men of several nationalities.) The ship carried a large and clearly painted American flag on its side and had its name and the hailing port of New York painted in letters that could be read from miles away.

The *City of Memphis* had been on a return trip from Cardiff, bound for New York, when a German submarine shelled and sank her on March 17 off the coast of Ireland. The ship did not carry any cargo but sailed in ballast after having delivered her cargo of baled cotton to Le Havre, France. The submarine sailors fired warning shots, instructed the *City of Memphis* crew to abandon ship in lifeboats, and then sank the empty cargo ship with 10 or 11 more gunshots. Eventually, all 57 members of the crew of the *City of Memphis* reached land safely.

The tanker *Illinois,* returning in ballast from London and destined for Port Arthur, Texas, sank on the afternoon of March 17. All 34 crew members of the *Illinois* reached land safely.

The *Vigilancia,* the *Illinois,* and the *City of Memphis* all sank within the German-designated war zone around Britain. Meanwhile, the Germans continued

A last-minute escape from a ship torpedoed by a German submarine. One survivor climbs down a line as the last lifeboat pulls away. *(National Archives)*

to sink many other ships registered to the British and French, with far worse effect. Two American women died on February 26 when a German submarine sank the British liner *Laconia*. The tonnage of ships sunk continued to mount, with dozens of British, French, and Italian ships sunk, including freighters, liners, fishing trawlers, and at least one ship under charter to the Belgian Relief Commission carrying food and supplies for hungry Belgian civilians.

MOUNTING PRESSURE FOR A WAR DECLARATION

With the sinking of three American ships announced on the same day, some newspapers commented that these incidents represented the specific overt act to which Wilson had alluded as necessary to represent a state of war, when he had announced the break in diplomatic relations with Germany. A massive rally held on March 22 at Madison Square Garden, attended by some 12,000, heard speeches from prowar advocates. Although Theodore Roosevelt could not attend, he sent a message to the rally in which he claimed that the sinking of the American ships amounted to an overt act on a par with the firing on Fort Sumter that had started the Civil War. Other speakers included Theodore Roosevelt's former secretary of state, Elihu Root, who gave an impassioned plea for war.

The cabinet agreed. On March 20, at a full cabinet meeting, Wilson asked each member his opinion as to whether he should ask Congress to convene in a special session. Congress had scheduled to reassemble on April 16, but every member of the cabinet agreed that Wilson should call Congress back into session earlier. Even the convinced neutralists in the cabinet, Postmaster Albert Burleson and Secretary of the Navy Josephus Daniels, reluctantly agreed that the time had come to ask for a congressional declaration that a state of war already existed between Germany and the United States. In fact, when the cabinet took that vote, every U.S. registered ship that had been sunk since February 1 had been within the announced war zone, and most of their crews had been warned to evacuate. The deaths of the five American merchant seamen aboard the *Vigilancia* had been the result of a lifeboat accident. Often the press had wrongly carried initial stories that submarines sank ships without warning or that temporarily missing seamen had been killed, before correcting the version in a smaller story tucked away on inside pages of the newspaper a few days later. So the attacks and the barrage of headlines about ships lost and crews missing created a sensational impression that reached a kind of peak in the week of March 18 to March 25.

The mounting toll of ships destroyed, combined with the impact on public opinion of the Zimmermann note, swung the cabinet over to advising war, no matter how scrupulously some submarine captains sought to follow cruiser rules. In the case of the ships registered to the belligerents, the U-boats demonstrated much less care. In March 1917, a total of 630 merchant seamen of various nationalities lost their lives in submarine attacks on ships flying under other flags. The press also followed the stories of attacks on completely innocent ships registered to other nations such as fishing boats, passenger liners, and the ship carrying relief supplies.

Despite the cabinet's unanimous and explicit advice to Wilson, the president did not confide to even his closest associates and friends what he planned to do. Some advisers recommended that his request for a declaration of war could be based on the fact that Germany had already made acts of war by attacking U.S.

ships. Therefore, they argued, the declaration of war could be cast as recognition of an existing state of affairs. Others pointed out that the war would pitch democracies against autocratic states and that the United States had ties of culture and heritage with the Allies. Some advisers, such as ambassador Page in Britain, already began planning administrative steps to be taken in the event of war. But Wilson did not discuss his intentions or ask for specific input or criticism of his speech draft. Nevertheless, he did issue a call to Congress to meet in special session on April 2.

The day Wilson issued the call, March 21, 1917, a submarine torpedoed another American ship, *Healdton*. The attack came entirely without warning, with two torpedoes striking the ship and sinking it quickly. Twenty-one of the crew died, and the survivors picked up off the coast of Holland included several who had suffered from exposure and burns. Some had been unable even to gather clothing. The 21 dead included seven Americans. Furthermore, the ship had been sailing in an area the Germans had declared a North Sea safe zone for neutral commerce, even in their blockade announcement of February 1. *Healdton,* a loaded oil tanker owned by Standard Oil Company, bore clear markings and American flags. The tanker mounted no armament. Although the survivors did not determine the nationality of the submarine, they, the press, and the American State Department believed it could only be German.

Even more clearly than the three sinkings announced on March 18, this attack showed the full effect of the ruthless campaign that Germany intended: no warning, no protection of the crew, no regard even for the safety lanes that had been announced, and a sudden attack on an unarmed ship. The accumulation of separate attacks on U.S. vessels made it clear that they would be targets. And, as in the destruction of British and French ships, some would be carefully warned and the crews provided for, while others, like *Healdton,* would simply be blown out of the water with no regard for the safety of those aboard. The destruction of *Healdton* caused more deaths than any prior sinking of an American ship by the Germans.

Two German decisions, first, to launch the submarine attacks, and, second, to attempt to build an alliance with Mexico and Japan, while seeming reasonable to German policy makers, had combined in their effects to bring the United States to the brink of war. In both cases, what appeared to hold a kind of tough-minded logic for the German leadership served only to convince many Americans who had supported neutrality that Germany was already conducting war on the United States.

DECLARING WAR

On April 2, Wilson addressed Congress and asked for a declaration that a state of war already existed. In the address, Wilson alluded only in an oblique way to the Zimmermann telegram and focused more especially on the attacks on American ships as direct attacks on the United States. He also pointed out that the United States had no quarrel with the German people but only with Germany's autocratic and unrepresentative government. The fact that the czar of Russia had abdicated two weeks before allowed Wilson to claim that the war now represented a conflict between democratic regimes (Britain, France, Italy, Russia, and now the United States) against the autocratic regimes of the Central Powers. He did not mention the total number of Americans killed in the shipping attacks.

When Wilson returned to the White House after his address, he appeared solemn, and his close associate Joseph Tumulty recorded in his diary that Wilson found it strange that the crowds lining Pennsylvania Avenue from Congress to the White House should cheer him as his car passed by. After all, he said, he had just asked Congress to send their sons to their deaths, and yet they cheered.

News that two other ships had been sunk reached the United States while Congress debated the war resolution. The *Aztec* sank on the night of April 1 near an island off Brest. At first, reports indicated that this ship, the first to be sunk while armed with the new guns and with a naval gun crew aboard, had been torpedoed. However, further reports revealed that the crew had not seen a submarine and that the captain believed the ship had struck a mine in the dark. Eleven Americans were among the 28 who died. The American steamer *Missourian* sank on April 5, 1917, in the Mediterranean by action of a submarine, with no casualties.

Thus, before the resolution came to a final vote, a total of nine American ships had been lost since the announcement of the submarine blockade, apparently eight of them to German submarines. A total of 12 American seamen were among the 36 crew members of many nationalities who lost their lives in the *Vigilancia* and *Healdton* submarine attacks. Due to the fact that some of the nine ships had been alerted by warning gunshots or by being hailed, that some sank only slowly from gunfire, and that one sank fairly slowly apparently after striking a mine, more than 80 percent of the crew members had survived the attacks.

Senator Robert La Follette prepared an impassioned speech opposing the declaration of war. *(Library of Congress)*

Clearly it was not the scale of American casualties that had tipped public opinion, the cabinet, and finally Wilson in favor of a declaration of war. A total of 128 American civilian passengers had died in the *Lusitania* tragedy in 1915 without the nation going to war. Rather than focusing on the 12 American merchant seamen lost from the *Vigilancia* and *Healdton,* the president and the press expressed outrage at the fact that the submarine blockade now led to a direct attack on American shipping and commerce, that some submarine captains made no provision for the safety of the crews, and that even ships in the safety zones in the Mediterranean and the North Sea faced the threat of attack.

The German leadership had decided that only a ruthless campaign would have a chance of success, and that very ruthless aspect of the submarine blockade shocked American opinion. The effort of four of the eight U-boat commanders to ensure that the crews safely evacuated the ships sunk by submarines in this period went almost unnoticed in the storm of anger, protest, and demands for war.

Senators George Norris and Robert La Follette gave impassioned speeches opposing the war resolution. Their arguments suggested that the United States had been lured into the war by profiteers and those with capital invested in the war industries. Why, they asked, should American young men be sent to die in the interest of capitalists who had already made millions by selling weapons, oil, and food to the Allies?

But, despite their pleas, the numbers went overwhelmingly in favor of war in two votes April 4 and 6, 1917. In the Senate on April 4, 82 favored war, with six opposed; on April 6, in the House of Representatives 373 voted for war and 50 were opposed. The lone woman who had been elected to the House of Representatives, Jeannette Rankin, member of Congress from Montana, spoke out among those opposing the declaration of war. Many women in the suffrage movement had contacted her urging her to support the war declaration, fearing that her opposition would turn the majority of men against suffrage for women. Nevertheless, she followed her conscience and joined with the 49 other opponents in the House of Representatives. Wilson signed the resolutions on April 7. Thus America joined the war.

CHRONICLE OF EVENTS

1916

November 2: Woodrow Wilson is reelected president, winning support in western states due to his strong neutralist position.

1917

January 9: The German high command meets at Pless Castle and decides on unrestricted submarine warfare to begin February 1, 1917. The calculation is that Britain will be reduced within a few months by the severance of all food and supplies from the United States, and that the risk of war with the United States is worth taking.

January 16: The Zimmermann telegram is sent, instructing German ambassador von Bernstorff in Washington to pass on to German minister H. von Eckhardt in Mexico City a proposal for a Mexican-German-Japanese alliance against the United States. The telegram is encrypted and sent over a line provided by Wilson for the exchange of diplomatic notes regarding a possible negotiated peace.

January 17: British Admiralty Room 40 (Naval Intelligence) intercepts the Zimmermann telegram but can read it only partially.

January 19: Bernstorff re-encodes the Zimmermann telegram and sends it to Eckhardt in Mexico City. The code Bernstorff uses to Eckhardt is easier for Room 40 to crack than the one used by Zimmermann to him.

January 22: Wilson delivers his Peace without Victory speech to Congress.

January 31: Germany announces that unrestricted submarine warfare is to begin February 1. The announcement declares a war zone around Britain, with arrangements for open lanes to Spain and Greece and a provision for a once-a-week passenger ship to Britain.

February 2: Wilson asks the cabinet what course of action they recommend; he asserts he prefers to remain neutral.

February 3: The U.S. steamship *Housatonic* is sunk by German submarine after a warning. Wilson announces a break of diplomatic relations with Germany. The British and the U.S. ambassador to Britain, W. H. Page, are appalled that Wilson still hopes to preserve neutrality.

February 3: Ambassador von Bernstorff is given his passport; that is, he is asked to leave the United States.

February 5: Zimmermann sends a message to Eckhardt to make the offer of an alliance with Mexico "even now," that is, before U.S. declaration of war. This message is not made public until after the war.

February 5: William Reginald ("Blinker") Hall of Room 40 delivers the complete text of the decoded Zimmermann telegram of January 17 to the British Foreign Office; Hall develops a version dated the 19th that appears to have been captured from Mexico, rather than decoded from the one sent from Europe.

February 6: Wilson offers to appoint Clifford Dodge to replace Page as U.S. ambassador in Britain, but Dodge turns him down.

February 7: The U.S. Senate passes a resolution endorsing Wilson's decision to break off relations with Germany.

February 9: The U.S. cabinet discusses the fact that very few ships have departed U.S. ports for the war zone, February 1–February 9.

February 12: A German submarine sinks the U.S. registered schooner *Lyman M. Law;* all crew members survive.

February 15: A German delegation of expelled diplomats sails from New York for Germany by way of Canada. They are delayed in Halifax, Canada, for more than a week.

February 19: Hall's group at Room 40 completes the decryption of the missing passages in the Zimmermann telegram and provides it to the Foreign Office.

February 22: Hall takes a copy of the Zimmermann telegram to Edward Bell, a secretary at the U.S. embassy, then both take it to U.S. ambassador Page. Page suggests it should be formally delivered to him and meanwhile prepares a cover note for transmission to the United States.

February 23: British prime minister Balfour officially delivers the Zimmermann telegram to Page.

February 23: At a cabinet meeting, W. G. McAdoo urges the arming of merchant ships, a plan supported by other cabinet members.

February 24: Page cables his cover note and the Zimmermann telegram to the U.S. State Department in Washington.

February 24: Counselor to the State Department Frank L. Polk takes the Zimmermann telegram to Wilson, who agrees to withhold it from public release until the return of Secretary of State Robert Lansing to Washington.

February 26: The British merchant ship *Laconia* is torpedoed, causing the death of two U.S. citizens, both women. Wilson asks Congress to pass the Armed Ship bill to provide antisubmarine weapons for merchant ships, because shipowners were interning many ships in port. Neutralist and pacifist senators plan a filibuster. Wilson says that there has not yet been an overt act of war.

February 26: Polk informs Colonel House of the Zimmermann telegram; House urges its immediate release.

February 27: U.S. State Department counselor Polk finds the original encrypted Zimmermann telegram in the files of cables that had been sent over a system that the United States had allowed Bernstorff to use for peace negotiations. Lansing shows the original encrypted version to Wilson, who is shocked that Germany used a diplomatic privilege he extended to plan the Mexican-Japanese alliance against the United States.

February 28: On Wilson's suggestion, Lansing calls in Senator Hitchcock (a neutralist) and shows him the Zimmermann telegram; Hitchcock agrees to support the Armed Ship bill. Lansing releases the telegram to the Associated Press bureau chief that evening with Wilson's permission.

February 28–March 4: A Senate group filibusters to prevent passage of the Armed Ship bill. Congress adjourns without Senate passage of the bill and schedules a special session for April 16 to deal with appropriations.

March 1: The Zimmermann telegram is published in all American newspapers that subscribe to the Associated Press service. Rumors as to how it was obtained are intentionally circulated by the British and U.S. governments. Doubts as to its authenticity are raised in the press. Because of an error in the A.P. story, it is widely believed that Wilson withheld release of the telegram for four weeks.

March 1: In response to a senatorial request, Lansing and Wilson send a note to the Senate to assure it that the telegram is genuine and that the United States has had it less than a week. The false impression is planted that the telegram was first decoded in the United States after a copy had been sold by a spy to the United States.

March 1: The House of Representatives passes the Armed Ship bill, on Wilson's request, to arm merchant ships, 403 to 13. The authenticity of the telegram is questioned for the next two days.

March 2: Zimmermann admits the authenticity of the telegram at a press conference. His statement will be printed the next day in U.S. newspapers. The German Foreign Ministry investigates whether the leak occurred in Mexico.

March 4: The German-American press has mixed reaction to Zimmermann's admission that the telegram was genuine, some newspapers continuing to believe it a forgery.

March 4: Wilson publicly criticizes the "little group of willful men representing no opinion but their own" for blocking the Armed Ship bill.

March 5: President Wilson is inaugurated for his second term; his speech hints that it may be necessary to go to war.

March 6–8: Secretary Lansing advises Wilson that he can arm merchant ships without the approval of Congress.

Shipping losses were used to stimulate bond sales. *(National Archives)*

March 9: Wilson provides for the arming of merchant ships by executive order.

March 12: The February Revolution in Russia establishes the Provisional Government and appears to move toward parliamentary democracy.

March 12: The U.S. steamship *Algonquin,* unarmed, is sunk by *U-38* after evacuation off the Scilly Islands in Cornwall, Britain. The crew survives 27 hours in open boats.

March 12: The State Department announces that all U.S. merchant ships entering the war zones will be armed.

March 13: The navy advises armed merchant ships to take action against submarines.

March 15: In Russia, the czar abdicates.

March 18: The sinking of three U.S. ships is announced: *City of Memphis, Illinois,* and *Vigilancia.* The three were sunk on March 16 and 17; 15 crewmen of *Vigilancia* were killed when their lifeboat capsized. All aboard the other ships survive.

March 19: U.S. pro-Allied newspapers generally regard the announced sinking of three ships as an overt act of war, and many explicitly call for a congressional declaration of a state of war.

March 20: Wilson asks the opinion of the cabinet as to whether to convene a special session of Congress, and they unanimously recommend that he do so.

March 21: The Standard Oil steamer *Healdton* is torpedoed without warning off the coast of Holland, causing 21 deaths. Wilson asks for a special session of Congress to convene on April 2, two weeks prior to schedule.

March 25: Wilson activates the National Guard.

April 1: A U.S. ship, *Aztec,* is sunk.

April 2: Wilson addresses Congress and asks for a declaration of war against Germany.

April 4: Speeches by Senators Robert La Follette and George Norris oppose the declaration resolution.

April 5: The American steamer *Missourian* is sunk in the Mediterranean.

April 6: Congress passes a declaration of war.

April 7: Wilson signs the declaration of war.

Eyewitness Testimony

The president's address to the Senate which was received to-day [January 16, 1917, to be delivered January 22] shows that he thinks he can play peace-maker. He does not at all understand (or if he do, so much the worse for him) that the Entente Powers, especially Great Britain and France, cannot make "peace without victory." If they do, they will become vassals of Germany. In a word the President does not know the Germans; and he is, unconsciously, under their influence in his thought. His speech plays into their hands.

This address will give great offense in England, since it puts each side in the war on the same moral level.

I immediately saw the grave danger to our relations with Great Britain by the Peace-without-Victory plan; and I telegraphed the President, venturing to advise him to omit that phrase—with no result.

> *U.S. ambassador Walter Hines Page, on receiving a draft of the "Peace without Victory" address of Woodrow Wilson on January 16, 1917, in a memorandum, reprinted in Burton Hendrick,* Life and Letters of Walter H. Page, *pp. 217–218.*

I vividly recall the day the Associated Press bulletin reached the White House. I took it immediately to the President who was at his desk in his private office. As I entered, he looked up from his writing, casual inquiry in his eyes. Without comment I laid the fateful slip of paper on his desk, and silently watched him as he read and then re-read it. I seemed to read his mind in the expressions that raced across his strong features: first, blank amazement; then incredulity that even Germany could be guilty of such perfidy; then gravity and sternness, a sudden grayness of colour, a compression of the lips and the familiar locking of the jaw which always characterized him in moments of supreme resolution. Handing the paper back to me, he said in quiet tones: "This means war. The break that we have tried so hard to prevent now seems inevitable."

> *Joseph Tumulty, recalling in his memoir the moment when Wilson heard of the announcement of German unrestricted submarine warfare, February 1, 1917, in* Woodrow Wilson as I Know Him, *p. 254.*

On Friday, February 2, 1917, when I went to Cabinet meeting, I realized that we might be facing the most momentous issue in our experience and in the history of the nation. I had heard a rumour that a German note had come or was on the way, renouncing all her partial pledges and recent practices and declaring her intention to engage in unrestricted submarine warfare.

The note announced that beginning February 1st, a new war zone would be established around Great Britain and along the coast of France and Italy, and that any ship found within it would be sunk without regard to life or property. . . . This was the last word of a mad war lord—the farthest limit of dictation. If we accepted it, we surrendered our sovereignty and self respect. When I heard its terms, I knew that Uncle Sam would begin to take off his coat and roll up his sleeves.

This note could have just one meaning for us. It meant war and meant the beginning of the end for Germany. There had been rumours for some time that she might pursue this course, but I could not believe that she would be so stupid. There was no ground for believing in any event, that she would take such a course before the beginning of spring. March 1st was the date suggested. Why did she set February 1st as the date, or why did she make the decision at all? . . .

As we sat down, the President asked what we thought should be done. "Shall I break off diplomatic relations with Germany?" . . .

Several of us immediately began to speak. McAdoo did much talking. He was for prompt action. We must act or swallow our brave words.

> *David Houston, Wilson's secretary of agriculture, recalling the cabinet meeting prior to the severance of diplomatic relations with Germany, February 2, 1917, in his memoir,* Eight Years with Wilson's Cabinet, 1913 to 1920, *vol. 1, pp. 227–229.*

On Tuesday, February 6, at Cabinet meeting, the situation of our American merchantmen occupied attention. Of course, they had a right to go to sea, but would they exercise it, or would they tie up in our ports? Would it be right to allow them to take risks if they wished to do so? Should we require ships to observe their mail contracts? It was suggested that the Postmaster General tell such ships to use their discretion. I said that, if this was done, they should be told that they might arm for defense and that the government should advise them of their rights—that it was necessary that they be told the policy of the government. Some said that the government ought not to give any advice. Others insisted that the situation was highly abnormal and that to the ship-owners should not be left the responsibility of deciding the course of action. It was decided that they be told that their rights were just the same as if Germany had said nothing, and that they could arm for defence.

David Houston, Wilson's secretary of agriculture, recalling cabinet discussions on the effect of the German submarine blockade, February 6, 1917, in his memoir, Eight Years with Wilson's Cabinet, 1913 to 1920, *vol. 1, p. 233.*

Most Secret. Decipher personally. Provided there is no danger of secret being betrayed to USA you are desired without further delay to broach the question of Alliance to the President [of Mexico, Carranza]. The definite conclusion of an Alliance, however, is dependent on the outbreak of war between Germany and USA. The President might, even now, on his own account, sound Japan. If the President declines from fear of subsequent revenge you are empowered to offer him a definitive alliance after the conclusion of peace providing Mexico succeeds in drawing Japan into the alliance.

German foreign minister Zimmermann, in follow-up note to Minister Eckhardt in Mexico City, February 8, 1917, cited in Peter Beesley, Room 40, *p. 215.*

At the meeting on Friday, the 9th [of February], it was clear that the shipping situation had not been cleared up. The ships were not sailing. They were showing every sign of interning. They wanted further assurances and protection. They wanted the United States to furnish arms and gun crews. They could not otherwise get satisfactory guns or efficient marksmen. It was suggested that we had power to sell, lend, or give guns to them and to furnish crews. The question of convoy was raised. Baker said that inoffensive merchantmen should not be exposed to danger. It would be better to send naval vessels along and have a clear test. It was customary to convoy and to guarantee the safety of goods. We had to adjourn without arriving at a final decision.

David Houston, Wilson's secretary of agriculture, recalling cabinet discussions on the effect of the German submarine blockade, February 9, 1917, in his memoir, Eight Years with Wilson's Cabinet, 1913 to 1920, *vol. 1, pp. 233–234.*

Wilson had long resisted the pressure to arm merchant ships. In a stormy Cabinet meeting on February 23, Houston, Lane, and McAdoo insisted upon immediate action. Wilson said, "You are trying to push us into war." He was irritated when Lane inquired whether it was true that German authorities had stripped the wives of

American consuls to "search for writings on their flesh." Lansing had no such reports, and Wilson regarded this as a suggestion that we should work up a propaganda of hatred against Germany. He said that Lane was appealing to the Code Duello. It was not these urgings by Cabinet members but the German attitude that caused Wilson to go before Congress and ask for the authority to arm merchant ships.

In the Cabinet meeting the President asked: "Daniels, has the Navy the gunners and the guns for this job?"

"We can arm them as fast as the ships are ready," I replied.

The sentiment was unanimous for arming them, but the question was debated whether in the absence of congressional authority, the President had the right to do so. Wilson believed that he had that authority but wished the power of Congress behind him—to be employed at the proper time.

Josephus Daniels, secretary of the navy, recalling the cabinet meeting of February 23, 1917, in his memoir, The Wilson Era: Years of Peace—1910–1917, *p. 594.*

February 24, 1917

Balfour has handed me the text of a cipher telegram from Zimmermann, German Secretary of State for Foreign Affairs, to the German Minister in Mexico which was sent via Washington and relayed by Bernstorff on January 19. You can probably obtain a copy of the text relayed by Bernstorff from the cable office in Washington. The first group is the number of the telegram 130 and the second is 13042 indicating the number of the code used. The last group but two is 97556 which is Zimmermann's signature. I shall send you by mail a copy of the cipher text and of the decode into German, and meanwhile I give you the English translation as follows.

The receipt of this information has so exercised the British Government that they have lost no time in communicating it to me to transmit to you in order that our Government may be able without delay to make such dispositions as may be necessary in view of the threatened invasion of our territory. The following paragraph is Strictly Confidential.

Early in the War the British Government obtained possession of a copy of the German cipher code used in the above message and have made it their business to obtain copies of Bernstorff's cipher telegrams to Mexico amongst others which are sent back to London and deciphered here. This accounts for their being able to decipher this telegram from the German Government to their representative in Mexico and also for the delay from January 19th until now in their receiving the information. This system has hitherto been a most jealously guarded secret and is only divulged now to you by the British Government in view of the extraordinary circumstances and their friendly feeling towards the United States. They earnestly request that you will keep the source of your information and the British Government's method of obtaining it secret but they put no prohibition on the publication of Zimmermann's telegram itself. The copies of this and other telegrams were not obtained in Washington but were bought in Mexico.

I have thanked Balfour for the service his Government has rendered us and suggest that a private official message of thanks from our Government to him would be appreciated. I am informed that this information has not yet been given to the Japanese Government but I think it is not unlikely that when it reaches them they will make a public statement on it in order to clear up their position regarding the United States and prove their good faith to their Allies.

The covering note prepared by Ambassador W. H. Page to accompany the transmission of the Zimmermann telegram to the State Department, sent February 24, 1917, cited in Peter Beesley, Room 40, *pp. 219–220.*

Washington to Mexico

We intend to begin on 1 February unrestricted submarine warfare. We shall endeavour in spite of this to keep the USA neutral. In the event of this not succeeding we make Mexico a proposal of alliance on the following terms:—

Make war together.

Make peace together.

Generous financial support and an undertaking on our part that Mexico is to reconquer the lost territory in Texas, New Mexico, and Arizona. The settlement in detail is left to you.

You will inform the President [of Mexico] of the above most secretly as soon as the outbreak of war with the USA is certain, and add the suggestion that he should on his own initiative invite Japan to immediate adherence and at the same time mediate between Japan and ourselves.

Please call the President's attention to the fact that the ruthless employment of our submarines now offers the prospect of compelling England in a few months to make peace.

German foreign minister Arthur Zimmermann, in his telegram relayed through Count Johann von Bernstorff in Washington to Minister Heinrich von Eckhardt in Mexico City, in the version released by the U.S. press, March 1, 1917 (actually sent January 16, 1917), reproduced in Peter Beesley, Room 40, *p. 216.*

The Senate of the United States is the only legislative body in the world which cannot act when the majority is ready for action. A little group of willful men, representing no opinion but their own, have rendered the great government of the United States helpless and contemptible. The only remedy is that the rules of the Senate should be altered so that it can act.

Woodrow Wilson, reacting to the filibuster that prevented the Senate from approving the Armed Ship bill, March 4, 1917, as quoted in David Houston, Eight Years with Wilson's Cabinet, 1913 to 1920, *p. 240.*

March 4, 1917

We who have sought in this country to balance sentiment, and to render less acute a situation created by those who have lauded the cause of the Allies to the skies and dragged the name of Germany through the mud of their senseless vilification, have done so only in the thought and confidence that Germany still honored "the heirloom of Frederick the Great"—America's friendship and friendship for America.

Viewed from any angle Dr. Zimmermann's instructions to the German Minister in Mexico constitute [such] a mistake that it renders the situation almost hopeless.

Bernard Ridder, publisher of the Staats-Zeitung, *a German-American publication, reacting to the news that Foreign Minister Zimmermann confirmed the authenticity of the telegram he sent to the German minister in Mexico City, quoted in "Ridder Repudiates Zimmermann Plot,"* New York Times, *March 4, 1917, p. 2.*

March 5, 1917

As some of the injuries done us have become intolerable we have still been clear that we wished nothing for ourselves that we were not ready to demand for all mankind,—fair dealing, justice, the freedom to live and be at ease against organized wrong.

It is in this spirit and with this thought that we have grown more and more aware, more and more certain that the part we wished to play was the part of those who mean to vindicate and fortify peace. We have been obliged to arm ourselves to make good our claim to a certain minimum of right and of freedom of action. We stand firm in armed neutrality since it seems that in no other way we can demonstrate what it is we insist upon and cannot forego. We may even be drawn on, by circumstances, not by our own purpose or desire, to a more active assertion of our rights as we see them and a more immediate association with the great struggle itself. But nothing will alter our thought or our purpose. They are too clear to be obscured. They are too deeply rooted in the principles of our national life to be altered. We desire neither conquest nor advantage. We wish nothing that can be had only at the cost of another people. We have always professed unselfish purpose and we covet the opportunity to prove that our professions are sincere.

Woodrow Wilson, commenting on the principles he believed had to be defended in the international arena, in his second inaugural address, March 5, 1917, from Ray Stannard Baker and William F. Dodd, The Public Papers of Woodrow Wilson: War and Peace, Presidential Messages, Addresses, and Public Papers, (1917–1924), *vol. 1, pp. 2–3.*

March 9, 1917

I find that continued delay in sending out American ships, especially American liners, is producing an increasingly unfavorable impression. . . . Delay is taken to mean the submission of our Government to the German blockade. . . . There is a tendency, even in high Government circles, to regard the reasons for delay which are published here as technicalities which a national crisis should sweep aside. British opinion couples the delay of our ships with the sinking of the *Laconia* and the Zimmermann telegram, and seems to be reaching the conclusion that our Government will not be able to take positive action under any provocation. The feeling which the newspaper despatches from the United States produce on the British mind, is that our Government is holding back our people until the blockade of our ships, the Zimmermann telegram, and the *Laconia* shall be forgotten and until the British navy shall overcome the German submarines. There is danger that this feeling harden into a conviction and interfere with any influence that we might otherwise have when peace comes.

So friendly a man as Viscount Grey of Fallodon writes me privately from his retirement: "I do not see how the United States can sit still while neutral shipping is swept off the sea. If no action is taken, it will be like a great blot in history or a failure that must grievously depress the future history of America."

Ambassador Walter Hines Page, in a letter to Colonel Edward House, March 9, 1917, cited in Charles Seymour, The Intimate Papers of Colonel House, *p. 459.*

March 12, 1917

We saw the submarine at 6 o'clock in the morning on Monday [March 12, 1917]. As soon as we saw her she started firing at us. I should say quite twenty shots came around us. While she was firing at us we got into the boats and left the steamer.

When the commander of the submarine saw that we were leaving the ship he seems to have given the order to cease firing, for it ceased as soon as we got into the boats and left the steamer. At that time the submarine had nothing but the periscope above water. In this fashion she cruised around the steamer six or

Those rescued at sea, like these survivors of a torpedo attack on the French liner *Sontay*, had harrowing tales to relate. *(National Archives)*

seven times and then came to the surface. Those on board her launched a small boat and went on board the *Algonquin*.

The first thing they did was to haul down the American flag and then they placed a bomb somewhere on board—I suppose in the engine room. There was a big explosion about two minutes after they left her, and the steamer sank in about ten minutes. The boat was then pulled over to us and an officer asked us where we were bound for, what was our cargo, and where we had come from. We asked him if he could give us a tow toward land, but the commander replied that he was too busy, as he expected two or three more steamers.

After the submarine left us to our own devices we commenced to pull for land. We got to land twenty-seven hours after the ship sunk. . . . There was absolutely no warning. Their first shot fell a little short, but each one afterward came a little nearer, until at last they got the exact range. I think the fifth shot hit the steamer's side. All the time we were on board we could hear shots whistling over our heads.

I am an American citizen.

> *Captain A. Norberg, reporting the attack on the steamer* Algonquin, *March 12, 1917, quoted in "Ship Shelled and Burned,"* New York Times, *March 15, 1917, p. 1.*

March 17, 1917

We saw two submarines. One disappeared, and the other fired two warning shots. We took to the boats. The submarines fired ten shells, and the *City of Memphis* finally was torpedoed and sunk flying the American colors.

When the ship rolled the submarine gunners aimed to hit below the ordinary water line. Some of the shells struck the water and leaped over the steamer like skimming stones. We were four hours in an open boat with biscuits and water, and were rescued by a trawler. The utmost kindness was shown to us by the crew. We are unspeakably grateful for the hospitality of Irish villagers and authorities.

> *Account by Dr. Robert J. Shea, ship's surgeon, of the sinking of the ship* City of Memphis, *March 17, 1917, reported in "15 Men Died on the Vigilancia—Captain Captured by U-Boat!"* New York Times, *March 20, 1917, p. 2.*

March 21, 1917

Voyage uneventful until 8:15, evening March 21, when ship lay twenty-three miles north by east of Terschelling Lightship; torpedoed twice without warning. First torpedo hit amidships; all lights went out. Second torpedo hit further aft, under flag painted on side port. Bunkers were ablaze and ship began to settle.

After first torpedo shock Captain ordered engine stopped and crew took boats. Vessel began list aport. Captain made farewell search for missing members crew. One boat tried pull away sinking vessel and capsized. Captain saw submarine approaching when he was lying off *Healdton* watch vessel sink. Nationality submarine impossible to determine, because it possessed no distinguishing marks and was seen from distance 100 feet forward. No words were exchanged with submarine. From action, Captain and crew believed submarine undoubtedly German. No other vessels were present or within sight when *Healdton* torpedoed.

Submarine made no effort to assist crew or officers to save their lives but disappeared immediately after *Healdton* sunk. Ship's papers were not demanded.

Captain and twelve men rowed and sailed in open boat for Terschelling Lightship. At 8 o'clock, morning March 22, boat was picked up by Dutch trawler, *Java,* about ten miles from Dutch coast. Another boat containing first mate and seven men picked up by a Dutch torpedo boat, *G-13,* near Terschelling, after seventeen hours exposure; rescued at 2 o'clock, afternoon March 22.

No details at hand concerning those drowned in capsized boat or on ship except one Norwegian with arms and legs frozen, brought Ymulden by steam trawler *Ocean.* Perils and hardship suffered by all survivors extraordinary. . . .

> *Report by U.S. consul G. H. Krogh, on the sinking of U.S.-registered Esso tanker* Healdton, *off the Dutch coast, March 21, 1917, reported in "Depicts Suffering of Healdton Crew,"* New York Times, *March 27, 1917, p. 4.*

March 25, 1917

It's very hard, not to say impossible, to write in these swiftly moving days. Anything written to-day is out of date to-morrow—even if it not be wrong to start with. The impression becomes stronger here every day that we shall go into the war "with both feet"—that the people have pushed the President over in spite of his vision of the Great Peacemaker, and that, being pushed over, his idea now will be to show he led them into a glorious war in defense of democracy. That's my reading of the situation, and I hope I am not wrong. At any rate, ever since the call of Congress for April

2nd, I have been telegraphing tons of information and plans that can be of use only if we go to war. Habitually they never acknowledge the receipt of anything at Washington. I don't know, therefore, whether they like these pieces of information or not. I have my staff of twenty-five good men getting all sorts of war-like information; and I have just organized twenty-five or thirty more—the best business Americans in London—who are also at work. I am trying to get the Government at Washington to send over a committee of conference—a General, an Admiral, a Reserve Board man, etc., etc. If they do half the things that I recommend we'll be in at the final lickin' big, and will save our souls yet. . . .

My mind keeps constantly on the effect of the war and especially of our action on our own country. Of course that is the most important end of the thing for us. I hope that—

1. It will break up and tear away our isolation;
2. It will unhorse our cranks and soft-brains;
3. It will make us less promiscuously hospitable to every kind of immigrant;
4. It will re-establish in our minds and conscience the policy of our true historic genesis, background, kindred and destiny—i.e., kill the Irish and the German influence.
5. It will revive our real manhood—put the molly-coddles in disgrace, as idiots and dandies are;
6. It will make our politics frank and manly by restoring our true nationality;
7. It will make us again a great sea-faring people. It is this that has given Great Britain its long lead in the world;
8. Break up our feminized education—make a boy a vigorous animal and make our education rest on a wholesome physical basis;
9. Bring men of a higher type into our political life.

We need waking up and shaking up and invigorating as much as the Germans need taking down.

There is no danger of "militarism" in any harmful sense among any English race or in any democracy.

By George! all these things open an interesting outlook and series of tasks—don't they?

U.S. ambassador to Britain Walter Hines Page, writing to his son, Arthur, from London, March 25, 1917, collected in Burton Hendrick, Life and Letters of Walter H. Page, *pp. 217–218.*

April 1, 1917

I asked [President Wilson] why he had not shown the Cabinet his address [asking for a declaration of war]. He replied that, if he had, every man in it would have had some suggestion to make and it would have been picked to pieces if he had heeded their criticism. He said he preferred to keep it to himself and take the responsibility. I feel that he does his Cabinet an injustice. . . . I have noticed recently that he holds a tighter rein over his Cabinet and that he is impatient of any initiative on their part.

Colonel Edward House, in a note for his diary, April 1, 1917, cited in Charles Seymour, The Intimate Papers of Colonel House, *p. 468.*

April 1, 1917

In these last days, before the United States is forced into war—by the people's insistence—the preceding course of events becomes even clearer than it was before; and it has been as clear all the time as the nose on a man's face.

The President began by refusing to understand the meaning of the war. To him it seemed a quarrel to settle economic rivalries between Germany and England. He said to me last September that there were many causes why Germany went to war. He showed a great degree of toleration for Germany; and he was, during the whole morning that I talked with him, complaining of England. The controversies we had with England were, of course, mere by-products of the conflict. But to him they seemed as important as the controversy we had with Germany. In the beginning he had made—as far as it was possible—neutrality a positive quality of mind. He would not move from that position.

That was his first error of judgement. And by insisting on this he soothed the people—sat them down in comfortable chairs and said, "Now stay there." He really suppressed speech and thought.

The second error he made was in thinking that he could play a great part as peacemaker—come and give a blessing to these erring children. This was strong in his hopes and ambitions. There was a condescension in this attitude that was offensive.

He shut himself up with these two ideas and engaged in what he called "thought." The air currents of the world never ventilated his mind.

This inactive position he has kept as long as public sentiment permitted. He seems no longer to regard himself nor to speak as a leader—only as a mouthpiece of public opinion after opinion has run over him.

He has not breathed a spirit into the people; he has encouraged them to supineness. He is *not* a leader, but rather a stubborn phrasemaker.

And now events and the aroused people seem to have brought the President to the necessary point of action; and even now he may act timidly.

Ambassador Walter H. Page, in a memorandum prepared April 1, 1917, while awaiting news of what the president would say to Congress on April 2, recorded in Burton Hendrick, Life and Letters of Walter H. Page, *pp. 222–223.*

We must go in with the Allies, not begin a mere single fight against submarines. We must sign the pact of London—not make a separate peace.

We musn't longer spin dreams about peace, nor leagues to enforce peace, nor the Freedom of the Seas. These things are mere intellectual diversions of minds out of contact with realities. Every political and social ideal we have is at stake. If we make them secure, we'll save Europe from destruction and save ourselves, too.

Ambassador Walter H. Page, in a letter to David Houston, secretary of agriculture, on April 1, 1917, outlining plans for war prior to Wilson's speech asking for a declaration of war, as reprinted in Burton Hendrick, Life and Letters of Walter H. Page, *pp. 226–227.*

April 2, 1917

The President began reading as soon as quiet prevailed; and, as he proceeded, I found myself watching Chief Justice [Edward Douglass] White, who sat a very short distance in front and to the left of me. I knew what his reaction would be, but I did not anticipate that he would show his emotions so strikingly. Several times I had talked to him about the war. Shortly after England entered the war, he came up to me one evening at a social gathering, put his hand on my shoulder, and said in a low voice: "I wish I were thirty years younger. I would go to Canada and volunteer." He listened with interest to the President's review of the submarine controversy. When the President said: "The present German submarine warfare against commerce is a warfare against mankind," he gave a vigourous nod. He repeated it when the President added: "It is a war against all nations. . . . The challenge is to all mankind." He listened with evident satisfaction to the statement characterizing armed neutrality as ineffectual, as "likely only to produce what it was meant to prevent," and as practically certain to draw us into the war without either the rights or the effectiveness of belligerents. But when the President said: "There is one choice we cannot make, we are incapable of making: We will not choose the path of submission," he did not wait to hear the rest of the sentence. He was on his feet instantly leading the Supreme Court and the entire assembly. His face was a study. It worked almost convulsively and great tears began to roll down his cheeks. From that moment to the end he was vigorously applauding everything. He had a profound realization of the issues at stake and particularly of the part England had played in the world, of the meaning of her institutions, and of the menace to the world of her overthrow by Germany. He knew what war meant, having been a soldier in the Civil War, and he was willing and anxious to stand the horrors of war again for vital principles.

David Houston, Wilson's secretary of agriculture, recalling Wilson's speech asking for a declaration of war, April 2, 1917, in his memoir, Eight Years with Wilson's Cabinet, 1913 to 1920, *vol. 1, pp. 254–255.*

I accompanied the President to Capitol Hill on the day of the delivery of his war message, and on that fateful day I rode with him from the Capitol back to the White House, the echo of applause still ringing in my ears.

For a while he sat silent and pale in the Cabinet Room. At last he said: "think what it was they were applauding." [He was speaking of the people who were lined along the streets on his way to the Capitol.] "My message to-day was a message of death for our young men. How strange it seems to applaud that." . . .

I shall never forget that scene in the Cabinet Room between the President and myself. He appeared like a man who had thrown off old burdens only to add new ones.

Joseph Tumulty, recalling the evening after Wilson delivered the war message to Congress, April 2, 1917, in his memoir, Woodrow Wilson as I Know Him, *p. 256.*

9

The Home Front in the United States
April 1917–November 1918

Although the United States had gone to war to defend democracy, democracy in 1917 did not extend to the right to oppose that war. America was torn by this and even more serious conflicts over the following months as the administration sought to reorganize the economy for war, raise and equip troops, and establish and enforce a patriotic fervor that would support the effort.

Although World War I raged in Europe, Asia, Africa, and on the oceans of the world for more than four terrible years, the United States participated in the war for only 19 months, from April 6, 1917, to November 11, 1918, and most American troops saw action only between February and November 1918. Altogether some 9 to 10 million soldiers and sailors of many nations perished in the war, but the United States lost only 53,500 men killed in combat, and another 63,000 to accidents and disease, out of the total of some 2 million American men and women who served in the American Expeditionary Force. Despite the brief engagement in the war and the relatively light casualties, the war had a deep and lasting impact on American society. The war marked the end of one era and the beginning of another. The deepest changes to American politics, economy, and society came about because of what transpired, not on the western front, but on the home front in the United States itself.

Until late 1916, Wilson had resisted the cry for preparedness mounted by leaders who believed the United States should join the battle earlier, particularly men like Walter Hines Page and Theodore Roosevelt. Roosevelt, who had served as president from 1901 to 1909 and had run as a Progressive for the presidency in 1912 to lose to Wilson, had publicly complained about Wilson's insistence on neutrality, openly charging that Wilson's position constituted a form of cowardice. Only reluctantly, facing reelection in 1916, had Wilson supported an expansion of the army and an increase in military budget. So when Wilson asked Congress for the declaration of war on April 2, 1917, the nation really had not prepared for war, just as Roosevelt had warned. To build a fleet of ships and effective numbers of aircraft and to train and equip an army would, in most estimates, take at least two or three years.

Furthermore, the Allies had exhausted their credit, and so the U.S. Treasury would be called upon to provide funding for British and French purchases of

Getting the troops to Europe required the construction of troopships like the *Henderson* (shown here). *(National Archives)*

ammunition, food, fuel, weapons, and transport equipment. As a consequence, the U.S. government's problems were compounded in that it had to organize the nation's industries to meet the demands of the Allies for a meaningful contribution to the war effort, organize and train an army, and find a way to finance both the American and Allied efforts. In April 1917, military and economic advisers viewed these tasks as daunting; even so, most believed that the American effort, once mounted, would eventually lead to an Allied victory, probably in 1919 or 1920.

Roosevelt volunteered to raise a division of troops that he would personally lead into battle in Europe. After being politely rebuffed by War Department officials several times, he appealed directly to Wilson, who put him off and finally rejected the offer, on the grounds that professional soldiers would be required. Furious, Roosevelt became even more bitter and remained a hostile and outspoken critic of Wilson's conduct of the war. Roosevelt quipped, "Mr. Wilson has been President when the urgent need of the nation has been for action; he has met the need purely by elocution."[1]

In general, Republicans, both the traditional conservatives and those who had joined Roosevelt in the Progressive movement, criticized the organization of supply, the management of industry, and the rate of training and shipment of troops to Europe. In Congress, Republicans sought to wrest control of the domestic organization of the war from Wilson by establishing a congressionally-appointed war cabinet; although Democrats defeated that measure, partisan bickering over such issues as industrial organization, military preparations, and battle strategy continued throughout the 19 months of the war. Joseph Tumulty, Wilson's personal secretary, believed that Republicans simply thought they alone knew how to run a government and fight a war and that Republicans thought all Democrats incompetent to handle those tasks. "The old myth sedulously cultivated by Republicans continued in 1917, that only Republicans are fit to govern, no matter how badly they govern. Direful prophecies and predictions of disaster to the country by reason of the Democratic auspices under which the war was to be conducted were freely made."[2]

Indeed, the view that Tumulty ascribed to the Republican leadership held an element of truth. The ideas about governance that Wilson and his type of progressive Democrat supported did not lend themselves well to the job of administering the government of a nation at war in the 20th century, and Wilson and his close advisers found it very difficult to construct a modern and efficient structure based on their views of proper government. Although Progressive Republicans including Roosevelt had argued for a centralizing and organizing government that would use boards of experts from industry and technical fields to regulate the economy even in peacetime, Democrats like Wilson tended to believe in a minimum of compulsory government regulation. Democrats trusted in voluntary systems of compliance and cooperation and a federal government that remained small and out of the way of the economy and the states. Wilson's approach had been dubbed the New Freedom during the presidential campaign of 1912, and, to a significant extent, his administration already embodied the small-government, voluntary approach. Reconciling Wilson's New Freedom views about free enterprise with the modern needs of total warfare, in which national resources of manpower and finance had to be channeled efficiently into the effort, proved a daunting task.

In order to find enough troops for a massive army, for example, Wilson and his colleagues did not like the concept of universal military training or conscription. Nevertheless, raising an army simply by calling for volunteers would not be sufficient, nor would it be fair, because it would allow less enthusiastic young men to shirk their duty. Yet advocates of small government abhorred the idea of a centralized system. The solution was a national selective service system administered locally, which would require all men between the ages of 21 and 30 to register, and then to be selected at random. To ensure that the draft not take the only means of support from young families by sending off to war the married fathers of children, exemptions would be granted. The release from military obligation on the grounds of financial hardship, medical disability, or work in a vital industry would be determined by local draft boards, established from among community leaders, county by county across the nation. Thus, in a paradox common to the New Freedom approach, a national system would be administered locally, and a compulsory system of obligation would be presented as a lottery that chose individuals for service to the country on a random basis.

The selective service system enacted in May 1917 and inaugurated with a mass registration on June 5, 1917, generated many inequities (such as white draft boards selecting a far higher proportion of blacks to meet local quotas than whites). Furthermore, while the draft represented a means to reconcile the need to meet national objectives with a locally based administration, no such dispersed mechanism could be effectively employed to deal with such pressing needs as industrial production, transportation coordination, shipping needs, and state financing. As the Wilson administration struggled to address these and other problems, it devised reforms and legislation that conformed as much as possible to the ideals of voluntary consent rather than federal government control. Instead of raising taxes, the government relied on voluntary purchase of bonds. Rather than restricting food consumption through rationing, the Food Administration adopted a policy of exhortation through publicity drives urging the public to conserve food and avoid waste. While those programs had some success, others simply broke down or had unintended consequences that led to conflicts, shortages, confusion, and disorganization.

The nation declared war quite unprepared militarily and economically for the demands of war. Furthermore, the public remained unready, psychologically and politically, to switch from the role of high-minded neutrality to a bloody and thorough commitment to war. So, at the same time as the Wilson administration attempted to organize funding and manpower, it also sought ways to win and solidify national support for the war. As a former college professor and president, Wilson had only limited experience or interest in mustering political support through the structure of the political party machinery. He had served only briefly as governor of New Jersey on a reform ticket before running for president, and he distrusted organized political machines; indeed, his reform approach in New Jersey had been to work against the old politicians who stood for patronage, payoffs, and inner-city ward campaigns to get out the reliable voters. Instead, Wilson relied on a combination of loyal journalists and established political figures, and his eloquent and impressive speaking manner to win popular support for his positions. As had become clear by 1916, his eloquence had some successes and some notable failures; however, his speeches alone would not be enough to effect an overnight conversion of the public persona from dispassionate neutral to passionate patriot.

The Food Administration urged voluntary conservation by depicting food as essential to the war effort. (*National Archives*)

A HOUSE DIVIDED

The disruption brought by the war ran far deeper than party politics or divisions over how to administer war agencies. Both Republicans and Democrats feared that the nation would be incapable of acting with unity. Wilson had spent two years arguing that the United States was above the fray and that it should be neutral in thought as well as action. Suddenly, he was asking the nation to unite behind a war because nine ships flying the American flag and crewed by a mix of American citizens and foreigners had been destroyed while carrying supplies and fuel to one side of that war. Clearly, American exporting businesses, ship owners, and oil companies found their profits endangered by the German unrestricted submarine blockade, but most Americans, including the northern urban voters and the rural white southerners who represented the core of the Democratic voting constituency, had little sympathy for corporations that drew their earnings from trade with the belligerents. Getting wholehearted support for the new course of action represented an urgent priority.

In his speech asking Congress to make a declaration of war, Wilson construed the war as a fight for democracy against autocracy, and, over the next months, he hoped to rally the people of America to this cause. Democracy could constitute a far nobler and far more high-minded battle cry than defending the right of ship-owners and corporations to make a profit from sales to the British and French. He understood that the American people might not rally to defend the flag that flew over merchant ships that supplied the Allies after years of believing that the United States as a nation had no stake in the conflict.

Although Congress had voted overwhelmingly for the declaration of war, the explicit opposition of six senators and 50 members of Congress like Progressive Robert La Follette and feminist Jeanette Rankin could readily denote a significant and widespread undercurrent of opposition. Even the leader of the Democratic majority, Claude Kitchin, opposed the resolution declaring a state of war. Had the vote in Congress been by secret ballot, many suspected that there would have been a far larger antiwar expression, ranging across party lines. Even without such guesswork, political observers knew that the political left, German-Americans, and many others strongly opposed the war.

Deep divisions ran through American society, already noted by Wilson in his public speeches and very familiar to all political leaders. Such divisions clearly could stand in the way of national unity in wartime. The first decade of the 20th century had seen unprecedented waves of immigrants to the United States, many of whom were barely assimilated, with cultural and loyalty ties to nations on both sides of the World War. Most Americans of Irish ancestry resented the British resistance to the movement for Home Rule and the suppression of the Easter Rebellion in Dublin in April 1916. The state of Missouri and other states in the upper Midwest had large populations of German Americans, and the loyalty of such "hyphenated" Americans in a war against Germany seemed problematic, not only to government officials, but also to fellow Americans who traced their ancestry to Britain or one of the other Allies. Immigrants and their children from Hungary, Austria, and even Mexico, since the alarm of the Zimmermann telegram and the suggestion of pro-German policies in Mexico, had reason to disagree with the war policy. Czechs and Poles eagerly awaited the collapse of the Austro-Hungarian Empire so that their national aspirations, like those of the Serbs, could be realized, and they naturally took a pro-Allied stand. But such facts confused many Americans who had only the foggiest notions about the geography and political upheavals of eastern Europe. The loyalty of even strongly pro-Allied subject peoples of the Habsburg and Ottoman empires more than once came into question in the United States during the war.

Through the lumber and mining regions of the West, the growing militant labor union, the Industrial Workers of the World (I.W.W.), seemed to echo the radical socialists of Russia in arguing that the war served only the interests of munitions makers, capitalists, and bankers. Socialists of a less radical type, who represented perhaps 8 or 10 percent of the total voting electorate, tended to view the war as contrary to the interests of the masses, and the American Socialist Party leadership voted explicitly to oppose the war and the draft.

In the southern states, many white Americans feared that African Americans would feel little loyalty or could not be relied upon during the war. Race prejudice ran so deep that most white army officers believed that any black troops should be entrusted only to labor units, while many white southern politicians viewed with alarm the concept of any blacks at all in military uniforms. Indeed, the claim that the war would be one to make the world safe for democracy did have a hollow ring for African Americans who constantly faced racial insult, lynching, and discriminatory laws. The fact that Wilson, a southerner, had instituted policies of racial segregation in federal facilities won him the enmity of many black spokesmen and leaders. Wilson clearly had no patience with African-American protests about racial conditions, and his position made it seem unlikely that black support for his war policies would be enthusiastic. Many black leaders regarded Wilson's claim to be defending democracy in the war as sheer hypocrisy, given the Democratic Party's abysmal record on race.

Still other divisions rumbled beneath the surface, focusing less on questions of loyalty to the war effort, but nevertheless reflective of a diverse political culture, rather than a simple, unified, American viewpoint. Rural, southern, and religiously fundamentalist sections of the country supported legislation that would outlaw the sale and consumption of alcohol. After years of crusading, Prohibitionists had won support in those sections and segments of the population on the grounds that alcohol not only contributed to crime, family abuse, and poverty but also that saloons and alcohol distributors had undue influence on corrupt city political machines and in state legislatures. Prohibitionists claimed that while a food shortage existed and while grain had to be supplied to help feed Britain, to divert grain to the production of alcohol represented a threat to the war effort. Arrayed against this sentiment, urban areas, Catholic regions, and many northern city politicians and labor leaders all protested that the individual should make the decision whether or not to consume beer, wine, or liquor and that their prohibition would lead only to smuggling and further criminality. Samuel Gompers, head of the American Federation of Labor, argued that support for prohibition of alcohol during the war would only exacerbate existing divisions at a time when the government sought national unity.

A growing movement to extend the right to vote to women had widespread support among progressives in both the Democratic and Republican parties; for the most part, the feminist and suffragist leaders had supported neutrality and pacifism in the period 1914–17. However, when the United States entered the war, most American suffragists, like their sisters in Britain, pledged their support to Wilson and the war effort, in hopes that their actions would win over the president and prowar men to their cause. Yet the war and the question of what strategy to pursue in winning suffrage continued to divide the leadership of the women's movement. Some suffragists had already turned to demonstrating for the right to vote by picketing the White House and other government facilities before the declaration of war, but after the war began, such activity could lead to arrest. Police and judges alike viewed such behavior as disruptive and disloyal in time of war. The most active male advocates of the war felt deeply suspicious of the feminist movement and highly critical of its leaders, since, for many years, leading feminists had been active in the peace movement. All of these crosscurrents made the search for a simple commitment to patriotic support for the war difficult.

Against this background of deep divisions, Wilson and his cabinet members sought ways to build loyalty and support for the war and to ensure that spokesmen for the Central Powers and advocates of continued neutrality not win a hearing. Exhorting the public at every opportunity with carefully wrought phrases had been Wilson's greatest strength. However, he and his advisers recognized that to get support for the war would take concerted public relations efforts on a much larger scale than simple presidential addresses to appreciative, preselected crowds of supporters. How to encourage the press and other media to support the war, through a voluntary approach, represented one of the first challenges faced by the administration after the declaration of war.

UNITY AT THE PRICE OF LIBERTY

In efforts to ensure unity, the Wilson administration took extraordinary steps. In response to a suggestion from the secretaries of war, treasury, and state, Wilson established the Committee on Public Information (C.P.I.) and placed at its head a colorful journalist who had been one of Wilson's political supporters, George Creel. Under Creel, the C.P.I. would go on to become a combination propaganda agency and censorship bureau that flooded the nation with speakers, posters, music, movies, books, and pamphlets all urging support for the war, support for bond drives to raise funds, support for the military draft, and suppression of any pro-German or peace-advocacy sentiments. The C.P.I. accepted and enlarged upon British propaganda issued in the form of the Bryce Report, which had collected and exaggerated unsubstantiated atrocity stories to whip up British public opinion against Germany. The agency provided copy and material free of charge to newspapers and magazines, using the method of press release and canned stories. Newspapers gladly received the material, which often contained elements of news and quotations from official government spokesmen. Since the law did not require a newspaper to print the stories, the system preserved in theory the principle of voluntarism. C.P.I. soon flooded the nation's media outlets with free material that supported the administration's position and methods.

James Montgomery Flagg is shown here with his most famous poster. *(National Archives)*

Creel took over an existing voluntary organization, the Four-Minute Men, made up of speakers who would deliver speeches limited to four minutes on a wide number of topics. He soon expanded the number of speakers, who worked furiously, delivering talks during intermissions at movie theaters, to church groups and club meetings, and even on street corners. In all, by Creel's own estimates, the Four-Minute Men gave more than 755,000 speeches in 18 months, urging support for the war, for the draft, for purchasing war bonds, and describing in horrible detail the supposed atrocities of the enemy.

The agency commissioned many of the famous posters that still survive in popular culture from the era, including the one by James M. Flagg depicting Uncle Sam pointing at the viewer and labeled "I want you." Eventually, C.P.I. released some propaganda movies to theaters for screening with a nominal charge that helped offset the cost to the government. A few of them, like *The Kaiser, the Beast of Berlin,* released in April 1918, became widely popular. In addition, the C.P.I. issued a daily periodical, the *Official Bulletin,* with a circulation of more than 100,000, containing news and propaganda from the government.

To further ensure unity of opinion, under the Espionage Act passed in the first months of the war, Postmaster Albert Burleson instituted a campaign of intimidation and censorship. By far the most aggressive and hostile member of Wilson's cabinet, Burleson specifically focused on foreign-language newspapers, as well as socialist and liberal publications that advocated continued neutrality or opposition to American participation in the war. Burleson would suspend a publication's mailing privileges, and he would then claim that it had failed to maintain its status as a regularly published periodical, using that as an excuse to then permanently cancel mailing privileges. Both the Justice Department's Bureau of Investigation (BI) and Army Military Intelligence (MI) assisted the Post Office Department in investigating complaints about specific newspapers and magazines, especially Socialist periodicals and the black press.

Burleson censored or suspended, among other publications, a Socialist newspaper, the *Milwaukee Leader;* a Socialist magazine, *Masses;* an Irish-American publication, *Bull;* a black-owned weekly newspaper, the *San Antonio;* and *The Messenger,* a Socialist African-American magazine published by A. Philip Randolph. The Post Office censors closely monitored several other black publications, including the *Boston Guardian, New York News, New York Age,* and the *Chicago Broad-Ax.* After numerous complaints and investigations, both the NAACP's *Crisis* and the widely circulated African-American newspaper the *Chicago Defender,* adopted a more loyal tone. Burleson suspended the mailing privileges of the liberal weekly *The Nation* for its criticism of labor leader Samuel Gompers, and, in this one instance, Wilson intervened to overturn the suspension. The Justice Department also went after anarchist publications, such as Emma Goldman's *Mother Earth.*

Domestic intelligence work by both the Justice Department's BI and by the Army's MI actively pursued Socialists, anarchists, assorted other radicals, conscientious objectors, and I.W.W. members. A volunteer group of self-appointed radical hunters, the American Protective League (A.P.L.), received a small amount of funding from the Justice Department's BI, and these vigilantes provided reports on tens of thousands of citizens, including unpopular schoolteachers, German Americans suspected of sympathy with the enemy, accused "slackers" who avoided the draft, and completely innocent individuals who had simply annoyed their neighbors or who seemed a bit strange. Armed with the Espionage Act of 1917, and later with expanded powers under the Trading with the Enemy Act and the so-called Sedition Act, the federal government had the power to arrest and imprison anyone who spoke out against the war, the draft, or the efforts to raise funds for the war. Together, these laws made any such speech an illegal act. The Justice Department and the Post Office Department particularly focused on Socialists and I.W.W. leaders. Coordinated raids on I.W.W. headquarters in 1917 netted more than 100 aliens who could be deported on political grounds, while several hundred conscientious objectors and Socialists faced arrest for their opposition to the war.

The combined efforts of the C.P.I. to whip up public support for the war and of the intelligence agencies and their volunteer assistants to stamp out opposition almost completely silenced criticism of the war and its goals. Most elected politicians and other leaders sought only to out-do each other in demonstrations of loyalty. Republican members of Congress could criticize the president for not conducting the war vigorously enough, but pacifists and others opposing the war simply could not get a public forum to express their ideas.

If politicians or leaders expressed opposition to the war itself, they could lose their position. When Robert La Follette delivered some extemporaneous remarks to a meeting of the Nonpartisan League on September 20, 1917, explaining his reasons for opposing the war resolution, he stated that he viewed the offenses of Germany against the United States as insufficient to justify war. The Minnesota Committee of Public Safety, a patriotic group, immediately petitioned the Senate to expel La Follette, and the Senate considered a resolution to that effect. The ensuing investigation dragged on until after the war, only then to be quietly dropped. However, other politicians who opposed the war could not only lose their positions but also face arrest. The government arrested, among others, Charles Schenck, general secretary of the Socialist Party (SP), Eugene Debs, former SP presidential candidate, and Victor Berger, former SP member of Congress and owner of the *Milwaukee Leader*. None faced charges of attempted overthrow of the government or any action more radical than voicing opposition to the war and the draft.

Charles Schenck, as general secretary of the SP, presided over the party's executive committee, which authorized the distribution of a leaflet comparing the draft to involuntary servitude or slavery. The Thirteenth Amendment to the Constitution, he pointed out, prohibited slavery. Schenck ran the Philadelphia headquarters of the party that sent out the leaflets. Federal authorities arrested Schenck and convicted him of violation of the Espionage Act on three counts, with three 10-year sentences to run concurrently. The Supreme Court confirmed the case against him early in 1919.

Authorities arrested Eugene Debs, who had won more than 900,000 votes in 1912 when he ran for president on the Socialist Party ticket, for a speech in Canton, Ohio, opposing the draft, delivered in June 1918. Still in prison in 1920, he again ran for president from his jail cell, as Prisoner 9653. He again garnered more than 900,000 votes. President Warren Harding, after painful deliberation, pardoned Debs on Christmas Eve 1921.

Victor Berger, the Socialist owner of the *Milwaukee Leader* and elected in 1910 as the first Socialist in the U.S. Congress, was indicted for his antiwar positions in February 1918 and found himself sentenced to 20 years in prison at his trial in December 1918. A month before his trial, however, he gained reelection to Congress in the off-year congressional elections of 1918, but when he sought to claim his seat, Congress rejected him on the grounds of his conviction. Berger did not serve time, and the Supreme Court dropped the charges on a technicality. Berger won eventual reelection to Congress and served there from 1923 to 1929.

The Justice Department arrested many besides the well-known Socialists Schenck, Debs, and Berger under the Espionage Act. Altogether, federal authorities charged some 1,600 war opponents under the espionage and sedition acts, getting convictions and sentences on about half of those charged. While the government did not incarcerate a vast number of people in this way, the use of federal law and courts to place limits on freedom of speech created an atmosphere of compulsory loyalty that had immediate political effects in the 1918 election, and deeper and more sinister effects that lasted on into the postwar period.

The hysteria induced by the pressure of propaganda from the C.P.I., the suppression of opposition, and the official support for A.P.L. citizen-spies had numerous ugly and immediate consequences. On July 12, the sheriff in Bisbee, Arizona, with funding from the Phelps-Dodge mining company, organized an armed, antiradical posse that forcibly expelled 1,200 striking miners from the community, sending them off into the desert. On July 31, 1917, in Butte, Montana, a mob mutilated and lynched Frank Little, an I.W.W. organizer. In Houston, Texas, on August 23, 1917, a group of black soldiers retaliated against racial insults by using their weapons to attack whites, killing 17. Later, the army court-martialed 13 of the soldiers and executed them before their lawyers could file appeals. On April 5, 1918, another mob lynched Robert Prager, a Socialist of German birth, in Collinsville, Illinois; the local court later acquitted identified members of his lynch mob. In 1917, lynch mobs killed 38 African Americans; in 1918, the total climbed to 58, including 10 black soldiers accused of wearing their uniforms too long after discharge. These and numerous other incidents, including army roundups of suspected draft evaders, supported by volunteers from the A.P.L., indicated that the surface unity and patriotic fervor whipped up by official and unofficial propaganda tapped into already existing, deep-seated divisions and prejudices.

On a less violent level, the spy hysteria and anti-German feeling led to flurries of rumor and harassment of law-abiding citizens and also to simple ignorant excesses. Loyal citizens suffering a bit of paranoia suspected people with lights on in houses in view of the seacoast of signaling submarines; rumors spread of armed uprisings of German Americans in St. Louis, Cincinnati, and Milwaukee, when nothing of the kind had happened. Some orchestras dismissed all German-born musicians, and many schools dropped German-language instruction on the grounds that such classes tended to spread German culture and values. In the Midwest, patriot thugs broke up meetings that had been intended to gather recruits among Czech Americans for the war against the Central Powers, because the self-appointed patriots did not understand Czech or quite realize which side of the war the volunteers preferred. Some saloons banned pretzels, while German terms such as *dachshund* and *sauerkraut* vanished, at least for a period, from the vocabulary, in favor of *sausage dog* and *liberty cabbage*.

The sudden rise of anti-German and spy-hunt hysteria during the short year and a half of the war reflected the effectiveness of the campaigns initiated by the federal government. The barrage of propaganda from the C.P.I., the censorship of opposition press by the Post Office, and the organized campaign by the BI, MI, and A.P.L. to track down draft dodgers, opponents of the war, Socialists, and pacifists combined to create the symptoms of a profound mass psychosis. Within a few years, shocked observers of the American scene, ranging from liberals like Walter Lippmann to conservatives like Alice Roosevelt Longworth and popular historian Mark Sullivan, looked aghast and with evident embarrassment at what had happened to the state of the American mind and public opinion.

ORGANIZING FOR WAR

Although the suppression of civil liberties represented an authoritarian method of thought-control, the Wilson administration started off the war effort with strictly voluntary measures. The Committee for Public Information, established on April 14, 1917, although a propaganda agency, worked at first by simply providing free material for the consumption of the nation's press. Three days later,

Boy Scouts helped in the drives for Liberty Bonds. *(National Archives)*

the government launched the first Liberty Bond drive. Wilson and his son-in-law and secretary of the treasury, William Gibbs McAdoo, chose to raise money for the war primarily by the voluntary method of selling and buying bonds rather than relying on compulsory taxation. In order to promote the sale, the treasury enlisted the C.P.I. in advertising and exhorting people to buy the bonds. The interest rate on the first issued bonds was set below the prevailing market rate for solid commercial loans, at 3.5 per cent. To make that rate attractive, any income tax on the gain was waived. This feature made the bonds financially attractive to wealthier individuals most concerned with income tax, rather than those in the lowest income ranks. The first issue of Liberty Bonds in April 1917 was set at $2 billion. Boy Scouts and Four-Minute Men urged the sale of bonds, and performers put on benefit entertainments. One session at Carnegie Hall, led by Enrico Caruso and Amelita Galli-Curci, raised $4.8 million in bonds.

Since banks could use Liberty Bonds as collateral for loans from the Federal Reserve System, the issuance of bonds eventually had the effect of placing more money in circulation. In effect, part of the war effort became funded, in this roundabout fashion, through the issuance of more currency, leading to rapid inflation. An unintended consequence of the voluntaristic bond sale, inflation represented an invisible compulsory tax on every consumer.

With inflation and climbing prices, workers of course demanded higher incomes, but the American Federation of Labor attempted to restrain any strike action for the duration of the war. However, in western lumbering and mining regions, numerous strikes broke out, some organized or led by the I.W.W., while in other areas unorganized workers began to form rudimentary independent organizations to demand higher wages. In Norfolk, Virginia, black women workers in the American Cigar Company tried to hold out for a living wage in September 1917. They and a local newspaper calculated that a bare minimum for food, fuel, and other necessities came to about $7.00 a week. Supported by others in the city in the beginning of a spontaneous general strike, the women soon faced police who assisted in breaking the strike. The white press joined in the strikebreaking effort, calling the strikers loafers or slackers.

Altogether, McAdoo pushed four bond drives during the war. He first estimated that the cost of the war effort would be $3.5 billion; by May 1918, he had raised the estimate to $13.7 billion with another $24 billion needed for the following year. In addition, the sale of bonds of the Allies in the United States totaled $9.5 billion. Eventually, selling bonds proved inadequate for all fund-raising, and the government imposed some new taxes, including an excess profits tax and adjusted income tax rates.

By 1918, many individuals began to sell their Liberty Bonds below face value, reflecting the hard times brought on by inflation. By contrast, however, some sectors enjoyed great profit levels, particularly mining, metals, and munitions. Bethlehem Steel made profits some 800 percent higher than prewar levels. McAdoo found two coal companies with profits of more than 1,000 percent per year, and an executive of American Metal Company got a bonus of $350,000 for 1917.

The disparity between the poverty of workers caught between rising prices and frozen wages and the great war profits among specific corporations would further divide the country during and after the war. In addition, those elements of the population on fixed incomes, like retirees who relied on returns from mortgages and bonds or academics working in institutions funded by regular returns from endowments, also suffered a drop in purchasing power. Such social conditions helped fuel the argument that the war had been fought in the interests of business, rather than for the higher goals that Wilson claimed.

INDUSTRIAL ORGANIZATION, FOOD, AND FUEL

The doctrine of voluntary cooperation and compliance had its limits, soon revealed in attempts to organize industry. Different purchasing agencies of the government soon found themselves bidding against each other for the same products. With shipowners reluctant to send freighters through the submarine blockade, goods piled up in railroad cars parked on sidings near East Coast ports. Coal prices climbed, and, despite increased production, fuel supplies dropped to dangerously low levels because of a severe winter in 1917–18 and vastly increased factory production. To meet these challenges, Wilson established several coordinating agencies. Although the agencies had few powers, they represented a step in the direction of a managed economy.

In the summer of 1917, Wilson established the War Industries Board and selected Bernard Baruch to head it up. A successful Wall Street financier, Baruch took on the task, resigning his position on several corporate boards of directors to avoid a conflict of interest. Baruch had already served in 1916 on the Advisory Commission of the Council of National Defense and as chair of the Commission on Raw Materials, Minerals, and Metals. Wilson first put Baruch in charge of coordinating all Allied purchasing in the United States. In addition to giving up his board memberships, Baruch sold his seat on the New York Stock Exchange and cashed in his corporate investments, using the proceeds to buy millions of dollars worth of Liberty Bonds. With enhanced powers, Baruch began to issue direct orders regulating aspects of the economy, all the while urging voluntary compliance. Nevertheless, in some industries,

Cooperation at home and putting off labor grievances was part of the teamwork required to win the war, according to this poster. *(National Archives)*

government orders became the only way to secure compliance. For example, the W.I.B. regulated the price of shoes, ordered that no platinum, gold, or silver be used in jewelry manufacture, and required that all automobile manufacture be devoted to government work by January 1, 1919.

Herbert Hoover, as food administrator, worked even more through exhortation to get enterprises and consumers to conform to certain voluntary rules, urging meatless days and reduction of wasted food by housewives and restaurant cooks and chefs. Hoover urged children to join a clean-plate league. Hoover proposed substitution of plentiful products for scarcer ones, such as corn for wheat, fish and beans for meat, and syrup for sugar, and the practice of voluntary conservation came to be called Hooverizing. Although Hoover held the power to close down businesses through the ability to withdraw federal licenses to operate, he very rarely used the penalty. Sometimes, when a corporation did not cooperate, Hoover would demand a contribution to the Red Cross and then let the business continue on promise of good behavior. He repeatedly called conferences of related industries, exhorted them to cooperation, and then relied on that cooperation.

The Lever Food and Fuel Act passed in August 1917 regularized Hoover's position and granted him federal authority, although he so preferred working through the voluntary method that he rarely employed the additional powers granted him. Under the Lever Act, Wilson appointed Harry Garfield as fuel administrator, and he, like Hoover, hoped to operate on a voluntary basis. However, as coal and oil stocks dropped in the severe winter of 1917–18, Garfield faced a crisis. Finally, on January 16, 1918, he issued an order shutting down all manufacturing plants east of the Mississippi for four days, January 18 to January 22. He supplemented that order with shutdowns on the following nine Mondays. The outcry against this decision, and the obvious failure of planning that it represented, led Republicans in Congress to attempt to pass legislation establishing a congressionally selected war cabinet to run the economy and the war effort. Democratic floor leaders successfully forestalled that attack on Wilson, pushing through the Overman Act, which gave the president the power to reorganize government departments without congressional approval. Democrats thus converted the clamor for more efficiency and more direct control into more administrative control in the hands of the president, quite the reverse of what the disgruntled leaders of the Republican opposition had been hoping to achieve.

The transportation problem was addressed separately at the end of December 1917, when Wilson appointed William Gibbs McAdoo director-general of the United States Railroads. Usually remembered as a federal takeover or nationalization of the railroads, in fact, the appointment act simply conferred on McAdoo the power to set and control rates and to override antitrust regulation that prohibited railroad collaboration on traffic management, pricing, and wage rates. McAdoo allowed for increased rates and worked with the existing companies to untangle the immense traffic jams that had developed.

With McAdoo's control of the railways, Baruch's management of industrial pricing, Hoover's gentle exhortation of food producers, and Garfield's sometimes draconian orders regarding coal and fuel consumption, the economy came under a form of government direction. While the power to regulate through license, order, and price setting had been established, the new agencies and administrators tended to operate through cooperation and coordination and relied largely on calls to patriotic duty. The calls did not always work, and prices on most commodities climbed partly because of currency inflation, reducing the value of the dollar by some 40 percent. Nevertheless, as a model for how to control the economy in a crisis, the foundation and principle of federal leadership had been established, despite the reluctance of Wilson and his appointees to use compulsory methods.

SOCIAL CHANGES: AFRICAN AMERICANS

The war years saw the greatest migration of African Americans from the South to the North since the Civil War, with about 500,000 (out of a total black population of about 10 million) relocating northward. About half of the migrants settled in a limited number of cities, including Chicago, Philadelphia, and New York City. At the time and over the decades since, observers have debated the extent to which the migration derived from the attractive pull of conditions in the North or from the push to leave generated by conditions in the South. The promise of jobs opened up by the cessation of European immigration and by the expansion of industry and commerce brought on by the war drew many African Americans from the farms, villages, and cities of the South. Employment agents scoured southern states for workers, offering free railroad tickets and other inducements to bring in a new labor supply. In addition, the lack of some of the outward signs of discrimination in the North, such as the ability to vote and to be relatively safe from racial violence, showed up in letters sent from the North to the South by new arrivals and published by the black-owned newspaper the *Chicago Defender,* widely circulated and read in the South.

On the other hand, continued racial violence, including dozens of lynchings per year, almost all in the South, made the North seem attractive by contrast. In most areas of the South common forms of discrimination such as denial of access to public facilities including parks, beaches, and libraries and concerted efforts to deny the vote to black citizens all made race conditions in the South deplorable.

The rapid migration created disruptions for North and South and especially for the African-American migrants themselves. In some southern rural counties, the shortage of labor became immediately apparent, even as early as 1916, and worsened through 1917 and 1918. Some local officials sought to prohibit the exodus, requiring the licensing of labor recruiters and otherwise attempting to discourage the migration. In the North, the promised land turned out to be less than a paradise for the African-American migrants. Housing discrimination usually forced the new arrivals to live in the most undesirable and worn-down neighborhoods, often extensions of the red-light districts where police winked at open prostitution and drug-dealing. Promised jobs, even at the bottom of the wage scale, did not always materialize or last very long. In East St. Louis, during July 1–3, 1917, a vicious race riot, in which whites slaughtered at least 39 black citizens including women and children, stemmed from tensions over black migration to the region in search of employment. In this and many other locations, the fairly sudden arrival of large numbers of blacks from the rural South created a white backlash that resulted in violence, some of it continuing to surface in bloody race riots and lynchings after the war ended.

Because of the labor shortage, African-American women were able to find factory work in defense industries. These women are preparing spiral puttees for bailing and shipment. *(National Archives)*

The Justice Department Bureau of Investigation and the army's Military Intelligence received thousands of complaints that German propagandists tried to woo African Americans, but investigators uncovered no such effort at all. The complaints reflected the fears and prejudices of those complaining, more than any reality. Nevertheless, the security services constantly watched black leaders, particularly those more outspoken in their advocacy of civil rights, such as W. E. B. DuBois, editor of the NAACP's journal *Crisis,* or the West Indian radical leader, Cyril Briggs. Both men, as well as many other black leaders, pointed out that the African American had little incentive to fight in a war to make the world safe for democracy when so little had been done to make America safe for democracy, a message that did not sit well with Burleson, Creel, or the officers in Military Intelligence. Nevertheless, in July 1918, DuBois published an editorial in *Crisis* entitled "Close Ranks" in which he urged his fellow African Americans to do their part as good citizens in the war effort. He suggested that such a course would strengthen the position of black Americans to demand more equal treatment when the war ended. The Post Office considered the editorial possibly inflammatory, but after a six-day holdup of delivery, allowed 100,000 copies of the magazine to be sent out. Although many black leaders and spokesmen criticized DuBois for adopting such a conciliatory position, his comments seemed to allay some of the suspicion leveled against him by the security agencies.

Black troops served in the 97th and 98th Army divisions in Europe, and, although French officers with whom they worked praised their performance, many white army officers reflected prejudices commonly held in the white American population. Some worried that black troops would be cowardly in the face of fire, while others felt that providing black men with uniforms and weapons and allowing them exposure to French women would have disastrous social consequences on the troops' return. White officers restricted a large number of the black troops sent to Europe to service in labor details. Incidents such as the court-martial and immediate execution three days later of 13 black troops for their participation in the race riot in Houston, Texas; the East St. Louis riots (which the federal government refused to investigate); and continued lynchings all helped convince black leadership that the Democratic administration of Woodrow Wilson showed almost no commitment to racial justice.

Although the war won no immediate social gains for black Americans, the fact that many leaders like DuBois and others pointed out the inconsistency between American claims to be the defender of democracy in Europe and the blatantly undemocratic racial repression in the United States lay the groundwork for later developments, such as the growth of a new black consciousness known as the Harlem Renaissance and the organized push for the protection of civil rights through the courts and legislatures over the next decades. A small number of influential whites, such as journalist Oswald Garrison Villard, who served on the NAACP board, heard and understood the arguments, supplemented later by alienated white intellectuals who found black culture attractive for psychological and cultural reasons. Although many administrators in Wilson's government shared the president's prejudices, a few, like Secretary of War Newton Baker made a concerted effort to limit incidents of racial injustice in the army during the war.

In the 1910 census, about 90 percent of the black population of the United States had lived in the South; by 1920, that percentage had been reduced to about 85 per cent, and the black migration to the North continued through the following years. Coupled with the political ferment brought about by the war and the linkage of democracy at home to the cause of democracy abroad, the simple demographic shift had vast political consequences. The new numbers meant that African-American voters in northern cities would begin to be a force to be reckoned with in national politics in the years to come.

SOCIAL CHANGES: WOMEN AND THE WAR

The fact that some 2 million men went out from the labor force to enter the A.E.F. created a shortage of workers on farms, in industry, and in service positions. While black men migrated from the South to take the places formerly occupied by waves of European immigrants, many women of all races also took new positions. However, contrary to popular impressions, the vast majority of women who went to work as factory hands, machinists, munitions workers, streetcar operators, telephone operators, and elevator attendants were not drawn from the ranks of middle-class housewives. Most women in these industrial and service jobs had worked before, many as low-paid domestic servants, seamstresses, or in textile industries. Many women did find themselves with better-paying jobs at least temporarily, even though the pay was not equal to that of male workers in the same positions. In general, organized labor leaders viewed the influx of women into new jobs very cautiously, believing the women would and should be short-time replacements for men who had gone into the military. As a consequence, women rarely organized, except in sporadic and spontaneous protests,

Defense jobs for women paid better than domestic work. These three women are stretching linen on aircraft wings. *(National Archives)*

such as that of the cigar makers in Norfolk, Virginia. In New York, women in the garment trades did organize and continued to hold some of their advances in pay and conditions after the war.

The women's suffrage movement had been severely divided by the war, with many women hoping that by pledging loyalty and support for the war and holding off from protest, they would win the approval of Congress for the suffrage amendment. The National Woman's Party, however, under the leadership of Alice Paul, a suffragist from New Jersey who had spent some time in Britain and had become familiar with demonstration tactics there, decided on a more direct approach. On January 10, 1917, three months before the declaration of war, Paul's group began picketing the White House. Politicians, for the most part, tried to ignore the protests.

However, a few weeks later, the District of Columbia police warned Ms. Paul that any further demonstrations would result in the arrest of the protesters. Alice Paul noted that, according to her lawyers, picketing remained perfectly legal, and no difference existed between picketing before and after the war began. Over the period June 22–June 26, police arrested a total of 29 women outside the White House. The court convicted six of them for obstructing traffic, and fined each $25. All six refused to pay the fine and were sent to jail. These arrests were followed in July with another 16 arrests, including the wife of a former ambassador to Great Britain and the wife of Wilson's New Jersey campaign manager.

The judge in their case considered charging the women with violation of the Espionage Act, but since they had restricted their picket signs to quotations from Wilson's own speeches about democracy, the women had forestalled that legal tactic and at the same time had given an ironic poke at the system. The women were sentenced to 60 days in the Occoquan Workhouse, the prison for offenders in the District of Columbia, on the charge of obstructing traffic. A lawyer whom Wilson had appointed as Collector of the Port of New York, Dudley Malone, threatened to resign his position and to offer his legal services to the women. Wilson pardoned all of the suffragists. Later, in October, the police arrested Alice Paul and 10 other women, but this time the women refused to even recognize the authority of the court, on the ground that they were completely unrepresented in the government that arrested them. After Paul and some of her fellow prisoners organized a hunger strike and requested to be treated as political prisoners, guards force-fed them and held them in solitary confinement.

Malone resigned his position and filed a writ of habeas corpus, finally obtaining the release of the suffragist prisoners in November 1917. By March 1918, the District of Columbia Court of Appeals ruled that the arrests had been illegal. The direct action of protesting and refusing to accept the justice system had set precedents for later civil disobedience and protest campaigns over other issues.

Although the protests, arrests, and appeals had proceeded during the hectic months of 1917 and early 1918, as the war effort dominated the news, the impact of the protests and the embarrassment to the administration apparently had an effect. Although disturbed at the willingness of women to picket and go to jail, many male politicians, like Malone, recognized the legitimacy of their point about disfranchisement. New York State extended suffrage to women on November 11, 1917. Energized both by Alice Paul's campaign and by more traditional lobbying efforts, the women's movement achieved congressional approval for the Nineteenth Amendment, which granted nationwide suffrage to women, on June 4, 1919. After a vigorous state-by-state campaign, 36 states approved the amendment and it went into effect in August 1920, in time for the November 1920 elections.

THE 1918 ELECTION

The Wilson administration had worked assiduously to suppress opposition to the war and to foster a sense of national unity and patriotism in the year and a half following the declaration of war. Yet many of the people attacked in that effort included some who had been among Wilson's earlier advocates. Much of Wilson's support in the elections of 1912 and 1916 had come from progressive Democrats, who increasingly called themselves liberals during this period. In general, liberal opinion had been in favor of women's rights, child labor protection, regulation of industry, and peaceful negotiation of international conflicts. Those opposed to the war and in favor of continued neutrality had mostly supported Wilson in 1916; however, through 1917 and 1918, his own administration made opposition to the war an illegal act and actively suppressed the voicing of that opinion. The instruments of government thus turned against the very core of Wilson's earlier voting base. Although a limited number of people had been arrested for violation of the Espionage Act on grounds of their opposition to the war and the draft, the broader effect had been to disillusion and silence liberal opinion.

Wilson's hold on the electorate had been slim in 1916. He had won reelection through the fact that many western states, traditionally Republican but also strongly Neutralist on the war, had swung by narrow majorities into his column. As the congressional elections of 1918 neared, Democrats urged Wilson to campaign or speak out in favor of the party, but he remained reluctant, withdrawing from partisan politics.

He made two strange exceptions to his silence on the election. In the first place, he endorsed the candidacy of Henry Ford, the automobile manufacturer usually assumed to be a Republican, to run as both a Democrat and a Republican in the election for the U.S. Senate from Michigan. Ford lost the Republican nomination and ran and lost as a Democrat, but the endorsement struck many faithful Democrats as peculiar, to say the least. Then, in another unwise political act, at the last minute on October 25, 1918, Wilson gave a speech in which he stated that his position in negotiating the peace abroad would be weakened if the American people did not show their support of him by returning Democrats to Congress. By not campaigning for particular candidates and then linking the popular vote for Congress to his own position on the war, Wilson adopted probably the worst set of tactics that could be imagined.

He had made it clear that he supported a peace that would not be vindictive against the Central Powers, but for 18 months the American people had been whipped into a frenzy of hatred for Germany. Now, it seemed, he expected them to follow him, by force of his rhetoric, in a course of action that would focus not on German war guilt, but on reconstructing a stable peace in Europe. While many opposed that course and believed Republicans would be more militant in their positions, others had more interest in local and particular issues, such as the prices of farm commodities, the sudden rise in the cost of living, the apparent profiteering in some industries, and distressed labor conditions. Statistically, the election turned out to be no more of a condemnation of the incumbent administration than usual in midterm elections, but after Wilson's plea for a popular endorsement of his positions, the outcome of the vote could be read as a repudiation of him. The Republicans won majorities with gains of six seats in the Senate and 30 seats in the House of Representatives, so that Democrats lost control of both houses. The Democratic Party losses ran greatest in western states, which largely returned to their traditional Republican position. The election took place six days before the end of the war.

CHRONICLE OF EVENTS

1917

April 6: Woodrow Wilson signs the declaration of war at 1:18 P.M. He issues a proclamation of a state of war and regulations limiting the rights of enemy aliens and requiring enemy aliens to register.

April 14: Wilson issues executive order 2594 establishing the Committee of Public Information to be headed by George Creel to take over the propaganda coordination function for various government agencies. Wilson predates the order to April 13.

April 17: The War Department establishes the Commission on Training Camp Activities (CTCA) with the function of looking after the moral welfare of newly recruited troops. The CTCA embodies many Progressive ideals and works to prevent venereal disease and alcohol consumption and to provide wholesome entertainment for troops.

April 23: The Justice Department Bureau of Investigation (forerunner of the FBI) provides funding for the American Protective League (A.P.L.), a nationwide organization of volunteer antiradical and anti-German vigilantes. The A.P.L. will suppress dissent with many clear abuses of civil liberties.

April 24: The Liberty Loan bond drive begins; the bond rate is set at 3.5 percent, causing the face value of bonds to drop over the next three years to about 80 percent of the original issue value. Since many bond buyers borrow funds to purchase bonds and since banks can use bonds as collateral to borrow from the Federal Reserve Banks, the system generates new money, causing very high inflation during the war.

May 13: The Selective Service Act becomes law.

May 15: Officers' training camps open, established along the lines of the Plattsburg Idea.

May 18: Wilson officially declines the offer of Theodore Roosevelt to organize a volunteer division to serve on the western front.

May 18: Wilson signs the proclamation establishing the draft and setting June 5 as the date for registration.

May 19: Wilson appoints Herbert Hoover as food administrator for war; Hoover obtains restrictions on consumption by voluntary cooperation and propaganda, rather than through rationing.

June: The Committee on Public Information (C.P.I.) takes over the Four-Minute Men organization, sending thousands of speakers out to support bond drives and to raise support for the war. Altogether more than 755,000 speeches are delivered.

June 5: All men between ages 21 and 30 are required to register for the draft on this day, by presidential proclamation; although more than 9 million register, an estimated 350,000 draft-evaders, known as slackers, fail to register.

June 15: The Espionage Act becomes law, allowing banning from the mail antiwar literature and any literature advocating resistance to any law.

June 28: An I.W.W.-led strike against copper mines begins; Sheriff Harry Wheeler organizes a posse to suppress the strike in Bisbee, Arizona.

July: Judge Learned Hand issues a temporary restraining order against Postmaster Burleson in the case of *Masses Publishing v. Patten;* the decision is reversed by the Circuit Court of Appeals, allowing suppression of the radical publication *Masses.*

The Selective Service System was supplemented by calls for volunteers, like this one for the tanks. *(National Archives)*

July 1: A race riot erupts in East St. Louis, Illinois. Although exact figures are never tallied, at least 39 African Americans and nine whites are killed.

July 12: An antiradical posse paid for by the Phelps-Dodge company expels 1,200 I.W.W. sympathizers from Bisbee, Arizona.

July 20: Secretary of War Baker hand-selects the first draft numbers for the call-up of those having registered the previous month.

July 28: The War Industries Board is reorganized by Wilson to be a more effective coordinator.

July 31: Industrial Workers of the World (I.W.W.) leader Frank Little is lynched in Butte, Montana.

August: The Lever Food and Fuel Act passed, providing for a system of price supports for certain agricultural products and establishing congressional approval for the Food Administration established by presidential action in May; Wilson names Harry Garfield as fuel administrator.

August 23: A race riot erupts in Houston, Texas; black soldiers of the 24th Infantry Division, 3rd Battalion, shoot to death 17 white civilians; the 3rd Battalion is disarmed and sent under arrest to New Mexico.

September 5: The Department of Justice raids I.W.W. offices nationwide with presidential approval; 113 leaders are arrested.

September 26: Canada passes a conscription act.

October: Congress passes the Trading with the Enemy Act.

October: Congress passes the War Revenue Act, which incorporates an excess-profits tax, after a bitter four-week debate in the Senate.

October 16: A U.S. Board of Censors is established; George Creel appoints Edgar Sisson as a C.P.I. representative, while Burleson appoints Robert L. Maddox. Other members are appointed from the War Trade Board, the army, and the navy.

October 18: Postmaster General Burleson suppresses the *Milwaukee Leader* despite disapproval by Woodrow Wilson.

November 11: New York State grants suffrage to women.

November 24: Jeremiah O'Leary, editor of *Bull,* the organ of the Irish-sponsored American Truth Society of which he was also president, is indicted for conspiracy to violate the Espionage Act on the grounds that he and others have advocated insubordination and disloyalty among members of the armed services.

December 4: Wilson asks Congress to declare that a state of war exists with Austria-Hungary.

December 7: Congress declares that a state of war exists with Austria-Hungary.

December 8: An explosion aboard a munitions ship destroys half of the port of Halifax, Nova Scotia; sabotage is suspected.

December 8: Thirteen black soldiers are condemned to death for participating in the Houston riots; they are executed December 11, before an appeal can be started.

December 9: C.P.I. issues a report, *German War Practices,* repeating propaganda created by the British in their Bryce Report.

December 11: Pursuant to the act of Congress on December 7, Wilson issues a proclamation that a state of war exists with Austria-Hungary and issues related regulations.

December 17: A pro-war coalition government defeats the Liberals in a Canadian election.

December 26: Wilson issues a proclamation announcing a takeover of U.S. railroads to be effective two days later. Wilson names W. G. McAdoo as director-general of railway administration.

December 28: The U.S. government takes control of all U.S. railroads; McAdoo raises charges to shippers to pay higher wages and salaries and to fund expansion.

1918

January 4: Wilson explains to Congress his decision to establish federal control of the railroads.

January 8: Wilson delivers his Fourteen Points speech, proposing his peace without victory terms and the reorganization of European states along lines of national self-determination.

January 10–13: The Senate Military Affairs Committee questions Secretary of War Newton Baker in an attempt to discredit the administration's handling of the war.

January 17: Fuel Administrator Harry Garfield orders all eastern factories closed for five days to conserve coal, which unleashes a storm of protest against government ineptitude in handling the economy.

January 19: Wilson supports and upholds the fuel curtailment order issued by Garfield.

January 19: Senator George Chamberlain introduces a bill to establish a three-man war cabinet that would take administration of the war from Wilson's hands.

January 28: Secretary of War Baker returns to the Military Affairs Committee to defend the actions of his department and those of Garfield and to oppose the Chamberlain War Cabinet bill.

March: Women are given the right to vote throughout Canada.

March 4: Bernard Baruch is appointed to head the War Industries Board.

March 19: The United States institutes daylight saving time, to go into effect April–October.

April: C.P.I. begins screenings of the propaganda film *The Kaiser, the Beast of Berlin,* which becomes a box-office hit.

April 5: Robert Prager, a Socialist of German birth, is lynched in Collinsville, Illinois; members of the lynch mob are later acquitted.

May 16: Wilson signs the Sedition Act, expanding the power of arrest of the Espionage Act. The Sedition Act prohibits "any disloyal, profane, scurrilous, or abusive language about the form of government of the United States, or the Constitution of the United States, or the flag of the United States, or the uniform of the Army or Navy" and further prohibits any language that would bring those institutions "into contempt, scorn, contumely, or disrepute."

May 20: The Overman Act becomes law, giving the president the power to reorganize executive agencies without consulting Congress. Wilson uses the act to reorganize the War Industries Board; this act disarms the congressional critics of inefficiency by giving the president more power at the expense of Congress.

May 23: General Enoch Crowder, director of Selective Service, issues a "work or fight order," introducing gradations in eligibility for the draft based on whether a worker was essential or could easily be replaced.

June 12: Wilson convinces Henry Ford to run for the Senate from Michigan; Ford enters both the Democratic and Republican primaries, losing first the Republican primary, then the general election in November, helping to discredit Wilson as a political leader.

June 16: Eugene Debs delivers a speech critical of the draft.

August: The Selective Service registers new 21-year-olds and later extends the draft age from the original 21–30 to 18–45, adding a potential pool of about 13 million new registrants to report for registration on September 12.

August 14–31: A worldwide pandemic of influenza, known as Spanish Flu, begins; it may have originated in Kansas.

Eugene Debs, former candidate for president, was arrested and imprisoned for opposing the draft, along with many other Socialists. *(Library of Congress)*

September: Postmaster Burleson suppresses the magazine the *Nation* for criticizing Samuel Gompers; in this one instance, President Wilson overrules Burleson's decision.

September 3–6: Slacker raids by the Department of Justice to round up men of apparent draft age to check their registration for the draft reach a peak when some 50,000 men are brought in for questioning in New York and northern New Jersey; more than 12,000 are detained in New Jersey alone.

September 16: President Wilson prohibits the production of beer on the grounds it calls for the consumption of grain, sugar, and transport equipment.

September 18: Eugene Debs is convicted and sentenced to 10 years in prison under the Sedition Act for a speech delivered to the Socialist convention in Canton, Ohio, June 16, 1918, in which he urged resistance to the draft and the war.

September 30: President Wilson asks the Senate to vote positively on the constitutional amendment granting suffrage to women.

October 25: In the congressional campaign, Wilson states that a return of a Republican majority to either house of Congress would represent a repudiation of his leadership. The speech leads to an outcry of protest from Republicans.

November 5: Republicans gain majorities in the congressional elections in both the House and Senate in the 66th Congress; Democrats lose six seats in the Senate and 30 in the House. Democratic Party losses are greatest in the western United States.

November 7: False rumors of a signed peace are printed in the United States, leading to a premature celebration in New York City.

November 11: The armistice is signed and goes into effect at 11:00 A.M. in Europe, ending World War I between Germany and the Allies and Associated powers.

EYEWITNESS TESTIMONY

The power against which we are arrayed has sought to impose its will upon the world by force. To this end it has increased armament until it has changed the face of war. In the sense in which we have been wont to think of armies there are no armies in this struggle. There are entire nations armed. Thus the men who remain to till the soil and man the factories are no less a part of the army that is in France than the men beneath the battle flags. It must be so with us. It is not an army that we must shape and train for war; it is a nation. To this end our people must draw close in one compact front against a common foe. But thus cannot be if each man pursues a private purpose. All must pursue one purpose. The Nation needs all men; but it needs each man, not in the field that will pleasure him, but in the endeavor that will best serve the common good. Thus, though a sharpshooter pleases to operate a trip hammer for the forging of great guns, and the expert machinist desires to march with the flag, the Nation is being served only when the sharpshooter marches and the machinist remains at his levers.

The whole Nation must be a team in which each man shall play the part for which he is best fitted.

To this end, Congress has provided that the Nation shall be organized for war by selection and that each man shall be classified for service in the place to which it shall best serve the general good to call him.

The significance of this cannot be overstated. It is a new thing in our history and a landmark in our progress. It is a new manner of accepting and vitalizing our duty to give ourselves with thoughtful devotion to the common purpose of us all. It is in no sense a conscription of the unwilling; it is rather selection from a nation which has volunteered in mass. It is no more a choosing of those who shall march with the colors than it is a selection of those who shall serve an equally necessary and devoted purpose in the industries that lie behind the battle line.

The day here named [June 5, 1917] is the time upon which all shall present themselves for assignment to their tasks. It is for that reason destined to be remembered as one of the most conspicuous moments in our history. It is nothing less than the day upon which the manhood of the country shall step forward in one solid rank in defense of the ideals to which this Nation is consecrated.

Woodrow Wilson, urging support for the draft on May 18, 1917, in Public Papers of Woodrow Wilson, *vol. 5,* War and Peace, *pp. 38–39.*

I have asked Mr. Herbert Hoover to undertake this all-important task of food administration. He has expressed his willingness to do so on condition that he is to receive no payment for his services and that the whole of the force under him, exclusive of clerical assistance, shall be employed so far as possible upon the same volunteer basis. He has expressed his confidence that this difficult matter of food administration can be successfully accomplished through the voluntary cooperation and direction of legitimate distributors of foodstuffs and with the help of the women of the country.

Woodrow Wilson, announcing the appointment of Herbert Hoover as food administrator, May 19, 1917, in Public Papers of Woodrow Wilson, *vol. 5,* War and Peace, *p. 43.*

Reckless journalism, regrettable enough in time of peace, is a positive menace when the Nation is at war. Victory rests upon unity and confidence, and those who imperil national solidarity by attack upon men and measures should be at infinite pains to establish their facts and to test their motives. In this day of high emotionalism and mental confusion, the printed word has immeasurable power, and the term traitor is not too harsh in application to the publisher, editor, or writer who wields this power without full and even solemn recognition of responsibilities.

George Creel, in a publication, Preliminary Statement to the Press of the United States, *issued shortly after his appointment as head of the Committee on Public Information, published at the end of May 1917, cited in Stewart Halsey Ross,* Propaganda for War: How the United States Was Conditioned to Fight the Great War of 1914–1918, *p. 227.*

This migration differs from all others in that it has no visible leader. To say that the negro is coming North for higher wages is grossly to misinterpret the spirit of the exodus. The negroes are leaving the South because life to them has been made miserable and unbearable. They are tired of being kept out of public parks and libraries, of being deprived of equal educational opportunities for their children, for which they are taxed, of reading signs, "Negroes and dogs not admitted"; the men are tired of disfranchisement, the women are tired of the insults of white hoodlums, and the whole race is sick of seeing mobs mutilate and burn unconvicted negro men. These migrating thousands are not seeking money, but manhood rights. All the people coming here are not poor. If the

350,000 negroes who have recently left the South were offered $5 a day and free transportation back, not 10 per cent,. would return in a whole year. If they were assured that these horrible injustices would be removed, especially the hellish institution of lynching, 80 per cent. of them would return almost as quickly as they came away.

African-American minister Rev. Clayton Powell, speaking at the Abyssinian Baptist Church, as quoted in "The South Blamed for Negro Exodus," New York Times, *July 2, 1917, p. 9.*

Eighteen colored women, the overflow from the colored dormitories, it was claimed, were assigned to sleep in our dormitory. I bathed my face today alongside of a colored woman sent down for drunkenness. We were forced to eat in the same dining room with petty thieves and habitual drunkards, white and colored. Our rest rooms were the same. The prison clothing was coarse and the toilet facilities were poor. Altogether it was a terrible experience, although we were willing to undergo it.

Mrs. Paul Reyneau, one of 16 white women suffragists arrested and briefly imprisoned at the Occoquan District of Columbia workhouse for demonstrating for the vote, commenting on conditions at the facility, quoted in "Militants Freed at Wilson's Word," New York Times, *July 20, 1917, p. 1.*

At the moment the papers devote much attention to the effort to safeguard the young conscripts against predatory country girls. Around every camp it appears, a "moral zone" is to be established, and it is apparently the intention to bar out from it every woman who cannot produce evidence that she has no desire to lead the soldiers astray. No enterprise, of course, could be more fantastically impossible of execution. . . . a great many innocent women will be abominably persecuted, and those who are not innocent will simply be scattered, and so made the more difficult to keep in order, and the more pertinacious and enterprising, and the more dangerous.

H. L. Mencken, commenting on the effort of the CTCA to close down red-light districts near army camps in September 1917, as quoted in Nancy K. Bristow, Making Men Moral: Social Engineering during the Great War, *p. 91.*

We have heard a good deal about the conscientious objector to serving in the war. Nineteen times out of twenty the conscientious objector is simply afraid or else he is lazy, but in the twentieth case, where the man is a conscientious objector, it is where he won't do anything to serve the country. If his conscience bothers him I would not do anything to interfere with this conscience, but I would understand that my conscience forbids him to vote in the country that my sons have to help save. I would hate to see the woman who does not raise her boy to be a soldier, but I hate to see the boy get the vote if he does not want to be a soldier. I hold that in each case the right to vote should be correlated with the performance of duty toward the state.

Again, people have said to me that we must not have women vote because they would all be pacifists. The Lord knows I despise a pacifist. And I have made no special effort to dissemble my feelings about that. But I have failed to notice that among them the shirking sisterhood of pacifists outnumbers the bleating brotherhood of pacifists. This white rabbit special that has been going around the country has not found a place for the soles of its feet to rest. It was perfectly impartial—it contained both sexes. Of course when we look at things rightly, we will hold that no one can be called a patriot unless he or she will perform any vital service that the nation needs, and there can be no more vital service than that of self-defense. The pacifist who won't fight for the nation is entitled to precisely the respect, and no more, that the man is entitled to who won't fight if his wife is slapped, or tries to rescue his daughter from the white slaver. He should defend one exactly as he should defend the other, and to no further extent.

On general grounds I have absolutely no question that suffrage must come, as a matter of right, if we are to continue our democratic experiment of Government—it must come.

Theodore Roosevelt, giving keynote address to the New York State Woman Suffrage Party, at its convention at his home in Oyster Bay, New York, September 8, 1917, reported in "Colonel Would Give Vote to Women Now," New York Times, *September 9, 1917, p. 8.*

In view of the present living conditions, the *Journal and Guide* is of the opinion that there are justice and reason in the demands of the women. We do not believe that under present conditions any adult laborer, man or woman, can subsist upon much less than the [$1.50 per day that the] factory women are asking. The average woman who works in the factory of the American

Cigar Company has to provide every week for house rent, for food, fuel, clothing, insurance, Church dues and incidentals. The items will run about ... $7.25 [per week]

At $1.25 a day, the women would earn $6.87 a week, as the working week at the factory is 5½ days....

Even if a woman is married or has other working members in her family, her pro rata of house rent cannot fall below $1.00 per week, nor fuel allowance less than 75 cents with slab wood selling at $8 per cord and coal at $9.50 a ton.... So in view of these conditions it appears to us that there are both justice and reason in the demands that the striking tobacco stemmers are making for a living wage.

Editorial in Norfolk Journal and Guide, *September 17, 1917, in support of black women strikers, who were later arrested as slackers and their Women Wage-Earners' Association disbanded, quoted in Philip Foner,* Women and the American Labor Movement, *vol. 2, p. 66.*

... if newspapers go so far as to impugn the motives of the Government and thus encourage insubordination, they will be dealt with severely.

For instance, papers may not say that the Government is controlled by Wall Street or munitions manufacturers, or other special interests. Publication of any news calculated to urge the people to violate law would be considered grounds for drastic action. We will not tolerate campaigns against conscription, sale of securities, or revenue collections. We will not permit the publication or circulation of anything hampering the war's prosecution or attacking improperly our allies.... We have files of [foreign language newspapers], and whether we license them or not depends on our inspection of the files.... Most Socialist papers do contain [treasonable or seditious] matter.

Postmaster General Albert Burleson, quoted in "Burleson Tells Newspaper, What They May Not Say," New York Times, *October 10, 1917, p. 1.*

We would rather see you shot by the highest tribunal of the United States Army because you dared to protect a Negro woman from the insult of a southern brute in the form of a policeman, than to have you forced to go to Europe to fight for a liberty you cannot enjoy. Negro women regret that you mutinied, and we are sorry that you spilt innocent blood, but we are not sorry that five southern policemen's bones now bleach in the graves of Houston, Texas.

It is far better that you be shot for having tried to protect a Negro woman, than to have you die a natural death in the trenches of Europe, fighting to make the world safe for a democracy that you can't enjoy. On your way to the Training Camps you are jim-crowed. Every insult that can be heaped upon you have to take, or be tried for court-martial if you resist it....

Be brave and face death fearlessly.

From an article by Clara L. Threadgill-Dennis, addressed to black men, published November 24, 1917, in the San Antonio Inquirer, *quoted in Theodore Kornweibel, Jr., "Investigate Everything": Federal Efforts to Compel Black Loyalty during World War I, pp. 170–171; the newspaper publisher, G. W. Bouldin, was arrested for violation of the Espionage Act for publishing the article and imprisoned for about one year.*

Dear "Governor" [President Woodrow Wilson]

The security markets in New York are very much demoralized. The declines in the past few days have produced a situation which contains very evil potentialities. Confidence has been badly impaired for various reasons. A great deal of unreasonable fear enters into the situation and wild rumors are in circulation. One of the contributing factors is the uncertainty about the railroad situation. The report of the Interstate Commerce Commission brought the issue to a head before provision could be made by the Administration to meet the situation which that report developed. I am told that rumors are in circulation that if the Government takes over the railroads, the rights of bondholders and stockholders will not be protected. Foolish as this is, it is making an impression.

I am inclined to think, therefore, that we ought to take action in the railroad matter at the very earliest possible moment, even before the holidays. Meanwhile, some sort of statement emanating from the Administration might have a very helpful effect in allaying apprehension, checking panic tendencies and reviving confidence in New York. I am concerned about the continued declines, because if they reach a point where a panic would set in, grave injury would result and the financial operations of the Government would be seriously imperiled. I think we might be able to arrest the existing demoralization if something reassuring could be said.

I have been asked to make a statement in reply to a telegram which may be sent to me and to which the enclosed would be responsive. Will you not be good

After William Gibbs McAdoo took control of the railroads, wages for railyard workers went up; some women like these three shared in the benefits, if only briefly. *(National Archives)*

enough to look over it and tell me if you would approve my saying something along these lines?

Affectionately yours, W G McAdoo

Enclosure:

In reply to your telegram, I see no reason for the pessimism which seems to prevail in the security markets of New York. The financial situation is inherently sound and strong and the operations of the Government will continue to be conducted with the utmost regard for the maintenance of prosperous conditions throughout the country. The railroad situation is going to be dealt with promptly, and the rights of stockholders and bondholders will, of course, be fully and justly protected. There is no ground for alarmist rumors about conditions here on the military fronts in Europe. This is no time for nerves or nervous people. We are going to win the war and solve all our difficulties if we keep our heads and courage.

P.S. I may not use this, I merely want to be armed for the Emergency. WGM

> *William Gibbs McAdoo, to Wilson, on the eve of announcement of the takeover of the railroads, December 14, 1917, quoted in Arthur Link, et al., eds.,* The Papers of Woodrow Wilson, *vol. 45, pp. 287–288.*

The advocates of the proposed prohibition amendment have disingenuously declared that the amendment is necessary as a war measure. How fraudulent is this pretense is best understood when it is known that the amendment cannot become effective until after the Legislatures of three-fourths of the States shall have ratified it, and as is known it is hoped that the war will have been successfully fought and won and come to an end long before the proposed constitutional amendment could come into operation.

But in the meantime, that is, between the time of the passage of the amendment by Congress (if it should pass) and until its ratification or defeat, covering a period of from six to seven years, and during the time when it is most essential that there shall be unity of spirit and action among the people of our country, the apple of discord will be thrown among them and the minds of the people will be diverted from the essential subject of winning the war to a proposition which can only become operative after the war has been concluded.

Beer is the general beverage of the masses of the people of the country. Light wines are used among large groups of our people. Many of them have acquired the habit by heritage of centuries and generations. The workers—the masses—no more than others in their indulgence in beers or light wines have found them a healthful part of their daily diet, particularly with their meals. With the cosmopolitan character of a large mass of our people, their divers habits and customs, I submit that it is neither wise, practical, nor beneficial to divide them into opposite camps upon a non-essential to the winning of the war, when its effectiveness—even if it is advantageous—could only become operative after the war is closed.

> *Samuel Gompers to Woodrow Wilson, December 14, 1917, in Arthur Link, et al., eds.,* The Papers of Woodrow Wilson, *vol. 45, p. 296.*

[I asked the president] if he ever thought how the roads of destiny turned. For instance, he was now in a position, to influence, for good or for evil, a large part of humanity and I wondered if he had followed the turn-

I find the President still antagonistic to Lansing. Lansing constantly does something to irritate him, and generally along the line of taking action without consultation. In this instance, it was sending a despatch to John W. Garrett at the Hague concerning the receiving of some peace overtures which Garrett thought the Germans were about to make, but in which the President had no confidence.

I have about come to the conclusion that it is George Creel who is prejudicing the President against Lansing.

Colonel Edward House, in his diary entry for
December 15, 1917, cited in Arthur Link, et al., eds.,
The Papers of Woodrow Wilson, *vol. 45, pp. 325, 327.*

There was no other way under the law to prevent profiteering except by voluntary agreement, as the food bill carried no power to fix prices. These agreements have of necessity been made with the old manufacturers, including the sugar trust. Independent refiners are represented by a majority on a committee whose duty it is to divide the imported sugar between all equitably. This committee has no price-fixing power; it has solely to do with distribution. The independent refiners who have been fighting the trust for years could be depended on to watch any unfair action.

Herbert Hoover, commenting on the shortage of sugar due
to increased European consumption and the shortage of
shipping, quoted in "Wilson Gives out Reply by Hoover
That Reed Barred," New York Times,
December 26, 1917, p. 1.

Labor leader Samuel Gompers cast his vote in his home district and spoke out as a strong opponent of Prohibition. *(Library of Congress)*

ing in the road which had brought him to this position. If he had not had the quarrel with the authorities at Princeton, he would not have [secured] the nomination for the Governorship of New Jersey. In ordinary years, New Jersey would have elected a republican rather than a democrat. If Roosevelt had not fallen out with Taft, Taft would probably have been re-elected. And so it goes.

The President thought these things were not chance, but were well worked out conclusions which had reached a conjunction. He admitted that there was such an element as chance. For example if one were walking down the street and a brick fell from a chimney on him that, he thought was purely chance. We finally decided that Providence had direction in human affairs because one could not account for the conjunction of circumstances otherwise. . . .

The Administration is not making a class war. Let it show that it isn't. It's no use resenting the imputation and pointing to scattered acts and facts which will set the Administration right in history. This is no time for argument and controversy. Act.

Accept openly the fact that there is this growing feeling. Say so. Call it by its names: doubt, confusion, suspicion, hate. And don't rebuke it. Understand it, sympathetically, and then—melt it into something akin to love and faith.

Ask the pro-war people to be more patient with the anti-war folk.

Ask the pacifists to be more considerate of the fighters; and to put their mind, not on peace, but the terms of a permanent peace.

Ask the soldiers again, as Baker did once, not to deal with the I.W.W.'s in the I.W.W. spirit. Ask this of the employers also.

Ask all editors, writers and speakers,—all—to remember that the war psychology is a little like a sickness; that it makes men's minds sensitive and sore; and that to say things that give pain to this state of mind is like being rough with the wounded.

Ask official prosecutors of war-time offenses to be fairer; they must do their duty, but they should do it less personally than some of them are doing it now; and more gently, much more justly. . . .

. . . certainly the President can repeat his assurance now that after the war, the war measures limiting our liberties will be repealed. And he can clinch this by letting us hope that some bad practices (notably in the Post Office) which grew up before the war, may be stopped when we make peace.

All these things should be done in one proclamation; and this also the most important of all:

Stop the appearance of "war on Labor." Stop or suspend labor prosecutions. Declare an amnesty in the class struggle and pardon all labor convicts in prison for "labor crimes"; all. . . .

Labor thinks this is a class war; that capital is getting the better of labor in it; that the employers are using the situation to gain advantages; and I heard groups of workers and one group of business men declaring that the Administration was in the "plot" to "fix" Organized Labor now for good and all!

I tried to reason with this state of mind, and failed. It's that terrible war psychology, which takes a few incidents that have no relation to one another, and darkens them into a conspiracy. Officials are doing the same thing. This is the day of "conspiracies." The prosecution of the I.W.W.'s is for conspiracy; a pro-German plot; and no doubt there are "proofs" which will appeal to a jury in war-time. . . .

If there was a conspiracy in the I.W.W. it was to use the war, as Labor thinks their bosses have, to raise prices and improve their condition.

Lincoln Steffens, in a memorandum for President Wilson forwarded to the president by Colonel Edward House, ca. December 28, 1917, quoted in Arthur Link, et al., eds., The Papers of Woodrow Wilson, *vol. 45, pp. 381–383.*

The Who, pre-eminently Who,
Is William Gibbs, the McAdoo,
(Whom I should like to hail but daren't,
A Royal Prince and Heir Apparent.)
The Greatest Son-in-Law on Earth—

With all the burdens thence accruing,
He's always up and McAdooing
From Sun to Star and Star to Sun,
His work is never McAdone.
He regulates our Circumstances,
Our Buildings, Industries, Finances,
And Railways, while the wires buzz
To tell us what he McAdoes . . .
I don't believe he ever hid
A single thing he McAdid!
His name appears on Scrip and Tissue
On bonds of each succeeding issue,
On coupons bright and posters rare,
And every Pullman Bill of Fare.
Poet Arthur Guiterman, writing in early 1918, quoted in Mark Sullivan, Our Times, *vol. 5,* Over Here, *pp. 462–463.*

Senator Chamberlain's statement as to the present inaction and ineffectiveness of the Government is an astonishing and absolutely unjustifiable distortion of the truth. As a matter of fact, the War Department has performed a task of unparalleled magnitude and difficulty with extraordinary promptness and efficiency. There have been delays and disappointments and partial miscarriages of plans, all of which have been drawn into the foreground and exaggerated by the investigations which have been in progress since the Congress assembled—investigations which drew indispensable officials of the department constantly away from their work and officers from their commands and contributed a great deal to such delay and confusion as had inevitably arisen. But, by comparison with what has been accomplished, these things, much as they were to be regretted, were insignificant, and no mistake has been made which has been repeated.

Nothing helpful or likely to speed or facilitate the war tasks of the Government has come out of such criticism and investigation. I understand that reorganizations by legislation are to be proposed—I have not been consulted about them and have learned of them only at second hand—but their proposal came after effective measures of reorganization had been thoughtfully and maturely perfected, and inasmuch as these measures have been the result of experience, they are much more likely than any others to be effective, if the Congress will but remove the few statutory obstacles of rigid departmental organization which stand in their way. The legislative proposal I have heard of would involve long additional delays and turn our experience into mere lost motion. My association and constant conference with the Secretary of War have taught me to regard him as one of the ablest public officials I have ever known. The country will soon learn whether he or his critics understand the business in hand.

To add, as Senator Chamberlain did, that there is inefficiency in every department and bureau of the Government is to show such ignorance of actual conditions as to make it impossible to attach any importance to his statement. I am bound to infer that the statement sprang out of opposition to the administration's whole policy rather than out of any serious intention to reform its practices.

Statement of Woodrow Wilson, published in the Official Bulletin, *January 22, 1918, #214, reproduced in Ray Stannard Baker and William E. Dodd, eds.,* The Public Papers of Woodrow Wilson, *vol. 1,* War and Peace, *pp. 167–168.*

I cannot thank you for your bread,
Because there wasn't any,
Nor any butter, either, though
Its substitutes were many.
But your pecan and fig croquettes;
Your muffins, flour- and eggless;
your beef-steak, raised in window-box,
Your mock duck, wing and legless;
Your near-fish wheedled from oat-meal;
Your butterine, from apple;
Your catnip salad, dressed with lard;
your porkless, parsnip scrapple
Composed a menu so conserved
That Mr. Hoover'd better
Commend my cheer in sending you
This meatless, wheatless letter!

Life magazine, *January 31, 1918, commenting humorously on wartime shortages, quoted in Mark Sullivan,* Our Times, *vol. 5,* Over Here, *p. 422.*

The war has so far disorganized the normal adjustment of industrial manpower as to prevent the enormous industrial output and national organization necessary to success. There is a popular demand for organization of manpower, but no direct draft could be imposed at present. Steps to prohibit idleness and non-effective occupation will be welcomed by our people. We shall give the idlers and men not effectively employed the choice between military service and effective employ-ment. Every man in the draft age, at least, must work or fight.

It is enough to ask what would happen if every man in the nation turned his hand to effective work. We must make ourselves effective. We must organize for the future. We must make vast withdrawals for the army and immediately close up the ranks of industry behind the gap with an accelerating production of every useful thing in necessary measure. How is this to be done?

The answer is plain. The first step toward the solution of the difficulty is to prohibit engagement by able bodied men (in idleness), or ineffectual employment, and thus induce and persuade the vast wasted excess into useful fields. . . . One of the unanswerable criticisms of the draft has been that it takes men from the farms and from all useful employments and marches them past crowds of idlers and loafers away to the army. The remedy is simple—to couple the industrial basis with other grounds for exemption and to require that any man pleading exemption shall also show that he is contributing effectively to the industrial welfare of the nation.

General Enoch Crowder, administrator of the Selective Service System, commenting on the granting of exemptions to the draft, as quoted in "Work or Fight, Warning to All on Draft Rolls," New York Times, *May 24, 1918, p. 1.*

. . . I welcome the opportunity to say that I agree without reservation that the full and sincere democratic reconstruction of the world for which we are striving and which we are determined to bring about at any cost, will not have been completely or adequately attained until women are admitted to the suffrage, and that only by that action can the nations of the world realize for the benefit of future generations the full ideal force of opinion or the full humane forces of action. The services of women during this supreme crisis of the world's history have been of the most signal usefulness and distinction. The war could not have been fought without them or its sacrifices endured. It is high time that some part of our debt of gratitude to them should be acknowledged and paid, and the only acknowledgment they ask is their admission to the suffrage. Can we justly refuse it? As for America, it is my earnest hope that the Senate of the United States will give an unmistakable answer to this question by passing the suffrage amendment to our federal Constitution before the end of this session.

Woodrow Wilson, in a letter dated June 13, 1918, to Carrie Chapman Catt, president of the International Woman Suffrage Alliance, in reference to a memorial of the French Union for Women Suffrage, reproduced in Ray Stannard Baker and William E. Dodd, eds., The Public Papers of Woodrow Wilson, *vol. 1, War and Peace, pp. 229–230.*

This is the crisis of the world. For all the long years to come men will point to the year 1918 as the great Day of Decision, the day when the world decided whether it would submit to military despotism and an endless armed peace—if peace it could be called—or whether they would put down the menace of German militarism and inaugurate the United States of the World.

We of the colored race have no ordinary interest in the outcome. That which the German power represents today spells death to the aspirations of Negroes and all darker races for equality, freedom and democracy. Let us not hesitate. Let us, while this war lasts, forget our special grievances and close our ranks shoulder to shoulder with our own white fellow citizens and the allied nations that are fighting for democracy. We make no ordinary sacrifice, but we make it gladly and willingly with our eyes lifted to the hills.

W. E. B. DuBois, in an editorial entitled, "Close Ranks," published in the NAACP journal Crisis, *July 1918.*

The department is in receipt of a telegram from one of the leading New York daily papers, the substance of which is as follows: "In handling such news as speech by John Reed, for which he was arrested the next day, or that of Debs some weeks ago, or that of Scott Nearing's repeated offenses, or of anti-war utterances, or Socialist Party, or German propaganda still circulating in library books, or The Nation being barred from the mails, there arises this problem: How shall we give the news of disloyalty without giving still further circulation to the words of sedition in our campaign against enemies within?

"It was necessary to reproduce examples of sedition literally in order to make loyal people aware of the acts of disloyalty and reconcile public sentiments to restraints upon free speech in wartime. Our feeling is that the necessity has passed. Therefore, we believe that in future it will be better to avoid literal treatment of seditious utterances and simply say, in such cases as Reed and Nearing and The Nation, that they attacked our Allies, or denounced the draft, or disparaged the war, adding at the end of a footnote that the text of the matter has been forwarded to the Government authorities." The Postmaster General coincides with the view expressed in the foregoing telegram and suggests that it will be in the interest of the country at the present time for publishers generally to pursue the course suggested.

Solicitor William Lamar of the Post Office Department, commenting on how censors are to handle reports of seditious speech, quoted in "Cut out Seditious Text," New York Times, *September 17, 1918, p. 15.*

My fellow countrymen,—The Congressional elections are at hand. They occur in the most critical period our country has ever faced or is likely to face in our time. If you have approved of my leadership and wish me to continue to be your unembarrassed spokesman in affairs at home and abroad, I earnestly beg that you will express yourselves unmistakably to that effect by returning a Democratic majority to both the Senate and the House of Representatives. I am your servant and will accept your judgment without cavil, but my power to administer the great trust assigned me by the Constitution would be seriously impaired should your judgment be adverse, and I must frankly tell you so because so many critical issues depend upon your verdict. No scruple of taste must in grim times like these be allowed to stand in the way of speaking the plain truth.

I have no thought of suggesting that any political party is paramount in matters of patriotism. I feel too keenly the sacrifices which have been made in this war by all our citizens, irrespective of party affiliations, to harbor such an idea. I mean only that the difficulties and delicacies of our present task are of a sort that makes it imperatively necessary that the Nation should give its undivided support to the Government under a unified leadership, and that a Republican Congress would divide the leadership.

The leaders of the minority in the present Congress have unquestionably been pro war, but they have been anti-administration. At almost every turn, since we entered the war they have sought to take the choice of policy and the conduct of the war out of my hands and put it under the control of instrumentalities of their own choosing. This is no time either for divided counsel or for divided leadership. Unity of command is as necessary now in civil action as it is upon the field of battle. If the control of the House and Senate should be taken away from the party now in power an opposing majority could assume control of legislation and oblige all action to be taken amidst contest and obstruction.

The return of a Republican majority to either House of the Congress would, moreover, certainly be interpreted on the other side of the water as a repudiation of my leadership. Spokesmen of the Republican Party are urging you to elect a Republican Congress in order to back up and support the President, but even if they should in this way impose upon some credulous voters on this side of the water, they would impose on no one on the other side. It is well understood there as well as here that the Republican leaders desire not so much to support the President as to control him. The peoples of the allied countries with whom we are associated against Germany are quite familiar with the significance of elections. They would find it very difficult to believe that the voters of the United States had consented to support their President by electing to Congress a majority controlled by those who are not in fact in sympathy with the attitude and action of the administration.

I need not tell you, my fellow countrymen, that I am asking your support not for my own sake or for the sake of a political party, but for the sake of the Nation itself, in order that its inward unity of purpose may be evident to all the world. In ordinary times I would not feel at liberty to make such an appeal to you. In ordinary times divided counsels can be endured without permanent hurt to the country. But these are not ordinary times. If in these critical days it is your wish to sustain me with undivided minds, I beg that you will say so in a way which it will not be possible to misunderstand either here at home or among our associates on the other side of the sea. I submit my difficulties and my hopes to you.

Woodrow Wilson, urging voters to elect a Democratic Congress, October 25, 1918, Baker and Dodd, eds., The Public Papers of Woodrow Wilson, *vol. 1,* War and Peace, *pp. 286–288.*

All the colored women like this work and want to keep it. We are making more money at this than any work we can get, and we do not have to work as hard as at housework which requires us to be on duty from six o'clock in the morning until nine or ten at night, with mighty little time off and at very poor wages. . . . What the colored women need is an opportunity to make money. As it is, they have to take what employment they can get, live in old tumbled down houses or resort to street walking, and I think a woman ought to think more of her blood than to do that. What occupation is open to us where we can make really good wages? We are not employed as clerks, we cannot all be school teachers, and so we cannot see any use in working our parents to death to get educated. Of course we should like easier work than this if it were opened to us, but this pays well and is no harder than other work open to us. With three dollars a day, we can buy bonds . . . , we can dress decently, and not be tempted to find our living in the streets. . . .

Helen Ross, an inspector for the Women's Service Section of the U.S. Railroad Administration, reporting on a conversation with an African-American woman worker, October 28, 1918, quoted in Maurine Weiner Greenwald, Women, War and Work: The Impact of World War I on Women Workers in the United States, *p. 27.*

10 The Calculus of Death
January 1917–November 1918

After the disasters of 1916, officers and soldiers of all nations on the western front realized that the war would not be quickly won. It seemed in early 1917 that few officers had learned any lessons from the fruitless slaughter of the previous two years. In a kind of bull-headed tenacity, they called for more artillery, more shells, more small arms ammunition, and, above all, more men to throw against the enemy. Signs that the method had ruined morale appeared in all the armies.

Even as Russian troops mutinied and turned to revolutionary ideas in the east, so British, French, and German troops grew sullen about advancing into meaningless, murderous gunfire. The British troops called the war the Great Sausage Machine, while the Germans called it the *Blutmühle* or blood-mill. By early 1917, open mutiny, in the form of refusal of troops to advance, spread dangerously through the French forces, coming close to outright revolution, while, in the British lines, explicitly stated hatred of ignorant staff officers stationed in the rear became endemic. In some cases, British troops simply refused to follow their officers out of the trenches, even when threatened with court-martial. In other battles, some troops would advance only a few yards, see their comrades fall dead or wounded, and return dispirited to the trench. Officers sent mounted cavalry into barbed wire entanglements and attempted attacks through deep mud even when clearly destined for failure, seemingly refusing to learn from past mistakes. Officers in the rear complained the men at the front lacked spirit; those at the front, like their troops, cursed the incompetence of the command that ordered ill-prepared and hopeless attacks while continuing to advocate the depressing concept of "acceptable losses" of men to take a few meaningless yards of ground.

After the disasters of the Somme and Verdun, both the British and French faced a paradox of staffing. Only officers with experience in the front lines understood the details of how and when an advance had a chance of success, which required close attention to the terrain, the defenses and strength of the defenders, available artillery and supplies, communication and transport, weather conditions, and actual strength of forces available for the attack. Yet with the slaughters, only small numbers of officers with frontline experience survived. If

Ambulances and supply trucks often got stuck moving through traffic jams such as this one in the American lines in the Argonne. *(National Archives)*

they relocated to the rear to help in staff planning of attacks, their experience would not be available at the front. On the other hand, if officers without front-line experience did the staff work in the rear, they had little or no understanding of what went into the practical details of an attack. As a consequence, staff work and planning was often chaotic, sloppy, and ill thought out, with multiple failures of communication and supply.

Several tactics, however, held out hope of changing the situation. The British put a great deal of faith in the introduction of tanks, developed as a secret weapon and then used to break the German lines in September 1916, at Flers. Officers did not follow up on the Flers advance, however, and German artillery destroyed some tanks while others broke down. Nevertheless, the British hoped that a massed introduction of tanks on drier ground and in better conditions could lead to a breakthrough, and, after producing more and more reliable tanks, that method showed some successes in breaching the trench lines and defenses. On the defense, rather than stationing heavy concentrations on the front line, the British adopted a method of defense-in-depth. This consisted of a network of strong points, machine-gun emplacements and fortified infantry positions connected with networks of trenches and barbed-wire screens, backed up with field artillery close behind and long-range heavy artillery farther to the rear, making the British defenses even harder to penetrate than they had been in the first years of the war.

The Germans also developed new defensive tactics, using defense-in-depth with three or more lines. The front lines were held with machine-gun emplacements in concrete pillboxes. Germans had invented the pillbox, which consisted of a buried reinforced concrete bunker with slits for the firing of machine guns and a steel door at the rear. Some of these pillboxes could hold out even when surrounded, sometimes being relieved by a counterattack. Impervious to hand-grenade attacks (unlike trenches and dugouts), the concrete pillboxes could be destroyed only by a direct artillery hit. With their rounded tops, only a few feet in diameter, they were difficult targets to acquire and hit. Behind the pillbox lines, the tactics called for reserve troops stationed in the rear lines of defense in well-protected concrete bunkers and, behind those lines, rapid light-rail and road connections that could bring forces and artillery to any endangered point in the line. Furthermore, the heavily fortified defense that the Germans called the Siegfried line and the British called the Hindenburg line, stretching through Flanders from Arras on the north to Soissons on the south, allowed for the shortening of the front, fewer troops, and more defensible positions. With the breakdown of the Russian front through late 1917 and into early 1918, the German position could be strengthened by the transfer of divisions from Russia to the western front.

It was on the Flanders front that the Allies witnessed the new German tactics on the offense: the use of highly experienced and well-trained storm-troops to lead an advance and cut through to the rear of Allied defenses, followed by mobile units of machine-gunners and troops carrying flame-throwers as well as small arms.

After disastrous slaughter of troops under the command of General Nivelle, the French also began to adopt new tactics, including open-maneuver advances (rather than the Napoleonic-era shoulder-to-shoulder march into deadly fire), coordination with aircraft and tanks, as well as massive rolling barrages coupled with registered or pre-aimed artillery fire calculated to take out specific targets identified from the air. By 1918, French and British aircraft regularly bombed and strafed German positions, sometimes in close coordination with planned attacks. French industrial production reached stupendous new levels with massive quantities of artillery shells and hundreds of effective aircraft thrown into the war in 1918. However, despite such changes in tactics developing in a series of battles through 1917 and into 1918, by March and April 1918 not even the most optimistic British or French generals believed that the war would end before late 1919.

CAPORETTO

Late in 1917 the Allies suffered a massive defeat on the Italian front that gave them every reason to expect a long and drawn-out war into the future. Since 1915, the major line between the Austro-Hungarian forces and the Italians had ranged between the Italian northeastern frontier and Gorizia on the Isonzo River, a line about 100 miles long but only about 10 to 20 miles into Austrian Slovenia at the farthest Italian advance. Since May of 1915, there had been 11 major battles on the Isonzo, with no clear advances. Then, on October 24, 1917, a combined German and Austro-Hungarian force decisively defeated the Italians at the town of Caporetto on the upper Isonzo River. The combined Central Power forces took more than 260,000 Italians prisoner, and more than 200,000 other Italian troops deserted the lines and sometimes their units altogether, scattering throughout Italy. The remnants of the Italian armies fell back toward Venice, crossing the Piave River and in some sections retiring to within 15 to 20 miles of Venice. The British and French rushed several divisions to Italy to help hold back the Austrian advance.

Caporetto, like Gallipoli earlier in the war, came to be a synonym for a great defeat. The Allies feared they might suffer another Caporetto on the road to Paris or in the fields of Flanders.

SUBMARINES AND CONVOYS

In mid-1917, the German officers, led by Ludendorff still in the role of quartermaster general, believed that their moment to win the war had arrived; and they pinned their hopes on the submarine. The German High Command had calculated that if 600,000 tons of shipping per month could be sunk by torpedo and gunfire under the unrestricted submarine warfare announced February 1, 1917, Britain would be forced, through lack of food and fuel, to sue for peace before any effective military support could arrive from the United States. The British did not publish all shipping losses, and the submarine captains sometimes reported a ship sunk when in fact it had been only damaged or failed to report the correct name of the ship sunk, thereby leading to some inaccurate guesses as to its tonnage. Some ships continued to be lost to mines and surface sea-raiders and to Austrian submarines in the Mediterranean.

All these factors meant that analysts and estimators produced somewhat different figures for the losses per month then and in the immediate postwar years. Even with more meticulous research in later years, precise tallies for tonnage sunk each month through 1917 and 1918 varied from source to source. Although both the British and German commands could only guess at the precise tonnage figures, they both knew that in the first few months of unrestricted submarine attack on British, Allied, and neutral shipping, the losses came very close to meeting, and sometimes exceeded, the German goals.

Every month from February through August 1917, losses of ships registered to the various countries of the British Empire ran to more than 300,000 tons, while worldwide losses of all Allied and neutral ships climbed from more than 500,000 in February to well more than 800,000 in April and did not shrink to much less than 500,000 per month through August and September of 1917.

Convoy escort: Using agile warships and convoys to protect cargo ships against submarines was finally accepted by the British Admiralty. *(National Archives)*

Although the British Admiralty resisted the concept of using transatlantic convoys to protect merchant shipping, a close study of the effect of local convoys led to a report approved by the Admiralty on April 26 to support the use of ocean convoys. Three days later, David Lloyd George met with the Admiralty; he later remained convinced that he had personally won the day for the convoy concept, although the decision had already been taken. Later support by Admiral William Sims of the U.S. Navy led to the contribution of U.S. destroyers and other ships to the convoy effort. Gradually, the British and Americans implemented the convoy system and it began to have an effect in reducing losses.

Convoys worked by assembling a group of merchant ships that traveled together at set distances from each other at the speed of the slowest ship in the group. The fleet of cargo ships, sometimes as few as four or five vessels or as many as 20 or more, were accompanied by destroyers or other sub-chasing vessels, sometimes tugs or trawlers converted to the purpose. If a submarine fired a torpedo at one of the cargo ships, the destroyers and sub-chasers immediately hunted down the submarine by tracing the track of the torpedo and subjecting the U-boat to depth charges, sometimes destroying it. Even if the submarine escaped destruction, survivors from the torpedoed ship would be rescued by other ships in the convoy or the ship itself would be taken in tow if it could be recovered in that fashion, and the whole flotilla would proceed on its way, while armed sub-chasers and destroyers hung back from the convoy and prevented the submarine from resurfacing or destroyed it. Some naval officers had feared that convoys would represent easy targets for submarines and believed that merchant ship masters and crews would be incapable of keeping their position in a group. Events proved that point of view to be incorrect.

The number of ships sunk while in convoy amounted to 1 or 2 percent of those crossing the Atlantic, well below the 10 to 20 percent or more sunk while sailing individually. British losses declined to little more than 250,000 tons by December 1917 and remained less than that through the end of the war. By April 1918, worldwide losses of merchant ships of all Allied and neutral nations fell to less than 300,000 tons per month and remained under that figure through the remaining months of the war. Even so, German and Austrian submarines continued to destroy some merchant ships, sinking a total of more than 5 million tons of British shipping in 1917 and 1918 and a total of more than 8 million tons worldwide. Later calculations by both German and British maritime experts confirmed the original German estimate that merchant ship losses in excess of 600,000 tons per month could have forced a British defeat by early 1918. However, such postwar calculations also confirmed the wisdom of the convoy system as a defense and it was adopted much more promptly in the Second World War.

FROM FRENCH ATTACK TO MUTINY, APRIL–JUNE 1917

In mid-March 1917, the French discovered that the Germans had evacuated a large area in their retreat to the Hindenburg-Siegfried Line. French troops moved out slowly across the devastated area, finally discovering that the Germans had set up seemingly impregnable defensive lines. Lines of concrete blockhouses and pillboxes confronted them, with dug-in artillery positions, deep dugouts to house infantry, and several lines of defense.

Motor transport could be detained by stubborn mules. *(National Archives)*

General Robert Nivelle nevertheless planned an attack, while officers and men in the front lines remained skeptical that it could be pulled off with success. Included in the troops to be thrown at the German lines were large numbers of French colonial troops from Morocco, Algeria, and Senegal. Nivelle hoped to make the attack in the beginning of April. After postponement due to weather, French guns bombarded a 30-mile front beginning April 16, but the German lines, well dug in, remained solid. The infantry attack began on April 22, led by 128 French tanks that moved about three miles per hour. Wave after wave of attacking troops on the front at Chemin des Dames were mowed down by German defenses. Despite repeated attacks, the French failed to penetrate the German defenses. By May 9, the French had suffered 140,000 casualties, including 30,000 dead. The troops refused to try again, and even his frontline generals and colonels told Nivelle that they would not order further slaughter.

By late May 1917 the refusals had mounted into a full-scale mutiny. Some 20,000 French troops deserted, and the French army suffered its most severe mutiny in the war. Although the mutineers did not shoot their officers, as Russian troops had done, they refused orders to advance during May and June 1917. In scattered areas, such as the town of Missy-aux-Bois near Soissons, troops declared an antiwar government.

Philippe Pétain took over from Nivelle as commander in chief of the French army in mid-May 1917, and it fell to him to attempt to restore order. With selective arrests, discipline, and a few reforms, the mutiny gradually died away. Officers and noncommissioned officers identified leaders and spokesmen of the mutiny, and more than 3,400 courts-martial were held. Although more than 550 soldiers were sentenced to death, only about 50 executions took place; others were given life sentences and sent to penal colonies. Pétain also began to listen to complaints, addressing issues of poor food and wine, clothing supplies, and living quarters. Most important, he decided against massed attacks in favor of taking limited objectives. Gradually, Pétain began to adopt new methods, including closer coordination with aircraft and tanks, employing much heavier supplies of artillery, as well as defense-in-depth with several lines of forces, somewhat like the new German defensive method. Furthermore, Pétain planned on holding off further major offensives until American troops began arriving in sufficient numbers to make a difference.

BRITISH TUNNELS AND TANKS

South of Ypres along the front near the towns of Wytschaete and Messines, the British and Germans had for two years fought a strange war beneath the ground. British, Australian, and Canadian soldiers, many of them former mine workers, tunneled under the line, listening with planted microphones for signs of enemy tunneling. Sometimes one tunnel would break into an enemy gallery, and a brief and fierce struggle underground would be followed by the detonation of an underground charge to close the passageways. Eventually, the Germans came to believe that the British Empire miners had given up tunneling.

But the British teams continued to work, advancing from 200 to 2,000 yards to points directly under the German lines in early 1917. There, at 21 sites, they planted huge charges of high explosives some 50 to 100 feet below the surface. Then, on June 7, 1917, the British opened their Flanders campaign of that year by setting off the mines. Two failed to work, but 19 of the charges detonated nearly simultaneously with about a million pounds of explosives, devastating the German trenches, dugouts, and fortifications and reportedly killing some 10,000 defenders. Another 7,000 were taken prisoner, many of them dazed by the explosions. Some of the survivors complained of the pure murderous nature of the sneak attack. Londoners, about 130 miles away, could clearly hear the near-simultaneous rumbling blast.

Tanks able to traverse trenches were beginning to break the stalemate on the front. *(Library of Congress)*

Artillery fire from 50 heavy guns and 2,000 field guns immediately followed the explosion of the tunnel-mines. English, Irish, and New Zealand troops moved forward, overwhelming the confused defenders and taking the towns of Wytschaete and Messines, moving on Messines Ridge just east of the towns. However, the British did not press their attack further, and the Germans prepared further defense in depth, with as many as nine layers of defensive lines in some areas.

The British, New Zealand, and Irish troops reached the Messines Ridge line beyond the towns of Messines and Wytschaete by June 15 and were able to hold that line into December 1917. Beginning at the end of July, just to the north, in front of Ypres, in what came to be known as the Third Battle of Ypres, or the Ypres campaign of 1917, British troops pushed forward in a series of violent engagements for a total of about five miles. However, with the rains that came in October and November, the battlefields became a nightmare of stagnant pools that could be crossed only on narrow duckboard passageways. Troops stumbling off the trails fell into mudholes up to their necks, where wounded soldiers drowned, their bodies left in place. By the beginning of November pools of mud constantly swallowed mules, guns, and wounded troops on the approach to the village of Passchendaele. The campaign, often remembered as Passchendaele rather than Third Ypres, came to represent a horrible disaster. Canadians and Australians grumbled, not quite fairly, that the British sacrificed Dominion troops, as they had at Anzac, rather than take the losses themselves. Passchendaele, like Gallipoli and Caporetto, became a name that took on ominous overtones of horror and defeat.

For the British, an encouraging bright spot came with the advance toward Cambrai, mounted on November 20, 1917. Although the British had used tanks on a small scale before without much success, officers planned this attack better, with relatively solid dry ground that could be traversed by the tanks chosen for the advance. Across a seven-mile-wide plain, some 381 British tanks moved toward the German lines of trenches and succeeded in pushing the front lines back more than six miles in places. The German infantry fought tenaciously, however, using artillery and a 12.98 mm. rifle with armor-piercing shells aimed at the tank's peepholes, effectively stopping the advance. Officers called off a British mounted cavalry attack that had been prepared to follow the tanks.

A swift counterattack by the Germans pushed the British line back on itself, in some areas even farther than their starting point on November 20. The Germans pushed ahead and took the town of Gouzecourt, then the British drove them back again. By December 7, the lines short of Cambrai had settled down with no spectacular gain on either side. Because the Germans stymied this massed tank attack, they may have concluded that the tank could never turn out to be a major factor in the war. However, the British had learned several lessons in the tank battles near Cambrai that they would apply the next year, and both France and Britain stepped up tank production.

GERMAN ADVANCES, MARCH–JULY 1918

At the beginning of 1918, Ludendorff and the rest of the German high command concluded that the submarine blockade would not be sufficient to bring

Gas attacks affected man and beast alike. *(Library of Congress)*

about British surrender or agreement to a negotiated settlement. Although the U-boats claimed more than 300,000 tons of Allied and neutral shipping per month, the tally fell far short of the 600,000 needed to bring about British collapse. American war planning seemed consumed in disarray, and the German command calculated that it would take at least another year for Americans to begin arriving in numbers sufficient to make a difference. Further, any American troops brought to the line, although freshly trained, would be inexperienced and probably no match for the hardened veterans of the German western front. Such reasoning and expectations constituted the German calculus of death.

In order to bring about an Allied defeat, Ludendorff planned several massive attacks using new tactics, intending to drive a wedge between the British and French units to force the British back to an enclave on the Channel coast. He anticipated that once the British retreated, the French would be willing to bargain for peace rather than risk an advance of German troops into Paris. Like so many earlier decisions, this calculated gamble entailed risk.

As a consequence, through the spring of 1918, the Germans launched several massive attacks, convincing Allied generals, enlisted men in the field, and civilians at home that the war would last another year or more. The first of the massed attacks, Operation Michael, began with an artillery barrage on March 21. Using gas, shock troops, and machine-gun units, together with German fighter aircraft to fend off Allied airplanes, German forces advanced in places as much as seven miles on the first day. Although the British regarded their 7,000 dead and 21,000 captured as a severe defeat, the Germans estimated their own casualties at 78,000. German bombers hit British ammunition dumps, and, in places, the British retreat became a confused rout, with inexperienced young troops simply running for the rear.

March 21, 1918, and the weeks that followed in Germany's Operation Michael turned into evil days for the British on the Flanders front, as the German offensive adopted the new method of infiltration that had worked at Caporetto in Italy with great success. The system operated by a penetration of the lines by wedges of storm troopers equipped with machine guns, reinforced and working inward, so that the defenders immediately found themselves taking flanking fire from right and left and in constant danger of being cut off.

Under cover of dense fog, the Germans made their way into the British Fifth Army front. Through gaps, great masses of German troops moved forward, and defending staffs lost touch with fighting units. Communications collapsed, and the British troops gave up ground they might have held, but they did not panic. Fortunately for the British, the Germans found it difficult to drag their heavy weapons through the desert they had created in their retreat the year before to the Hindenburg Line.

The line moved back to Péronne and Bapaume, then to a landmark windmill at Pozières, and finally to an old battle line in Delville Wood that the British Tommies called Devil Wood. Where refugees had moved back to reclaim their homes and villages, they now evacuated once again, with mothers gathering up their babies and packing bundles into baby carriages to move through shell fire and burning thatched roofs to the rear. The defense of Arras included the 3rd Division, known as the Iron Division, and the 56th Division, the London Division. A breathing space for the British came when the Germans directed their assault at the French sector of the line, at the Marne, once again threatening Paris.

The war had dragged into its fourth full year, and now, it seemed, before the Americans could arrive in numbers, the slaughter might culminate in disaster for the Allies. Yet the defense lines pulled back and held.

As a consequence of the desperate situation, General Douglas Haig, leading the British, agreed to accept the appointment of French chief of staff Ferdinand Foch as supreme allied commander, or generalissimo, on March 23, 1918. The Germans continued to press their attack toward Amiens and Arras, driving a wedge as planned between British and French troops as they advanced in a broad curve between Amiens and Paris. During this period the Germans brought up giant long-range guns that could fire shells some 70 to 75 miles, raining down a barrage on Paris. Although more a terror weapon than a true weapon of war, the six so-called Paris Guns killed some 256 civilians over a period of three months.

Gradually, the united Allied command under Foch was able to hold a line, and, by April 1, Operation Michael ground to a halt. German troops, after advancing in places up to 40 miles, underfed and demoralized, took up plundering the villages and British equipment they found in their push toward Amiens.

An elderly French couple greets American troops as they liberate their ruined village. *(National Archives)*

In places the troops became so drunk on wine or liquor that they ignored their officers, drove livestock to the rear, and, burdened with loot, simply walked away from the attack.

Although the different armies calculated casualty figures in different ways, the Germans counted more than 100,000 men killed or missing. The demoralization of the surviving troops appeared to be even more disturbing to German officers than the raw casualty figures. Coupled with the loss of some of the most experienced and well-trained storm troopers, German commanders faced the spring months of 1918 with far less optimism than they had expressed at the end of 1917.

AMERICANS AT WAR

American troops began to arrive in numbers in February 1918. The 26th Division, made up of troops of the New England National Guard, fought a bloody battle in late April in lines around the village of Seicheprey.

African-American troops made up the four regiments of the 93rd Division, and the French army completely integrated these regiments into their forces. Wearing American uniforms, they carried French weapons and wore French helmets and gear. One of the four regiments, the 369th, moved into the Argonne Forest and took over a three-mile sector of the line by mid-April. At the time, American forces held a total of only 15 miles, and the African-American 369th made up one-fifth of that. The men of the 369th eventually saw extensive rugged combat and earned the admiration of the French officers with whom they worked.

Ludendorff planned a second attack, this against the French army moving from the Chemin des Dames Ridge toward Paris, some 70 miles distant. The attack began on May 27, and, by May 30, German troops advanced on the Marne, about 55 miles from the outskirts of Paris. As French troops moved into defensive positions, Foch put the U.S. Third Division at Château-Thierry and the U.S. Second Division, which included the U.S. Marine Brigade, into the line at Belleau Wood.

The appearance of fresh American troops in the line by early summer of 1918 made it clear to the German command that their timetable for victory had suddenly shortened. The Marine Brigade battle at Belleau Wood extended over June 6 to June 12 and, after a short respite, included another hand-to-hand battle on June 17. During a three-week period, the Marine Brigade lost 5,600 casualties out of the total 13,500-man force, partly because they fought in massed groups, rather than in open formation. They had not learned to take cover one by one as they advanced, as had the veterans on both sides on the western front. As a consequence, like the troops of 1914, they were easily cut down by massed machine-gun fire. Nevertheless, after bitter fighting, the marines doggedly pushed the German forces out of the wood, with help from the 369th Regiment.

Ludendorff ordered other attacks, including a push on July 15 with 52 German divisions aimed directly toward Paris. Allied forces turned this drive back with French colonials and large American divisions, the 1st and 2nd. Using combined attacks involving infantry, artillery, aircraft, and tanks, the Allies forced the Germans back across the Marne River.

After a total of five major assaults by the Germans through early and mid-1918, the German army lost nearly a million men wounded, captured, dead, or deserted. At the same time as American troops began to make their presence known on the front, the French began throwing more tanks and aircraft into the battles, while supplies of both equipment and manpower dwindled on the German side. Furthermore, German morale collapsed in many units, with word of the despair reaching back to headquarters.

In early August, British troops pushed ahead on the old Somme battlefield, and an American force attacked the long-standing St. Mihiel salient near Verdun in mid-August. The American forces included a large Army Air Force, with at least half of its planes of French manufacture. The German command had already planned to evacuate the St. Mihiel salient, so when the American attack came, the Germans had already started pulling away from their fortified positions. Americans nipped off the salient and took more than 13,000 prisoners.

By September, as the Allied armies planned attacks, they had not only superior numbers of troops but also clear superiority in equipment including tanks, artillery, and aircraft. As commander of all the Allied forces on the front, Foch could count on 220 divisions altogether, including 42 large-sized American divisions, against a depleted and weakened 197 divisions of German troops. Most of those were worn down or demoralized, and the German forces could count on only about 50 divisions ready for combat.

In some of the last and most bloody battles fought by the Americans in the war, American troops pushed back German defenses in the Argonne Forest, north of Verdun. Unseasoned American troops went through some terrifying experiences. Sergeant William Triplet calculated that his unit suffered more than 80 percent casualties, and he suffered a wound in the shoulder and stayed in a hospital briefly before returning to the front. Corporal Alvin York, a true sharpshooter from Tennessee, killed 25 German soldiers and personally captured 132 more, earning him a Medal of Honor. The 1st Battalion of the 308th Regiment, 77th Division, which was completely cut off, became known as the Lost Battalion. More than 400 men out of the original 600 died before the 200 survivors saw relief on October 7.

The explanation for what stopped the German advances in mid-1918 has been the subject of intense historical debate. The British stressed their tenacity and their successful use of tanks in several battles. French accounts emphasized their use of new tactics and massive industrial output of artillery, supplies, and aircraft. The arrival of American troops, their rapid training, and their willingness to plunge into battle has also been credited with tipping the battle, a factor recognized as important by Ludendorff himself and of course the focus of many American-authored studies of the topic.

A deeper cause of the fairly rapid collapse of the German advances in 1918 lay in the exhaustion of

General John "Black Jack" Pershing commanded U.S. troops in Europe from his headquarters at Chaumont. *(National Archives)*

manpower and the destruction of the morale of the German troops. Some of the collapse in morale sprang from widespread starvation, coupled with reports of smuggling, black markets, and profiteering on the German home front. Even when the Germans made successful advances in the region of the Somme across lands that had been thoroughly destroyed more than once, German officers watched in horror as their troops broke away from command to loot food, clothing, wine, liquor, and even notebook paper from the English storage dumps and damaged villages and towns they conquered. Starved and dispirited, the German troops simply gave up the battle in places and settled in to enjoy their booty or began to simply melt away and go home, rather than continuing their advance. Letters to and from the homes of German soldiers revealed that the starvation blockade and the years of fruitless warfare had destroyed the confidence of the German population in their leadership as well as the esprit of the troops and their trust in their officers. By August 1918, after the loss of hundreds of thousands of troops, German commanders prepared to ask the civilian leadership to open negotiations toward a peace.

GERMAN COLLAPSE

Woodrow Wilson had clarified American war goals in a carefully crafted speech delivered on January 8, 1918, in which he spelled out what came to be known as the Fourteen Points. Later speeches amplified these points until he had come up with more than 20. Most of Wilson's points dealt with proposed territorial settlements based on the ethnicity and preference of the populations in question, but four of the points were more general. The United States wanted guarantees of freedom of the seas, abandonment of secret treaties in favor of "open covenants, openly arrived at," no reparations based on war guilt but only compensation for war damage, and commitment to a League of Nations to enforce future peace. Seemingly based on a set of ideals rather than a desire for revenge or territorial gain, the war goals had been made public and won some popular support in the United States, although strongly anti-German politicians like Theodore Roosevelt argued that the proposed peace terms were too generous to Germany.

After the defeats of August 1918, the German command concluded that the war could not be won. Ludendorff recommended that peace be negotiated on the basis of the Fourteen Points. When confronted with the collapse of troop morale and the unwillingness of the army to throw more troops into the slaughter, the kaiser appointed a new premier, the liberal Prince Maximilian, on October 4. In a series of diplomatic notes, Prince Max, as the American press called him, opened negotiations with Wilson in October. By negotiating with Wilson rather than with the other Allies, Max no doubt hoped to obtain an armistice on terms that Germany could accept. The Fourteen Points, it may have seemed, would save Germany from being forced to suffer complete defeat and surrender.

In August, although German troops fell back, their defense-in-depth still slowed Allied advances. Furthermore, German troops still occupied most of Belgium and a swath of French territory between the German frontier and the Meuse River, and the retreat had not gotten close to the original German boundary. The exchange of notes between Wilson and Prince Max continued through October 27, as Wilson insisted on a number of details, including full independence for Czechoslovakia and the South Slavs who wanted to join with

Serbia. These demands required the dismemberment of the Austro-Hungarian Empire. Wilson also demanded that the government of Germany be responsive to the will of the German people, a not-too-subtle demand for regime change. Only after Wilson had secured a commitment to most of the points did he open discussions with the other Allies to ensure that they would accept an armistice based on the same points.

In order to secure that agreement, Wilson dispatched Colonel Edward House, his personal confidant and political adviser, to negotiate with the British, French, and Italians. House had a difficult time in these discussions because the British at first rejected any endorsement of the vague concept of freedom of the seas, the French insisted on an occupation of German territory as well as heavy reparations, and the Italians wanted guarantees that lands promised them in the secret treaty with Britain would not fall to the newly created Serbian-dominated South Slav state. House extracted a sort of compromise, in which the British agreed to discuss the meaning of freedom of the seas at the peace conference, the French agreed that the exact reparations would be left until later, and the French prime minister Georges Clemenceau made a personal promise that occupation of German territory would be temporary to ensure German compliance with the armistice terms and the terms of military occupation would be worked out by the military commanders. House also suggested that treaty obligations would be honored.

As these discussions proceeded, the German admirals in charge of the surface fleet, which had been largely bottled up in harbors since the early battles of 1915, planned a desperate raid on the British fleet. Apparently the admirals felt that the honor of the German navy would be preserved by a suicide mission that had little chance of success, and they planned the attack at the very time that Prince Max attempted to work out the terms of an armistice. Clearly the attack would lead not only to the deaths of many sailors in a war that Germany had already lost but would also provide the Allies with even more justification for demanding not an armistice but an outright surrender.

Meanwhile, during the last week of October and the first two weeks of November, the war suddenly wound down through a rapid series of military, diplomatic, and political events. The Allies made a successful push at Vittorio Veneto on the Italian front, driving back the Austrian troops from the Piave River on October 24. Within days, the Austro-Hungarian officers on that front demanded that their government seek an armistice. On the 26th, when Ludendorff learned the terms of Wilson's peace demands, especially including the subordination of the military to civilian authority and the civilian authority to a democratically selected government, he publicly urged the army to reject the terms. The kaiser then demanded Ludendorff's resignation and replaced him with General William Groener on October 26. Groener informed the admirals that the military was to be subject to the direction of the civilian prime minister, Prince Max. Thus the planned naval suicide mission, or *Flottenvortoss,* became now clearly illegal, lacking endorsement from the civilian authority.

Sailors began to mutiny in Kiel and other port cities on October 28 and 29 when they received the orders to get up steam for the secretly planned naval mission. The mutinies spread rapidly over the next few days. In ports and nearby cities, sailors released prisoners, raised red flags, selected local leaders, and pressured officers into granting leave and ignoring the sailors' seizure of

Due to a leak of information, Americans celebrated the "false armistice" on November 7, 1918, four days early. *(National Archives)*

ships, shore facilities, and weapons. The officers saw the mutinies as abortive Bolshevik uprisings, but in fact they appeared to consist of simple refusals to obey the illegal orders to steam into battle. These mutinies resulted in very little bloodshed, with only scattered incidents of gunfire. To the extent that the mutinies had any political side, they demonstrated that the naval enlisted men wanted an armistice as soon as possible and that they rejected the attempted coup by the admirals.

On October 30, Turkey surrendered, and, on November 1, the Austro-Hungarian Empire offered an armistice on the basis of the Fourteen Points. The Italians accepted that offer on November 4. By November 5, House had secured his compromises with the other Allies, and Secretary of State Lansing informed the German government that General Foch would present the terms of the armistice to representatives of the Germans at a specified meeting place at Campiègne, near the battle lines. On November 7, the German team, led by Matthias Erzberger, met with General Foch and learned the terms of the armistice. Erzberger was stunned to see that the Allies demanded evacuation of German territory on the German east bank of the Rhine and the surrender of heavy weapons. The German delegates recognized that the terms constituted surrender rather than the cease-fire that they expected.

Erzberger explained that he would need further instructions from the German government at Spa. Meanwhile, word of the peace negotiation was leaked out by a newspaper press service, leading to a false celebration on November 7 in New York and other American cities on the assumption that the war had ended.

Before Erzberger could return to Campiègne with his instructions, a general strike in Berlin led to clashes between loyal and mutinous troops. Prematurely, Prince Max announced the abdication of the kaiser, and he turned the government over to the majority Socialists, who then proclaimed that Germany had become a republic. The legislature proclaimed Philipp Scheidemann prime minister. The next day, the kaiser fled to Holland, where he remained in exile. Later, he confirmed his abdication. The Scheidemann government sent Erzberger back to Foch with instructions to sign the armistice, which he did at 5 A.M. on the morning of November 11, with the armistice to take effect at 11:00 A.M. At that hour, the guns fell silent and the war ended. In a curious postscript, the word of the armistice did not reach German troops in Africa until two days later, and the last German army there surrendered to British troops at Abercorn, Northern Rhodesia, on November 25.

Almost too suddenly for the generals to accept, the war that they expected to last well into 1919 had come to an abrupt end. Unraveling from the tangle of treaties, agreements, understandings, and lists of points, what kind of peace should emerge became the difficult task for the Great Power statesmen over the following months.

CHRONICLE OF EVENTS

1917

January–March: Hunger riots and strikes break out across Germany as a result of severe winter food shortages.

April 9: The British begin an attack at Arras toward Vimy Ridge.

April 16–May 9: French general Robert Nivelle orders a suicidal attack at Soissons (Chemin des Dames) that costs 30,000 dead and another 110,000 wounded or captured. The Germans had already pulled back to the fortified Hindenburg Line, which the Germans called the Siegfried Line, and that line held against the French.

April 26: After months of severe losses, the British Admiralty adopts the convoy system proposed by Admiral A. L. Duff.

April 30: Prime Minister Lloyd George meets with the Admiralty and thereafter takes credit for adoption of the convoy system.

May: The Poles demand an independent and united Poland.

May 15: Pétain succeeds Nivelle in charge of French army, and he gradually changes tactics to reflect new conditions, including defense in depth, open formation advances, coordinated attacks, rolling barrages, and integrated use of aircraft and tanks.

May 27–June 7: Fifty-four French divisions mutiny, refusing to advance. An estimated 20,000 soldiers desert the army. Mutineers take over the town of Missy-aux-Bois, near Soissons, in early June. Eventually there are 3,400 courts-martial and 49 to 55 executions for dereliction of duty.

June 7: The British Flanders campaign begins with the explosion of 19 tunnel-mines at Messines Ridge.

July: Admiral Sims of the U.S. Navy endorses the convoy system; henceforth many ships cross the Atlantic safely in convoy. The system will be largely in place by November, reducing British losses to about 200,000 tons monthly by January 1918.

July 31: The British renew the offensive at Ypres (known as Third Ypres). They lose thousands of men; Germans use mustard gas. Each side suffers 35,000 killed. Some 25,000 Germans are taken prisoner.

August: Canada introduces conscription.

October 22–November 8: Third Ypres continues, but the British are stopped by German defenses and by deep mud at Passchendaele. The British suffer 70,000 dead and 147,000 wounded.

October 24–27: Joint German-Austrian forces make a breakthrough at Caporetto under German general von Bülow. Ten Italian regiments surrender en masse. The Central Power forces push the Isonzo front back 70–80 miles. More than 300,000 Italian troops desert and 265,000 are taken prisoner.

November 5–7: A conference at Rapallo establishes the Allied Supreme War Council.

November 11: At a staff conference in Mons, Belgium, Hindenburg and Ludendorff agree that the submarine tactic is insufficient to defeat the Allies and that an offensive should be mounted in March 1918, before the arrival of American troops. Ludendorff plans an attack to focus on the British line, at the point of juncture of the French and British forces.

November 16: Poincaré appoints Clemenceau as the head of the French government.

November 20: British mass 381 tanks at Cambrai. The initial advances until November 29 will turn to losses of ground by December 5.

November 30: German troops and African auxiliaries cross from German East Africa into Portuguese East Africa.

December: The Austrian advance after Caporetto is halted on a line between the Piave River and Venice after the arrival of British and French troops transferred from the western front.

December 27: Jellicoe resigns as first sea lord because the convoy system had not completely stopped severe losses to merchant shipping.

1918

January 8: Woodrow Wilson delivers his Fourteen Points speech.

January 28–February 4: A wave of strikes protesting continuance of the war sweeps Germany with demonstrations in Danzig, Berlin, Dresden, Munich, and at least 10 other cities.

February: Britain passes the Representation of the People Act, enfranchising property-holding married women, mothers older than 30, all men 21 and older, and men in service aged 19 and 20; conscientious objectors are denied the vote for five years.

February: Polish troops in the Austro-Hungarian army mutiny at Czernowitz.

March 3: The Treaty of Brest Litovsk is signed, ending formal Russian participation in the war.

March 21: Operation Michael, Ludendorff's offensive against the British to push them to the sea, is launched, leading to a British retreat. Ultimately the offensive costs the Germans 300,000 casualties, including 105,000 killed. The British suffer 150,000 dead and the French, 60,000 dead.

March 23: German guns start to shell Paris. The shells weigh 250 pounds each and will later be fired from a total of six guns with a range of 75 miles. During the next six months, they will kill 256 people.

March 26: General Douglas Haig agrees to work under General Ferdinand Foch.

April: The African-American U.S. 369th Regiment, integrated into a French unit, fights in the Argonne.

April 14: General Ferdinand Foch becomes commander in chief (generalissimo) of all Allied forces.

May 27–30: Germans advance across the Marne to within 37 miles of Paris.

May 27–June 5: American forces at Chateau-Thierry help the French halt the German advance.

June 6, 9, and 12: At the Battles of Belleau Wood 27,500 American troops repulse the German advance and retake the wood.

June–July: Flu begins to hit troops of both sides in the front lines; eventually the influenza pandemic will claim the lives of 21.5 million worldwide, more than twice the total of all soldiers killed in combat in the war.

July 15–17: Germans begin an offensive in the Second Battle of the Marne (the Hagen offensive); German losses in the March and July offensives total about 1 million, with 125,000 dead and 100,000 missing.

July 18: The French begin a counteroffensive. Nine American divisions participate.

July 22: The Allies cross the Marne.

African-American troops fought well in the Argonne, winning praise from the French. *(Library of Congress)*

August 8: The Allied offensive at Amiens combines air, tanks, and artillery; 54,000 American troops participate.

August 31: Woodrow Wilson endorses the Balfour Declaration, which favors establishing a Jewish national home in Palestine.

September 12–14: Americans take the St. Mihiel salient, capturing 15,000 to 16,000 prisoners.

September 20–29: Bulgarian troops mutiny and demand an end to the war; they march on Sofia.

September 26: American Expeditionary Force begins the Meuse-Argonne offensive that will continue through November 11. After initial setbacks, total gains are 34 miles forward, occupying 580 square miles.

September 26: Bulgaria asks for an armistice after its defeat at the Battle of Monastir-Doiron and troop mutinies.

September 29–October 30: Allied troops advance from Macedonia through Serbia to Belgrade.

September 30: The German chancellor, Georg Graf von Hertling, resigns with his cabinet.

October: Hungarian troops mutiny at Asiago in Italy.

October 1–2: The British take St. Quentin, Lens, and Armentieres.

October 4: Prince Maximilian von Baden, a liberal, is selected new chancellor in Germany.

October 6: Chancellor Maximilian von Baden opens negotiations with Wilson based on the Fourteen Points. The correspondence will continue, with three diplomatic notes from Wilson, to October 27, when Max agrees to Wilson's terms.

October 12: The last liner sunk in the war, *Leinster,* is torpedoed by a U-boat on its regular mail run between England and Ireland. Losses total 176, including women and children. The sinking may have contributed to Wilson stiffening his demands on Prince Maximilian.

October 18: Wilson notifies Austria-Hungary that autonomy for Czechoslovaks and Jugo-Slavs (as stated in the Fourteen Points) is no longer sufficient, but that their territories will need to be recognized as independent national states.

October 19: The Czech national council demands absolute independence for the Czech fatherland.

October 21: As a show of good faith during armistice negotiations, the kaiser orders that submarines are to suspend attacks against passenger ships. Admiral Scheer claims to recall all submarines.

October 22–28: The German "admirals' revolt" develops, in which Admiral Reinhard Scheer and Captains Magnus von Levetzow and Adolf von Trotha plan a final surface battle between the High Seas Fleet and the British navy.

October 23: Wilson informs the German government that there must be a government responsive to the people in Germany, not an autocratic one.

October 23–November 5: Colonel House negotiates with the Allies to get them to agree to Wilson's terms. The British reject freedom of the seas, and the French demand German disarmament and the occupation of German territory. House regards terms as acceptance of the Fourteen Points with compromise.

October 24: A successful Italian-British-French offensive is launched at Vittorio Veneto, pushing back from the River Piave.

October 26: The kaiser demands Ludendorff's resignation, after Ludendorff urges the army command to reject Wilson's peace terms. Ludendorff will be succeeded in office by General William Groener the next day. Groener will inform Scheer that the military is subject to Prince Maximilian.

October 27: The kaiser informs Wilson that the military authorities are now subject to the civilian representatives of the German people.

October 27–29: The admirals attempt their *Flottenvorstoss,* or attack on the British fleet by the High Seas Fleet.

October 28: Thomas Masaryk, Eduard Beneš, and Milan Stefanik proclaim the independence of the Republic of Czechoslovakia.

October 28: Austro-Hungarian generals on the Italian front demand that the empire negotiate an armistice.

October 28: The German Reichstag approves the subordination of the military to the civilian authority.

October 28–29: German sailors begin to mutiny after being ordered to sea under the admirals' plot.

October 29: The Independent Kingdom of the Serbs, Croats, and Slovenes—later known as Jugo-Slavia or Yugoslavia—is proclaimed at Zagreb.

October 30: Turkey surrenders unconditionally.

November 1: British forces move into the Mosul district of Mesopotamia (now Iraq).

November 1: The AEF First Army resumes its offensive through Meuse-Argonne, advancing more than five miles.

November 1: The Austro-Hungarian Empire offers an armistice.

November 2: German forces in Africa leave Portuguese East Africa and enter Northern Rhodesia.

November 3–4: German navy mutineers free prisoners and, after exchanging gunfire with guards, take control of the city of Kiel and of all ships in port.

November 4: The Italians accept the Austro-Hungarian offer of an armistice.

November 5: U.S. secretary of state Lansing informs the German government that Foch will present the terms of the armistice to German representatives.

November 7: Order is restored in Kiel under a Reichstag deputy selected as Socialist governor Gustav Noske, but over the next days the mutiny spreads throughout the navy and to other cities, including Hamburg and Bremen.

November 7: Bavaria is declared an independent Bolshevik Free State; the king of Bavaria abdicates.

November 7: German negotiator Matthias Erzberger meets with Foch in a railway car at Compiègne. Foch presents punitive military terms of withdrawal that bear little resemblance to the Fourteen Points.

November 8: Erzberger and his delegation ask for instructions from German Imperial Headquarters at Spa.

November 8–9: Uprisings, often led by sailors, spring up in Cologne, Hanover, Magdeburg, and several other German cities.

November 9: A general strike in Berlin leads to clashes between loyal and mutinous troops. Prince Maximilian announces the abdication of the kaiser. A republic is proclaimed in Berlin, dominated by the Socialists and led by Philippe Scheidemann.

November 10: Kaiser Wilhelm flees to Holland.

November 11: At 5 A.M. the German republic sends instructions to Matthias Erzberger to sign the armistice, which goes into effect at 11 A.M., ending the war in Europe. Poland declares its independence. Karl, emperor of Austria-Hungary, abdicates.

November 13: General Paul von Lettow-Vorbeck, in Africa, learns of the armistice.

November 25: German troops and civilians under Lettow-Vorbeck in Africa surrender at Abercorn, Northern Rhodesia.

EYEWITNESS TESTIMONY

. . . we saw our divisional general, "Dicky" Fanshawe, standing alone on a little knoll. He also was interested in the attack which started soon afterwards. It was a very pretty sight, and for a moment we were thrilled by the line of galloping horses and pointed swords in perfect order, but the excitement was soon spent for we knew that there were no enemy in front. We saw one or two fellows whirl out of their saddles from long-range machine gun fire, but then came a pitiful anticlimax, for on meeting with a few thin strands of wire, they were thrown into confusion and as Fanny mounted and rode away, we started off too, leaving a line of dismounted troopers leading their frightened horses across the entanglement.

> *Entry for April 2, 1917, in the diary of Lieutenant Edwin Campion Vaughan, describing a cavalry charge published in his* Some Desperate Glory: The World War I Diary of a British Officer, *p. 78.*

The battle of Arras, in which the British army was engaged, began on April 9th, an Easter Sunday, when there was a gale of sleet and snow. From ground near the old city of Arras I saw the preliminary bombardment when the Vimy Ridge was blasted by a hurricane of fire and the German lines beyond Arras were tossed up in earth and flame. From one of old Vauban's earthworks outside the walls I saw lines of our men going up in assault beyond the suburbs of Blangy and St.-Laurent to Roclincourt, through a veil of sleet and smoke. Our gun-fire was immense and devastating, and the first blow that fell upon the enemy was overpowering. The Vimy Ridge was captured from end to end by the Canadians on the left and the 51st Division of Highlanders on the right. By the afternoon the entire living German population, more than seven thousand in the tunnels of Vimy, were down below in the valley on our side of the lines, and on the ridge were many of their dead as I saw them afterward horribly mangled by shell-fire in the upheaved earth. . . .

That night masses of German prisoners suffered terribly from a blizzard in the barbed-wire cages at Etrun, by Arras, where Julius Caesar had his camp for a year in other days of history. They herded together with their bodies bent to the storm, each man sheltering his fellow and giving a little human warmth. All night through a German commandant sat in our Intelligence hut with his head bowed on his breast. Every now and then he said: "It is cold! It is cold!" And our men lay out in the captured ground beyond Arras and on the Vimy Ridge, under harassing fire and machine-gun fire, cold, too, in that wild blizzard, with British dead and German dead in the mangled earth about them.

> *Philip Gibbs, British war correspondent, describing the British advance toward Vimy Ridge as part of the late winter offensive in Flanders in April 1917, in his memoir,* Now It Can Be Told, *pp. 459–460.*

I was in the village below Observatory Ridge on the morning of April 11th when cavalry was massed on that ground, waiting for orders to go into action. The headquarters of the cavalry division was in a ditch covered by planks, and the cavalry generals and their staffs sat huddled together with maps over their knees. "I am afraid the general is busy for the moment," said a young staff officer on top of the ditch. He looked about the fields and said, "It's very unhealthy here." I agreed with him. The bodies of many young soldiers lay about. Five-point-nines (5.9's) were coming over in a haphazard way. It was no ground for cavalry. But some squadrons of the 10th Hussars, Essex Yeomanry, and the Blues were ordered to take Moncy, and rode up the hill in a flurry of snow and were seen by German gunners and slashed by shrapnel. Most of their horses were killed in the village or outside it, and the men suffered many casualties, including their general—Bulkely Johnson—whose body I saw carried back on a stretcher to the ruin of Thilloy, where crumps were bursting.

> *Philip Gibbs, British war correspondent, describing a fruitless cavalry charge as part of the late winter offensive in Flanders in April 1917, in his memoir,* Now It Can Be Told, *p. 462.*

The submarine issue is very much more serious than the people realize in America. The recent success of operations and the rapidity of construction constitute the real crisis of the war. The morale of the enemy submarines is not broken, only about fifty-four are known to have been captured or sunk and no voluntary surrenders have been recorded. . . .

Supplies and communications of forces on all fronts, including the Russians, are threatened and control of the sea actually imperiled.

German submarines are constantly extending their operations into the Atlantic, increasing areas and the difficulty of patrolling. Russian situation critical. Baltic fleet mutiny, eighty-five admirals, captains, and commanders murdered, and in some armies there is insubordination.

The amount of British, neutral and Allied shipping lost in February was 536,000 tons, in March 571,000 tons, and in the first ten days of April 205,000 tons. With short nights and better weather these losses are increasing.

U.S. admiral William S. Sims, in a cablegram to Josephus Daniels, April 14, 1917, quoted in Josephus Daniels, The Wilson Era: Years of War and After, *p. 69. (The tonnage figures for the months mentioned were later revised upward.)*

I had seen the working of the tunnelers up by Hill 70 and elsewhere. I had gone into the darkness of the tunnels, crouching low, striking my steel hat with sharp, spine-jarring knocks against the low beams overhead, coming into galleries where one could stand upright and walk at ease in electric light, hearing the vibrant hum of great engines, the murmur of men's voices in dark crypts, seeing numbers of men sleeping on bunks in the gloom of caverns close beneath the German lines, and listening through a queer little instrument called a microphone, by which I heard the scuffle of German feet in German galleries a thousand yards away, the dropping of a pick or shovel, the knocking out of German pipes against charcoal stoves. It was by that listening instrument, more perfect than the enemy's, that we had beaten him, and by the grim determination of those underground men of ours, whose skin was the color of the chalk in which they worked, who coughed in the dampness of the caves, and who packed high explosives at the shaft-heads,—hundreds of tons of it—for the moment when a button should be touched far away, and an electric current would pass down a wire, and the enemy and his works would be blown into dust.

That moment came at Hill 60, and sixteen other places below the Wytschaet and Messines Ridge at three-thirty on the morning of June 7th, after a quiet night of war, when a few of our batteries had fired in a desultory way and the enemy had sent over some flocks of gas-shells and before dawn I heard the cocks crow on Kemmel Hill. I saw the seventeen mines go up, and earth and flame gush out of them as though the fires of hell had risen. A terrible sight, as the work of men against their fellow creatures.

Philip Gibbs, British war correspondent, describing mining works at Messines Ridge in June 1917, in his memoir, Now It Can Be Told, *pp. 468–469.*

A few days after the battle [of Third Ypres, which began on July 31] the rains began, and hardly ceased for four months. Night after night the skies opened and let down steady torrents, which turned all that country into one great bog of slime. Those little rivers or "beeks," which ran between the knobby fingers of the claw like a range of ridges, were blown out of their channels and slopped over into broad swamps. The hurricanes of artillery fire which our gunners poured upon the enemy positions for twenty miles in depth churned up deep shell-craters which intermingled and made pits which the rains and floods filled to the brim. The only way of walking was by "duck-boards," tracks laid down across the bogs under enemy fire, smashed up day by day, laid down again under cover of darkness. Along a duck-board men must march in single file, and if one of our men, heavily laden in his fighting-kit, stumbled on those greasy boards (as all of them stumbled at every few yards) and fell off, he sank up to his knees, often up to his waist, sometimes up to his neck, in mud and water. If he were wounded when he fell, and darkness was about him, he could only cry to God or his pals, for he was helpless otherwise. One of our divisions of Lancashire men—the 66th—took eleven hours in making three miles or so out of Ypres across that ground on their way to attack, and then, in spite of their exhaustion, attacked. . . .

I say now that nothing that has been written is more than the pale image of the abomination of those

American casualties were extraordinarily high. Here a group of wounded await evacuation from a partially destroyed church in Neuvilly. *(National Archives)*

battlefields, and that no pen or brush has yet achieved the picture of that Armageddon in which so many of our men perished.

British correspondent Philip Gibbs, describing the British advance in the first days of the Third Battle of Ypres offensive in Flanders in August 1917, in his memoir, Now It Can Be Told, *pp. 472–474.*

Re-entering the pillbox I found the Boche officer quite talkative. He told me how he had kept his garrison fighting on, and would never have allowed them to surrender. He had seen us advancing and was getting his guns on to us when a shell from the tank behind had come through the doorway, killed two men and blown his leg off. His voice trailed away and he relapsed into a stupor. So I went out again into the open and walked along our line; a few heavies were still pounding about us, but a more terrible sound now reached my ears.

From the darkness on all sides came the groans and wails of wounded men; faint, long, sobbing moans of agony, and despairing shrieks. It was too horribly obvious that dozens of men with serious wounds must have crawled for safety into new shell-holes, and now the water was rising about them, and powerless to move, they were slowly drowning. Horrible visions came to me with those cries—of Woods and Kent, Edge and Taylor, lying maimed out there trusting that their pals would find them, and now dying terribly, alone amongst the dead in the inky darkness. And we could do nothing to help them; Dunham was crying quietly beside me, and all the men were affected by the piteous cries.

How long, I wondered, could this situation last.

Diary entry for August 27, 1917, describing mud conditions during the Third Battle of Ypres offensive, Lieutenant Edwin Campion Vaughan, published in his Some Desperate Glory: The World War I Diary of a British Officer, *p. 228.*

"Why do you think we volunteered?" I asked sarcastically, when the testimony was complete.

Monsieur le Ministre was evidently rather uncomfortable. He writhed a little in his chair, and tweaked his chin three or four times. The rosette and the moustache were exchanging animated phrases. At last Noyon, motioning for silence and speaking in an almost desperate tone, demanded:

"*Est-ce-que vous détestez les boches?* [Is it that you detest the Germans?]"

I had won my own case. The question was purely perfunctory. To walk out of the room a free man I had merely to say yes. My examiners were sure of my answer. The rosette was leaning forward and smiling encouragingly. The moustache was making little *oui's* in the air with his pen. And Noyon had given up all hope of making me out a criminal. I might be rash, but I was innocent; the dupe of a superior and malign intelligence. I would probably be admonished to choose my friends more carefully next time and that would be all. . . .

Deliberately, I framed the answer:

"*Non. J'aime beaucoup les français.* [No. I like the French more.]"

Agile as a weasel, Monsieur le Ministre was on top of me: "It is impossible to love Frenchmen and not to hate Germans."

I did not mind his triumph in the least. The discomfiture of the rosette merely amused me. The surprise of the moustache I found very pleasant. . . .

And my case was lost, forever lost. . . .

At the conclusion of a short conference I was told by Monsieur:

"I am sorry for you, but due to your friend you will be detained a little while."

Poet E. E. Cummings, describing the hearing at which he was remanded to a French detention center in September 1917 for neutrals and Allies who had come under suspicion of sedition, as described in his autobiographical novel, The Enormous Room, *pp. 19–20.*

Don't Worry, Boys!

If the War doesn't end next month, of two things one is certain: Either you will be sent across the big pond or you will stay on this side.

If you stay at home there is no need to worry. If you go across, of two things one is certain: Either you will be put on the firing line or kept behind the lines.

If you are behind the lines there is no need to worry. If you are at the front, of two things one is certain: Either you are resting in a safe place or you're exposed to danger.

If you are resting in a safe place there is no need to worry. If you are exposed to danger, of two things one is certain: Either you're wounded or not wounded.

If you are not wounded there is no need to worry. If you are wounded, of two things one is certain: Either you're wounded seriously or you're wounded slightly.

If you are wounded slightly there is no need to worry. If you are wounded seriously, of two things one is certain: Either you recover or you don't.

If you recover there is no need to worry. If you don't recover you can't worry.

"A famous syllogism," from The Camp Dodger, *September 28, 1917, quoted in Mark Sullivan,* Our Times, *vol. 5,* Over Here, *p. 326.*

All depended on the surprise of the tanks. If they were discovered before the assault the whole adventure would fail at the start.

They had been brought up secretly by night, four hundred of them, with supply tanks for ammunition and petrol lying hidden in woods by day. So the artillery and infantry and cavalry had been concentrated also. The enemy believed himself secure in his Hindenburg line, which had been constructed behind broad hedges of barbed wire with such wide ditches that no tank could cross.

How then, would tanks cross? Why, that was a little trick which would surprise the Germans mightily. Each tank would advance through the early morning mists with a bridge on its nose. The bridge was really a big "fascine," or bundle of fagots about a yard and a half in diameter, and controlled by a lever and chain from the interior of the tank. Having plowed through the barbed wire and reached the edge of the Hindenburg trench, the tank would drop the fascine into the center of the ditch, stretch out its long body, reach the bundle of fagots, find support on it, and use it as a stepping-stone to the other side. Very simple in idea and effect! So it happened, and the mists favored us, as I saw on the morning of the attack at a little place called Beaumont, near Villers Pluich. The enemy was completely surprised, caught at breakfast in his dugouts, rounded up in batches. The tanks went away through the breach they had made, with the infantry swarming round them, and captured Havrincourt, Hermies, Ribecourt, Gouzeaucourt, Masnières, and Marcoing, and a wide stretch of country forming a cup or amphitheater below a series of low ridges south of Bourlon Wood, where the ground rose again.

Philip Gibbs, British correspondent, describing the first massed tank attack at Cambrai, November 20, 1917, in his memoir, Now It Can Be Told, *p. 487.*

I have just come across the first English prisoners, companies of English and Irish regiments of different divisions. They are all magnificently equipped with leather jerkins, good puttees, and excellent boots. An awfully good-looking young English captain is just waiting, with a smiling, interested face, for me to speak to him; I do so. It appears they had been expecting the attack for the past twenty days, but did not expect it to-day; the preliminary bombardment by our guns seemed to him much too mild for that!!! . . . This officer wore the most wonderful riding-boots. When I looked him up and down he apologized for not being dressed for marching. He said he had just been going for a ride. He appeared to take it rather amiss that our attack had not left him time to dress himself in proper style with boots and puttees to be taken prisoner.

German aide de camp Rudolf Binding, from his diary, March 1, 1918, A Fatalist at War, *translated by Ian F. D. Morrow, p. 205.*

March 26, 1918

There was the corner of a little wood where the English put up a desperate resistance, apparently with a few machine-guns, and finally with only one. When the defence was broken down, out from the lines of our advancing infantry, which I was following, appeared an English General, accompanied by a single officer. He was an extraordinary sight. About thirty-five years old, excellently—one can almost say wonderfully—dressed and equipped, he looked as if he had just stepped out of a Turkish bath in Jermyn Street. . . .

I said, "Good morning," and he came to a stop with his companion. By way of being polite, I said with intention: "You have given us a lot of trouble; you stuck it for a long time." To which he replied: "Trouble! Why, we have been running for five days and five nights!" It appeared that when he could no longer get his brigade to stand he had taken charge of a machine-gun himself, to set an example to his retreating men. All his officers except the one with him had been killed or wounded, and his brigade hopelessly cut up. I asked for his name, to remind me of our meeting, and he gave it. He was General Dawson, an Equerry of the King.

We have now spent two nights in the crater-field of the old Somme battle. No desert of salt is more desolate. Last night we slept in a hole in the crumbly, chalky soil, and froze properly. It is impossible to sleep for excitement. Really one would like to be after them day and night, and only longs that there shall be no rest until one can feel the first breath of the Atlantic in Amiens. To-morrow we hope to be on a level with Albert, where there will be villages again. Here the villages are merely names. Even the ruins are ruined. Yesterday I was looking for Bouchavesnes, which used to be quite a large place.

There was nothing but a board nailed to a low post with the inscription in English, "This was Bouchavesnes."

German aide de camp Rudolf Binding, March 26, 1918, describing German advance in the Somme, from his diary, A Fatalist at War, translated by Ian F. D. Morrow, pp. 207–208.

March 28, 1918

To-day the advance of our infantry suddenly stopped near Albert. Nobody could understand why. Our air-men had reported no enemy between Albert and Amiens. . . .

As soon as I got near the town I began to see curi-ous sights. Strange figures, which looked very little like soldiers, and certainly showed no signs of advancing, were making their way back out of the town. There were men driving cows before them on a line; others who carried a hen under one arm and a box of notepaper under the other. Men carrying a bottle of wine under their arm and another one open in their hand. Men who had torn a silk drawing-room curtain from off its rod and were dragging it to the rear as a useful bit of loot. More men with writ-ing-paper and coloured note-books. Evidently they had found it desirable to sack a stationer's shop. Men dressed up in comic disguise. Men with top-hats on their heads. Men staggering. Men who could hardly walk. . . . When I got into the town the streets were running with wine. . . . Had not I seen yesterday an officer younger than myself sitting beside me in the car suddenly call out to the driver to stop at once, without so much as asking my leave. When I asked him in astonishment what he meant by stopping the car when we were on an urgent mission, he answered, "I must pick up that English waterproof [raincoat] lying beside the road." The car stopped. He jumped out, seized an English waterproof which lay on the bank, and then jumped joy-fully back again, as if refreshed and waked to new life.

If this lack of restraint seized an officer like that, one can imagine what effect it must have on the private soldier to have craved and hungered and thirsted for months on end. Where in the case of the officer it was the waterproof which tempted him so irresistibly as to make him forget his most important duties, with the private soldiers, according to taste, it was the coloured picture-postcard, the silk curtain, the bottle of wine, the chicken, or the cow, but in most cases the wine.

German aide de camp Rudolf Binding, March 28, 1918, from his diary, commentary on the collapse of morale among German troops, in A Fatalist at War, translated by Ian F. D. Morrow, pp. 209–211.

Come on, you sons-of-bitches. Do you want to live forever?

Gunnery Sergeant Daniel J. Daley to his platoon, U.S. Marine Corps, at Belleau Wood, June 6, 1918, as quoted in John Morrow, The Great War, p. 238.

August 17, 1918

I am in the grip of the fever. Some days I am quite free; then again a weakness overcomes me so that I can barely drag myself in a cold perspiration on to my bed and blankets. Then pain, so that I don't know whether I am alive or dead. I can neither eat nor drink, and yet have constantly a bitter taste in my mouth from thirst. My bowels suddenly revolt as though I were poisoned, then subside again, but the weakness lasts. So it has been going on for weeks.

German aide de camp Rudolf Binding, August 17, 1918, from his diary, A Fatalist at War, translated by Ian F. D. Morrow, p. 243.

September 26, 1918

There was a company moving slowly up to our left rear in lozenge squad columns so I went over to their head-quarters group and reported to the tall, sandy-haired captain who was mopping the sweat from his freckled forehead. "Sergeant Triplet, D Company, 140th Infantry, sir. Can you tell me where I can find the 140th?"

"They ought to be somewhere back there but with that fog, I don't know. Just got here myself."

"Well, captain, I've got a platoon over there, and we're lost. I sure don't want to backtrack to find my outfit. And I don't want to be court-martialed for deser-tion either. So I wonder if you could use another pla-toon until I can locate my own company?"

"Glad to have you sergeant. We're in lozenge now so tack your lot on behind my fourth platoon like the tail of a kite, fifty-yard distance. And send me a runner."

So we tagged along as the fifth platoon, E Company, 138th Infantry. Sure was nice to belong to somebody again after our lonesome trek through that fog.

We went right through the monstrous crater in the center of the hill after crossing through the wreckage of the most beautiful trench system I'd ever seen. The Jerries didn't have a chance, of course, but they'd done well while they lasted.

American army sergeant William Triplet, describing confused conditions during the American offensive in the Argonne, September 26, 1918, quoted in Robert Ferrell, ed., A Youth in the Meuse-Argonne, p. 167.

September 28, 1918

Couldn't sleep so I did some mental mathematics. We'd started over the top with fifty-one men. Lost twelve yesterday, that left thirty-nine. We'd had eleven hit today, that left twenty-eight. At this rate we'd be finished in two or three days. But we'd gained Offenbacher's squad from the 138th so we had thirty-six now. Elfield and his shorthanded auto teams on outpost added up to ten. That left a sort of Mexican army, Kay, Robbie, and I commanding three squads, twenty-six-man total counting us. Hadn't had time to think about it before but the last couple of days had been pretty hard on us.

Longest night I've ever spent. The chaplains tell us that hell is hot. I know better—it's freezing cold and perpetually wet. We dozed and shivered, heard an occasional shell whooshing down and didn't even wince. They were mixing gas with the explosive shells now and when the onion smell got too strong we'd wake each other, put masks on, and shudder off to another nightmare. A very long night.

> *American army sergeant William Triplet, describing casualty rates during the American offensive in the Argonne, September 28, 1918, as quoted in Robert Ferrell, ed.,* A Youth in the Meuse-Argonne, *p. 217.*

We all stood frozen and gazed and drooled at the sight of this beautiful "bit of fluff" as she arranged her bottles, bandages, and shiny tools.

The vision turned and crooked her finger invitingly at me. I took a firm grip on my pitiful little beltless, buttonless toga and moved forward.

"Where were you wounded?" Asked my ministering angel in a husky whisper.

"At Exermont, ma'am, about ten miles north of Mont Vauquois."

"Don't get funny with me, soldier," she rasped. Evidently she was inquiring from an anatomical rather than a geographical viewpoint. But before I could start a correction she went into action. "Here, lets have a look at that arm," and she deftly swept the robe from my clutching fingers.

Gosh, I hadn't been treated like that since I was five years old. I knew now how the Circassian slave girl feels when she's shown on the auction block in the Turkish market. Blushed a hot bright pink clear to my toes, frantically grabbing for the robe. Got it in part and too late.

The Florence Nightingale of Base Hospital 37 was now kneading my swollen shoulder and pulling the arm

hither and yon, apparently hoping to hear the grating of bone fragments or a piercing scream. She gave up on that approach, selected a foot-long, round-pointed needle of about .22 caliber with an eye near the rear end, and jerked her head toward a stool.

"You'd better sit down."

I sat down.

"This is going to hurt," she promised pleasantly, starting the rounded point into the bullet hole in front and lining it up with the exit hole in rear. She pushed and wiggled the needle but was having trouble getting it through.

"Mmmmmmmmmm." She was dead right, it did hurt.

"Raise your arm a little, slowly." I raised and she pushed and wiggled that crowbar again.

"More." Finally the muscles must have got lined up like they'd been when I got hit, the shaft found the bullet track, and the blunt point came out the rear.

"Whoosh." I mopped some of the sweat off with my sleeve.

"Oh it really wasn't all that bad was it?" she inquired brightly, threading a small cloth through the eye of the needle like a gun patch in the end of a cleaning rod. She swabbed the exposed shaft and doused the patch with iodine.

"Now this is really going to hurt," she prophesized with a winning smile, or was it a ghoulish grin? She pushed the shaft farther, almost up to the patch. Since it was in the right channel that was practically painless. But then she shifted her grip to the rear, pulled slowly, and the patch disappeared.

"Holy Mmmoses on the flaming Mmmountain!" I felt like she was dragging a cedar sapling through the hole sideways. It finally came clear and she examined the gory patch hopefully for bits of cloth, raincoat, lead, cupro-nickle, or bone. Don't know what she found. I drooped, sweated profusely, and swallowed repeatedly to keep my breakfast down. That woman was no angel of mercy, she was a damned coldhearted, sadistic witch with the hands of a blacksmith and the soul of Torquemada. Probably pulled wings off flies when she was a baby.

But the rest was a "piece of kyke" as the Limeys say.

> *American army sergeant William Triplet, describing medical treatment for a bullet wound in October 1918, quoted in Robert Ferrell, ed.,* A Youth in the Meuse-Argonne, *pp. 241–242.*

The President then spoke with great frankness relative to the note in question. He said that he had studied it with the utmost care—that he had not relied on the official translation, but had taken the German text and had even gotten out his dictionaries to make sure of the precise meaning of the note. He said it was exceedingly frank in terms and that if it had come from any civilized nation it would have been necessary to accept it, but knowing the German situation, he was forced into the course that he had pursued. He said,

"You may not know it, and it is not generally known, but some of our Allies are very anxious for peace, and if I had followed the course that Senator Lodge seems to desire, and had slammed the door, it might well have been possible that someone else amongst our friends would have put his foot in the door."

He said we are the real fighting nation now, and he said, "You will also observe that the war is still going on." He said the difficulty with Senator Lodge is that he wants me to be a Hun and dictate a Hun peace.

Homer S. Cummings, chairman of Democratic National Committee, recording a conversation with President Wilson, October 11, 1918, in a memorandum, quoted in Link, et al., eds., The Papers of Woodrow Wilson, *vol. 51, p. 303.*

I ascertained that [David Lloyd] George and [Georges] Clemenceau believed that the terms of the armistice, both naval and military, were too severe and that they should be modified. George stated that he thought it might be unwise to insist on the occupation of the east bank of the Rhine. Clemenceau stated that he

By the fall of 1918, U.S. troops had advanced on St. Mihiel through St. Baussant. *(National Archives)*

could not maintain himself in the Chamber of Deputies unless this was made a part of the armistice to be submitted to the Germans, and that the French army would also insist on this as their due after the long occupation of French soil by the Germans; but he gave us his word of honor that France would withdraw after the peace conditions had been fulfilled. I am inclined to sympathize with the position taken by Clemenceau.

I pointed out the danger of bringing about a state of Bolshevism in Germany if the terms of the armistice were made too stiff, and the consequent danger to England, France, and Italy. Clemenceau refused to recognize that there was any danger of Bolshevism in France. George said it was possible to create such a state of affairs in England, and both agreed that anything might happen in Italy.

> *Edward House, reporting to Wilson on his discussions regarding the armistice, October 30, 1918, in Charles Seymour,* The Intimate Papers of Colonel House, The Ending of the War, *pp. 118–119.*

I sent for William Wiseman immediately upon my return from Versailles, and told him that unless Lloyd George would make some reasonable concessions in his attitude upon the "Freedom of the Seas," all hope of Anglo Saxon unity would be at an end; that the United States went to war with England in 1812 on the question of her rights at sea, and that she had gone to war with Germany in 1917 upon the same question. I did not believe that even if the President wished to do so, he could avoid this issue; and if Lloyd George expressed the British viewpoint as he indicates, there would be greater feeling against Great Britain at the end of the war than there had been since our Civil War. I again repeated, with as much emphasis as I could, that our people would not consent to allow the British Government, or any other Government, to determine upon what terms our ships should sail the seas either in time of peace or in time of war.

> *Edward House, in a note in his diary on November 1, 1918, in Charles Seymour,* The Intimate Papers of Colonel House, The Ending of the War, *pp. 179–180.*

In the last weeks of the war, the United States deployed naval guns mounted on railroad flatcars. This 14-inch railroad gun is being fired by men of the 35th Coast Artillery. *(National Archives)*

November 10 may perhaps turn out to be the most significant day of this war. At least this is the way I felt on Sunday morning as I gazed down upon a mob of "a hundred thousand." For the first time I felt somewhat solemn. A springlike sun was shining and the happy and gay faces of the men indicated that they welcomed the arrival of the new era with open arms. Although the procession had already lasted two hours, a constant stream of new battalions of sailors and soldiers came streaming from the center of town. Amidst wild cheering Stoker First Class Kuhnt introduced himself as the first president of the Republic of Oldenburg. Low-flying aircraft dropped down bundles of handbills. To the thunderous applause of the mob, the huge Imperial war flag was lowered and the red flag of liberty, equality and fraternity rose up over the barracks. I could no longer resist and was swept along by the mass hysteria.

All my qualms of conscience evaporated when the Kaiser abdicated and my Bavaria proclaimed itself a Republic.

> *German seaman Richard Stumpf, describing his reaction to the German naval mutiny, November 10, 1918, from* War, Mutiny and Revolution in the German Navy: The World War I Diary of Seaman Richard Stumpf, *Daniel Horn, ed., pp. 426–427*

11

The Peace Conference and the Treaty of Versailles
November 11, 1918– March 4, 1921

Although the guns on the western front had fallen silent at 11:00 A.M. on November 11, 1918, the leaders of the Allied powers remained severely divided as they faced the complex questions surrounding a peace treaty with Germany. Colonel House, Wilson's personal emissary, had obtained reluctant agreement from France and Britain to develop a peace based on the Fourteen Points despite grave reservations. The British regarded the point relating to freedom of the seas as open to discussion because they did not want to commit to any agreement that would limit their use of naval blockades in the future, while the French sought

The armistice is celebrated in Philadelphia, November 11. *(National Archives)*

276

a peace that would weaken Germany to the point that it could never again represent a threat to French national security.

Within Germany, the new republican government inherited a military that firmly believed the war had been lost because of collapse on the home front. A small but passionate communist party dreamed of following Russia into a Bolshevik future, and a bitter, disillusioned, and starving civilian population resented Allied claims that the German people should shoulder responsibility for the war. The German republic had accepted the armistice as sketched out by U.S. secretary of state Robert Lansing as at least allowing Germany to avoid invasion and was willing to settle the war based on the Fourteen Points.

Through November and December, leaders drew up plans for the peace conference to be convened in Paris in January 1919. Britain would be represented by David Lloyd George, a Liberal who had organized a coalition government that included Conservatives. He was committed to making Germany pay for the war; in the December elections, Lloyd George had campaigned on a platform that called the kaiser a criminal and advocated squeezing Germany for the total cost of the war. The Tiger, Premier Georges Clemenceau, who would represent France, had also just emerged from a national election based on much the same principles. The Italian premier, Vittorio Orlando, came to the conference prepared to argue aggressively for Italian territorial gain. In the United States, Woodrow Wilson decided that he should attend personally, over the objections of Secretary of State Lansing.

Unlike Lloyd George and Clemenceau, Wilson held the dual position of chief of state and head of government. As the newspapers reported it, Wilson would attend in his capacity as "prime minister" of the United States. Lansing objected to Wilson's attendance on more personal grounds, suggesting that attending the conference would only diminish Wilson's prestige and that he would be put in the difficult position of reaching agreements that would then have to be ratified by the U.S. Senate before becoming binding on the United States. While both Lloyd George and Clemenceau (and the other prime ministers or heads of government who attended the conference) represented the majority party or coalition governments of their countries and could be presumed to speak for their ratifying parliaments, Wilson by contrast headed the Democratic Party, which had just lost the November 1918 elections to Republican majorities in both houses of Congress. Thus, while attending the peace conference and nominally representing the U.S. government, he did not in fact represent the party that controlled the legislature of that government. This difficulty would come back to haunt Wilson later in 1919 and the world more broadly in the years to come.

Wilson apparently had other reasons for not sending Lansing as the head of the delegation to Paris. Although Lansing attended as part of the staff to support Wilson, the president later made the pointed statement that he

French prime minister "Tiger" Clemenceau was vigorous before and after being shot by an assassin with poor aim. *(Library of Congress)*

did not intend to have lawyers framing the treaty. Since Lansing was the only lawyer in the room, he took the comment personally, and, in his memoirs, he traced the division between Wilson and himself both to his advice that Wilson should not attend Paris personally and to Wilson's belief that statesmen, not attorneys, should be drawing up the treaty. Lansing also disagreed with many of Wilson's policies and ideals, particularly the concept that the boundaries of the former Central Power empires should be redrawn on the basis of self-determination. Lansing visualized the day when the claim to the right of self-determination would spell the end of all the colonial empires and would lead to interminable national civil wars and international conflicts over jurisdiction and sovereignty of peoples. Lansing correctly anticipated issues that continued to cause conflict into the 21st century, including struggles over Irish and Israeli sovereignty.

Wilson not only decided to attend the conference personally but he also decided not to include in the delegation any representatives of the U.S. Senate, either Republicans or Democrats. He believed that the senators would have an opportunity to vote on the treaty when it came before the Senate for ratification, and, that if any of them attended the negotiations, they would get the opportunity to vote twice on the same document. Wilson sailed for Europe in December; prior to the convening of the conference, he went on a brief tour, speaking in Paris, London, Manchester, Rome, Milan, and Turin. After the opening of the Peace Conference he gave further addresses in Paris and elsewhere in Europe. In these speeches, he outlined his hopes that the peace treaty would be linked to the creation of a League of Nations. He believed that the treaty could work out new boundaries and security arrangements in Europe, but that later adjustment of the boundaries would have to be negotiated through the League,

The Big Four: Prime Minister David Lloyd George, Vittorio Orlando, Georges Clemenceau, and President Woodrow Wilson at the Hotel Crillon in Paris. *(National Archives)*

which would be empowered to investigate and study the issues in greater depth and to resolve difficulties.

The outpouring of popular support for Wilson stunned the journalists in attendance as well as the officials who greeted him on his Italian tour. Vast crowds assembled in Rome, Milan, and Turin, where the throngs acclaimed him and demanded that he address them, which he did numerous times, without loudspeakers, from the balconies of hotels and town halls. Despite the language barrier, the mobs cheered resoundingly, causing some embarrassment to Wilson's hosts, whose own political campaigns had never drawn such crowds. Journalists and later commentators believed that the tumultuous welcome convinced Wilson that his Fourteen Points, particularly the concepts of a peace without war guilt, self-determination, and a plan for a future League of Nations, had the support of the mass of the populations in Britain, France, and Italy. Whether or not the outpouring of affection strengthened his conviction, he entered the Peace Conference in January firmly committed to fighting for his beliefs.

DIFFERENT VISIONS

Five principal Allies, Britain, France, Italy, the United States, and Japan dominated the conference from the beginning. The Japanese, however, tended to focus only on decisions affecting their own interests in the Pacific and Asia. Soon, the press adopted the convention of referring to Lloyd George, Clemenceau, Orlando, and Wilson, as the Big Four. The terminology of a Big Three or Big Four would survive into history as so-called summits met in later decades, attended by three or four heads of government.

Critics complained that the Paris Peace Conference, which lasted from January until June 1919, took far too long to reach decisions, and, at the same time, that the conference reached too many decisions hastily. Both criticisms appear justified. At the heart of the problem lay the fact that the Allies, although in the position to dictate the terms of peace to the Germans, did not have an agreed-upon agenda or program among themselves, nor any shared vision of what the war had been about. Membership in the alliance had changed with events since 1914. Serbia had helped form a joint Serb-Croat-Slovene state (already called Jugo-Slavia in the press) that had been carved from pieces of the Austro-Hungarian Empire and Bulgaria. Russia, which had been one of the original Allies, had dropped out of the war and did not have an official delegation at the conference. In fact, Russia's former allies had dispatched troops into Russia, with different goals, but largely opposed to the emerging Soviet state there. Austria-Hungary had already dissolved, and Czechs, Poles, and Hungarians hoped that their claims would be met and resolved at the conference.

The Japanese wanted their claim to German territories in the Pacific and China honored. France and Britain had promised the lands to them as a price for entry into the war. Furthermore, the Japanese wanted the other Allies to recognize the principle of racial equality, so that Japanese immigrants to other nations would not be exposed to racial discrimination. In the United States, racial discrimination against Japanese (as well as against African Americans, Native Americans, Chinese, and other groups) tended to be established by state law, rather than national law. The Japanese failed to get their motion opposing racial discrimination incorporated into the final covenant of the league.

Some of the most severe disagreements came up between and among the Big Four. Britain wanted to acquire the German fleet and to prevent Germany from ever developing as a maritime power. Further, Britain desired to strip Germany of its overseas colonies. Britain also planned to extract from Germany not only the cost of actual physical damage (Britain had suffered rather limited damage from zeppelin bombing and naval shelling of seaports) but also the cost of veterans' benefits, including pensions.

France sought not only the restoration of Alsace-Lorraine (under German rule since 1871) but also territory on the west side of the Rhine and payment for the actual extensive war damage to property in northern France from Flanders through the Marne region. Furthermore, France sought to reduce German military and economic power so that Germany could not represent a future threat to France's security. For this reason, France supported the establishment of the boundaries of Poland, including not only the Polish regions of the Austro-Hungarian Empire but also territory formerly under German sovereignty. Clemenceau also expected that the secret Sykes-Picot agreement, granting France control over Syria and Lebanon, would be honored.

Orlando expected that Italy's secret treaty with Britain and the other Allies, the Treaty of London of April 26, 1915, would grant Italy sovereignty over the Tyrol, inhabited by German- speaking Austrians, up to the Brenner Pass through the Alps. Similarly, Italy expected to gain control over the port city of Trieste. Italy had further goals, hoping to establish control over at least a section of Albania, coastal islands along the Dalmatian side of the Aegean Sea, the port city of Fiume (which had formerly been the Hungarian enclave of Rijeka), and a share in the distribution of Ottoman territories. Fiume had an ethnically mixed population about 50 percent Italian, although Slovenes made up a clear majority in the nearby suburbs. Such claims ran directly counter to the interests of the Jugo-Slavs, the direct inheritors of the Serbian dream of South-Slav unity.

The old port of Fiume, whose waterfront is shown here, became a major sticking point at the Paris Peace Conference. Italy and the new Kingdom of Serbs, Croats, and Slovenes both laid claim to it. *(Library of Congress)*

The United States had entered the war over infringement of neutral rights and freedom of the seas, and the nation brought no territorial ambitions to the war. Americans believed that the peace that emerged should put an end to future wars and make the world safe for democracy. Such words did not seem empty slogans to Wilson or to many Americans. Rather, Wilson hoped the ideals would form the basis for a machinery or program to create an international league that would accept representatives of governments supported by their peoples. He hoped and planned that the league would be structured to work out through discussion and compromise and the force of world opinion, any further international disputes before they would erupt into war. Wilson recognized that in order to get approval of the league and the treaty by the U.S. Senate, that the league covenant would have to include a provision that protected the Monroe Doctrine, which precluded the expansion of European control into the nations of the Western Hemisphere. Furthermore, one of Wilson's Fourteen Points had been the opposition to secret treaties. Clearly, Italy, Japan, and France expected their secret treaties, regarding territorial change, to be honored, whether or not such changes required violation of the principle of ethnic self-determination.

Even regarding the proposed league, Wilson and the other members of the Big Four found little agreement. Britain, France, and Italy conceived of the league as very similar to the Concert of Europe which had arranged many of the boundary disputes in Europe in the 19th century through intermittently called special Congresses of the Great Powers. In effect, the European Allies visualized the league as a permanent version of the Great Power Congresses. Wilson, on the other hand, believed that the smaller powers should be equally represented in the league, thus reflecting world opinion and giving the league's decisions the force of a world voice. The covenant finally worked out represented a compromise between these two views, with a small group of Five Great Powers on an Executive Council, smaller states represented by four other nations on that council, and all member nations represented in a larger assembly.

With all of these differing views among the Allies regarding what should be accomplished at the Paris Peace Conference, the conference represented a negotiating session between and among the Allies over the peace terms to offer the Germans and the structure of the league, rather than a negotiating session between the Allies on one side and the Germans on the other. Most of the drama and intrigue at the conference revolved around inter-Allied disputes and compromises. In fact, it was so difficult to work out the settlements among the Allies that, once agreed upon, they had to be presented to the Germans as a single take-it-or-leave-it package, because a modification of one or another territorial provision could unravel the bargains that had been struck among the Allied powers.

After the armistice, Britain had acquired the German merchant fleet. The existing war blockade had been extended by severing shipments across the Baltic from Norway and Sweden, and the food blockade became a major weapon to force Germany to sign whatever treaty the Allies generated at Paris. So when the Allies presented the final treaty to the German representatives, the Germans faced the choice of signing or starvation and possibly a humiliating invasion and occupation by the Allies.

THE CONFERENCE

The Paris Peace Conference convened on January 18, and, at its second plenary session a week later, the delegates accepted a resolution proposed by Wilson to make the covenant of the League of Nations an integral part of the peace treaty. Wilson believed the League of Nations to be more important than the specific geographic boundary issues and the specific economic aspects of the reparations agreements. In his numerous speeches throughout this period he made it clear that he believed the specifics could be altered on a more just basis later with a league in place to make the adjustments.

Although he studied the maps of Europe and ethnic statistics in great detail before agreeing to boundary changes, none of those changes reflected an interest of the United States; from his point of view, the American objective was a lasting peace. In one sense, the bargain he struck with the other delegates exchanged his consent to boundaries that they desired for the other Powers' acceptance, at least in part, of the principle of self-determination and their agreement to a permanent league. The precise redrawing of the maps of Europe and the Middle East and the parceling out of former German colonies as league mandates to the other colonial powers had very little bearing on American interests.

Considering that the United States had no territorial claims, one might have expected the settlements to go rather quickly. However, in the months from January through June, the conference struggled through several highly charged debates, at first in public session, and then, at more length, behind closed doors. Despite the fact that the conference barred newsmen from many separate meetings and discussions, the later publication of dozens of memoirs, diaries, and collections of letters reveal some of the complex exchanges.

Several of the issues came very close to breaking up the conference. These included the French demand for German territory on the western side of the Rhine and then later the Saar mining region, Italian demands for control over the port of Fiume, and Japanese claims to Tsingtao (Shantung). Other boundary disputes regarding Poland, Jugo-Slavia, and Romania, as well as the American insistence on a clause regarding the Monroe Doctrine in the league covenant, produced long, drawn-out debates. Several delegations threatened or made actual walkouts. On April 7, in order to move the French along to a decision that would limit their occupation of the German Rhineland, Wilson threatened to return to the United States. That threat helped produce an agreement. Then, two weeks later, when Wilson appealed to the Italian people to reject their government's claim to Fiume, the Italian delegation walked out, boycotting the next few weeks of the conference.

In exchange for a commitment on the part of the French to limit their occupation of the Rhineland to a maximum of 15 years, with some zones to be occupied for lesser periods of five or 10 years, Wilson agreed to a separate treaty in which the United States and Britain would come to the aid of France if invaded by Germany. The status of Fiume shifted several times over the next years, finally taken over by Italy in 1924. The Japanese obtained concessions in China, but did not acquire the remaining years of the German "lease" on Shantung as they had expected under their agreement with the British.

The French expected that damage to their cities, towns, and villages, like this one in Varennes, would be fully paid for by German reparations. *(National Archives)*

PROVISIONS REGARDING GERMANY

In addition to ceding Alsace-Lorraine to France, Germany had to accept several other losses of territory. The treaty shifted a section of German land to Poland so that Poland gained access to the sea through a corridor. The delegates at the conference agreed that Danzig, formerly a German port on the Baltic, should become a free city, through which Poland could gain access to the sea, but where the German population could govern locally. The Polish Corridor had the effect of isolating East Prussia from the rest of Germany. The treaty terms required that Austria, although made up of a German-speaking population, not be allowed to join with Germany nor have more than a very small army. The treaty also limited Germany's army, allowing no aircraft or tanks, and the German navy could have only up to 12 ships and no submarines. Germany had already turned over to the Allies all its artillery, tanks, aircraft, naval ships, most of the merchant marine and larger fishing vessels, and much of its railroad equipment. On top of these armistice transfers, Article 231 of the treaty required that Germany accept both responsibility and guilt for the loss and damage that its aggression had caused and reparations for damages, which would entail cash transfers. From the point of view of France and Britain, which had each lost more than a million men to German arms, the limitations on German rearmament seemed appropriate, perhaps even mild.

Reparations themselves posed an even more difficult issue, and the resolution, in the view of some observers, such as economist John Maynard Keynes, could destroy the German economy and lead to further international disasters. The armistice included only a vague statement that Germany would accept responsibility for reparation of damage done. But at the peace conference, Britain and France claimed that Germany should be responsible for the total cost of the war incurred by them, including pensions and benefits to their veterans.

The Paris conference delegates summoned German representatives to Versailles on June 16 and presented them with the treaty. Although clearly outraged at its provisions, the Germans had little choice and, after a week's delay, signed the Treaty of Versailles June 23, 1919.

LINGERING DISSATISFACTION

Because the Versailles Treaty represented a series of rough compromises, all the major participants in the peace conference had reason to be disappointed. From the point of view of idealists in the United States who believed that the Fourteen Points should be the basis of peace, the conference fell far short of expectations. The Versailles Treaty itself had been worked out behind closed doors, rather than openly arrived at, as promised in the Fourteen Points. The geographical settlements repeatedly violated the principle of self-determination, most notoriously in honoring the secret treaties granting the German-speaking Tyrol to Italy and Arab lands under mandates to Britain and France and in denying Austrians the possibility of unification with Germany. The war-guilt clause in the treaty, Article 231, clearly violated the spirit ozilson's prearmistice agreement with Germany that the peace would be based on the Fourteen Points.

On the other hand, both conservatives and liberals in the United States believed that American troops, who had fought and died in an effort to create a new order under which peace would be preserved, had died in vain. Many believed the treaty and the league covenant served only to strengthen the old order. The British had successfully stopped any treaty protection of freedom of the seas, the original cause for American participation. Republican leaders in the

Two French refugees return home and consider the war cost. (*National Archives*)

United States, already frustrated at Wilson's idealism and his exclusion of them from the conference, believed he had been duped by the British and French into accepting a treaty based on old-order, Great Power politics, rather than a new and just arrangement.

British conservatives who believed Germany should be made to pay for the war felt dissatisfied because Germany remained a major power in central Europe, while British liberals believed the treaty too harsh in ceding territories to France, in preventing the union of German-speaking Austria with Germany, and in other provisions. French conservatives fumed because they saw no guarantee of French security in the treaty, while liberals viewed some of the territorial transfers as unjust to Germany. And, of course, the German population resented the terms of the treaty and its assignment of war guilt and costs to Germany. Furthermore, the boundary rearrangements left German-speaking populations under foreign control in Austria, Poland, Czechoslovakia, Lithuania, Danzig, and the Rhineland. Altogether, Germany lost some 13 percent of its prewar territory to other powers. Japan and Italy also believed they had been cheated of rights and territory promised as the price of their participation in the war.

The delegates to the Paris conference left the exact calculation of the appropriate amount to be paid as reparations to an international Reparations Commission, which first scheduled payments of some $56 billion by Germany, later reduced to more manageable amounts. Even though stripped of many of its resources, Germany had emerged from the war with only insignificant war damage compared with such nations as Belgium, France, and Serbia. Trade barriers tended to prevent Germany from paying its reparations through profits on international trade, in effect, forcing Germany into making its payments with any remaining reserves of bullion or outstanding international credits. Furthermore, the new German republic did not impose a tough balanced-budget policy, and, as a consequence, Germany suffered hyperinflation in the immediate postwar years. Critics of the treaty in Germany, Britain, and the United States have tended to blame the harsh reparations terms for the economic crisis in Germany and the subsequent rise of the Nazi party. Closer analysis by some later economic historians has suggested that, with different policies, the German republic might have been able to meet its reparation payment schedule and could have prevented the hyperinflation that destroyed the savings of the German middle class.

AMERICA AND THE LEAGUE

Wilson returned to the United States determined to secure senatorial ratification of the treaty and the covenant of the league, despite clear opposition that developed even before his return. In a round-robin letter signed by 39 senators and senators-elect, the opposition had made it clear that they found the treaty and league likely to engage the United States even more deeply in European politics.

Wilson sent the treaty and the covenant to the Senate on July 10, 1919. Under the U.S. Constitution, ratification of treaties requires a two-thirds vote, but the Senate had divided into three different groups, making debates and votes on the treaty over the next months quite complex. Democrats loyal to Wilson represented a pro-league group. Most Republicans followed the lead of Henry Cabot Lodge, believing that the league could be accepted with modifications or reservations. A smaller group, made up of Republicans, some of whom had been Progressives, such as Robert La Follette and Hiram Johnson, opposed the league with or without reservations. This later group, *the irreconcilables,* although rejecting the treaty and the league entirely, sided with the Wilson faction to defeat the treaty with Lodge reservations attached.

Wilson insisted that the treaty and the league be voted on together in a single package, which seemed illogical to Robert Lansing and to other Wilson supporters. Wilson, however, had made it clear that he regarded the treaty with its boundary adjustments as a temporary settlement that could be effective only if coupled with a league that could revise and adjust its terms as required over the coming years. Wilson also presented, independently of the league and covenant package, the separate treaty with France that offered protection in case of an invasion by Germany, which he had promised to Clemenceau. That treaty never came to a vote before the Senate.

In order to win popular support for the Versailles Treaty, Wilson began a speaking tour through the midwestern and western states on September 3, 1919, starting in Indiana and moving on to Iowa and eventually to Colorado by late September. Altogether he gave 37 speeches in 29 different cities. Although respectful and interested crowds greeted Wilson as he appealed over the heads of the senators directly to their constituents, the divisions within the Senate seemed largely unchanged. On September 25, after speaking at Pueblo, Colorado, Wilson experienced a breakdown, and his personal doctor, Admiral Cary Grayson, ordered him back to Washington. A week later, on October 2, Wilson suffered a stroke that left him partially paralyzed and from which he never fully recovered.

A minor difficulty then developed in early October when Robert Lansing asked the other cabinet members to consider whether they should declare the president incapacitated. Several cabinet members, as well as Dr. Grayson, opposed any such move, scandalized that Lansing should suggest it. Later, when Wilson heard of the discussion, he asked for Lansing's resignation. Meanwhile, from his confinement in the White House, Wilson continued to direct the strategy for gaining ratification of the treaty and the covenant by the Senate. However, he insisted that Democrats loyal to him refuse any reservations to, or modifications of, the treaty, on the grounds that it had already been negotiated and that any adjustment would require that the other Allies be consulted. In fact, British and French diplomats made it clear that minor reservations or clarifications by the Senate would not prevent admission of the United States to the league or require reconsideration of the treaty by their own legislatures.

As a consequence of Wilson's policy of no reservations, each time the treaty came to a vote, it failed to get the two-thirds support required. When put up for a vote on November 19, 1919, without reservations, only the Wilson Democrats supported it. When proposed with reservations on March 19, 1920, some 21 Democrats deserted the Wilson position to vote with the Lodge Republicans. Even so, they could not muster enough votes to ratify the treaty and league with the two-thirds majority required. The loyalty of about 20 Democrats to Wilson's no-reservation position, coupled with the vote of their die-hard irreconcilable opponents, prevented the United States from signing the treaty or joining the League of Nations.

In the election of 1920, the Democratic candidate, James Cox (with Franklin Roosevelt as running mate for vice president), promised that he would make every effort to join the league if elected. However, Republican Warren Harding, who expressed no position on the league, defeated Cox in the general election. After Harding's election, he remarked that the issue of the league was as dead as slavery, and then he declared in February 1923 that the United States would not be interested in joining. The league convened and met in Geneva, Switzerland, without U.S. representation, although, gradually, through the 1920s, American representatives did participate in some league-sponsored meetings and organizations.

A PEACE WITHOUT PEACE OR DEMOCRACY

Although many Americans had believed, with Wilson, that the Great War would bring an end to wars, the peace settlement of 1919 left so many nations dissatisfied and so many issues unresolved that Europe, Asia, and the Middle East rumbled with war, revolution, land-grabs, passive resistance strikes, and bloody disruptions over the next decades. In a continuing legacy of boundary disputes and conflicts, the 20 years between 1919 and 1939, while often perceived as the interwar years, became in fact a period of continuing wars. No great alliances fought against each other, but frequent, short wars between two nations flared up. Several specific issues and territorial adjustments in the Versailles Treaty lay at the heart of these disputes, while dozens of other conflicts arose, as Lansing had predicted, out of conflicting claims of self-determination.

In 1919 Greek occupation of Izmir (Smyrna) in Turkey helped bring Kemal Ataturk to power in Turkey. In 1920, Turkey seized the region around Kars from the Republic of Armenia, and the remaining territory of the short-lived Armenian republic came under Soviet control. Under Ataturk's leadership, Turkey expelled the Greeks in 1922. Under the 1923 Treaty of Lausanne, Greeks from Smyrna moved to Greece, while some of the Turkish population of Greek territory moved to Turkey.

Armed intervention by Japan, France, Britain, and the United States into the Soviet Union continued during the period 1918–21. The Russo-Polish war of 1920–21 ended with the Peace of Riga on March 21, 1921, which temporarily resolved some of the boundary questions by dividing the Ukraine and Belorussian areas between the two countries. Clearly, the war to end wars had left a legacy of new wars.

Some other bitter disputes simmered, but did not immediately lead to pitched battles between armies. In 1921, a League of Nations plebiscite divided Upper Silesia between Poland and Germany, with the industrial southern section joining Poland. The German province of Posen became Polish Poznan. In 1923, in order to enforce control, the French occupied the Ruhr district of Germany. Italy obtained Fiume in January 1924 under a treaty in which it abandoned to Yugoslavia (or Jugoslavia as it was then known) its claims to Dalmatia. In 1925, French troops evacuated Westphalia in Germany and in the same year bombarded Damascus in Syria to suppress Arab resistance. After a decade of turbulence and resistance to British governance of Mesopotamia (now Iraq), Britain accepted Iraqi independence in 1930.

From the American viewpoint, the war had also been fought to make the world safe for democracy. The effect seemed almost the opposite. Across Europe and the Middle East, a host of dictatorships emerged in the years following the

Versailles Treaty, often drawing their strength from the nationalistic conflicts unresolved by the treaty. The list of autocratic and dictatorial regimes that thrived on such nationalistic claims included, among others, those of King Ibn Saud in Arabia (1919), Admiral Horthy as regent in Hungary (1920), Mussolini in Italy (1922), Ataturk in Turkey (1923), Pilsudski in Poland (1926), Stalin in the Soviet Union (1927), King Zog in Albania (1928), King Alexander in Yugoslavia (1929), and of course Hitler in Germany (1933). France and Britain, while retaining representative government at home, administered their mandates over the former German colonies much as they did their other colonies, with a minimum of consultation with the local population, and frequently with the application of armed force. With few exceptions, autocratic regimes also ruled the independent states in Latin America and Asia through these years. The world had become *unsafe* for democracy after Versailles.

Although negotiation, plebiscite, and other mechanisms envisaged under League of Nations auspices solved some territorial sovereignty issues, others continued to rankle, leaving a legacy of bitterness and conflict. Disputes over ethnic Germans living in Austria and Czechoslovakia, and over the situation of Danzig, Memel in Lithuania, and in the Polish Corridor provided a basis for claims by Germany in the 1930s. Efforts to appease those demands by liberals in Britain and France only infuriated conservatives who saw in them a pattern of unjustified aggression by Nazi Germany. The conflicts over Poland led, in 1939, to the outbreak of World War II in Europe. Meanwhile, Japan evacuated the Tsingtao region (Shangtung) in 1922 in accord with the Versailles Treaty. However, Japan fortified the Pacific islands acquired from Germany as a League of Nations mandate through the 1920s and 1930s, and then seized the Chinese province of Manchuria in 1931 and much of northeastern China by 1937.

When viewed in the light of such events, the period of the 1920s and 1930s did not represent a peaceful interlude between the First World War and the Second, but an era of unresolved territorial disputes, dictatorships that thrived on bitterness, and simmering conflicts. Some of those disputes flared into short wars, while others glowed like embers, ready to ignite another vast future conflagration.

CHRONICLE OF EVENTS

1918

November 11: The Allies and Germany sign the armistice at Compiègne.

December 13: Woodrow Wilson arrives at Brest, France, to participate in the peace conference.

December 30: Wilson delivers a speech at Manchester, Britain.

1919

January 3: Wilson delivers a speech in Rome and is made an honorary citizen of the city.

January 4: Wilson is made a member of the Academy of the Lencei, Rome.

January 5: At Genoa, Italy, Wilson delivers a speech at the monument to Mazzini, another at the town hall on being made a citizen of the city, and another at the monument to Columbus.

January 5: Wilson delivers four speeches in Milan, Italy.

January 6: Wilson delivers five speeches at Turin, Italy. Several of these speeches in Italy are spontaneously delivered from balconies to crowds gathered in the plazas below.

January 18: Allied leaders meet in Paris to decide on the terms of the peace treaty with the Central Powers. Wilson addresses the first plenary session.

January 20: Wilson speaks to the senate of the French republic at the Luxembourg Palace in Paris.

January 25: The Paris conference second plenary session votes to include the League of Nations covenant in the peace settlement. Wilson is selected to head the commission to draft the covenant.

January 25: Wilson addresses the working women of France.

February 3: Wilson addresses the French chamber of deputies.

February 3–14: Wilson heads the commission at the peace conference to draft the covenant of the League of Nations.

February 14: Wilson presents the draft covenant of the league to the peace conference.

February 19: A would-be assassin shoots French prime minister Clemenceau but fails to kill him.

February 24: Wilson arrives in Boston on his first return to the United States and delivers a public speech in favor of the League of Nations.

March 2: Thirty-nine U.S. senators (including two senators-elect) sign a round-robin rejecting the League of Nations.

March 4: Wilson addresses a public meeting at the Metropolitan Opera House in New York regarding the League of Nations.

March 13: Wilson returns to France. He works out a compromise with the French in which the United States and Britain agree to defend France if France is attacked by Germany; in exchange, France agrees to a term-limit to its occupation of the Rhineland: The French defense treaty will never be approved by the U.S. Senate.

March 21: Hungary is declared a Soviet republic, headed by Bela Kun. The socialist regime will be overthrown by outside intervention in August. The restored monarchy will be governed by a dictatorship, with Admiral Nicholas Horthy de Nagybanya as regent, from 1920 to 1944.

April 7: Wilson threatens to leave the conference.

April 11: Geneva, Switzerland, is chosen as headquarters for the League of Nations.

April 14: Wilson asks the Italian delegation to the peace conference to renounce claims to Fiume.

April 23–May 5: The Italian delegation leaves the conference because its claims to Fiume are not accepted.

April 23: Wilson appeals directly to the Italian people to insist that they renounce claims to Fiume.

April 28: Wilson accepts Japanese demands to acquire all German rights in Shantung. At the Peace Conference fifth plenary session, Wilson moves the adoption of the covenant of the league as amended. The treaty incorporates so many compromises that changes negotiated by the Germans or in the process of ratification by the Allies are made difficult.

April 29: The German delegation to Versailles is brought to Paris and confined behind barbed wire; the delegation is headed by Count Ulrich von Brockdorff-Rantzau.

May: Ibn Saud, leader of the Muslim Wahabi movement in Arabia, defeats Hussein, king of Hejaz.

May 7: The Germans are presented with the Versailles Treaty and ordered to respond only in writing.

May 7: German colonies in the Pacific north of the equator are distributed to Japan and those south of the equator to Britain, New Zealand, and Australia.

May 15: Greek troops occupy Smyrna, and Italian troops land on the Anatolian mainland of Turkey.

June 16: Germans are told they have seven days to sign the peace treaty or face resumption of hostilities.

June 19: Wilson delivers four addresses in Brussels, Belgium.

June 23: Germans agree to sign the Treaty of Versailles.

June 28: The Treaty of Versailles is signed in the Hall of Mirrors at Versailles, establishing a Reparations Commission, declaring German responsibility for the war, and establishing limitations on German armaments.

July 8: Wilson returns to the United States.

July 10: Woodrow Wilson sends the Treaty of Versailles and the League of Nations covenant to the U.S. Senate. The final treaty version strips Germany of all overseas colonies. Germany loses Alsace-Lorraine, the Saar Basin (subject to a plebiscite scheduled for 1935), Posen, and parts of Schleswig and Silesia. Reparations will later be set at $56 billion and reduced in later agreements.

The war's devastation was ultimately felt at the personal level. *(Library of Congress)*

July 10–Nov 19: The U.S. Senate debates the league, dividing into three groups: pro-league Democrats; moderates; irreconcilables. Moderates, led by Henry Cabot Lodge, propose a series of reservations.

July 29: Wilson presents a treaty to preserve France against unprovoked attack by Germany (which he had agreed to on March 13 in order to limit French occupation of German territory to a period of years). This treaty never comes to a vote.

September: The Italian poet Gabriele D'Annunzio leads a force that seizes control of the city of Fiume.

September 3: Woodrow Wilson begins a speaking tour through the western United States to promote the Versailles Treaty and the League of Nations. The first cities on the tour will be Columbus, Ohio, and Richmond and Indianapolis, Indiana (September 4) and St. Louis, Missouri (September 5).

September 6: Continuing his tour, Wilson speaks in Des Moines, Iowa.

September 10: By the Treaty of St. Germain-en-Laye, the Austro-Hungarian Empire is abolished, and the Republic of Austria is established; Austria recognizes the new states of Poland, Czechoslovakia, Yugoslavia, and Hungary; Austria's army is limited to 30,000, with no air force or navy; Austria is prohibited from joining with Germany; Austria accepts partial war guilt.

September 25: Wilson suffers a breakdown at Pueblo, Colorado, while on a speaking tour promoting the league and the Versailles Treaty.

October 2: Wilson suffers a stroke; he makes no further public appearances.

October 6: Robert Lansing calls a cabinet meeting to consider disqualifying Wilson to serve as president. Dr. Cary Grayson, Wilson's physician, and other cabinet members reject Lansing's suggestion.

October 13: France ratifies the Treaty of Versailles.

October 15: Britain and Italy ratify the Treaty of Versailles.

October 28: Over Wilson's veto, the Volstead Act is passed, enforcing the 18th Amendment to the U.S. Constitution prohibiting the sale of alcoholic beverages.

October 30: Japan ratifies the Treaty of Versailles.

November 6: Senator Henry Cabot Lodge proposes 14 reservations to the covenant of the League of Nations.

November 18: Wilson urges Democrats to reject the treaty with the proposed Lodge reservations.

November 19: The U.S. Senate rejects the Treaty of Versailles (without reservations) by a vote of 38-53;

the Lodge reservationists and the irreconcilables vote together.

November 27: Under the Treaty of Neuilly, Bulgaria gives up its access to the Aegean Sea to Greece.

December 10: Romanian troops withdraw from Hungary after suppressing the Hungarian Socialist Republic under Bela Kun.

1920

January 20: A British mandate over German East Africa is established as Tanganyika; German colonists are deported and their lands confiscated.

February: Admiral Nicholas Horthy is appointed regent for the king under a restored monarchy in Hungary.

February 15: U.S. secretary of state Lansing resigns; he is replaced by Bainbridge Colby.

March 11: The national congress in Syria proclaims Feisal I as monarch.

March 19: Twenty-one Wilson Democrats agree to vote for the treaty with the Lodge reservations, over the objections of Wilson; the treaty with the Lodge amendments is defeated. Loyal Wilson Democrats and the irreconcilables join in voting against the treaty.

April 18: The Conference of San Remo sets the terms for the peace treaty with Turkey.

April 24: The British are granted a mandate over Palestine and Trans-Jordan by the Supreme Allied Council.

May 20: Congress, by a joint resolution, declares the World War over. Wilson vetoes the resolution.

June 4: Under the Treaty of Trianon, Hungary loses most of its land and population to Romania and other lands to Czechoslovakia and Yugoslavia. Its army is limited to 35,000, and it accepts partial war guilt.

June 22: The Greek-Turkish war begins with Greek attacks in European Turkey and Anatolia.

July–December: Insurgents fight against British occupation of Mesopotamian territory (now Iraq).

July 24: French troops occupy Damascus and depose Feisal I as king of Syria.

August: Under the Treaty of Sèvres, Turkey accepts the loss of Arab lands to British and French mandates, and of lands in Europe to Greece, accepts Armenian independence, and renounces claims to non-Turkish lands. This treaty will be superseded by the Treaty of Lausanne in 1923, which will recognize Turkish control of Armenia and Greek departure from Smyrna.

August 26: The Nineteenth Amendment to the U.S. Constitution goes into effect, granting women suffrage.

November 2: Warren Harding, Republican, defeats Democratic nominee James Cox in presidential elections in the United States. Cox's running mate as candidate for vice president is Franklin D. Roosevelt.

November 12: Under the Treaty of Rapallo, Italy obtains Zara, renounces claims to other Dalmatian lands, and recognizes the independence of Fiume. The Fiume state is taken over by Mussolini for Italy in 1924.

December 2: By the Treaty of Alexandropol, Armenia cedes half its territory to Turkey.

December 3: The remnants of Armenia are declared a Soviet republic.

December 15–22: The Brussels conference establishes the rate of German war reparations, which will extend over 42 years.

1921

March 4: Warren G. Harding is inaugurated as president of the United States.

EYEWITNESS TESTIMONY

I had a conference this noon with the President at the White House in relation to the Peace Conference. I told him frankly that I thought the plan for him to attend was unwise and would be a mistake. I said that I felt embarrassed in speaking to him about it because it would leave me at the head of the delegation, and I hoped that he understood that I spoke only out of a sense of duty. I pointed out that he held at present a dominant position in the world, which I was afraid he would lose if he went into conference with the foreign statesmen; that he could practically dictate the terms of peace if he held aloof; that he would be criticized severely in this country for leaving at a time when Congress particularly needed his guidance; and that he would be greatly embarrassed in directing domestic affairs from overseas. . . . While this difference of opinion apparently in no way affected our cordial relations, I cannot but feel, in reviewing this period of our intercourse, that my open opposition to his attending the Conference was considered by the President to be an unwarranted meddling with his personal affairs and was none of my business. It was, I believe, the beginning of his loss of confidence in my judgment and advice which became increasingly marked during the Paris negotiations.

Secretary of State Robert Lansing, on November 12, 1918, in his memoir, The Peace Negotiations, *pp. 23–25.*

There is a great voice of humanity abroad in the world just now which he cannot hear is deaf. There is a great compulsion of the common conscience now in existence which if any statesman resist he has gained the most unenviable eminence in history. We are not obeying the mandates of parties or of politics. We are obeying the mandates of humanity. That is the reason why it seems to me that the things that are most often in our minds are the least significant. I am not hopeful that the individual items of the settlements which we are about to attempt will be altogether satisfactory. One has but to apply his mind to any one of the questions of boundary and of altered sovereignty and of racial aspirations to do something more than conjecture that there is no man and no body of men who know just how it ought to be settled. Yet if we are to make unsatisfactory settlements, we must see to it that they are rendered more and more satisfactory by the subsequent adjustments which are made possible.

So we must provide a machinery of readjustment in order that we may have a machinery of good will and of friendship. Friendship must have a machinery.

President Wilson in his address at the Free Trade Hall, Manchester, England, to the Lord Mayor and assembled guests, regarding the impending peace conference, December 30, 1918, in R. S. Baker and William E. Dodd, eds., The Public Papers of Woodrow Wilson: War and Peace: Presidential Messages, Addresses, and Public Papers by Woodrow Wilson, *p. 354.*

December 30, 1918
The more I think about the President's declaration as to the right of "self-determination," the more convinced I am of the danger of putting such ideas into the minds of certain races. It is bound to be the basis of impossible demands on the Peace Congress and create trouble in many lands.

What effect will it have on the Irish, the Indians, the Egyptians, and the nationalists among the Boers? Will it not breed discontent, disorder, and rebellion? Will not the Mohammedans of Syria and Palestine and possibly of Morocco and Tripoli rely on it? How can it be harmonized with Zionism, to which the President is practically committed?

The phrase is simply loaded with dynamite. It will raise hopes which can never be realized. It will, I fear, cost thousands of lives. In the end it is bound to be discredited, to be called the dream of an idealist who failed to realize the danger until too late to check those who attempt to put the principle in force. What a calamity the phrase was ever uttered! What misery it will cause.

Robert Lansing, quoting from his own notes of December 30, 1919, in his memoir, The Peace Negotiations, *pp. 98–99.*

There is a widespread feeling here that the events of the last month greatly cleared the air as regards the Peace Conference, which is now looked forward to much more hopefully than it was at the beginning of December.

It may now be admitted that considerable anxiety then existed as to President Wilson's attitude, which many persons feared would be difficult to accord with the views known to be held by the French Government.

At the same time Clemenceau's own position was thought to be insecure, and there were rumors of a possible difficulty with England over the Syrian question, which a strongly imperialist article on the subject in

Briand's review, La France, and the confident prognostications of his friends that the ex-Premier would be soon a member of the Cabinet did not tend to allay. The situation was further complicated by the uncertainty about the result of the British election, so to speak generally, the best-informed opinion was decidedly tinged with pessimism.

Now things are very different. The President's broadmindedness has created a favorable impression here, and the French were delighted to find that there was no tendency on his part to assume the role of dictator, as some of them had feared.

Clemenceau's striking victory in the Chamber, coupled with Lloyd George's overwhelming majority, has settled the doubts whether they could come to the

British prime minister David Lloyd George came to the peace conference after just winning a vote of confidence in Britain, in contrast to President Woodrow Wilson, whose party had been defeated a week before the armistice. *(Library of Congress)*

Peace Conference armed with mandates from their own peoples.

American journalist Walter Duranty, reporting from Paris on hopes for the upcoming peace conference, January 2, 1919, in "Paris Reassured on Peace Parleys," New York Times, January 3, 1919, p. 1.

I was saying playfully to Mr. Orlando and Baron Sonnino this afternoon that in trying to put the peoples of the world under their proper sovereignties we would not be willing to part with the Italians in the United States. We would not be willing unless they desired it, that you should resume possession of them, because we too much value the contribution that they have made, not only to the industry of the United States but to its thought and to many elements of its life. This therefore, is a very welcome occasion upon which to express a feeling that goes very deep. I was touched the other day to have an Italian, a very plain man, say to me that we had helped to feed Italy during the war, and it went to my heart, because we had been able to do so little. . . . My heart goes out to the little poor families all over this great kingdom who stood the brunt and the strain of the war and gave their men gladly to make other men free and other women and children free.

Woodrow Wilson, January 3, 1919, in Rome, in a toast to the king of Italy and an address of January 3, 1919, as collected in R. S. Baker and William E. Dodd, eds., The Public Papers of Woodrow Wilson: War and Peace: Presidential Messages, Addresses, and Public Papers by Woodrow Wilson, pp. 357–358.

I want to make it clear at the very beginning that we Zionists are animated by no thought of territorial greed or national ambition. Our claims are of the most modest character, and in formulating them we have done the utmost to avoid anything that may cause friction with our prospective neighbors in the Near East.

We ask not for the greater Palestine of Solomon, but simply for the tract of country between our ancient boundaries and to Beersheba, or in modern terms from the River Littoni [Litani, now in southern Lebanon] to El Arish. Westward our limit will be the sea. Eastward it may well be that the new Arabian Kingdom will preclude our extension beyond the River Jordan, which would thus form our eastern boundary.

Otherwise, we feel that the region around Hauran and the desert tract southeastward in the direction of the Gulf of Akaba [the modern Negev] might well be included in our territory. At present it is barren and practically uninhabited, but with irrigation and cultivation it could be restored to its ancient richness and fertility.

In any event, we are on good terms with the King of Hedjaz [Arabia], with whom we have concluded an entente, and it is one of our greatest hopes that a Jewish commonwealth will be a link between the Arabs and Occidental civilization.

Dr. Nahum Sokolow, Jewish Zionist leader [spelled "Sokoloff" in this interview], as interviewed by Walter Duranty in "Plans of Zionists for the New State," New York Times, January 4, 1919, p. 12.

At this meeting . . . the President took up the provisions of his original draft of a Covenant, which was at the time in typewritten form, and indicated the features which he considered fundamental to the proper organization of a League of Nations. I pointed out certain provisions which appeared to me objectionable in principle or at least of doubtful policy. Mr. Wilson, however, clearly indicated—at least so I interpreted his words and manner—that he was not disposed to receive these criticisms in good part and was unwilling to discuss them. He also said with great candor and emphasis that he did not intend to have lawyers drafting the treaty of peace. Although this declaration was called forth by the statement that the legal advisors of the American Commission had been at my request, preparing an outline of [a] treaty, a "skeleton treaty" in fact, the President's sweeping disapproval of members of the legal profession participating in the treaty-making seemed to be, and I believe was, intended to be notice to me that my counsel was unwelcome. Being the only lawyer on the delegation I naturally took this remark to myself, and I know that the other American Commissioners held the same view of its purpose.

Robert Lansing, reporting on a meeting of Wilson with the American Peace Commissioners, January 10, 1919, in Paris, in his memoir, The Peace Negotiations, p. 107.

The American delegation was the only one to present any definite scheme of reparation. The other delegations merely filed general statements to the effect that the war being a wrongful act by Germany, Germany was responsible for all the loss and damage, direct and indirect, which resulted therefrom. . . . The Americans stressed the fact that Germany's capacity of payment could scarcely extend appreciably beyond that needed to meet the American program. Nevertheless the delegations of France, Serbia, and to an extent even of Belgium, did not openly espouse this program, which afforded them a particularly favorable position, chiefly because the program seemed to involve a sparing of Germany against which their public opinion revolted.

Bernard Baruch, economic adviser to the American delegation to the peace conference, comparing the American plan for reparations by Germany with that of Britain on February 2, 1919, in his memoir, The Making of the Reparation and Economic Sections of the Treaty, pp. 20–22.

February 4, 1919

To the supreme Council to hear Venizelos conclude his statement. He talks of Greek claims in Asia Minor. He is again extremely good, but not so logical and effective as he was yesterday. The Italians say a few nice words when it is all over, which is applauded by P.W. [President Wilson]. "Hear! Hear!" says P.W. clapping silent palms. Clemenceau as usual wears the half-smile of an irritated, sceptical and neurasthenic gorilla.

I stay behind a few minutes while they discuss whether they shall appoint a Committee of Experts to examine the Greek claims. Lloyd George proposes it, P.W. seconds it. Clemenceau concludes abruptly— "Objections? . . . Adopté." The Italians gasp, as they do not want a Committee of Experts in the least.

Harold Nicolson, member of the British delegation to the peace conference, in the diary portion of his memoir, February 4, 1919, Peacemaking 1919, pp. 216–217.

Gordon wrote a cable to Tumulty for the President's approval, inviting the Foreign Relations Committee of both the Senate and the House to dine with him as soon as practicable after his arrival, and requesting them to refrain from comment in Congress upon the League of Nations until he had an opportunity to discuss it with them. When I first proposed this several days ago, he declared he would not do it and that the most he would do would be to make an address to Congress. This seemed wholly inadequate because it would not please Congress, since they would take it that he had called them together as a schoolmaster, as they claim he usually does. There would be no chance for discussion, consultation, or explanation, and they would not regard it as a compliment but rather the contrary.

He read the cable [to Tumulty inviting the senators and members of Congress to dinner] that had been prepared and changed only one word. It was sent immediately.

Colonel Edward House, reflecting on Wilson's decision to invite key senators to discuss the peace treaty, February 14, 1919, in his memoir, The Intimate Papers of Colonel House: The Ending of the War, *p. 316.*

I had ample opportunity this morning to go over the entire situation with the President and to get from him his story of his visit to the United States. He said, "Your dinner to the Senate Foreign Relations Committee was a failure as far as getting together was concerned." He spoke with considerable bitterness of the manner in which he was treated by some of the Senators. Knox and Lodge remained perfectly silent, refusing to ask any questions or to act in the spirit in which the dinner was given. However, I said to the President that the dinner was a success from my viewpoint, which was that it checked criticism as to his supposed dictatorship and refusal to consult the Senate about foreign affairs. He admitted this. I said that it also had a good effect upon the people, even if it had failed to mollify the Senators themselves.

Colonel Edward House, March 14, 1919, in his memoir, The Intimate Papers of Colonel House: The Ending of the War, *pp. 385–386.*

. . . when I urged again that some positive report be given out, [Wilson] replied:

"How can we? We have nothing to report. We have accomplished nothing definite, and if I were to tell the truth, I should have to put the blame exactly where it belongs—upon the French."

The pressure was steadily growing heavier—and the President, desperately driven, was beginning to show the physical strain. He was not only sitting with the others in two long sessions daily but he was also trying to meet the criticisms of delay, so far as the Americans were concerned, by holding night sessions of the League of Nations Commission at the Crillon to drive to a conclusion the drafting of the Covenant.

Ray Stannard Baker, head of the American Press Bureau, commenting on the delays in late March 1919 at the peace conference, in his account, Woodrow Wilson and World Settlement: Written from his Unpublished and Personal Material, *vol. 2, p. 27.*

The League for peace, disarmament, and friendly council will take up its residence very shortly in the ancient city of Calvin, and from Geneva on the historic lake the new world polity will be formulated and broadcast to a world that is weary of the old procedures. General Smuts made the motion by arrangement with House and neither a voice was raised nor a vote cast in opposition. The Colonel is pleased with the result and above all with the speed at which it has been reached. As he says, it is "these long talky-talky sessions of the Commission that sap my vitality and bear me down." The President did not open his mouth, but it is evident he is pleased to have the matter settled as it was becoming a breeder of ill feeling. In the early discussion bouts the President opposed the choice of The Hague, which enjoyed support in many quarters, because, as he said, it would revive memories none too happy of the Russian peace movement in the last century. He was more outspoken in his opposition to the choice of Brussels, and many of the things he said have, as usual, leaked out and given great offense.

Colonel Stephen Bonsal, staff member of the U.S. delegation at Paris, March 29, 1919, in his memoir, Unfinished Business, *p. 168.*

On April 7th, the President struggled to his feet and faced the [Paris Peace Conference Supreme] Council in what everyone recognized as a final test of strength. There must be an end to this dreary, interminable business of making agreements only to break them. An agreement must be reached once for all. If a peace of justice, he would remain; if a peace of greed, then he would leave. He had been second to none in recognizing the wrongs of the Allies, the state of mind of their peoples, and he stood as firmly as any for a treaty that would bring guilt home to the Germans, but he could not, and would not, agree to the repudiation of every war aim or to arrangements that would leave the world worse off than before. The *George Washington* was in Brooklyn. By wireless the President ordered it to come to Brest at once.

The gesture was conclusive as far as England and France were concerned. Lloyd George swung over instantly to the President's side. . . .

Wilson's director of the Committee on Public Information, George Creel, reporting on April 7, 1919, quoted in Joseph Tumulty's Wilson as I Know Him, *pp. 350–351.*

When in April the negotiations bogged down and the Paris press, always voicing governmental opinion, was critical of Wilson and his insistence upon the League, which Clemenceau never desired, Wilson almost stunned Paris when he directed me to send the *George Washington* to Brest to take him to the United States. It not only stunned Paris but shocked the people in the United States. Acting Secretary of State Polk understood Wilson better than Private Secretary Tumulty and cabled, "Papers playing up order signifies President's determination to end peace delays." Tumulty had cabled Admiral Grayson that it was accepted at home "as an act of petulance and impatience. . . . withdrawal would be desertion. He should remain until the very last demanding an acceptance of his Fourteen Points. . . . Any necessary sacrifice should be made to get League." Dr. Grayson replied, "The French are the champion time-killers of the world. The *George Washington* has had a castor-oil effect on them all. More progress has been made in the last two days than in two weeks, and if the President's health holds out I am confident he will win handsomely."

Josephus Daniels, April 7, 1919, explaining Wilson's threat to walk out of the peace conference, in his memoir, The Wilson Era, 1917–1923, *pp. 360–361.*

I went up to see President Wilson at 6:30—the first time since he fell ill—and had a long talk. I found him fully dressed in his study, looking still thin and pale. A slight hollowness around the eyes emphasized a characteristic I had often noted before—the size and luminosity of his eyes. . . .

He has reached the point where he will give no further.

"Then Italy will not get Fiume?" I asked.

"Absolutely not—as long as I am here," he said sharply.

"Nor France the Saar?"

"No."

I told him, in urging again that a statement of his position be issued at once, that I believed the great masses of the people were still strongly with him, but were confused and puzzled by hearing every case in the world but ours, and that they would rally again to his support if he told them exactly what the situation was and the nature of his opposition.

"I believe so, too," he said. . . .

I told the President about the effect of his announcement regarding the *George Washington*.

"The time has come to bring this thing to a head," he said. ". . . The whole course of the Conference has

been made up of a series of attempts, especially by France, to break down this agreement, to get territory and to impose punishing indemnities. The only real interest of France in Poland is in weakening Germany by giving Poland territory to which she has no right."

Ray Stannard Baker, commenting on Wilson's view of French and Italian demands at the peace conference. April 7, 1919, in his memoir of the peace conference, Woodrow Wilson and World Settlement: Written from his Unpublished and Personal Material, *vol. 2, pp. 59–60.*

. . . I was called into another conference over Fiume. The President had received our personal letter protesting against any compromise which would give it to the Italians even under nominal form, and sent us a very cordial answer. But it was rather vague. He thanked us for "reinforcing his judgment," but didn't say that he approved our advice. The situation is complex. The three Commissioners—Lansing, White, and Bliss—are kept out of the matter entirely. They feel very strongly against granting Italian sovereignty over Fiume and yesterday sent a memorandum to Wilson to this effect. But whether or not this will have any impact remains to be seen. Actually they are exercising little more influence on events than we are, if as much. House claims that he agrees with us in principle, but that his hands are tied. Actually, I think that he is behind the President in making any sacrifice in order to get full support from Italy for the League.

So you have Wilson and House deciding everything, the six of us territorial specialists and the three Commissioners being bitterly opposed to yielding. The French and British are simply waiting on Wilson's decision.

Historian and staff member of the U.S. delegation to the Paris Peace Conference, Charles Seymour, in a letter dated April 19, 1919, describing pressures regarding Fiume in his collection of correspondence, Letters from the Paris Peace Conference, *pp. 206–207.*

The President's famous public statement had been most carefully prepared—written out on his own typewriter. On the afternoon of April 23, Admiral Grayson brought it by hand to the Press Bureau and told me that the President wished it given the widest possible publicity. We put it out at once. . . .

This statement which was about 1,200 words in length, set forth with great clarity the President's position. He said that while Italy had entered the war on "a definite but private understanding ... now known as the Pact of London," the whole circumstances had now changed. ... He then cited the fact that the nations had adopted "certain clearly defined principles" at the Armistice upon which "the whole structure of peace must rest." On the basis of those principles "Fiume must serve as the outlet and inlet of the commerce, not of Italy, but of ... Hungary, Bohemia, Roumania, and the states of the new Jugo-Slavic group."

The memorandum contained nothing that the President had not been long struggling for in the Councils; but the sensation caused by its publication was tremendous. The Old Order gasped, while a shiver of reviving hope swept through the drooping ranks of the supporters of the New. ...

The Italians declared loudly that Wilson was not playing the game, that he was going over the heads of the authorized representatives of the Italian nation in a demagogic appeal subversive of all principles of organized government.

Ray Stannard Baker, on the reaction to Wilson's April 23, 1919, appeal regarding Fiume, in his account, Woodrow Wilson and World Settlement: Written from his Unpublished and Personal Material, *vol. 2, pp. 168–169.*

On April 23 [Wilson] issued to the Press a statement of his own views on the Fiume problem, in which he appealed, not without his old eloquence, to the heart of Italy against the brain of the Italian Delegation in Paris. The next day Signor Orlando left Paris in dramatic, although somewhat prearranged, indignation. And the emotions of the Italian people founted in passionate abuse of President Wilson. "Either Fiume," they yelled, "or death." The President had appealed both to his principles and to The People. And the latter gnashed their teeth at him in rage. He was much discouraged. From that moment he seems to have abandoned all hope of imposing his doctrines on the false democracies of Europe.

Harold Nicolson, commenting on the Italian reaction to Wilson's rejection of Italian claims to Fiume on April 23, 1919, in his memoir, Peacemaking, 1919, *p. 182.*

Orlando's departure has caused a flutter. The Japanese are also threatening to go. The *"Temps"* heads its leading article, *"Le voyage de M. Orlando."* In effect he will come back. The Italians have made the mistake of being obstructive and untruthful. They hoped by opposing everything all along the line to obtain a snap decision at the end. The snap has come all right—but not of the sort they wanted. They must now either climb down and creep back to Paris or else break with their allies. The whole business in the end will increase the prestige of the Conference and of Wilson personally. Of course the Italian feeling against the latter is now almost hysterical, and I gather that at the Gare de Lyon when Orlando left there were cries of "Abasso [down with] Wilson!"

Harold Nicholson, April 25, 1919, in the diary section of his memoir, Peacemaking, 1919, *p. 315.*

We are thinking about little except the declaration of the President on the Adriatic and the withdrawal of the Italians from the Conference. I am hoping that you have enough facts about the problem at home to get the right and wrong of it; but everything that I have seen in the press is so confused that I am worried as to public opinion in America.

As I wrote last week, the gist of the matter is that the Italians have tried to blackmail the Conference into granting unjust demands which if approved would certainly lead to war with the Jugoslavs. Part of the Italian claims had been promised in the Treaty of London by France and England, and they have to keep to their promise, although their representatives have told us that they regard the bargain as iniquitous and hoped that we could get them out of it. Fiume was not included in the promise and France and England are standing with us in refusing it to Italy; but they are letting us take all the blame for the trouble with Italy. Still this cannot be helped and I am glad that our nation is the one that takes its public stand for what is right.

Charles Seymour, in a letter dated April 25, 1919, in his collection of correspondence, Letters from the Paris Peace Conference, *pp. 209–210.*

One question is on every lip: have we made the world safe for Democracy? Time alone will bring the answer. Fresh from my contacts with the peacemakers, I am not optimistic. I recall the eloquent words with which the President announced to Congress in February 1918 the purpose and the plan of his world crusade. He said: "We fight for a new International Order; without that new Order at the end of the war the world would be without peace." Well it can only be asserted while the battle is not won the struggle continues.

Col. Stephen Bonsal, staff member of the U.S. delegation, April 30, 1919, commenting on whether the peace treaty will make the world safe for democracy, in his memoir of his missions to Europe after World War I, Unfinished Business, *p. 217.*

. . . a secretary had placed before Count Brockdorff-Ranzau a copy of the . . . Treaty. He gave it a single glance but let it lie untouched. Although actual discussion of the terms was to be entirely in writing the leader of the German delegation had this one opportunity to address the former enemies of Germany face to face. He did not, for some inexplicable reason, rise from his seat as Clemenceau had done, and thus, at the very start, offended the proprieties and placed himself and the German delegation at a disadvantage. He spoke slowly, and sentence by sentence his words were interpreted.

"We are under no illusion as to the extent of our defeat and the degree of our want of power. We know that the power of the German arms is broken."

Beginning upon this sullen and defiant note he insured the worst possible reception for his remarks. It was a remarkable exhibition of the want of tact. He called into question the good faith of the statesmen opposite him at the start, referring to the "power of the hatred which we encounter here" and the "passionate demand that the vanquishers may make us pay." Then he attacked the whole basis of the Peace as drafted by denying Germany's responsibility for the war. Admitting that the former government "have certainly contributed to the disaster," he added: "But we energetically deny that Germany and its people, who were convinced that they were making a war of defence, were alone guilty."

Ray Stannard Baker, May 7, 1919, in his account of the position of the German signatories to the peace treaty, in Woodrow Wilson and World Settlement: Written from his Unpublished and Personal Material, *vol. 2, p. 27.*

You have made me deeply happy by the generous welcome you have extended to me. But I do not believe that the welcome you extend to me is half as great as that which I extend to you. Why, Jerseyman though I am, this is the first time I ever thought Hoboken beautiful. I really have, though I have tried on the other side of the water to conceal it, been the most homesick man in the American Expeditionary Force, and it is with feel-

ings that it would be vain for me to try to express that I find myself in this beloved country again.

Wilson's address in Carnegie Hall, New York, July 8, 1919, after his return from the Paris Peace Conference, in "City Gives Warm Greeting," New York Times, *July 9, 1919, p. 1.*

The only people I owe any report to are you and the other citizens of the United States.

And it has become increasingly necessary, apparently, that I should report to you. After all the various angles at which you have heard the treaty held up, perhaps you would like to know what is in the treaty. I find it very difficult in reading some of the speeches that I have read to form any conception of the great document. It is a document unique in the history of the world for many reasons, and I think I cannot do you a better service, or the peace of the world a better service, than by pointing out to you just what this treaty contains and what it seeks to do.

In the first place, my fellow countrymen, it seeks to punish one of the greatest wrongs ever done in history, the wrong which Germany sought to do to the world and to civilization; and there ought to be no weak purpose with regard to the application of the punishment. She attempted an intolerable thing, and she must be made to pay for the attempt. The terms of the treaty are severe, but they are not unjust. I can testify that the men associated with me at the Peace Conference in Paris had it in their hearts to do justice and not wrong. But they knew, perhaps, with a more vivid sense of what had happened than we could possibly know on this side of the water, the many solemn covenants which Germany had disregarded, the long preparation she had made to overwhelm her neighbors, and the utter disregard which she had shown for human rights, for the rights of women, of children, of those who were helpless. . . .

Look even into the severe terms of reparation—for there was no indemnity. No indemnity of any sort was claimed, merely reparation, merely paying for the destruction done, merely making good the losses so far as such losses could be made good which she had unjustly inflicted, not upon the governments, for the reparation is not to go to the governments, but upon the people whose rights she had trodden upon with absolute absence of everything that even resembled pity. . . .

. . . this treaty was not intended merely to end this war. It was intended to prevent any similar war. I wonder if some of the opponents of the League of Nations have forgotten the promises we made to our people before we went to that peace table. We had taken by process of law the flower of our youth from every household, and we told those mothers and fathers and sisters and wives and sweethearts that we were taking those men to fight a war which would end business of that sort; and if we do not end it, if we do not do the best that human concert of action can do to end it, we are of all men the most unfaithful, the most unfaithful to the loving hearts who suffered in this war, the most unfaithful to those households bowed in grief and yet lifted with the feeling that the lad laid down his life for a great thing and, among other things, in order that other lads might never have to do the same thing. That is what the League of Nations is for, to end this war justly, and then not merely to serve notice on governments which would contemplate the same things that Germany contemplated that they will do it at their peril but also concerning the combination of power which will prove to them that they will do it at their peril. . . . The League of Nations is the only thing that can prevent the recurrence of this dreadful catastrophe and redeem our promises.

Woodrow Wilson, addressing the public about the need to obtain Senate ratification of the peace treaty and league covenant at the opening of his western tour, at Columbus, Ohio, September 4, 1919, collected in R. S. Baker and William E. Dodd, eds., The Public Papers of Woodrow Wilson: War and Peace: Presidential Messages, Addresses, and Public Papers by Woodrow Wilson, *pp. 590–593.*

The Bernstorff who stood before me was far from being the "glass of fashion and the mold of form" he had undoubtedly been during the long years of his mission in Washington. His shoes were cracked, his cuffs were frayed, and his trousers—how they needed pressing! Those who were in Washington during the last tense months of his mission (I was in foreign parts) are in agreement that the vast propaganda sums that were placed at Bernstorff's disposal were not all wasted in printing pamphlets or even in blowing up munition plants. Much was spent in furnishing his table with delicacies, and it was conceded that his wines and his cigars were superb. With this reputation in mind I had some natural hesitancy in offering the Ambassador one of my army cigars, a crime of the Service of Supplies, and indeed I only did it in answer to his silent but hungry appeal. (When later, I turned over to him a box more than half full of these stogies, Bernstorff, though long trained to conceal his feelings went to pieces, and the thanks he proffered bordered on the hysterical. . . .)

"The German revolution," explained Bernstorff, "was after all but a disease of demobilization, and we cannot be sure that maladies of this nature have run their course or that our people can be said to be immune to a recurrence in the near future. . . ."

Stephen Bonsal, September 25, 1919, reporting on a meeting with the former German ambassador to the United States, Count Johann Bernstorff, in his memoir of his missions to Europe after World War I, Unfinished Business, *p. 222.*

President Warren G. Harding regarded the League of Nations to be as dead as slavery. *(Library of Congress)*

Uncomplainingly the President applied himself to the difficult tasks of the Western trip. While the first meeting at Columbus was a disappointment as to attendance, as we approached the West the crowds grew in numbers and the enthusiasm became boundless. The idea of the League spread and spread as we neared the coast. Contrary to the impression in the East, the President's trip West was a veritable triumph for him and was so successful that we had planned, upon the completion of the Western trip, to invade the enemy's country, Senator Lodge's own territory, the New England States, and particularly Massachusetts. This was our plan, fully developed and arranged, when about four o'clock in the morning of September 26, 1919, Doctor Grayson knocked at the door of my sleeping compartment and told me to dress quickly, that the President was seriously ill. As we walked toward the President's car, the Doctor told me in a few words of the President's trouble and said that he greatly feared it might end fatally if we should attempt to continue the trip and that it was his duty to inform the President that by all means the trip must be cancelled; but that he did not feel free to suggest it to the President without having my cooperation and support. When we arrived at the President's drawing room I found him fully dressed and seated in his chair. With great difficulty he was able to articulate. His face was pale and wan. One side of it had fallen, and his condition was indeed pitiful to behold. . . . Turning to both of us, he said, "Don't you see that if you cancel this trip, Senator Lodge and his friends will say that I am a quitter and that the Western trip was a failure, and the Treaty will be lost." . . . He then tried to move over nearer to me to continue his argument against the cancellation of the trip; but he found he was unable to do so. His left arm and leg refused to function.

Joseph Tumulty, reporting on the collapse of the president after his speech at Pueblo, Colorado, on September 25, 1919, in his memoir, Wilson as I Know Him, *pp. 446–447.*

This volume goes to press as the Allies have concluded a conference with the Germans at Spa. The deliberations there showed the impossibility of having arrived at a perfect solution of reparations in the Paris conference. It is becoming increasingly plain that the reparation clauses were framed to make possible a successful future solution of the problems involved.

As the needs of the Allies are better understood, as Germany's ability to pay is more definitely disclosed, as her willingness to meet her obligations is increasingly manifested, and, above all, as the anger and hatred engendered by the war cool, a wiser solution becomes possible. The final outcome must carry with it the sanction of a public opinion awakened to the needs of the world. The machinery of the Reparation Commission awaits this aroused opinion.

Bernard Baruch, July 1920, commenting on the continuing debate over just reparations by Germany, in his memoir, The Making of the Reparation and Economic Sections of the Treaty, *p. 74.*

12

Lost Generation in the 1920s
1919–1927

The legacy of the war weighed heavily on Wilson, but it also changed the nation and the world. The legacy of World War I could be described in many ways. The most immediate and most tragic came in tallying the sad statistics of war casualties. Each of the major belligerent countries used somewhat different ways to gather casualty statistics, resulting in a wide range of estimates of war dead and wounded. Most estimates placed the direct war dead at about 10 million, with another 21 million dead from the influenza pandemic that spread across the planet. The disease hit India particularly heavily, but millions died in Europe and an estimated 500,000 died in the United States.

The war casualty totals do not include civilian deaths, heavy in both the Armenian holocaust and in the Russian civil war. The fact that the 115,000 American soldiers who died in the war represented a small fraction of the total was of course a result of the short participation of the United States, most of it during the period from February to November 1918.

Some regions of Europe, particularly northwestern France and Belgium, lay in devastated ruin from battles, with whole towns and villages destroyed entirely. Returning veterans included not only the physically wounded but millions whose psychic scars would never heal; what a later generation called post-traumatic stress syndrome, doctors and the public in that era simply called shell shock. Troubled by nightmarish flashbacks to the scenes of horror they had witnessed, many veterans in all the combatant nations could not participate normally in social and economic life.

Even for those who had not fought in the war but who had only witnessed the conflict as noncombatant ambulance drivers, journalists, or even as civilians at home, the horrors of the war left lasting marks. The slaughter had been so widespread and grotesque, and its reasons so illogical and incomprehensible, that a whole generation in Europe and the United States saw the war itself as the most significant event of their lives. As late as the 1970s, for people who lived through the experience, the expression "before the War" meant "before 1914." Even though the casualty figures for the United States seemed quite minor by comparison to the loss of a whole generation of youth in Germany, Austria-Hungary, France, and Britain, America reverberated with profound social, political, and cultural impacts from the war.

301

For Americans and Europeans alike, the war represented the dividing line between a past gone forever and an unfamiliar new order. That new order disturbed and pained some, while to others it represented a liberation or release from constraints. For many of the younger generation, the war freed them from a set of values they called variously "Victorian," "Puritan," or "bourgeois."

A whole generation seemed disillusioned with the Wilsonian ideals, and that disillusionment lay at the heart of the sense of departure from the past in the United States. When Wilson rode away from the White House on the inauguration of Harding in March 1921, it seemed that Wilson's ideas and ideals went with him into the cold. Rather than making the world safe for democracy, governments everywhere seemed attracted to autocratic, centralist methods directly in opposition to the goals of democracy. Furthermore, rather than ending wars, the Great War had produced boundary readjustments and claims to self-determination across Europe and the Middle East that led directly to several bitter wars and appeared to set the stage for another world clash of the major powers.

A War to Make the World Safe for Autocracy

Liberal regimes in Europe and North America had adopted total-war methods: in Germany, Britain, France, and Russia traditions of economic liberalism and laissez-faire gave way to statism; free-enterprise yielded to state control; and, in country after country, the total economy and population became dedicated, through laws and propaganda, to serving national interests. While the transformation to state control that had begun in the war years started later and did not go so far in the United States as in Europe, even so, the Committee on Public Information, the U.S. Railway Commission, the Food Administration, and other federal agencies represented steps in the same direction. In Russia, Germany, and Italy, advocates of state control of the economy (whether Marxist, fascist, or simply autocratic) after the war could point to the precedent of war-induced national administration of the economy. The revolutionary and statist principles of ideologues seemed far less revolutionary in the light of the fact that laissez-faire and the freedom to express varied political viewpoints had already been abandoned by all the major countries participating in the war, even by staunch liberals.

After the war, in many countries, the appeal of state control of the economy and the public mind in the national interest continued to flourish. In the Soviet Union and Italy in particular, the change to a national regime based on such principles came within a few years, under the guise of Marxism-Leninism in the former and Fascism in the latter. When the Great Depression hit in the 1930s, France, Britain, and the United States turned back to state control of the economy in one fashion or another. After struggling through the 1920s under a weak and divided regime, Germany also turned to the statist model in the 1930s. The German people, however, embittered by what they perceived as an unjust and imposed peace that stripped the nation of land, population, and colonies and saddled it with debts, and believing the military had been "stabbed in the back" by socialist politicians, turned to an extreme form of statism in the militaristic, centralized, and totalitarian regime of the Nazi state. Even if Hitler had never emerged as the criminal mastermind of that regime, Germany seems to have been destined to take a militarized and nationalistic course as a consequence of the war.

A War to Spawn Future Wars

In the fields of military and international relations, World War I gave birth to a revanchist Germany, left with much of its industry intact and a bitter population that had heard the message of Ludendorff and other generals and admirals. They had claimed in their memoirs and in their postwar support of the Nazi alternative that with only a better and more concentrated effort on the homefront and a more thorough Prussianism, Germany could have won the war and could win the next. In Italy, Mussolini played on the sense of betrayal at Versailles, arguing that legitimate national aspirations had been stymied by Wilson and the other Allies. In Britain and France, liberals seemed partially convinced that German and Italian claims of injustice in the territorial settlements had fair grounds and gave widespread support to the concept of offering adjustments that would appease the demands of German and Italian leaders. Thus in Europe, World War I clearly gave birth to a set of discontents that would coalesce into World War II. In Asia, many Japanese believed themselves empowered to replace the European colonial regimes in Southeast Asia and their control of China that had been exercised through the policy of spheres of influence, and, by the early 1930s, under an increasingly militant leadership, Japan had embarked on that course.

In the Mideast, the British and French struggled to maintain control of their mandates from the Ottoman Empire. However, Britain departed Iraq after nearly a decade of insurgency in 1932 and used force to try to prevent wholesale Jewish settlement into Israel in the 1930s. The French continued to apply force to keep Syria subservient to French policy. The region remained ripe for struggles among the contending ethnic and religious groups and against the European colonial style of administration of the mandates, leaving a legacy that would simmer and sometimes boil over in the decades to come.

The United States remained aloof from the League of Nations in the 1920s and 1930s, but, nevertheless, even in its isolation the nation still echoed with political, social, and cultural changes brought by the war. With autocratic and dictatorial regimes flourishing in Europe, Wilson's goals and words seemed hollow and naïve. Those who had favored joining the League were disappointed with the failure of the Senate to approve the treaty and the covenant; those who opposed it believed the continuing conflicts in Europe demonstrated only that, if the United States had joined, it would have been immersed in entangling alliances and further sacrifice of American military lives for foreigners' ambitions.

War Legacy in American Politics

Politically, American idealists and liberals found their message had been perverted, their liberties suppressed and replaced by a strident and sometimes mindless patriotic nationalism by the very regime they had elected during the war. The censorship, suppression of civil liberties, and arrest of leaders such as Debs resulted in the left's becoming even more disillusioned in and alienated from the American political scene. The liberal, pro-peace sentiment that had been suppressed and silenced during the war remained embittered. The crackdown on political dissidents, begun during the war years by the Post Office censorship of radical publications and the Justice Department investigation and arrest of socialists and pacifists under the Alien and Sedition Acts, continued through 1919 in what has been described as the first red scare.

Attorney General A. Mitchell Palmer organized a series of simultaneous raids on socialist, Bolshevik, and anarchist political offices and homes on November 7, 1919, and then, in January 1920, in an even wider sweep, officials arrested some 2,700 individuals. This manifestation of an official clampdown on radical thought led to the deportation from the United States of 249 foreign-born radicals (some of whom had become naturalized U.S. citizens), including the anarchists Emma Goldman and Alexander Berkman, aboard the U.S. transport ship *Buford* on December 22, 1919. After a 28-day trip, the deportees landed at Hango, Finland and went by a locked train to the Russian border. Palmer hoped to deport all the others arrested, and, after a series of hearings arranged by the Labor Department, the government deported a total of 600 more. State and local authorities backed up the federal raids (New York State, for example, prosecuted 75 radicals), while in Centralia, Washington, a lynch mob murdered a leader of the I.W.W., Wesley Everett. New York State arrested Benjamin Gitlow, the author of a *Left Wing Manifesto,* and convicted him on a charge of criminal anarchy. In an unrelated case, two Italian immigrants with anarchist backgrounds, Nicola Sacco and Bartolomeo Vanzetti, were arrested and convicted in 1921 of a murder during a payroll robbery. They both claimed to be innocent. The case seemed to represent the hostility of the American establishment to immigrants and radicals, and public debate over the case reflected the bitter persistence of those issues. In the United States and abroad, thousands of supporters firmly believed in Sacco and Vanzetti's innocence, but despite pleas for their pardon and worldwide agony over their apparently unjust conviction, the state of Massachusetts executed them both in 1927.

Although progressives had won their objectives of woman suffrage and Prohibition through constitutional amendments, the women's vote appeared to split much as the male vote had done, although in elections throughout the 1920s, women in most of the country went to the polls in lower percentages than did men. Through the decade, women activists remained divided over whether to push for a broader Equal Rights Amendment to the Constitution to guarantee equality in all spheres of public life or to simply work on using the right to vote.

Prohibition, although it succeeded in reducing access to alcohol by the poor, led to a crime wave as smugglers, bootleggers, and speakeasy operators profited from supplying illegal beer and liquor to those who could afford their prices. The two constitutional amendments, the Eighteenth and Nineteenth, which represented the achievement of specific Progressive goals, had the ironic effect of converting many of the activists who had fought for those changes into conservatives dedicated only to preserving the status quo, which now included votes for women and prohibition of alcohol. In effect, the loose progressive coalition of different reform groups had been stripped of two of its most vocal and well-organized segments by the very fact that those specific goals had been achieved.

In the 1920 election, Harding won the presidency, after expressing no opinion on the treaty or the covenant of the League. He made it clear after his inauguration that he would not support any move to revive those measures. Born and raised in the small town of Blooming Grove, Ohio, Harding came to represent the old-fashioned values of small town America, both for those who admired those values and for intellectuals bent on demonstrating their distance from them.

Harding received credit for inventing he word *normalcy* to define the state to which he sought to return the nation. Writers Sinclair Lewis, Samuel Hopkins Adams, and F. Scott Fitzgerald all used him as a model for characters in later plays or novels. An apparently easygoing, hail-fellow-well-met manner that represented a sharp contrast to the schoolmasterly, intellectual style of Wilson, Harding remained convinced that the defeat of Wilson's cherished League in the Senate meant that, even when his own party held a majority in Congress, a president would be relatively powerless in the field of foreign affairs. Harding's brief administration suffered a tarnished reputation from the exposure of major corruption scandals and influence-peddling. He died of a heart attack and coronary thrombosis in 1923 after a summer trip to Alaska. Vice President Calvin Coolidge succeeded him. The dour former governor of Massachusetts, known as Silent Cal, had earned national fame because he had used the state militia and volunteers to suppress a police strike in Boston.

President Calvin Coolidge, known as Silent Cal, had won fame for putting down a strike by police in Boston. *(Library of Congress)*

Coolidge ran for the presidency in 1924, easily defeating Democrat John W. Davis and Robert La Follette, who ran on a third-party Progressive ticket. For the Democrats, Davis had been the compromise choice after a long, divisive, and bitter battle at the nominating convention between June 24 and July 9, 1924, which took 103 ballots, between Wilson's son-in-law, William McAdoo, and the governor of New York, Al Smith. Davis, with a reputation as a corporate attorney, held little appeal for the Democratic base. The Republicans spent most of their 1924 campaign energies denouncing the third-party candidacy of Robert La Follette by calling him, quite erroneously, an American Bolshevik.

Herbert Hoover, the former mining engineer who had established an international reputation as director of Belgian relief and then as food administrator under Wilson and as director of international relief to Europe after the war, served as secretary of commerce under both Harding and Coolidge. Hoover ran as a Republican for the presidency in 1928, defeating the liberal Democratic Party governor of New York, Al Smith. Although conservative in many regards, Hoover showed ability as a very capable administrator and an exponent of efficient and effective regulation of the economy through impartial commissions of experts selected from industry and academia. He also earned a reputation as a workaholic, and, perhaps unfairly, as unfeeling toward those suffering economic distress.

ISOLATION WITH ENTANGLEMENTS

Together, Harding, Coolidge, and Hoover represented a 12-year conservative Republican regime dedicated to supporting big business, opposing organized labor, restricting immigration, and adopting only moderate programs to help preserve the status quo. These Republican presidents and their supporters called their administration *The New Era,* but the term smacked of considerable irony, for their opponents believed that Republicans looked backward, not forward, for the model for their policies. For the most part, the three Republican presidents of the 1920s did not take an aggressive stand on either domestic or foreign policy. To a great extent their reluctance to be aggressive on international affairs stemmed from their personal predilections. However, the legacy of Wilson's failed effort to manage foreign affairs haunted them and certainly gave grounds and support to any individual reluctance they each may have felt to engage overseas or to manage foreign policy personally. The fact that the Senate had thwarted Wilson on the Versailles Treaty and the League made it clear in the postwar years that presidents alone could not dictate foreign policy. Henry Cabot Lodge chaired the Senate Foreign Relations Committee until his death in 1924; thereafter, through the 1920s, Senator William Borah of Idaho served as chair. Borah and Lodge had very different personalities, but Borah also staunchly opposed the League and any other international agreements that might infringe on his perception of American sovereignty.

Standing aloof from the League and faced with a public opinion highly critical of any entanglements with Europe, America in the 1920s took an isolationist stance. Despite the refusal of the United States to become involved in the League, the legacy of World War I left important issues in the realm of international affairs that the Republican administrations of the era could not entirely ignore. The United States became heavily involved in a series of international conferences devoted to limitations on armaments, beginning with the Washington Naval Conference that took place from November 1921 to February 1922, followed by one in Geneva in 1927 and another in London in 1930. In the United States, advocates of disarmament, many of whom had previously regarded themselves as pacifists, focused on reducing expenditures for naval ships. By contrast, without the major capital investments in weapons platforms such as ships, reductions in army costs could be easily achieved by returning troops to civilian life and reducing payrolls to prewar levels.

Ironically, the advocates of isolation and disarmament had to take the position of demanding that the administration enter into international agreements to get other leading naval powers to reduce their expenditures on ships. The only way to be isolated required diplomatic engagement, it appeared. Senator Borah took the lead in demanding an agreement that would reduce the naval budgets of Britain, France, and the United States by 50 percent. Arrayed against Borah and the isolationists, pro-navalists feared that Japan could represent a threat to American interests in the Pacific, requiring a strong American navy to protect those interests. The Versailles Treaty had confirmed the hold of the Japanese not only in former German holdings in China at Tsingtao (Shantung) but also in the former German-held islands that lay directly between American bases in Hawaii and the Philippines. Faced with isolationists demanding a reduction in the American navy and navalists fearing a threat from Japan, President Harding issued an invitation to Britain, Japan, France, and Italy to a meeting in Washington to discuss both naval disarmament and affairs in the Far East. One of several minor but nagging issues surfaced as part of the agenda for the conference. Wilson believed he had asked at Versailles that the former German-held island of Yap in the Pacific be made an exception to the Japanese control over the mandated islands, because it served as an important cable center. Japan insisted and Great Britain agreed that no such reservation regarding Yap had been stated at Versailles.

At the opening of the Washington Conference in November 1921, Harding's secretary of state, Charles Evans Hughes, who had run for the presidency against Wilson in 1916, proposed a massive reduction in ships. He described a formula to which the conference members eventually agreed after two months of difficult negotiation. Under the formula, the United States and Britain would each have roughly 500,000 tons of major ships, Japan would have 300,000 tons, while Italy and France got the ratio of 1.75 each as compared to the 5 to 5 to 3 for the other major powers. To get to those levels, the United States would scrap or discontinue the construction of more than 800,000 tons of shipping, while Britain would give up more than 580,000 tons and Japan almost 450,000 tons. In one stroke, observers noted, Hughes sank more ships than all the admirals had sunk over several centuries of sea battles. After his stunning proposal, in a process of give-and-take similar to the negotiations at Paris four years earlier, the parties compromised on the limitations on ships and signed several collateral agreements regarding Japanese holdings in Asia and the Pacific, as well as recognition of the right of Japan to retain several specific ships that Hughes had originally scheduled for destruction.

Another international issue that could not be entirely ignored in the United States remained the complex problem of war debts and reparations. Britain and France had specifically tied their schedule of repayment of loans and war credits to the United States to the payment of German reparations, which had been set at the figure of $32 billion by early 1921. Faced with soaring inflation and economic chaos, the German government made it clear by 1922 that it would go into default on the reparations payments. Both Britain and France threatened that, if Germany did not meet the war reparations schedule, they would be forced to occupy Germany and administer its economy to ensure the payments. But, politically, neither country could expect its population to support the sending of an army of occupation into Germany. Temporary French occupation of the Ruhr Valley had led to a general strike and passive resistance on the part of the German population that led the French to seek other sorts of solutions.

The American press and public opinion went into a frenzy of outrage when British and French diplomats suggested that a resolution of the financial mess might be a cancellation or severe reduction of war debts to the United States. Altogether, various foreign government agencies owed the United States more than $12 billion. Politicians, editorialists, and the general public believed that a debt was a debt, due and payable no matter what problems the British and French might be having over reparations. However, because the United States had high tariffs which tended to prevent the import of European goods, payment of such debts had to be made with hard currency or gold, rather than the profits deriving from trade.

In 1924, Secretary Hughes dispatched the American banker, Charles Dawes, to Germany to head a commission that made practical, rather than political, suggestions for resolution of the problem. The group worked from January 14 to April 9, 1924, and generated a proposal known as the Dawes Plan. Without ever explicitly acknowledging the relationship between German reparations payments to Britain and France and their ability to pay their war debts to the United States, Dawes proposed a scheme that all major powers accepted through the following few years. American investors were encouraged to finance public projects through investment in German state and municipal bonds designed to help in the restoration of a viable German economy. To ensure that the system would get off to a good start, President Coolidge personally got the agreement of J.P. Morgan and Company to begin the loans with $110 million of the first $200 million to start the system working. Due to the flow of capital from the U.S. investment community, a circular arrangement was developed that appeared to satisfy all parties: American investors bought apparently solid German bonds with good yields; this money flowed through the German economy and then became available for meeting the reparations schedules; and Britain and France made regular payments on the war debts back to the United States. Over the period 1924–28, Germany borrowed about $1.5 billion and paid reparations of about $1.25 billion. The circular system, which few investors or officials publicly recognized, appeared to work out fine for a few years.

Under a plan established early in 1929 under the chairmanship of Owen D. Young, France and Britain accepted a scaling back of total reparations and a reduction of interest rates. The Young Plan barely got under way, however, when it was overtaken by events. After the Great Crash of 1929, when American capital dried up and German investments appeared less sound, the circular scheme collapsed. Early in the 1930s, Germany defaulted on the reparations, and Britain and France defaulted on the loans.

WAR LEGACY: AMERICAN SOCIAL SHIFTS

During the war, some 10 percent of the African-American population had left the South in a wave of great migration brought on by the labor demand of northern industries and the closing of European immigration. Concentrated in a relatively limited number of northern cities, the swelling population of African Americans began to make itself felt politically by the end of the 1920s. In Chicago, and later in New York and other cities, both Republican and Democratic political machines nominated black candidates for local positions and for Congress, and those candidates began to win office. Republican Oscar De Priest, who ran and won in Chicago in 1928, was the first black man to serve in Congress since 1901.

The consequences of the northward migration for Afro-American cultural and intellectual life ran much deeper than political effects. Through the early 1920s, the Jamaican-born Marcus Garvey revived a form of black nationalism that had great appeal among recent arrivals in northern cities, while less widely known cult and sect leaders built small but devoted followings based on messianic, Muslim, or Jewish religious ideas. Garvey soon fell afoul of federal authorities when he sought to sell shares in a black-owned shipping company, the Black Star Line, and failed to ensure proper handling and administration of the funds that he raised. Arrested in 1923, he served time in the federal penitentiary in Atlanta before being pardoned and deported back to Jamaica in 1927. But Garvey and the minor cult leaders left a legacy of black nationalist thinking that would remain alive in the following decades.

In a very different way, black intellectuals and performers appealed to a growing black population that earned enough to spend money on literature and

entertainment. The consequent Harlem Renaissance and the spread of African-American musical styles and literature gave the era one of its names: the Jazz Age. Black writers, musicians, performers, and artists, including James Weldon Johnson, Countee Cullen, Paul Robeson, and Langston Hughes, soon gained interracial audiences. Intellectuals and other alienated members of the white middle class identified with the African-American sense of being cut off from the mainstream of American life and responded to the alternative culture that black writers and musicians offered. In New York, white writers and artists expressing their rebellion against traditional cultural restraints flocked to speakeasies and Harlem night clubs (as well as to art colonies in New Mexico and California) as recorded in great detail in a diary by the white writer Carl Van Vechten, published years later as *The Splendid Drunken Twenties*. The loose and hectic cultural alliance thus formed between black and white intellectuals would later have political consequences as white liberals gradually came to support the civil-rights goals of black leaders and spokesmen over the next decades.

African-American troops of the 369th Regiment are shown here returning home. Black veterans brought new energy to the quest for equal rights. *(National Archives)*

For women who had advocated the recognition of their status as citizens, the war had a tangible and positive result in the Nineteenth Amendment. However, simply achieving the right to vote did not guarantee social equality, equal legal rights, or equal pay for equal work. Those goals would remain on the agenda of women activists who supported an equal rights amendment for decades to come.

Although the war had provided temporary opportunities for women in new jobs, many of the industrial and service jobs that had opened to women during the labor shortages of the war vanished with the peace. Many women who had worked as bus drivers, aircraft factory hands, railroad employees, and delivery truck drivers during the war had moved up from less well-paying jobs as domestic servants or seamstresses. Many had simply been able to temporarily improve their earning power with higher-paid jobs less susceptible to economic exploitation. When the war ended and men returned from military service, employers simply fired many women in industry, transportation, and the trades. Most had no choice but to return to their former occupations or to unpaid parenting. Nevertheless, the fact that so many young women had been at least temporarily liberated from the control of parents or husbands did leave a psychological legacy of liberation that found expression in such phenomena as the "flapper" image—a young woman whose hair style and clothing reflected an androgynous, rather than traditionally feminine, appearance. Flappers were sufficiently liber-

Ice delivery jobs for women melted away after the men returned from the war. *(National Archives)*

Detroit police break up an illegal brewery in this photo. The criminalization of alcohol consumption had unintended consequences. *(National Archives)*

ated from convention to smoke cigarettes in public and to flout old-fashioned standards of proper behavior in other ways. The older generation expressed shock and dismay.

The great progressive reform of Prohibition soon revealed itself as a failure. Although later analysis has shown that the amendment and the Volstead Act designed to enforce it did have the effect of reducing total alcohol consumption, the widespread flouting of the law and attempts to enforce it created a complex backlash. Since obtaining alcohol required that the consumer break the law by dealing with an illegal enterprise, the amendment had the effect of putting great numbers of otherwise law-abiding individuals in defiance of the law. From 1920 until 1933, Prohibition generated an odd alliance between middle- and upper-class drinkers and elements of the criminal underworld. For those who supported the law, the flouting of Prohibition seemed to demonstrate decadence and collapse of morality; for those who opposed it by continuing to obtain alcohol, the law and its attempted enforcement demonstrated the futility of legislating moral reform and gave their personal habits the imprimatur of a clearly illegal form of rebellion against authority.

WAR LEGACY: CULTURAL DEPARTURES

For Europeans and Americans, the war years represented the end of innocence, a transition from one cultural era to another. Defining that change was no simple matter, partly because of the diversity of reactions against the old order and partly because some of the intellectual and cultural trends that marked the 1920s had been under way well before the war. The postwar generation of young intellectuals and writers included in the United States such diverse individuals as

E. E. Cummings (he began to spell his name "e.e.cummings" in the mid-1920s), Ernest Hemingway, and F. Scott Fitzgerald. Cummings came to represent the hostility to convention and authority, growing out of his experiences during the war when he had been unjustly imprisoned in France. Hemingway, who served in the ambulance corps in Italy, adopted a highly personal literary style stripped of any decoration, and which focused on the courage of individuals facing physical and mental challenges. F. Scott Fitzgerald represented the voice of the liberated young elite generation of the 1920s. Although very different in their experiences and in their literary styles and subjects, in their varied ways each represented a departure from the standards of propriety and good taste that had dominated literature in the prewar era. The hundreds of prominent writers and artists who emerged in the 1920s in Europe and America and who represented the voices of the Lost Generation, like these three, reflected a wide variety of styles of rebellion and reaction.

Across Europe and the Americas, new styles of art, architecture, and music caught the flavor of a new era. The styles ranged from the German Bauhaus movement promoting functional decor and architecture to the monumental styles of art moderne in public buildings in Europe and the United States to the socialist realism of Soviet artists and the powerful work of Mexican muralists and illustrators. Avant-garde artists founded new schools of work during and after the war decade, including, among others, cubism, post-impressionism, and surrealism. Prominent artists in each of these styles made it clear that they intended their work to break with tradition and to capture the essence of rebellion against the standards of the previous generation. Many artists and writers frankly sought through their work to mark a sharp break with the past and its conventions. Painters, sculptors, graphic designers, musicians, cinematographers, playwrights, and commercial artists all moved in new directions, seemingly liberated from the rules and expectations of prewar styles in bursts of creativity that went in many directions. Some of their creations became classics, well-remembered, studied, and often emulated in later decades by appreciative future generations.

Yet much of that liberation and departure from the constraints of 19th-century standards had nothing whatever to do with the war but sprang from other sources. Young rebels had been shaking literary and artistic standards since the 1890s. Informed readers had already learned that the findings of Albert Einstein undermined the rules of Newtonian physics, that the latest researches of biologists required a rethinking of the gradual evolution suggested by Charles Darwin, and that Sigmund Freud showed sexuality as a far more powerful force than polite society cared to admit. Social commentators like Thorstein Veblen and H. L. Mencken had scorned the values and mores of the mainstream before the war came along, and Pablo Picasso and others had started their revolutionary movement in the pictorial arts well before the death of the archduke in Sarajevo. These sources of new thinking and rejection of past certitudes already flourished by 1913; the crises, disasters, and disillusionment of the war, however, did give a sharper psychological dividing line with the past and provided a ready audience for rebellion against old thinking. The war gave a whole generation deep and well-justified reasons to be skeptical about the wisdom of traditional political and military leadership, and that skepticism of authority spilled over into all realms of creative work.

World War I and its tragedies represented the end of many of the values and ideals of 19th-century Western civilization and brought in its wake decades of dictatorship and further war. However, a lasting and in the long run apparently positive legacy of World War I showed up in the surviving generation of the war, the creative rebels of the 1920s, who set the tone of modernity for the rest of the 20th century.

CHRONICLE OF EVENTS

1919

Greece occupies Izmir in Turkey, sparking a Greco-Turkish war that will last until 1922.

April: German architect Walter Gropius establishes Bauhaus in Weimar. Bauhaus teachers include Paul Klee, Mies van der Rohe, Wassily Kandinsky, Marcel Breuer, and Laszlo Moholy-Nagy.

September 9: Boston, Massachusetts, police go on strike.

October 28: The Volstead Act is passed over Wilson's veto.

November 7: The Palmer raids bring in radicals for possible federal charges or deportation.

November 11: A lynch mob in Centralia, Washington, kills I.W.W. member Wesley Everett.

December 22: The ship *Buford* departs from the United States with 249 radical deportees, including Emma Goldman and Alexander Berkman. The deportees will be landed in January in Finland and sent overland in a sealed train to the Russian border.

1920

January 2: Palmer raids in 33 cities net 2,700 radicals.

January 16: The Volstead Act goes into effect.

January 30–February 5: Benjamin Gitlow, author of the *Left Wing Manifesto,* is convicted of criminal anarchy. His conviction is later upheld by the U.S. Supreme Court.

Anarchists Emma Goldman and Alexander Berkman are shown here. After their arrest for opposing the draft during the war, they were deported to Russia via Finland. "Sasha" Berkman's foot was injured prior to his arrest. *(National Archives)*

February 13: Secretary of State Robert Lansing resigns after Wilson discovers Lansing had sought to open discussions regarding the disqualification of Wilson, due to his health, from serving as president. Wilson appoints Bainbridge Colby as Lansing's successor.

April: American novelist F. Scott Fitzgerald publishes *This Side of Paradise,* his first successful work.

August 20: The Turkish government signs the Treaty of Sevres, renouncing claims to all non-Turkish territory outside the Anatolian peninsula (but retaining claims to Armenian and Kurdish areas within Anatolia).

August 26: The Nineteenth Amendment to the Constitution granting woman suffrage is declared ratified.

November 2: Republican Warren Harding defeats James Cox in the election for president.

The first U.S. radio station, KDKA in Pittsburgh, broadcasts for the first time.

1921

Gertrude Saunders opens in New York in the musical *Shuffle Along,* presumably the origin of the Harlem Renaissance.

March 5: Warren Harding is inaugurated as president. His secretary of state is Charles Evans Hughes and his secretary of commerce is Herbert Hoover.

May 31–July 14: The trial of Nicola Sacco and Bartolomeo Vanzetti is held; both are found guilty of murder and sentenced to the death penalty.

November 12: The Washington Naval Conference opens and runs to February 6, 1922.

1922

American poet E. E. Cummings publishes *The Enormous Room.*

September 9: Turkish general Kemal's forces drive Greeks from Turkey, including Smyrna (Izmir).

October: Benito Mussolini becomes prime minister of Italy as head of a coalition government.

November 27: The stage show *Liza* premieres in New York; it is credited with introducing the Charleston to white audiences.

1923

May 18–June 19: Black nationalist leader Marcus Garvey is tried for using the mails to defraud in connection with his investment plans for the Black Star Line. He is sentenced to five years in prison.

July 23: The Treaty of Lausanne recognizes the end of the Ottoman sultanate and settles the Greek-Turkish conflict. The destiny of the oil-rich Mosul district is left to the League of Nations, which awards it to Iraq in 1925.

August 2: Warren Harding dies in San Francisco after a heart attack on his return from a trip to Alaska; Calvin Coolidge is sworn in by his father on August 3, 1923.

1924

February 3: Woodrow Wilson dies.

April 9: The Dawes Plan, providing for American loans to stimulate the German economy, is announced.

November 4: Calvin Coolidge defeats John Davis for the presidency. Third-party candidate Robert La Follette receives about 16 percent of the popular vote. The Republicans retain control of both houses of Congress.

November 9: Henry Cabot Lodge dies and is succeeded as chair of the Senate Foreign Relations Committee by William Borah.

1925

January 3: Benito Mussolini assumes dictatorial powers in Italy.

April 1: Bauhaus moves to Dessau, Germany.

April 10: F. Scott Fitzgerald publishes *The Great Gatsby.*

July 10–July 21: John Scopes is tried in Dayton, Tennessee, for violating a law against teaching the theory of evolution in public schools. He is defended by Clarence Darrow, and the prosecution is aided by William Jennings Bryan. Scopes is found guilty and fined $100.

October 25–December 17: Colonel Billy Mitchell is tried for criticizing the military's neglect of air power. Mitchell is suspended from the service for a term of five years, during which he resigns.

1927

August 23: Sacco and Vanzetti are executed.

Eyewitness Testimony

Architects, painters, and sculptors must once more acquaint themselves with and come to understand that many-membered entity, the building, as a whole and in its parts, for then their works will, of themselves, again become infused with the architectonic spirit which, as salon art, they have lost.

The old art schools were unable to achieve this unity and, after all, how could they, since art cannot be taught? They must be absorbed once more by the workshop. This world of designers and decorators who only draw and paint must finally become one of builders again. . . .

Let us, therefore, establish a new guild of craftsmen, free of that class-dividing arrogance which seeks to erect a haughty barrier between craftsmen and artists! Let us desire, conceive, and create together the new building of the future, which will embrace everything—architecture, sculpture, and painting—in one entity, and which will mount toward heaven from the hands of a million craftsmen as the crystal symbol of a new and coming faith.

German architect Walter Gropius, in the initial four-page brochure announcing the foundation of the Bauhaus, April 1919, translated and published in Howard Dearstyne, Inside the Bauhaus, *pp. 38–39.*

My mail had again been held up for ten days. The contents of two letters I had written had been found to be of a treasonable nature. I had ridiculed in them the Congressional committee that was investigating bolshevism in America; I had also attacked the high-handed autocracy of Attorney General A. Mitchell Palmer and his regime, as well as Messrs. Lusk and Overman, the New York State Senators delving into radicalism. Those Rip van Winkles had suddenly awakened to find that some of their countrymen had actually been thinking and reading about social conditions, and that other subversive elements had even dared to write books on the subject. It was a crime to be nipped in the bud if American institutions were to be saved.

Anarchist Emma Goldman, May 1919, commenting on suppression of civil liberties in the United States in her memoir, Living My Life, *vol. 2, p. 680.*

We of this less favored race realize that our future lies chiefly in our own hands. On ourselves alone will depend the preservation of our liberties and the transmission of them in their integrity to those who will come after us. And we are struggling on, attempting to show that knowledge can be obtained under difficulties; that poverty may give place to affluence; that obscurity is not an absolute bar to distinction, and that a way is open to welfare and happiness to all who will follow the way with resolution and wisdom; that neither the old-time slavery nor continued prejudice need extinguish self-respect, crush manly ambition or paralyze effort. . . . In order for us to successfully do all these things it is necessary that you of the favored race catch a new vision and exemplify in your actions this new American spirit. A fraternity must be established in which success and achievement are recognized, and those deserving receive the respect, honor and dignity due them. We too have a part in this new American Idealism. We too have felt the great thrill of what it means to sacrifice for other than the material. We revere our honored ones as belonging to the martyrs who died, not for personal gain, but for adherence to moral principles, principles which through the baptism of the blood reached a fruitage otherwise impossible, giving as they did a broader conception to our national life.

May I not appeal to you who also revere their memory to join us in continuing to fight for the great principles for which they contended, until in all sections of this fair land there will be equal opportunities for all, and character shall be the standard of excellence; until men by constructive work aim toward Solon's definition of the ideal government—where an injury to the meanest citizen is an insult to the whole Constitution; and until black and white shall clasp friendly hands in the consciousness of the fact that we are brethren and that God is the father of us all.

African-American singer and actor Paul Robeson, in his Rutgers commencement day address, June 18, 1919, quoted in Paul Robeson, Jr., The Undiscovered Paul Robeson: An Artist's Journey, 1898–1939, *pp. 37–38.*

Deep snow lay on the ground; the air was cut by a biting wind. A row of armed civilians and soldiers stood along the road to the bank. Dimly the outlines of a barge were visible through the morning mist. One by one the deportees marched, flanked on each side by the uniformed men, curses and threats accompanying the thud of their feet on the frozen ground. When the last man had crossed the gangplank, the girls and I were ordered to follow, officers in front and in back of us.

We were led to a cabin. A large fire roared in the iron stove, filling the air with heat and fumes. We felt suffocating. There was no air nor water. Then came a violent lurch; we were on our way.

I looked at my watch. It was 4:20 a.m. on the day of our Lord, December 21, 1919. On the deck above us I could hear the men tramping up and down in the wintry blast. I felt dizzy, visioning a transport of politicals doomed to Siberia, the *etapé* of former Russian days. Russia of the past rose before me and I saw the revolutionary martyrs being driven into exile. But no, it was New York, it was America, the land of liberty! Through the port-hole I could see the great city receding into the distance, its sky-line of buildings traceable by their rearing heads. It was my beloved city, the metropolis of the New World. It was America, indeed, America repeating the terrible scenes of tsarist Russia. I glanced up—the Statue of Liberty!

Dawn was breaking when our barge pulled up alongside of the large ship. We were quickly transferred and assigned to a cabin.

Emma Goldman, describing her deportation on December 21, 1919, in her memoir, Living My Life, *vol. 2, p. 717.*

The war and its emotions passed with extraordinary suddenness. To see the full meaning of the story that ended in 1917 it is necessary to look beyond the wartime enthusiasm and beyond the complementary, savage disillusion of the postwar years. At some time long after the Armistice whistles had stopped blowing, it became apparent that a profound change had taken place in American civilization, a change that affected all the contenders in the prewar cultural strife. This was the end of American innocence. Innocence, the absence of guilt and doubt and the complexity that goes with them, had been the common characteristic of the older culture and its custodians, of most of the progressives, most of the relativists and social scientists, and of the young leaders of the pre-war Rebellion. This innocence had often been rather precariously maintained. Many had glimpsed a world whose central meaning was neither clear nor cheerful, but very few had come to live in such a world as a matter of course. . . . The most obvious aspect of change was the complete disintegration of the old order, the set of ideas which had dominated the American mind so effectively from the mid-nineteenth century until 1912. The nineties had undermined this set of beliefs; the Rebellion had successfully defied it;

the twenties hardly had to fight it. After the war it was hard to find a convincing or intellectually respectable spokesman for the prewar faith. The old moral idealism had become a caricature of Woodrow Wilson.

Historian Henry F. May, regarding the roots of disillusionment in the period 1912–17, in his social commentary, The End of American Innocence: A Study of the First Years of Our Time, 1912–1917, *pp. 393–394.*

There was great excitement in [Moscow], due to the arrival of a number of foreign delegates for the Second Congress of the Red Trade-Union International. Among them we were delighted to find some Anarcho-Syndicalists from Spain, France, Italy, Germany, and Scandinavia. . . . The clearest minds among them were two anarchists, Pistania from Spain and Augustin Souchy from Germany, representing the Anarcho-Syndicalist labour bodies of their respective countries. These two men were entirely with the Revolution and sympathetic with the Bolsheviki. They were, however, not the kind who could be feted into seeing everything in roseate colours. They came as earnest students of the situation, desirous of getting the facts at first and of observing the Revolution in action. They inquired, among other things, how our comrades were faring under the Communist State. All sorts of rumours had filtered to Europe about the persecution of anarchists and other revolutionists. The comrades abroad, they told us, had refused to credit such reports as long as they had not heard from us about the matter. They had asked that we send back word through Souchy and Pistania about the actual state of affairs. Sasha [Alexander Berkman] explained that the rumours were unfortunately not unfounded. Anarchists, Left Socialist Revolutionists, militant workers and peasants were imprisoned in Soviet jails and detention camps, denounced as bandits and counter-revolutionists. They were nothing of the kind, of course, but sincere comrades, most of whom had taken an active part in the October days. Our efforts had been effective for but few of them. Possibly the Anarcho-Syndicalist delegates, as representatives of large left labour organizations abroad, would be more successful with the Soviet authorities. They should insist on their right to visit the prisons and talk to the prisoners. Sasha also suggested that the delegates demand redress for our people. But he was reluctant to talk to the men of the general situation. . . . They would have to learn for themselves.

I felt differently on the matter. . . . To the oppressed of the world the Bolsheviki had become the synonym of the Revolution itself. The revolutionists outside of Russia could not easily credit how far that was from the truth. One seldom learns from the experience of others. Nevertheless I did not regret having talked frankly to the delegates.

Emma Goldman, on her disillusionment with the Soviet regime and her attempts to explain conditions to visiting anarchists, July 10–15, 1920, while awaiting in Moscow paperwork for a train tour of Central Asia, described in her autobiography, Living My Life, *vol. 2, pp. 799–800.*

The Liberal-Democratic government quite naturally put difficulties in the way of the Fascist movement. It relied principally on the royal guards—Guardia Regia—blind instrument of anti-national hatred. But we, who had sane courage, resource and ability, accepted the fact of facing ambush, traps and death. When instead we were taken to prison, we remained there long periods waiting for trial. I had an effect on my soldiers which seemed to me almost mystical. The boys saw in me the avenger of our wronged Italy. The dying said, "give us our black shirts for winding sheets." I could not remain unmoved when I knew that their last thoughts were of "Our native land and the Duce." Love and songs bloomed. A revival of youth, filled with Italian boldness, swamped by its virile male beauty and the unrestrained rages of the irresponsibles, painted out the fear of the Socialists, obliterated the ambiguity of the Liberals. The poesy of battle, the voices of an awakening race were multiplying, in those years of revival, the energies of our nation.

Italian Fascist leader Benito Mussolini, commenting on events in Italy in early 1921 regarding the rise of the Fascist Party, in My Autobiography, *pp. 125–126.*

I speak for administrative efficiency, for lightened tax burdens, for sound commercial practices, for adequate credit facilities, for sympathetic concern with all agricultural problems, for the omission of unnecessary interference of government with business, for an end of government's experiment in business, and for more efficient business in government administration. With all of this must attend a mindfulness for the human side of all activities, so that social, industrial and economic justice will be squared with the purposes of a righteous people.

From Warren G. Harding's inaugural address, in "Text of President Harding's Inaugural Address," New York Times, *March 5, 1921, p. 4.*

"As for controlling conditions with chaperones," continued the Dean [of Morningside College, Iowa], "we'd just be wasting our time, because frankly, the girls no longer care what their elders think of them. Through their fault or our fault, we've lost the respect for our generation. The modern young girl values no censorship under heaven save the public opinion of her contemporaries."

For all that, the Older Generation is trying to mold her. Mrs. Grundy has begun to do something. Why else were glaring electric lights put outside the garages of a Hoboken country club? To chaperon the young things that sit in the cars between dances, explained the shocked Mrs. Grundy. Why else did the Principal of a high school in Pittsburgh ban the use of powder and rouge and lip stick? Why else has the Catholic Archbishop of the Ohio diocese issued a warning against the toddle and shimmy and also against "bare female shoulders"? And why else should the city fathers of Syracuse positively forbid jazz dancing in public dance places? And the college authorities of the same town forbid hiking army breeches for co-eds outside of the college campus—and right after they had banned smoking, too?

These are general cases—a panoramic view of flapper reform.

Social commentator and journalist Helen Bullitt Lowry, offering her views on the attempt to enforce an older style of morality on the youth of the 1920s, in "Mrs. Grundy on the Job of Reforming the Flapper," March 27, 1921, New York Times, *sec. BRM, p. 4.*

In a later conversation with the British Ambassador, it appeared that the British Government had agreed with Japan in 1916 to favor the awarding to Japan of the islands in the North Pacific. I asked if President Wilson was acquainted with this agreement and the Ambassador said that Mr. Balfour had given him a copy when he was here. I inquired if Mr. Balfour had called President Wilson's attention to it. The Ambassador replied that he did not know as to that but understood it was left with a number of papers. He added that President Wilson knew of it when he reached Paris.

Evidently Japan in view of the agreement with the British Government expected to get the islands and when the scheme of mandates was substituted for absolute cession, she nevertheless contemplated doing what she pleased with the mandated territory. The mandates, however, prohibited fortifications. . . .

Harding's secretary of state Charles Evans Hughes, recalling his conversation with the British ambassador in which he learned of the secret Japanese-British agreement regarding disposition of German territory, on April 12, 1921, in The Autobiographical Notes of Charles Evans Hughes, *p. 233.*

Among the most embarrassing situations in history is that of being a *"revolté"* and having nobody so much as aware of the existence of a revolt. Such was almost the case of our passionately throbbing literary insurgents until just a few months ago. They were calling themselves the "Young Intelligencia" and nobody knew it. They were railing against the "American Bourgeoisie" and the past and present and flivvers and bridge clubs and Ohio and Minnesota and Red Cross drives, and nobody was taking note of the fact except the few subscribers to the circulating fiction libraries who read their novel a day.

Now all that is changed. The Atlantic Monthly, the Bookman, the Freeman and The New Republic have suddenly begun to run articles about the "Young Intellectual"—to attack and to defend him. Overnight the group has become articulate and is having the grandest time. "The problem of America versus the Young Intellectual" is the earnest way one of them labels the intermagazine debate—the young intellectual versus the anti-vice societies and the tired business man.

Some half dozen young writers are always mentioned when the group is referred to, though the fringes are rather indefinite. Of some particularly "deserving" novelist like, for instance, Wharton, a member of the "revoltés" proper will kindly allow, "Her spirit is young, she isn't smug about the perfections of American life. She even writes better than some of us. Therefore we may fairly count her as one of us."

Of course there are some of them that "everybody" concedes "belong." There is Sherwood Anderson with his "Poor White," Waldo Frank who has written "The Dark Mother," Floyd Dell in "Moon Calf," and of course, Sinclair Lewis in "Main Street," while the Flapper-Intellectual of the crowd is Scott Fitz-Gerald with his "This Side of Paradise." Sometimes, too, Zona Gale is included among them with "Miss Lulu Bett." Around these financially more successful pessimists are grouped some few dozen of our minor pessimists who don't get so well paid. All in all, there are perhaps some fifty young and youngish writers and editors who consider themselves a part of the "movement." Somebody has labeled them the Now It Can Be Told School.

Most of them know each other, too, for the literary world is small, in mentioning one another they're apt to say "Hal" when they are referring to Lewis, and you always have to be guessing which of each other they're talking about. But they are not a formal organization, nor do they meet together to discuss the revolt. They have not done it yet anyway. For all that the group has two grave responsibilities that all of them seem to recognize. One is to expose the meanness of our middle classes and our Middle West from double beds to Fatty Arbuckle fans. And the other is to sell books—their own and other people's. The Young Intelligencia are issuing manifestos about each other's works, even as Lillian Russell issues testimonials to cold creams of super excellency.

There is nothing to restrain them but the supply of adjectives.

Helen Bullitt Lowry, "Mutual Admiration Society of Young Intellectuals," New York Times, *May 8, 1921, p. 42.*

If Great Britain will take my advice she would call a conference tomorrow morning, and say to all Englishmen leave India, leave Africa and go back to England because we want peace. If France takes my advice she will call out her white colonists from her African dominions, because so long as this injustice is perpetrated against weaker peoples there is going to be wars and rumors of wars. It is human nature and the world knows it. . . . The new Negro is going to strike back or is going to die; and if David Lloyd George, Briand and the different statesmen believe they can assemble in Washington, in London, in Paris, or anywhere and dispose of black people's property without first consulting them they make a big mistake, because we have reared many Fochs between 1914 and 1918 on the battlefields of France and Flanders.

Black nationalist leader Marcus Garvey in a speech regarding the Washington Disarmament Conference, delivered in New York, November 5, 1921, reprinted in Amy Jacques Garvey, Philosophy and Opinions of Marcus Garvey, *pp. 114–115.*

My own disappointment with the public estimate of me lies in the fact that so many seem to think I can take a whip and show Congress where to head in. It was possible for my predecessor to follow such a course during the war when men ofttimes put aside their petty interests to

Black nationalist Marcus Garvey at work, before his arrest and later deportation. His ideas about black liberation offended the establishment. *(Library of Congress)*

After running two blocks the fugitive was captured at Thomas Street. He said he was Harry Cohen, 35 years old, a shoe salesman, of 272 South Ninth Street, Brooklyn. He was locked up at the Old Slip Police Station, charged with violation of the State Prohibition law and of the Sullivan law and felonious assault.

The detectives were Frederick Franklin and Thomas Burns of Inspector Thomas V. Underhill's staff. They charged that Cohen conducted a "speak-easy" in Greenwich Street, near Record, and reported the seizure of fourteen pint flasks of alleged liquor and a loaded revolver in the place.

Cohen, the detectives said, admitted them to a room on the second floor of a tenement in response to their knocks on the door. "You have no search warrant and you have no business here," Cohen is reported to have said when the detectives made known their identity.

News story headlined "Shots in Rum Chase Frighten Crowd—Detectives Capture an Alleged 'Speak-Easy' Proprietor in Greenwich Street," New York Times, *February 24, 1922, p. 12.*

The first year of our activities for the Black Star Line added prestige to the Universal Negro Improvement Association. Several hundred thousand dollars worth of shares were sold. Our first ship, the steamship Yarmouth, had made three voyages to the West Indies and Central America. The white press had flashed the news all over the world. I, a young Negro, as President of the corporation, had become famous. My name was discussed on five continents. The Universal Negro Improvement Association gained millions of followers all over the world. By August, 1920, over 4,000,000 persons had joined the movement. A convention of all the Negro peoples of the world was called to meet in New York that month. Delegates came from all parts of the known world. Over 25,000 persons packed the Madison Square Garden on August 1 to hear me speak to the first International Convention of Negroes. It was a record-breaking meeting, the first and the biggest of its kind. The name of Garvey had become known as a leader of his race.

Such fame among Negroes was too much for other race leaders and politicians to tolerate. My downfall was planned by my enemies. They laid all kinds of traps for me.

Marcus Garvey, on the birth of opposition to him among African-American leaders, in an article published in Current History, *September, 1923, reprinted in* Philosophy and Opinions of Marcus Garvey, *p. 130.*

perform what was believed to be a patriotic service. Conditions are not quite the same now. Probably I am lacking in the domineering traits which Mr. Wilson possessed and found himself able to exercise for considerable time. In the end he came to failure because of the practices followed.

Warren Harding, in a confidential letter to his friend, Morris Jennings, January 6, 1922, quoted in Andrew Sinclair, The Available Man: The Life behind the Masks of Warren Gamaliel Harding, *p. 238.*

An exchange of revolver shots between two detectives and the alleged owner of a "speak-easy" in a tenement was followed by an exciting chase along Greenwich Street late yesterday afternoon as thousands of persons were homeward bound from downtown office buildings. The sight of the two detectives with drawn revolvers pursuing a third man caused the throngs to seek shelter.

Dear Comrade [Alice Stone] Blackwell:

I bit my tongue 'til now, not to tell you a thing which will make you sorry, but I cannot help but tell it. They took me away from the hospital and brought me in the east north ward, the worst of the wards, for the most dangerous or the punished. While other patients enjoy all day long the sunshine and open air in spacious yards, we have one hour of yard in the morning, and one in the afternoon, and our yard is narrow and shadowy; closing the sight, except to the sky. The door of my room is kept open during the day, and I have a chair and books in my room. But I stay in because the other prisoners are kept in.

Now, they cannot say that I am dangerously insane, nor can they claim that I deserved punishment by my conduct. Two weeks ago Mr. Thompson was here, and they . . . said that they cannot give me more liberty because I am a dangerous man. After that, I was declared by the Prison authorities "A model prisoner;" the best one, and after my conduct here, really exemplar.

They believe me guilty; they believe my principles to be aberration and insanity; they believe my friends (I mean the comrades and Italians) arch-criminals; they believe (and told me so) that the Americans in our behalf are fools and cheaters. But what is worse, they asked me if I believed in God, in the golden rule; if the murderers shall not be punished. If they do not nail me, I will answer.

Bartolemeo Vanzetti, April 16, 1925, to one of his and Sacco's supporters, collected in Marion Denman Frankfurter, The Letters of Sacco and Vanzetti, *pp. 147–148.*

While he was executive secretary of the NAACP, James Weldon Johnson's famous "God's Trombones" was published and he wrote "Saint Peter Relates an Incident of the Resurrection Day," as well as "Along this Way," one of the earlier portions of his autobiography. Both Johnson and Jessie Fauset held many cultural soirees at their apartments in Harlem. Celebrities of both races who often attended included the Carl Van Vechtens, the Clarence Darrows, and the young Paul Robesons; Miguel Covarrubias and Aaron Douglas, the artists; Charles S. Johnson, the sociologist; Rebecca West, the English novelist; and Salvador Madariaga, the Spanish philosopher. Walter White's parties too, on Edgecombe Avenue in what was then Harlem's most fashionable apartment building, brought together brilliant company—Sinclair Lewis, Willa Cather, Rudolph Fisher, Heywood Broun, George Gershwin—and perhaps included more stars of the theater than the other gatherings did.

Langston Hughes, describing the flowering of the Harlem Renaissance about 1926 in his autobiography, Fight for Freedom, *reprinted in* The Collected Works of Langston Hughes, *vol. 10,* Fight for Freedom and Other Writings on Civil Rights, *pp. 78–79.*

Very often I turn around my mind's eyes to see, contemplate and study the world even and mankind. The spectacle is extremely repugnant and heart tearing. At it, one does not know if to love or if to hate, if to sympathize or if to despise humanity. Things are going from bad to worse. War in China, Nicaragua, revolution in Java, Mexico, Brazil; the Balkans on foot of war; France and Italy mobilizing one against the other; England, United States, France and Japan in a crazy rivalry of armament; South America and United States in danger of war; Italy under the fascist dictatorship; Russia under the Bolsheviki one; scandals, corruption, crimes, diseases, degeneration, greed, hatred, unconsciousness, prejudices, and insanity sweeping the earth. I wonder how it will all end. There is but one system, one philosophy through which I can explain to myself the causes of this universal tragedy and the possible remedies, which of course, should be prompted by the human voluntarism: It is the *Philosophy of the Miseria* by Proudhon.

Bartolomeo Vanzetti to Alice Stone Blackwell, January 10, 1927, from Charlestown prison, reprinted in Marion Denman Frankfurter, The Letters of Sacco and Vanzetti, *p. 230.*

I feel that the music of my race is the happiest medium of expression for what dramatic and vocal skill I possess. In the first place, Negro music is more and more taking its place with the music of the world. It has its own distinctive message and philosophy. Many critics say it is the only folk music of America. Negro music portrays the hopes of our people who faced the hardships of slavery. They suffered. They fled to God through their songs. They sang to forget their chains and misery. Even in darkness they looked to their songs to work out their destiny and carve their way to the promised land.

There is no expression of hate or revenge in their music. That a race which had suffered and toiled as the

Negro had did not express bitterness but expressed love is strong evidence of the influence of Christianity. I am not ashamed of the Spirituals. They represent the soul of my people. White and colored people react alike to the songs. Differences are forgotten and prejudices vanish when mixed audiences meet at the concerts. Humanity is helped and lifted to higher levels.

Paul Robeson, in an interview with the YMCA magazine, Association Men, *July 1927, quoted in Paul Robeson, Jr.,* The Undiscovered Paul Robeson: An Artist's Journey, 1898–1939, *pp. 140–141.*

APPENDIX A
Documents

1. Francis Joseph's proclamation of the annexation of Bosnia and Herzegovina, October 6, 1908
2. The Constitution of the Ujedinjenje ili Smrt—Unification or Death (the "Black Hand"), May 9, 1911
3. Note confirming the "blank check," July 6, 1914
4. The note of Austria-Hungary to Servia, presented July 23, 1914, in Belgrade
5. The Serbian reply to the Austrian ultimatum, July 25, 1914
6. The German request for free passage through Belgium note, August 2, 1914
7. The Belgian refusal of free passage note, August 3, 1914
8. Excerpts from the Treaty of London, April 26, 1915
9. Bernstorff *Arabic* Pledge, October 5, 1915
10. Husain-McMahon letter on Commitment to the Arabs, October 24, 1915
11. Memorandum of the German government on the treatment of armed merchant ships as ships of war, February 10, 1916
12. Tirpitz memorandum on the advisability of unrestricted submarine warfare, February 13, 1916
13. Wilson on the *Sussex* incident, April 19, 1916
14. Sykes-Picot Agreement, May 16, 1916
15. Zimmermann note, January 19, 1917
16. Wilson's Peace Without Victory note, January 22, 1917
17. Order No. 1 of the Petrograd Soviet, March 14, 1917
18. Robert Lansing's Memorandum on the Cabinet Meeting of March 20, 1917
19. Wilson's War Message to Congress, April 2, 1917
20. Opposition to the Declaration of War, April 5, 1917
21. War Resolution, April 6, 1917
22. Balfour Declaration (statement of Foreign Secretary Balfour to Lord Rothschild), November 8, 1917
23. Wilson's Fourteen Points speech, delivered January 8, 1918
24. Brest-Litovsk Peace Treaty, March 3, 1918
25. Armistice terms proposed by Woodrow Wilson to Germany, October 13, 1918
26. Allies' Conditions, November 5, 1918
27. Covenant of the League from the Versailles Treaty, June 28, 1919
28. Reparations clauses of the Versailles Treaty, June 28, 1919

1. Francis Joseph's Proclamation of the Annexation of Bosnia and Herzegovina, October 6, 1908

We, Francis Joseph, Emperor of Austria, King of Bohemia, and Apostolic King of Hungary, to the inhabitants of Bosnia and Herzegovina:

When a generation ago our troops crossed the borders of your lands, you were assured that they came not as foes, but as friends, with the firm determination to remedy the evils from which your fatherland had suffered so grievously for many years. This promise given at a serious moment has been honestly kept. It has been the constant endeavour of our government to guide the country by patient and systematic activity to a happier future.

To our great joy we can say that the seed then scattered in the furrows of a troubled soil has richly thrived. You yourselves must feel it a boon that order and security have replaced violence and oppression, that trade and traffic are constantly extending, that the elevating influence of education has been brought to bear in your country, and that under the shield of an orderly administration every man may enjoy the fruits of his labours.

It is the duty of us all to advance steadily along this path. With this goal before our eyes, we deem the moment come to give the inhabitants of the two lands a new proof of our trust in their political maturity. In order to raise Bosnia and Herzegovina to a higher level of political life, we have resolved to grant both of those lands constitutional governments that are suited to the prevailing conditions and general interests, so as to create a legal basis for the representation of their wishes and needs. You shall henceforth have a voice when decisions are made concerning your domestic affairs, which, as hitherto, will have a separate administration. But the necessary premise for the introduction of this provincial constitution is the creation of a clear and unambiguous legal status for the two lands.

For this reason, and also remembering the ties that existed of yore between our glorious ancestors on the Hungarian throne and these lands, we extend our suzerainty over Bosnia and Herzegovina, and it is our will that the order of succession of our House be extended to these lands also. The inhabitants of the two lands thus share all the benefits which a lasting confirmation of the present relation can offer. The new order of things will be a guarantee that civilization and prosperity will find a sure footing in your home.

2. The Constitution of the Ujedinjenje ili Smrt—Unification or Death (The "Black Hand"), May 9, 1911

I. Purpose and Name

Article 1. For the purpose of realising the national ideals—the Unification of Serbdom—an organization is hereby created, whose members may be any Serbian irrespective of sex, religion, place or birth, as well as anybody else who will sincerely serve this idea.

Article 2. The organisation gives priority to the revolutionary struggle rather than relies on cultural striving, therefore its institution is an absolutely secret one for wider circles.

Article 3. The organization bears the name: *"Ujedinjenje ili Smrt."*

Article 4. In order to carry into efect its task the organization will do the following things:

(1) Following the character of its *raison d'être* it will exercise its influence over all the official factors in Serbia—which is the Piemont of Serbdom—as also over all the strata of the State and over the entire social life in it;

(2) It will carry out a revolutionary organisation in all the territories where Serbians are living;

(3) Beyond the frontiers, it will fight with all means against all enemies of this idea;

(4) It will maintain friendly relations with all the States, nations, organisations, and individual persons who sympathise with Serbia and the Serbian race;

(5) It will give every assistance to those nations and organisations who are fighting for their own national liberation and unification.

II. Official Departments of the Organisation

Article 5. The supreme authority is vested in the Supreme Central Directorate with its headquarters at Belgrade. Its duty will be to see that the resolutions are carried into effect.

Article 6. The number of members of the Supreme Central Directorate is unlimited—but in principle it should be kept as low as possible.

Article 7. The Supreme Central Directorate shall include, in addition to the members from the Kingdom of Serbia, one accredited delegate from each of the organisations of all the Serbian regions: (1) Bosnia and Herzegovina, (2) Montenegro, (3) Old Serbia and Macedonia, (4) Croatia, Slovenia and Symria (Srem), (5) Voyvodina, (6) Sea-coasts.

Article 8. It will be the task of the Supreme Central Directorate to carry out the principles of the organisation within the territory of the Kingdom of Serbia.

Article 9. The duty of each individual Provincial Directorate will be to carry out the principles of the organisation within the respective territories of each Serbian region outside the frontiers of the Kingdom of Serbia. The Provincial Directorate will be the supreme authority of the organisation within its own territory.

Article 10. The subdivisions of the organisation into District Directorates and other units of authority shall be established by the By-Laws of the organisation which shall be laid down, and if need be, from time to time amended and amplified by the Supreme Central Directorate.

Article 11. Each Directorate shall elect, from amongst its own members, its President, Secretary and Treasurer.

Article 12. By virtue of the nature of his work, the Secretary may act as a Deputy President. In order that he may devote himself entirely to the work of the organisation, the Secretary's salary and expenses shall be provided by the Supreme Central Directorate.

Article 13. The positions of President and Treasurer shall be un-salaried.

Article 14. All official business questions of the organisation shall be decided in the sessions of the Supreme Central Directorate by a majority of votes.

Article 15. For the execution of such decisions of the organisation, the absolute executive power shall be vested in the President and the Secretary.

Article 16. In exceptional and less important cases the President and the Secretary shall make the decisions and secure their execution, but they shall report accordingly at the next following session of the Supreme Central Directorate.

Article 17. For the purpose of ensuring a more efficient discharge of business, the Supreme Central Directorate shall be divided into sections, according to the nature of the work.

Article 18. The Supreme Central Directorate shall maintain its relations with the Provincial Directorates through the accredited delegates of the said provincial organisations, it being understood that such delegates shall be at the same time members of the Supreme Central Directorate; in exceptional cases, however, these relations shall be maintained through special delegates.

Article 19. Provincial Directorates shall have freedom of action. Only in cases of the execution of broader revolutionary movements will they depend upon the approval of the Supreme Central Directorate.

Article 20. The Supreme Central Directorate shall regulate all the signs and watchwords, necessary for the maintenance of secrecy in the organisation.

Article 21. It shall be the Supreme Central Directorate's duty punctually and officially to keep all the members of the organisation well posted about all the more important questions relative to the organisation.

Article 22. The Supreme Central Directorate shall from time to time control and inspect the work of its own departments. Analogically, the other Directorates shall do likewise with their own departments.

III. The Members of the Organisation

Article 23. The following rule, as a principle, shall govern all the detailed transactions of the organisation: All communications and conversations to be conducted only through specially appointed and authorised persons.

Article 24. It shall be the duty of every member to recruit new members, but it shall be understood that every introducing member shall vouch with his own life for all those whom he introduces into the organisation.

Article 25. The members of the organisation as amongst themselves shall not be known to one another. Only the members of Directorates shall be known personally to one another.

Article 26. In the organisation the members shall be registered and known by their respective numbers. But the Supreme Central Directorate must know them also by their respective names.

Article 27. The members of the organisation must unconditionally obey all the commands given by their respective Directorates, as also all the Directorates must obey unconditionally the commands which they receive direct from their superior Directorate.

Article 28. Every member shall be obliged to impart officially to the organisation whatever comes to his knowledge, either in his private life or in the discharge of his official duties, in as far as it may be of interest to the organisation.

Article 29. The interest of the organisation shall stand above all other interests.

Article 30. On entering into the organisation, every member must know that by joining the organisation he loses his own personality; he must not expect any glory for himself, nor any personal benefit, material or moral.

Consequently the member who should dare to try to exploit the organisation for his personal, or class, or party interests shall be punished by death.

Article 31. Whosoever has once entered into the organisation can never by any means leave it, nor shall anybody have the authority to accept the resignation of a member.

Article 32. Every member shall support the organisation by his weekly contributions. The organisations, however, shall have the authority to procure money, if need be, by coercion. The permission to resort to these means may be given only by the Supreme Central Directorate within the country, or by the regional Directorates within their respective region.

Article 33. In administering capital punishment the sole responsibility of the Supreme Central Directorate shall be to see that such punishment is safely and unfailingly carried into effect without any regard for the ways and means to be employed in the execution.

IV. The Seal and the Oath of Allegiance

Article 34. The Organisation's official seal is thus composed: In the centre of the seal there is a powerful arm holding in its hand an unfurled flag on which—as a coat of arms—there is a skull with crossed bones; by the side of the flag, a knife, a bomb and a phial of poison. Around, in a circle, there is the following inscription, reading from left to right: "Unification or Death," and in the base: "The Supreme Central Directorate."

Article 35. On entering into the organisation the joining member must pronounce the following oath of allegiance:

"I (the Christian name and surname of the joining member), by entering into the organisation "Unification or Death," do hereby swear by the Sun which shineth upon me, by the Earth which feedeth me, by God, by the blood of my forefathers, by my honour and by my life, that from this moment onward and until my death, I shall faithfully serve the task of this organisation and that I shall at all times be prepared to bear for it any sacrifice. I further swear by God, by my honour and by my life, that I shall unconditionally carry into effect all its orders and commands. I further swear by my God, by my honour and by my life, that I shall keep within myself all the secrets of this organisation and carry them with me into my grave. May God and my comrades in this organisation be my judges if at any time I should wittingly fail or break this oath!"

V. Supplementary Orders

Article 36. The present Constitution shall come into force immediately.

Article 37. The present Constitution must not be altered.

Done at Belgrade this 9th day of May, 1911 A.D.

Signed:

Major Ilija Radivojevitch
Vice-Consul Bogdan Radenkovitch
Colonel Cedimilj A. Popovitch
Lt.-Col. Velimir Vemitch
Journalist Ljubomir S. Jovanovitch
Col. Dragutin T. Dimitrijevitch
Major Vojin P. Tanksoitch
Major Milan Vasitch
Col. Milovan Gr. Milovanovitch

3. NOTE CONFIRMING THE "BLANK CHECK," JULY 6, 1914

Telegram from the Imperial Chancellor, von Bethmann-Hollweg, to the German Ambassador at Vienna. Tschirschky, July 6, 1914

Confidential. For Your Excellency's personal information and guidance

The Austro-Hungarian Ambassador yesterday delivered to the Emperor a confidential personal letter from the Emperor Francis Joseph, which depicts the present situation from the Austro-Hungarian point of view, and describes the measures which Vienna has in view. A copy is now being forwarded to Your Excellency.

I replied to Count Szagyeny today on behalf of His Majesty that His Majesty sends his thanks to the Emperor Francis Joseph for his letter and would soon answer it personally. In the meantime His Majesty desires to say that he is not blind to the danger which threatens Austria-Hungary and thus the Triple Alliance as a result of the Russian and Serbian Pan-Slavic agitation. Even though His Majesty is known to feel no unqualified confidence in Bulgaria and her ruler, and naturally inclines more toward our old ally Rumania and her Hohenzollern prince, yet he quite understands that the Emperor Francis Joseph, in view of the attitude of Rumania and of the danger of a new Balkan alliance aimed directly at the Danube Monarchy, is anxious to bring about an understanding between Bulgaria and the Triple alliance. . . . His Majesty will, furthermore, make an effort at Bucharest, according to the wishes of the Emperor Francis Joseph, to influence King Carol to the fulfilment of the duties of his alliance, to the renunciation of Serbia, and to the suppression of the Rumanian agitations directed against Austria-Hungary.

Finally, as far as concerns Serbia, His Majesty, of course, cannot interfere in the dispute now going on between Austria-Hungary and that country, as it is a matter not within his competence. The Emperor Francis Joseph may, however, rest assured that His Majesty will faithfully stand by Austria-Hungary, as is required by the obligations of his alliance and of his ancient friendship.

BETHMANN-HOLLWEG

4. THE NOTE OF AUSTRIA-HUNGARY TO SERVIA, PRESENTED JULY 23, 1914, IN BELGRADE

On March 31st, 1909, the Royal Servian Minister to the Court of Vienna made the following statement, by order of his Government: "Servia declares that she is not affected in her rights by the situation established in Bosnia, and that she will therefore adapt herself to the decisions which the Powers are going to arrive at in reference to Art. 25 of the Berlin Treaty. By following the councils of the Powers, Servia binds herself to cease the attitude of protest and resistance which she has assumed since last October, relative to the annexation, and she binds herself further to change the direction of her present policies towards Austria-Hungary, and, in the future, to live with the latter in friendly and neighbourly relations."

The history of the last years, and especially the painful events of June 28th, have demonstrated the existence of a subversive movement in Servia whose aim it is to separate certain territories from the Austro-Hungarian monarchy. This movement, which developed under the eyes of the Servian Government, has found expression subsequently beyond the territory of the kingdom, in acts of terrorism, a series of assassinations and murders.

Far from fulfilling the formal obligations contained in the declaration of March 31st, 1909, the Royal Servian Government has done nothing to suppress this movement. She suffered the criminal doings of the various societies and associations directed against the monarchy, the unbridled language of the Press, the glorification of the originators of assassinations, the participation of officers and officials in subversive intrigues; she suffered the unwholesome propaganda in public education, and lastly permitted all manifestations which would mislead the Servian people into hatred of the monarchy and into contempt for its institutions.

This sufferance of which the Royal Servian Government made itself guilty, has lasted up to the moment in which the events of June 28th demonstrated to the entire world the ghastly consequences of such sufferance.

It becomes plain from the evidence and confessions of the criminal authors of the outrage of June 28th, that the murder at Sarajevo was conceived in Belgrade, that the murderers received the arms and bombs with which they were equipped, from Servian officers and officials who belonged to the Narodna Odbrana, and that, lastly, the transportation of the criminals and their arms to Bosnia was arranged and carried out by leading Servian frontier officials.

The cited results of the investigation do not permit the Imperial and Royal Government to observe any longer the attitude of waiting, which it has assumed for years towards those agitations which have their centre in Belgrade, and which from there radiate into the territory of the monarchy. These results, on the contrary, impose upon the Imperial and Royal Government the duty to terminate intrigues which constitute a permanent menace for the peace of the monarchy.

In order to obtain this purpose, the Imperial and Royal Government is forced to demand official assurance from the Servian Government that it condemns the propaganda directed against Austria-Hungary, i.e. the entirety of the machinations whose aim it is to separate parts from the monarchy which belong to it, and that she binds herself to suppress with all means this criminal and terrorizing propaganda.

In order to give to these obligations a solemn character, the Royal Servian Government will publish on the first page of its official organ of July 26th, 1914, the following declaration:—

"The Royal Servian Government condemns the propaganda directed against Austria-Hungary, i.e., the entirety of those machinations whose aim it is to separate from the Austro-Hungarian monarchy territories belonging thereto, and she regrets sincerely the ghastly consequences of these criminal actions.

"The Royal Servian Government regrets that Servian officers and officials have participated in the propaganda, cited above, and have thus threatened the friendly and neighbourly relations which the Royal

Government was solemnly bound to cultivate by its declaration of March 31st, 1909.

"The Royal Government, which disapproves and rejects every thought or every attempt at influencing the destinations of the inhabitants of any part of Austria-Hungary, considers it its duty to call most emphatically to the attention of its officers and officials, and of the entire population of the kingdom, that it will henceforward proceed with the utmost severity against any persons guilty of similar actions to prevent and suppress which it will make every effort."

This explanation is to be brought simultaneously to the cognisance of the Royal Army through an order of H.M. the King, and it is to be published in the official organ of the Army.

The Royal Servian Government binds itself, in addition, as follows:

1. to suppress any publication which fosters hatred of, and contempt for, the Austro-Hungarian monarchy, and whose general tendency is directed against the latter's territorial integrity;

2. to proceed at once with the dissolution of the society Narodna Odbrana, to confiscate their entire means of propaganda, and to proceed in the same manner against the other societies and associations in Servia which occupy themselves with the propaganda against Austria-Hungary. The Royal Government will take the necessary measures, so that the dissolved Societies may not continue their activities under another name or in another form;

3. without delay to eliminate from the instruction in Servia, so far as the corps of instructors, as well as the means of instruction are concerned, that which serves, or may serve, to foster the propaganda against Austria-Hungary;

4. to remove from military service and the administration in general all officers and officials who are guilty of propaganda against Austria-Hungary, and whose names, with a communication of the material which the Imperial and Royal Government possesses against them, the Imperial and Royal Government reserves the right to communicate to the Royal Government;

5. to consent that in Servia officials of the Imperial and Royal Government co-operate in the suppression of a movement directed against the territorial integrity of the monarchy;

6. to commence a judicial investigation against the participants of the conspiracy of June 28th who are on Servian territory. Officials, delegated by the Imperial and Royal Government will participate in the examinations;

7. to proceed at once with all severity to arrest Major Voja Tankosic and a certain Milan Ciganowic, Servian State officials, who have been compromised through the result of the investigation;

8. to prevent through effective measures the participation of the Servian authorities in the smuggling of arms and explosives across the frontier and to dismiss those officials of Shabatz and Loznica who assisted the originators of the crime of Sarajevo in crossing the frontier.

9. To give to the Imperial and Royal Government explanations in regard to the unjustifiable remarks of high Servian functionaries in Servia and abroad who have not hesitated, in spite of their official position, to express themselves in interviews in a hostile manner against Austria-Hungary after the outrage of June 28th.

10. The Imperial and Royal Government expects a reply from the Royal Government at the latest until Saturday, 25th inst., at 6 p.m. A memoir concerning the results of the investigations at Sarajevo, so far as they concern points 7 and 8, is enclosed with this note.

Enclosure.

The investigation carried on against Gabrilo Princip and accomplices in the Court of Sarajevo, on account of the assassination on June 28th has, so far, yielded the following results:

1.   The plan to murder Archduke Franz Ferdinand during his stay in Sarajevo was conceived in Belgrade by Gabrilo Princip, Nedeljko, Gabrinowic, and a certain Milan Ciganowic and Trifko Grabez, with the aid of Major Voja Tankosic.

2.   The six bombs and four Browning pistols which were used by the criminals were obtained by Milan Ciganowic and Major Tankosic, and presented to Princip and Gabrinowic in Belgrade.

3.   The bombs are hand grenades, manufactured at the arsenal of the Servian Army in Kragujevac.

4.   To insure the success of the assassination, Milan Ciganowic instructed Princip and Gabrinowic in the use of the grenades and gave instructions in shooting with Browning pistols to Princip and

Grabez in a forest near the target practice field of Topshider—(outside Belgrade).

5. In order to enable the crossing of the frontier of Bosnia and Herzegovina by Princip and Gabrinowic and Grabez, and the smuggling of their arms, a secret system of transportation was organised by Ciganowic. The entry of the criminals with their arms into Bosnia and Herzegovina was effected by the frontier captains of Shabatz (Rade Popowic) and of Loznica, as well as by the custom house official Rudivoy Grbic of Loznica with the aid of several other persons.

5. THE SERBIAN REPLY TO THE AUSTRIAN ULTIMATUM, JULY 25, 1914

This declaration will be brought to the knowledge of the Royal Army in an order of the day, in the name of His Majesty the King, by his Royal Highness the Crown Prince Alexander, and will be published in the next official army bulletin.

The Royal Government will undertake:—

1. To introduce at the first regular convocation of the Skuptchina a provision into the press law providing for the most severe punishment of incitement to hatred or contempt of the Austro-Hungarian Monarchy, and for taking action against any publication the general tendency of which is directed against the territorial integrity of Austria-Hungary. The Government engage at the approaching revision of the Constitution to cause an amendment to be introduced into article 22 of the Constitution of such a nature that such publication may be confiscated, a proceeding at present impossible under the categorical terms of article 22 of the Constitution.

2. The Government possesses no proof, nor does the note of the Imperial and Royal Government furnish them with any, that the "Narodna Odbrana" and other similar societies have committed up to the present any criminal act of this nature through the proceedings of any of their members. Nevertheless, the Royal Government will accept the demand of the Imperial and Royal Government, and will dissolve the "Narodna Odbrana" Society and every other society which may be directing its efforts against Austria-Hungary.

3. The Royal Servian Government undertake to remove without delay from their public educational establishments in Servia all that serves or could serve to foment propaganda against Austria-Hungary, whenever the Imperial and Royal Government furnish them with facts and proofs of this propaganda.

4. The Royal Government also agree to remove from military service all such persons as the judicial enquiry may have proved to be guilty of acts directed against the integrity of the territory of the Austro-Hungarian Monarchy, and they expect the Imperial and Royal Government to communicate to them at a later date the names and acts of these officers and officials for the purposes of the proceedings which are to be taken against them.

5. The Royal Government must confess that they do not clearly grasp the meaning or the scope of the demand made by the Imperial and Royal Government that Servia shall undertake to accept the collaboration of the organs of the Imperial and Royal Government upon their territory, but they declare that they will admit such collaboration as agrees with the principle of international law, with criminal procedure, and with good neighbourly relations.

6. It goes without saying that the Royal Government consider it their duty to open an enquiry against all such persons as are, or eventually may be, implicated in the plot of the 15th June, and who happen to be within the territory of the kingdom. As regards the participation in this enquiry of Austro-Hungarian agents or authorities appointed for this purpose by the Imperial and Royal Government, the Royal Government cannot accept such an arrangement, as it would be a violation of the Constitution and of the law of criminal procedure; nevertheless, in concrete cases communications as to the results of the investigation in question might be given to the Austro-Hungarian agents.

7. The Royal Government proceeded, on the very evening of the delivery of the note, to arrest Commandant Voislav Tankossitch. As regards Milan Ziganovitch, who is a subject of the Austro-Hungarian Monarchy and who up to the 15th June was employed (on probation) by the directorate of railways, it has not yet been possible to arrest him. The Austro-Hungarian Government are requested to be so good as to supply as soon as possible, in the customary form, the presumptive evidence of guilt, as well as the eventual proofs of guilt which have been collected up to the present, at the enquiry.

8. The Servian Government will reinforce and extend the measures which have been taken for preventing the illicit traffic of arms and explosives across the frontier. It goes without saying that they will immediately order an enquiry and will severely punish the frontier [officials] on the Schabatz-Loznitza line who have failed in their duty and allowed authors of the crime of Serajevo to pass.

6. THE GERMAN REQUEST FOR FREE PASSAGE THROUGH BELGIUM NOTE, AUGUST 2, 1914

The German Ambassador at Brussels, Herr von Below Saleske, delivered the following note to M. Davignon, Belgian Minister for Foreign Affairs.

Kaiserlich Deutsche Gesandschaft in Belgien-Brüssel August 2, 1914

(Very Confidential)

RELIABLE information has been received by the German Government to the effect that French forces intend to march on the line of the Meuse by Givet and Namur. This information leaves no doubt as to the intention of France to march through Belgian territory against Germany.

The German Government cannot but fear that Belgium, in spite of the utmost goodwill, will be unable, without assistance, to repel so considerable a French invasion with sufficient prospect of success to afford an adequate guarantee against danger to Germany. It is essential for the self-defence of Germany that she should anticipate any such hostile attack. The German Government would, however, feel the deepest regret if Belgium regarded as an act of hostility against herself the fact that the measures of Germany's opponents force Germany, for her own protection, to enter Belgian territory.

In order to exclude any possibility of misunderstanding, the German Government make the following declaration:—

1. Germany has in view no act of hostility against Belgium. In the event of Belgium being prepared in the coming war to maintain an attitude of friendly neutrality towards Germany, the German Government bind themselves, at the conclusion of peace, to guarantee the possessions and independence of the Belgian Kingdom in full.

2. Germany undertakes, under the above-mentioned condition, to evacuate Belgian territory on the conclusion of peace.

3. If Belgium adopts a friendly attitude, Germany is prepared, in cooperation with the Belgian authorities, to purchase all necessaries for her troops against a cash payment, and to pay an indemnity for any damage that may have been caused by German troops.

4. Should Belgium oppose the German troops, and in particular should she throw difficulties in the way of their march by a resistance of the fortresses on the Meuse, or by destroying railways, roads, tunnels, or other similar works, Germany will, to her regret, be compelled to consider Belgium as an enemy.

In this event, Germany can undertake no obligations towards Belgium, but the eventual adjustment of the relations between the two States must be left to the decision of arms.

The German Government, however, entertain the distinct hope that this eventuality will not occur, and that the Belgian Government will know how to take the necessary measures to prevent the occurrence of incidents such as those mentioned. In this case the friendly ties which bind the two neighbouring States will grow stronger and more enduring.

7. THE BELGIAN REFUSAL OF FREE PASSAGE NOTE, AUGUST 3, 1914

…This note [asking free passage] has made a deep and painful impression upon the Belgian Government. The intentions attributed to France by Germany are in contradiction to the formal declarations made to us on August 1, in the name of the French Government. Moreover, if, contrary to our expectation, Belgian neutrality should be violated by France, Belgium intends to fulfil her international obligations and the Belgian army would offer the most vigorous resistance to the invader. The treaties of 1839, confirmed by the treaties of 1870 vouch for the independence and neutrality of Belgium under the guarantee of the Powers, and notably of the Government of His Majesty the King of Prussia.

Belgium has always been faithful to her international obligations, she has carried out her duties in a spirit of loyal impartiality, and she has left nothing undone to maintain and enforce respect for her neutrality.

The attack upon her independence with which the German Government threaten her constitutes a flagrant violation of international law. No strategic interest justifies such a violation of law.

The Belgian Government, if they were to accept the proposals submitted to them, would sacrifice the honour of the nation and betray their duty towards Europe.

Conscious of the part which Belgium has played for more than eighty years in the civilisation of the world, they refuse to believe that the independence of Belgium can only be preserved at the price of the violation of her neutrality.

If this hope is disappointed the Belgian Government are firmly resolved to repel, by all the means in their power, every attack upon their rights.

8. EXCERPTS FROM THE TREATY OF LONDON, APRIL 26, 1915

Great Britain, Parliamentary Papers, London, 1920, LI Cmd. 671, Miscellaneous No. 7, 2–7.

ARTICLE 1. A military convention shall be immediately concluded between the General Staffs of France, Great Britain, Italy, and Russia. This convention shall settle the minimum number of military forces to be employed by Russia against Austria-Hungary in order to prevent that Power from concentrating all its strength against Italy, in the event of Russia deciding to direct her principal effort against Germany. . . .

ARTICLE 2. On her part, Italy undertakes to use her entire resources for the purpose of waging war jointly with France, Great Britain, and Russia against all their enemies.

ARTICLE 3. The French and British fleets shall render active and permanent assistance to Italy. . . .

ARTICLE 4. Under the Treaty of Peace, Italy shall obtain the Trentino, Cisalpine Tyrol with its geographical and natural frontier, as well as Trieste, the counties of Gorizia and Gradisca, all Istria as far as the Quarnero and including Volosca and the Istrian islands of Cherso and Lussin, as well as the small islands of Plavnik, Unie, Canidole, Palazzuoli, San Pietro di Nembi, Asinello, Gruica, and the neighbouring islets. . . .

ARTICLE 5. Italy shall also be given the province of Dalmatia within its present administrative boundaries. . . .

ARTICLE 6. Italy shall receive full sovereignty over Valona, the island of Saseno and surrounding territory. . . .

ARTICLE 7. Should Italy obtain the Trentino and Istria in accordance with the provisions of Article 4, together with Dalmatia and the Adriatic islands within the limits specified in Article 5, and the Bay of Valona (Article 6), and if the central portion of Albania is reserved for the establishment of a small autonomous neutralised State, Italy shall not oppose the division of Northern and Southern Albania between Montenegro, Serbia, and Greece. . . .

ARTICLE 8. Italy shall receive entire sovereignty over the Dodecanese Islands which she is at present occupying.

ARTICLE 9. Generally speaking, France, Great Britain, and Russia recognise that, . . . in the event of total or partial partition of Turkey in Asia, she ought to obtain a just share of the Mediterranean region adjacent to the province of Adalia. . . .

ARTICLE 11. Italy shall receive a share of any eventual war indemnity corresponding to their efforts and her sacrifices.

ARTICLE 13. In the event of France and Great Britain increasing their colonial territories in Africa at the expense of Germany, those two Powers agree in principle that Italy may claim some equitable compensation. . . .

ARTICLE 14. Great Britain undertakes to facilitate the immediate conclusion, under equitable conditions, of a loan of at least 50,000,000 pounds. . . .

ARTICLE 16. The present arrangement shall be held secret.

9. BERNSTORFF *ARABIC* PLEDGE, OCTOBER 5, 1915

The German Ambassador to the Secretary of State
Washington, October 5, 1915.
Mr. Dear Mr. Secretary:

Prompted by the desire to reach a satisfactory agreement with regard to the *Arabic* incident, my Government has given me the following instructions:

The orders issued by His Majesty the Emperor to the commanders of the German submarines—of which I notified you on a previous occasion—have been made so stringent that the recurrence of incidents similar to the *Arabic* case is considered out of the question.

According to the report of Commander Schneider of the submarine that sank the *Arabic,* and his affidavit as well as those of his men, Commander Schneider was convinced that the *Arabic* intended to ram the submarine. On the other hand, the Imperial Government does not doubt the good faith of the affidavits of the British officers of the *Arabic,* according to which the *Arabic* did not intend to ram the submarine. The attack of the submarine, therefore, was undertaken against the instructions issued to the commander. The Imperial Government regrets and disavows this act and has notified Commander Schneider accordingly.

Under these circumstances my Government is prepared to pay an indemnity for the American lives which, to its deep regret, have been lost on the *Arabic.* I am authorized to negotiate with you about the amount of this indemnity.

I remain [etc.]

J. von Bernstorff

10. Husain–McMahon Letter on Commitment to the Arabs, October 24, 1915

I have received your letter of the 29th Shawal, 1333, with much pleasure and your expression of friendliness and sincerity have given me the greatest satisfaction.

I regret that you should have received from my last letter the impression that I regarded the question of limits and boundaries with coldness and hesitation; such was not the case, but it appeared to me that the time had not yet come when that question could be discussed in a conclusive manner.

I have realised, however, from your last letter that you regard this question as one of vital and urgent importance. I have, therefore, lost no time in informing the Government of Great Britain of the contents of your letter, and it is with great pleasure that I communicate to you on their behalf the following statement, which I am confident you will receive with satisfaction.—

The two districts of Mersina and Alexandretta and portions of Syria lying to the west of the districts of Damascus, Homs, Hama and Aleppo cannot be said to be purely Arab, and should be excluded from the limits demanded.

With the above modification, and without prejudice to our existing treaties with Arab chiefs, we accept those limits.

As for those regions lying within those frontiers wherein Great Britain is free to act without detriment to the interests of her ally, France, I am empowered in the name of the Government of Great Britain to give the following assurances and make the following assurances and make the following reply to your letter:

(1) Subject to the above modifications, Great Britain is prepared to recognise and support the independence of the Arabs in all the regions within the limits demanded by the Sherif of Mecca.

(2) Great Britain will guarantee the Holy Places against all external aggression and will recognise their inviolability.

(3) When the situation admits, Great Britain will give to the Arabs her advice and will assist them to establish what may appear to be the most suitable forms of government of those various territories.

(4) On the other hand, it is understood that the Arabs have decided to seek the advice and guidance of Great Britain only, and that such European advisers and officials as may be required for the formation of a sound form of administration will be British.

(5) With regard to the vilayets of Bagdad and Basra, the Arabs will recognise that the established position and interests of Great Britain necessitate special administrative arrangements in order to secure these territories from foreign aggression to promote the welfare of the local populations and to safeguard our mutual economic interests.

I am convinced that this declaration will assure you beyond all possible doubt of the sympathy of Great Britain towards the aspirations of her friends the Arabs and will result in a firm and lasting alliance, the immediate results of which will be the expulsion of the Turks from the Arab countries and the freeing of the Arab peoples from the Turkish yoke, which for so many years has pressed heavily upon them.

I have confined myself in this letter to the more vital and important questions, and if there are any other matters dealt with in your letters which I have omitted to mention, we may discuss them at some convenient date in the future.

It was with very great relief and satisfaction that I heard of the safe arrival of the Holy Carpet and the accompanying offerings which, thanks to the clearness of your directions and the excellence of your arrangements, were landed without trouble or mishap in spite of the dangers and difficulties occasioned by the present sad war. May God soon bring a lasting peace and freedom of all peoples.

I am sending this letter by the hand of your trusted and excellent messenger, Sheikh Mohammed ibn Arif ibn Uraifan, and he will inform you of the various matters of interest, but of less vital importance, which I have not mentioned in this letter.

(Compliments).

(Signed): A. HENRY McMAHON.

11. MEMORANDUM OF THE GERMAN GOVERNMENT ON THE TREATMENT OF ARMED MERCHANT SHIPS AS SHIPS OF WAR, FEBRUARY 10, 1916

I

1. Even before the outbreak of the present war the British Government had given English shipping companies the opportunity to arm their merchant vessels with guns. On March 26, 1913, Winston Churchill, then First Lord of the Admiralty, made the declaration in the British Parliament . . . that the Admiralty had called upon the shipowners to arm a number of first-class liners for protection against danger menaced in certain cases by fast auxiliary cruisers of other powers; the liners were not, however, to assume the character of auxiliary cruisers themselves. The Government desired to place at the disposal of the shipowners the necessary guns, sufficient ammunition, and suitable personnel for the training of the gun crews.

2. The English shipowners have readily responded to the call of the Admiralty. Thus Sir Owen Philipps, president of the Royal Mail Steam Packet Company, was able to inform the stockholders of his company in May 1913, that the larger steamers of the company were equipped with guns. . . .

II

1. With regard to the legal character of armed merchantmen in international law, the British Government has taken the position in respect of its own merchantmen that such vessels retain the character of peaceable merchant vessels as long as they carry arms for defensive purposes only. In accordance with this, the British Ambassador at Washington in a note dated August 25, 1914 . . . gave the American Government the fullest assurances that British merchant vessels were never armed for purposes of attack, but solely for defense, and that they consequently never fire unless first fired upon. On the other hand, the British Government set up

the principle for armed vessels of other flags that they are to be treated as war vessels. No. 1 of Order 1 of the prize court rules, promulgated by the order in council of August 5, 1914, expressly provides [as a matter of definition] "ship of war shall include armed ship."

2. The German Government has no doubt that a merchantman assumes a warlike character by armament with guns, regardless of whether the guns are intended to serve for defense or attack. It considers any warlike activity of an enemy merchantman contrary to international law, although it accords consideration to the opposite view by treating the crew of such a vessel not as pirates but as belligerents. The details of its position are set forth in the memorandum on the treatment of armed merchantmen in neutral ports . . . communicated to the American Government in October 1914, the contents of which were likewise communicated to other neutral powers.

3. Some of the neutral powers have accepted the position of the British Government and therefore permitted armed merchantmen of the belligerent powers to stay in their ports and shipyards without the restrictions which they had imposed on ships of war through their neutrality regulations. Some, however, have taken the contrary view and subjected armed merchantmen of belligerents to the neutrality rules applicable to ships of war.

III

1. During the course of the war the armament of English merchantmen has been more and more generally carried out. From reports of the German naval forces numerous cases became known in which English merchantmen not only offered armed resistance to the German war vessels, but proceeded to attack them on their own initiative, and in so doing they frequently even made use of false flags. A list of such cases is found in Exhibit 4, which from the nature of the matter can include only a part of the attacks which were actually made. It is also shown by this list that the practice described is not limited to English merchantmen, but is imitated by the merchantmen of England's allies.

2. The explanation of the action of the armed English merchantmen described is contained

in Exhibits 5 to 12, which are photographic reproductions of confidential instructions of the British Admiralty found by German naval forces on captured ships. These instructions regulate in detail artillery attack by English merchantmen on German submarines. They contain exact regulations touching the reception, treatment activity, and control of the British gun crews taken on board merchantmen; for example, they are not to wear uniform in neutral ports and thus plainly belong to the British navy. Above all, it is shown by these instructions that these armed vessels are not to await any action of maritime war on the part of the German submarines, but are to attack them forthwith. In this respect the following regulations are particularly instructive:

(a) The instructions [to armed merchant ships] . . . provide in the section headed "Action," in paragraph 4: "It is not advisable to open fire at a range greater than 800 yards unless the enemy has already opened fire." From this it is the duty of the merchantman in principle to open fire without regard to the attitude of the submarine.

(b) The instructions regarding submarines applicable to vessels carrying a defensive armament . . . prescribe under No. 3: "If a submarine is obviously pursuing a ship by day and it is evident to the master that she has hostile intentions, the ship pursued should open fire in self-defense, notwithstanding the submarine may not have committed a definite hostile act such as firing a gun or torpedo." From this also the mere appearance of a submarine in the wake of the merchantman affords sufficient occasion for an armed attack.

In all these orders, which do not apply merely to the zone of maritime war around England, but are unrestricted as regards their validity . . . the greatest emphasis is laid on secrecy, plainly in order that the action of merchantmen, in absolute contradiction of international law and the British assurances . . . might remain concealed from the enemy as well as the neutrals.

3. It is thus made plain that the armed English merchantmen have official instructions to attack the German submarines treacherously wherever they come near them; that is, orders to conduct relentless warfare against them. Since England's rules of maritime war are adopted by her allies without question, the proof must be taken as demonstrated

in respect of the armed merchantmen of the other enemy countries also.

IV

In the circumstances set forth above, enemy merchantmen armed with guns no longer have any right to be considered as peaceable vessels of commerce. Therefore the German naval forces will receive orders, within a short period, paying consideration to the interests of the neutrals, to treat such vessels as belligerents. The German Government brings this state of things to the knowledge of the neutral powers in order that they may warn their nationals against continuing to entrust their persons or property to armed merchantmen of the powers at war with the German Empire.

12. TIRPITZ MEMORANDUM ON THE ADVISABILITY OF UNRESTRICTED SUBMARINE WARFARE, FEBRUARY 13, 1916

Secretary of State of the Imperial Marine Service v. Tirpitz to Imperial Chancelor v. Bethmann-Hollweg:

Berlin, February 13, 1916.

[Admiral von Tirpitz provides answers to questions posed by Chancellor Bethmann-Hollweg.]

Can England be forced to sue for peace by means of a U-boat war?

I. The most important and surest means which can be adopted to bring England to her knees is the use of our U-boats at the present time. We shall not be able to defeat England by a war on land alone. The unrestricted carrying out of the U-boat war, supported by our other naval craft and by our air fleet—all under a unified and determined leadership—is of the most decisive importance in obtaining the desired result. England will be cut to the heart by the destruction by U-boats of every ship which approaches the English coast. The ocean's commerce is the very elixir of life for England, its interruption for any length of time a deadly danger, its permanent interruption absolutely fatal within a short time. Every attack upon England's transoceanic communication is therefore a blow in the direction of the termination of the war. The more the losses take place with merciless regularity at the very gates of the island kingdom, the more powerful will be the material and moral effect on the English people. In spite of its former resources, England will not be able to make a successful defense against the attacks of submarines directed against its transoceanic commerce, provided they are well planned. That is precisely why a timely U-boat war is the most dangerous and, if vigorously carried on, the form of warfare which will unconditionally decide the war to England's disadvantage.

II. The prerequisites of a successful carrying out of an unrestricted U-boat war are military and economic In both respects they are noticeably more favorable than in February, 1915. . . .

III. In order to get the correct view of America's attitude in the U-boat question, it is necessary to go back over its development during the course of the war.

From the very beginning, the attitude of the United States toward us has not been a friendly one. The close racial feeling which bound the greater part of the population to England, together with the combinations of English and American economic forces which have constantly resulted in more and more intimate relations in this direction, necessarily resulted in the antagonism referred to. In spite of this, there existed in the beginning, at least so far as the government was concerned, a certain objection against openly taking sides with either party. If from the date of the February note onward, we could have afforded to pay no attention at all to the objections urged by the United States against the U-boat war, the unrestricted conduct of this war would not, in my opinion, have led to a break with the United States. In view of the restrictions imposed upon the conduct of the U-boat war and of the enormous deliveries of ammunition and war material of every kind which was made possible thereby, the whole economic life of the United States, and the American policy as well, came to be connected with the British cause in a manner quite different from that existing at the beginning of the war. America is directly interested in the fate of England's economic existence, and, as a logical consequence, in England's intention to crush Germany. As a result, the conviction on the part of Americans of the growing dangers involved in Japan's hostile attitude, and that sooner or later differences with Japan will be bound to ensue, has become stronger as the war has run its course. Understandings unquestionably exist today, if not between the two governments, at least, in any case, between the leaders of the trusts in England and America, whose purpose is to give Japan a very definite setback by means of the combined forces of England and the United States after the war. But this is possible only if England can be absolutely secured against any

danger emanating from Europe, that is, if Germany is overpowered. It follows that the United States, whether they desire to be so or not, are directly interested in our defeat, and have become a direct enemy of Germany.

If the United States intends to push this position to its logical conclusion and to let matters come to a break with us, the resulting circumstances would suffer no material change, provided this break were limited to a refusal to maintain diplomatic relations. But if the United States should go as far as to declare war against us, then the problem of shipping space would occupy a prominent place among those questions on which we would have to pass in connection with the then newly created situation. The assistance in men and material with which the United States would then be in a position to provide England and our other opponents would, as a practical proposition, be measured by the amount of tonnage for commercial purposes actually at their disposal.

The attempt on the part of the United States to increase this tonnage to any appreciable extent through a retaliatory seizure of the German commercial tonnage within their reach would, in the first place, be confronted with quite substantial obstacles and, in the second place, be useless in any case.

The gross tonnage of German steamers now in the United States [interned by the war] amounts to 440,000 tons, according to my estimate. There are about 116,850 gross tons in the American colonies. . . .

But assuming that, in spite of all this, the United States should succeed in placing the German merchant ships in their service, the personal interests of the country would make it necessary for these ships to be held for their own purposes. So that an advantage to England or a lightening of England's burdens would not result from this situation.

Were America, after a break with us, to provide financial support in ever-increasing volume to England and our opponents, the only result for the latter would be that they would become more and more dependent upon the United States. And moreover, the practical effect of such financial support would, for the most part, take the form of possibly providing them with increased shipments of war material of all kinds which were not obtainable in their own country, and of supplying them with those articles essential to their economic life. But this possibility can only become an established fact if the shipments in question can actually be delivered. For instance, an increase in Italy's financial resources for the purpose of obtaining coal does not actually bring coal to the country. And so an increased financial support of our opponents by America would, in the last analysis, for its effective working out, be inseparably and mainly dependent upon the problem of tonnage. . . .

V. With regard to supplementing the tremendous results of the war on land, we have the following:

1. The entrance of America into the list of our opponents would be of no definite assistance to England.
2. It is only by making the fullest use of all of our instrumentalities adapted to warfare on the sea, amongst which the U-boats will play an important part by shutting England off from all intercourse by sea, that it will be possible to bring about England's defeat.

Berlin, February 8, 1916.

13. WILSON ON THE *SUSSEX* INCIDENT APRIL 19, 1916

United States, 64th Cong., 1st Sess., House Document 1034.

[Excerpts from President Wilson's remarks before Congress concerning the German attack on the unarmed Channel steamer *Sussex* on March 24, 1916.]

. . . I have deemed it my duty, therefore, to say to the Imperial German Government, that if it is still its purpose to prosecute relentless and indiscriminate warfare against vessels of commerce by the use of submarines, notwithstanding the now demonstrated impossibility of conducting that warfare in accordance with what the Government of the United States must consider the sacred and indisputable rules of international law and the universally recognized dictates of humanity, the Government of the United States is at last forced to the conclusion that there is but one course it can pursue; and that unless the Imperial German Government should now immediately declare and effect an abandonment of its present methods of warfare against passenger and freight carrying vessels this Government can have no choice but to sever diplomatic relations with the Government of the German Empire altogether.

This decision I have arrived at with the keenest regret; the possibility of the action contemplated I am sure all thoughtful Americans will look forward to with unaffected reluctance. But we cannot forget that we are in some sort and by the force of circumstances the responsible spokesmen of the rights of humanity, and that we cannot remain silent while those rights seem in process of being swept utterly away in the maelstrom of this terrible war. We owe it to a due regard to our own rights as a nation, to our sense of duty as a representative of the rights of neutrals the world over, and to a just conception of the rights of mankind to take this stand now with the utmost solemnity and firmness. . . .

14. SYKES-PICOT AGREEMENT, MAY 16, 1916

The Sykes-Picot Agreement: 1916

It is accordingly understood between the French and British governments:

That France and Great Britain are prepared to recognize and protect an independent Arab state or a confederation of Arab states (a) and (b) marked on the annexed map, under the suzerainty of an Arab chief. That in area (a) France, and in area (b) Great Britain, shall have priority of right of enterprise and local loans. That in area (a) France, and in area (b) Great Britain, shall alone supply advisers or foreign functionaries at the request of the Arab state or confederation of Arab states.

That in the blue area France, and in the red area Great Britain, shall be allowed to establish such direct or indirect administration or control as they desire and as they may think fit to arrange with the Arab state or confederation of Arab states.

That in the brown area there shall be established an international administration, the form of which is to be decided upon after consultation with Russia, and subsequently in consultation with the other allies, and the representatives of the sheriff of Mecca.

That Great Britain be accorded (1) the ports of Haifa and Acre, (2) guarantee of a given supply of water from the Tigres and Euphrates in area (a) for area (b). His Majesty's government, on their part, undertake that they will at no time enter into negotiations for the cession of Cyprus to any third power without the previous consent of the French government.

That Alexandretta shall be a free port as regards the trade of the British empire, and that there shall be no discrimination in port charges or facilities as regards British shipping and British goods; that there shall be freedom of transit for British goods through Alexandretta and by railway through the blue area, or (b) area, or area (a); and there shall be no discrimination, direct or indirect, against British goods on any railway or against British goods or ships at any port serving the areas mentioned.

That Haifa shall be a free port as regards the trade of France, her dominions and protectorates, and there shall be no discrimination in port charges or facilities as regards French shipping and French goods. There shall be freedom of transit for French goods through Haifa and by the British railway through the brown area, whether those goods are intended for or originate in the blue area, area (a), or area (b), and there shall be no discrimination, direct or indirect, against French goods on any railway, or against French goods or ships at any port serving the areas mentioned.

That in area (a) the Baghdad railway shall not be extended southwards beyond Mosul, and in area (b) northwards beyond Samarra, until a railway connecting Baghdad and Aleppo via the Euphrates valley has been completed, and then only with the concurrence of the two governments.

That Great Britain has the right to build, administer, and be sole owner of a railway connecting Haifa with area (b), and shall have a perpetual right to transport troops along such a line at all times. It is to be understood by both governments that this railway is to facilitate the connection of Baghdad with Haifa by rail, and it is further understood that, if the engineering difficulties and expense entailed by keeping this connecting line in the brown area only make the project unfeasible, that the French government shall be prepared to consider that the line in question may also traverse the Polgon Banias Keis Marib Salkhad tell Otsda Mesmie before reaching area (b).

For a period of twenty years the existing Turkish customs tariff shall remain in force throughout the whole of the blue and red areas, as well as in areas (a) and (b), and no increase in the rates of duty or conversions from ad valorem to specific rates shall be made except by agreement between the two powers.

There shall be no interior customs barriers between any of the above mentioned areas. The customs duties leviable on goods destined for the interior shall be collected at the port of entry and handed over to the administration of the area of destination.

It shall be agreed that the French government will at no time enter into any negotiations for the cession of their rights and will not cede such rights in the blue area to any third power, except the Arab state or confederation of Arab states, without the previous agreement of his majesty's government, who, on their part, will give a similar undertaking to the French government regarding the red area.

The British and French governments, as the protectors of the Arab state, shall agree that they will not themselves acquire and will not consent to a third power acquiring territorial possessions in the Arabian peninsula, nor consent to a third power installing a naval base either on the east coast, or on the islands, of the Red Sea. This, however, shall not prevent such adjustment of the Aden frontier as may be necessary in consequence of recent Turkish aggression.

The negotiations with the Arabs as to the boundaries of the Arab states shall be continued through the same channel as heretofore on behalf of the two powers.

It is agreed that measures to control the importation of arms into the Arab territories will be considered by the two governments.

I have further the honor to state that, in order to make the agreement complete, His Majesty's government are proposing to the Russian government to exchange notes analogous to those exchanged by the latter and Your Excellency's government on the 26th April last. Copies of these notes will be communicated to Your Excellency as soon as exchanged. I would also venture to remind Your Excellency that the conclusion of the present agreement raises, for practical consideration, the question of claims of Italy to a share in any partition or rearrangement of Turkey in Asia, as formulated in article 9 of the agreement of the 26th April, 1915, between Italy and the allies.

His Majesty's government further consider that the Japanese government should be informed of the arrangements now concluded.

15. ZIMMERMANN NOTE, JANUARY 19, 1917

Note: various alternative translations of the original German note, with slightly different phrasing of the points, have been published.

To the German Minister to Mexico:

On the first of February we intend to begin submarine warfare unrestricted. In spite of this, it is our intention to endeavor to keep neutral the United States of America.

If this attempt is not successful, we propose an alliance on the following basis with Mexico: That we shall make war together and together make peace. We shall give generous financial support, and it is understood that Mexico is to reconquer the lost territory in New Mexico, Texas, and Arizona. The settlement in detail is left to you.

You will inform the President [of Mexico] of the above in the greatest confidence as soon as it is certain that there will be an outbreak of war with the United States and suggest that the President of Mexico, on his initiative, should communicate with Japan suggesting adherence at once to this plan; at the same time, offer to mediate between Germany and Japan.

Please call to the attention of the President of Mexico that the employment of ruthless submarine warfare now promises to compel England to make peace in a few months.

Zimmermann

16. Wilson's Peace Without Victory Note, January 22, 1917

Senate, January 22, 1917

Gentlemen of the Senate:

On the 18th of December last, I addressed an identical note to the governments of the nations now at war requesting them to state, more definitely than they had yet been stated by either group of belligerents, the terms upon which they would deem it possible to make peace. I spoke on behalf of humanity and of the rights of all neutral nations like our own, many of whose most vital interests the war puts in constant jeopardy.

The Central Powers united in a reply which states merely that they were ready to meet their antagonists in conference to discuss terms of peace. The Entente powers have replied much more definitely and have stated, in general terms, indeed, but with sufficient definiteness to imply details, the arrangements, guarantees, and acts of reparation which they deem to be the indispensable conditions of a satisfactory settlement. We are that much nearer a definite discussion of the peace which shall end the present war. We are that much nearer the definite discussion of the international concert which must thereafter hold the world at peace.

In every discussion of peace that must end this war, it is taken for granted that the peace must be followed by some definite concert of power which will make it virtually impossible that any such catastrophe should ever overwhelm us again. Every love of mankind, every sane and thoughtful man must take that for granted.

I have sought this opportunity to address you because I thought that I owed it to you, as the counsel associated with me in the final determination of our international obligations, to disclose to you without reserve the thought and purpose that have been taking form in my mind in regard to the duty of our Government in the days to come when it will be necessary to lay afresh and upon a new plan the foundations of peace among the nations.

It is inconceivable that the people of the United States should play no part in that great enterprise. To take part in such a service will be the opportunity for which they have sought to prepare themselves by the very principles and purposes of their polity and the approved practices of their government ever since the days when they set up a new nation in the high and honorable hope that it might, in all that it was and did, show mankind the way to liberty.

They cannot in honor withhold the service to which they are now about to be challenged. They do not wish to withhold it. But they owe it to themselves and to the other nations of the world to state the conditions under which they will feel free to render it.

That service is nothing less than this, to add their authority and their power to the authority and force of other nations to guarantee peace and justice throughout the world. Such a settlement cannot now be long postponed. It is right that before it comes this Government should frankly formulate the conditions upon which it would feel justified in asking our people to approve its formal and solemn adherence to a League for Peace. I am here to attempt to state those conditions.

The present war must first be ended; but we owe it to candor and to a just regard for the opinion of mankind to say that, so far as our participation in guarantees of future peace is concerned, it makes a great deal of difference in what way and upon what terms it is ended. The treaties and agreements which bring it to an end must embody terms which will create a peace that is worth guaranteeing and preserving, a peace that will win the approval of mankind, not merely a peace that will serve the several interests and immediate aims of the nations engaged. . . .

No covenant of cooperative peace that does not include the peoples of the New World can suffice to keep the future safe against war; and yet there is only one sort of peace that the peoples of America could join in guaranteeing. The elements of that peace must be elements that engage the confidence and satisfy the principles of the American governments, elements consistent with their political faith and with the practical convictions which the peoples of America have once for all embraced and undertaken to defend.

I do not mean to say that any American government would throw any obstacle in the way of any terms of peace the governments now at war might agree upon or seek to upset them when made, whatever they might be. I only take it for granted that mere terms of peace between the belligerents will not satisfy even the belligerents themselves. Mere agreements may not make peace secure. It will be absolutely necessary that a force be created as a guarantor of the permanency of the settlement so much greater than the force of any nation now engaged or any alliance hitherto formed or projected that no nation, no probable combination of nations could face or withstand it. If the peace presently to be made is to endure, it must be a peace made secure by the organized major force of mankind.

The terms of the immediate peace agreed upon will determine whether it is a peace for which such a guarantee can be secured. The question upon which the whole future peace and policy of the world depends is this: Is the present war a struggle for a just and secure peace, or only for a new balance of power? If it be only a struggle for a new balance of power, who will guarantee, who can guarantee the stable equilibrium of the new arrangement? Only a tranquil Europe can be a stable Europe. There must be, not a balance of power, but a community of power; not organized rivalries, but an organized common peace.

Fortunately we have received very explicit assurances on this point. The statesmen of both of the groups of nations now arrayed against one another have said, in terms that could not be misinterpreted, that it was no part of the purpose they had in mind to crush their antagonists. But the implications of these assurances may not be equally clear to all—may not be the same on both sides of the water. I think it will be serviceable if I attempt to set forth what we understand them to be.

They imply, first of all, that it must be a peace without victory. It is not pleasant to say this. I beg that I may be permitted to put my own interpretation upon it and that it may be understood that no other interpretation was in my thought. I am seeking only to face realities and to face them without soft concealments. Victory would mean peace forced upon the loser, a victor's terms imposed upon the vanquished. It would be accepted in humiliation, under duress, at an intolerable sacrifice, and would leave a sting, a resentment, a bitter memory upon which terms of peace would rest, not permanently, but only as upon quicksand. Only a peace between equals can last. Only a peace the very principle of which is equality and a common participation in a common benefit. The right state of mind, the right feeling between nations, is as necessary for a lasting peace as is the just settlement of vexed questions of territory or of racial and national allegiance.

The equality of nations upon which peace must be founded if it is to last must be an equality of rights; the guarantees exchanged must neither recognize nor imply a difference between big nations and small, between those that are powerful and those that are weak. Right must be based upon the common strength, not upon the individual strength, of the nations upon whose concert peace will depend. Equality of territory or of resources there of course cannot be; nor any sort of equality not gained in the ordinary peaceful and legitimate development of the peoples themselves. But no one asks or expects anything more than an equality of rights. Mankind is looking now for freedom of life, not for equipoises of power.

And there is a deeper thing involved than even equality of right among organized nations. No peace can last, or ought to last, which does not recognize and accept the principle that governments derive all their just powers from the consent of the governed, and that no right anywhere exists to hand peoples about from sovereignty to sovereignty as if they were property. I take it for granted, for instance, if I may venture upon a single example, that statesmen everywhere are agreed that there should be a united, independent, and autonomous Poland, and that henceforth inviolable security of life, of worship, and of industrial and social development should be guaranteed to all peoples who have lived hitherto under the power of governments devoted to a faith and purpose hostile to their own.

I speak of this, not because of any desire to exalt an abstract political principle which has always been held very dear by those who have sought to build up liberty in America but for the same reason that I have spoken of the other conditions of peace which seem to me clearly indispensable—because I wish frankly to uncover realities. Any peace which does not recognize and accept this principle will inevitably be upset. It will not rest upon the affections or the convictions of mankind. The ferment of spirit of whole populations will fight subtly and constantly against it, and all the world will sympathize. The world can be at peace only if its life is stable, and there can be no stability where the will is in rebellion, where there is not tranquillity of spirit and a sense of justice, of freedom, and of right.

So far as practicable, moreover, every great people now struggling towards a full development of its resources and of its powers should be assured a direct outlet to the great highways of the sea. Where this cannot be done by the cession of territory, it can no doubt be done by the neutralization of direct rights of way under the general guarantee which will assure the peace itself. With a right comity of arrangement no nation need be shut away from free access to the open paths of the world's commerce.

And the paths of the sea must alike in law and in fact be free. The freedom of the seas is the sine qua non of peace, equality, and cooperation. No doubt a somewhat radical reconsideration of many of the rules of international practice hitherto thought to be established may be necessary in order to make the seas indeed free and common in practically all circumstances for the use of mankind, but the motive for such changes is convincing and compelling. There can be no trust or intimacy between the peoples of the world without them. The free, constant, unthreatened intercourse of nations is an essential part of the process of peace and of development. It need not be difficult either to define or to secure the freedom of the seas if the governments of the world sincerely desire to come to an agreement concerning it.

It is a problem closely connected with the limitation of naval armaments and the cooperation of the navies of the world in keeping the seas at once free and safe. And the question of limiting naval armaments opens the wider and perhaps more difficult question of the limitation of armies and of all programs of military preparation. Difficult and delicate as these questions are, they must be faced with the utmost candor and decided in a spirit of real accommodation if peace is to come with healing in its wings, and come to stay.

Peace cannot be had without concession and sacrifice. There can be no sense of safety and equality among the nations if great preponderating armaments are henceforth to continue here and there to be built up and maintained. The statesmen of the world must plan for peace and nations must adjust and accommodate their policy to it as they have planned for war and made ready for pitiless contest and rivalry. The question of armaments, whether on land or sea, is the most immediately and intensely practical question connected with the future fortunes of nations and of mankind.

I have spoken upon these great matters without reserve and with the utmost explicitness because it has seemed to me to be necessary if the world's yearning desire for peace was anywhere to find free voice and utterance. Perhaps I am the only person in high authority amongst all the peoples of the world who is at liberty to speak and hold nothing back. I am speaking as an individual, and yet I am speaking also, of course, as the responsible head of a great government, and I feel confident that I have said what the people of the United States would wish me to say.

May I not add that I hope and believe that I am in effect speaking for liberals and friends of humanity in every nation and of every program of liberty? I would fain believe that I am speaking for the silent mass of mankind everywhere who have as yet had no place or opportunity to speak their real hearts out concerning the death and ruin they see to have come already upon the persons and the homes they hold most dear.

And in holding out the expectation that the people and government of the United States will join the other civilized nations of the world in guaranteeing the permanence of peace upon such terms as I have named I speak with the greater boldness and confidence because it is clear to every man who can think that there is in this promise no breach in either our traditions or our policy as a nation, but a fulfillment, rather, of all that we have professed or striven for.

I am proposing, as it were, that the nations should with one accord adopt the doctrine of President Monroe as the doctrine of the world: that no nation should seek to extend its polity over any other nation or people, but that every people should be left free to determine its own polity, its own way of development, unhindered, unthreatened, unafraid, the little along with the great and powerful.

I am proposing that all nations henceforth avoid entangling alliances which would draw them into competitions of power; catch them in a net of intrigue and selfish rivalry, and disturb their own affairs with influences intruded from without. There is no entangling alliance in a concert of power. When all unite to act in the same sense and with the same purpose all act in the common interest and are free to live their own lives under a common protection.

I am proposing government by the consent of the governed; that freedom of the seas which in international conference after conference representatives of the United States have urged with the eloquence of those who are the convinced disciples of liberty; and that moderation of armaments which makes of armies and navies a power for order merely, not an instrument of aggression or of selfish violence.

These are American principles, American policies. We could stand for no others. And they are also the principles and policies of forward looking men and women everywhere, of every modern nation, of every enlightened community. They are the principles of mankind and must prevail.

17. ORDER NO. I OF THE PETROGRAD SOVIET, MARCH 14, 1917

March 1 (14 N.S.),1917.

To the garrison of the Petrograd District. To all the soldiers of the Guard, army, artillery and fleet for immediate and precise execution, and to the workers of Petrograd for information.

The Soviet of Workers' and Soldiers' Deputies has decided:

1. In all companies, battalions, regiments, depots, batteries, squadrons and separate branches of military service of every kind and on warships immediately choose committees from the elected representatives of the soldiers and sailors of the above mentioned military units.

2. In all military units which have still not elected their representatives in the Soviet of Workers' Deputies elect one representative to a company, who should appear with written credentials in the building of the State Duma at ten o'clock on the morning of March 2.

3. In all its political demonstrations a military unit is subordinated to the Soviet of Workers' and Soldiers' Deputies and its committees.

4. The orders of the military commission of the State Duma are to be fulfilled only in those cases which do not contradict the orders and decisions of the Soviet of Workers' and Soldiers' Deputies.

5. Arms of all kinds, as rifles, machine-guns, armored automobiles and others must be at the disposition and under the control of the company and battalion committees and are not in any case to be given out to officers, even upon their command.

6. In the ranks and in fulfilling service duties soldiers must observe the strictest military discipline; but outside of service, in their political, civil and private life soldiers cannot be discriminated against as regards those rights which all citizens enjoy. Standing at attention and compulsory saluting outside of service are especially abolished.

7. In the same way the addressing of officers with titles: Your Excellency, Your Honor, etc., is abolished and is replaced by the forms of address: Mr. General, Mr. Colonel, etc. Rude treatment of soldiers of all ranks, and especially addressing them as "thou," is forbidden; and soldiers are bound to bring to the attention of the company committees any violation of this rule and any misunderstandings between officers and soldiers. This order is to be read in all companies, battalions, regiments, marine units, batteries and other front and rear military units.

PETROGRAD SOVIET OF WORKERS' AND SOLDIERS' DEPUTIES.

18. ROBERT LANSING'S MEMORANDUM ON THE CABINET MEETING OF MARCH 20, 1917

Tuesday, March 20, 1917, 2.30–5 p.m.

The Cabinet Meeting of today I consider the most momentous and therefore, the most historic of any of those which have been held since I became Secretary of State, since it involved, unless a miracle occurs, the question of war with Germany and the abandonment of the policy of neutrality which has been pursued for two years and a half....

The corridors of the State Department and Executive Office swarmed with press correspondents seeking to get some inkling of what would be done from passing officials. It was through these eager crowds of news-gatherers that I forced my way at half-past two Tuesday afternoon under a bombardment of questions, to which I made no reply, and entered the Cabinet room where all the other members had arrived.

Three minutes later the President came in and passed to his place at the head of the table shaking hands with each member and smiling as genially and composedly as if nothing of importance was to be considered. Composure is a marked characteristic of the President. Nothing ruffles the calmness of his manner or address. It has a sobering effect on all who sit with him in council. Excitement would seem very much out of place at the Cabinet table with Woodrow Wilson presiding.

. . . the President said that he desired advice from the Cabinet on our relations with Germany and the course which should be pursued. He began with a review of his actions up to the present time pointing out that he had said to Congress on February 3rd that, while the announced policy of Germany had compelled the severance of diplomatic relations, he could not bring himself to believe that the German Government would carry it out against American vessels, but that, if an "overt act" occurred, he would come before them again and ask means to protect Americans on the high seas even though he thought he possessed the constitutional power to act without Congress. He said that the situation compelled him to do this on February 23rd and Congress had desired to adopt the measures, which he sought, but had been prevented, and that he had then acted on his own authority and placed armed guards on American vessels intending to proceed to the German barred zone.

He went on to say that he did not see from a practical point of view what else could be done to safeguard American vessels more than had already been done unless we declared war or declared that a state of war existed, which was the same thing; and that the power to do this lay with Congress.

He said that the two questions as to which he wished to be advised were—

Should he summon Congress to meet at an earlier date than April 16th, for which he had already issued a call?

Second. What should he lay before Congress when it did assemble?

He then spoke in general terms of the political situations in the belligerent countries particularly in Russia where the revolution against the autocracy had been successful, and in Germany where the liberal element in the Prussian Diet was grumbling loudly against their rulers. He also spoke of the situation in this country, of the indignation and bitterness in the East and the apparent apathy of the Middle West.

After the President had finished McAdoo was the first to speak. He said that war seemed to him a certainty and he could see no reason for delay in saying so and acting accordingly; that we might just as well face the issue and come out squarely in opposition to Germany, whose Government represented every evil in history; that, if we did not do so at once, the American people would compel action and we would be in the position of being pushed forward instead of leading, which would be humiliating and unwise. He further said that he believed that we could best aid the Allies against Germany by standing back of their credit, by underwriting their loans, and that they were sorely in need of such aid. He felt, however, that we could do little else, and doubted whether we could furnish men.

McAdoo spoke with great positiveness in advocating an immediate call of Congress. His voice was low and his utterance deliberate, but he gave the impression of great earnestness.

Houston, who followed, said that he agreed with McAdoo that it would create a most unfortunate, if not disastrous, impression on the American public as well as in Europe if we waited any longer to take a firm stand now that Germany had shown her hand. He said that he doubted whether we should plan to do more than to use our navy and to give financial aid to the Allies; that to equip an army of any size would divert the production of our industrial plants and so cut off from the Allies much needed supplies; and he thought that we ought to be very careful about interfering with their efficiency. He concluded by urging the President to summon Congress at once because he felt that a state of war already existed and should be declared.

Redfield followed Houston with his usual certainty of manner and vigor of expression. He was for declaring war and doing everything possible to aid in bringing the Kaiser to his knees. He made no points which particularly impressed me; and, as he had so often shown his strong pro-Ally sentiments, I was sure his words made little impression upon the President.

Baker was the next to express an opinion and he did so with the wonderful clearness of diction of which he is master. He said that he considered the state of affairs called for drastic action with as little delay as possible, and that he believed Congress should meet before April 16th. He said that the recent German outrages showed that the Germans did not intend to modify in the least degree their policy of inhumanity and lawlessness, and that such acts could mean only one thing, and that was war.

Since we were now forced into the struggle he favored entering it with all our vigor. He advocated preparing an army at once to be sent to Europe in case the Allies became straightened in the number of their men. He said that he believed the very knowledge of our preparations would force the Central Powers to realize that their cause was hopeless. He went on to discuss the details of raising, equipping and training a large force.

I followed Baker and can very naturally remember what I said better and more fully than I can the remarks of others.

I began with the statement that in my opinion an actual state of war existed today between this country and Germany, but that, as the acknowledgment of such a state officially amounted to a declaration of war, I doubted the wisdom as well as the constitutional power of the President to announce such fact or to act upon it; that I thought that the facts should be laid before Congress and that they should be asked to declare the existence of a state of war and to enact the laws necessary to meet the exigencies of the case. I pointed out that many things could be done under our present statutes which seriously menaced our national safety and that the Executive was powerless to prevent their being done. I referred in some detail to the exodus of Germans from this country to Mexico and Cuba since we severed diplomatic relations, to the activities of German agents here, to the transference of funds by Germans to Latin American countries, to the uncensored use of the telegraph and the mails, &c.

For the foregoing reasons I said that I felt that there should be no delay in calling Congress together and securing these necessary powers.

In addition to these reasons which so vitally affected our domestic situation I said that the revolution in Russia, which appeared to be successful, had removed the one objection to affirming that the European War was a war between Democracy and Absolutism; that the only hope of a permanent peace between all nations depended upon the establishment of democratic institutions throughout the world; that no League of Peace would be of value if a powerful autocracy was a member, and that no League of Peace would be necessary if all nations were democratic; and that in going into the war at this time we could do more to advance the cause of Democracy than if we failed to show sympathy with

the democratic powers in their struggle against the autocratic government of Germany.

I said that the present time seemed to me especially propitious for action by us because it would have a great moral influence in Russia, because it would encourage the democratic movement in Germany, because it would put new spirit in the Allies already flushed with recent military successes and because it would put an end to the charges of vacillation and hesitation, which were becoming general and bring the people solidly behind the President. . . .

The President said that he did not see how he could speak of a war for Democracy or of Russia's revolution in addressing Congress. I replied that I did not perceive any objection but in any event I was sure that he could do so indirectly by attacking the character of the autocratic government of Germany as manifested by its deeds of inhumanity, by its broken promises, and by its plots and conspiracies against this country.

To this the President only answered, "Possibly."

Whether the President was impressed with the idea of a general indictment of the German Government I do not know. I felt strongly that to go to war solely because American ships had been sunk and Americans killed would cause debate, and that the sounder basis was the duty of this and every other democratic nation to suppress an autocratic government like the German because of its atrocious character and because it was a menace to the national safety of this country and of all other countries with liberal systems of government. Such an arraignment would appeal to every liberty-loving man the world over. This I said during the discussion, but just when I do not remember.

When I had finished, Secretary Wilson in his usual slow but emphatic way said: "Mr. President, I think we must recognize the fact that Germany has made war upon this country and, therefore, I am for calling Congress together as soon as possible. I have reached this conviction with very great reluctance, but having reached it I feel that we should enter the war with the determination to employ all our resources to put an end to Prussian rule over Germany which menaces human liberty and peace all over the world. I do not believe we should employ half-measures or do it half-heartedly."

Gregory, who had been listening with much attention although on account of his deafness I am sure only heard his neighbors at the table, gave it as his opinion that it was useless to delay longer, that the possibility of peace with Germany was a thing of the past, and that he was in favor of assembling Congress as soon as possible, of enacting all necessary legislation, and of pursuing as aggressive action toward Germany as we were able. He went on to speak of German intrigues here, of the departure of German reservists and of the helplessness of his Department under existing laws. He said that every day's delay increased the danger and Congress ought to be called on to act at once.

After Gregory had given his views the President said, "We have not yet heard from Burleson and Daniels."

Burleson spoke up immediately and said: "Mr. President, I am in favor of calling Congress together and declaring war, and when we do that I want it to be understood that we are in the war to the end, that we will do everything we can to aid the Allies and weaken Germany with money, munitions, ships, and men, so that those Prussians will realize that, when they made war on this country, they woke up a giant which will surely defeat them. I would authorize the issue of five billions in bonds and go the limit." He stopped a moment and then added, "There are many personal reasons why I regret this step, but there is no other way. It must be carried through to the bitter end."

The President then turned his head toward Daniels who sat opposite Burleson and said: "Well, Daniels?" Daniels hesitated a moment as if weighing his words and then spoke in a voice which was low and trembled with emotion. His eyes were suffused with tears. He said that he saw no other course than to enter the war, that do what we would it seemed bound to come, and that, therefore, he was in favor of summoning Congress as soon as possible and getting their support for active measures against Germany.

Burleson had at previous meetings resisted an aggressive policy toward Germany, and he had, as late as the Cabinet meeting on Friday, the 16th, advocated very earnestly taking a radical stand against Great Britain on account of detention of the mails. Whenever I had called attention to the illegal acts of Germany he would speak of British wrong doings, I felt sure that he did this to cause a diversion of attention from the German violations of law. Possibly I misjudged him, and there was no such motive. His words at this meeting indicated hostility to Germany and a desire for drastic action, so I may have been mistaken.

As for Daniels his pacifist tendencies and personal devotion to Mr. Bryan and his ideas were well known.

It was, therefore, a surprise to us all when he announced himself to be in favor of war. I could not but wonder whether he spoke from conviction or because he lacked strength of mind to stand out against the united opinion of his colleagues. I prefer to believe the former reason, though I am not sure.

The President said, as Daniels ceased speaking: "Everybody has spoken but you, Lane."

Lane answered that he had nothing to add to what had been said by the other members of the Cabinet, with whom he entirely agreed as to the necessity of summoning Congress, declaring war and obtaining powers. He reviewed some of the things which had been said but contributed no new thought. He emphasized particularly the intensity of public indignation against the Germans and said that he felt that the people would force us to act even if we were unwilling to do so. . . .

When at last every Cabinet officer had spoken and all had expressed the opinion that war was inevitable and that Congress ought to be called in extraordinary session as soon as possible, the President in his cool, unemotional way said "Well, gentlemen, I think that there is no doubt as to what your advice is. I thank you."

The President, during the discussion or at the close, gave no sign what course he would adopt. However as we were leaving the room he called back Burleson and me and asked our views as to the time of calling a session if he so decided. After some discussion we agreed that to prepare the necessary legislation for submission to Congress would take over a week and that, therefore, Monday, April 2nd, would be the earliest day Congress could conveniently be summoned. I asked the President if he would issue a proclamation that afternoon so it would appear in the morning papers on Wednesday. He replied smilingly: "Oh, I think I will sleep on it."

Thus ended a Cabinet meeting the influence of which may change the course of history and determine the destinies of the United States and possibly of the world. The possible results are almost inconceivably great. I am sure that every member of the Cabinet felt the vital importance of the occasion and spoke with a full realization of the grave responsibility which rested upon him as he advised the President to adopt a course which if followed can only mean open and vigorous war against the Kaiser and his Government. The solemnity of the occasion as one after another spoke was increasingly impressive and showed in every man's face as he rose from the council table and prepared to leave the room. Lane, Houston and Redfield, however, did not hide their gratification, and I believe we all felt a deep sense of relief that not a dissenting voice had been raised to break the unanimity of opinion that there should be no further parley or delay. The ten councillors of the President had spoken as one, and he—well, no one could be sure that he would echo the same opinion and act accordingly.

19. WILSON'S WAR MESSAGE TO CONGRESS, APRIL 2, 1917

Gentlemen of the Congress:

I have called the Congress into extraordinary session because there are serious, very serious, choices of policy to be made, and made immediately, which it was neither right nor constitutionally permissible that I should assume the responsibility of making.

On the 3d of February last I officially laid before you the extraordinary announcement of the Imperial German Government that on and after the 1st day of February it was its purpose to put aside all restraints of law or of humanity and use its submarines to sink every vessel that sought to approach either the ports of Great Britain and Ireland or the western coasts of Europe or any of the ports controlled by the enemies of Germany within the Mediterranean. That had seemed to be the object of the German submarine warfare earlier in the war, but since April of last year the Imperial Government had somewhat restrained the commanders of its undersea craft in conformity with its promise then given to us that passenger boats should not be sunk and that due warning would be given to all other vessels which its submarines might seek to destroy, when no resistance was offered or escape attempted, and care taken that their crews were given at least a fair chance to save their lives in their open boats. The precautions taken were meagre and haphazard enough, as was proved in distressing instance after instance in the progress of the cruel and unmanly business, but a certain degree of restraint was observed. The new policy has swept every restriction aside. Vessels of every kind, whatever their flag, their character, their cargo, their destination, their errand, have been ruthlessly sent to the bottom without warning and without thought of help or mercy for those on board, the vessels of friendly neutrals along with those of belligerents. Even hospital ships and ships carrying relief to the sorely bereaved and stricken people of Belgium, though the latter were provided with safe-conduct through the proscribed areas by the German Government itself and were distinguished by unmistakable marks of identity, have been sunk with the same reckless lack of compassion or of principle.

I was for a little while unable to believe that such things would in fact be done by any government that had hitherto subscribed to the humane practices of civilized nations. International law had its origin in the attempt to set up some law which would be respected and observed upon the seas, where no nation had right of dominion and where lay the free highways of the world. By painful stage after stage has that law been built up, with meagre enough results, indeed, after all was accomplished that could be accomplished, but always with a clear view, at least, of what the heart and conscience of mankind demanded. This minimum of right the German Government has swept aside under the plea of retaliation and necessity and because it had no weapons which it could use at sea except these which it is impossible to employ as it is employing them without throwing to the winds all scruples of humanity or of respect for the understandings that were supposed to underlie the intercourse of the world. I am not now thinking of the loss of property involved, immense and serious as that is, but only of the wanton and wholesale destruction of the lives of noncombatants, men, women, and children, engaged in pursuits which have always, even in the darkest periods of modern history, been deemed innocent and legitimate. Property can be paid for; the lives of peaceful and innocent people can not be. The present German submarine warfare against commerce is a warfare against mankind.

It is a war against all nations. American ships have been sunk, American lives taken, in ways which it has stirred us very deeply to learn of, but the ships and people of other neutral and friendly nations have been sunk and overwhelmed in the waters in the same way. There has been no discrimination. The challenge is to all mankind. Each nation must decide for itself how it will meet it. The choice we make for ourselves must be made with a moderation of counsel and a temperateness of judgment befitting our character and our motives as a nation. We must put excited feeling away. Our motive will not be revenge or the victorious assertion of the physical might of the nation, but only the vindication of right, of human right, of which we are only a single champion.

When I addressed the Congress on the 26th of February last, I thought that it would suffice to assert our neutral rights with arms, our right to use the seas against unlawful interference, our right to keep our people safe against unlawful violence. But armed neutrality, it now appears, is impracticable. Because submarines are in effect outlaws when used as the German submarines have been used against merchant shipping, it is impossible to defend ships against their attacks as the law of nations has assumed that merchantmen would defend themselves against privateers or cruisers, visible craft giving chase upon the open sea. It is common prudence in such circumstances, grim necessity indeed, to endeavour to destroy them before they have shown their own intention. They must be dealt with upon sight, if dealt with at all. The German Government denies the right of neutrals to use arms at all within the areas of the sea which it has proscribed, even in the defense of rights which no modern publicist has ever before questioned their right to defend. The intimation is conveyed that the armed guards which we have placed on our merchant ships will be treated as beyond the pale of law and subject to be dealt with as pirates would be. Armed neutrality is ineffectual enough at best; in such circumstances and in the face of such pretensions it is worse than ineffectual; it is likely only to produce what it was meant to prevent; it is practically certain to draw us into the war without either the rights or the effectiveness of belligerents. There is one choice we can not make, we are incapable of making: we will not choose the path of submission and suffer the most sacred rights of our nation and our people to be ignored or violated. The wrongs against which we now array ourselves are no common wrongs; they cut to the very roots of human life.

With a profound sense of the solemn and even tragical character of the step I am taking and of the grave responsibilities which it involves, but in unhesitating obedience to what I deem my constitutional duty, I advise that the Congress declare the recent course of the Imperial German Government to be in fact nothing less than war against the Government and people of the United States; that it formally accept the status of belligerent which has thus been thrust upon it, and that it take immediate steps not only to put the country in a more thorough state of defense but also to exert all its power and employ all its resources to bring the Government of the German Empire to terms and end the war.

What this will involve is clear. It will involve the utmost practicable cooperation in counsel and action with the governments now at war with Germany, and, as incident to that, the extension to those governments of the most liberal financial credits, in order that our resources may so far as possible be added to theirs. It will involve the organization and mobilization of all the material resources of the country to supply the materials of war and serve the incidental needs of the nation in the most abundant and yet the most economical and efficient way possible. It will involve the immediate full equipment of the Navy in all respects but particularly in supplying it with the best means of dealing with the enemy's submarines. It will involve the immediate addition to the armed forces of the United States already provided for by law in case of war at least 500,000 men, who should, in my opinion, be chosen upon the principle of universal liability to service, and also the authorization of subsequent additional increments of equal force so soon as they may be needed and can be handled in training. It will involve also, of course, the granting of adequate credits to the Government, sustained, I hope, so far as they can equitably be sustained by the present generation, by well conceived taxation. . . .

While we do these things, these deeply momentous things, let us be very clear, and make very clear to all the world what our motives and our objects are. My own thought has not been driven from its habitual and normal course by the unhappy events of the last two months, and I do not believe that the thought of the nation has been altered or clouded by them. I have exactly the same things in mind now that I had in mind when I addressed the Senate on the 22d of January last; the same that I had in mind when I addressed the Congress on the 3d of February and on the 26th of February. Our object now, as then, is to vindicate the principles of peace and justice in the life of the world as against selfish and autocratic power and to set up amongst the really free and self-governed peoples of the world such a concert of purpose and of action as will henceforth ensure the observance of those principles. Neutrality is no longer feasible or desirable where the peace of the world is involved and the freedom of its peoples, and the menace to that peace and freedom lies in the existence of autocratic governments backed by organized force which is controlled wholly by their will, not by the will of their people. We have seen the last of neutrality in such circumstances. We are at the beginning of an age in which it will be insisted that the same standards of conduct and of responsibility for wrong done shall be observed among nations and their governments that are observed among the individual citizens of civilized states.

We have no quarrel with the German people. We have no feeling towards them but one of sympathy and friendship. It was not upon their impulse that their Government acted in entering this war. It was not with their previous knowledge or approval. It was a war determined upon as wars used to be determined upon in the old, unhappy days when peoples were nowhere consulted by their rulers and wars were provoked and waged in the interest of dynasties or of little groups of ambitious men who were accustomed to use their fellow men as pawns and tools. Self-governed nations do not fill their neighbour states with spies or set the course of intrigue to bring about some critical posture of affairs which will give them an opportunity to strike and make conquest. Such designs can be successfully worked out only under cover and where no one has the right to ask questions. Cunningly contrived plans of deception or aggression, carried, it may be, from generation to generation, can be worked out and kept from the light only within the privacy of courts or behind the carefully guarded confidences of a narrow and privileged class. They are happily impossible where public opinion commands and insists upon full information concerning all the nation's affairs.

A steadfast concert for peace can never be maintained except by a partnership of democratic nations. No autocratic government could be trusted to keep faith within it or observe its covenants. It must be a league of honour, a partnership of opinion. Intrigue would eat its vitals away; the plottings of inner circles who could plan what they would and render account to no one would be a corruption seated at its very heart. Only free peoples can hold their purpose and their honour steady to a common end and prefer the interests of mankind to any narrow interest of their own.

Does not every American feel that assurance has been added to our hope for the future peace of the world by the wonderful and heartening things that have been happening within the last few weeks in Russia? Russia was known by those who knew it best to have been always in fact democratic at heart, in all the vital habits of her thought, in all the intimate relationships of her people that spoke their natural instinct,

their habitual attitude towards life. The autocracy that crowned the summit of her political structure, long as it had stood and terrible as was the reality of its power, was not in fact Russian in origin, character, or purpose; and now it has been shaken off and the great, generous Russian people have been added in all their naive majesty and might to the forces that are fighting for freedom in the world, for justice, and for peace. Here is a fit partner for a league of honour.

One of the things that has served to convince us that the Prussian autocracy was not and could never be our friend is that from the very outset of the present war it has filled our unsuspecting communities and even our offices of government with spies and set criminal intrigues everywhere afoot against our national unity of counsel, our peace within and without our industries and our commerce. Indeed it is now evident that its spies were here even before the war began; and it is unhappily not a matter of conjecture but a fact proved in our courts of justice that the intrigues which have more than once come perilously near to disturbing the peace and dislocating the industries of the country have been carried on at the instigation, with the support, and even under the personal direction of official agents of the Imperial Government accredited to the Government of the United States. Even in checking these things and trying to extirpate them we have sought to put the most generous interpretation possible upon them because we knew that their source lay, not in any hostile feeling or purpose of the German people towards us (who were, no doubt, as ignorant of them as we ourselves were), but only in the selfish designs of a Government that did what it pleased and told its people nothing. But they have played their part in serving to convince us at last that that Government entertains no real friendship for us and means to act against our peace and security at its convenience. That it means to stir up enemies against us at our very doors the intercepted [Zimmermann] note to the German Minister at Mexico City is eloquent evidence.

We are accepting this challenge of hostile purpose because we know that in such a government, following such methods, we can never have a friend; and that in the presence of its organized power, always lying in wait to accomplish we know not what purpose, there can be no assured security for the democratic governments of the world. We are now about to accept gage of battle with this natural foe to liberty and shall, if necessary, spend the whole force of the nation to check and nullify its pretensions and its power. We are glad, now that we see the facts with no veil of false pretence about them, to fight thus for the ultimate peace of the world and for the liberation of its peoples, the German peoples included: for the rights of nations great and small and the privilege of men everywhere to choose their way of life and of obedience. The world must be made safe for democracy. Its peace must be planted upon the tested foundations of political liberty. We have no selfish ends to serve. We desire no conquest, no dominion. We seek no indemnities for ourselves, no material compensation for the sacrifices we shall freely make. We are but one of the champions of the rights of mankind. We shall be satisfied when those rights have been made as secure as the faith and the freedom of nations can make them.

Just because we fight without rancour and without selfish object, seeking nothing for ourselves but what we shall wish to share with all free peoples, we shall, I feel confident, conduct our operations as belligerents without passion and ourselves observe with proud punctilio the principles of right and of fair play we profess to be fighting for.

I have said nothing of the governments allied with the Imperial Government of Germany because they have not made war upon us or challenged us to defend our right and our honour. The Austro-Hungarian Government has, indeed, avowed its unqualified endorsement and acceptance of the reckless and lawless submarine warfare adopted now without disguise by the Imperial German Government, and it has therefore not been possible for this Government to receive Count Tarnowski, the Ambassador recently accredited to this Government by the Imperial and Royal Government of Austria-Hungary; but that Government has not actually engaged in warfare against citizens of the United States on the seas, and I take the liberty, for the present at least, of postponing a discussion of our relations with the authorities at Vienna. We enter this war only where we are clearly forced into it because there are no other means of defending our rights.

It will be all the easier for us to conduct ourselves as belligerents in a high spirit of right and fairness because we act without animus, not in enmity towards a people or with the desire to bring any injury or disadvantage upon them, but only in armed opposition to an irresponsible government which has thrown aside all considerations of humanity and of right and is running amuck. We are, let me say again, the sincere friends of the German people, and shall desire nothing so much as the early reestablish-ment of intimate relations of mutual advantage between us—however hard it may be for them, for the time being, to believe that this is spoken from our hearts. We have borne with their present government through all these bitter months because of that friendship—exercising a patience and forbearance which would otherwise have been impossible. We shall, happily, still have an opportunity to prove that friendship in our daily attitude and actions towards the millions of men and women of German birth and native sympathy, who live amongst us and share our life, and we shall be proud to prove it towards all who are in fact loyal to their neighbours and to the Government in the hour of test. They are, most of them, as true and loyal Americans as if they had never known any other fealty or allegiance. They will be prompt to stand with us in rebuking and restraining the few who may be of a different mind and purpose. If there should be disloyalty, it will be dealt with with a firm hand of stern repression; but, if it lifts its head at all, it will lift it only here and there and without countenance except from a lawless and malignant few.

It is a distressing and oppressive duty, gentlemen of the Congress, which I have performed in thus addressing you. There are, it may be, many months of fiery trial and sacrifice ahead of us. It is a fearful thing to lead this great peaceful people into war, into the most terrible and disastrous of all wars, civilization itself seeming to be in the balance. But the right is more precious than peace, and we shall fight for the things which we have always carried nearest our hearts—for democracy, for the right of those who submit to authority to have a voice in their own governments, for the rights and liberties of small nations, for a universal dominion of right by such a concert of free peoples as shall bring peace and safety to all nations and make the world itself at last free. To such a task we can dedicate our lives and our fortunes, everything that we are and everything that we have, with the pride of those who know that the day has come when America is privileged to spend her blood and her might for the principles that gave her birth and happiness and the peace which she has treasured. God helping her, she can do no other.

20. OPPOSITION TO THE DECLARATION OF WAR, APRIL 5, 1917
[Speech by Robert M. LaFollette]

I had supposed until recently that it was the duty of senators and representatives in Congress to vote and act according to their convictions on all public matters that came before them for consideration and decision. Quite another doctrine has recently been promulgated by certain newspapers, which unfortunately seems to have found considerable support elsewhere, and that is the doctrine of "standing back of the President" without inquiring whether the President is right or wrong.

For myself, I have never subscribed to that doctrine and never shall. I shall support the President in the measures he proposes when I believe them to be right. I shall oppose measures proposed by the President when I believe them to be wrong. The fact that the matter which the President submits for consideration is of the greatest importance is only an additional reason why we should be sure that we are right and not to be swerved from that conviction or intimidated in its expression by any influence of power whatsoever. . . .

It is unfortunately true that a portion of the irresponsible and war-crazed press, feeling secure in the authority of the President's condemnation of the senators who opposed the armed-ship bill, have published the most infamous and scurrilous libels on the honor of the senators who opposed that bill. It was particularly unfortunate that such malicious falsehoods should fill the public press of the country at a time when every consideration for our country required that a spirit of fairness should be observed in the discussions of the momentous questions under consideration. . . .

Just a word of comment more upon one of the points in the President's address. He says that this is a war "for the things which we have always carried nearest to our hearts—for democracy, for the right of those who submit to authority to have a voice in their own government." In many places throughout the address is this exalted sentiment given expression.

It is a sentiment peculiarly calculated to appeal to American hearts and, when accompanied by acts consistent with it, is certain to receive our support; but in this same connection, and strangely enough, the President says that we have become convinced that the German government as it now exists—"Prussian autocracy" he calls it—can never again maintain friendly relations with us. His expression is that "Prussian autocracy was not and could never be our friend," and repeatedly throughout the address the suggestion is made that if the German people would overturn their government, it would probably be the way to peace. So

true is this that the dispatches from London all hailed the message of the President as sounding the death knell of Germany's government.

But the President proposes alliance with Great Britain, which, however liberty-loving its people, is a hereditary monarchy, with a hereditary ruler, with a hereditary House of Lords, with a hereditary landed system, with a limited and restricted suffrage for one class and a multiplied suffrage power for another, and with grinding industrial conditions for all the wage-workers. The President has not suggested that we make our support of Great Britain conditional to her granting home rule to Ireland, or Egypt, or India. We rejoice in the establishment of a democracy in Russia, but it will hardly be contended that if Russia was still an autocratic government, we would not be asked to enter this alliance with her just the same.

Italy and the lesser powers of Europe, Japan in the Orient; in fact, all the countries with whom we are to enter into alliance, except France and newly revolutionized Russia, are still of the old order—and it will be generally conceded that no one of them has done as much for its people in the solution of municipal problems and in securing social and industrial reforms as Germany.

Is it not a remarkable democracy which leagues itself with allies already far overmatching in strength the German nation and holds out to such beleaguered nation the hope of peace only at the price of giving up their government? I am not talking now of the merits or demerits of any government, but I am speaking of a profession of democracy that is linked in action with the most brutal and domineering use of autocratic power. Are the people of this country being so well-represented in this war movement that we need to go abroad to give other people control of their governments?

. . . In the sense that this war is being forced upon our people without their knowing why and without their approval, and that wars are usually forced upon all peoples in the same way, there is some truth in the statement; but I venture to say that the response which the German people have made to the demands of this war shows that it has a degree of popular support which the war upon which we are entering has not and never will have among our people. The espionage bills, the conscription bills, and other forcible military measures which we understand are being ground out of the war machine in this country is the complete proof that those responsible for this war fear that it has no popular support and that armies sufficient to satisfy the demand of the Entente Allies cannot be recruited by voluntary enlistments. . . .

Now, I want to repeat: It was our absolute right as a neutral to ship food to the people of Germany. That is a position that we have fought for through all of our history. The correspondence of every secretary of state in the history of our government who has been called upon to deal with the rights of our neutral commerce as to foodstuffs is the position stated by Lord Salisbury. . . . He was in line with all of the precedents that we had originated and established for the maintenance of neutral rights upon this subject.

In the first days of the war with Germany, Great Britain set aside, so far as her own conduct was concerned, all these rules of civilized naval warfare.

According to the Declaration of London, as well as the rules of international law, there could have been no interference in trade between the United States and Holland or Scandinavia and other countries, except in the case of ships which could be proven to carry absolute contraband, like arms and ammunition, with ultimate German destination. There could have been no interference with the importation into Germany of any goods on the free list, such as cotton, rubber, and hides. There could have properly been no interference with our export to Germany of anything on the conditional contraband list, like flour, grain, and provisions, unless it could be proven by England that such shipments were intended for the use of the German Army. There could be no lawful interference with foodstuffs intended for the civilian population of Germany, and if those foodstuffs were shipped to other countries to be reshipped to Germany, no question could be raised that they were not intended for the use of the civilian population.

It is well to recall at this point our rights as declared by the Declaration of London and as declared without the Declaration of London by settled principles of international law, for we have during the present war become so used to having Great Britain utterly disregard our rights on the high seas that we have really forgotten that we have any, as far as Great Britain and her allies are concerned.

Great Britain, by what she called her modifications of the Declaration of London, shifted goods from the free list to the conditional contraband and contraband lists, reversed the presumption of destination for civilian population, and abolished the principle that a blockade to exist at all must be effective. . . .

It is not my purpose to go into detail into the violations of our neutrality by any of the belligerents. While Germany has again and again yielded to our protests, I do not recall a single instance in which a protest we have made to Great Britain has won for us the slightest consideration, except for a short time in the case of cotton. I will not stop to dwell upon the multitude of minor violations of our neutral rights, such as seizing our mails, violations of the neutral flag, seizing and appropriating our goods without the least warrant or authority in law, and impressing, seizing, and taking possession of our vessels and putting them into her own service. . . . But those are individual cases. There are many others. All these violations have come from Great Britain and her allies, and are in perfect harmony with Britain's traditional policy as absolute master of the seas. . . .

I find all the correspondence about the submarines of Germany; I find them arrayed; I find the note warning Germany that she would be held to a "strict accountability" for violation of our neutral rights; but you will search in vain these volumes for a copy of the British order in council mining the North Sea.

I am talking now about principles. You cannot distinguish between the principles which allowed England to mine a large area of the Atlantic Ocean and the North Sea in order to shut in Germany, and the principle on which Germany by her submarines seeks to destroy all shipping which enters the war zone which she has laid out around the British Isles.

The English mines are intended to destroy without warning every ship that enters the war zone she has proscribed, killing or drowning every passenger that cannot find some means of escape. It is neither more nor less than that which Germany tries to do with her submarines in her war zone. We acquiesced in England's action without protest. It is proposed that we now go to war with Germany for identically the same action upon her part. . . .

I say again that when two nations are at war any neutral nation, in order to preserve its character as a neutral nation, must exact the same conduct from both warring nations; both must equally obey the principles of international law. If a neutral nation fails in that, then its rights upon the high seas—to adopt the President's phrase—are relative and not absolute. There can be no greater violation of our neutrality than the requirement that one of two belligerents shall adhere to the settled principles of law and that the other shall have the advantage of not doing so. The respect that German naval authorities were required to pay to the rights of our people upon the high seas would depend upon the question whether we had exacted the same rights from Germany's enemies. If we had not done so, we lost our character as a neutral nation and our people unfortunately had lost the protection that belongs to neutrals. Our responsibility was joint in the sense that we must exact the same conduct from both belligerents. . . .

The failure to treat the belligerent nations of Europe alike, the failure to reject the unlawful "war zones" of both Germany and Great Britain is wholly accountable for our present dilemma. We should not seek to hide our blunder behind the smoke of battle, to inflame the mind of our people by half truths into the frenzy of war in order that they may never appreciate the real cause of it until it is too late. I do not believe that our national honor is served by such a course. The right way is the honorable way.

One alternative is to admit our initial blunder to enforce our rights against Great Britain as we have enforced our rights against Germany; demand that both those nations shall respect our neutral rights upon the high seas to the letter; and give notice that we will enforce those rights from that time forth against both belligerents and then live up to that notice.

The other alternative is to withdraw our commerce from both. The mere suggestion that food supplies would be withheld from both sides impartially would compel belligerents to observe the principle of freedom of the seas for neutral commerce.

Source: Record, 65 Cong., 1 Sess., pp. 212–214, 223–236.

21. WAR RESOLUTION, APRIL 6, 1917

Joint Resolution Declaring that a state of war exists between the Imperial German Government and the Government and the people of the United States and making provision to prosecute the same.

Whereas the Imperial German Government has committed repeated acts of war against the Government and the people of the United States of America; Therefore be it Resolved by the Senate and the House of Representatives of the United States of America in Congress Assembled, that the state of war between the United States and the Imperial German Government

which has thus been thrust upon the United States is hereby formally declared; and that the President be, and he is hereby, authorized and directed to employ the entire naval and military forces of the United States and the resources of the Government to carry on war against the Imperial German Government; and to bring the conflict to a successful termination all of the resources of the country are hereby pledged by the Congress of the United States.

CHAMP CLARK
Speaker of the House of Representatives
THOS. R. MARSHALL
Vice President of the United States and President of the Senate
Approved, April 6, 1917
WOODROW WILSON

22. BALFOUR DECLARATION (STATEMENT OF FOREIGN SECRETARY BALFOUR TO LORD ROTHSCHILD), NOVEMBER 8, 1917

Foreign Office
November 2, 1917
Dear Lord Rothschild,

I have much pleasure in conveying to you, on behalf of His Majesty's Government, the following declaration of sympathy with the Jewish Zionist aspirations which has been submitted to, and approved by, the Cabinet.

"His Majesty's Government view with favor the establishment in Palestine of a national home for the Jewish people, and will use their best endeavors to facilitate the achievement of this object, it being clearly understood that nothing shall be done which may prejudice the civil and religious rights of existing non-Jewish communities in Palestine, or the rights and political status enjoyed by Jews in another country."

I should be grateful if you would bring this declaration to the knowledge of the Zionist Federation.

23. WILSON'S FOURTEEN POINTS SPEECH, DELIVERED JANUARY 8, 1918

Once more, as repeatedly before, the spokesmen of the Central Empires have indicated their desire to discuss the objects of the war and the possible bases of a general peace. Parleys have been in progress at Brest-Litovsk between representatives of the Central Powers to which the attention of all the belligerents has been invited for the purpose of ascertaining whether it may be possible to extend these parleys into a general conference with regard to terms of peace and settlement. The Russian representatives presented not only a perfectly definite statement of the principles upon which they would be willing to conclude peace but also an equally definite program of the concrete application of those principles. The representatives of the Central Powers, on their part, presented an outline of settlement which, if much less definite, seemed susceptible of liberal interpretation until their specific program of practical terms was added. That program proposed no concessions at all either to the sovereignty of Russia or to the preferences of the populations with whose fortunes it dealt, but meant, in a word, that the Central Empires were to keep every foot of territory their armed forces had occupied,—every province, every city, every point of vantage,—as a permanent addition to their territories and their power. It is a reasonable conjecture that the general principles of settlement which they at first suggested originated with the more liberal statesmen of Germany and Austria, the men who have begun to feel the force of their own peoples' thought and purpose, while the concrete terms of actual settlement came from the military leaders who have no thought but to keep what they have got. The negotiations have been broken off. The Russian representatives were sincere and in earnest. They cannot entertain such proposals of conquest and domination.

The whole incident is full of significance. It is also full of perplexity. With whom are the Russian representatives dealing? For whom are the representatives of the Central Empires speaking? Are they speaking for the majorities of their respective parliaments or for the minority parties, that military and imperialistic minority which has so far dominated their whole policy and controlled the affairs of Turkey and of the Balkan states which have felt obliged to become their associates in this war? The Russian representatives have insisted, very justly, very wisely, and in the true spirit of modern democracy, that the conferences they have been holding with the Teutonic and Turkish statesmen should be held within open, not closed, doors, and all the world has been audience, as was desired. To whom have we been listening, then? To those who speak the spirit and intention of the Resolutions of the German Reichstag of the ninth of July last, the spirit and intention of the liberal leaders and parties of Germany, or to those who resist and defy that spirit and intention and insist upon conquest and subjugation? Or are we listening, in fact, to both, unreconciled and in open and hopeless contradiction? These are very serious and pregnant questions. Upon the answer to them depends the peace of the world.

But, whatever the results of the parleys at Brest-Litovsk, whatever the confusions of counsel and of purpose in the utterances of the spokesmen of the Central Empires, they have again attempted to acquaint the world with their objects in the war and have again challenged their adversaries to say what their objects are and what sort of settlement they would deem just and satisfactory. There is no good reason why that challenge should not be responded to, and responded to with the utmost candor. We did not wait for it. Not once, but again and again, we have laid our whole thought and purpose before the world, not in general terms only, but each time with sufficient definition to make it clear what sort of definitive terms of settlement must necessarily spring out of them. Within the last week Mr. Lloyd George has spoken with admirable candor and in admirable spirit for the people and Government of Great Britain. There is no confusion of counsel among the adversaries of the Central Powers, no uncertainty of principle, no vagueness of detail. The only secrecy of counsel, the only lack of fearless frankness, the only failure to make definite statement of the objects of the war, lies with Germany and her Allies. The issues of life and death hang upon these definitions. No statesman who has the least conception of his responsibility ought for a moment to permit himself to continue this tragical and appalling outpouring of blood and treasure unless he is sure beyond a peradventure that the objects of the vital sacrifice are part and parcel of the very life of Society and that the people for whom he speaks think them right and imperative as he does.

There is, moreover, a voice calling for these definitions of principle and of purpose which is, it seems to me, more thrilling and more compelling than any of the many moving voices with which the troubled air of the world is filled. It is the voice of the Russian people. They are prostrate and all but helpless, it would seem, before the grim power of Germany, which has hitherto known no relenting and no pity. Their power, apparently, is shattered. And yet their soul is not subservient. They will not yield either in principle or in action. Their conception of what is right, of what it is humane and honorable for them to accept, has been stated with a frankness, a largeness of view, a generosity of spirit, and a universal human sympathy which must challenge the admiration of every friend of mankind; and they have refused to compound their ideals or desert others that they themselves may be safe. They call to us to say what it is that we desire, in what, if in anything, our purpose and our spirit differ from theirs; and I believe that the people of the United States would wish me to respond, with utter simplicity and frankness. Whether their present leaders believe it or not, it is our heartfelt desire and hope that some way may be opened whereby we may be privileged to assist the people of Russia to attain their utmost hope of liberty and ordered peace.

It will be our wish and purpose that the processes of peace, when they are begun, shall be absolutely open and that they shall involve and permit henceforth no secret understandings of any kind. The day of conquest and aggrandizement is gone by; so is also the day of secret covenants entered into in the interest of particular governments and likely at some unlooked-for moment to upset the peace of the world. It is this happy fact, now clear to the view of every public man whose thoughts do not still linger in an age that is dead and gone, which makes it possible for every nation whose purposes are consistent with justice and the peace of the world to avow now or at any other time the objects it has in view.

We entered this war because violations of right had occurred which touched us to the quick and made the life of our own people impossible unless they were corrected and the world secured once for all against their recurrence. What we demand in this war, therefore, is nothing peculiar to ourselves. It is that the world be made fit and safe to live in; and particularly that it be made safe for every peace-loving nation which, like our own, wishes to live its own life, determine its own institutions, be assured of justice and fair dealing by the other peoples of the world as against force and selfish aggression. All the peoples of the world are in effect partners in this interest, and for our own part we see very clearly that unless justice be done to others it will not be done to us. The program of the world's peace, therefore, is our program; and that program, the only possible program, as we see it, is this:

I. Open covenants of peace, openly arrived at, after which there shall be no private interna-

tional understandings of any kind but diplomacy shall proceed always frankly and in the public view.

II. Absolute freedom of navigation upon the seas, outside territorial waters, alike in peace and in war, except as the seas may be closed in whole or in part by international action for the enforcement of international covenants.

III. The removal, so far as possible, of all economic barriers and the establishment of an equality of trade conditions among all the nations consenting to the peace and associating themselves for its maintenance.

IV. Adequate guarantees given and taken that national armaments will be reduced to the lowest point consistent with domestic safety.

V. A free, open-minded, and absolutely impartial adjustment of all colonial claims, based upon a strict observance of the principle that in determining all such questions of sovereignty the interests of the populations concerned must have equal weight with the equitable claims of the government whose title is to be determined.

VI. The evacuation of all Russian territory and such a settlement of all questions affecting Russia as will secure the best and freest cooperation of the other nations of the world in obtaining for her an unhampered and unembarrassed opportunity for the independent determination of her own political development and national policy and assure her of a sincere welcome into the society of free nations under institutions of her own choosing; and, more than a welcome, assistance also of every kind that she may need and may herself desire. The treatment accorded Russia by her sister nations in the months to come will be the acid test of their good will, of their comprehension of her needs as distinguished from their own interests, and of their intelligent and unselfish sympathy.

VII. Belgium, the whole world will agree, must be evacuated and restored, without any attempt to limit the sovereignty which she enjoys in common with all other free nations. No other single act will serve as this will serve to restore confidence among the nations in the laws which they have themselves set and determined for the government of their relations with one another. Without this healing act the whole structure and validity of international law is forever impaired.

VIII. All French territory should be freed and the invaded portions restored, and the wrong done to France by Prussia in 1871 in the matter of Alsace-Lorraine, which has unsettled the peace of the world for nearly fifty years, should be righted, in order that peace may once more be made secure in the interest of all.

IX. A readjustment of the frontiers of Italy should be effected along clearly recognizable lines of nationality.

X. The peoples of Austria-Hungary, whose place among the nations we wish to see safeguarded and assured, should be accorded the freest opportunity of autonomous development.

XI. Rumania, Serbia, and Montenegro should be evacuated; occupied territories restored; Serbia accorded free and secure access to the sea; and the relations of the several Balkan states to one another determined by friendly counsel along historically established lines of allegiance and nationality; and international guarantees of the political and economic independence and territorial integrity of the several Balkan states should be entered into.

XII. The Turkish portions of the present Ottoman Empire should be assured a secure sovereignty, but the other nationalities which are now under Turkish rule should be accorded an undoubted security of life and an absolutely unmolested opportunity of autonomous development, and the Dardanelles should be permanently opened as a free passage to the ships and commerce of all nations under international guarantees.

XIII. An independent Polish state should be erected which should include the territories inhabited by indisputably Polish populations, which should be assured a free and secure access to the sea, and whose political and economic independence and territorial integrity should be guaranteed by international covenant.

XIV. A general association of nations must be formed under specific covenants for the purpose of affording mutual guarantees of political independence and territorial integrity to great and small states alike.

In regard to these essential rectifications of wrong and assertions of right we feel ourselves to be intimate partners of all the governments and peoples associated together against the Imperialists. We cannot be separated in interest or divided in purpose. We stand together until the end.

For such arrangements and covenants we are willing to fight and to continue to fight until they are achieved; but only because we wish the right to prevail and desire a just and stable peace such as can be secured only by removing the chief provocations to war, which this program does remove. We have no jealousy of German greatness, and there is nothing in this program that impairs it. We grudge her no achievement or distinction of learning or of pacific enterprise such as have made her record very bright and very enviable. We do not wish to injure her or to block in any way her legitimate influence or power. We do not wish to fight her either with arms or with hostile arrangements of trade if she is willing to associate herself with us and the other peace-loving nations of the world in covenants of justice and law and fair dealing. We wish her only to accept a place of equality among the peoples of the world,—the new world in which we now live,—instead of a place of mastery.

Neither do we presume to suggest to her any alteration or modification of her institutions. But it is necessary, we must frankly say, and necessary as a preliminary to any intelligent dealings with her on our part, that we should know whom her spokesmen speak for when they speak to us, whether for the Reichstag majority or for the military party and the men whose creed is imperial domination.

We have spoken now, surely, in terms too concrete to admit of any further doubt or question. An evident principle runs through the whole program I have outlined. It is the principle of justice to all peoples and nationalities, and their right to live on equal terms of liberty and safety with one another, whether they be strong or weak. Unless this principle be made its foundation no part of the structure of international justice can stand. The people of the United States could act upon no other principle; and to the vindication of this principle they are ready to devote their lives, their honor, and everything that they possess. The moral climax of this the culminating and final war for human liberty has come, and they are ready to put their own strength, their own highest purpose, their own integrity and devotion to the test.

24. BREST-LITOVSK PEACE TREATY, MARCH 3, 1918

[List of plenipotentiaries deleted]

Article I.

Germany, Austria-Hungary, Bulgaria, and Turkey, for the one part, and Russia, for the other, declare that the state of war between them has ceased. They are resolved to live henceforth in peace and amity with one another.

Article II.

The contracting parties will refrain from *any* agitation or propaganda against the Government public and military institutions of the other party. In so far as this obligation devolves upon Russia, it holds good also for the territories occupied by the Powers of the Quadruple Alliance.

Article III.

The territories lying to the west of the line agreed upon by the contracting parties which formerly belonged to Russia, will no longer be subject to Russian sovereignty; the line agreed is traced on the map submitted as an essential part of this treaty of peace (Annex 1). The exact fixation of the line will be established by a Russo-German commission.

No obligations whatever toward Russia shall devolve upon the territories referred to, arising from the fact that they formerly belonged to Russia.

Russia refrains from all interference in the internal relations of these territories. Germany and Austria-Hungary propose to determine the future status of these territories in agreement with their population.

Article IV.

As soon as a general peace is concluded and Russian demobilization is carried out completely, any [Russian troops] will evacuate the territory lying to the east of the line designated in paragraph 1 title III, in so far as Article VI does not determine otherwise.

Russia will do all within her power to insure the immediate evacuation of the provinces of eastern Anatolia and their lawful return to Turkey.

The districts of Erdehan, Kars, and Batum will likewise and without delay be cleared of Russian troops. Russia will not interfere in the reorganization of the national and rational relations of these districts, but leave it to the population of these districts, to carry out this reorganization in agreement with the neighboring States, especially with Turkey.

Article V.

Russia will, without delay, carry out the full demobilization of her army inclusive of those recently organized by the present Government.

Furthermore, Russia will either bring her warships into Russian ports and there detain until the day of the conclusion of a general peace, or disarm them forthwith. Warships of the States which continue in the state of war with the Powers of the Quadruple Alliance, insofar as they are within Russian sovereignty, will be treated as Russian warships.

The barred zone in the Arctic Ocean continues as such until the conclusion of a general peace. In the Baltic sea, and, as far as Russian power extends within the Black sea, removal of mines will be proceeded with at once. Merchant navigation within these maritime regions is free and will be resumed at once. Mixed commissions will be organized to formulate the more detailed regulations, especially to inform merchant ships with regard to restricted lanes. The navigation lanes are always to be kept free from floating mines.

Article VI.

Russia obligates herself to conclude peace at once with the Ukrainian People's Republic and to recognize the treaty of peace between that State and the Powers of the Quadruple Alliance. The Ukrainian territory will, without delay, be cleared of Russian troops and the Russian Red Guard. Russia is to put an end to all agitation or propaganda against the Government or the public institutions of the Ukrainian People's Republic.

Esthonia and Livonia will likewise, without delay, be cleared of Russian troops and Russian Red Guard. The eastern boundary of Esthonia runs, in general, along the river Narwa. The eastern boundary of Livonia crosses, in general, lakes Peipus and Pskow, to the southwestern corner of the latter, then across Lake Luban in the direction of Livenhof on the Dvina. Esthonia and Livonia will be occupied by a German police force until security is insured by proper national institutions and until public order has been established. Russia will liberate at once all arrested or deported inhabitants of Esthonia and Livonia, and insure the safe return of all deported Esthonians and Livonians.

Finland and the Aaland Islands will immediately be cleared of Russian troops and Russian Red Guard, and the Finnish ports of the Russian fleet and of the Russian naval fort. So long as the ice prevents the transfer of warships into Russian ports, only limited forces will remain on board the warships. Russia is to put an end to all agitation or propaganda against the Government or the public institutions of Finland.

The fortresses built on the Aaland Islands are to be removed as soon as possible. As regards the permanent non-fortification of these islands as well as their further treatment in respect to military and technical navigation matters, a special agreement is to be concluded between Germany, Finland, Russia, and Sweden; there exists an understanding to the effect that should Germany desire, still other countries bordering upon the Baltic Sea would be consulted in this matter.

Article VII.

In view of the fact that Persia and Afghanistan are free and independent States, the contract parties obligate themselves to respect the political and economic independence and territorial integrity of these States.

Article VIII.

The prisoners of war of both parties will be released to return to their homeland. The settlement of the questions connected therewith will be effected through the special treaty provided for in Article XII.

Article IX.

The contracting parties mutually renounce compensation for their war expenses, i.e., of public expenditures for the conduct of the war, as well as compensation for war losses, such losses as were caused them and their nationals within the war zones by military measures, inclusive of all requisitions effected in enemy country.

Article X.

Diplomatic and consular relations between the contracting parties will be resumed immediately upon the ratification of the treaty of peace. As regards the reciprocal admission of consuls, separate agreements are reserved.

Article XI.

As regards the economic relations between the Powers of the Quadruple Alliance and Russia the regulations contained in Appendices II–V are determinative, namely Appendix II for Russo-German, Appendix III for the Russo-Austro-Hungarian, Appendix IV for the Russo-Bulgarian, and Appendix V for the Russo-Turkish relations.

Article XII.

The reestablishment of public and private legal relations, the exchange of war prisoners and interned civilians, the question of amnesty as well as the question anent the treatment of merchant ships which have come into the power of the opponent, will be regulated in separate treaties with Russia which form an essential part of the general treaty of peace, and, as far as possible, go into force simultaneously with the latter.

Article XIII.

In the interpretation of this treaty, the German and Russian texts are authoritative for the relations between Germany and Russia; the German, the Hungarian, and Russian texts for the relations between Austria-Hungary and Russia; the Bulgarian and Russian texts for the relations between Bulgaria and Russia; and the Turkish and Russian texts for the relations between Turkey and Russia.

Article XIV.

The present treaty of peace will be ratified. The documents of ratification shall, as soon as possible, be exchanged in Berlin. The Russian Government obligates itself, upon the desire of one of the Powers of the Quadruple Alliance, to execute the exchange of the documents of ratification, within a period of two weeks. Unless otherwise provided for in its articles, in its annexes, or in the additional treaties, the treaty of peace enters into force at the moment of its ratification.

In testimony whereof the Plenipotentiaries have signed this treaty with their own hand. Executed in quintuplicate at Brest-Litovsk, 3 March, 1918.

25. ARMISTICE TERMS PROPOSED BY WOODROW WILSON TO GERMANY, OCTOBER 13, 1918

Message to the GOVERNMENT THROUGH MR. FREDERICK OEDERLIN, CHARGE D'AFFAIRES OF SWITZERLAND, SIGNED BY SECRETARY LANSING, OCTOBER 23, 1918.

I have the honor to acknowledge the receipt of your note of the twenty-second transmitting a communication under date of the twentieth from the German

Government and to advise you that the President has instructed me to reply thereto as follows:

"Having received the solemn and explicit assurance of the German Government that it unreservedly accepts the terms of peace laid down in his address to the Congress of the United States on the eighth of January, 1918, and the principles of settlement enunciated in his subsequent addresses, particularly the address of the twenty-seventh of September, and that it desires to discuss the details of their application, and that this wish and purpose emanate, not from those who have hitherto dictated German policy and conducted the present war on Germany's behalf, but from ministers who speak for the majority of the Reichstag and for an overwhelming majority of the German people; and having received also the explicit promise of the present German Government that the humane rules of civilized warfare will be observed both on land and sea by the German armed forces, the President of the United States feels that he cannot decline to take up with the Governments with which the Government of the United States is associated the question of an armistice.

"He deems it his duty to say again, however, that the only armistice he would feel justified in submitting for consideration would be one which should leave the United States and the powers associated with her in a position to enforce any arrangements that may be entered into and to make a renewal of hostilities on the part of Germany impossible. The President has, therefore, transmitted his correspondence with the present German authorities to the Governments with which the Government of the United States is associated as a belligerent, with the suggestion that, if those Governments are disposed to effect peace upon the terms and principles indicated, their military advisers and the military advisers of the United States be asked to submit to the Governments associated against Germany the necessary terms of such an armistice as will fully protect the interests of the peoples involved and insure to the associated Governments the unrestricted power to safe-guard and enforce the details of the peace to which the German Government has agreed, provided they deem such an armistice possible from the military point of view. Should such terms of armistice be suggested, their acceptance by Germany will afford the best concrete evidence of her unequivocal acceptance of the terms and principles of peace from which the whole action proceeds.

"The President would deem himself lacking in candor did he not point out in the frankest possible terms the reason why extraordinary safeguards must be demanded. Significant and important as the constitutional changes seem to be which are spoken of by the German Foreign Secretary in his note of the twentieth of October, it does not appear that the principle of a government responsible to the German people has yet been fully worked out or that any guarantees either exist or are in contemplation that the alterations of principle and of practice now partially agreed upon will be permanent. Moreover, it does not appear that the heart of the present difficulty has been reached. It may be that future wars have been brought under the control of the German people, but the present war has not been; and it is with the present war that we are dealing. It is evident that the German people have no means of commanding the acquiescence of the military authorities of the Empire in the popular will; that the power of the King of Prussia to control the policy of the Empire is unimpaired; that the determining initiative still remains with those who have hitherto been the masters of Germany.

"Feeling that the whole peace of the world depends now on plain speaking and straightforward action, the President deems it his duty to say, without any attempt to soften what may seem harsh words, that the nations of the world do not and cannot trust the word of those who have hitherto been the masters of German policy, and to point out once more that in concluding peace and attempting to undo the infinite injuries and injustices of this war the Government of the United States cannot deal with any but veritable representatives of the German people who have been assured of a genuine constitutional standing as the real rulers of Germany. If it must deal with the military masters and the monarchical autocrats of Germany now, or if it is likely to have to deal with them later in regard to the international obligations of the German Empire, it must demand, not peace negotiations, but surrender. Nothing can be gained by leaving this essential thing unsaid."

26. ALLIES' CONDITIONS, NOVEMBER 5, 1918

The Allied Governments have given careful consideration to the correspondence which has passed between the President of the United States and the German Government. Subject to the qualifications which follow they declare their willingness to make peace with the Government of Germany on the terms of peace laid down in the President's address to Congress of January, 1918, and the principles of settlement enunciated in his subsequent addresses. They must point out, however, that clause 2, relating to what is usually described as the freedom of the seas, is open to various interpretations, some of which they could not accept. They must, therefore, reserve to themselves complete freedom on this subject when they enter the peace conference. Further, in the conditions of peace laid down in his address to Congress of January 8, 1918, the President declared that invaded territories must be restored as well as evacuated and freed, the Allies feel that no doubt ought to be allowed to exist as to what this provision implies. By it they understand that compensation will be made by Germany for all damage done to the civilian population of the Allies and their property by the aggression of Germany by land, by sea and from the air.

27. Covenant of the League from the Versailles Treaty, June 28, 1919

Part I

THE COVENANT OF THE LEAGUE OF NATIONS.

THE HIGH CONTRACTING PARTIES, In order to promote international co-operation and to achieve international peace and security by the acceptance of obligations not to resort to war by the prescription of open, just and honourable relations between nations by the firm establishment of the understandings of international law as the actual rule of conduct among Governments, and by the maintenance of justice and a scrupulous respect for all treaty obligations in the dealings of organised peoples with one another Agree to this Covenant of the League of Nations.

Article 1.

The original Members of the League of Nations shall be those of the Signatories which are named in the Annex to this Covenant and also such of those other States named in the Annex as shall accede without reservation to this Covenant. Such accession shall be effected by a Declaration deposited with the Secretariat within two months of the coming into force of the Covenant. Notice thereof shall be sent to all other Members of the League. Any fully self-governing State, Dominion, or Colony not named in the Annex may become a Member of the League if its admission is agreed to by two-thirds of the Assembly provided that it shall give effective guarantees of its sincere intention to observe its international obligations, and shall accept such regulations as may be prescribed by the League in regard to its military, naval, and air forces and armaments. Any Member of the League may, after two years notice of its intention so to do, withdraw from the League, provided that all its international obligations and all its obligations under this Covenant shall have been fulfilled at the time of its withdrawal.

Article 2.

The action of the League under this Covenant shall be effected through the instrumentality of an Assembly and of a Council, with a permanent Secretariat.

Article 3.

The Assembly shall consist of Representatives of the Members of the League. The Assembly shall meet at stated intervals and from time to time as occasion may require at the Seat of the League or at such other place as may be decided upon. The Assembly may deal at its meetings with any matter within the sphere of action of the League or affecting the peace of the world. At meetings of the Assembly each Member of the League shall have one vote, and may not have more than three Representatives.

Article 4.

The Council shall consist of Representatives of the Principal Allied and Associated Powers, together with Representatives of four other Members of the League. These four Members of the League shall be selected by the Assembly from time to time in its discretion. Until the appointment of the Representatives of the four Members of the League first selected by the Assembly, Representatives of Belgium, Brazil, Spain, and Greece shall be members of the Council. With the approval of the majority of the Assembly, the Council may name additional Members of the League whose Representatives shall always be members of the Council; the Council with like approval may increase the number of Members of the League to be selected by the Assembly for representation on the Council. The Council shall meet from time to time as occasion may require, and at least once a year, at the Seat of the League, or at such other place as may be decided upon. The Council may deal at its meetings with any matter within the sphere of action of the League or affecting the peace of the world. Any Member of the League not represented on the Council shall be invited to send a Representative to sit as a member at any meeting of the Council during the consideration of matters specially affecting the interests of that Member of the League. At meetings of the Council, each Member of the League represented on the Council shall have one vote, and may have not more than one Representative.

Article 5.

Except where otherwise expressly provided in this Covenant or by the terms of the present Treaty, decisions at any meeting of the Assembly or of the Council shall require the agreement of all the Members of the League represented at the meeting. All matters of procedure at meetings of the Assembly or of the Council, including the appointment of Committees to investigate particular matters, shall be regulated by the Assembly or by the Council and may be decided by a majority of the Members of the League represented at the meeting. The first meeting of the Assembly and the first meeting of the Council shall be summoned by the President of the United States of America.

Article 6.

The permanent Secretariat shall be established at the Seat of the League. The Secretariat shall comprise a Secretary General and such secretaries and staff as may be required. The first Secretary General shall be the person named in the Annex; thereafter the Secretary General shall be appointed by the Council with the approval of the majority of the Assembly. The secretaries and staff of the Secretariat shall be appointed by the Secretary General with the approval of the Council. The Secretary General shall act in that capacity at all meetings of the Assembly and of the Council. The expenses of the Secretariat shall be borne by the Members of the League in accordance with the apportionment of the expenses of the International Bureau of the Universal Postal Union.

Article 7.

The Seat of the League is established at Geneva. The Council may at any time decide that the Seat of the League shall be established elsewhere. All positions under or in connection with the League, including the Secretariat, shall be open equally to men and women. Representatives of the Members of the League and officials of the League when engaged on the business of the League shall enjoy diplomatic privileges and immunities. The buildings and other property occupied by the League or its officials or by Representatives attending its meetings shall be inviolable.

Article 8.

The Members of the League recognise that the maintenance of peace requires the reduction of national armaments to the lowest point consistent with national safety and the enforcement by common action of international obligations. The Council, taking account of the geographical situation and circumstances of each State, shall formulate plans for such reduction for the consideration and action of the several Governments. Such plans shall be subject to reconsideration and revision at least every ten years. After these plans shall have been adopted by the several Governments, the limits of armaments therein fixed shall not be exceeded without the concurrence of the Council. The Members of the League agree that the manufacture by private enterprise of munitions and implements of war is open to grave objections. The Council shall advise how the evil effects attendant upon such manufacture can be prevented, due regard being had to the necessities of those Members of the League which are not able to manufacture the munitions and implements of war necessary for their safety. The Members of the League undertake to interchange full and frank information as to the scale of their armaments, their military, naval, and air programmes and the condition of such of their industries as are adaptable to war-like purposes.

Article 9.

A permanent Commission shall be constituted to advise the Council on the execution of the provisions of Articles 1 and 8 and on military, naval, and air questions generally.

Article 10.

The Members of the League undertake to respect and preserve as against external aggression the territorial integrity and existing political independence of all Members of the League. In case of any such aggression or in case of any threat or danger of such aggression the Council shall advise upon the means by which this obligation shall be fulfilled.

Article 11.

Any war or threat of war, whether immediately affecting any of the Members of the League or not, is hereby declared a matter of concern to the whole League, and the League shall take any action that may be deemed wise and effectual to safeguard the peace of nations. In case any such emergency should arise the Secretary General shall on the request of any Member of the League forthwith summon a meeting of the Council. It is also declared to be the friendly right of each Member of the League to bring to the attention of the Assembly or of the Council any circumstance whatever affecting international relations which threatens to disturb international peace or the good understanding between nations upon which peace depends.

Article 12.

The Members of the League agree that if there should arise between them any dispute likely to lead to a rupture, they will submit the matter either to arbitration or to inquiry by the Council, and they agree in no case to resort to war until three months after the award by the arbitrators or the report by the Council. In any case under this Article the award of the arbitrators shall be made within a reasonable time, and the report of the Council shall be made within six months after the submission of the dispute.

Article 13.

The Members of the League agree that whenever any dispute shall arise between them which they recognise to be suitable for submission to arbitration and which cannot be satisfactorily settled by diplomacy, they will submit the whole subject-matter to arbitration. Disputes as to the interpretation of a treaty, as to any question of international law, as to the existence of any fact which if established would constitute a breach of any international obligation, or as to the extent and nature of the reparation to be made for any such breach, are declared to be among those which are generally suitable for submission to arbitration. For the consideration of any such dispute the court of arbitration to which the case is referred shall be the Court agreed on by the parties to the dispute or stipulated in any convention existing between them. The Members of the League agree that they will carry out in full good faith any award that may be rendered, and that they will not resort to war against a Member of the League which complies therewith. In the event of any failure to carry out such an award, the Council shall propose what steps should be taken to give effect thereto.

Article 14.

The Council shall formulate and submit to the Members of the League for adoption plans for the establishment of a Permanent Court of International Justice. The Court shall be competent to hear and determine any dispute of an international character which the parties thereto submit to it. The Court may also give an advisory opinion upon any dispute or question referred to it by the Council or by the Assembly.

Article 15.

If there should arise between Members of the League any dispute likely to lead to a rupture, which is not submitted to arbitration in accordance with Article 13, the Members of the League agree that they will submit the matter to the Council. Any party to the dispute may effect such submission by giving notice of the existence of the dispute to the Secretary General, who will make all necessary arrangements for a full investigation and consideration thereof. For this purpose the parties to the dispute will communicate to the Secretary General, as promptly as possible, statements of their case with all the relevant facts and papers, and the Council may forthwith direct the publication thereof. The Council shall endeavour to effect a settlement of the dispute, and if such efforts are successful, a statement shall be made public giving such facts and explanations regarding the dispute and the terms of settlement thereof as the Council may deem appropriate. If the dispute is not thus settled, the Council either unanimously or by a majority vote shall make and publish a report containing a statement of the facts of the dispute and the recommendations which are deemed just and proper in regard thereto. Any Member of the League represented on the Council may make public a statement of the facts of the dispute and of its conclusions regarding the same. If a report by the Council is unanimously agreed to by the members thereof other than the Representatives of one or more of the parties to the dispute, the Members of the League agree that they will not go to war with any party to the dispute which complies with the recommendations of the report. If the Council fails to reach a report which is unanimously agreed to by the members thereof, other than the Representatives of one or more of the parties to the dispute, the Members of the League reserve to themselves the right to take such action as they shall consider necessary for the maintenance of right and justice. If the dispute between the parties is claimed by one of them and is found by the Council, to arise out of a matter which by international law is solely within the domestic jurisdiction of that party, the Council shall so report, and shall make no recommendation as to its settlement. The Council may in any case under this Article refer the dispute to the Assembly. The dispute shall be so referred at the request of either party to the dispute, provided that such request be made within fourteen days after the submission of the dispute to the Council. In any case referred to the Assembly, all the provisions of this Article and of Article 12 relating to the action and powers of the Council shall apply to the action and powers of the Assembly, provided that a report made by the Assembly, if concurred in by the Representatives of those Members of the League represented on the Council and of a majority of the other Members of the League, exclusive in each case of the Representatives of the parties to the dispute shall have the same force as a report by the Council concurred in by all the members thereof other than the Representatives of one or more of the parties to the dispute.

Article 16.

Should any Member of the League resort to war in disregard of its covenants under Articles 12, 13, or 15, it shall ipso facto be deemed to have committed an act of war against all other Members of the League, which hereby undertake immediately to subject it to the severance of all trade or financial relations, the prohibition of all intercourse between their nations and the nationals of the covenant-breaking State, and the prevention of all financial, commercial, or personal intercourse between the nationals of the covenant-breaking State and the nationals of any other State, whether a Member of the League or not. It shall be the duty of the Council in such case to recommend to the several Governments concerned what effective military, naval, or air force the Members of the League shall severally contribute to the armed forces to be used to protect the covenants of the League. The Members of the League agree, further, that they will mutually support one another in the financial and economic measures which are taken under this Article, in order to minimise the loss and inconvenience resulting from the above measures, and that they will mutually support one another in resisting any special measures aimed at one of their number by the covenant-breaking State, and that they will take the necessary steps to afford passage through their territory to the forces of any of the Members of the League which are co-operating to protect the covenants of the League. Any Member of the League which has violated any covenant of the League may be declared to be no longer a Member of the League by a vote of the Council concurred in by the Representatives of all the other Members of the League represented thereon.

Article 17.

In the event of a dispute between a Member of the League and a State which is not a Member of the League, or between States not Members of the League, the State or States, not Members of the League shall be invited to accept the obligations of membership in the League for the purposes of such dispute, upon such conditions as the Council may deem just. If such invitation is accepted, the provisions of Articles 12 to 16 inclusive shall be applied with such modifications as may be deemed necessary by the Council. Upon such invitation being given the Council shall immediately institute an inquiry into the circumstances of the dispute and recommend such action as may seem best and most effectual in the circumstances. If a State so invited shall refuse to accept the obligations of membership in the League for the purposes of such dispute, and shall resort to war against a Member of the League, the provisions of Article 16 shall be applicable as against the State taking such action. If both parties to the dispute when so invited refuse to accept the obligations of membership in the League for the purpose of such dispute, the Council may take such measures and make such recommendations as will prevent hostilities and will result in the settlement of the dispute.

Article 18.

Every treaty or international engagement entered into hereafter by any Member of the League shall be forthwith registered with the Secretariat and shall as soon as possible be published by it. No such treaty or international engagement shall be binding until so registered.

Article 19.

The Assembly may from time to time advise the reconsideration by Members of the League of treaties which have become inapplicable and the consideration of international conditions whose continuance might endanger the peace of the world.

Article 20.

The Members of the League severally agree that this Covenant is accepted as abrogating all obligations or understandings inter se which are inconsistent with the terms thereof, and solemnly undertake that they will not hereafter enter into any engagements inconsistent with the terms thereof. In case any Member of the League shall, before becoming a Member of the League, have undertaken any obligations inconsistent with the terms of this Covenant, it shall be the duty of such Member to take immediate steps to procure its release from such obligations.

Article 21.

Nothing in this Covenant shall be deemed to affect the validity of international engagements, such as treaties of arbitration or regional understandings like the Monroe doctrine, for securing the maintenance of peace.

Article 22.

To those colonies and territories which as a consequence of the late war have ceased to be under the sovereignty of the States which formerly governed them and which are inhabited by peoples not yet able to stand by themselves under the strenuous conditions of the modern world, there should be applied the principle that the well-being and development of such peoples form a sacred trust of civilisation and that securities for the performance of this trust should be embodied in this Covenant. The best method of giving practical effect to this principle is that the tutelage of such peoples should be entrusted to advanced nations who by reason of their resources, their experience or their geographical position can best undertake this responsibility, and who are willing to accept it, and that this tutelage should be exercised by them as Mandatories on behalf of the League. The character of the mandate must differ according to the stage of the development of the people, the geographical situation of the territory, its economic conditions, and other similar circumstances. Certain communities formerly belonging to the Turkish Empire have reached a stage of development where their existence as independent nations can be provisionally recognised subject to the rendering of administrative advice and assistance by a Mandatory until such time as they are able to stand alone. The wishes of these communities must be a principal consideration in the selection of the Mandatory. Other peoples, especially those of Central Africa, are at such a stage that the Mandatory must be responsible for the administration of the territory under conditions which will guarantee freedom of conscience and religion, subject only to the maintenance of public order and morals, the prohibition of abuses such as the slave trade, the arms traffic, and the liquor traffic, and the prevention of the establishment of fortifications or military and naval bases and of military training of the natives for other than police purposes and the defence of territory, and will also secure equal opportunities for the trade and commerce of other Members of the League. There are territories, such as South-West Africa and certain of the South Pacific Islands, which, owing to the sparseness of their population, or their small size, or their remoteness from the centres of civilisation, or their geographical contiguity to the territory of the Mandatory, and other circumstances, can be best administered under the laws of the Mandatory as integral portions of its territory, subject to the safeguards above mentioned in the interests of the indigenous population. In every case of mandate, the Mandatory shall render to the Council an annual report in reference to the territory committed to its charge. The degree of authority, control, or administration to be exercised by the Mandatory shall, if not previously agreed upon by the Members of the League, be explicitly defined in each case by the Council. A permanent Commission shall be constituted to receive and examine the annual reports of the Mandatories and to advise the Council on all matters relating to the observance of the mandates.

Article 23.

Subject to and in accordance with the provisions of international conventions existing or hereafter to be agreed upon, the Members of the League:

1. will endeavour to secure and maintain fair and humane conditions of labour for men, women, and children, both in their own countries and in all countries to which their commercial and industrial relations extend, and for that purpose will establish and maintain the necessary international organisations;

2. undertake to secure just treatment of the native inhabitants of territories under their control;

3. will entrust the League with the general supervision over the execution of agreements with regard to the traffic in women and children, and the traffic in opium and other dangerous drugs;

4. will entrust the League with the general supervision of the trade in arms and ammunition with the countries in which the control of this traffic is necessary in the common interest;

5. will make provision to secure and maintain freedom of communications and of transit and equitable treatment for the commerce of all Members of the League. In this connection, the special necessities of the regions devastated during the war of 1914–1918 shall be borne in mind;

6. will endeavour to take steps in matters of international concern for the prevention and control of disease.

Article 24.

There shall be placed under the direction of the League all international bureaux already established by general treaties if the parties to such treaties consent. All such international bureaux and all commissions for the regulation of matters of international interest hereafter constituted shall be placed under the direction of the League. In all matters of international interest which are regulated by general conventions but which are not placed under the control of international bureaux or commissions, the Secretariat of the League shall, subject to the consent of the Council and if desired by the parties, collect and distribute all relevant information and shall render any other assistance which may be necessary or desirable. The Council may include as part of the expenses of the Secretariat the expenses of any bureau or commission which is placed under the direction of the League.

Article 25.

The Members of the League agree to encourage and promote the establishment and co-operation of duly authorised voluntary national Red Cross organisations having as purposes the improvement of health, the prevention of disease, and the mitigation of suffering throughout the world.

Article 26.

Amendments to this Covenant will take effect when ratified by the Members of the League whose representatives compose the Council and by a majority of the Members of the League whose Representatives compose the Assembly. No such amendment shall bind any Member of the League which signifies its dissent therefrom, but in that case it shall cease to be a Member of the League.

ANNEX.
I. ORIGINAL MEMBERS OF THE LEAGUE OF NATIONS SIGNATORIES OF THE TREATY OF PEACE.

UNITED STATES OF AMERICA, BELGIUM, BOLIVIA, BRAZIL, BRITISH EMPIRE, CANADA, AUSTRALIA, SOUTH AFRICA, NEW ZEALAND, INDIA, CHINA, CUBA, ECUADOR, FRANCE, GREECE, GUATEMALA, HAITI, HEDJAZ, HONDURAS, ITALY, JAPAN, LIBERIA, NICARAGUA, PANAMA, PERU, POLAND, PORTUGAL, ROUMANIA, SERB-CROAT-SLOVENE STATE, SIAM, CZECHO-SLOVAKIA, URUGUAY

STATES INVITED TO ACCEDE TO THE COVENANT. ARGENTINE REPUBLIC, CHILE, COLOMBIA, DENMARK, NETHERLANDS, NORWAY, PARAGUAY, PERSIA, SALVADOR, SPAIN, SWEDEN, SWITZERLAND, VENEZUELA.
II. FIRST SECRETARY GENERAL OF THE LEAGUE OF NATIONS.
The Honourable Sir James Eric Drummond, K.C.M.G., C.B.

28. REPARATIONS CLAUSES OF THE VERSAILLES TREATY, JUNE 28, 1919

Article 231.

The Allied and Associated Governments affirm and Germany accepts the responsibility of Germany and her allies for causing all the loss and damage to which the Allied and Associated Governments and their nationals have been subjected as a consequence of the war imposed upon them by the aggression of Germany and her allies.

Article 232.

The Allied and Associated Governments recognise that the resources of Germany are not adequate, after taking into account permanent diminutions of such resources which will result from other provisions of the present Treaty, to make complete reparation for all such loss and damage.

The Allied and Associated Governments, however, require, and Germany undertakes, that she will make compensation for all damage done to the civilian population of the Allied and Associated Powers and to their property during the period of the belligerency of each as an Allied or Associated Power against

Germany by such aggression by land, by sea and from the air, and in general all damage as defined in Annex l hereto.

In accordance with Germany's pledges, already given, as to complete restoration for Belgium, Germany undertakes, in addition to the compensation for damage elsewhere in this Part provided for, as a consequence of the violation of the Treaty of 1839, to make reimbursement of all sums which Belgium has borrowed from the Allied and Associated Governments up to November 11, 1918, together with interest at the rate of five per cent (5) per annum on such sums. This amount shall be determined by the Reparation Commission, and the German Government undertakes thereupon forthwith to make a special issue of bearer bonds to an equivalent amount payable in marks gold, on May 1, 1926, or, at the option of the German Government, on the 1st of May in any year up to 1926. Subject to the foregoing, the form of such bonds shall be determined by the Reparation Commission. Such bonds shall be handed over to the Reparation Commission, which has authority to take and acknowledge receipt thereof on behalf of Belgium.

Article 233.

The amount of the above damage for which compensation is to be made by Germany shall be determined by an Inter-Allied Commission, to be called the Reparation Commission and constituted in the form and with the powers set forth hereunder and in Annexes II to VII inclusive hereto.

ANNEX I.

Compensation may be claimed from Germany under Article 232 above in respect of the total damage under the following categories:

1. Damage to injured persons and to surviving dependents by personal injury to or death of civilians caused by acts of war, including bombardments or other attacks on land, on sea, or from the air, and all the direct consequences thereof, and of all operations of war by the two groups of belligerents wherever arising.

2. Damage caused by Germany or her allies to civilian victims of acts of cruelty, violence or maltreatment (including injuries to life or health as a consequence of imprisonment, deportation, internment or evacuation, of exposure at sea or of being forced to labour), wherever arising, and to the surviving dependents of such victims.

3. Damage caused by Germany or her allies in their own territory or in occupied or invaded territory to civilian victims of all acts injurious to health or capacity to work, or to honour, as well as to the surviving dependents of such victims.

4. Damage caused by any kind of maltreatment of prisoners of war.

5. As damage caused to the peoples of the Allied and Associated Powers, all pensions and compensation in the nature of pensions to naval and military victims of war (including members of the air force), whether mutilated, wounded, sick or invalided, and to the dependents of such victims, the amount due to the Allied and Associated Governments being calculated for each of them as being the capitalised cost of such pensions and compensation at the date of the coming into force of the present Treaty on the basis of the scales in force in France at such date.

6. The cost of assistance by the Government of the Allied and Associated Powers to prisoners of war and to their families and dependents.

7. Allowances by the Governments of the Allied and Associated Powers to the families and dependents of mobilised persons or persons serving with the forces, the amount due to them for each calendar year in which hostilities occurred being calculated for each Government on the basis of the average scale for such payments in force in France during that year.

8. Damage caused to civilians by being forced by Germany or her allies to labour without just remuneration.

9. Damage in respect of all property wherever situated belonging to any of the Allied or Associated States or their nationals, with the exception of naval and military works or materials, which has been carried off, seized, injured or destroyed by the acts of Germany or her allies on land, on sea or from the air, or damage directly in consequence of hostilities or of any operations of war.

10. Damage in the form of levies, fines and other similar exactions imposed by Germany or her allies upon the civilian population.

. . . . .

ANNEX III.

1. Germany recognises the right of the Allied and Associated Powers to the replacement, ton for ton (gross tonnage) and class for class, of all merchant ships and fishing boats lost or damaged owing to the war.

Nevertheless, and in spite of the fact that the tonnage of German shipping at present in existence is much less than that lost by the Allied and Associated Powers in consequence of the German aggression, the right thus recognised will be enforced on German ships and boats under the following conditions:

The German Government, on behalf of themselves and so as to bind all other persons interested, cede to the Allied and Associated Governments the property in all the German merchant ships which are of 1,600 tons gross and upwards; in one-half, reckoned in tonnage, of the ships which are between 1,000 tons and 1,600 tons gross; in one-quarter, reckoned in tonnage, of the steam trawlers; and in one-quarter, reckoned in tonnage, of the other fishing boats.

2. The German Government will, within two months of the coming into force of the present Treaty, deliver to the Reparation Commission all the ships and boats mentioned in paragraph 1.

3. The ships and boats mentioned in paragraph 1 include all ships and boats which (a) fly, or may be entitled to fly, the German merchant flag; or (b) are owned by any German national, company or corporation or by any company or corporation belonging to a country other than an Allied or Associated country and under the control or direction of German nationals; or (c) are now under construction (1) in Germany, (2) in other than Allied or Associated countries for the account of any German national, company or corporation.

APPENDIX B
Biographies of Major Personalities

Ataturk, Mustafa Kemal (1881–1938) *Turkish army officer, statesman*

Ataturk was a Turkish soldier, leader, and statesman, who served as a general during World War I in the Ottoman army and later emerged as president of Turkey. Although he was victorious in several of his battles, with the defeat of the Central Powers, Greece began occupying part of Anatolia. In response, Ataturk simultaneously set up a provisional government in opposition to the sultan, and led decisive battles against Greece in 1921 and 1922. The sultanate was abolished in 1922, and Ataturk emerged as the leader of the single-party, republican government of Turkey.

Born in Salonica (now part of Greece), the son of a customs official and businessman, Mustafa earned the second name Kemal, meaning "perfection," from his excellent performance in school. He went by the name of Mustafa Kemal during his youth. In 1934, when Turkey established the western practice of surnames, the national legislature officially bestowed on him the name Ataturk ("Father of the Turks").

Mustafa Kemal pursued a military career, graduating from the War Academy in 1905, and entering the Ottoman army as a staff captain. He organized a clandestine society to oppose the sultan's despotic rule. In 1915, with the rank of colonel, Mustafa Kemal led the troops who repelled the invaders at a crucial battle at the Dardanelles. After serving in the army during the war commanding Ottoman armies in Palestine and Syria, in May 1919, he convened a congress and raised an army to overthrow the sultanate and secure Turkey's national sovereignty. In 1920, the Grand National Assembly elected him, now known as Mustafa Kemal Pasha, president. With the complete liberation of the Anatolian homeland in 1922, Mustafa Kemal Pasha led the government. Under his leadership, Turkey signed the 1923 Lausanne Treaty, which formally brought an end to World War I for that nation. In October 1923,

Turkey was proclaimed a republic and Kemal Pasha was unanimously elected president. He continued to rule the one-party state until his death in 1938. Although autocratic, his government was widely recognized as modernizing the country, elevating the status of women, and instituting a broad variety of other social, legal, and economic reforms.

Baker, Newton D. (1871–1937) *U.S. lawyer, mayor, secretary of war*

Newton Baker served as secretary of war in Woodrow Wilson's cabinet in the period 1916–21. Baker was born in West Virginia, attended law school in Virginia, and practiced in West Virginia. He moved to Cleveland, Ohio, where he worked as city solicitor under reform mayor Tom Johnson. The city elected Baker as a Democrat to succeed Johnson. He served from 1912–16. As mayor, he earned a reputation as one of the nation's progressive and reformist local leaders. He attended the national nominating convention of the Democratic Party in 1912, working to help nominate Woodrow Wilson. Wilson appointed him secretary of war in 1916, partly because of Baker's reputation as a pacifist.

When the United States entered the war in April 1917, Republicans criticized Baker for the nation's lack of preparedness, and he faced a congressional investigation. Despite his opposition to participation in the World War, he committed himself to the effort, stating that as a pacifist, he would fight for peace. He submitted a plan to Congress for the draft, reorganized the War Department, and efficiently administered a greatly expanded budget.

After the war, Baker continued to stand for American participation in the League of Nations and the World Court. Partly because of this repute, President Calvin Coolidge appointed Baker to the Permanent Court of Arbitration at The Hague in 1928. In 1936, Baker published *Why We Went to War* in defense of Wilson's decision to abandon neutrality in 1917. Like many other Democrats of his era, he questioned the expansion of government authority under the New Deal.

Balfour, Arthur James (1848–1930) *British statesman, foreign secretary*

Arthur Balfour served as British foreign minister during the last years of World War I and is most remembered for his support for the establishment of a Jewish homeland in Palestine. A member of the British aristocracy, Balfour entered political life immediately upon completion of his education at Cambridge University, beginning in the House of Commons in 1874. From 1885 to 1906, he represented a constituency in East Manchester as a member of the Conservative Party. He served in the cabinet as Irish chief secretary, earning a reputation for strict repression of Irish insurrection and opposition to Irish Home Rule. In the period 1902–05, Balfour served as prime minister of Great Britain. During his tenure as prime minister, he worked out the Entente Cordiale, a bilateral defense treaty with France and the core of the later three-nation Triple Entente that included Russia. He remained head of the Conservative opposition party in the period 1906–11.

Balfour's participation in British foreign affairs during World War I began with his joining a reorganized national unity or bipartisan government under Herbert Henry Asquith in 1915. In that government, Balfour succeeded Winston Churchill as first lord of the admiralty after Churchill's resignation over the Gallipoli campaign. A new coalition government established in 1916 under David Lloyd George as prime minister gave Balfour the position of foreign secretary. When the United States entered the war in 1917, Balfour visited America as head of a British commission to work on details of cooperation in the war effort.

In November 1917, on the urging of Chaim Weizmann, Balfour sent a note to Baron Rothschild, the British representative of the Rothschild international banking family. The note, remembered in history as the Balfour Declaration, pledged British support for the establishment of a homeland for Jews in Palestine. The note also stipulated that such a homeland not prejudice the rights of the non-Jewish population in Palestine and that in no way should it diminish the rights and political status of Jews living in other countries. Later, Woodrow Wilson and the League of Nations endorsed the terms of the Balfour Declaration.

Balfour participated in the Paris Peace Conference and worked to mitigate some of the harsher terms of the Treaty of Versailles signed in 1919.

Balfour continued to hold office in several postwar positions, and, in 1922, he was created a peer with the title of 1st Earl of Balfour, Viscount Traprain. In 1926, he engaged in the negotiations that led to the definition of the relations between Great Britain and the Dominions (Canada, Australia, New Zealand, and the Union of South Africa) documented in the Balfour Report. That relationship was established in law the year after his death in the Statute of Westminster. In addition to his career as a political leader and statesman, Balfour earned a reputation as an author on philosophical topics, including a defense of religion in the science-religion debates of the era.

Baruch, Bernard Mannes (1870–1965) *U.S. businessman, presidential adviser*

Bernard Baruch served as a close adviser to Woodrow Wilson in World War I and member of the U.S. delegation to the Paris Peace Conference. Baruch was born in Camden, South Carolina, and graduated from the College of the City of New York in 1889. He soon took up a position as an office boy in a Wall Street brokerage firm. There he learned the investment business, and, by age 30, he had amassed a multimillion-dollar fortune. An active Democrat who made numerous contributions to political campaigns, in 1916 he came to the attention of Woodrow Wilson, who appointed him to several advisory and administrative positions during the war.

In 1916, Baruch served as a member of the Advisory Commission of the Council of National Defense and as chair of the Commission on Raw Materials, Minerals, and Metals. Wilson put Baruch in charge of all allied purchasing in the United States, and, in 1918, Wilson appointed Baruch to serve as chairman of the War Industries Board. In order to avoid any appearance of conflict of interest, Baruch resigned his positions on the boards of corporations and his seat on the New York stock exchange, liquidated his corporate investments, and purchased millions of dollars of Liberty Bonds. Later, the wartime organization of the American economy under Baruch would be viewed as a precursor to the government engagement in the economy under Franklin Roosevelt's New Deal.

Baruch served as an economic adviser to the Peace Commission and as a member of the Supreme Economic Council at the Paris Peace Conference. He especially dealt with the economics and reparations clauses of the peace treaty, which he detailed in a work published after the war, *The Making of the Reparations and Economic Sections of the Treaty*. During the peace negotiations, Baruch met Winston Churchill and they became lifelong friends.

In later years, Baruch remained an informal adviser to presidents, especially Roosevelt and Harry Truman. In 1946, he presented the American plan for the international control of atomic energy to the United Nations. Although developed by David Lilienthal and Dean Acheson in its preliminary form, the plan was known as the Baruch Plan and called for a system of international inspections to ensure that no nation developed atomic weapons. In effect, the Baruch Plan called for a system of world government over one area of scientific and weapons development. The Soviet Union rejected the plan.

In addition to giving advice to every president from Wilson to John F. Kennedy, Baruch was often spotted discussing his views with members of the public while sitting on a park bench in Lafayette Square, across from the White House. Baruch became known as an elder statesman and park-bench philosopher, remaining active in his later years.

Bernstorff, Count Johann-Heinrich (1862–1939) *German diplomat*

Count Johann Bernstorff served as Germany's ambassador to the United States, 1908–17. During the period of American neutrality, Bernstorff worked both to keep the United States neutral and to assist in the efforts of President Woodrow Wilson to bring about a negotiated end to the war.

Bernstorff had entered the German diplomatic service in 1899, serving in Serbia, Holland, Russia, Bavaria, and Britain, before being posted as consul general to Egypt in 1906. In 1908, he was appointed ambassador to the United States, where his charm and his American wife helped win him a reputation as a genial member of the diplomatic corps. Although he worked to support the mediating role of the United States in the World War, his position as a moderate was made tenuous by the fact that members of the diplomatic delegation were deeply involved in espionage, especially the military attach Franz von Papen and the naval attaché Karl Boy-Ed. When Germany declared unrestricted submarine warfare early in 1917, over

Bernstorff's opposition, Bernstorff found himself fully isolated from German policy. He was recalled to Berlin, where he was appointed as ambassador to the Ottoman Empire. Because of his open opposition to several German policies, he was cut off from the inner circle of German diplomatic and military leadership in the last years of the war. At the end of the war he was offered the post of minister of foreign affairs, but he declined.

Bernstorff served as a deputy to the Reichstag during the Weimar Republic, from 1921 to 1928, and was an active supporter of the League of Nations. When Hitler came to power, Bernstorff went into exile in Switzerland, where he published his memoirs. In that work he claimed that if Germany had followed a more careful policy, it could have avoided war with the United States.

Bettignies, Louise de (1880–1918) *Belgian spy for the British*

Louise de Bettignies served as the head of an espionage ring in Lille, Belgium, providing information to both the French and the British for nearly a year from 1914 to 1915. The daughter of a porcelain manufacturer in Lille, Bettignies received a good education, and became fluent in several languages, including German, English, Italian, and French. Before World War I she worked as a governess and language teacher in the families of wealthy patrons. When Germany invaded Belgium, she fled as a refugee to Britain, where she provided a detailed account of the German invasion to British intelligence. She was then enlisted as an agent and returned to Lille under the code name Alice Dubois. For the French, her codename was Pauline.

In Lille, she recruited Marie-Leonie Van Houtte (code-named Charlotte), a shopkeeper. Working out of the shop, the two established a network of spies, known to British intelligence as the "Alice Ring." Bettignies smuggled much of her information out by way of neutral Holland, crossing at unguarded points, or by swimming across a canal. She and Van Houtte worked out many ingenious ways of concealing messages inside ordinary commercial products, such as toys, candy bars, or balls of wool. Bettignies recruited others to her ring, including young boys as couriers, an expert cartographer, and an ink-chemist and forger. Her ring rescued escaped prisoners of war and provided them with forged German passports, which they used to flee into Holland.

The ring operated for less than a year, when German counterintelligence began to track down its members. Both Bettignies and Van Houtte were arrested and court-martialed, but neither admitted anything about the network. The Germans condemned both to death but, apparently remembering the negative worldwide publicity that came out of their execution of Edith Cavell, commuted the sentences to prison terms. Bettignies contracted pneumonia in prison and died in a Cologne hospital in September 1918. Van Houtte was released following the armistice. Bettignies was honored with medals by the British and French governments, and she was buried with full military honors in Lille. A statue was erected there in her memory.

Borden, Robert (1854–1937) *Canadian politician, prime minister*

Robert Borden served as prime minister of Canada from 1911 to 1920. Borden's policies during World War I helped establish Canada as an independent partner with Britain, within the empire, in the prosecution of the war against the Central Powers. Borden's formal education ended before he turned 15, but he studied law and became a prominent lawyer in Halifax. He entered politics in 1896, entering the Canadian Parliament as a Conservative member from that city. In 1900, Borden was chosen to head the Conservative Party, and, with the defeat of the Liberal government in 1911, Borden became prime minister. In 1914, King George of Britain knighted him.

Before the war began, Borden supported a Canadian grant of $35 million to Britain to pay for the construction of three battleships. When the war began, Borden urged that Canada be consulted on major war decisions, but it was not until the establishment of the government of David Lloyd George that his views prevailed. Borden's position was that if Canada were to contribute a half-million or more men to the war, it should have a role in the policies that directed their fate.

In 1917, Lloyd George established the Imperial War Cabinet, and Canada gained a voice in the Allies' war policy. Under Borden's government, nearly a half-million Canadians volunteered for the military, but to maintain the forces at level, conscription was put in place. Bringing Liberals into his government, Borden headed a Unionist government from 1917 to develop unity over the conscription issue. The draft was strongly opposed among French Canadians, and Borden's support was based largely among English-speaking Canadians. As a consequence of his position on conscription and the Union government, no representative of the province of Quebec served in his cabinet. During the war, numerous scandals over wartime profiteering, graft, and the minister of Militia and Defense surrounded his administration. The Wartime Elections Act, which he supported, denied German Canadians and others the right to vote on ethnic grounds. At the Versailles conference, Borden supported the American interpretation of the reparation clauses.

After the war, Borden advocated sending Canadian troops as part of the international force intervening in the Russian civil war, but after a public outcry, he brought the troops back from the Russian far east. In 1919, he ordered the arrest of leaders of the Winnipeg general strike, earning him strong opposition from labor. He resigned the government in 1920. He served as representative of Canada at the Washington Naval Disarmament Conference in 1921.

The fact that Canada was independently represented at the Paris peace conference and that Borden's signature was on the Versailles Treaty is often taken as representing the independence of Canada as a sovereign nation within the British Commonwealth. In retirement, Borden authored works on Canada's constitution and its place in the British Commonwealth. He remained active in business and law until his death in 1937.

Brooke, Rupert (1887–1915) *British poet, soldier*

Rupert Brooke, a casualty of World War I, became a symbol of the loss of a promising generation of youth. Brooke had already earned a reputation as a poet, an aesthete, and a charming member of British society when World War I broke out. His father had been headmaster of the Rugby School, which Brooke attended before going on to King's College at Cambridge. In 1911, a volume of his poetry was published. In 1912, he edited, with Edward Marsh, an anthology, *Georgian Poetry, 1911–1912.* The Georgian poets were known for their evocation of rustic themes and romantic subjects such as friendship and love. Although he had fallen in love with at least three different young women, in each case the relationship had broken up. Brooke spent a year during 1913–14 traveling in the United States and in the South Pacific, sending back travel accounts and poetry for publication in the *Westminster Gazette.*

In 1914, he enlisted in the British navy as an officer and saw limited action at the evacuation of Antwerp. Later in 1915, while en route to Gallipoli, he died at sea from blood poisoning of a minor wound, reportedly a mosquito bite. He was buried on the Greek island of Skyros in the Aegean Sea.

Brooke was a minor celebrity as a romantic figure: youthful, handsome, and a sentimental poet. Following his death, his friends and the British public made him into an immediate legend. His obituary, written by Winston Churchill, appeared in the London *Times* and contributed to the establishment of Brooke as a symbol for the generation of promising youth sacrificed during the war. The internationally known novelist D. H. Lawrence also published a eulogy on Brooke's death. As a troubled youth, only 28 years old at his death, popular, well-liked, and born into a prestigious family, Brooke's death caught the popular imagination as representing the tragedy of the war at the individual level.

Brooke's *1914 and Other Poems,* published posthumously, also contributed to his role as an exemplar of the slaughtered generation. However, his poetry was criticized as reflecting a sentimental and romantic view of the war, which those poets and authors who experienced more of it soon abandoned in favor of a harder, less innocent tone. Nevertheless, his work retained popularity even in a more cynical age. These lines from one of his sonnets, "The Soldier," were often quoted:

> If I should die, think only this of me.
> That there's some corner of a foreign field
> That is for ever England.

Bryan, William Jennings (1860–1925) *U.S. politician, journalist, secretary of state*

William Jennings Bryan served as Woodrow Wilson's first secretary of state who broke with the president over the neutrality policy toward Germany. Born in Illinois, Bryan attended law school in Chicago, and, after a visit to Nebraska, relocated there in 1887. He entered politics and ran for Congress as a Democrat, adopting many ideas of the Populist Party and movement in his campaign. He was elected to Congress as the first Democratic member of Congress in Nebraska, earning national recognition. In 1894, he ran for the U.S. Senate, but was defeated and became the editor of a Democratic newspaper in Omaha, Nebraska. In 1896, he delivered the keynote address at the Democratic national convention, known as the Cross of Gold

speech, in which he supported a policy of monetary inflation to offset the long-term depression in commodity prices which had led to difficult conditions for farmers. That speech and his flair for oratory won him the Democratic nomination for the presidency at that convention, and again in 1900 and 1908. Although he lost all three presidential elections to the Republican candidate, he firmly established himself as a national figure, representing "the common man" and the progressive wing of the Democratic Party.

In 1912, Bryan threw his support to Woodrow Wilson, who won the presidency after the Republican party split into two factions, with progressives campaigning for Theodore Roosevelt and conservatives standing by the incumbent Republican president, William Howard Taft. In recognition of Bryan's help, Wilson appointed him secretary of state. It was in that role that Bryan would play a significant part in the history of World War I.

Although Bryan had warmly supported the American position during the Spanish-American War of 1898 and had even raised a regiment to participate, he had established himself as an advocate of international negotiation rather than war as a solution to international disputes. One of his first efforts as secretary of state was to work for an international treaty that would establish a process of arbitration and a cooling-off period in case of international disputes. He was in the process of securing agreements to this arrangement in the summer of 1914 when World War I broke out following the assassination in Sarajevo.

Bryan continued to advocate strict American neutrality during that war. Among other measures, he sought to prohibit Americans from traveling as passengers on the ships of belligerent nations. Further, he sought to prohibit the granting of loans to belligerent nations. Both such measures would have prevented to a large extent the slide from neutrality to a pro-Allied position that characterized American policy during the period 1915–17.

When a German submarine sank the British passenger ship *Lusitania* on May 17, 1915, Bryan disagreed with Wilson over the American response. Wilson demanded that the United States respond to the sinking with a formal note of protest, drafted by Wilson, that required that Germany be held "to strict accountability" for the loss of some 128 American lives aboard that ship. Rather than submit the note, Bryan resigned his position as secretary of state, to be replaced by Robert Lansing, who had served under Bryan as counselor to the department.

Despite their disagreements, Bryan gave his support to Wilson for reelection in 1916. However, in the postwar period, Bryan's position became associated with the isolationist foreign policy that was adopted by many former progressives of both the Democratic and Republican Parties. Although no longer a major political figure, Bryan threw himself into the campaign to prohibit the teaching of the theory of evolution in public schools, and, in 1925, he volunteered to assist in the prosecution of public high-school teacher John T. Scopes in Tennessee. Immediately after that trial, Bryan suffered a fatal heart attack. His wife, Mary Baird Bryan, collaborated in editing his memoirs, which were published in 1925.

Casement, Roger (1864–1916) *Irish diplomat, nationalist leader*

Roger Casement, who had been knighted by the British government for his work in developing reports revealing the exploitation of native workers in the Congo, was an Irish nationalist who during World War I supported plans for an armed Irish rebellion against British rule. Arrested and tried for treason, Casement was executed in London on August 2, 1916.

Casement was born in Dublin county, son of a Protestant father and Catholic mother. He left school at age 16 to work in a shipping company in Liverpool, England. He joined the British consular service, working first in Nigeria (1892–95), and then in Portuguese East Africa. Further assignments included a posting to Angola (1898–1900), and then to the Belgian Congo (1901–04). Appalled at the treatment of workers in the Congo where plantation owners treated the laborers like slaves, even inflicting corporal punishment, including mutilation for disobedience, he wrote a report exposing the conditions. As a consequence, King Leopold of Belgium appointed a commission, which confirmed the conditions, and then the king instituted a series of reforms. For his work in this effort, Casement received international recognition as a crusader against exploitation in the antislavery tradition. During a year's leave of absence in Ireland, he grew interested in the Irish independence movement.

In 1906–08, he served as British consul in Brazil, and then, in 1910, he was asked to investigate allegations that a British firm was exploiting workers on rubber plantations in a remote area of the Putamayo River on the Peruvian-Brazilian border. He investigated these charges, and, as a result of his report, he was knighted.

In 1912, he retired from the British consular service to Ireland. He worked for Irish home rule and assisted in organizing the Irish National Volunteers. In July 1914, he traveled to New York to try to raise money for the effort. On the outbreak of war in August, he traveled to Germany by way of Scandinavia. There, from among prisoners of war held by the Germans, he sought to raise a brigade of Irish troops committed to returning to fight against British rule. However, he had little or no success in this effort. He learned that the Germans would provide rifles for a projected uprising but no German officers, nor any heavier weapons. Convinced that German support would be insufficient for a successful revolution, he returned to Ireland to attempt to convince his colleagues to postpone the uprising. He returned by way of a German submarine.

British intelligence learned of his arrival and arrested him a few days after he landed in Ireland. He was taken to Britain where he was tried for treason and hanged, despite a petition campaign by leading British reformers who believed his prior service should mitigate the charge. Nevertheless it was clear he had conspired with German officials and had attempted to get German help in support of the Irish cause. The British government published a set of diaries written by Casement that detailed homosexual liaisons that he had in Africa and Brazil. He was given no chance to review the diaries or to answer the charges, so it was widely assumed that the diaries were fabrications intended to discredit him. However, when the diaries were released for examination decades later, experts concluded that they were in his handwriting and were probably genuine.

Catt, Carrie Chapman (1859–1947) *U.S. suffragist*

Known during the period of World War I as a leader of the movement for women's suffrage in the United States and for women's rights more generally on an international level, Carrie Chapman Catt carried her ideals into other spheres of political action in the years following the war. Her leadership came at a time when the status of women in the United States and in western Europe was rapidly changing, and her practical approach to the specific question of suffrage was crucial in embodying the new status in specific institutional change. She was active in the formation of the League of Women Voters; she advocated American membership in the League of Nations, and she worked in the world peace movement. Most remembered for her activities in the suffrage arena, she represented many of the crosscurrents and concerns of the Progressive era, including political reform, child labor, and international peace, as well as women's rights.

Carrie Chapman Catt was born in Ripon, Wisconsin, the daughter of Lucius and Maria Lane. Her family moved to a rural area of Iowa where she attended public schools and later graduated from the Iowa Agricultural College in Ames, now Iowa State University. Despite working her way through college, she graduated as the only woman in her class and earned high honors. She worked briefly as a law clerk and then as a teacher, principal, and one of the first women to serve as a superintendent of schools in the United States. Carrie Lane married Leo Chapman, the editor of a newspaper in Mason City, Iowa, and together they moved to San Francisco. Her husband died there, and she made a living working as a newspaper reporter in that city before returning to Iowa City where she joined the Iowa State Woman Suffrage Association. She worked as a writer and lecturer with that organization, later serving as secretary and then state organizer in the period 1890–92.

During this period she married her second husband, George Catt, and then began working for the National American Woman Suffrage Association (NAWSA). She spoke at the 1890 national convention of the organization. Impressed with her work, the national association president, Susan B. Anthony asked Carrie Chapman Catt to address the United States Congress, which she did in 1892. In 1900, she was selected as president of NAWSA and served until 1904. Following the death of her husband and other family members, she traveled abroad, speaking on the topic of women's rights and promoting equal suffrage.

During her absence, the NAWSA divided over tactics, and, on her return in 1915, she once again took up the leadership of the organization. In 1916, she announced a plan under which NAWSA would work for both state and national suffrage for women, compromising by accepting state suffrage in those states offering the most resistance to suffrage in federal elections. As the movement spread, women's votes began to count more and more in the selection of state legislature members, helping to ensure a positive vote for the U.S. constitutional amendment when it came before the legislatures for ratification. One of the most notable victories was the winning of woman suffrage in New York State in 1917.

In 1920, the Nineteenth Amendment to the U.S. Constitution was ratified, and Catt resigned her position with NAWSA. She was a cofounder of the League of Women Voters and was the honorary president of that organization until her death in 1949. She also founded an organization for world peace, the National Committee on the Cause and Cure of War, attempting to harness the dividing women's movement to the cause of world peace.

Cavell, Edith (1865–1915) *British nurse, underground operative in Belgium*
Edith Cavell was a British nurse serving in Belgium when World War I began. She then began working to help Allied soldiers escape to Holland through an underground network that involved the Red Cross hospital where she worked. She and several collaborators were arrested and she was sentenced to death. Her execution by the Germans became a worldwide sensation and a symbol of Germany's ruthless conduct of the war.

Edith Cavell was born in Swardeston, Britain, where her father served as vicar of a Church of England parish. She attended boarding schools and became fluent in French. After a brief tour of Austria and Bavaria, she developed an interest in nursing. In 1890, she became a governess for a brief period in Brussels, Belgium, and in 1896 she entered a nurse-training program at London Hospital. After graduation, she held several nursing positions in Britain. In 1907, she visited Belgium to serve as a private nurse to a child patient there and was soon recruited to help administer a nursing program at a new school for nonreligious nurses opened on the outskirts of Brussels, the Berkendael Medical Institute.

In her position as head of the school, she soon gained responsibilities. Her school regularly provided nurses for three hospitals, and numerous communal schools and kindergartens. At the outbreak of the war on August 3, 1914, Cavell sent home the Dutch and German nurses at the school and converted the clinic into a Red Cross hospital dedicated to providing care to wounded soldiers from both Allied and German armies. After the fall of Brussels to the Germans, the German command moved its own wounded troops to a separate hospital, and most of the British nurses were sent back to Britain.

In fall 1914, Cavell began providing shelter to fugitive British troops who had been cut off behind the lines. Working with a variety of prominent Belgians, Cavell cooperated in an underground escape line. In July 1915, two members of the escape network were arrested, and, early in August 1915, Cavell was interned. The Germans interrogated her and falsely stated that all the other members of the network had confessed. Naively, she made a complete confession and freely admitted that she had helped soldiers escape so that they would not be taken prisoner or shot. The Germans charged her with personally helping some 200 escape to Holland. Under the German penal code, helping Allied troops to escape and fight again was a capital crime. Both American and Spanish ministers to Germany argued for clemency, to no avail. She was executed October 12 by firing squad.

The international outcry of protest came as a shock to the German authorities. From their point of view, Cavell had abused her position as head of a Red Cross hospital and had freely admitted committing a capital crime. The execution immediately became a major propaganda victory for the Allies, who treated her as a martyr. Her own view was that her action was not heroic but simply that of a nurse trying to do her duty. Such comments and her stoic resolve while in prison only added to her legend. According to some accounts, the flow of volunteers into the British army doubled for a period of two months after the announcement of her execution. The news of Cavell's execution had an immense impact in the United States as well, where editorialists and commentators held it up as proof of German barbarity. What the Germans defined as a crime, her admirers regarded as an extension of the feminine role of caregiver.

No doubt part of the intense international outcry derived from the contemporary view, widely held in English-speaking countries, of the values then associated with the role of women. As a single, religious, middle-aged woman nurse, Cavell represented many of the virtues ascribed in an idealistic fashion to women in the era. Her execution by the Germans indicated, in both a symbolic and very practical way, that the German command in Belgium did not regard such qualities as more significant than the violation of her status as a noncombatant.

Clemenceau, Georges (1841–1929) *French journalist, politician, prime minister*
Georges Clemenceau was a French journalist and statesman who served as premier of France from 1917 to 1920. Under his leadership, France emerged as one of the victorious Allies in World War I, and he led the French delegation to the peace negotiations that produced the Treaty of Versailles. During those negotiations, he argued strongly for a peace that would render Germany incapable of starting another war, a position that was largely successful over the more lenient and idealistic proposals of the American delegation.

Clemenceau was born in the Vendée region and was educated as a medical doctor. During the American Civil War he worked as a war correspondent for the *Paris Temps*. In 1869, he returned to France, practiced medicine briefly, and then entered politics. In 1871, he was elected mayor of the 18th arrondissement, the Montmartre district of Paris, and in 1876 he was elected to the Chamber of Deputies. There he emerged as a leader of the Radical Party and an outspoken opponent of the government. He stood for several radical positions including full separation of church and state and opposed the expansion of French colonies in Africa and Asia. Although he was defeated for reelection in 1893, he remained active in politics through journalism. In 1894, when Alfred Dreyfus was convicted of treason, Clemenceau became one of the leaders in the defense, helping to secure a pardon for Dreyfus in 1899. In 1902, Clemenceau was elected to the French Senate, and he served in the cabinet as minister of the interior. He served as prime minister from 1906 to 1909. In the Senate Clemenceau urged military preparedness and warned of the menace of German aggression both as a politician and as a journalist.

He continued his militant stance, and, in 1917, he was again selected as premier at the head of a coalition government. Known as the Tiger for his tenacity and toughness, he became immensely popular in France and among the other Allies for a period. In the position of premier he worked to raise French morale and cooperated with David Lloyd George to establish a unified military command. He made General Ferdinand Foch marshal of France and organized France on a wartime footing. He persisted in an uncompromising position in the peace negotiations after the war. During the Paris Peace Conference, an attempted assassin wounded Clemenceau, but he continued his duties, scoffing at the poor aim of the shooter. Oddly enough, he was defeated for election as the president of France in 1920 on the grounds that he had been too lenient toward Germany, and Alexander Millerand succeeded him. Clemenceau retired and wrote his memoirs and other works. His explanation of his actions during the war is found in his autobiography, *Grandeur and Misery of Victory,* published after his death.

Creel, George (1876–1953) *U.S. journalist, director of propaganda, politician*

George Creel served as Woodrow Wilson's director of propaganda, as head of the Committee of Public Information (CPI) during World War I. In this position, he demonstrated the powerful effect on public opinion of what a later generation would call a concerted multimedia campaign.

Creel was born in Kansas and worked as a newspaper reporter on the *Kansas City World.* By 1899, he had established his own newspaper, the *Kansas City Independent,* and began to receive recognition as a muckraking journalist. He supported Woodrow Wilson in the campaigns of 1912 and 1916, and, after the United States entered the war, Wilson selected Creel to head the CPI. Creel not only worked with newspapers to spread Wilson's positions, he also oversaw the creation of posters, music, motion pictures, paintings, cartoons, distribution networks for handbills and publications, and a network of public speakers. Perhaps the most famous poster that his committee supported was the Uncle Sam recruiting poster labeled "I WANT YOU" by James Montgomery Flagg, although many others became classics of poster art. The network of propaganda speakers included more than 75,000 "four minute men and women" who would give brief speeches in movie theaters and at other public locations, delivering hundreds of thousands of speeches in less than two years.

Creel's work was controversial, for several reasons. Republican opponents of Wilson felt it was inappropriate to use federal funds to so clearly support a political platform and set of policies. Indeed, Creel's mottoes "a war to end all wars" and "making the world safe for democracy" would come back to haunt Wilsonian Democrats in the period of disillusionment following the war.

Creel wrote a book justifying and explaining his activities in 1920, *How We Advertised America,* and wrote several other books over the next few years. In 1934, he ran for the Democratic nomination for the position of governor of California, but lost to the somewhat more radical Upton Sinclair.

Daniels, Josephus (1862–1948) *U.S. journalist, secretary of navy*

Josephus Daniels served as Woodrow Wilson's secretary of the navy from 1913 to 1921, overseeing the expansion of the navy in response to the war. Controversial for many of his positions and decisions, Daniels, like some others in Wilson's early cabinet, was a committed pacifist and reformer as well as an advocate of racial segregation. The appointment of a pacifist to head the Navy Department, struck preparedness advocates and big-navy proponents as ironic and wrong-headed.

Daniels was born in Washington, North Carolina, during the Civil War. His father died at the end of the war, and his mother, who eventually took a position as postmistress of the town of Wilson, North Carolina, supported him and his brothers. As a youth, Daniels took a job in a printing office, and then, with a brother, went into the newspaper business. By age 18, he was editor of a local newspaper and strongly voicing the views of the Democratic Party. His outspoken support for Grover Cleveland in 1882 cost his mother her political appointment.

Daniels entered the law school of the University of North Carolina in 1885 and was admitted to the bar but never practiced. He continued his career in journalism and was elected state printer in the period 1887–93 and briefly served during the Cleveland administration in a minor post in the U.S. Department of Interior. While in Washington at that position, he purchased the Raleigh *News and Observer,* which soon earned a national reputation for its Democratic Party positions, including antitrust campaigns, support for racial segregation, and opposition to the U.S. policy in the Philippines.

He threw his newspaper support to Wilson for the presidential nomination in 1912, and Wilson rewarded him, as he did some of his other major political supporters, with a cabinet appointment. As secretary of the navy, Daniels was criticized by naval officers and preparedness advocates for his reluctance to build up the navy, as well as for his policies of supporting government-owned factories, rather than the private sector, to produce munitions. His criticism of the steel companies that produced armor plate reflected his antitrust values. Despite his initial opposition to an armaments program, by 1915, he began to support expansion of the navy. However, the battleship program begun under his administration did not produce ships until after the war was over. Some new destroyers and other antisubmarine craft were helpful in providing aid to convoys of goods to Britain in 1917–18. Other policies that did not always sit well with sailors and officers included increasing the number of chaplains and prohibiting alcohol aboard ship. The latter provision particularly irked officers who had long been accustomed to the maritime traditions surrounding wine and liquor at sea. Franklin D. Roosevelt served under Daniels as assistant secretary of the navy.

After the war, Daniels returned to his newspaper business and published a biography of Wilson. In 1932, after vigorously supporting Franklin Roosevelt for President, Daniels was appointed U.S. ambassador to Mexico. He served in that post from 1933 to 1941. In addition to his *Life of Woodrow Wilson* and *The Wilson Era,* he published three autobiographical memoirs.

Debs, Eugene V. (1855–1926) *U.S. Socialist Party leader, candidate for U.S. presidency*

Eugene Debs was a leading member of the American Socialist Party, and campaigned vigorously against American participation in World War I. In June 1918, Debs was arrested for sedition because he gave a speech denouncing the draft and began his 10-year sentence in the Atlanta Penitentiary five months after the Armistice, in April 1919. President Harding pardoned him in 1921.

Debs was born in Terre Haute, Indiana, and dropped out of high school to work for the railroad. He joined the Brotherhood of Locomotive Firemen. He mixed labor union politics and local electoral politics, serving as city clerk in 1879 and as state legislative representative in 1884. During that time, he became editor of the Brotherhood's national journal and became national secretary-treasurer of the union in 1885. He became disappointed, however, both in electoral politics, with its round of compromises, and with trade-unionism, which he believed was a divisive program. In 1893, he founded the American Railway Union (ARU), an industrial rather than craft union that accepted as members anyone who worked for any American railroad in any capacity. After some initial successes that vastly increased the ARU's membership, the union called for a national strike in support of the Pullman workers in 1894. As a result, Debs was arrested for obstructing the mails and for contempt of court. On his release in 1895, he was hailed as a national hero and martyr to the cause of labor.

While in prison, Debs studied Marxist literature, and, with reservations, joined with others in forming the Socialist Party of the United States. He ran as candidate for president on the Socialist ticket in 1900, 1904, 1908, 1912, and 1920. He polled more than 900,000 votes in 1912. He sought to be arrested with his antiwar rhetoric, making the point that American Socialists, unlike their European comrades, chose loyalty to the class war over loyalty to the nation during the World War. Although he was in prison on the sedition charge in 1920, he campaigned for the presidency from his cell, again winning more than 900,000 votes. His supporters were proud to wear a button stating "Vote for Prisoner 9653."

President Warren Harding pardoned Debs on Christmas 1921. At age 66, his health impaired, Debs retired from active political life.

Denikin, Anton (1872–1947) *Russian anti-Bolshevik army officer*

Anton Denikin was a Russian army officer who rose through the ranks. He emerged as commander of the anti-Bolshevik forces in the south of Russia during the Russian Civil War in 1918. He was successful in leading the antirevolutionary forces for several months, coming within about 250 miles of capturing Moscow.

Denikin was born near Warsaw, in a part of Poland then controlled by Russia. He was born to a relatively poor family and attended military school. He served in the Russo-Japanese war in 1904–05 and had just been appointed to the rank of major general when the First World War started in August 1914. He served as deputy chief of staff to General Brusilov, and then worked with Brusilov in action with Romania, then Russia's ally. Following the February 1917 revolution, Denikin served as chief of staff to three commanders in chief of the army, M. V. Alexeev, Alexei Brusilov, and L. G. Kornilov. When Kornilov attempted a coup against the revolutionary government, Denikin served with him and then was imprisoned. In the October revolution, both Kornilov and Denikin escaped to join with Alexeev to help organize the so-called White Army that represented the anti-Bolshevik armed forces in the south.

Kornilov died in the spring of 1918, and Denikin then emerged as commander of the White Army in the south. He led the army in several actions in the Caucasus, and, by the end of 1918, he appeared to be on the road to success. In early 1919, Denikin led several attacks on the way toward Moscow but was defeated at Orel in October 1919. Part of the reason for his failure was his inability to secure the territories to his rear, due to his apparent support for landlords and other members of the upper classes. Lack of Allied support for the White Army, peasant uprisings, and desertions among his troops further weakened his cause. He was forced back to the Crimea by March 1920. He then resigned his post and was succeeded by General Pyotor Wrangel. Denikin then went into exile, first in France, and, in the last year of his life, in the United States. He published a memoir of his experiences, *History of the Civil Strife in Russia,* in five volumes, published over the years 1923–27.

Dzerzhinsky, Felix (1877–1926) *Polish founder of Soviet secret police*

Dzerzhinsky was appointed by V. I. Lenin in 1917 to head the Russian secret police, establishing the forerunner organization of the later KGB. In that position, Dzerzhinsky presided over the Red Terror that increased in intensity following an attempt on the life of Lenin.

Dzerzhinsky was born in what is now Belarus into a prosperous Polish land-owning family. He was arrested at age 20 for his political activity in helping to establish the Polish Social Democratic Party. After serving two years of his sentence in Siberia, he escaped but was arrested again in 1905 and was released in 1912. He was arrested again and sentenced to a nine-year term, but he was released during a political amnesty proclaimed by the Kerensky government in 1917. Later that year he was active in the October Revolution in Russia.

In December 1917, Lenin appointed Dzerzhinsky to establish the All-Russian Extraordinary Commission for Combating Counter-Revolution and Sabotage, abbreviated in Russian as *Cheka*. Although the state secret police would undergo many reorganizations and renamings in future years, dedicated agents, no matter what the agency was later called, were known as Chekists.

In September 1918, following an attempt on Lenin's life, Dzerzhinsky began a series of mass arrests. Later, when sailors aboard the battleship *Kronstadt* mutinied against the Bolshevik government in support of the Left Social Revolutionary Party, Dzerzhinsky directed the arrest and execution of many of the sailors. The political repression of the 1918–19 period in which opponents of the Bolsheviks on both the left and right were rounded up, tortured, and executed became known as the Red Terror. Many accounts of the period attribute the terror directly to Dzerzhinsky.

Dzerzhinsky was known for his dedicated support for the Bolshevik cause and for his ruthless approach to politics and administration. In 1919, he purged the Cheka itself by having many of its members executed. In 1922, he converted the Cheka into the State Political Administration (GPU), reorganized the next year as the Combined (or Unified) State Political Administration (OGPU), by which name the organization continued until 1934. Dzerzhinsky served on the Supreme Council of National Economy and was appointed by Stalin to a position on the central decision-making body of the Soviet state, the Politburo. Dzerzhinsky died of a heart attack in July 1926.

Goldman, Emma (1869–1940) *Lithuanian-born U.S. anarchist leader*

Emma Goldman was an anarchist and freethinker whose opposition to American participation in World War I and to the draft led to her arrest and imprisonment.

Emma Goldman was born in what is now Lithuania to Jewish parents and immigrated to the United States in 1885. She worked in a clothing factory in Rochester, New York, before moving to New York City. She was influenced by the writings of Johann Most and became an anarchist, working closely with her lover, Alexander Berkman. Berkman was later arrested for attempting the assassination of Henry Frick of the Carnegie Steel Corporation. During the 1890s, Goldman campaigned for women's suffrage and the publication of birth control information. In 1901, she was blamed for inspiring Leon Czolgosz, the assassin of U.S. president William McKinley, although by that time, she had moved away from advocacy of assassination in the direction of political education as the means to advance her ideas.

From 1906 to 1917, she published the anarchist magazine *Mother Earth*. After the United States entered the war, she spoke out against the draft. As a result, she was imprisoned for two years in the Missouri State Penitentiary. As a symbol of radicalism and feminist ideas, Goldman proved useful to the repressive administration of Attorney General A. Mitchell Palmer. She and Berkman were deported to Russia, along with more than 260 other foreign-born radicals in 1919. In the Soviet Union, she soon became disillusioned by the Bolshevik version of socialism, and she moved first to Berlin and then on to Britain. She married a British citizen and obtained a British visa. In the 1930s, she represented the Spanish anarchists in an office in London and toured, speaking on a variety of topics, including criticism of the Soviet Union.

With the defeat of the Spanish Loyalist government in 1939, she toured Canada, hoping to win aid for Spanish anarchist refugees. While in Toronto, she died of a stroke, but authorities granted permission for her body to be transported to the United States for burial near Chicago. Her published works include *Anarchism and Other Essays* (1911), *My Disillusionment in Russia* (1923), and *Living My Life* (1931).

Grey, Edward (1862–1933) *British statesman, foreign secretary*
Edward Grey served as British foreign secretary in the period 1905–16, and he is credited with establishing the Triple Alliance that linked Britain to France and Russia as allies in World War I. Grey attempted a mediated solution to the war crisis in July 1914, and when that failed, he convinced the Liberal government of Herbert Asquith to support the declaration of war against Germany.

Educated at Balliol College in Oxford, Grey was elected to Parliament as a Liberal in 1892 and served as foreign minister under Gladstone in 1892–95 and later under the administrations of Henry Campbell Bannerman and Herbert Asquith from 1905–16. He conducted much of his international diplomacy in secret, and the exact nature of the Triple Alliance established in 1907 was not publicly known. During the Balkan wars of 1912–13, Grey called a Great Power conference, which prevented those wars from exploding into a broader Great War. He attempted the same tactic in 1914, but events moved too rapidly in July 1914 to prevent the crisis initiated by the assassination from turning into full-scale war. It has been argued that if Grey had made it clear that Britain was prepared to come to the aid of France if France were attacked, then Germany might have put pressure on Austria-Hungary to find a compromise solution to the dispute with Serbia following the assassination of the archduke. When Germany declared war on France and invaded through Belgium, Grey convinced a reluctant Liberal cabinet to support going to war in defense of Belgium, on the grounds of an old European guarantee of Belgium's neutrality.

Unknown to the public and to Germany, French and British officers had met secretly under Grey's sponsorship to work out strategies in case a rapid infusion of British force should be needed to offset a German invasion. Later critics suggested that Grey's methods, which ignored the force of public opinion and the impact of open pledges, contributed directly to the disastrous engagement of all the major European powers in World War I. Grey's preference for secret treaties and behind-the-scenes agreements between the great powers led to his concluding the Treaty of London with Italy, which brought that nation into the war, as well as to supporting other efforts to win allies with territorial promises, including most notably Russia and Japan.

Grey's opponents blamed his policies for driving both Turkey and Bulgaria into the camp of the Central Powers. When Asquith established a War Cabinet in 1915, he excluded Grey from membership. In July 1916, Grey was ennobled, becoming Sir Edward Grey, First Viscount Grey of Fallodon. He later became leader of the House of Lords.

When David Lloyd George came to power as prime minister in December 1916, he dismissed Grey as foreign secretary and replaced him with Arthur Balfour.

Grey published his memoirs in 1925 as *Twenty-Five Years, 1892–1916*.

Haig, Douglas (1861–1928) *British army officer, commander of British Expeditionary Force*
General Douglas Haig was the leading British advocate of the military doctrine of attrition during World War I. In command of the First Army corps in the British Expeditionary Force (BEF) and later as commander in chief of the BEF, Haig was a firm proponent of the idea of massed attacks, apparently ignoring the combined impact of barbed wire, machine guns, and modern transport equipment in strengthening defense.

Haig was born in Edinburgh and studied at Oxford before attending the Royal Military Academy, Sandhurst. He served as a cavalry officer in India, fought with Kitchener in reconquering the Sudan in 1898, and served as chief of staff in the Boer War in 1899–1902 under John French. In 1909, Haig became chief of staff of the Indian army. At the outbreak of World War I, he was in charge of the British army training facility at Aldershot. Leading the First Army corps of the BEF during the first months of the war, his troops performed well in actions at Mons and Ypres. In December 1915, he was appointed commander in chief of the BEF. Haig's reputation for stubborn adherence to outmoded tactics derives mostly from his leadership during the Battle of the Somme in 1916 and from the attacks launched in 1917 known as "Third (Battle of) Ypres" or Passchendaele.

Called on to relieve the pressure of the Germans attacking at Verdun, Haig launched the Somme attack, utilizing the New Army of conscripts. On the first day of the battle, July 1, 1916, the British suffered about 20,000 dead and about 40,000 wounded, the greatest losses ever incurred in a single day to British troops. In the period July to November 1917, while the French held defensive positions and awaited the arrival of American troops, Haig planned a massive attack without corresponding French advances near Ypres at Passchendaele. The horrors of that campaign, in which thousands of troops from British Commonwealth countries perished by drowning in mud after being wounded, further damaged Haig's reputation. David Lloyd George opposed Haig's tactics but could not remove him because of the support Haig had from King George V.

In 1918, Haig supported the appointment of the French general, Ferdinand Foch, as supreme allied commander, or "generalissimo." Haig retained full control over the British forces and was in command of British forces in the final Allied assaults that began in August 1918. Contemporary and later criticisms of Haig have focused on his willingness to sacrifice great numbers of his own troops in battles of attrition that gained little territory or any strategic objective. Nevertheless, his leadership was credited with contributing to the final battles that convinced the German side to seek an armistice.

After the war, he worked to raise funds for veterans and instituted the British fund-raising tactic of Poppy Day.

Hall, William Reginald (Blinker Hall) (1870–1943) *British naval intelligence officer*

William R. Hall, known as "Blinker" because of a facial twitch, served as director of British naval intelligence during World War I. He was responsible for establishing the British "Room 40," which decrypted German naval messages, and, most famously, the Zimmermann note, which proved important in convincing the United States to enter the war on the side of the Allies.

Hall had joined the navy at age 14, reaching the rank of captain in 1905. He served as an inspector of mechanical training, and then, in the period 1911–13, he was assistant controller of the Royal Navy. At the outbreak of the war, he served as commander of the

battle cruiser *Queen Mary,* but by November 1914 he had to give up his command because of ill health.

He was immediately named director of naval intelligence, and it was in that post that he played a crucial role in Britain's war effort. He organized and consolidated the Royal Navy's cryptographic section and moved it into Room 40 of the old Admiralty Building in London. The office was known by the designation Room 40 for decades, even after it had moved several times.

Room 40 acquired captured naval codebooks and used them to crack the regular transmissions to and from the German ships. With this information, the exact location of many German ships and submarines, as well as their orders, could be tracked. Nevertheless, the information was not always put to good use. Several important decrypts of information regarding German moves during the May 1916 Battle of Jutland, for example, had little impact on British tactics. Hall established the practice of sharing information with other intelligence agencies, including MI-5 (domestic counterintelligence) and MI-6 (overseas intelligence), as well as with Scotland Yard's Special Branch.

Early in 1917, Hall's office obtained through intercepts the January 17 note from German foreign minister Arthur Zimmermann to the German ambassador to the United States, Count von Bernstorff, instructing Bernstorff to forward to the German minister in Mexico instructions to open negotiations with Mexico to join Germany in the event of war with the United States. In exchange for such a commitment, Germany would support Mexico for claims of territory in Texas, California, and the other states that occupied the lands lost by Mexico in its 1846 war with the United States. After verifying the contents of the message, Hall withheld it from use until the timing was right, and, when released on March 1, 1917, it had an electrifying effect upon the U.S. Congress and American public opinion. Hall was able to conceal the pathway by which the message had been intercepted, and Zimmermann himself admitted its authenticity.

Hall was knighted in recognition for his wartime service and was promoted to rear admiral. He retired from the Royal Navy in 1919 and entered Parliament as a member of the Conservative Party. In later years, Hall traveled to the United States where he gave lectures on intelligence issues. The achievements of Room 40 in monitoring the German navy's communications, in cracking the Zimmermann note, and in concealing the sources and methods of their work, set famous precedents for intelligence work in many nations throughout the rest of the 20th century.

Hemingway, Ernest (1899–1961) *U.S. ambulance driver, novelist*
Well known as an author of fiction in the 1930s and later, with several major novels to his credit, Ernest Hemingway's career was influenced by his short service as a volunteer ambulance driver in Italy during World War I.

Hemingway was born in Oak Park, Illinois, where he attended public schools. After graduation from high school, he worked briefly as a cub reporter for the *Kansas City Star.* At age 18 he sought to enlist in the U.S. Army but was rejected because of poor vision. He then signed up for the Red Cross ambulance service and was accepted in December 1917. He shipped to Europe in May 1918 and traveled to Milan, Italy, by way of Paris. In Milan he immediately assisted in removing casualties from a munitions plant explosion, then was assigned to the front at Schio, where he drove ambulances. On July 18, shortly after beginning his work, he was wounded at the Piave River front while distributing cigarettes and chocolate to troops in the trenches. He was knocked unconscious, while others nearby were wounded or killed. On the way back to an aid station with shrapnel in his legs, he was further wounded by machine-gun fire. The Italian government awarded him the Silver Medal for Valor, citing the fact that he had provided assistance to the other wounded before allowing himself to be carried out.

Some of the details of his experiences found their way into his novel *A Farewell to Arms,* published in 1929. An earlier novel, *The Sun Also Rises,* reflected the life of others of his generation, many of whom had died in the war. With that work, he was widely recognized as a literary spokesman for what Gertrude Stein called "the lost generation." Most of his novels reflect similar themes; in them, central male characters deal with pain and crises with tough, stoic courage, facing difficulties and getting through them, seemingly extrapolations of his own brief warfront experience. His direct and terse style, which many critics found repetitive and even monotonous, reflected his background in journalism and his effort to reduce complex emotional situations to their elements.

Hemingway went on to publish other celebrated works, including the novel *For Whom the Bell Tolls* (1940), based on the Spanish civil war of the late 1930s. Other works include the play *The Fifth Column,* the novel *To Have and to Have Not,* and the short novel *The Old Man and the Sea,* among others. After World War II, he lived in Cuba for a period and then relocated to Idaho. Troubled by poor health and depression, he committed suicide in 1961.

Hindenburg, Paul von (1847–1934) *German army officer, chief of staff*
Paul von Hindenburg was the general in charge of the German Eighth Army, and he was credited with the overwhelming victory over Russian forces at the Battle of Tannenberg in 1914. He was promoted to field marshal and succeeded General Erich von Falkenhayn in 1916 as chief of the German general staff, responsible for the direction of all German forces during the war. Hindenburg's success on the eastern front and as chief of staff was largely due to his own chief of staff and quartermaster-general, Erich von Ludendorff, who, most analysts agree, was the mastermind of German military organization.

Hindenburg was born in Posen and was educated at military cadet schools. He fought in the Franco-Prussian War and was promoted to the rank of general in 1903. He retired from the army in 1911, but, on the outbreak of World War I, he was recalled to service. Victories under his command at Tannenberg and Masurian Lakes in 1914 established his reputation. Under his nominal leadership, Erich von Ludendorff organized the military governance of Poland and the Baltic states and pushed the Russian army to the edge of defeat. From his appointment as army chief of staff in August 1916 until September 29, 1918, Hindenburg, Ludendorff, and other senior officers and industrialists virtually ruled Germany under the Third Supreme Command.

Hindenburg and Ludendorff established the defensive line on the western front known to the Allies as the Hindenburg line, which the Germans had designated the Siegfried line. With this fortified front holding back Allied advances, German forces were able to shift quickly to defeat Rumania when it entered the war on the Allied side. Hindenburg and Ludendorff planned and executed several major offensives in early 1918, but when U.S. troops began to arrive, and with vast quantities of French equipment and aggressive tactics on the Allied side, the Germans pulled back and sought an armistice.

Hindenburg retired from the army in June 1919, and he escaped indictment as a war criminal because of his immense popularity in Germany. He published his memoirs, *Out of My Life,* in 1920. Like Ludendorff, he blamed the defeat of Germany, not on the military, but on politicians and radicals on the home front. Hindenburg was chosen as president of the Weimar Republic in 1925, was reelected in 1932, and served until his death in 1934. As president, he appointed Adolf Hitler as chancellor in January 1933, who soon used the post to establish the Nazi dictatorship.

Hoover, Herbert (1874–1964) *U.S. mining engineer, relief administrator, president*

Herbert Hoover, who had already established a worldwide reputation as an engineer, served during World War I, first as director of Belgian relief and, after the United States entered the war, Food Administrator for War. Immediately after the war, he directed food relief to central and eastern Europe, including Russia.

Hoover was born in Iowa and was brought up by relatives in Oregon. He entered Stanford University in 1891, the year it opened, and worked his way through the institution by setting up small businesses. Graduating with a degree in mining engineering, his first jobs were as a mining laborer in Nevada. He was selected at a young age to assist in the management of mines in Australia, and then in China. He married a classmate from Stanford, and they were resident in China in 1900 when the Boxer Rebellion broke out, trapping many foreign nationals in Tientsin. He assisted in organizing the food supply for the isolated group and in constructing barricades from which a small detachment of legation troops was able to hold out until the arrival of a relief expedition.

Hoover and his wife, the former Lou Henry, moved to London, where he was offered a partnership in an international mining company at age 27. He soon established his own consulting engineering firm, reorganizing mining companies and reviving unproductive mines. His articles on mining were collected and published as *Principles of Mining,* which was widely used as a college text on the subject. His wife collaborated with him in the translation into English of a Latin text on mining, *De Re Metallica.*

In 1914, Hoover was resident in London, where many of his businesses were located. The U.S. ambassador asked Hoover to assist in arranging the transport of Americans back to the United States. Hoover resigned his executive positions and for the next five years worked as a volunteer without compensation. He chaired the Belgian Relief Commission, organizing food supplies to Belgium, constantly meeting with military and civil authorities not only in England and France but in Germany and in neutral countries as well.

After the U.S. entry into the war in April 1917, Woodrow Wilson asked Hoover to return to the United States and help organize U.S. food consumption. Hoover established and administered the U.S. Grain Corporation, the Food Purchase Board, and the Sugar Equalization Board. Immediately after the war, Hoover was appointed chairman of the American Relief Administration, which provided aid to Germany, Russia, and another 19 countries. He directed railways, controlled shipping, and organized the reopening of ports and canals that had been closed by the war. He also established the European Children's Fund.

In 1921, President Warren Harding appointed Hoover secretary of commerce, a post that he held until 1928. As secretary, he increased the importance of the department, bringing his abilities as an organizer to bear on the internal restructuring of boards and commissions and assisting industry in setting standards for products. His ability as a former businessman and engineer to work with growing technical issues, such as regulation of radio and air travel, further cemented his reputation. He received the Republican nomination for president and was elected president in 1928.

During his term of office, the stock market crash and the beginnings of the Great Depression presented challenges. Although some of the governmental responses that he initiated, such as the Reconstruction Finance Corporation and federal public works projects such as major water conservation dams, were continued during the New Deal, the public came to associate Hoover with the dire economic conditions, and he was defeated for reelection by Franklin Roosevelt in 1932. In later years, Hoover developed plans for reorganization of government agencies to avoid waste and duplication during the Truman and Eisenhower administrations.

Hoover's published works included *America's First Crusade* (1942), *The Problem of Lasting Peace* (1942), and his *Memoirs* (1951–52). His papers are collected and organized by the National Archives and Records Administration at the Hoover Presidential Library in West Branch, Iowa.

House, Edward M. (Colonel House) (1858–1938) *U.S. presidential adviser*

Edward House served as a close personal adviser to President Woodrow Wilson during World War I. Wilson sent House on several missions to Britain and Europe in hopes of securing a negotiated peace, and House served as a member of the delegation to negotiate the armistice. He was a member of the U.S. peace commission and a representative of the United States at the Versailles Conference, where he assisted in drafting the terms of the treaty and the Covenant of the League of Nations.

House was born in Texas to a wealthy ranching family, and after studies at Cornell University he returned to Texas in 1880 and entered politics. He was close adviser to three Texas governors during the period 1895–1907, and, by virtue of his staff appointment, earned the state title of Colonel, but he never served in a military position. He worked for Wilson in the nomination campaign of 1912. After Wilson took office, House worked with members of Congress and with Cabinet officers to implement Wilson's legislative program.

On the outbreak of war in Europe, Wilson sent House on several missions to Europe, where he visited foreign ministers and heads of state in hopes of getting the warring parties to state their war goals and to work toward a negotiated peace. After U.S. entry into the war, House served as a coordinator of supplies and manpower with the Allied powers. He worked with Wilson in drafting the Fourteen Points, and then served at the Paris Peace Conference. He was more willing to compromise than was Wilson and broke sharply with the president in 1919.

After the war House cooperated with historian Charles Seymour in publishing two works: *What Really Happened at Paris* (1921) and the two-volume *The Intimate Papers of Colonel House* (1926–28).

Joffre, Joseph (1852–1931) *French army officer*

Joseph Jacques Césaire Joffre was born in Rivesaltes in the eastern Pyrénées near the border with Spain and was educated at the École Polytechnique in Paris. He served as a junior officer during the Franco-Prussian War and later in French colonial possessions in Africa and Asia. He was appointed chief of staff of the French army in 1911 and was commander in chief when war was declared in 1914.

Joffre's first battle plan, known as Plan XVII, called for a direct attack by French forces through Alsace-Lorraine. This attack turned into a disaster due to strong German resistance and in light of the unexpected invasion by Germany through Luxembourg and Belgium that threatened to bring a strong German army toward Paris. With German troops advancing through the Marne River region to the outskirts of Paris, Joffre hastily organized a new French army, which together with the British army slowed the German advance. In the period September 6–9, 1914, Joffre planned and executed the First Battle of the Marne, which drove the Germans back to the Somme. Thereafter, the lines of battle in France settled into the form they held for the most part until late 1917.

On December 2, 1915, Joffre was named commander in chief of all the French armies. However, in 1916, Joffre's reputation suffered because of the German attack at Verdun and the failure of Anglo-French efforts on the Somme. He was held responsible for these failures, relieved from command on December 13, 1916, and replaced by General Robert Nivelle as French commander in chief. Joffre resigned his nominally advisory position on December 26, 1916. Despite the fact that the war proved his policies of offense were unsuited to the new conditions, he was still regarded as a great hero and the savior of Paris in 1914. So, to meliorate his removal from command, he was appointed marshal of France on the same day he resigned. He later traveled to the United States as head of the French mission to familiarize Americans with conditions of the war in early 1917 and was the nominal head of the Supreme Allied War Council in 1918.

He died in 1931, and his two-volume memoir was published in 1932.

Kerensky, Alexander Fyodorovich (Aleksandr Kerenski) (1881–1970) *Russian lawyer, provisional government prime minister*

Alexander Kerensky was a member of the Russian Social Revolutionary Party who served as head of the Russian Provisional Government from July to October 1917.

Kerensky was born in Simbirsk, Russia, into a middle-class family. His father was a teacher, and Kerensky attended St. Petersburg University, where he studied law and grew interested in political issues. He became a lawyer in 1904 and gained a reputation for the defense of individuals against political repression. In 1912, he was elected to the Fourth Duma, or national legislative body, as a member of a loosely organized pro-labor group. He continued his work as a defense lawyer and gained fame in a case in which he defended a Jewish man who faced a false charge of murder. He argued for the St. Petersburg bar to condemn the charges as a slanderous attack on the Jewish people and was imprisoned for criticizing the justice system. A forceful speaker, his fame grew as a spokesman of the left.

In February 1917, he advocated the abdication of the czar for failing to organize the military effort during the war. Following the February revolution in which the czar abdicated, the Petrograd Soviet elected Kerensky as one of two vice chairmen, and he also accepted a post as minister of justice in the Provisional Government formed by the Duma. He was the only individual to serve in both the Soviet and the Duma-selected government, and he was able to work as liaison between the two governing organizations. In May, Kerensky accepted the post of minister of war and of the navy and emerged as the key leader in the Provisional Government. He organized a major offensive against the Germans in June 1917, and, after its failure, he was selected as prime minister.

During his brief administration in 1917, he was responsible for the promulgation of protections of civil rights, freedom of speech, freedom of the press, and rights for women. At the same time, he continued to advocate a vigorous prosecution of the war, even in the face of mass desertions of troops. Attacked on both the political left and right, he strove to maintain power. He ordered the arrest of Lenin and Trotsky. Lenin fled to Finland, where he was able to maintain contact with the Bolshevik leaders in Petrograd. Kerensky appointed General Lavr Kornilov as supreme commander of the army and ordered troops to Moscow to help protect order in September. However, when he heard of Kornilov's plans to establish a military dictatorship, he dismissed the officer. The Bolsheviks temporarily rallied to support his regime, and they gained an increased following for their apparent service in preventing the counterrevolution. In September, Kerensky released radical leaders from prison and established a socialist government.

On October 24 (in the Old Style calendar, but November 6 in the New Style used in western Europe), the Bolsheviks led a coup against Kerensky's government after he had ordered the arrest of the Bolshevik revolutionary committee. Kerensky fled to the front in order to organize troops to oppose the Bolshevik takeover, but he could not gain a following

there. He went into hiding and then escaped from Russia in disguise on a French warship. He sought support from the British and French, but, instead, they sent aid to the White Army. Meanwhile, the Bolsheviks under Lenin's leadership began purging the Socialist Revolutionaries and Menshevik Social Democrats from the government in order to establish one-party rule.

Kerensky lived in exile in Paris until 1940, where he edited the émigré newspaper, *Dni*. In 1940, he moved to the United States, where he continued to write and lecture. After 1956, he was associated with the Hoover Institution on War, Revolution, and Peace at Stanford University in California. Among his published works were *Prelude to Bolshevism* (1919), *The Catastrophe* (1927), The *Crucifixion of Liberty* (1934), and his memoirs, *Russia and History's Turning Point* (1965).

King, William Mackenzie (Mackenzie King) (1874–1950) *Canadian politician, prime minister*

A Liberal Canadian political leader. Mackenzie King spent most of the World War I years studying labor relations in the United States with the Rockefeller Foundation. He had served in the Canadian House of Commons prior to the war and served as minister of labor under the Liberal government of Wilfrid Laurier. In 1917 King ran unsuccessfully for the House of Commons again. In 1919, he emerged as the leader of the Liberal party.

After graduating from the University of Toronto and pursuing graduate work at the University of Chicago and Harvard University, Mackenzie King started work as a journalist in 1897, with the *Toronto Mail and Empire,* writing about conditions in the garment industry. When he discovered that postmen's uniforms were made in sweatshops, he recommended to the postmaster general that a fair-wage clause be required in all contracts. After the postmaster took his advice, King, at age 25, was asked to serve as deputy minister of labor in Canada's first department of labor, thereby beginning his career as a civil servant and budding politician. Over the period 1900–08, he helped settle more than 40 labor disputes. He won national recognition for these efforts and for his election as a Liberal to the House of Commons in 1908, from a usually Conservative district in Ontario. He lost his seat in 1911, and he continued to work in the Liberal Party before accepting the Rockefeller Foundation post as director of industrial relations during World War I.

In that same period, Mackenzie King supported former prime minister Wilfrid Laurier in his opposition to conscription, although most English-speaking Liberals had supported it. This policy was popular in Quebec and, combined with his strong support for labor, helped establish King's position as a national leader. His unsuccessful bid for election in 1917 reflected his continuing loyalty to Laurier. In 1918, he published *Industry and Humanity,* which explained his positions on capitalism and labor, spelling out a position somewhat more socially liberal than that of the mainstream of his party. Following the war, his experience as a negotiator in labor disputes helped him in healing severe divisions within the Canadian Liberal Party. In 1921, he became prime minister of Canada. He served in that post through 1930, and again from 1935 through 1948.

During World War II, Mackenzie King led the Canadian government in cooperating closely with both Britain and the United States. He was on personal friendly terms with both Winston Churchill and Franklin Roosevelt. King, noted for his ability to reconcile and accommodate conflicting viewpoints, was an ideal leader to evoke a sentiment of national unity out of the politically and culturally diverse nation of Canada during both the Great Depression and the World War II years.

Kitchener, Horatio Herbert (Lord Kitchener)
(1850–1916) *British army officer, minister of war*
Horatio Kitchener was British minister of war from August 1914 until his death in June 1916. Widely revered by the British public for prior service in India, Egypt, and South Africa, Kitchener recognized that the war would demand vast numbers of troops and that it would be a long struggle. In these predictions he ran against conventional wisdom, but he turned out to be quite correct. His reputation was damaged, however, by his agreeing to the Gallipoli campaign and by dissatisfaction among other cabinet members who found him extremely difficult to work with.

Kitchener was born in County Kerry, in Ireland, of British parents and educated at the Royal Military Academy. He received a commission in the Royal Engineers at age 21 and spent the next several years in survey work in Cyprus, Turkey, and Palestine. In 1883 he was posted to Egypt to serve with the British cavalry there and won international recognition for his work in suppressing a rebellion by a religious leader, the Mahdi in Sudan. His unsuccessful attempt to rescue General Gordon from the siege at Khartoum made him a popular hero, a reputation further enhanced when he arranged a settlement with the French. In 1892, he was made commander in chief of the Egyptian army. In 1898, he led a force of some 28,500 troops against the Mahdist fortress at Omdurman, defeating an army estimated at twice that size. With this victory, he was made Lord Kitchener of Khartoum.

In 1899 he went to South Africa, first as chief of staff to General Frederick Roberts, and then in command of British forces there in the Boer War. His effective but ruthless tactics finally succeeded in suppressing the Boer uprising after the Boers resorted to guerrilla methods. He then participated in reorganizing the army in India, and, after a dispute with the viceroy, Lord Curzon, in which his own views prevailed, he was appointed to serve as the British ruler over Egypt and the Sudan. He helped organize the modernization of Egypt, with new roads and railroads, irrigation systems, and land reform.

At the outbreak of World War I, he was recalled from his field marshal post to serve as minister of war in the war cabinet under Herbert Asquith. Over the next two years, he organized the expansion of the British army from 20 divisions to 70 divisions, by calling for volunteers. Although he believed that a draft system would be needed, Asquith and others argued that it would not be publicly supported. Nevertheless, Kitchener's personal call for volunteers was quite successful. He endorsed the plans for the invasion of Gallipoli and reluctantly added more troops to that effort after the first landings on the beachheads did not result in success. Used to administration by command, he soon established a reputation for failing to delegate responsibility and for reluctance to work cooperatively with other members of the cabinet. When a shortage of artillery ammunition developed in Europe, Kitchener was blamed, and responsibility for supply was taken from him. Then, after the failure at Gallipoli, planning of strategy was removed from his control.

In June 1916, he left on a mission to Russia to attempt to encourage Russian forces. However, on June 16, his transport vessel, H.M.S. *Hampshire,* struck a mine off the Orkney Islands and Kitchener was drowned.

Lansing, Robert **(1864–1928)** *U.S. international lawyer, secretary of state*
Robert Lansing served as Woodrow Wilson's second secretary of state, taking office after William Jennings

Bryan resigned over sending a protest note to Germany regarding the sinking of the *Lusitania* in June 1915.

Born in Watertown, New York, Lansing earned a bachelor's degree at Amherst College, and then married into a prominent diplomatic family. His father-in-law was John W. Foster, who had served as secretary of state under President Benjamin Harrison and, incidentally, was the grandfather of the later secretary of state, John Foster Dulles. As head of the American delegation to an arbitration commission to settle a controversy over the Bering Sea in 1892–93, John Foster secured the appointment of Lansing as counsel for the delegation, getting the young lawyer launched on a career in the field of international law. With that start, Lansing served on several arbitration commissions, building a reputation in the field. His background made him a natural selection to serve as counselor to the State Department in April 1914. Wilson's first secretary of state, William Jennings Bryan, generally disdained the niceties of diplomatic and international legal precedent, so the position of counselor held by Lansing evolved into a quite responsible post similar to that of an under-secretary. Thus on Bryan's resignation, the appointment of Lansing to replace Bryan was a natural choice, despite the fact that he was not nationally prominent in a political sense.

Even though Lansing officially served as secretary of state from 1915 until 1920, during this period, Woodrow Wilson made all crucial foreign policy decisions, often not even consulting with Lansing. Lansing had to put his name to numerous international communications, but Wilson usually made the actual decisions, often with the advice of Colonel Edward House.

Although decisions regarding neutrality and war remained in Wilson's hands, Lansing received personal credit for a few diplomatic moves during his tenure of office. He arranged the sale of the Danish West Indies to the United States in 1916, and they became the U.S. Virgin Islands. Lansing was concerned that should Germany win the war, Denmark would fall under German dominance and the islands would represent a German outpost in the Western Hemisphere. Lansing also may be recognized for negotiating the Lansing-Ishii agreement in 1917, in which the United States accepted Japan's interests in China, with Japan agreeing that all nations would retain equal trading rights there. With these major exceptions, however, Lansing tended to be simply an administrator and nominal figurehead of the department.

In negotiating the U.S. entry into World War I, and then at the peace negotiations, Lansing in fact played quite a negligible role. Against Lansing's advice, Wilson attended the Paris negotiations and personally participated in the discussions about the disposition of territory and the covenant of the League of Nations. Frequently, Lansing was even excluded from such discussions and had to learn about them from other delegates. Critics have suggested that he should have resigned under these circumstances, but Lansing, apparently out of loyalty and concern that no action of his should disrupt the proceedings, went along with the subordination of his role. Privately, he disagreed with many of Wilson's policies and ideals, particularly the endorsement of the principle of ethnic self-determination, which he predicted would lead to numerous future conflicts. In effect, Wilson was his own secretary of state, a fact noted by contemporaries and historians alike.

Lansing advised Wilson not to link acceptance of the Versailles Peace Treaty with acceptance of the League of Nations in Senate ratification proceedings, but Wilson rejected the advice. Consequently, Lansing was put in the difficult position of arguing for both documents together before the Senate.

After Wilson fell ill in the summer of 1919, Lansing began to convene cabinet meetings. At one such early meeting, he raised the question of whether Wilson should be removed from office for disability, which would have transferred presidential authority to Vice President Thomas Marshall. When Wilson heard of these actions, he regarded them as presumptuous. Wilson asked for Lansing's resignation, and Lansing left office in February 1920. He wrote several works on international law and two memoirs of the peace settlements: *The Peace Negotiations* and *The Big Four and Others of the Peace Conference,* both of which were published in 1921. In these memoirs he made clear the way in which he had been shut out from the decision-making process at Paris, but did not suggest that he considered tendering his resignation under the circumstances.

Lawrence, T. E. (Thomas Edward Lawrence, Lawrence of Arabia) (1888–1935) *British army officer, adviser to Arabian leaders of revolt against Turks*

A British scholar-soldier, Thomas Edward Lawrence emerged during World War I as adviser and leader of the Arab Revolt against the Turks. His use of what is now called asymmetric guerrilla tactics and his methods of destroying rail communications held down thousands of Turkish troops in Saudi Arabia and Jordan. After receiving official approval from General Edmund Allenby, Lawrence assisted in leading an advance from Aqaba north through the Jordan valley to Damascus, on the right flank of Allenby's advance to Jerusalem. Although ambivalent about his own role in the victories over the Turks, he was widely hailed and became known as Lawrence of Arabia.

Lawrence had been born in Wales, the illegitimate son of Sir Thomas Chapman, an Anglo-Irish baronet. He was educated at Oxford and in 1910 joined an archaeological expedition in Turkey and traveled in the Sinai desert. He became fluent in local dialects of Arabic. Prior to the outbreak of World War I, he gathered military intelligence in the Ottoman Empire, and, when the war broke out, Lawrence entered the British army as a second lieutenant. With the rank of captain he served as an intelligence officer in Cairo. Growing restless in the staff position, he accepted an assignment to work with Arab forces under Prince Feisal al Husayn (Hussein) of Mecca. In November 1916, he was posted to serve Feisal in a staff advisory position. He also led raids of camel cavalry, gaining the respect of the desert warriors by sharing their diet, long periods without water, and their style of clothing. With a large camel corps, he assisted when the Arab forces took Aqaba in June 1917, and, in July, General Allenby, recently promoted to head the Allied effort in the Middle East, agreed to provide funds and arms assistance on a larger scale to the Arab revolt. Lawrence, working with these funds and personally leading a camel-mounted company-sized force of his own bodyguard (sometimes supported by aircraft and armored cars), then helped coordinate mobile raids from Allenby's right flank through the Jordan River valley and along the Dead Sea. During the raids, he was wounded several times, and at Deraa he was briefly captured, sexually assaulted and tortured, but succeeded in concealing his British identity from his Turkish captors before escaping back to his own lines.

He helped establish Feisal in control of Damascus, but the British had made the commitment under the Sykes-Picot Agreement that Syria was to fall within the French sphere of influence. Disillusioned at the various contradictory promises made by the British to different parties, including not only the French and Italians, but also the various Arab factions and the Zionist settlers, and exhausted by his own experiences, Lawrence resigned the service with the rank of lieutenant colonel.

Lawrence attended the Paris Peace Conference, where he argued for Arab independence. However, of the Arab territories he helped to liberate, only Saudi Arabia (much of which had been outside of Ottoman control before the war) became fully independent. Syria and Lebanon were made into French mandates, while Palestine, Trans-Jordan, and Mesopotamia (now Iraq) became British mandates. Feisal, deposed from rule in Syria by the French, was given the monarchy of Mesopotamia as a form of compensation. Lawrence criticized the British occupation of Mesopotamia as mismanaged and inappropriate.

While in Paris, Lawrence began to write an account of his wartime experiences, but the manuscript was either lost or stolen, and he had to write it all over again. At first, it was printed in a limited edition of less than 10 copies, and then, in 1927, a short version appeared under the title *Revolt in the Desert*. In the account, Lawrence revealed his own mixed feelings about the Arab revolt, his irreverent attitude toward those in the British military he found officious or small-minded, his admiration for Allenby, and his approach to guerrilla war. The full version of his memoirs was published commercially in 1935 under the title *Seven Pillars of Wisdom*. The longer version contained many more philosophical and political digressions, as well as much more detail regarding the specific events and military engagements. Both the short and the long books reflect a unique mix of romantic elitism, admiration for aspects of Arab culture, undertones of suppressed sexuality, contempt mixed with reluctant admiration for bureaucratic procedures, a pragmatic engineering and cartographic background, as well as other apparently contradictory values.

In his postwar years, Lawrence's career was even more enigmatic than his adventures during the war. He joined the newly formed British Royal Air Force as an enlisted man under the assumed name John Hume Ross. When he was found out, he resigned and entered the tank corps, again as an enlisted man, rejoining the RAF in 1925. In 1928, he legally changed his name to T. E. Shaw. He authored several other works, including an autobiographical account of his postwar military service. He was discharged from the RAF in 1935 and died in a motorcycle accident later that year. His accounts of the Arab revolt are among the most detailed and fascinating eyewitness accounts of the World War I period published in English.

Lenin, Vladimir Ilyich (Vladimir Ilyich Ulanov) (1870–1924) *Russian founder of Communist Party, head of Soviet state*

Lenin emerged as the leader of the Bolshevik branch of the Russian Social Democrats in the years before the Russian Revolution, and head of the Russian and the Soviet government from 1917 to 1924. A compelling speaker and forceful writer, he brought his powers of logic and legal training to bear on organizing an elite core of radicals to lead a successful Russian revolutionary movement. After seizing power in 1917, he headed the government that signed the peace treaty with the German government, known as the Treaty of Brest Litovsk. Lenin was head of the Soviet state until his death in 1924.

Named Vladimir Ilyich Ulanov, Lenin was born into a prosperous family in Simbirsk, in central Russia, where his father held a supervisory post in the provincial educational department. After being expelled from law school for participating in a student demonstration, Lenin returned home to continue his studies, reading radical works and at the same time completing his law degree as an external student at St. Petersburg University. He earned the degree in 1892. After briefly working in a law firm, Lenin resigned and moved to St. Petersburg, where he joined a group of young radicals who were interested in Marxist thought.

The St. Petersburg radicals distributed literature among factory workers. Labor unions had been outlawed, and Lenin was arrested for attempting to organize one. He was sentenced to three years' exile in Siberia. In 1900, he moved first to Switzerland and then to Munich, Germany, where he became one of the editors of the revolutionary newspaper, *Iskra* (The Spark). In 1901, he adopted the revolutionary name Lenin, which he chose based on the name of a peaceful Siberian river, the Lena.

Through his pamphlets and books, Lenin became a leader of the Russian Social Democrat Labor Party. At a 1903 party meeting, he emerged as the head of a group arguing that the party should act as an exclusive vanguard of the revolution, rather than as wide open to all members who wanted to join. A bare majority supported his elitist leadership argument, and his wing became known as the Bolsheviks, Russian for *majority*. Oddly enough, however, the Bolshevik wing stood for a very limited, rather than widespread, party membership.

In exile in Switzerland in 1912, Lenin worked with the Bolsheviks to organize a separate party conference, held in Prague. After that meeting the Bolshevik Party was independent of the other Russian Social Democrat Labor groups. Remaining in Switzerland during the World War, Lenin continued to write and published *Imperialism, The Highest Stage of Capitalism*. In that book, he argued that the war was an inevitable consequence of capitalism and its tendency to imperial expansion. He called himself a defeatist, arguing openly for the defeat of Russia in the war, as a prelude to revolution. His position horrified other Russian radicals who saw it as unpatriotic, but when the defeat came and revolutionary uprisings and mutinies spread among the troops and sailors, his position seemed at least partially vindicated.

In March 1917 the czar abdicated and yielded power to a provisional government. The next month, Lenin traveled by sealed train, as had been arranged by the German government, to St. Petersburg (by that time renamed Petrograd). In October, after an abortive try by Lenin in July at seizing power, armed workers, soldiers, and sailors took over government buildings in Petrograd and arrested members of the Provisional Government. Working with another party, the Left Socialist Revolutionaries, the Bolsheviks formed a government, with Lenin as chairman. A planned constitutional convention to be held early in 1918 would have been dominated by Left Socialist Revolutionaries had it been able to proceed, but Bolshevik guards disbanded the meeting before that threat to power materialized. It was the Soviet government that worked out the peace treaty with Germany in March 1918, yielding a huge swath of territory to the enemy. Faced with desertion of the troops and their headlong flight from the front, the government had little choice.

The Bolsheviks dismissed their former allies, the Left Socialist Revolutionaries, from the government early in 1918 and renamed themselves the Russian Communist Party (Bolshevik). In August 1918, Lenin was wounded in an assassination attempt, which left him weakened. During the civil war in Russia, which lasted from 1918 to 1921, Lenin adopted more and more ruthless means to squash the forces opposed to the revolution.

Lenin suffered several strokes and died in 1924. His legacy consisted not only of the Soviet state and the international communist movement, but also a body of ideas known as Marxism-Leninism, which dominated leftist thinking and communist activities for decades afterward.

Lloyd George, David (1863–1945) *British lawyer, politician, prime minister*
David Lloyd George became prime minister of Great Britain in 1916 in a coalition, or national unity, government formed after the resignation of the Liberal prime minister Herbert Asquith. Lloyd George, who had already established a reputation as a reformer, powerful orator, and good organizer, reduced the size of the policy-making cabinet from 20 members to five and also worked for a unified command of the Allied forces in Europe. His government represented a new approach to the war that, for some, served to lift British morale. After the war he participated in the peace conference and in framing the Treaty of Versailles.

Lloyd George was born in Manchester, England, of Welsh parents and moved to Wales as a child. He excelled in school and trained in law. Very early in his legal career, he entered local politics and soon earned repute for crusading for the poor. His fiery orations tended to attract popular support but sometimes offended other leaders of the Liberal Party. As a member of Parliament, he opposed the Boer War. In 1906, with the election of a Liberal government in Britain, Lloyd George was selected president of the Board of Trade, and, in 1908, Asquith appointed him chancellor of the exchequer. In that post he introduced legislation that established a graduated income tax for the first time in Britain, as well as other taxes that fell more heavily on the rich, such as inheritance taxes and capital gains taxes. He also instituted a system of tax deductions for dependents. In order to enact these liberal reforms, Lloyd George toured the country giving speeches and attacking those in the House of Lords who used their position to protect their own wealth and stop aid for the poor. Partly as a consequence of his campaign, in 1911, the system was reformed to reduce the power of the House of Lords to affect tax policy.

British Fabian socialists such as George Bernard Shaw had influenced Lloyd George, and his reforms won support from leaders of the Labour Party as well as Liberals. Along with other Liberals, Lloyd George opposed the entry of Britain into World War I, but when several other members of the government resigned on the declaration of war, Lloyd George did

not resign. He soon emerged as a voice for an even more forceful prosecution of the war. In 1915, he was selected minister of munitions, and he attracted the attention of Conservatives who agreed that the war should be fought more vigorously. In December 1916, he sided with Conservatives and forced the resignation of Asquith. Lloyd George was selected by the coalition of disaffected Liberals and Conservatives to head the unity or coalition government.

As prime minister, Lloyd George was instrumental in convincing the Royal Navy to support the concept of convoys to protect shipping against submarine attacks. Although Liberals and former Labour supporters opposed Lloyd George, he won wide support for his vigorous leadership of the war effort. He supported the unification of Allied armies on the western front under General Foch.

At the Versailles Conference, Lloyd George argued for a more moderate and less vengeful treaty than that supported by the French prime minister, Georges Clemenceau.

After the war, he fell out with Conservatives over social policy, and, in 1920, he introduced a bill for Home Rule in Ireland. The Irish Free State was established under his leadership, but, in 1922, Conservatives withdrew their support from his government. Although no longer prime minister, he continued to serve as a member of Parliament and was leader of the opposition until 1931.

He authored a number of books, including *The Truth about the Peace Treaty,* published in 1938.

Lodge, Henry Cabot (1850–1924) *U.S. senator from Massachusetts, opponent of League of Nations*
Henry Cabot Lodge was a conservative Republican senator from Massachusetts and a prominent leader of his party while Woodrow Wilson was president. Although Lodge supported U.S. entry into World War I, he was highly critical of Wilson's methods, ideas, and personality. Most notably, Lodge led the Senate opposition to the ratification of the peace treaty and the Covenant of the League of Nations, helping to prevent their acceptance. Partly as a consequence of his leadership, the United States never joined the League of Nations.

Lodge was born to a wealthy Boston family and was educated at Harvard. He earned a Ph.D. in political science in 1876 and was admitted to the bar in the same year. Lodge served as an editor on the *North American*

Review and briefly served as a lecturer in U.S. history at Harvard. In 1880, he was elected to the Massachusetts state legislature, and, in 1887, he was elected as a member of the U.S. House of Representatives. In 1893, he was selected by the Massachusetts legislature as U.S. senator from Massachusetts, and he was reelected in later years, serving until his death in 1924.

As one of the leading intellectuals in the Senate, Lodge may have personally disliked the idea of a fellow former academic and Ph.D., in the person of Woodrow Wilson, leading the other party and securing the White House. In any case, Lodge's politics were quite the opposite of Wilson's on many counts, and Lodge and Wilson became clear political and personal opponents in Wilson's first term.

In 1918, Republicans gained control of the U.S. Senate, and Lodge was selected Senate majority leader, as well as serving as chair of the powerful Foreign Relations Committee. In that position, he led the opposition to the League of Nations and the peace treaty, arguing that the two should be voted on separately, rather than in a single package. Despite the fact that many of Wilson's supporters, including Colonel Edward House and Robert Lansing, both thought that tactic might be more successful, Wilson continued to insist that the two be ratified jointly. Lodge was able to bring about defeat of the ratification by proposing amendments to the covenant that imposed reservations on the U.S. acceptance of the league. Under the reservation amendments, the U.S. Congress would in some circumstances independently decide whether a decision of the league was binding on the United States. Although some Democratic senators were willing to accept the league with these reservations, Wilson insisted that Democrats loyal to him should reject such terms as insulting; Wilson believed that the Lodge amendments represented an attack on his own ability to protect American interests in the drafting of the covenant language. Thus the ratification, which required a two-thirds majority, never received sufficient votes, either with or without the reservations. Wilson bitterly attacked Lodge and his small group of colleagues who, he believed, intentionally manipulated the reservation issue to block the league and the Versailles Treaty. In 1921, Lodge served as one of the American representatives at the Washington conference on the limitation of naval armaments. Lodge published numerous works during his life, including a defense of his position: *The Senate and the League of Nations* (1925).

Ludendorff, Erich (1865–1937) *German army officer; chief architect of German war economy*

A German general staff officer, Erich Ludendorff emerged as the leading military strategist in Germany during World War I. He supported those naval officers who advocated the use of unrestricted submarine warfare against the British, the policy that eventually brought the United States into the war in 1917. By early 1918, he was in charge of strategy on the western front and organized the last great offensives by which Germany came close to defeating the Allies. In 1918, when the United States demanded unconditional surrender from Germany, Ludendorff opposed accepting those terms, and, as a result, he was dismissed from the army. In the postwar years he continued to argue that Germany had been betrayed by those who accepted surrender and by the Allies, who had used the armistice to impose a vengeful peace. In the postwar period, he at first worked with the Nazi Party and was elected to the Reichstag as a member of that party in the years 1924–28.

Ludendorff was born near Posen, Prussia (now Poznan in Poland), and joined the army at age 18. He won distinction in the first days of World War I, when he took command of an army infantry brigade after the death of its general and successfully led the defeat of the fortified city of Liège in Belgium. Paul von Hindenburg, who commanded German forces on the eastern front, appointed Ludendorff as his quartermaster general. Ludendorff served well in that position and provided crucial advice to Hindenburg in the Battles of Tannenberg and Masurian Lakes. When Hindenburg was promoted to chief of staff of the German army in August 1916, he brought Ludendorff along as quartermaster general. Ludendorff worked with industrial leaders in establishing and engineering the whole German war effort. He pressured the kaiser and others who were reluctant to adopt unrestricted submarine warfare, and he also played an important role in the Treaty of Brest Litovsk, which ended the war with Russia. In the spring of 1918, he organized the last great offensive on the Marne, which almost succeeded in reaching Paris.

Ludendorff resigned on October 26, 1918, when faced with the imminent armistice. He fled to Sweden and began to write articles and books arguing that Germany had been stabbed in the back by its own domestic left-wing politicians. He returned to Germany in 1920 and entered politics. Although he worked with Hitler and served in the Reichstag as a member of the

Nazi Party from 1924 to 1928, he had a falling out with Hitler. Even so, Hitler attended his funeral in 1937.

Mata Hari (Margaretha Geertruida Zelle)
(1876–1917)   *Dutch-born exotic dancer, spy for Germany*
Mata Hari was the stage name of a Dutch woman, Margaretha Geertruida, who was tried, convicted, and shot for espionage by the French in 1917. Her name became almost a synonym for the legend of the alluring and exotic female spy. Her life, although shrouded in mystery, did not quite match the myth.

Margaretha Zelle was born in Holland to a well-off hat dealer and had attended teachers' college before marrying a Scotsman by the name of Campbell Macleod. Macleod served in the Dutch army and his wife accompanied him to the Dutch East Indies. They lived there during the period 1897 to 1902. Apparently the marriage was troubled, for when Margaretha returned to Holland she divorced Macleod. In 1905, she moved to Paris and adopted her stage name, Mata Hari (said to be a Malay term for *Eye of Dawn*). She performed exotic dances in skimpy costumes and was regarded at the time as extremely seductive and sensual. It was doubtful if the dances had any basis in the culture of Java or Sumatra where she had lived, but her combination of beauty, exotic costume and music, and her good looks seemed to work magic on her male audiences.

She established a reputation for having numerous lovers, and, by some accounts, her affairs verged on prostitution, as she soon established a small fortune. As a citizen of Holland, a neutral country, she was free to travel during World War I between the belligerent countries. According to her own account, she was living in The Hague in 1916 when a German official offered to pay her for information she might be able to gather on her next visit to France. She admitted that she later gave him some outdated information. Perhaps to test her reliability or to entrap her, the French recruited her to gather information or to act in their interests in German-occupied Belgium. She said that one of her missions was to attempt to recruit the allegiance of Ernest Augustus, a German duke, to the Allied cause.

Perhaps because British intelligence learned of her prior contacts with German agents, the French moved against her. She was arrested in Paris on February 13, 1917, tried before a military court July 24–25, 1917, and executed on October 15, 1917, by a firing squad. According to some interpretations, she had become a scapegoat for the French obsession with spies and disloyalty during the war. Coupled with anxiety over the changing status of women brought on by the war, those sentiments may have contributed to the decision to arrest her and charge her with espionage.

Maugham, Somerset (William Somerset Maugham)   (1874–1965)   *British author, espionage agent*
William Somerset Maugham became renowned as a prolific and popular British author from the 1900s through the 1940s. Maugham served briefly as a British espionage agent during World War I.

Born in Paris as the youngest son of the attorney for the British embassy, Maugham learned French before he learned English. Educated in Britain, he studied in Heidelberg and then at medical school in London, qualifying as a doctor in 1897. After writing several successful plays produced in London, he joined a Red Cross ambulance unit at age 40 at the outbreak of the war. While serving in France, he met a young American, Gerald Haxton, and they reputedly became lovers, living together for the next 30 years. Such a relationship in that era would usually remain covert, and Haxton had the open role of personal secretary to Maugham. In another relationship, Maugham fathered a child by Mrs. Syrie Wellcome, then married her after her divorce, but continued to live with Haxton. One of Syrie's friends was the mistress of a British intelligence officer, Captain John Wallinger.

Wallinger, the director of British MI-6 efforts in France, after meeting Maugham socially, asked him to serve as an agent. Maugham worked in Switzerland, where his fame as a popular author served as an excellent cover, and his fluency in several languages assisted in his work. He acted as a contact or courier between the Special Intelligence Service headquarters and agents in Europe, and he was instrumental in exposing several double agents who pretended to serve Britain while actually working for the Central Powers. Maugham's own espionage work during the war yielded the inspiration for episodes in the collection of short stories, *Ashenden, or The British Agent* (1928). Details of transmittal of messages, working with intermediaries, safe houses, demands for pay from fraudulent agents, and other authentic elements from his own experiences have been identified in the *Ashenden* stories. Alfred Hitchcock used elements of the work in the film *Secret Agent*. Some commentators regard *Ashenden* as the first in the genre of the modern spy story, setting precedents with its cynical distance from issues of idealistic politics and its close descriptions of exotic locales, ideas, and themes followed by Eric Ambler, John LeCarre, and others.

Maugham was the author of numerous novels, short stories, and plays, among the most famous of which were *Of Human Bondage* (1915), *The Moon and Sixpence* (1919), and *The Razor's Edge* (1944). The short story "Rain," set in the South Pacific, was made into a play and several movies. Maugham lived many years in the south of France and continued his prolific writing career during and after World War II.

Nicholas II (1868–1918) *Russian czar*

Nicholas II was the last emperor of Russia, reigning from 1894 to 1917. He abdicated his position during the March 1917 revolution and was later murdered with his wife and children by Bolshevik soldiers when in captivity. His regime saw social turmoil, nominal adoption of constitutional government, incompetent administration, and two disastrous wars, first against Japan in 1904–05 and then against the Central Powers in World War I.

Nicholas lived in the shadow of his powerful and autocratic father, Czar Alexander III, who reigned from 1881 to 1894. Perhaps because his mother was possessive and protective, Nicholas matured late. Educated by tutors and fascinated by courses in military science, Nicholas followed his education with travels in the middle and far east. At the age of 26, and well aware of his own inexperience and lack of qualifications, he succeeded as czar on the death of his father. Shortly thereafter he married a minor German princess, a granddaughter of Queen Victoria, who took the Russian name Alexandra.

Alexandra eventually bore five children, four girls and a boy. The boy Alexis, heir to the throne, suffered from hemophilia. Alexandra turned to Grigori Rasputin, a mystic healer, in hopes that he could cure Alexis, and increasingly came under his influence. Meanwhile, Nicholas faced severe problems of governance, including widespread strikes and uprisings after the disastrous defeat of Russia in the Russo-Japanese War in 1905. Nicholas reluctantly accepted a plan to establish parliamentary government with an elected Duma but insisted on regarding himself as the autocrat. After dismissing competent reformers and closing the Duma, in effect he instituted a coup d'état from above by introducing a new electoral law. With a new and more

subservient Duma in place after 1907, Nicholas tended to withdraw from direct administration.

After the assassination of Archduke Franz Ferdinand in Sarajevo, Nicholas mobilized the Russian army, and Germany declared war. At first, Nicholas was immensely popular as a wave of patriotism swept the country, but with military defeats, food shortages, and labor unrest, he soon lost support. In 1915, Nicholas dismissed his uncle, Nikolai, as commander in chief of the army, and Nicholas personally assumed command. Although he made few military decisions, he moved from the capital at Petrograd (St. Petersburg) to the military general headquarters at Mogilev, while Alexandra remained at the capital. Through 1915 and 1916, the government fell into disarray, as Alexandra, on Rasputin's advice, ordered the dismissal of competent ministers. Nicholas was informed of the collapse of government morale but refused to override his wife's decisions.

In December 1916, a group of conservative leaders, including a nephew of Nicholas, murdered Rasputin. Although the Duma expected an improvement in conditions, two months later in February 1917 minor strikes and disturbances in Petrograd resulted in an uprising against authority. The ministers fled the government, and a provisional authority, representing both the Duma and the local Soviet, insisted upon the abdication of Nicholas. After wavering, he signed the abdication on March 15 (March 3 under the older Russian calendar then in force) in favor of his younger brother, who refused the position.

The Provisional Government imprisoned the czar and his family and eventually transferred them to western Siberia. Later, Soviet authorities moved the family to Yekaterinburg (Sverdlovsk). There, on the night of July 16–17, 1918, local Bolshevik troops murdered Nicholas, his wife, and their five children to prevent their rescue.

Forces far beyond the power of any czar to resist had confronted Nicholas. Nevertheless, his personal failure to recognize the need for change and his capitulation to the domination of his wife by Rasputin contributed to the downfall of his regime and the chaos that produced the Bolshevik takeover of the Russian Empire.

Orlando, Vittorio Emanuele (1860–1952) *Italian law professor, prime minister*

Vittorio Orlando was premier of Italy from October 1917 to June 1919 and was the head of the Italian delegation to the Paris Peace Conference in early 1919.

Orlando was born in Palermo in Sicily, graduated from the University of Palermo in the field of constitutional law in 1883, and later taught at the university level in Rome and Modena. He was elected to the Chamber of Deputies in 1897 and held several cabinet posts as a member of the Liberal Party, serving as minister of education (1903–05) and minister of justice (1907–09 and 1914–17). He was a strong advocate of Italy's entry into the war. In October 1917, after the defeat of Italian forces at the Battle of Caporetto, he became prime minister and worked to rally the country's morale.

At the Paris Peace Conference, Orlando emerged as one of the so-called Big Four, along with Georges Clemenceau, Woodrow Wilson, and David Lloyd George. Orlando soon had a falling out with Wilson, as Orlando argued for the inclusion of Fiume (Rijecka) in the territories transferred to Italian jurisdiction from the defeated Austro-Hungarian Empire. Wilson, who had accepted Italian claims to the Tyrol region up to the Brenner Pass, argued against the transfer of Fiume on the grounds that there was no treaty obligation or any justification on the grounds of self-determination. Orlando, on the other side, argued that Italy needed control over Fiume for security reasons and that the majority of the population of the city was Italian in ethnicity and loyalty. Closer examination of the issue by outside experts confirmed that the largest ethnic group in Fiume was indeed Italian, but that they were a minority in the surrounding suburbs and region. When Wilson appealed to the Italian people over the head of Orlando to reject the claim to Fiume, Orlando walked out of the conference on April 23, 1919. After receiving a vote of confidence from the Italian parliament, Orlando returned to sign the Versailles Treaty the next month.

However, he was disappointed at his failure to obtain more favorable terms at the conference and resigned as prime minister on June 19, 1919. His successor was Francesco Nitti, who sought to assure Italian acceptance of the Versailles terms.

In the early 1920s, Orlando supported Benito Mussolini and his coalition government. In 1924, however, after Fascists murdered the Socialist leader, Giacomo Matteotti, Orlando withdrew his support from the regime. He resigned from the Chamber of Deputies in 1927.

After the death of Mussolini in 1944, Orlando emerged as the leader of the Conservative Democratic Union and was elected president of the Constituent Assembly in 1946. In 1948 he was elected to the Italian senate where he held office until 1952, the year of his death.

Pankhurst, Emmeline (Emmeline Goulden) (1858–1928) *British suffragist*

Emmeline Pankhurst was a leader of the British movement for woman suffrage before and after World War I. Under her leadership, the movement suspended its program of civil disobedience and agitation for women's rights during the war years and converted the organization into an enthusiastic and patriotic agency in support of the British effort in the war.

Emmeline Pankhurst was born in Manchester, England, the daughter of a successful businessman, Robert Goulden, who was a campaigner for several radical and liberal causes in the mid-19th century. Sophia Goulden, Emmeline's mother, took her to women's suffrage meetings as a child. After being educated in France, Emmeline Goulden returned to Manchester where she met Richard Pankhurst, who was a dedicated socialist and advocate of women's rights. He drafted an amendment to the British voting law that extended the local franchise to unmarried women who were property holders, passed into law in 1870. Emmeline married Richard Pankhurst in 1878, and she then had four children, including Christabel Pankhurst (born in 1880) and Sylvia (born in 1882) who also became advocates for women's suffrage. Emmeline and Richard Pankhurst were both active in the Independent Labour Party, but, despite several attempts, Richard was never elected to the House of Commons.

After the death of her husband in 1898, Emmeline Pankhurst continued to advocate the extension of women's suffrage to all women. In 1903, she founded the Women's Social and Political Union (WPSU), dedicated both to suffrage issues and to questions of social justice. In 1905, Christabel Pankhurst and a colleague created a disturbance at a public meeting being addressed by Sir Edward Grey, a leader of the Liberal Party then serving as foreign secretary. When asked to leave the meeting, the two women refused. Their arrest catapulted the issue of women's rights into the news, and the organization decided that the only way to maintain public interest and concern was to create similar minor acts of civil disobedience that would lead to arrest. In 1907, Emmeline Pankhurst moved into London and began a campaign that led to her imprisonment at least a dozen times.

She and her fellow protesters developed the use of the hunger strike in prison. When force-feeding of the prisoners by restraining them and forcing soup through their clenched teeth further shocked the public, the government enacted a special provision that allowed prisoners to be temporarily released for their own health. After giving up the hunger strike and being restored to health, the protester would be rearrested to serve out the sentence. This so-called cat-and-mouse procedure backfired on the government, for it only succeeded in keeping many of the suffrage advocates in the news.

For a period, the WPSU called its publication *The Suffragette,* a term which was later applied, often derogatorily, to all women advocates of the right to vote. After the outbreak of war, the WPSU negotiated a settlement with the government. In exchange for the release from prison of all women's suffrage protesters, the organization agreed to suspend civil disobedience for the duration of the war and to support the war effort. The name of the organization's paper was changed to *Britannia,* and its editorials took on a militantly patriotic tone. In the publication, Liberal or Labour critics of the war were criticized as disloyal or pro-German, and women were encouraged to support the war in numerous ways.

Emmeline Pankhurst and her daughter Christabel formed the Women's Party in 1917, with a program of more vigorous war measures, the purging of disloyal individuals and those with alien ancestry from government, and the abolition of trade unions (many of which had resisted women working in occupations traditionally reserved for men). At the same time the party stood for a program of equal rights and maternity benefits.

Meanwhile, Sylvia Pankhurst remained dedicated to more radical Socialist principles, including the rejection of marriage as an institution. Sylvia had established a working-class women's organization, the East London Federation of Suffragettes, which had its own publication, *The Women's Dreadnaught,* later called *The Worker's Dreadnaught.* In this periodical and in her own speeches and organizational efforts, Sylvia Pankhurst continued to link women's causes to her view of the class struggle. The WPSU expelled Sylvia from membership in 1914, and, unlike her mother and older sister, she continued the strongly feminist campaign for the right to vote during the war. In 1917, she visited Russia and met with Lenin. In Britain, she spoke in favor of the Bolshevik revolution and was imprisoned for several months on

sedition charges. Meanwhile, Emmeline and Christabel continued their stridently patriotic and prowar position in their publications. The split between Emmeline and her younger daughter became even more pronounced after the war.

After living in Canada and the United States for a few years, Emmeline returned to Britain in 1925 and accepted the nomination of the Conservative Party as a candidate for Parliament in East London. In 1927 Sylvia bore an illegitimate son, whom Emmeline refused to recognize or visit. She died in 1928 without reconciling her differences with her daughter.

Emmeline wrote *My Own Story* (1914), and, in later years, Sylvia published a biography of her mother. Sylvia lived on to campaign for women's rights, for support for Ethiopia against its invasion by Fascist Italy, and in favor of the Loyalist regime in Spain during the Spanish civil war. Sylvia Pankhurst moved to Ethiopia and died there in 1960.

Pašić, Nikola (Nicola Pasik, Nicola Pasitch) (1845–1926) *Serbian leader of Radical Party, prime minister of Serbia and Yugoslavia*

Nikola Pašić was prime minister of Serbia during World War I, and, after the war, served as prime minister of the Kingdom of the Serbs, Croats, and Slovenes, the country that would later be called Yugoslavia. Before the war, he was internationally known as the leader of the pan–South Slav movement and he served several times as prime minister of Serbia between 1891 and 1914. His terms of office as prime minister of Serbia were 1891–92, 1904–05, 1906–08, 1909–11, and 1912–18.

Pašić was born into a middle-class family and studied engineering, graduating from a polytechnic institute in Zurich, Switzerland, where he became interested in anarchism and socialism. He returned to Serbia in 1873, where he edited a Socialist newspaper and became a leader of the opposition to the authoritarian monarchy of King Milan Obrenović. He was elected to the Serbian parliament, and, in 1881, he was a cofounder of the Radical Party, devoted to Serbian nationalism, the pan–South Slav movement, and parliamentary government. After a brief period of exile for his political views, Pašić returned to Serbia, where he served in several positions, including president of the parliament (Skupština), mayor of Belgrade, premier, and foreign minister. In the last position, he established personal contacts as well as diplomatic ties with czarist Russia.

After the coup and assassination of King Alexander (son of Milan) in 1903, Pašić became the leading political figure in Serbian politics. He was the head of the Radical Party and continued to serve terms through the first years of the 20th century as prime minister and sometimes as foreign minister as well. Under his regime, Serbia successfully fought in the two Balkan wars, against Turkey in 1912 and against Bulgaria in 1913. Although Pašić attempted to meet the terms of the Austrian ultimatum that came after Serbian nationalists assassinated the Austrian archduke in June 1914, the refusal of his government to accept Austrian participation in the police investigation into the plot within Serbia precipitated the Austrian attack on Serbia that set off World War I. During the war, Pašić formed a coalition government, which operated first out of the town of Niš and then from the Greek island of Corfu, as Austrian forces took over most of Serbia. Pašić hoped to establish a pan-Serbian state, but because of the necessity of working with representatives of Croats and Slovenes, he briefly compromised in supporting the Corfu Declaration of July 1917, which proposed a postwar federal state. In the years after the war, the division in viewpoint persisted. While Pašić and Serb Radicals believed the South Slav state should be centralized with Serbian control, representatives of other regions believed the nation should be federal in nature with equal rights to self-government by the provinces of Slovenia, Croatia, and Bosnia-Herzegovina, acquired from the collapse of the Austro-Hungarian Empire, and Macedonia, acquired from Turkey and Bulgaria.

Pašić attended the Paris Peace Conference as a delegate to represent the newly formed Kingdom of Serbs, Croats, and Slovenes. When he was selected as premier in 1921, he established a unitary and centralized constitution and set up a cabinet entirely composed of Radicals. With only brief interruptions, he was premier of the new nation from 1921 to 1926. Throughout the 1920s until his death at age 80, Pašić continued to work against the federalized approach to the Yugoslav state that tended to be preferred by Croats and Slovenes.

Paul, Alice (1885–1977) *U.S. suffragist*
Alice Paul became a dedicated champion for women's rights, in particular the right to vote, and during World War I, her protests in front of the White House led to her arrest several times. Many of the tactics of protest and demonstration she developed became permanent parts of the American political scene. After the war, she worked for an equal rights amendment to the U.S. constitution and campaigned for world peace.

Alice Paul was born on a farm in Moorestown, in southern New Jersey. She earned an impressive education, with a B.A. degree from Swarthmore College in 1905 and a master's degree in sociology from the University of Pennsylvania. She studied in Britain at the University of Birmingham and received a Ph.D. in economics from the University of Pennsylvania.

While in Britain, she attended a speech by Christabel Pankhurst at the University of Birmingham and was inspired and impressed. She joined the Women's Social and Political Union (WSPU) in Britain and participated in many of the direct action efforts of that organization. As a result, she was imprisoned three times in Britain and, following the tactics of the WSPU, went on a hunger strike; like other suffragists using the same protest method, she was force-fed.

After her return to the United States, the National American Woman Suffrage Association agreed to appoint her cochair of their Congressional Committee in Washington, with the stipulation that she could lobby for a constitutional amendment granting suffrage to women if she could raise her own funds. Her cochair was another American suffragist she had met in Britain, Lucy Burns, and they set up office in December 1912. Paul organized a large Washington demonstration, consisting of about 8,000 delegates who marched in costumes and with banners, the day before the inauguration of President Woodrow Wilson.

In several western states, women already had the vote, and, in 1915, Alice Paul and a group of like-minded suffragists organized the National Woman's Party (NWP) to mobilize their vote. Partly through her personal efforts, the question of support for the constitutional amendment became a major campaign and election issue in 1914 and 1916.

Many of the ideas and tactics used by Alice Paul and the NWP were based on the more militant style of the British WSPU, including campaigning against the party in power, targeting particular legislators who opposed their position, and picketing key buildings, including the White House. When told that picketing the White House was prohibited, the suffragists continued, leading to arrests on the grounds of obstructing a sidewalk. Many of those arrested were sent to the District prison near Lorton, Virginia, then known as the Occoquan Workhouse. Revelations of the sordid conditions there added to public support for their cause. Paul herself was treated as a psychiatric case in prison, but she persisted in both her hunger strike and her protest.

Picketing of the White House and civil disobedience were unheard of before Paul introduced these methods, and to conduct such protests against the president during the war was viewed by many patriotic men as tantamount to treason. As a consequence, there were several scuffles and near-riots surrounding the suffrage effort in Washington during the war years, involving not only the police against the suffragists, but groups of male bystanders and the suffragists.

Congress passed the Nineteenth Amendment in 1919, and, during the next year, in a heated campaign to secure state legislative ratification, Alice Paul and the WPU organized campaigns. The necessary three-quarters of the legislatures ratified the amendment the next year, and American women voted in the presidential election of 1920.

In the postwar period, Alice Paul continued her work for women's rights, organizing a world party for equal rights and attempting to influence the League of Nations. The organization took responsibility for the establishment of the United Nations Commission on the Status of Women in 1946. Paul was also instrumental in helping several Jewish refugees escape the Holocaust through Switzerland. Like other members of her generation, she saw women's issues in a larger context of social justice and after achieving a partial victory for her cause in the United States, continued to work for women's rights, an end to sex discrimination, and world peace.

Pershing, John Joseph (Black Jack Pershing)
(1860–1948) *U.S. army officer, head of American Expeditionary Force*

General John J. Pershing led the American Expeditionary Force in Europe during World War I, and was noted for his insistence that U.S. troops be deployed to their own sectors of the front, rather than being integrated as replacements into British and French divisions.

Pershing was born on a farm near Laclede, Missouri, and, after a brief teaching career, entered the U.S. Military Academy. He graduated in 1886, and over the next few years he served in Indian campaigns in the Southwest and Northern Plains. In 1895–96, he was assigned to command a unit of the 10th Cavalry, the so-called Buffalo Soldiers, of African-American troops. In this position, he earned the nickname "Black Jack" Pershing. He commanded troops in Cuba during the Spanish-American War and served in the occupation of the Philippines from 1899 to 1903. He was promoted to the rank of brigadier general in 1906 over many more senior officers in a storm of controversy, springing from the fact that his father-in-law was the chairman of the Senate Committee on Military Affairs.

In 1909, Pershing was appointed military governor of Moro Province in the Philippines, charged with restoring order over the Moro Insurrection there. In 1913, he returned to the United States and, in April 1914, took command of Fort Bliss, an infantry post near El Paso, Texas. Over the next two years, as the Mexican Revolution led to violence over the border and threats of American intervention, Pershing built up a strong force. After raids by Mexican forces under Pancho Villa across the border into New Mexico, Pershing received orders to pursue Villa and apprehend him. On March 16, 1916, he led an expedition into Mexico, encountering problems of transport and never catching the elusive Villa. Derisively, the press began to call his effort, "The Perishing Expedition." In fact, Pershing introduced several new tactics, including aerial surveillance and mapping by small planes and extensive use of railroad transport.

Recalled from Mexico in January 1917, Pershing was put in charge of Fort Sam Houston in San Antonio, and, when war was declared April 6, 1917, Pershing enthusiastically congratulated President Wilson. The War Department selected Pershing to head the American Expeditionary Force in May.

Eventually Pershing mobilized more than 2 million troops for the force. Although he did compromise his position that U.S. troops would operate only under American command (except for the assignment of several African-American units to fight under French command), for the most part, American troops operated in independent sectors. Notable successes included the reduction of the St. Mihiel salient and a bloody advance in the Meuse-Argonne region. Allied commanders believed that the lack of experience with prevailing wartime conditions led to reckless charges and excessive casualties among American troops, who did not understand the changes that had been brought about by trench, barbed wire, and the machine gun. Even so, the presence of large numbers of fresh American troops with relatively high morale was one of the factors that led the German high command to seek an armistice.

After the war, Pershing became U.S. Army chief of staff, and, in 1924, Congress awarded him the rank of general of the armies, a rank held previously only by George Washington. Pershing published his autobiography in 1931, *My Experience of War.*

Pétain, Henri Philippe (1856–1951) *French army officer, war hero, premier of Vichy France*
Pétain was a French general who gained the admiration of the French people for leading the defense of Verdun in 1916. With considerable irony, in later life he was convicted of collaborating with the German enemy in World War II and spent the last years of his life in prison.

Pétain was born to a peasant family in Cauchy à la Tour and graduated from the St. Cyr military academy in 1887. He later attended the French equivalent of the Army War College, where he later taught. In 1914, he was nearing retirement and had advanced only to the rank of colonel, perhaps due to his arguments against the tactic of infantry attack against defended positions.

During the first year of the war, Pétain earned recognition for leadership and received promotion to general in command of the Second Army. In February 1916, he was ordered to defend Verdun, where he organized a resupply system and led the troops in a costly, but eventually successful defense. His succinct mottoes, such as "They shall not pass," were widely repeated and came to symbolize the spirit of French defense of the homeland.

In May 1917, he was promoted to commander in chief of the army and instituted reforms and ordered courts-martial in response to the wave of mutinies that swept the French army that spring. When Foch was appointed generalissimo over all Allied armies in the west, Pétain received command of the French forces and led them during the final offensives that ended the war. At the end of the war in November 1918, he was promoted to marshal of France.

In the mid-1920s, he was sent to North Africa, where he led French and Spanish forces in putting down a rebellion in Morocco. He served in the cabinet in the mid-1930s and as ambassador to Spain in 1939–40, then under the regime of Francisco Franco. Franco had served under Pétain in Morocco. Pétain supported the development of a strong defensive line of fortresses for France, the Maginot line, retaining his belief that strongly defended positions could readily hold off the offensive. He joined the cabinet again in

1940 during the German invasion, and, when he concluded that further French resistance to the German invasion was fruitless, he advocated an armistice. He was named premier on June 16, 1940, and, within a week, France and Germany signed an armistice. He moved with the government to Vichy, where he served both as head of government and head of state in a government that cooperated with the German conquest. Under his regime, the Vichy government became more and more a puppet state controlled by Nazi Germany.

After the defeat of Germany in World War II, Pétain voluntarily returned from Germany to be tried in Paris, where he was sentenced to death for the crime of collaborating with the enemy. However, Charles de Gaulle commuted Pétain's sentence to life in prison, and Pétain spent the remaining years of his life imprisoned on an island off the coast of Brittany.

Princip, Gavrilo (1894–1918) *Serbian nationalist, assassin*
Gavrilo Princip was one of the assassins sent to Sarajevo and fired the shots that killed Archduke Franz Ferdinand and his wife, Sophie, on June 28, 1914. Like several of the other conspirators, Princip suffered from tuberculosis, and he knew he did not have long to live when he volunteered for the mission.

Princip was born in Bosnia, then a province of the Ottoman Empire, under the mandate and control of Austria-Hungary. After attending schools in Sarajevo and Tuzla, Princip, then 18 years old, moved to Belgrade, Serbia, in 1912. There he joined the society known informally as the Black Hand and more formally as Ujedinjenje ili Smrt (Unification or Death), a militant organization devoted to Serbian nationalism, with the goal of uniting Serbs, Slovenes, and Croats together into a larger Serbian nation. Princip was recruited by Dragutin Dimitrijevic, then serving as head of the Intelligence Department of the Serbian Government, who was a founding member of the Black Hand. Along with his fellow conspirators, Princip was provided with pistols, pistol training, small grenades, and cyanide pills to take after the assassination. Some of the weapons were later traced back to Serbian sources. The assassination plot was only the last of a number of such attempts against officials of the Austro-Hungarian regime by young Slav nationalists in the first few years of the 20th century.

One conspirator threw a grenade that bounced off the lead car in the procession from the Sarajevo rail station to the town hall. Alarmed by the episode, the driver sped on to the town hall. Later, however, the archduke asked to visit the hospital where one staff member injured in the grenade attack was being treated. On the return, the archduke's car passed down the Appel Quay along the river, and, after making a wrong turn near a bridge, backed up to resume the correct route to the hospital. At that moment, Princip, who happened to be resting in a nearby outdoor café, stepped forward, closed his eyes, and fired two shots. The archduke was struck in the neck and his wife was hit in the abdomen. The driver proceeded on to the governor's residence, but both the archduke and his wife died from their wounds shortly thereafter. Princip was seized by police and detained.

After some hesitation, the Austro-Hungarian government sent an ultimatum to the Serbian government, demanding that the Black Hand organization be prohibited, and that parties responsible for the assassination in Serbia be arrested. They also demanded that Austrian officials participate in the investigation. Serbia refused the ultimatum and Austro-Hungarian artillery fired on Belgrade, leading to the invoking of alliances and the outbreak of World War I. Princip was tried on October 24, 1914, some 10 weeks after the war began. Princip, along with others under the age of 21, was found guilty and sentenced to 20 years in prison, the maximum for a minor under Austro-Hungarian law. Princip's tuberculosis infected his arm, and, after an amputation, he died in April 1918 in a hospital in Theresienstadt, Austria.

Although the Austro-Hungarian government took the position that Princip's act had been planned and supported by officials of the Serbian government, those charges were never definitively proven. Several years later the former head of Serbian intelligence, Dragutin Dimitrijevic confessed that he had provided the assassins with support, but that confession was criticized as either self-aggrandizing or made under duress, or both. Whether or not Princip's crime represented an incident of state-supported terrorism or the act of a martyr in the cause of Serbian nationalism has remained a subject of debate.

Rankin, Jeannette (1880–1973) *First woman member of U.S. Congress, opponent of war*
Jeannette Rankin was the first woman elected to the U.S. Congress and one of 50 members who voted against the declaration of war in April 1917. Rankin grew up in Montana and graduated from Montana University in 1902. She worked as a teacher and then entered the New York School of Philanthropy in 1908, where she studied the field later known as social work, practicing in Montana, California, and Washington State. She also attended the University of Washington, where she became active in the suffrage movement. She visited New Zealand in 1915, and she briefly worked as a seamstress to gain more knowledge of the conditions of working-class women.

In 1916, she ran for Congress from Montana on the Republican ticket, supporting universal suffrage, prohibition, and child labor reform, as well as continued neutrality in World War I. When the vote came on the declaration of war in April 1917, other women active in the suffrage movement asked her to support the war vote, believing their movement would be damaged if she did not. However, she stuck with her position and joined 49 other Members of Congress in opposing the war. She hoped to be elected to the Senate in 1918, but she did not gain her party's nomination. She ran as an independent, but lost.

After the war, Rankin continued to fight for equal citizenship for women, for child labor reform, and for international peace. She was active in several antiwar organizations through the 1920s and 1930s. She was reelected to Congress in 1940 on an antiwar platform, and she was the only member of Congress to vote against the declaration of war against Japan after the attack on Pearl Harbor. She was defeated for reelection in 1942. She remained active in her later years, forming a woman's cooperative in Watkinsville, Georgia, and campaigning against the Vietnam War. At the age of 87, she led a protest march against that war in Washington.

Reed, John (1887–1920) *U.S. journalist, supporter of Russian Bolsheviks*
John Reed was an American journalist who befriended Lenin in Petrograd, Russia, and witnessed the Russian Revolution. His book, *Ten Days That Shook the World,* published in 1919, was widely read as one of the best eyewitness accounts of the revolution.

Reed was born in Portland, Oregon, and graduated from Harvard College in 1910. He began his career as a journalist, and, beginning in 1913, worked with the radical magazine, *The Masses.* He grew famous for his coverage of the Paterson, New Jersey, silk workers' strike in 1913 and, later, Pancho Villa's rebel army in Mexico. In reporting both struggles, he demonstrated his sympathy for revolutionary politics.

Serving as a reporter during World War I, he first published an account, *The War in Eastern Europe* (1916), before meeting Lenin in Petrograd. After the Russian Revolution, Reed returned to the United States, where he was expelled from the National Socialist Convention held in August 1919, along with others who supported the Bolshevik position. He helped organize a splinter group, the Communist Labor Party, which later became one of the factions organized into the Communist Party of the United States. Reed was twice indicted for sedition, but those charges were dropped. He returned to Russia, where he shared in representing the American communist movement with the leader of a rival faction. On a mysterious mission, he was arrested in Finland with a reputed $1.5 million in gems and cash. Although the purpose of his trip was unclear, some observers suggested that the money was intended to help him establish the Communist Party in the United States. While attending a conference in the city of Baku, he contracted typhus and died in 1920. He was buried in the Kremlin and was treated as a hero of the revolution. His name lived on in American radical circles, where organized writers' and artists' groups of the Communist Party were known as John Reed Clubs, which operated from 1929 to about 1935.

Sims, William (1858–1936) *U.S. naval officer*
William Sims, as rear admiral and vice admiral during World War I, coordinated U.S. naval forces with those of the Allies and is credited with advocating and helping to arrange the convoy system that effectively protected merchant shipping to Britain and France against submarine attack after the U.S. entry into the war.

Sims graduated from the U.S. Naval Academy in 1880 and rose through the officer ranks. During the Spanish-American war, he was appalled at the American gunnery performance, and, as a consequence of his criticisms, he was appointed inspector of naval gunnery. During the Russo-Japanese War, 1904–05, Sims served as an official U.S. naval observer and continued to advocate improving U.S. standards of gunnery. Despite official policy, Sims was explicitly pro-British in the first decade of the 20th century. In 1911, he was promoted to captain and was appointed an instructor

at the Naval War College. In 1916, he was promoted to rear admiral.

When the United States declared war on Germany, Sims was en route to Britain to serve as liaison officer to the Royal Navy. In May 1917, Sims was promoted to vice admiral and given command over all U.S. naval forces operating in Europe. Unlike General John Pershing, who insisted that U.S. Army forces operate in separate sectors under separate command, Sims worked to integrate the U.S. naval forces with those of the Allies. He quickly argued for stepped up antisubmarine forces, and, at his urging, Secretary of the Navy Josephus Daniels approved the rapid fitting out of more than 400 antisubmarine craft, including 273 destroyers. Due to the convoy system, in which dozens of merchant ships steamed together, screened by antisubmarine warships, the record of losses to submarines declined month by month through mid- and late 1917 and into 1918, foiling the German plan to starve Britain into submission by unrestricted submarine warfare.

Sims remained outspoken throughout his career and, after the war, was critical of both Secretary Daniels and Chief of Naval Operations Benson for their conduct of the war. He returned to his post as president of the War College and retired from the navy in 1922.

Smuts, Jan Christian (1870–1950) *South African army officer, statesman, prime minister*
A South African leader of Afrikaans ancestry, Smuts was responsible for suppressing a Boer uprising against British rule during World War I and for defeating the German forces in South-West Africa (Namibia). While attending the 1917 Imperial War Conference, Smuts was recruited by David Lloyd George to serve directly in the Imperial War Cabinet. Smuts was given command of the Royal Flying Corps, which he reorganized as the Royal Air Force.

Smuts had been born in Cape Colony with British citizenship. He attended Victoria College in Stellenbosch and studied law at Christ's College, in Cambridge University in Britain. He was admitted to the British bar in 1894. He returned to South Africa in 1895 and began a law practice, but he was soon caught up in the growing dispute between the Dutch-settler-descended Boers and the British. At first he advocated compromise, but when the regime of Cecil Rhodes supported the Jameson Raid to suppress Boer independence, Smuts renounced his British citizenship and moved to the Boer republic of Transvaal. He was made state attorney there, and he continued to strive for a peaceful solution.

However, after the Boer War broke out in 1899, Smuts joined the Boer army and led a contingent of guerrilla fighters raiding into Cape Colony. While conducting a siege of British forces, he was called from the line to help work on the peace settlement that ended the Boer War in May 1902.

Smuts worked with General Louis Botha to form a new political party, *Het Volk* (The People), which continued to strive for reconciliation between British and Boer in South Africa. After achieving British recognition of self-government in the Orange Free State and Transvaal, Smuts then worked successfully to help establish the Union of South Africa, which included those two states and the colonies of Natal and Cape Colony. Smuts served as minister of defense in the South African government from 1910 to 1920.

In 1914, with the outbreak of World War I, Smuts took direct command of the South African army. Those forces suppressed a German-sponsored Boer uprising, and also defeated German forces in South-West Africa. Smuts also commanded the South African forces in their pursuit of German troops in German East Africa. Brought to Britain in 1916 for the Imperial War Conference, he was appointed to serve on the Imperial War Cabinet and to organize the British air force.

After the war, Smuts served with Botha as a South African representative at the Paris Peace Conference, where his position was considerably less vindictive toward Germany than that of his British and French counterparts. In the postwar years, Smuts continued his career as a statesman and politician, serving as South African prime minister during 1919–24. Defeated for office in 1924 by a coalition of Nationalist and Labour parties under James Hertzog, Smuts turned to his scientific interests, publishing a work on evolution entitled *Holism and Evolution*. In 1933, during the Great Depression, Smuts worked with Hertzog, forming a coalition government, and then, in 1939, he emerged as prime minister again, defeating Hertzog's pro-neutrality faction. Smuts was commander in chief of South African forces during World War II and later was instrumental in the formation of the United Nations. He was defeated for reelection as prime minister in 1948 by a more nationalist and pro-Apartheid slate, and he died two years later.

Swinton, Ernest (1868–1951) *British army officer, advocate of tank development*

Ernest Swinton served as an officer in the British army during World War I, both as a provider of information from the front as the official "Eyewitness" and as the officer credited with conceiving and advocating the idea of the tank. It is in the latter capacity that he is most remembered by later generations, as the armored, tracked vehicle would play a significant role in breaking the deadlock on the western front and would become a regular feature of land warfare throughout the rest of the 20th century.

Swinton was born in Bangalore, India, and joined the Corps of Royal Engineers in 1888. He served in India in the period 1889–94, receiving a commission as lieutenant in 1891. He served in the Boer War (1899–1902) and in a number of other capacities over the next few years, including that of official army historian of the Russo-Japanese War. By 1914, he had achieved the rank of lieutenant colonel.

Kitchener, as war minister, appointed Swinton to his post as Eyewitness, or official war correspondent. Since at that point journalists were barred from the front, Swinton's official stories, approved personally by Kitchener, were for a time the only direct material released to the press.

The story of how he was inspired to develop the tank has several versions. He saw a Holt tractor, towing a gun, during Christmas 1914 and that may have served as the germ of the idea. According to other accounts, he had seen Holt caterpillar tractors in South Africa, and, when considering the devastation wrought by the machine gun, both during the Russo-Japanese War and in the trenches of the western front, he developed the concept. In any case, he presented his suggestions through army channels, and the concept was at first rejected. However, Winston Churchill, as First Lord of the Admiralty, thought the principle had merit and encouraged Lloyd George to adopt it. The Landships Committee was formed and a prototype tank was produced. Its battlefield debut was at Flers, in September 1916, with more effective use at the Battle of Cambrai in 1917.

Swinton retired after the war with the honorary rank of major general. He continued to serve the British defense establishment, however, first in the Air Ministry, and later as professor of military history at Oxford University, from 1925 to 1939. Under several pseudonyms, he published works of fiction centered on military themes. He published *Eyewitness,* based on his war experiences, in 1932 and his autobiography in 1951.

Tirpitz, Alfred von (Alfred Tirpitz) (1849–1930) *German naval officer*

Alfred von Tirpitz was the chief advocate of a strong German navy in the years before World War I, and he served as secretary of state of the Imperial Navy Department from 1897 and as grand admiral from 1911 until his resignation in March 1916.

He was born Alfred Tirpitz and acquired the "von" in 1900, when he was granted noble rank. Tirpitz was the son of a Prussian civil servant, and he enlisted in the Prussian navy in 1865. After attending the Kiel Naval School, he was commissioned in 1869, and then served in a torpedo-boat flotilla. He became chief of staff of the Navy High Command and was promoted to rear admiral in 1895. After commanding the German cruiser squadron in the Far East, he returned to Germany to begin the buildup of the German navy in the two decades that followed 1897. With the passage of naval laws that funded German warship building, the fleet of major capital ships increased to 29 by 1914.

Although the British fleet was still stronger than the German on the eve of World War I, the publicity surrounding the German fleet buildup may have had an adverse effect on British public opinion by threatening an arms race or creating a war scare. At least to some extent, the formation of the British-French-Russian alliance may have been due to concerns over increasing German sea power. Tirpitz was disappointed to realize that the High-Seas Fleet could not hope to take on the British fleet during the war and that the submarine force was not strong enough to determine the course of the war. He was an early advocate of unrestricted submarine warfare and sought direct command of the fleet, but, facing mounting opposition to his positions from more cautious members of the naval staff and from Chancellor von Bethmann-Hollweg, he resigned his post in 1916.

Following the war, he briefly entered politics, serving in the Reichstag from 1924 to 1928, representing the German National People's Party. He published his memoirs in 1919 and a more thoroughly argued defense of his policies, *Politische Dokumente,* in 1924–26. Like Erich Ludendorff, Tirpitz believed that Germany could have won the war if his more determined policies had not been thwarted by bureaucrats, a view which became popular among the embittered postwar generation in Germany. He died in retirement near Munich in 1930.

Trotsky, Leon (Lev Davidovich Bronstein) (1879–1940) *Russian revolutionary leader*

Leon Trotsky was a major leader of the Russian revolution and commissar of foreign affairs in the first communist government of Soviet Russia in 1917–18. In that post, he helped negotiate the Treaty of Brest Litovsk, which ended the war between Russia and the Central Powers. Trotsky resigned that post and became commissar of war, leading the Red Army during the Russian Civil War that was fought between the communist government and its counterrevolutionary opponents, particularly the White armies.

Trotsky was born Lev Davidovich Bronstein, the son of a prosperous Jewish farmer in the Ukraine. He attended school in and near Odessa, where he always excelled as a student. He finished secondary school in 1897. He was influenced by the wave of Marxist organizations sweeping the Russian Empire at the time, joining the Social Democrats and working with the South Russian Workers' Union. He was arrested for his labor activities in 1898 and was sentenced to prison and then to Siberian exile. In 1902, he escaped from exile and went to London, where he met and worked with Lenin and other Russian Social Democrats. Trotsky was present at the 1903 meeting of the Russian Social Democratic Labor Party that later split into Mensheviks and Bolsheviks, with Lenin leading the Bolshevik faction. Trotsky sided with the Mensheviks until 1917, when he broke with them and joined with the Bolsheviks.

In the period between 1903 and 1917, Trotsky, like many other Russian radicals, lived abroad. He established his reputation by writing and publishing articles and several books on the topics of political organization and revolution. In July 1917, Trotsky joined with Lenin in the Bolshevik Central Committee and worked to oppose the newly established Provisional Government in Russia. After the Bolsheviks gained power in October 1917, Trotsky first served as commissar of foreign affairs. He was disgusted at the treatment that Russia received from Germany, but the Russian representatives were powerless to oppose a vindictive treaty that ceded a huge swath of territory to the Central Powers in the Treaty of Brest Litovsk.

Trotsky organized the Red Army and was widely credited with the victories against the counterrevolutionary forces in the Civil War that lasted from 1918 to 1921. Stalin began to emerge through manipulation as head of the Communist Party in 1922, and, gradually, Trotsky was pushed into the background, losing his position as commissar of war and his post in the Politburo. Stalin had Trotsky expelled from the party in 1927, and then exiled to Central Asia. In 1929, he was exiled from the Soviet Union entirely and lived abroad in Turkey, in European countries, and finally settled in Mexico. There he organized the Fourth International, a group of anti-Stalinist communist organizations around the world, which believed that the world revolution should proceed. Stalin ordered Trotsky assassinated, and, after a failed attempt, he was killed at his home near Mexico City in 1940 by a Spanish communist, Ramon Mercader, who was working for the Soviet secret police.

Wilson, Woodrow (Thomas Woodrow Wilson) (1856–1924) *U.S. college president, New Jersey governor, president of the United States*

Woodrow Wilson served as president of the United States from 1913 to 1921. In his first term, he worked to maintain the neutrality of the United States in the First World War, and he was reelected in 1916 by a bare majority. However, in early 1917, when the Germans launched unrestricted submarine warfare against shipping headed to Britain and France, including the sinking of American ships, Wilson first asked Congress for authorization to provide arms and gun crews for privately owned merchant ships. Later, after several more ships were sunk, he convened Congress on April 2, 1917, and asked it to declare war against Germany. During his second administration, he oversaw the reorganization of the national defense and led in the planning of a wartime economy. Immediately after the war, he headed the American delegation to the peace negotiations in Paris, where he argued for a less vindictive peace settlement and one that recognized the right of self-determination of peoples.

Wilson was born Thomas Woodrow Wilson in Virginia, where his father was a Presbyterian minister. The family moved to Georgia, living there during the Civil War. After that war, the family moved to South Carolina and then to North Carolina. Wilson attended Davidson College in 1873, where his father served as trustee of the Presbyterian college, and then transferred to the College of New Jersey (Princeton), where he completed his bachelor's degree. An undergraduate paper he authored was published in 1879, drawing attention to his writing style and abilities. He entered the University of Virginia and studied law, then practiced in 1882 and 1883. However, he became disillusioned with the practice of law and entered Johns Hopkins University in Baltimore to earn a graduate degree in history. His dissertation on congressional government earned him a Ph.D. in 1885. He taught briefly at Bryn Mawr College outside Philadelphia, and then at Wesleyan College in Connecticut. He was offered several teaching positions and accepted one at the College of New Jersey in 1890. (The institution changed its name from the College of New Jersey to Princeton University in 1896.)

During these teaching years, Wilson published several works on American history and politics, earning him a national reputation. In 1902, he was unanimously selected to serve as president of Princeton University. As president of the university, he advocated several reforms that attracted national attention, particularly the abolition of the notorious eating clubs and their replacement with a more democratic system of university housing, which resembled the system in place in Britain, in which study and residence were combined. Furthermore, he raised the admission standards and sought to establish a more discussion-based education. Wilson ran into severe opposition to some of these changes, but his advocacy of reform was widely noticed.

The Democratic machine in New Jersey sought a candidate for the governorship of the state who would be dissociated from the long-standing corruption of the party, hoping to capitalize on nationwide pressures for reform by nominating an inexperienced but well-known person to serve as a figurehead. Wilson accepted the nomination and was elected but soon made it clear that he took his mandate for reform seriously. He not only opposed the head of the machine, but also was able to push a number of state reforms through the legislature.

Thus, in 1912, Wilson was widely recognized as an up-and-coming progressive Democrat, and he received the nomination of the party for the presidency. That year, the Republican Party split, with incumbent president William Howard Taft running as a Republican and Theodore Roosevelt running as a Progressive. In state after state, Roosevelt drew enough votes away from Taft for Wilson to win the electoral vote by a plurality. He had a clear majority in the electoral college, but less than 42 percent of the popular vote nationwide. As a result of the split in Republican ranks, Democrats also came out of the election with control of both houses of Congress.

Wilson's program, dubbed the New Freedom, represented an attempt to achieve progressive goals with a minimum of centralized administration, in contrast to the progressive vision of Theodore Roosevelt, which called for strong regulatory boards of experts. As president in his first term, Wilson supported a wide variety of measures that captured the Progressive reform aspirations, including the establishment of a Federal Trade Commission, the Federal Reserve System, lowered tariffs, passage of the Clayton Anti-Trust Act, and legislation to limit the hours of work of children. Some observers believed that Wilson's support for these reforms was intended to win to the Democratic Party at least some of those Republicans who had followed Theodore Roosevelt in his third-party attempt at the presidency in 1912.

Nevertheless, Wilson continued to reflect several conservative Democratic traditions. He appointed several southern Democrats to positions of influence, including Josephus Daniels as secretary of the navy and Walter Hines Page as ambassador to Great Britain. Furthermore, he endorsed the reintroduction of racial segregation in the lunch facilities in federal office buildings and refused to endorse African-American appeals for federal legislation outlawing lynching.

In foreign affairs, Wilson took a strong line with Mexico, ordering a punitive expedition under General John Pershing to pursue the forces of Pancho Villa after they had conducted a provocative raid across the border in March 1916. The failure of the troops to apprehend Villa and continuing difficulties with the government of Mexico almost led to a full-scale war, but Wilson recalled the expedition late in 1916. He was also unsuccessful in his effort to find a pathway through the difficult dilemmas presented by the mutual blockades of Germany by Britain and of Britain by Germany. Although each side used methods deemed to threaten the rights of neutral states, American trade with Britain flourished to the point that German leaders decided that no further damage to their position could be done by outright attack on American ship-

ping. Wilson's attempt to mediate between the warring parties came to nothing.

Although widely hailed for his idealistic stance on the question of neutrality and, after U.S. entry into the war, for his advocacy of a just peace without revenge against the losers, Wilson failed to achieve either goal. The Versailles Treaty recognized the dissolution of the Austro-Hungarian Empire and stripped Germany not only of its colonies, but also of much of its financial and industrial resources. The League of Nations, which Wilson had supported as a means of preserving the peace, was established, but Wilson failed to win acceptance for the treaty in the United States Senate.

Many contemporary observers and historians have placed responsibility for these failures directly on Wilson, noting his stubborn personality, his unwillingness to compromise, and his reliance on a very limited set of advisers for ideas and opinions. Others, however, have viewed his lack of success in these areas with more objectivity, suggesting that larger conditions made neutrality impossible, that the peace arrangements in Europe would have been even more draconian had not Wilson attempted to moderate the positions of the British and French, and that the failure of the League in the U.S. Senate was more the result of willful opposition by a handful of bitter Republican opponents than due to Wilson's own positions.

Wilson suffered a stroke while attempting to win support for the league in a nationwide speaking tour in September 1919. For the last 18 months of his administration, Wilson lived in seclusion. It was during this period that the final votes on the league went against his position. He did not choose to resign, and his vice president, Thomas Marshall, had neither the precedent nor the ambition to attempt to force his resignation. After the inauguration of Warren Harding, Wilson retired from public view entirely and died at his home in Washington in 1924.

His extensive papers were collected at Princeton University, where a definitive edition of them was published under the chief editorship of Arthur Link in the 1980s.

Yardley, Herbert O. (1889–1958) *U.S. cryptanalyst, author*

Herbert Yardley is often regarded as the father of American cryptography, although he was one of several specialists in World War I and the years that followed who perfected methods of decoding enciphered messages. His later fame rested to a great extent on his publication in 1931 of *The American Black Chamber*, his personal account of his work during and immediately after the war.

After graduating from high school in 1907, Yardley spent a few years drifting from job to job, playing poker, and seeing the United States. In 1912, he got a job as a telegraph operator in the U.S. State Department in Washington. He soon found that coded messages sent to the president could be easily decoded and that secret and encrypted American diplomatic messages sent in code from Britain could easily be read by the employees of the British-controlled cable office. On his own time, he prepared a lengthy report proving how easily the codes could be cracked. When the United States entered the war, Yardley, despite the fact that his position was unpopular, was sent to the Signal Corps from the State Department, given the rank of lieutenant, and put in charge of MI-8, that is, section 8 of Military Intelligence. In that small bureau, Yardley and his group began to break German codes, including a key message that identified Lothar Witzke, a German agent, as one who had plotted sabotage.

During the war, Yardley met and discussed cryptological methods with William Hall, the director of Britain's Room 40, which had cracked the Zimmermann telegram. At the end of the war, despite plans to disband the office, Yardley helped convince his superiors to continue funding the work, performed by an official group jointly financed by the State Department and the army. In 1919, Yardley set up shop in a brownstone building in New York City, which continued to provide decryptions through the 1920s. This so-called American Black Chamber, which operated secretly, broke numerous codes, including the Japanese diplomatic code. At the Washington Naval Conference held in 1921–22, American officials knew the secret bargaining position of the Japanese because of the work of the Black Chamber.

In 1928, Henry Stimson, now secretary of state, decided that the operation should be closed down, and Yardley found himself without a job. In order to raise funds, he wrote the account describing his work, which was first published in serial form in the *Saturday Evening Post* and then as a book in 1931. *The American Black Chamber* was an immediate best seller, causing intense distress in some government circles over the secrets it revealed. Under a law passed in 1933, such publication became a federal crime, and the book was withdrawn from publication, but not before it had been widely sold and translated into several languages, including Japanese. Yardley went on to write spy novels and other works and later worked for both the Canadian and Chinese governments in code cracking. His account of his Chinese experience was published as *The Chinese Black Chamber: An Adventure in Espionage*. His other publications include the novels *The Blonde Countess* and *The Red Sun of Nippon*, and an autobiographical account, *The Education of a Poker Player*. *The Blonde Countess* was made into a movie, *Rendezvous*, starring William Powell and Rosalind Russell, in 1935.

Yardley worked briefly for the government in World War II in a noncryptographic job in the Office of Price Administration. He died in 1958, the year after the publication of his book on poker.

York, Alvin C. (Alvin Cullum York) (1887–1964) *U.S. Army noncommissioned officer, war hero*

Alvin Cullum York, although a pacifist, became the most famous American war hero of World War I, due to his heroic performance in the Argonne in October 1918.

York was born in Pall Mall, Tennessee, one of 11 children. As a youth, he learned to shoot a rifle for hunting and won several prizes at county turkey-shoots for his marksmanship. In 1915, he met his future wife, Gracie Williams, and became converted to the strictly pacifist Church of Christ in Christian Union. When the Selective Service Act required registration, York requested an exemption on the ground that his religion made him a conscientious objector. That request was denied and he was drafted.

After basic training, he was shipped to France in June 1918. On October 8, 1918, in the Battle of the Meuse-Argonne, Corporal York was ordered to lead his squad in an attack against a group of German machine guns. In the first rush, they captured a group of about 15 Germans, including a major. However, the major called out to the other machine-gun emplacements, and the squad came under fire from a nearby ridge. With most of his squad killed, York began picking off the machine gunners one by one. When a German officer and several soldiers charged to attack him, York aimed carefully and brought them down as they ran. Finally, the major offered to surrender the whole command, if York would stop killing them. The machine gunners surrendered, and, as York and his prisoners returned to his lines, they accumulated more prisoners, for a total of 132. The next day, it was determined that York had killed 28 Germans and that the emplacement contained 35 machine guns, ammunition, and small arms. York prayed for both the Germans and Americans killed in the engagement.

York was promoted to sergeant and later received numerous medals and honors for his part in the battle, including the Congressional Medal of Honor, the Distinguished Service Cross, and high honors from the French and Italian governments.

York returned home after the war, and the state of Tennessee granted him a farm. He married Gracie Williams and together they raised seven children. He made appearances to collect funds to found a Bible school and an industrial high school and continued to preach, farm, hunt, and do blacksmithing work. Royalties from a film about his life made in 1941 were also used to help fund the school that he founded. After a cerebral hemorrhage that left him an invalid for the last 10 years of his life, he died in 1964.

Zeppelin, Count Ferdinand von (1838–1917) *German developer of the dirigible*

Zeppelin developed the first successful, lighter-than-air, rigid airship that could operate under its own power. A number of these aircraft, called zeppelins, were employed by the Germans in bombing raids in Europe and over Britain in World War I. Although susceptible to antiaircraft fire and to attack from fighter planes, the fact that the zeppelins could operate at extremely high altitudes and that they could operate over Britain foreshadowed the strategic and terror bombing of World War II.

Count Zeppelin was born in Constance, Württemberg, to a minor member of the Württemberg nobility and was educated at both a military academy and at university. In 1859, he received a commission in the Prussian army and was assigned as an observer to the Union army in the American Civil War. There he witnessed the use of balloons for artillery observation, and he became convinced that the potential of lighter-than-air aircraft for military use had not been fully exploited. While serving as a Prussian army officer, he continued to work on his concepts and, on retirement, established a plant on the German shore of Lake Constance at Friedrichshafen. His first successful demonstration of a self-propelled, rigid-framed airship in 1900 won public

support and eventual funding from the German Imperial government.

Zeppelin's factory turned out some 115 airships for use by German forces, and many conducted raids over Britain. Although their bombing was quite inaccurate, they spread fear in the British population and demonstrated one aspect of German technical superiority. Zeppelin had plans to establish regular intercontinental air travel in the postwar years, but he did not live to see the realization of his dream.

Zimmermann, Arthur (1864–1940) *German diplomat, foreign minister*

Arthur Zimmermann served briefly as the German secretary of state for foreign affairs, November 1916 to August 1917. During that period Zimmermann became world-renowned for authoring a memorandum instructing the German minister in Mexico to approach the Mexican government about a possible wartime alliance against the United States. The Zimmermann Note, as it came to be called, helped arouse American public opinion in favor of joining the war on the side of the Allies.

Zimmermann had first served as counselor in the German foreign office from 1908, and then as an undersecretary from 1911 to 1916. The infamous note that he authored was sent to Mexico by way of a cable line between Berlin and Washington that the United States had made available to the German government to discuss Woodrow Wilson's mediation attempts. Thus the encoded telegram planning a conspiracy against the United States was communicated by way of a facility that the United States had made available as a goodwill gesture. That particular aspect of the affair appeared to be the most offensive to Wilson, as a violation of a trust.

The telegram was intercepted and deciphered in Britain by a group in Naval Intelligence under William ("Blinker") Hall, in Room 40 of the Admiralty Building. After the note was fully deciphered, Hall's group arranged that a copy of the telegram be obtained in Mexico, so that it would appear that the interception had occurred there. The British provided a deciphered and translated version to the United States, and the note was published in the United States on March 1, 1917, about five weeks before Wilson asked for a declaration of war against Germany.

The note asked Mexico to approach Japan about a possible alliance against the United States in exchange for a promise to support Mexico's claims to lands lost to the United States in the war with Mexico (including most of the far west). The note had a major impact on American public opinion, particularly in the western states, which had tended to be more opposed to entry into the war. Confronted with the note, Zimmermann admitted its authenticity. As several American-registered ships were sunk by German and Austrian submarines during the period March 1–April 5, 1917, the repeated attacks, cou-pled with the note, helped convince a majority of members of Congress that war was the appropriate response.

Zimmermann admitted that the note was authentic in several discussions with journalists, in March 1917. Zimmermann remained in office until the summer of 1917, when he resigned with a change in the German cabinet in August. He never held such a high post again and spent the remainder of his life in retirement. He died in 1940.

APPENDIX C
Maps and Table

1. Steps Leading to World War I, 1914
2. German Advance on the Western Front, August–September 1914
3. First Battle of the Marne, September 6–10, 1914
4. World War I in the Western Pacific, 1914
5. German Naval Action in the Pacific, 1914–1915
6. Cruise of the German Raider *Emden,* September–November 1914
7. World War I on the Eastern Front, 1914
8. World War I in Africa, 1914–1918
9. Abortive Anglo-French Naval Attack on the Dardanelles, March 1915
10. Allied Dardanelles-Gallipoli Campaign, 1915
11. Armenian Holocaust, 1915–1922
12. Arab Revolt, 1916–1917
13. Major Naval Engagements in the North Sea, 1914–1916
14. U.S. Ships Sunk, February 3, 1917–April 5, 1917
15. Habsburg Territories, 1814–1914
16. Dissolution of the Habsburg Empire, after 1918
17. Redrawing the Map of Central Europe, 1920
18. Realization of Serbian Nationalism, 1918–1929

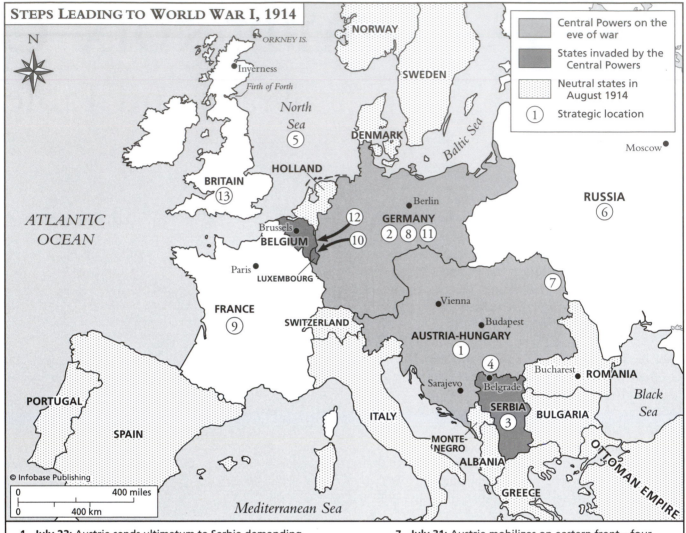

STEPS LEADING TO WORLD WAR I, 1914

Legend:
- Central Powers on the eve of war
- States invaded by the Central Powers
- Neutral states in August 1914
- ① Strategic location

1. **July 23:** Austria sends ultimatum to Serbia demanding suppression of anti-Austrian propaganda and arrest of those implicated in plot to assassinate archduke.

2. **July 25:** Germany supports Austrian position.

3. **July 25:** Serbia mobilizes its army.

4. **July 29:** Austria shells Belgrade and invades.

5. **July 29:** British fleet is mobilized in North Sea. Ships are readied for action at Scapa Flow in the Orkney Islands, in Inverness, and at Firth of Forth in Scotland.

6. **July 30:** Russia mobilizes its army.

7. **July 31:** Austria mobilizes on eastern front—four armies along the Russian-Poland border and two along the Serbian border.

8. **August 1:** Germany mobilizes in response to Russian mobilization and declares war on Russia.

9. **August 1:** France mobilizes.

10. **August 2:** German troops invade Luxembourg.

11. **August 3:** Germany declares war on France.

12. **August 4:** German troops invade Belgium.

13. **August 4:** Britain declares war on Germany.

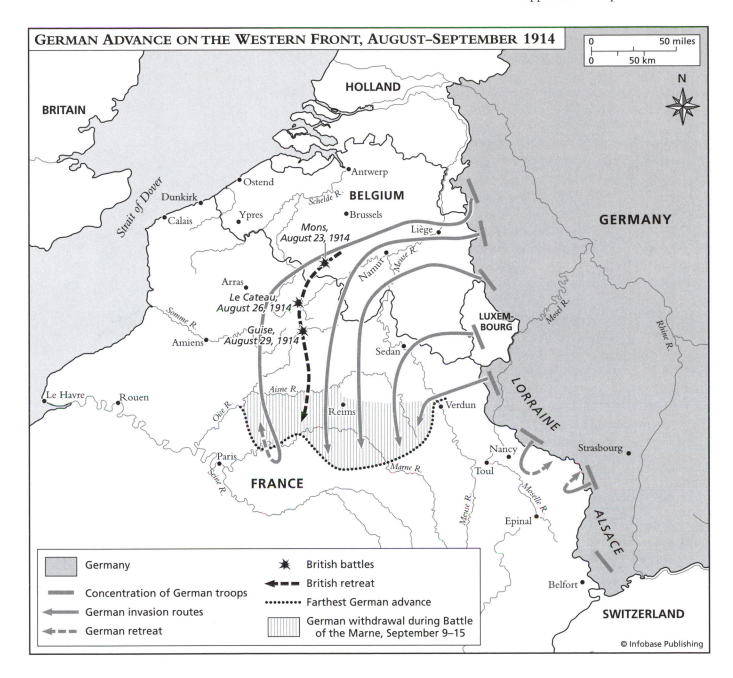

GERMAN ADVANCE ON THE WESTERN FRONT, AUGUST–SEPTEMBER 1914

0   50 miles
0   50 km

N

BRITAIN

HOLLAND

Strait of Dover

Dunkirk
Ostend
Calais
Ypres

Antwerp

Schelde R.   BELGIUM

Brussels

Mons,
August 23, 1914

Liège

GERMANY

Arras

Le Cateau,
August 26, 1914

Namur   Meuse R.

Guise,
August 29, 1914

Somme R.

Amiens

LUXEM-
BOURG

Sedan

Mosel R.

Rhine R.

LORRAINE

Le Havre   Rouen

Aisne R.

Oise R.

Reims

Verdun

Nancy

Strasbourg

Paris

Marne R.

Toul

Meuse R.

Moselle R.

Seine R.

FRANCE

Epinal

ALSACE

Belfort

SWITZERLAND

▨	Germany	✴ British battles
▰▰	Concentration of German troops	▰▰► British retreat
◄──	German invasion routes	••••• Farthest German advance
◄▰▰	German retreat	▦ German withdrawal during Battle of the Marne, September 9–15

© Infobase Publishing

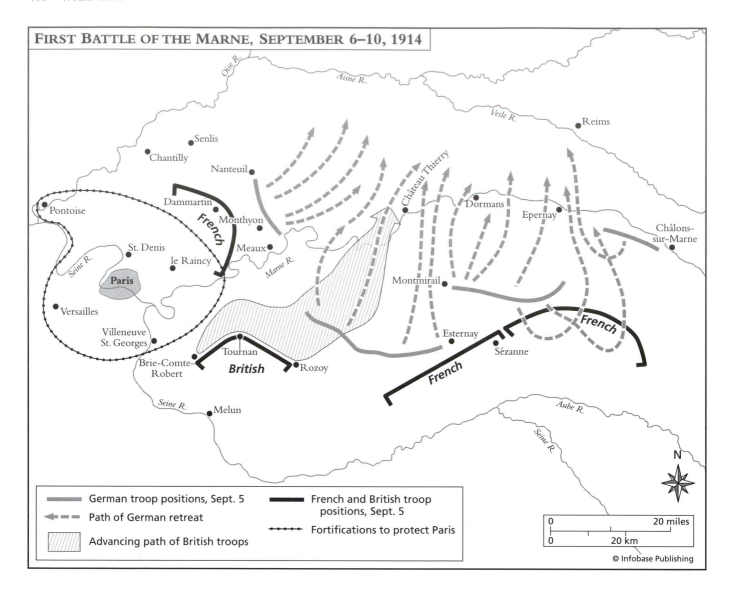

FIRST BATTLE OF THE MARNE, SEPTEMBER 6–10, 1914

Oise R.

Aisne R.

Vesle R.

Reims

Senlis

Chantilly

Nanteuil

Château Thierry

Dormans

Epernay

Châlons-sur-Marne

Dammartin

Monthyon

French

Pontoise

Meaux

Marne R.

St. Denis

le Raincy

Seine R.

Montmirail

French

Paris

Versailles

Esternay

Sézanne

Villeneuve St. Georges

Tournan

French

Brie-Comte-Robert

British

Rozoy

Seine R.

Melun

Aube R.

Seine R.

N

German troop positions, Sept. 5

French and British troop positions, Sept. 5

Path of German retreat

Fortifications to protect Paris

Advancing path of British troops

0   20 miles

0   20 km

© Infobase Publishing

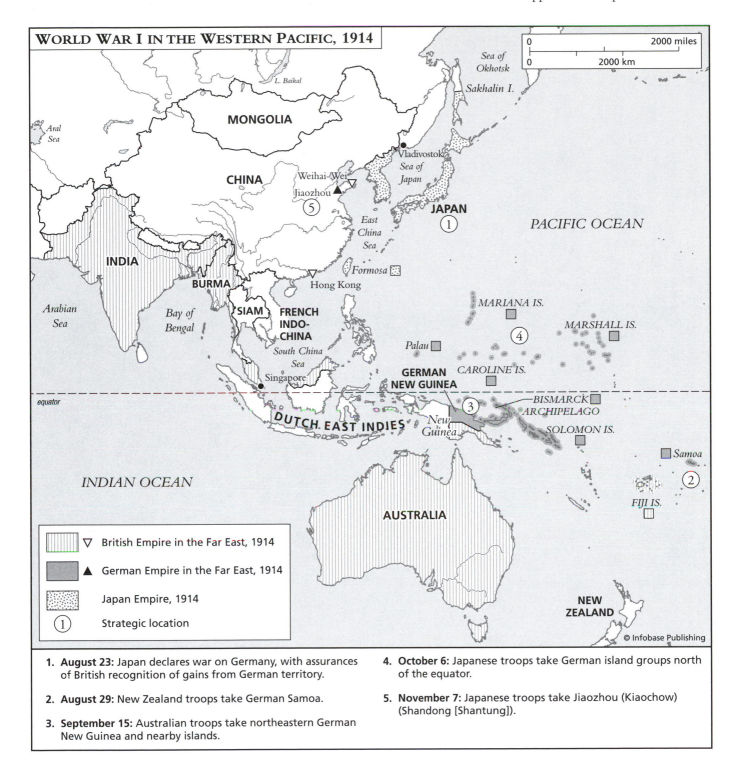

WORLD WAR I IN THE WESTERN PACIFIC, 1914

Legend:

- ▽ British Empire in the Far East, 1914
- ▲ German Empire in the Far East, 1914
- Japan Empire, 1914
- ① Strategic location

© Infobase Publishing

1. **August 23:** Japan declares war on Germany, with assurances of British recognition of gains from German territory.

2. **August 29:** New Zealand troops take German Samoa.

3. **September 15:** Australian troops take northeastern German New Guinea and nearby islands.

4. **October 6:** Japanese troops take German island groups north of the equator.

5. **November 7:** Japanese troops take Jiaozhou (Kiaochow) (Shandong [Shantung]).

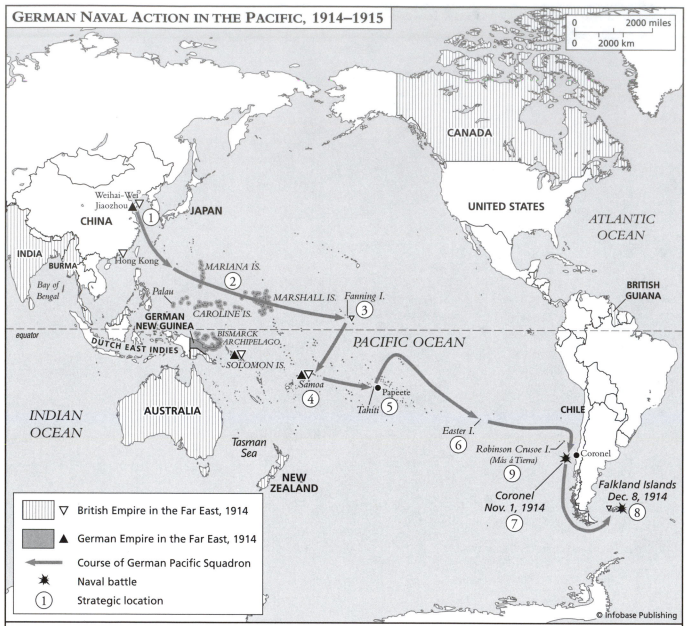

GERMAN NAVAL ACTION IN THE PACIFIC, 1914–1915

British Empire in the Far East, 1914

▲ **German Empire in the Far East, 1914**

← **Course of German Pacific Squadron**

✸ **Naval battle**

① **Strategic location**

1. **August 6, 1914:** German squadron avoids Japanese and British forces and flees to Pacific.

2. **August 11–13, 1914:** Squadron takes on coal and water.

3. **September 7, 1914:** Squadron destroys British cable station.

4. **September 13, 1914:** Squadron takes on more fuel and supplies.

5. **September 22, 1914:** Squadron shells French station.

6. **October 12–18, 1914:** Squadron takes shore leave and resupplies.

7. **November 1, 1914:** Battle of Coronel off Chilean coast. German squadron sinks two British cruisers; British losses are more than 1,400 sailors.

8. **December 8, 1914:** Falkland Islands battle. Four German cruisers destroyed; German losses are 1,800.

9. **March 14, 1915:** The *Dresden* is scuttled at Robinson Crusoe Island (Más a Tierra) in the Juan Fernández Islands.

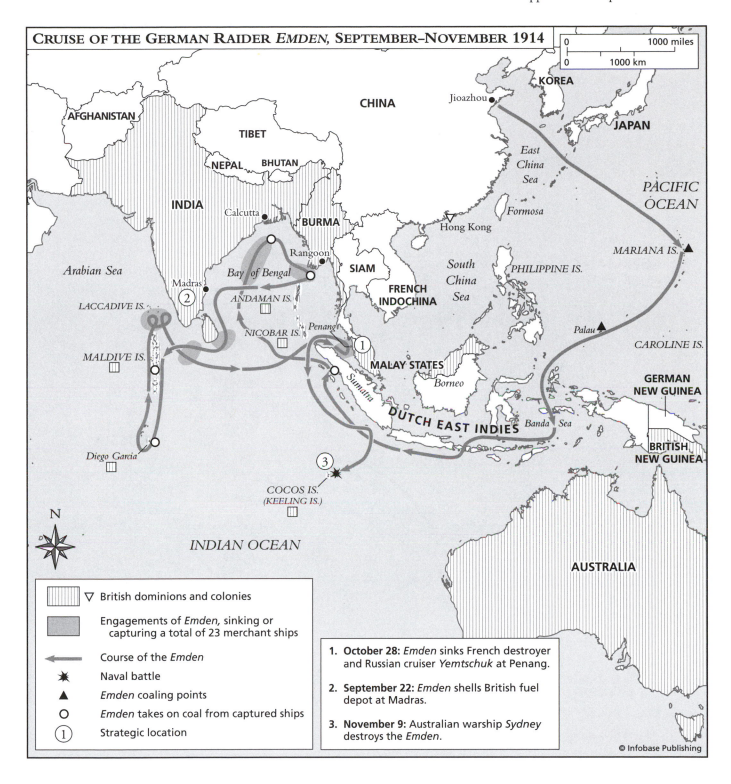

CRUISE OF THE GERMAN RAIDER *Emden*, SEPTEMBER–NOVEMBER 1914

Legend:

- ▽ British dominions and colonies
- Engagements of *Emden*, sinking or capturing a total of 23 merchant ships
- ← Course of the *Emden*
- ✳ Naval battle
- ▲ *Emden* coaling points
- ○ *Emden* takes on coal from captured ships
- ① Strategic location

1. **October 28:** *Emden* sinks French destroyer and Russian cruiser *Yemtschuk* at Penang.

2. **September 22:** *Emden* shells British fuel depot at Madras.

3. **November 9:** Australian warship *Sydney* destroys the *Emden*.

© Infobase Publishing

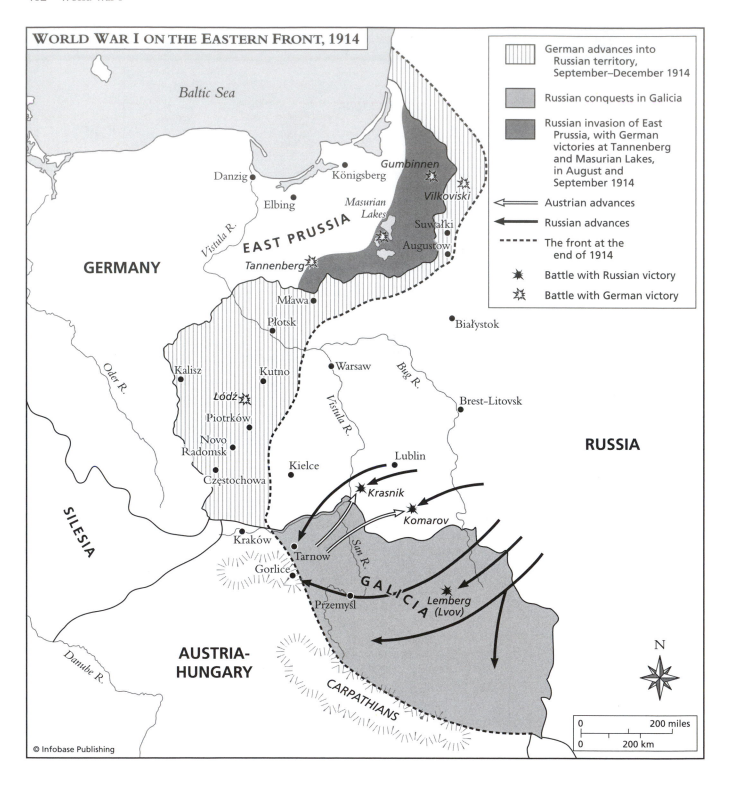

WORLD WAR I ON THE EASTERN FRONT, 1914

Baltic Sea

German advances into Russian territory, September–December 1914

Russian conquests in Galicia

Russian invasion of East Prussia, with German victories at Tannenberg and Masurian Lakes, in August and September 1914

Austrian advances

Russian advances

The front at the end of 1914

Battle with Russian victory

Battle with German victory

Danzig •
Königsberg •
Gumbinnen
Vilkoviski

Elbing •
Masurian Lakes
Suwałki •
Augustow

GERMANY

EAST PRUSSIA

Vistula R.

Tannenberg

Mława •

Płotsk •

• Białystok

Oder R.

Kalisz •
Kutno •
• Warsaw
Bug R.

Łódź

Vistula R.

• Brest-Litovsk

Piotrków •

Novo Radomsk •

• Kielce

RUSSIA

Częstochowa •

SILESIA

• Lublin

Krasnik

Komarov

Kraków •

Tarnow •

San R.

Gorlice •

G A L I C I A

Przemyśl •

Lemberg (Lvov)

AUSTRIA-HUNGARY

Danube R.

CARPATHIANS

N

0   200 miles
0   200 km

© Infobase Publishing

WORLD WAR I IN AFRICA, 1914–1918

German colonial holdings

① Strategic location

Note: Map shows colonial borders as of 1914.

FRENCH WEST AFRICA

ANGLO-EGYPTIAN SUDAN

NORTHERN NIGERIA

FRENCH EQUATORIAL AFRICA

GOLD COAST ①

SOMALILAND

EMPIRE OF ETHIOPIA (neutral)

SOUTHERN NIGERIA

CAMEROONS (KAMERUN)

Duala ③

TOGOLAND

UGANDA

BRITISH EAST AFRICA

SPANISH GUINEA

FRENCH EQUATORIAL AFRICA

BELGIAN CONGO

INDIAN OCEAN

CABINDA

GERMAN EAST AFRICA ⑥

ATLANTIC OCEAN

ANGOLA

NORTHERN RHODESIA

NYASALAND

MOZAMBIQUE

MADAGASCAR

GERMAN SOUTH-WEST AFRICA ②

SOUTHERN RHODESIA

Walvis Bay (BRITAIN)

BECHUANALAND

SWAZILAND

UNION OF SOUTH AFRICA ④ ⑤

BASUTOLAND

N

© Infobase Publishing

1. **August 1914:** Two hundred German troops surrender.

2. **September 1914:** More than 10,000 South African troops desert to the German side.

3. **September 27, 1914:** Main German force defeated at Duala. A small German contingent holds out in the hinterland until mid-February 1916.

4. **October 14, 1914–February 4, 1915:** Boer uprising put down by pro-Allied regime.

5. **July 1915:** South African troops loyal to the Allied side defeat German-Boer forces.

6. **November 1917–November 1918:** German forces, supported by 20,000 African troops, make advances into Rhodesia and Portuguese Mozambique. The German troops did not surrender in Africa until 12 days after the Armistice in Europe.

ABORTIVE ANGLO-FRENCH NAVAL ATTACK ON THE DARDANELLES, MARCH 1915

The abortive attack on the Dardanelles in March 1915 signaled the Turks that an invasion was imminent; the ships turned back after three battleships struck mines in the lower passage. The failure to use submarines with commando raids or aircraft to attack the shore installations of the Turks allowed the Turkish batteries and mines to prevent the fleet from steaming up through the Sea of Marmara to threaten Constantinople.

Aegean Sea

Sari Fort
Agh Bashi Fort
Ak Fort
Sestos Point
Kilia Lodos
Abydos Point
Nagara Baba Fort
Nagara Kalesi
Maidos
Mal Tepe Fort
Anadolu Mejidie Fort
Cham Burnu
Mejidie Avan Fort
Derma Burnu
Namazieh
Kilid Bahr
Chanak
Hamidieh II
Chemenlik
Rumli Mejidieh
Hamidiehi
Yildiz
The Narrows
Messudieh
Sari Sighlar Bay
Kephez Bay
Dardanos

Minefield damages three battleships—Irresistible, Bouvet, and Ocean, causing all three to sink

Cape Helles
Sedd-el-Bahr
Majestic
Prince George
Queen Elizabeth
Agamemnon
Lord Nelson
Inflexible
Vengeance
Gaulois
Triumph
Irresistible
Charlemagne
Bouvet
Albion
Suffren
Ocean
Swiftsure
Kum Kale
Eren Keui Bay

N

	Major Turkish gun emplacement
▲	Minor Turkish gun emplacement
▽	Mobile artillery
◎	Search light
- - -	Minefield
⬭	First-line Allied battleships
◯	Second-line Allied battleships
◼	Turkish forts and batteries

0   3 miles
0   3 km

© Infobase Publishing

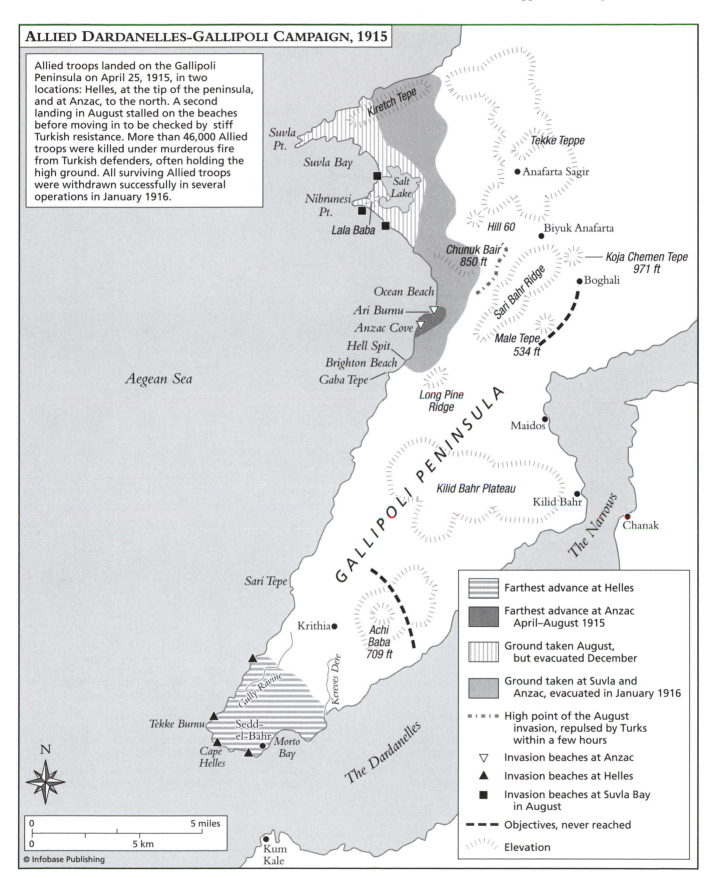

ALLIED DARDANELLES-GALLIPOLI CAMPAIGN, 1915

Allied troops landed on the Gallipoli Peninsula on April 25, 1915, in two locations: Helles, at the tip of the peninsula, and at Anzac, to the north. A second landing in August stalled on the beaches before moving in to be checked by stiff Turkish resistance. More than 46,000 Allied troops were killed under murderous fire from Turkish defenders, often holding the high ground. All surviving Allied troops were withdrawn successfully in several operations in January 1916.

Kiretch Tepe

Suvla Pt.

Suvla Bay

Salt Lake

Nibrunesi Pt.

Lala Baba

Tekke Teppe

Anafarta Sagir

Hill 60

Biyuk Anafarta

Chunuk Bair 850 ft

Koja Chemen Tepe 971 ft

Sari Bahr Ridge

Boghali

Ocean Beach

Ari Burnu

Anzac Cove

Hell Spit

Brighton Beach

Gaba Tepe

Male Tepe 534 ft

Long Pine Ridge

Maidos

Aegean Sea

GALLIPOLI PENINSULA

Kilid Bahr Plateau

Kilid Bahr

The Narrows

Chanak

Sari Tepe

Krithia

Achi Baba 709 ft

Tekke Burnu

Sedd-el-Bahr

Cape Helles

Morto Bay

Gully Ravine

Kereves Dere

The Dardanelles

N

Kum Kale

0   5 miles
0   5 km

© Infobase Publishing

Legend:

- Farthest advance at Helles
- Farthest advance at Anzac April–August 1915
- Ground taken August, but evacuated December
- Ground taken at Suvla and Anzac, evacuated in January 1916
- — · — · High point of the August invasion, repulsed by Turks within a few hours
- ▽ Invasion beaches at Anzac
- ▲ Invasion beaches at Helles
- ■ Invasion beaches at Suvla Bay in August
- - - - Objectives, never reached
- Elevation

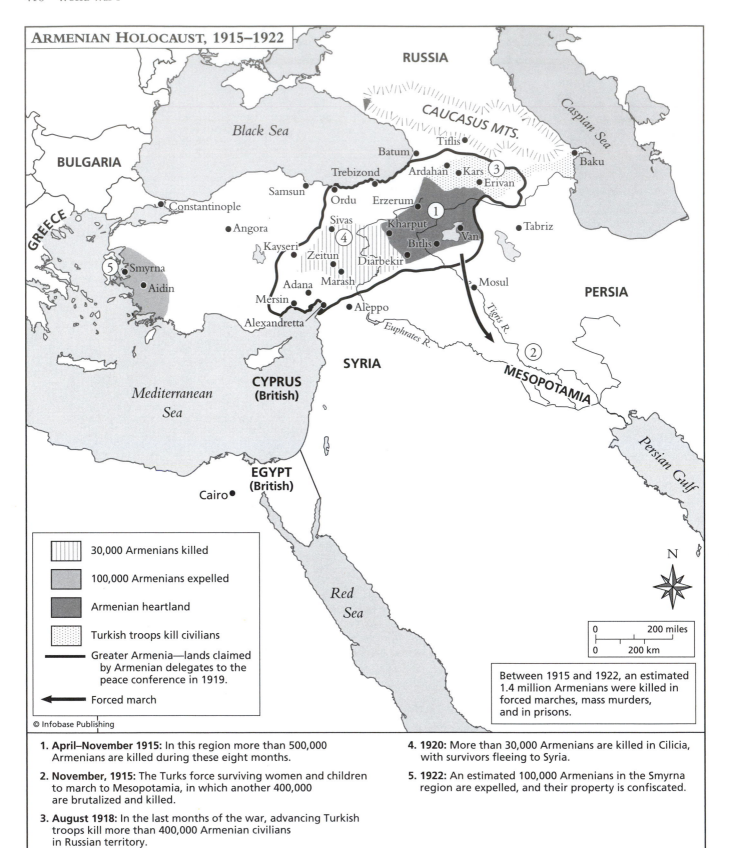

ARMENIAN HOLOCAUST, 1915–1922

RUSSIA

Black Sea

BULGARIA

CAUCASUS MTS.

Caspian Sea

Tiflis

Batum

Ardahan   Kars   ③

Baku

GREECE

Trebizond

Samsun

Constantinople

Ordu

Erzerum   ①

Erivan

Angora

Sivas

Kharput

Tabriz

Kayseri

④

Van

Bitlis

Zeitun

Smyrna

⑤

Diarbekir

Marash

Adana

Aidin

Mersin

Aleppo

Mosul

PERSIA

Alexandretta

Euphrates R.

②

MESOPOTAMIA

SYRIA

CYPRUS
(British)

*Mediterranean
Sea*

EGYPT
(British)

Cairo

*Red
Sea*

Persian Gulf

N

30,000 Armenians killed	
100,000 Armenians expelled	
Armenian heartland	
Turkish troops kill civilians	

Greater Armenia—lands claimed
by Armenian delegates to the
peace conference in 1919.

Forced march

© Infobase Publishing

0   200 miles
0   200 km

Between 1915 and 1922, an estimated
1.4 million Armenians were killed in
forced marches, mass murders,
and in prisons.

1. April–November 1915: In this region more than 500,000 Armenians are killed during these eight months.

2. November, 1915: The Turks force surviving women and children to march to Mesopotamia, in which another 400,000 are brutalized and killed.

3. August 1918: In the last months of the war, advancing Turkish troops kill more than 400,000 Armenian civilians in Russian territory.

4. 1920: More than 30,000 Armenians are killed in Cilicia, with survivors fleeing to Syria.

5. 1922: An estimated 100,000 Armenians in the Smyrna region are expelled, and their property is confiscated.

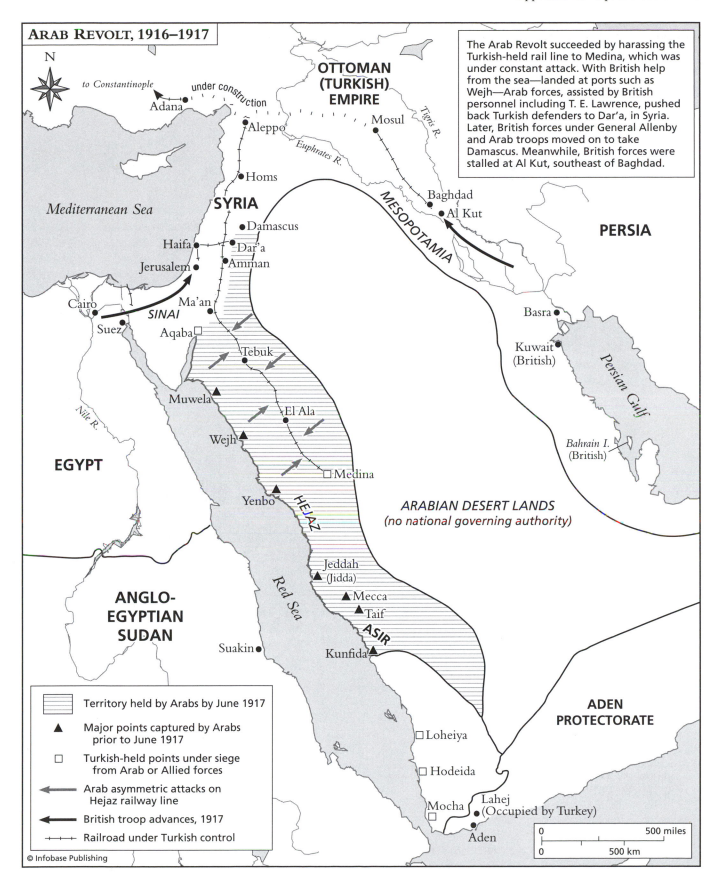

ARAB REVOLT, 1916–1917

N

to Constantinople

under construction

Adana

OTTOMAN (TURKISH) EMPIRE

Aleppo

Mosul

Tigris R.

Euphrates R.

Homs

MESOPOTAMIA

SYRIA

Baghdad

Al Kut

PERSIA

Mediterranean Sea

Damascus

Haifa

Dar'a

Jerusalem

Amman

Basra

Cairo

Ma'an

SINAI

Kuwait (British)

Suez

Aqaba

Persian Gulf

Tebuk

Nile R.

Muwela

El Ala

Bahrain I. (British)

EGYPT

Wejh

Medina

ARABIAN DESERT LANDS
(no national governing authority)

Yenbo

HEJAZ

Red Sea

ANGLO-EGYPTIAN SUDAN

Jeddah (Jidda)

Mecca

Taif

ASIR

Suakin

Kunfida

ADEN PROTECTORATE

The Arab Revolt succeeded by harassing the Turkish-held rail line to Medina, which was under constant attack. With British help from the sea—landed at ports such as Wejh—Arab forces, assisted by British personnel including T. E. Lawrence, pushed back Turkish defenders to Dar'a, in Syria. Later, British forces under General Allenby and Arab troops moved on to take Damascus. Meanwhile, British forces were stalled at Al Kut, southeast of Baghdad.

Loheiya

Hodeida

Mocha

Lahej (Occupied by Turkey)

Aden

Territory held by Arabs by June 1917

▲ Major points captured by Arabs prior to June 1917

☐ Turkish-held points under siege from Arab or Allied forces

← Arab asymmetric attacks on Hejaz railway line

← British troop advances, 1917

+—+ Railroad under Turkish control

0   500 miles

0   500 km

© Infobase Publishing

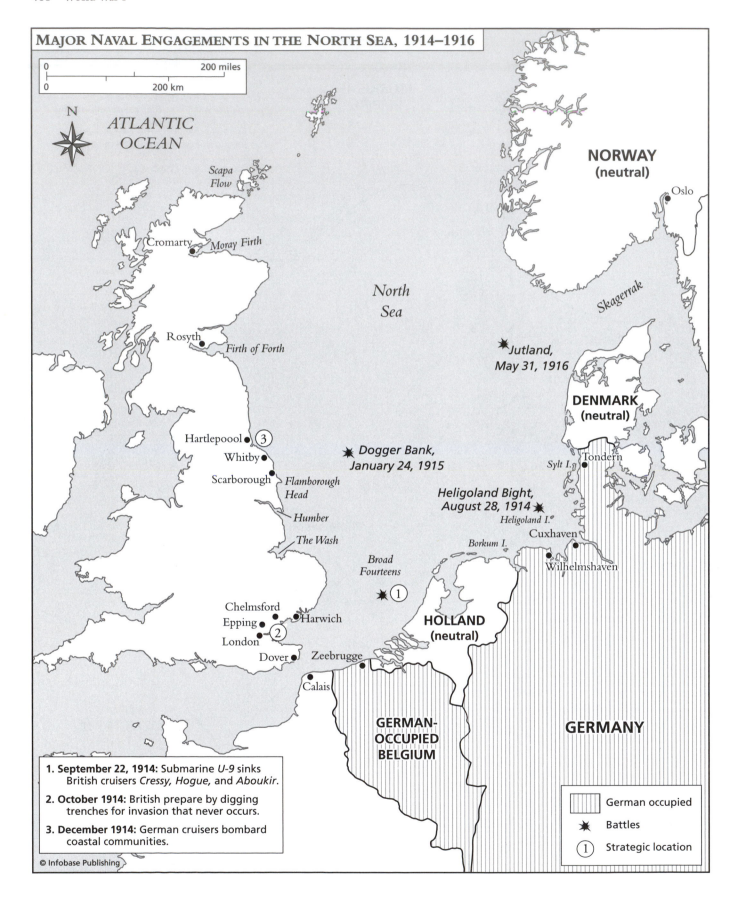

MAJOR NAVAL ENGAGEMENTS IN THE NORTH SEA, 1914–1916

ATLANTIC
OCEAN

NORWAY
(neutral)

Oslo

Scapa
Flow

Cromarty Moray Firth

North
Sea

Skagerrak

Rosyth Firth of Forth

Jutland,
May 31, 1916

DENMARK
(neutral)

Hartlepoool ③
Whitby
Scarborough Flamborough
Head

Dogger Bank,
January 24, 1915

Tondern
Sylt I.

Heligoland Bight,
August 28, 1914
Heligoland I.

Humber
The Wash

Cuxhaven
Borkum I.
Wilhelmshaven

Broad
Fourteens

①

Chelmsford
Epping   Harwich
London ②
Dover Zeebrugge
Calais

HOLLAND
(neutral)

GERMANY

GERMAN-
OCCUPIED
BELGIUM

1. **September 22, 1914:** Submarine *U-9* sinks British cruisers *Cressy, Hogue,* and *Aboukir.*

2. **October 1914:** British prepare by digging trenches for invasion that never occurs.

3. **December 1914:** German cruisers bombard coastal communities.

© Infobase Publishing

German occupied
✳ Battles
① Strategic location

U.S. Ships Sunk, February 3, 1917–April 5, 1917

Date	Ship	G.tons	Location	Number in Crew	Details of Episode
February 3	*Housatonic*	3,143	Off Scilly Islands	37	All crew towed to safety by sub; in barred zone; carrying contraband. Warned.
February 12	*Lyman M. Law*	1,300	Off Sardinia	10	All crew of schooner reached land; ship sunk by German sub. Warned.
March 12	*Algonquin*	2,832	English Channel	26	Crew all reached land safely. Warned.
March 16	*Vigilancia*	4,115	Off Plymouth	43	15 members of crew drowned, including 5 Americans. No warning.
March 17	*City of Memphis*	5,252	Off Ireland	58	All crew abandoned ship safely. Warned.
March 17	*Illinois*	5,225	Off Alderney	34	Tanker in ballast; all crew abandoned ship safely. Warning shots.
March 21	*Healdton*	4,488	Off Holland	41	21 of loaded tanker crew killed by torpedo attack, including 7 Americans; ship steamed in safety zone. No warning.
April 1	*Aztec* (armed)	3,727	Near Brest	51	Struck mine; 28 died, including 11 Americans
April 5	*Missourian*	7,924	In Mediterranean	53	All crew survived; torpedoed without warning.
Totals	**38,006 gross tons**			**353 crew**	**64 deaths, including 23 American deaths**

Source: Compiled from reports in *New York Times,* February 4–April 6, 1917.

HABSBURG TERRITORIES, 1814–1914

Habsburg territory, 1814

Territory regained after Congress of Vienna, 1815

Territory acquired, 1815–1914

—— Austro-Hungarian Empire, 1914

- - - Kingdom of Hungary, 1866

Republic of Kraków
Kraków
Bohemia
Prague
Moravia
Galicia and Lodomeria
Dniester R.
ARCHDUCHY OF AUSTRIA
Bukovina
Lake Constance
Vienna
Danube R.
Budapest
Salzburg
KINGDOM OF HUNGARY
Tyrol
Lake Como
VENETIA
Sava R.
Transylvania
Lombardy
Venice
Trieste
Milan
Lake Garda
CROATIA
Slavonia
Banat
Po R.
Drava R.
Genoa
Bosnia (protectorate, 1878; annexed 1908)
Belgrade
Bucharest
Modena
Danube R.
ITALY
Sarajevo
Sanjak of Novipazar (Occupied, 1878–1909)
Adriatic Sea
Mitrovica

0   100 miles
0   100 km

© Infobase Publishing

DISSOLUTION OF THE HABSBURG EMPIRE, AFTER 1918

Four new states

Territory acquired by Italy

Territory acquired by Poland

Territory acquired by Romania

Territory acquired by Yugoslavia

POLAND
Bohemia
Prague
Moravia
Kraków
Lemberg (Lvov)
Przemyśl
Galicia
Dniester R.
CZECHOSLOVAKIA
GERMANY
Vienna
Danube R.
Bukovina
AUSTRIA
Budapest
SWITZERLAND
Salzburg
HUNGARY
ROMANIA
Lake Constance
Tyrol
ITALY
Lake Como
Venice
Sava R.
Drava R.
Arad
Transylvania
Lake Garda
Trieste
Zagreb
Subotica
Backa
Banat
Po R.
Croatia
Fiume
Slavonia
Bosnia
Belgrade
Bucharest
Dalmatia
Sarajevo
YUGOSLAVIA
Danube R.
Hercegovina
(from 1929; formerly the Kingdom of the Serbs, Croats, and Slovenes)
Adriatic Sea
BULGARIA

The Austro-Hungarian Empire was dissolved at the end of World War I. Four new states were created out of the territories once controlled by the Habsburgs: Austria, Hungary, Czechoslovakia, and the Kingdom of the Serbs, Croats, and Slovenes (changed in 1929 to Yugoslavia). The latter represented the Greater Serbia that had been the aspiration of Narodna Obrana and other Serbian nationalists. Independent Poland gained the territory around Kraków and Galicia. In addition, Romania gained Transylvania, and Italy gained the South Tyrol province and Trieste as rewards for their participation on the Allied side in the war.

0   100 miles
0   100 km

© Infobase Publishing

REDRAWING THE MAP OF CENTRAL EUROPE, 1920

Legend:
- Habsburg territory ceded to Romania and to Serbia
- New states established with the support of the Allied Powers
- Separate countries created from the core of the Habsburg Empire
- Ceded by Russia to Romania

* The Serb-Croat-Slovene kingdom becomes Yugoslavia

0 — 120 miles
0 — 120 km

N

FINLAND (formerly part of Russian Empire)

Lake Ladoga

SWEDEN

ESTONIA

Baltic Sea

LATVIA

LITHUANIA

Free City of Danzig

EAST PRUSSIA

RUSSIA

North Sea

Vistula R.

HOLLAND

GERMANY

POLAND

Elbe R.

Oder R.

Dnieper R.

BELGIUM

LUXEM-BOURG

CZECHOSLOVAKIA (formerly part of the Austro-Hungarian Empire)

Dniester R.

BESSARABIA

FRANCE

Rhine R.

Danube R.

Prut R.

SWITZER-LAND

AUSTRIA

HUNGARY

ROMANIA

Po R.

Free City of Fiume

Sava R.

Black Sea

ITALY

Adriatic Sea

YUGOSLAVIA*

Danube R.

BULGARIA

Corsica

ALBANIA

Sardinia

GREECE

TURKEY

Mediterranean Sea

© Infobase Publishing

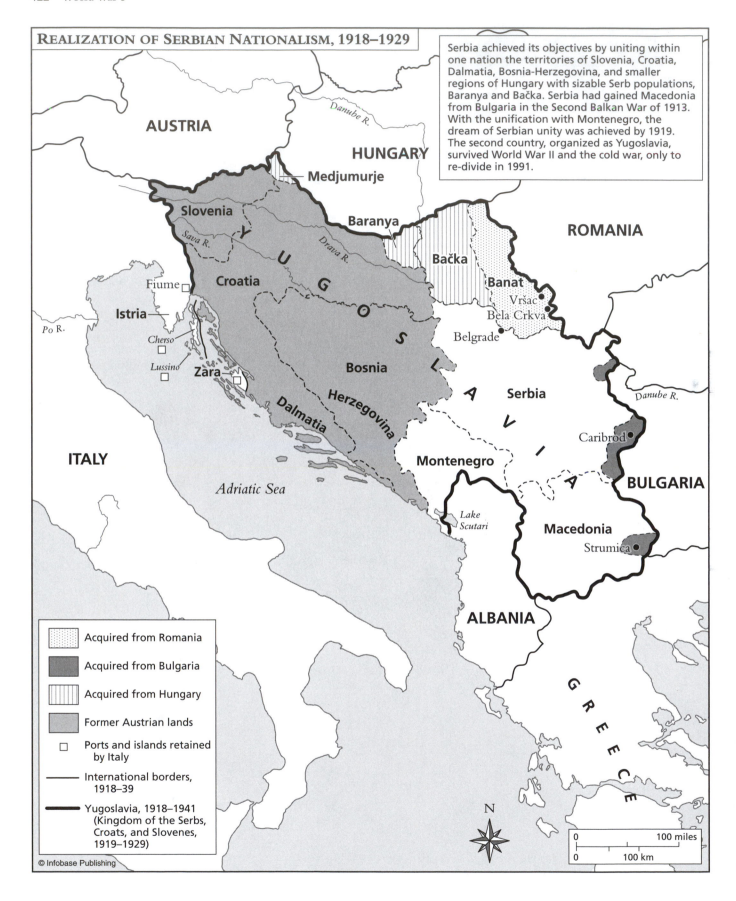

REALIZATION OF SERBIAN NATIONALISM, 1918–1929

Serbia achieved its objectives by uniting within one nation the territories of Slovenia, Croatia, Dalmatia, Bosnia-Herzegovina, and smaller regions of Hungary with sizable Serb populations, Baranya and Bačka. Serbia had gained Macedonia from Bulgaria in the Second Balkan War of 1913. With the unification with Montenegro, the dream of Serbian unity was achieved by 1919. The second country, organized as Yugoslavia, survived World War II and the cold war, only to re-divide in 1991.

AUSTRIA

HUNGARY

ROMANIA

Danube R.

Medjumurje

Slovenia

Baranya

Bačka

YUGOSLAVIA

Sava R.

Drava R.

Croatia

Banat

Vršac

Fiume

Bela Crkva

Istria

Belgrade

Po R.

Cherso

Lussino

Zara

Bosnia

Serbia

Danube R.

Dalmatia

Herzegovina

Caribrod

ITALY

Montenegro

Adriatic Sea

BULGARIA

Lake Scutari

Macedonia

Strumica

ALBANIA

GREECE

Legend:

- Acquired from Romania
- Acquired from Bulgaria
- Acquired from Hungary
- Former Austrian lands
- ☐ Ports and islands retained by Italy
- International borders, 1918–39
- Yugoslavia, 1918–1941 (Kingdom of the Serbs, Croats, and Slovenes, 1919–1929)

N

0　　　　100 miles
0　　　　100 km

© Infobase Publishing

APPENDIX D
Glossary

Allies   The nations arrayed against the Central Powers, beginning with the Triple Entente consisting of Russia, France, and Britain. Eventually included Serbia, Italy, and Japan. The United States, after 1917, was classified as an "Associated Power."

ambulance   A vehicle for carrying wounded, but also a term employed during World War I for a clinic or way-station for the walking wounded.

archies   Anti-aircraft weapons, with shrapnel-loaded shells set to detonate at preset altitudes.

armed neutrality   Doctrine adopted by the United States from March 9, 1917, to April 6, 1917, in which the United States would remain neutral in World War I, but would provide weapons of defense against submarine attacks aboard merchant ships.

asparagus   (German, *der Spargel*)   U-boat crews' slang for the periscope.

Associated Powers   After the United States joined in the war, the American position was that the country would not be officially an ally among the Allies, but rather associated with them in the war effort. Thus in some official documents the Allies after April 1917 were referred to as "The Allied and Associated Powers."

Balkan Peninsula   The section of southeastern Europe comprising the modern nations of Romania, Bulgaria, Greece, Albania, Macedonia, Serbia, Montenegro, Bosnia-Herzegovina, Croatia, and Slovenia. The small section of Turkey known as Thrace that lies on the western, or European, side of the Dardanelles waterway is also part of the Balkan Peninsula. Collectively the countries and provinces of the peninsula are known as "the Balkans."

Ballplatz   The location of the foreign office of the Habsburg Empire in Vienna; colloquially, the foreign policy viewpoint of the empire (similar to the usage of *Quai d'Orsay* for France, *Westminster* for Britain).

batman   In the British army, an officer's servant.

black chamber   A secret office devoted to the decoding of secret diplomatic and military correspondence of foreign powers, deriving from the Cabinet Noir established in France in the reign of King Louis XIII (1601–43), the first regular French intelligence service.

Blighty   British slang for being wounded sufficiently to be sent back to Britain, as in "going to Blighty" or "got Blighty."

Blutmühle   German term for the nature of war on the western front; literally, "blood-mill."

Boche   Contemptuously, the Germans, as used by Allied writers and personnel. From the French *alboche*, derived from the phrase *allemand caboche*, "German thickhead."

Central Powers   Germany, Austria-Hungary, Bulgaria, and the Ottoman Empire.

comitadjis   (*komitadschis*)   Irregular Serbian militias or "free corps" organized after 1910, effective in raids into Macedonia and serving alongside Serbian army units in the Balkan Wars of 1912–13.

communication trench   A trench dug between two defensive trenches or forward into no-man's–land through which troops could advance without being exposed to enemy fire.

contraband   Goods that are prohibited by a blockading state from shipment to the blockaded state. The traditional contraband of war included weapons, transport equipment, and ammunition. Britain added food and all other goods to the contraband list, declaring a total blockade of Germany in early 1915.

cordite   Smokeless powder used for small arms, such as rifles.

Cyrillic alphabet   By tradition, this alphabet was developed by Saint Cyril (827–869), Apostle to the Slavs, but more likely it was developed in the 10th century by Bulgarian scholars. The alphabet is used by Russians, Bulgarians, Serbs, Ukrainians, and Macedonians.

dreadnought   A battleship; named after the British 1906 *Dreadnought* that set a new standard as a heavily armored ship carrying only large guns. Both Britain and Germany launched several ships of the dreadnought class between 1906 and 1914.

dug-out   An underground shelter connected by trenches to the front line, held up by timbers and usually covered with a foot or more of earth; later, the term applied ironically to more luxurious commandeered quarters, including palaces and other fine buildings; by the end of the war, the term was used derogatorily to refer to officers who had been stationed in relative comfort to the rear of the front line.

éclopé   French term for the walking wounded from the front.

fire-step   In the trenches, a step above the floor that allowed standing soldiers to peer over the front edge of the trench and fire their weapons at the enemy.

Flammenwerfer   German flame throwers that spouted ignited gasoline from hoses attached to petrol tanks carried on the backs of infantrymen.

foc'sle   Abbreviated expression for *forecastle,* the most forward compartment of a ship, often used as the crew's quarters.

Fritz   A German; term employed by the British.

Fritzies   German 42-cm shells, fired from "Jack Johnsons."

gelignite   A high-explosive nitroglycerine-nitrocellulose combination employed in artillery shells and bombs in World War I.

Gouslars   The legendary minstrels of the Serbian people; according to nationalist legend, the Gouslars conveyed views of liberty and equality.

guerre d'usure   The French term for the tactic of war by attrition.

Huns   The Germans; term employed by the French and later by all the Allies, with reference to the fact that the invasion of the Huns (Magyars) was stopped in western Europe more or less where the German invasion of 1914–15 was stopped in modern France. Since the Magyar invasion was remembered as "barbaric," the term implied similar behavior on the part of the Germans.

irredentism   The political movement to incorporate ethnic members of a national group, living under foreign rule, into the borders of the home state; so named after the 19th-century Italian movement to incorporate the "*irredenta,*" meaning "unredeemed" Italian nationals, into a single state.

mandate   Under international agreements, the recognized right to run the civil and military affairs of a territory without acquiring sovereignty over it; thus the Habsburg Empire had a mandate over Bosnia-Herzegovina from 1878 to 1908 while the Ottoman Empire retained nominal sovereignty there. The mandate principle was utilized after World War I, for League of Nations-recognized mandates over former territories of the Ottoman Empire and colonies of the German Empire.

Materialschlachten   The German word for the tactic of war by attrition, literally "battles of material."

mitrailleuse   A multi-barreled machine gun or, more generally, any type of machine gun.

morganatic marriage   In royal marriages, one that involved a prenuptial agreement that in the event of the death of the monarch, the title and other rights inherent by right of birth would not be passed to the children of the marriage, usually because of the lower-ranking birth of one member of the couple. The marriage of Ferdinand and Sophie was such a marriage; while Ferdinand was slated to inherit the throne from his childless uncle Franz Josef, Ferdinand's own children born by Sophie would not be in the line of succession.

nap   A card game popular with the troops in World War I in which the highest bidder named the trump suit; named for Napoleon.

New Army   The British force built up through conscription, rather than volunteers, that began to see service on the western front in 1916.

no-man's-land   The area between the forwardmost trenches of enemy sides, usually devastated by shell holes and strung with barbed-wire coils or strands to slow an attack from the other side.

Old Serbia   *(Old Servia)*   The province of Kosovo, ruled out of Albania by the Ottoman Empire prior to 1912; regarded as the ancestral home of Serbians.

panne   A forced landing of an aircraft.

parapet   The leading edge of a trench, facing toward the enemy lines, from which troops would fire at the enemy; usually banked higher than the rear edge.

Piedmont   The province of Italy that was the base for Italian nationalism in the 19th century; as the original homeland for irredentism, the name of the province became synonymous with revolutionary nationalism. Hence, the *Ujedinjenji ili Smrt* (Black Hand) movement adopted the name of the province in the Serb language, *Pijemont* (also spelled *Piemont*), for its newspaper, implying that Serbia would be the "Piedmont" province of South-Slav unification, intended to echo the province around which Italy had united in the 19th century.

pillbox   A small concrete fortification, shaped like the round box used to carry pills, developed by German engineers.

poilus   French term of endearment refering to unshaven French enlisted men in the trenches, and more generally any French soldier; literally, the hairy or unshaven ones.

Porte, The (short for *The Sublime Porte—"The High Gate"*)   The location of the courts and government of the Ottoman Empire; colloquially, the viewpoint of the Ottoman Empire, similar to the usage of *Ballplatz* to refer to the foreign ministries of the Austro-Hungarian Empire.

portside   The left side of a ship when facing forward.

Q-ship   British steamers and schooners that were outfitted with concealed weapons; used as decoys to lure German submarines into attack, when the British fighting flag (ensign) would be raised and the submarine fired on and sometimes destroyed.

Quai d'Orsay   The location of the French foreign office, hence used to refer to the French position in international affairs.

regicide   The act of killing a monarch; an individual guilty of such a crime.

revanche   A political movement that expressed the urge for national revenge; particularly applied to French anger at the loss of Alsace-Lorraine to Germany in 1871. More generally applied to national revenge movements, such as Serbian revenge for the establishment of Austro-Hungarian sovereignty over Bosnia-Herzegovina.

Room 40   British Naval Intelligence office, headed by William ("Blinker") Hall, maintained in Room 40 of the Old Admiralty Building in London, devoted to deciphering foreign diplomatic and military codes.

ruse de guerre   French term for a ruse or deception of war, applied particularly to the use of false neutral flags and markings by merchant ships to avoid being identified as British by German U-boats. More generally, any deception used in war, such as the planting of false documents, or mounting a pretense of attack on one point while quietly moving to retreat or attack another point.

salient   An advanced position achieved by one side that is ahead of the general line on a battle front, thus exposing flanks to counterattack. Germany maintained a pronounced salient into the French lines at St. Mihiel for most of World War I.

sanjak   Within the Ottoman Empire, provinces were known as vilayets, and sanjaks were administrative subdivisions within vilayets. The Sanjak of Novi Pazar was militarily occupied by the Habsburgs from 1878 to 1908 as a possible route for a railroad and as a geopolitical barrier between Serbia and Montenegro.

sap-head   The front or fathermost point of a trench or tunnel, where the digging had stopped.

seventy-five (*soixante-quinze*)   75-caliber cannon, part of the French arsenal.

shipperke   A breed of small dog in Belgium, often used to guard canal boats; Frederick Palmer compared Belgian national character and resistance to the German invasion to the *shipperkes'* vigorous defense of their boats.

shrapnel   Metal balls loaded in artillery shells as antipersonnel weapons, or in antiaircraft shells. Named after a British artillery officer who developed the concept, Henry Shrapnel (1761–1842).

Territorials   British troops originally organized to defend the home territory, that is, the British Isles.

Tommy Atkins   Collective name for the British soldier. In later years, reduced to "Tommy." The name originated in the use of the name "Thomas Atkins" on sample forms in official British army regulations after 1815.

Triple Alliance   A shaky alliance between the German Empire, the Austro-Hungarian Empire, and Italy. Italian resentment at Austria had so damaged the alliance by 1914, that Italy was at first neutral in the Great War, then sided with the Triple Entente against her former allies, Germany and Austria-Hungary.

Triple Entente   Consisting of France, Russia, and Britain, the Triple Entente was an offset to the Triple Alliance; the Entente formed the core of the group later known as "the Allies," which fought against Germany, Austria-Hungary, and the Ottoman Empire, known as the "Central Powers."

uhlan   The German lance-carrying cavalry; a cavalryman.

U-boat (*Unterseeboot*, undersea boat)   German submarine.

Ujedinjenji ili Smrt (Unification or Death)   Informally called *Crna Ruka,* the Black Hand, apparently after a popular novel of the period with a cover that showed a black hand clutching a pistol.

western front   The battle line between German forces and those of England, Belgium, and France, which extended from the English Channel through Belgium and France to the border of neutral Switzerland.

W/T   Wireless telegraph. Radio that used Morse code for sending messages.

NOTES

(Citations to sources are presented here only for direct quotations that appear in the chapter narratives. Sources for Eyewitness Testimony material are presented at the end of each testimony selection and in the general bibliography.)

CHAPTER 1

1. Lavender Cassells, *The Archduke and the Assassin* (Stein and Day, 1985), p. 176.

CHAPTER 3

1. As quoted in Edwyn A. Gray, *The Killing Time* (Scribners, 1972), p. 6.

CHAPTER 7

1. George Washington's Farewell Address is widely reproduced. An authoritative source is James D. Richardson, ed., *The Compilation of the Messages and Papers of the Presidents, 1789–1897,* Vol. I (Washington, D.C.: By Authority of Congress, 1899), pp. 222–223.
2. Woodrow Wilson, Message to Congress, 63rd Congress, 2nd Session, Senate Doc. No. 566 (Washington, D.C.: 1914), pp. 3–4.
3. W. G. McAdoo, *Crowded Years: The Reminiscences of William Gibbs McAdoo* (Houghton Mifflin, 1931), pp. 333–336.

4. Edwyn A. Gray, *The Killing Time* (Scribners, 1972), p. 87.
5. The Sussex note is reproduced in many sources, for example, W. G. McAdoo, *Crowded Years: The Reminiscences of William Gibbs McAdoo* (Houghton Mifflin, 1931), p. 367.
6. James's campaign rhetoric is quoted in McAdoo, *Crowded Years: The Reminiscences of William Gibbs McAdoo* (Houghton Mifflin, 1931), p. 365.

CHAPTER 8

1. Woodrow Wilson, March 4, 1917, as quoted in David Houston, *Eight Years with Wilson's Cabinet, 1913 to 1920* (Doubleday, Page & Company, 1926), p. 240.
2. Bernard Ridder, publisher of the *Staats-Zeitung,* quoted in "Ridder Repudiates Zimmermann Plot," *New York Times,* March 4, 1917, p. 2.

CHAPTER 9

1. Mark Sullivan, *Our Times, 1900–1925,* Vol. 5 (Scribners, 1926), p. 280.
2. Joseph Tumulty, *Wilson as I Know Him* (Doubleday, Page & Company, 1921), p. 266.

BIBLIOGRAPHY

OFFICIAL GOVERNMENT DOCUMENT COLLECTIONS RELATING TO THE CAUSES OF THE WAR

"Austrian Red Book": Austro-Hungarian Monarchy. *Austrian Red Book—Official Files Pertaining to Pre-War History.* London: G. Allen & Unwin, Ltd., 1920.

Collected Diplomatic Documents Relating to the Outbreak of the European War. London: Harrison and Sons, 1915.

"French Yellow Book": France, Ministry of Foreign Affairs. *"French Yellow Book": France and the European War: Full text of diplomatic documents/authorized translation by the Paris correspondent of the* Times *for the French government, relating to the negotiations which preceded the declaration of war by Germany (August 1, 1914) and by France (August 4, 1914).* London: Times Publishing Company, 1914.

"German White Book": Oxford University Press. *German White Book Concerning the responsibility of the authors of the war, translated by the Carnegie Endowment for International Peace, Division of International Law.* New York: Oxford University Press, 1924.

Oxford University Press. *Official German Documents Relating to the World War, Translated under the supervision of the Carnegie Endowment for International Peace.* New York: Oxford University Press, 1923.

MEMOIRS, DIARIES, LETTER COLLECTIONS, AND SELECTED SECONDARY WORKS

Adams, Bernard. *Nothing of Importance: A Record of Eight Months at the Front with a Welsh Battalion, October 1915 to June 1916.* 1917. Reprint, Stevenage, England: Strong Oak Press, 1988.

Aldrich, Mildred. *On the Edge of the War Zone: From the Battle of the Marne to the Entrance of the Stars and Stripes.* Boston: Small, Maynard, 1917.

Aldridge, Olive M. *The Retreat from Serbia through Montenegro and Albania.* London: Minerva, 1916.

Allen, Frederick Lewis. *Only Yesterday—An Informal History of the 1920s.* New York: Harper and Brothers, 1931.

Andrew, Christopher. *Her Majesty's Secret Service: The Making of the British Intelligence Community.* New York: Penguin, 1987.

Andreyev, Leonid. *The Confessions of a Little Man during Great Days.* Translated by R. S. Townsend. New York: Alfred A. Knopf, 1917.

Ashmead-Bartlett, E. *Some of My Experiences in the Great War.* London: George Newnes, 1918.

Aubrey, Herbert. *Mons, Anzac and Kut.* London: Edward Arnold, 1919.

Baker, Ray Stannard. *Woodrow Wilson and World Settlement: Written from His Unpublished and Personal Material.* Vol. 2. Garden City, N.Y.: Doubleday, Page, 1923.

Baker, Ray Stannard, and William F. Dodd, eds. *The Public Papers of Woodrow Wilson: War and Peace, Presidential Messages, Addresses, and Public Papers, (1917–1924).* Vol. 1. New York: Harper & Brothers, 1927.

Baruch, Bernard M. *The Making of the Reparation and Economic Sections of the Treaty.* New York: Harper & Brothers, 1920.

Beatson, A. M. *The Motor-Bus in War: Being the Impressions of an A.S.C. Officer during Two and a Half Years at the Front.* London: T. Fisher Unwin, 1918.

Beesly, Patrick. *Room 40: British Naval Intelligence, 1914–1918.* New York: Harcourt Brace Jovanovich, 1982.

Ben-Horin, Eliahu. *The Middle East: Crossroads of History.* New York: W.W. Norton, 1943.

Berman, Ronald. *Fitzgerald, Hemingway, and the Twenties.* Tuscaloosa: University of Alabama Press, 2001.

Betts, Ernest. *The Bagging of Baghdad.* London: John Lane, 1920.

Binding, Rudolf. *A Fatalist at War.* Translated by Ian F. D. Morrow. Boston: Houghton Mifflin, 1929.

Bonsal, Stephen. *Suitors and Suppliants: The Little Nations at Versailles.* Port Washington, N.Y.: Kennikat Press, 1969.

———. *Unfinished Business.* Garden City, N.Y.: Doubleday, Doran, 1944.

Bristow, Nancy K. *Making Men Moral: Social Engineering during the Great War.* New York: New York University Press, 1996.

Browder, Robert Paul, and Alexander Kerensky. *The Russian Provisional Government, 1917: Documents.* Stanford, Calif.: Hoover Institution Publications, Stanford University Press, 1961.

Brown, Carrie. *Rosie's Mom: Forgotten Women Workers of the First World War.* Boston: Northeastern University Press, 2002.

Bryan, William Jennings, and Mary Baird Bryan, *The Memoirs of William Jennings Bryan.* Philadelphia: John C. Winston, 1925.

Buswell, Leslie. *Ambulance No. 10: Personal Letters from the Front.* Boston: Houghton Mifflin, 1916.

Campbell, Rear Admiral Gordon. *My Mystery Ships.* London: Hodder and Stoughton, 1928.

Cassells, Lavender. *The Archduke and the Assassin: Sarajevo, June 28, 1914.* New York: Stein and Day, 1985.

Cavill, H. W. *Imperishable Anzacs: A Story of Australia's Famous First Brigade.* Sydney, Australia: William Brooks, 1916.

Chapman, Guy. *A Passionate Prodigality.* New York: Holt Rinehart Winston, 1933, 1966.

Coben, Stanley. *Rebellion against Victorianism: The Impetus for Cultural Change in 1920s America.* New York: Oxford University Press, 1991.

Cowley, Robert. *1918: Gamble for Victory: The Greatest Attack of World War I.* New York: Macmillan, 1964.

Creighton, Rev. Oswin. *With the 29th Division in Gallipoli.* London: Longmans, Green, 1916.

Cummings, E. E. *The Enormous Room.* New York: Modern Library, 1934.

Danelski, David J., and Joseph S. Tulchin. *The Autobiographical Notes of Charles Evans Hughes.* Cambridge, Mass.: Harvard University Press, 1973.

Daniels, Josephus. *The Wilson Era: Years of Peace—1910–1917.* Chapel Hill: University of North Carolina Press, 1946.

———. *The Wilson Era: Years of War and After—1917–1923.* Chapel Hill: University of North Carolina, 1946.

Dawson, Coningsby. *Living Bayonets: A Record of the Last Push.* London: John Lane, 1919.

Dearstyne, Howard. *Inside the Bauhaus.* New York: Rizzoli International, 1986.

Dragnich, Alex N. *Serbia, Nikola Pašić, and Yugoslavia.* New Brunswick, N.J.: Rutgers University Press, 1974.

Early, Frances. H. *A World without War: How U.S. Feminists and Pacifists Resisted World War I.* Syracuse, N.Y.: Syracuse University Press, 1997.

Einstein, Lewis. *Inside Constantinople: A Diplomatist's Diary during the Dardanelles Expedition.* New York: E. P. Dutton, 1918.

Ellis, L. Ethan. *Republican Foreign Policy, 1921–1933.* New Brunswick, N.J.: Rutgers University Press, 1968.

Ellis, Mark. *Race, War, and Surveillance: African Americans and the United States Government during World War I.* Bloomington: Indiana University Press, 2001.

Ewing, William. *From Gallipoli to Baghdad.* London: Hodder and Stoughton, 1917.

Fay, Sidney Bradshaw. *The Origins of the World War.* 2nd ed. New York: Macmillan, 1947.

Fitzsimons, Bernard, ed. *Warships and Sea Battles of World War I.* London: BPC Publishing, 1973.

Foner, Philip S. *Women and the American Labor Movement: From World War I to the Present.* New York: Free Press, 1980.

Forstner, G. G. von. *The Journal of Submarine Commander Von Forstner.* Translated by Mrs. Russell Codman. Boston and New York: Houghton Mifflin, 1917.

Fox, Henry L., ed. *What the "Boys" Did over There—By "Themselves."* New York: Allied Overseas Veterans' Stories, 1919.

Frothingham, Thomas Goddard. *Naval History of the World War.* Cambridge, Mass.: Harvard University Press, 1925.

Gallishaw, John. *Trenching at Gallipoli: The Personal Narrative of a Newfoundlander with the Ill-Fated Dardanelles Expedition.* New York: Century, 1916.

Garvey, Amy Jacques, ed. *Philosophy and Opinion of Marcus Garvey.* 2nd ed. London: Frank Cass, 1967.

Gavin, Lettie. *American Women in World War I: They Also Served.* Niwot: University Press of Colorado, 1997.

Gibbs, Philip. *Now It Can Be Told.* New York: Harper & Brothers, 1920.

Gillam, Major John Graham. *Gallipoli Diary.* London: George Allen & Unwin, 1918.

Goldman, Emma. *Living My Life.* Vol. 2. New York: Knopf, 1931. Reprint, New York: Dover, 1970.

Goodspeed, D. J. *The Conspirators: A Study of the Coup d'Etat.* Toronto: Macmillan of Canada, 1962.

Graves, Robert. *Goodbye to All That.* New York: Blue Ribbon Books, 1930.

Greenwald, Maurine Weiner. *Women, War and Work: The Impact of World War I on Women Workers in the United States.* Ithaca, N.Y.: Cornell University Press, 1990.

Grey, Viscount, of Fallodon (Edward Grey). *Twenty-Five Years, 1892–1916.* Vol. 2. New York: Stokes, 1925.

Hall, James Norman. *Kitchener's Mob; The Adventures of an American in the British Army.* Boston: Houghton Mifflin, 1916.

Harbaugh, William H., ed. *The Writings of Theodore Roosevelt.* Indianapolis: Bobbs-Merrill, 1967.

Harries, Meiron, and Susie Harries. *The Last Days of Innocence: America at War, 1917–1918.* New York: Random House, 1997.

Held, Joseph, ed. *The Columbia History of Eastern Europe in the Twentieth Century.* New York: Columbia University Press, 1992.

Hendrick, Burton J., ed. *The Life and Letters of Walter H. Page.* Vol. 2. Garden City, N.Y.: Doubleday, Page, 1922.

Herrmann, David G. *The Arming of Europe and the Making of the First World War.* Princeton, N.J.: Princeton University Press, 1996.

Heywood, Chester D. *Negro Combat Troops in the World War: The Story of the 37th Infantry.* Worcester, Mass.: Commonwealth Press, 1929. Reprint, New York: AMS Press, 1969.

Hockley, A. H. Farrar. *The Somme.* London: Pan Books, 1964.

Horn, Daniel. *The German Naval Mutinies of World War I.* New Brunswick, N.J.: Rutgers University Press, 1969.

———. *War, Mutiny and Revolution in the German Navy: The World War I Diary of Seaman Richard Stumpf.* Edited and translated by David Horn. New Brunswick, N.J.: Rutgers University Press, 1967.

Horne, Charles F., and Walter F. Austin, eds. *Source Records of the Great War.* Vols. 2, 3, and 6. New York: Victor Scott, 1923.

Houston, David F. *Eight Years with Wilson's Cabinet: 1913 to 1920.* Vol 1. Garden City, N.Y.: Doubleday, Page, 1926.

Howe, Mark Anthony De Wolfe. *The Harvard Volunteers in Europe: Personal Records of Experience in Military, Ambulance, and Hospital Service.* Cambridge, Mass.: Harvard University Press, 1916.

Hughes, Langston. *The Collected Works of Langston Hughes.* Vol. 10, *The Fight for Freedom and Other Writings on Civil Rights.* Edited by Christopher C. DeSantis. Columbia: University of Missouri Press, 2001.

Isaacs, Edouard Victor. *Prisoner of the U-90.* Boston and New York: Houghton Mifflin, 1919.

Jannen, William, Jr. *The Lions of July: Prelude to War, 1914.* Novato, Calif.: Presidio, 1996.

Jaszi, Oscar. *The Dissolution of the Habsburg Monarchy.* Chicago: University of Chicago Press, 1929.

Jellicoe, John. *The Grand Fleet, 1914–1916.* New York: George H. Doran, 1919.

Jensen, Joan M. *Army Surveillance in America, 1775–1980.* New Haven, Conn.: Yale University Press, 1991.

Jordan, William G. *Black Newspapers and America's War for Democracy, 1914–1920.* Chapel Hill: University of North Carolina Press, 2001.

Kahn, David. *The Codebreakers: The Story of Secret Writing.* New York: Macmillan, 1967.

Kautz, John Iden. *Trucking to the Trenches.* Boston and New York: Houghton Mifflin, 1916.

Kennedy, David M. *Over Here: The First World War and American Society.* New York: Oxford University Press, 1980.

King, Jere Clemens. *The First World War.* New York: Walker, 1972.

Kornweibel, Theodore, Jr. *"Investigate Everything": Federal Efforts to Compel Black Loyalty during World War I.* Bloomington: Indiana University Press, 2002.

Kreisler, Fritz. *Four Weeks in the Trenches: The War Story of a Violinist.* Boston and New York: Houghton Mifflin, 1917.

Lansing, Robert. *The Peace Negotiations: A Personal Narrative.* Boston: Houghton Mifflin, 1921.

Lawrence, T. E. *Revolt in the Desert.* New York: George H. Doran, 1927. Republished in a longer version as *Seven Pillars of Wisdom.* New York: Doubleday, 1935.

Lepsius, Johannes, Albrecht Mendelssohn-Bartholdy, and Friedrich Thimme, eds. *Die große Politik der europäischen Kabinette, 1871–1914; Sammlung der diplomatischen Akten des Auswärtigen Amtes.* 40 vols. Berlin: Deutsche Verlagsgesellschaft für Politik und Geschichte, 1922–1927.

Lincoln, W. Bruce. *Passage through Armageddon: The Russians in War and Revolution, 1914–1918.* New York: Simon and Schuster, 1986.

Link, Arthur, et al., eds. *The Papers of Woodrow Wilson.* Vols. 45, 46, and 51. Princeton, N.J.: Princeton University Press, 1982.

Lloyd George, David. *War Memoirs of David Lloyd George: 1918.* Boston: Little, Brown, 1937.

Ludendorff, Erich Von. *Ludendorff's Own Story.* Vol. 1, *August 1914–November 1918.* New York: Harper & Brothers, 1919.

Lussu, Emilio. *Sardinian Brigade.* Harrisburg, Pa.: Stackpole Books, 1967.

Mack, Arthur. *Shellproof Mack: An American's Fighting Story.* Boston: Small, Maynard, 1918.

Masefield, John. *Gallipoli.* New York: Macmillan, 1916.

May, Ernest R., ed. *The Coming of War, 1917.* The Berkeley Series in American History. Chicago: Rand McNally, 1963.

May, Henry F. *The End of American Innocence: A Study of the First Years of Our Own Time, 1912–1917.* New York: Alfred A. Knopf, 1959.

McAdoo, William Gibbs. *Crowded Years: The Reminiscences of William Gibbs McAdoo.* Boston and New York: Houghton Mifflin, 1931.

McCustra, "Trooper" L. *Gallipoli Days and Nights.* London: Hodder and Stoughton, 1916.

Moorehead, Alan. *Gallipoli.* New York: Harper, 1956.

Morgenthau, Henry. *Ambassador Morgenthau's Story.* Garden City, N.Y.: Doubleday, 1918.

Morison, Elting E., and John M. Blum. *The Letters of Theodore Roosevelt.* Vol. 8. Cambridge, Mass.: Harvard University Press, 1951–54.

Mussolini, Benito. *My Autobiography.* New York: Charles Scribner's Sons, 1928.

Nevinson, Henry W. *The Dardanelles Campaign*. New York: Henry Holt, 1919.

Nicholson, Harold. *Peacemaking, 1919*. New York: Grosset and Dunlap, 1965.

Noble, George Bernard. *Policies and Opinions at Paris, 1919: Wilsonian Diplomacy, the Versailles Peace, and French Public Opinion*. New York: Howard Fertig, 1968.

Page, Walter Hines. *The Life and Letters*. 8 vols. London: Heinemann, 1923–25.

Palmer, Frederick. *My Second Year of the War*. New York: Dodd, Mead, 1917.

———. *My Year of the Great War*. New York: Dodd, Mead, 1917.

———. *With My Own Eyes*. Indianapolis: Bobbs-Merrill, 1932.

Patterson, A. Temple. *The Jellicoe Papers: Selections from the Private and Official Correspondence of Admiral of the Fleet Earl Jellicoe of Scapa*. Shortlands, Kent: Navy Records Society, 1966.

Price, Alan. *The End of the Age of Innocence: Edith Wharton and the First World War*. New York: St. Martin's Press, 1996.

Purdom, C. B., ed. *Everyman at War: Sixty Personal Narratives of the War*. London: J. M. Dent, 1930.

Reed, John. *Ten Days That Shook the World*. Edited by Bertram Wolfe. New York: Modern Library, 1960.

Richards, Frank. *Old Soldiers Never Die*. New York: Berkley Publishing, 1966.

Richardson, James D., ed. *The Compilation of the Messages and Papers of the Presidents, 1789–1897*. Vol. 1. Washington, D.C.: By Authority of Congress, 1899.

Riddell, George. *Lord Riddell's War Diary, 1914–1918*. London: Ivor Nicholson & Watson, 1933.

Robeson, Paul, Jr. *The Undiscovered Paul Robeson: An Artist's Journey, 1898–1939*. New York: John Wiley, 1991.

Robien, Louis de. *The Diary of a Diplomat in Russia, 1917–1918*. Translated by Camilla Sykes. New York: Praeger, 1969.

Ross, Stewart Halsey. *Propaganda for War: How the United States Was Conditioned to Fight the Great War of 1914–1918*. Jefferson, N.C.: Macfarland, 1996.

Sanders, Liman von. *Five Years in Turkey*. Annapolis, Md.: Naval Institute Press, 1928.

Scheer, Reinhard. *Germany's High Seas Fleet in the World War.* London: Cassell, 1920.

Schreiner, George Abel. *From Berlin to Bagdad: Behind the Scenes in the Near East.* New York: Harper & Brothers, 1918.

Seaman, L. C. B. *Post-Victorian Britain, 1902–1951.* London: Methuen University Paperbacks, 1967.

Seymour, Charles. *Letters from the Paris Peace Conference.* Edited by Harold B. Whiteman, Jr. New Haven, Conn.: Yale University Press, 1965.

———. *Woodrow Wilson and the World War.* New Haven, Conn.: Yale University Press, 1921.

Seymour, Charles, ed. *The Intimate Papers of Colonel House.* Boston and New York: Houghton Mifflin, 1926, 1928.

Sharp, Alan. *The Versailles Settlement: Peacemaking in Paris, 1919.* New York: St. Martin's Press, 1991.

Sinclair, Andrew. *The Available Man: The Life Behind the Masks of Warren Gamaliel Harding.* New York: Macmillan, 1965.

Smith, Munroe, ed. *Out of Their Own Mouths.* New York: D. Appleton, 1917.

Stephenson, Graham. *Russia from 1812 to 1945, A History.* New York: Praeger, 1970.

Stone, Ralph A. *Wilson and the League of Nations.* New York: Holt Rinehart Winston, 1967.

Strachan, Hew, ed. *World War I: A History.* New York: Oxford University Press, 1998.

Sukanov, Nikolai Nikolayevich (Himmer). *The Russian Revolution.* 3 vols. Translated by Joel Carmichael. New York: Harper, 1962.

Sullivan, Mark. *Our Times, 1900–1925.* New York: Scribner, 1926.

Tabachnick, Stephen Ely. *T. E. Lawrence.* Rev. ed. New York: Twayne, 1997.

Taylor, A. J. P. *The First World War: An Illustrated History.* New York: Perigree Books, 1970.

Thomas, Lowell. *Raiders of the Deep.* Garden City, N.Y.: Garden City Publishing, 1928.

Triplett, William S. *A Youth in the Meuse-Argonne: A Memoir, 1917–1918*. Edited by William Ferrell. Columbia: University of Missouri Press, 2000.

Tuchman, Barbara W. *The Guns of August*. New York: Macmillan, 1962.

———. *The Zimmermann Telegram: The Astounding Historic Espionage Operation That Propelled America into World War I*. New York: Random House, 1966.

Tumulty, Joseph P. *Woodrow Wilson as I Know Him*. Garden City, N.Y.: Doubleday, Page, 1921.

Van Vechten, Carl. *The Splendid Drunken Twenties: Selections from the Daybooks, 1922–1930*. Edited by Bruce Kellner. Urbana: University of Illinois Press, 2003.

Vaughan, Edwin Campion. *Some Desperate Glory: The World War I Diary of a British Officer, 1917*. New York: Simon and Schuster, 1981.

Wade, Rex, ed. *Documents of Soviet History*. Vol. I, *The Triumph of Bolshevism, 1917–1919*. Gulf Breeze, Fla.: Academic International Press, 1991.

Werfel, Franz. *The Forty Days of Musa Dagh*. Translated by Geoffrey Dunlop. New York: Viking, 1934.

Wharton, Edith. *The War on All Fronts: Fighting France, from Dunkerque to Belfort*. New York: Charles Scribner's Sons, 1918.

Williams, Frank. *Old Soldiers Never Die*. London: Faber and Faber, 1936.

Wolfe, Tom. *From Bauhaus to Our House*. New York: Farrar Strauss Giroux, 1981.

Yardley, Herbert O. *The American Black Chamber*. Introduction by David Kahn. New York: Ballantine Books, 1981.

INDEX

Locators in *italics* indicate illustrations. Locators in **boldface** indicate main entries, topics, and biographies. Locators follow by *m* indicate maps. Locators followed by *t* indicate tables. Locators followed by *g* indicate glossary entries. Locators followed by *c* indicate chronology entries.